Mexican Multinationals

Over the past two decades, emerging market multinationals have become an important force in international business. This book provides a better understanding of the actions and strategies used by firms from mid-sized emerging markets to upgrade their capabilities and become successful multinationals. It is the first book to provide an in-depth look at Mexican multinationals, or 'Multimexicans'. These include some of the leading firms in the world, such as the construction materials producer Cemex and the tortilla maker Grumasa, as well as smaller but innovative firms such as the theme park operator Kidzania and the cinema multicomplex chain Cinepolis. This comprehensive analysis contains case studies written by local industry experts on these and other firms, across twenty-two industries. The lessons drawn are of interest to researchers, students, and consultants, as well as managers and executives of firms in other emerging markets looking to upgrade capabilities and expand abroad.

ALVARO CUERVO-CAZURRA is Professor of International Business and Strategy at Northeastern University, Boston. He was elected a Fellow of the Academy of International Business and to the Executive Committee of the International Management Division of the Academy of Management. He is co-editor of *Global Strategy Journal*.

MIGUEL A. MONTOYA is Professor of International Business and Economics at Tecnologico de Monterrey, Mexico. He is a member of the Academy of International Business and the National Council for Technology and Science (CONACYT-Mexico). He is also a member of the editorial board of *Competition and Regulation in Network Industries*.

Mexican Multinationals

Building Multinationals in Emerging Markets

Edited by

ALVARO CUERVO-CAZURRA
Northeastern University

MIGUEL A. MONTOYA
Instituto Tecnologico y de Estudios Superiores de Monterrey

CAMBRIDGE
UNIVERSITY PRESS

CAMBRIDGE
UNIVERSITY PRESS

University Printing House, Cambridge CB2 8BS, United Kingdom

One Liberty Plaza, 20th Floor, New York, NY 10006, USA

477 Williamstown Road, Port Melbourne, VIC 3207, Australia

314-321, 3rd Floor, Plot 3, Splendor Forum, Jasola District Centre, New Delhi - 110025, India

103 Penang Road, #05-06/07, Visioncrest Commercial, Singapore 238467

Cambridge University Press is part of the University of Cambridge.

It furthers the University's mission by disseminating knowledge in the pursuit of education, learning and research at the highest international levels of excellence.

www.cambridge.org
Information on this title: www.cambridge.org/9781108456104
DOI: 10.1017/9781108616843

First published 2018
First paperback edition 2022

A catalogue record for this publication is available from the British Library

Library of Congress Cataloging in Publication data
Names: Cuervo-Cazurra, Alvaro, editor. | Montoya Bayardo, Miguel A., editor.
Title: Mexican multinationals : how to build multinationals in emerging markets / edited by Alvaro Cuervo-Cazurra, Northeastern University, Boston, Miguel A. Montoya Bayardo, Tecnologico de Monterrey, Guadalajara.
Description: Cambridge, United Kingdom ; New York, NY : Cambridge University Press, 2018.
Identifiers: LCCN 2017061454 | ISBN 9781108480611
Subjects: LCSH: International business enterprises – Mexico. | Mexico – Commerce.
Classification: LCC HD2811 .M49 2018 | DDC 338.8/8972–dc23
LC record available at https://lccn.loc.gov/2017061454

ISBN 978-1-108-48061-1 Hardback
ISBN 978-1-108-45610-4 Paperback

To Alvaro Cuervo for his continued guidance
—Alvaro Cuervo-Cazurra

To Celina Zaragoza for her support
—Miguel A. Montoya

Contents

Figures

Tables

Contributors

Jorge L. Alcaraz is Professor of International Business at the University of the Americas Puebla. His research interests are foreign direct investment (inward and outward) and multinational enterprises in emerging economies, the latter focusing on internationalization. He received a Ph.D. in international business from Michoacan University of Saint Nicholas of Hidalgo.

Leticia Armenta Fraire is a professor of microeconomics at Monterrey Institute of Technology and Higher Education's Mexico City Campus. She received a Ph.D. in economics from the National Autonomous University of Mexico. Her research field is industry analysis, with a focus on the petrochemical complex in Mexico. She is also a consultant for private and public organizations such as the Mexican Congress, the Agriculture Ministry, and the Public Finance Ministry.

L. Arturo Bernal is a professor of international finance at Monterrey Institute of Technology and Higher Education's Guadalajara Campus, where he also received a Ph.D. He studies risk management using derivatives and also analyzes real options valuation. He has published articles in various academic journals.

Verónica Ilián Baños-Monroy is Professor of Entrepreneurship and Family Business at Monterrey Institute of Technology and Higher Education, and holds a Ph.D. from the National Autonomous University of Mexico and a second Ph.D. from the Autonomous University of Madrid. She studies the succession process and innovation in SMEs. She has also published articles in a range of different academic journals. She is a Family Business Consultant in the Entrepreneurship Division at Monterrey Institute of Technology and Higher Education's Guadalajara Campus.

Alfonso Brown del Rivero is a professor of international economics and international business at Anáhuac University, Mexico and holds a Ph.D. from the Autonomous University of Barcelona, and a second Ph.D. from Monterrey Institute of Technology and Higher Education. His research interests are international business, especially foreign direct investment and economic regional integration in America and Europe.

Daniel Carrasco Brihuega is a professor at the University of Guadalajara. He studies comparative politics and public policy and also analyzes the governance of cities and the democratization process. He has published articles in various academic journals and is the author of a book about ministerial careers. He was Director of the School of Government at Monterrey Institute of Technology and Higher Education's Guadalajara Campus. He received a Ph.D. from the Grenoble Institute of Political Studies.

Mauricio Cervantes-Zepeda is Professor of Corporate Finance and Investment at Monterrey Institute of Technology and Higher Education's Guadalajara Campus. His research interests are microfinance, base of the pyramid, and cultural finance. He is Executive Director of the Asia Pacific Institute at Monterrey Institute of Technology and Higher Education. He is a consultant in the areas of international finance, portfolio theory, risk coverage, and business in China. He has been a visiting professor at the University of International Business and Economics in Beijing, China; Portland State University, USA; Universidad San Francisco de Quito, Ecuador; and ESAN University, Graduate School of Business, Peru. He holds a Ph.D. in finance from the University of Texas at Austin and Monterrey Institute of Technology and Higher Education, an MBA, and a Bachelor's degree in electronic engineering.

Alvaro Cuervo-Cazurra is Professor of International Business and Strategy at Northeastern University. He is an expert on the internationalization of firms, with a special interest in emerging market multinationals; capability upgrading, particularly technological capabilities; and governance issues, focusing on corruption in international business. He was elected a Fellow of the Academy of International Business, and to the Executive Committee of the International Management Division of the Academy of Management. He is coeditor of *Global Strategy Journal*. He was awarded a Ph.D. from the Massachusetts Institute of Technology.

Eileen Daspro is an associate professor of international business at Monterrey Institute of Technology and Higher Education's Guadalajara Campus. Her research focuses on the international competitiveness of emerging market firms and multinational corporate policy implementation across global markets. She is the Chair of the Department of International Business at Monterrey Institute of Technology and Higher Education's Guadalajara Campus, and Director of the Americas Competitiveness Center. She received her Ph.D. from Argosy University.

Mario Adrián Flores Castro is the Vice-President of Monterrey Institute of Technology and Higher Education's Guadalajara Campus. He leads the team representing Mexico in the Global Entrepreneurship Monitor (GEM). He has conducted research in the UK, USA, and Latin America. Before joining the academic world, he worked for over ten years at companies such as The Goodyear Tire and Rubber Company and Continental Tires. He holds a Ph.D. in business administration with a specialization in operations. He also holds an M.Sc. degree in industrial engineering and is a mechanical engineer.

Hugo Javier Fuentes Castro is a professor of microeconomics and economics of organization at Monterrey Institute of Technology and Higher Education's Mexico City Campus. His research fields are economics of organization, frontier analysis, and evaluation of public policies. He is a consultant to public and private institutions such as the World Bank, CEPAL, and the Secretary of Economy. He received a Ph.D. from the Autonomous University of Barcelona.

Jorge E. Gómez is Director of the Management and Marketing Department, and Director of the Center of Excellence for Family Business and Corporate Governance, at Monterrey Institute of Technology and Higher Education's Guadalajara Campus. He holds a Ph.D. in creation, strategy, and business management from the Autonomous University of Barcelona, and an MBA and Bachelor's degree in industrial and systems engineering from Monterrey Institute of Technology and Higher Education.

Isai Guizar is Professor of Finance at the University of Guadalajara. His primary research field is development economics and finance. His current research areas include financial services in developing countries, interest rate restrictions, and the effects of credit rationing on microenterprises. He holds a Ph.D. from The Ohio State University.

Andreas M. Hartmann is an associate professor at Monterrey Institute of Technology and Higher Education's Monterrey Campus, where he teaches in the fields of strategic management, cross-cultural management, and international negotiation. His research focuses on multinational companies, knowledge-based firms, and cross-cultural aspects of management. A native German, he is also fluent in English, Spanish, and French. He holds a Ph.D. in international business and an MBA from the Monterrey Institute of Technology and Higher Education as well as a double Master's degree in translation and conference interpreting from the University of Heidelberg.

Olivia Hernández-Pozas is an associate professor at Monterrey Institute of Technology and Higher Education's Monterrey Campus. She is certified as an advanced cultural intelligence facilitator by the Cultural Intelligence Center. She is a member of the AOM, ACACIA, and SIETAR USA, and is the founder of SIETAR México. She serves as an associate editor of *GABC Journal*.

Daniel Lemus-Delgado is Professor of International Relations at Monterrey Institute of Technology and Higher Education. He studies national and regional innovation systems, specifically in emerging countries. He also analyzes the relationship between building innovation capacities and culture, with a special interest in East Asia. He is a member of National System of Researchers in Mexico. He received his Ph.D. from the University of Colima.

Joan Llonch Andreu is Professor of Business at the Autonomous University of Barcelona and a professor of commercialization and market research in the Business Department of that institution. He studies strategic marketing with a special interest in emerging markets, market orientation, international marketing, and services marketing. He is a member of the Board of Directors of the Sabadell Bank and of BancSabadell d'Andorra, S.A. He holds a Ph.D. in economics and business from the Autonomous University of Barcelona.

Miguel A. López-Lomelí is Professor of Sales and Marketing at Monterrey Institute of Technology and Higher Education's Guadalajara Campus. He studies branding with a special interest in global, local, and glocal brand strategies. He also has a special interest in marketing strategy, focused on consumers of the middle and base of the socioeconomic pyramid in emerging markets and on sales management. He participates in the Executive Education Division as instructor and consultant at the Monterrey Institute of Technology and Higher Education. He holds a Ph.D. from the Autonomous University of Barcelona.

Raúl Montalvo is Professor of Microeconomics, Entrepreneurial Economics, and Macroeconomics at the Monterrey Institute of Technology and Higher Education. His research is focused on analyzing business models for competition. He also studies consumer behavior in the base of the pyramid. He is Director of EGADE Business School at Monterrey Institute of Technology and Higher Education's

Guadalajara Campus. He received his Ph.D. from the University of Essex.

Miguel A. Montoya is Professor of International Economics and Business at Monterrey Institute of Technology and Higher Education's Business School. He studies the regulation of Latin-American telecom companies. He also analyzes multinational companies and innovations at the base of the pyramid in emerging markets. He has published articles in various academic journals, and book chapters. He received his Ph.D. from the Autonomous University of Barcelona.

Jose F. Moreno is an associate professor of finance at the University of the Incarnate Word in San Antonio, Texas. He received his Ph.D. in finance from the University of Texas Pan-American.

Edgar Muñiz Ávila is Professor of Business Creation and Director of Entrepreneurship and Innovation at Monterrey Institute of Technology and Higher Education's Guadalajara Campus. He studies entrepreneurship with special interests in social entrepreneurship, and creation and development of enterprises and family businesses. For the last nine years he has directed the Business Incubator and the Enterprise Acceleration programs. He received his Ph.D. from Antonio de Nebrija University.

Edgar Rogelio Ramírez-Solís is Professor of International Strategic Management and Family Business at Monterrey Institute of Technology and Higher Education, and holds a Ph.D. from the National Autonomous University of Mexico and a second Ph.D. from the Autonomous University of Madrid. He studies the best practices in designing and executing strategies. He has published articles in various different academic journals, and is also a Family Business Consultant in the Marketing and Business Department at Monterrey Institute of Technology and Higher Education's Guadalajara Campus.

Mauricio Ramírez Grajeda is a full professor in the Department of Quantitative Methods at the University of Guadalajara, and a lecturer in economics at Monterrey Institute of Technology and Higher Education. He is editor of the scientific *journal EconoQuantum*. He has published in journals such as *The Spatial Economic Analysis, Asian Journal of Latin American Studies*, and *The Journal of Mathematics and System Science*. Since 2008 he has belonged to the National System of Researchers of Mexico. He has been a speaker at international academic events in the USA, Canada, the Netherlands, Argentina, Brazil, and Ecuador. He obtained his Ph.D. in development economics from The Ohio State University.

Angel E. Rivera is Professor of Management, Quality Systems, and Research Methodology at the National Polytechnic Institute of Mexico. He studies knowledge management practices and the innovation process in organizations, with a special interest in using mixed methods to study these dynamic processes. He also has a special interest in using social network analysis to measure the dynamics and collaboration process between significant agents. He participates in the Economic Development Network at the National Polytechnic Institute of Mexico. He received his Ph.D. in business administration from the EGADE Business School of Monterrey Institute of Technology and Higher Education.

Lucía Rodríguez-Aceves is Professor of Entrepreneurship at Monterrey Institute of Technology and Higher Education's Guadalajara Campus. She studies knowledge management and strategy, with a special interest in using social network analysis to measure collaboration in knowledge-based networks. She participates in the Global Knowledge Research Network and the Ibero-American Knowledge Systems Community. She received her Ph.D. in business administration from the EGADE Business School of Monterrey Institute of Technology and Higher Education.

José Manuel Saiz-Álvarez is a visiting research professor in the Entrepreneurship Division at Monterrey Institute of Technology and Higher Education's Guadalajara Campus. He has taught courses on entrepreneurship and family business at the graduate level. He has edited the *Handbook of Research on Social Entrepreneurship and Solidarity Economics* and has coauthored several books on this topic. He holds a Ph.D. in economics and business administration from the Autonomous University of Madrid and a Ph.D. in sociology from the Pontifical University of Salamanca.

Adriana Sánchez is a professor at Monterrey Institute of Technology and Higher Education's Business School, León Campus. She is a coauthor of two books on the fundamentals of marketing and has published various articles on intelligent environments. She has also collaborated with international research projects measuring entrepreneurial activity in Mexican enterprises. She has a Ph.D. in business administration science from the University of Alcalá.

Francisco J. Valderrey is a professor at Monterrey Institute of Technology and Higher Education's León Campus. His research focuses on strategy in the tourism industry, as well as marketing in China, and negotiation strategy in multicultural environments. He has published several articles on Asia Pacific topics, and most recently he started a research group analyzing technology and global business. He has coauthored two textbooks on the fundamentals of marketing. He earned a Ph.D. in administration and marketing from the University of Valencia.

Maria E. Vázquez is Professor of Marketing and Retailing at Monterrey Institute of Technology and Higher Education's Business School, Guadalajara Campus. Her research includes retail strategy and service marketing with a special interest in branding and marketing strategy. For the last nine years, she has been Director of the Center for Retailing and the School of Business and Humanities. She received a DBA from the University of Phoenix.

Xiomara Vázquez Guillén is an associate professor at Monterrey Institute of Technology and Higher Education's Guadalajara Campus. She has published in the microfinance field and has been a speaker at international academic events in the USA, Canada, Brazil, Argentina, and Spain. She has been the Accounting and Finance Department Director since 2007, Master in Finance Director since 2012, and from 2011 to 2015 was the National Academic Coordinator of the Bachelor in Finance for all the Monterrey Institute of Technology and Higher Education Campuses. She received her Ph.D. in economics and management sciences at the University of Guadalajara in 2011, and holds Master degrees in Finance and Business Administration, and a Bachelor's degree in Accounting, from Monterrey Institute of Technology and Higher Education.

Laura Zapata is an associate professor in the Management Department at EGADE Business School and has been Director of MBA Programs at Monterrey Institute of Technology and Higher Education's Monterrey Campus since 2011. She teaches business strategy for the MBA program and methodology and strategy for the DBA program. Her research work focuses on strategic management and knowledge management processes: generation and transfer. She has been distinguished with the 2008 Teaching and Research Award from Monterrey Institute of Technology and Higher Education, and The Carolina Foundation Postdoctoral Fellowship. From 2009 to 2014 Dr. Zapata was head of European Studies for the Development and Competitiveness Research Chair, and since 2006 she has been a member of Mexico's National Researchers System (CONACyT).

Preface

This book is the result of a large collaborative effort between Alvaro Cuervo-Cazurra of Northeastern University and Miguel A. Montoya of the Monterrey Institute of Technology and Higher Education ("Monterrey Tec") in Guadalajara. We first met in 2008, when Alvaro was a faculty member at the University of South Carolina, which had a joint MBA program with Monterrey Tec in Guadalajara, where Miguel was the Dean of Graduate Studies. The initial teaching relationship evolved into a research collaboration, and since 2010, Alvaro has been working with a group of professors and Ph.D. students at the Center for Asia Pacific, led by Miguel, to gain a better understanding of Mexican firms. The outcome of this collaboration was a series of papers presented at academic conferences and published in academic journals. As the research progressed, it became apparent that a collaborative volume would be one way to deepen the understanding already gained about Mexican firms. Hence, at a meeting in late August 2014, we decided to organize a book that would facilitate the dissemination of the insights gained beyond the academic community. Alvaro and Miguel acted as coordinators of chapters written by authors from Monterrey Tec and their collaborators. In September–December 2014, the authors of each chapter gathered secondary data on the companies and industry that served as the basis for the comparative cases. We had a conference in early January 2015 to determine progress and improve the content and presentation of the cases, and to gain new ideas from the insights developed by other coauthors. In January–March 2015, once the cases had been created using secondary data, the authors of each chapter conducted interviews with current and past managers of the companies to understand in more detail the reasons behind the actions taken, and gather additional information that was not publicly available. We had another conference in May 2015 to integrate the completion of the cases with the interview data and draw conclusions. We worked on the drafts of the chapters throughout 2016 and 2017 to ensure consistency in the arguments, and to draw comparison across cases. What you are now reading is the outcome of this collaboration.

We are grateful to the people who supported us during this process:

- To the co-authors of the chapters for being responsive to our continual demands for improvement to the manuscripts, and for juggling the research requirements with their teaching responsibilities;
- To the managers and owners of the MultiMexicans for their willingness to provide candid explanations of not just the successes but also the failures that accompanied the transformation and international expansion of their firms;
- To the Center for Asia Pacific at Monterrey Tec in Guadalajara, Mexico, and the Center for Emerging Markets at Northeastern University in Boston, USA, for financial support to meet managers and periodically share ideas and discuss progress in person;
- To the staff at Monterrey Tec in Guadalajara, who helped coordinate the meetings: in particular, Omar Robledo. We appreciate all the research support of Eduardo Schcolnik, Miguel A. Montoya-Zaragoza, S. Raúl Silva and Karol Padilla.

And finally – and most importantly – we express our thanks to our families, who had to bear our absences and long hours of working on this project.

1 MultiMexicans
An Introduction

Alvaro Cuervo-Cazurra

INTRODUCTION

When one asks students to name a few Mexican multinationals, which in this book we call MultiMexicans, many struggle. Some may have read the case studies of the cement producer Cemex or the bakery giant Bimbo. However, the vast majority tend to mention brands of tequila and beer, which in most cases are foreign owned, or talk about the exports by contract manufacturers, i.e., *maquilas*, but without being able to name the firms. This lack of awareness is not limited to students, however. Many academics and a fair number of managers only know about a few MultiMexicans. This is partly a result of lack of knowledge or misperceptions about the competitiveness of local Mexican firms, and partly a result of lack of exposure to the brands of MultiMexicans, because many of these multinationals operate in industrial sectors or acquire foreign brands in their international expansion.

However, there is an increasing number of Mexican firms that are not only exporting but also establishing operations abroad, and some of them have already achieved regional and global leadership. For example, of the 122 Latin American multinationals, i.e., MultiLatinas, that the magazine *AmericaEconomía* identified among the 500 largest firms in Latin American in 2016, 45 were from Mexico. This placed the number of MultiMexican firms well ahead of other Latin American countries such as Brazil with 31, Chile with 24, Colombia with nine, or Argentina with six (AmericaEconomia, 2016). Some MultiMexicans have become leaders in their industries, like the baked goods firm Bimbo (1st in the world), the tortilla maker Gruma (1st in the world), the construction materials producer Cemex (5th largest in the world),

1

the telecommunications firm América Móvil (1st in Latin America), and the chemical firm Mexichem (1st plastic tube producer in Latin America). However, not all MultiMexicans are large firms. Some are *mini-multinationals*: successful multinationals with a limited global presence, such as the car components firm Nemak or the cinema chain Cinépolis.

Surprisingly, given their growing importance in global markets, we have a limited number of studies of MultiMexicans, with no books providing a systematic analysis. Instead, we have a few articles and book chapters that explain the internationalization of a few large MultiMexicans. These include, for example, the study of the cement producer Cemex by Lessard & Lucea (2009), the analysis of the competitiveness of Mexican business groups in Grosse & Mesquita (2007), the description of some Mexican firms in the study of MultiLatinas by Santiso (2013), or the description of the conglomerate Grupo Carso, the cement producer Cemex, the baked goods firm Bimbo, and the brewer Grupo Modelo in Casanova (2009). This is surprising, as Mexico by 2016 had become the 11th largest economy in the world, with US$2.3 trillion in PPP terms, ahead of Italy, Korea, and Spain (World Bank, 2017). Its GDP per capita in PPP terms was 18 thousand, ahead of China and Brazil, with 15 thousand each, and India, with 6 thousand, although below the 25 thousand of Russia, to establish a comparison with the so-called BRIC countries. Thus, it appears that the time is ripe to analyze MultiMexicans comprehensively, covering a multitude of industries and a variety of sizes; that is what this book offers.

Hence, this book differs from others by being the first to provide a systematic analysis of MultiMexicans. What also differentiates the book is the approach we take, providing a contextual analysis of their global expansion, in which the internationalization of firms is placed within the particular conditions of the industry and especially of the home country. This contextual analysis provides both a deep understanding of the historical situation that enabled Mexican firms to upgrade their competitiveness to international levels, and a sophisticated understanding of the strategies they used to conquer foreign markets. With this dual approach, we aim to generate insights that are useful for managers, not only of other Mexican firms but also of firms in other emerging markets, who are considering how to transform their firms into global competitors.

Now, the question is, is there something special about these firms for our understanding of multinationals? Can current models and analyses of multinationals be used to explain their expansion? The answer is yes and no. Yes, in the sense that good models are applicable and previous insights and approaches can be used to understand their internationalization, and no, in the sense that the context of operation of MultiMexicans plays a large role in their transformation into international competitors and subsequent internationalization, and existing models do not accommodate this role well. Thus, to better understand the insights that we derive from the analysis of MultiMexicans, in the following paragraphs I briefly review the core models of the multinational. I then discuss the phenomenon of multinationals from emerging markets, and how their analysis highlights the importance of studying the impact of the home country on internationalization. I conclude with an overview of the themes that we cover in the book and the insights that are identified in the conclusions.

TRADITIONAL MODELS OF THE MULTINATIONAL

The international business literature has offered several explanations for the existence of the multinational and the process of internationalization. These models were developed in the 1970s and 1980s by analyzing multinationals from advanced economies (mostly European and American companies and later Japanese firms) as these firms set up wholly owned operations around the world. Their behavior did not fit well with economic explanations of foreign investment that assumed it was a financial flow (for a good historical overview of the literature see Dunning, 2009, and Hennart, 2009a). The result of these theoretical advances was the development of two types of multinational model. One type sought to explain the existence of multinationals, firms that controlled assets abroad and managed cross-border transactions. Another type of model sought to explain the process by which firms expanded across countries.

Why Multinationals Exist

The first type of model explains why multinationals exist. Among the models we have the OLI framework, the internalization theory of the multinational, and the knowledge-based explanation of the multinational, which I briefly explain now.

The OLI framework, introduced by Dunning (1977), describes the existence of a multinational, i.e., a firm with foreign direct investments (FDI), as the result of the combination of three advantages: Ownership, Location, and Internalization. Ownership advantages refer to the situation in which the company has particular resources or capabilities that enable it to do things better than competitors, that is, that provide it with a competitive advantage. These same resources and capabilities that the firm owns can then be used in other countries to achieve a competitive advantage there. Location advantages refer to the situation in which the company invests abroad to benefit from the better conditions of inputs or factors of production, i.e., the comparative advantage of a location, or to serve new markets. Finally, internalization advantages refer to the situation in which managers decide to internalize cross-border transactions, i.e., manage transactions within the company rather than using contracts with third parties, because doing so is more efficient or effective. This paradigm, which was initially developed from the study of British and later US firms, has been refined and extended over the years to adapt it to new realities of international business and theoretical advances. These highlight different subtypes of ownership advantage, which include asset-based advantages from the ownership of particular resources, transactional advantages from the capability to coordinate operations, and institutional advantages from the capability to manage institutions and norms (Eden & Dai, 2010).

A modification of the OLI paradigm is the FSA/CSA model of the multinational (Rugman & Verbeke, 1992). This model discusses the existence of a multinational as the result of the combination of two types of advantage: (1) firm-specific advantages (FSAs), which only the company can access and which include the ownership and internalization advantages of the OLI framework; and (2) country-specific advantages (CSAs), which not only the company but also other companies in the same location can access and that include the location advantages of the OLI framework. One contribution of this model is highlighting that some of these advantages are tied to a place and are not transferable across countries, i.e., they are location bound, hence limiting the ability of a company to engage in international operations. In contrast, other advantages are not location bound and support the ability of a company to become a multinational by transferring them across borders. Similar to the OLI framework, the FSA/CSA model is a general framework that focuses attention on those resources and capabilities that provide the multinational with an advantage. However, both tend to assume that the advantages exist and do not get into an analysis of how resources and associated advantages emerge.

The internalization model of the multinational (Buckley & Casson, 1976) and the related transaction cost analysis of the multinational (Hennart, 1982; Teece, 1986) explain the conditions under which a multinational will use different governance modes when engaging in cross-border transactions. This theory focuses on the 'I' of the 'OLI' paradigm, and provides detailed descriptions of the governance modes and the reasons for using contracts, alliances, or the firm as the mechanism to manage cross-border transactions based on the characteristics of the assets and ability to contract effectively (Anderson & Gatignon, 1986). In this model, it is better to use the market when engaging in cross-border transactions because markets tend to be more efficient transaction systems; the price mechanism provides appropriate signals and competition among providers ensures better quality. However, it may be better to internalize cross-border relationships when the multinational: (a) has assets that have low secondary uses, i.e., are specific to a relationship; (b) cannot find appropriate contract partners; and (c) cannot specify a clear contract that governs the use of those assets because of problems of information asymmetry and uncertainty, and ineffective contract protection and contract dispute settling mechanisms. This approach has been extended to incorporate the notion that there are several contracting parties with alternative objectives and that complementary assets and their access play a role in determining the appropriate transaction mode (Hennart, 2009b). This model provides a deep understanding of the scope of the multinational and the conditions under which it internalizes cross-border transactions or uses alliances or contracts to manage them. However, at the same time, this model tends to assume that the company has resources and capabilities that provide it with a competitive advantage in the first place.

In contrast to these, the knowledge-based view of the multinational (Kogut & Zander, 1992), which builds on the broader resource-based view (Barney, 1991), argues that knowledge is the key asset of a company. It studies how the development, transfer, use, and protection of knowledge across borders enable domestic companies to become multinationals. In the resource-based view, a firm is a collection of resources and capabilities (Penrose, 1959). Among those, some provide the firm with an advantage when they are (Barney, 1991): (a) valuable because they can be used to create value for customers; (b) rare because only the company or few companies have them; (c) difficult to imitate by competitors because other firms cannot replicate them easily; and (d) difficult to substitute by competitors because other firms cannot find alternative ways to achieve the same function. Among the resources that a firm can control, knowledge is the key one because it enables the firm to obtain and manage all the other resources and capabilities (Kogut & Zander, 1992). However, at the same time, knowledge is a difficult resource to manage (Nonaka, 1994). Its tacit nature – i.e., much knowledge is not codified in manuals and websites that can easily be retrieved and shared, but rather is embedded in the minds of employees – makes it a resource that is more difficult to imitate as competitors cannot easily observe the knowledge. It also makes it a resource that is more difficult for the firm to transfer and use across borders. As a result, firms become multinationals to effectively manage the transfer and use of knowledge across borders, as well as to benefit from the knowledge that is created from the management of these cross-border relationships. This knowledge-based view, and the underlying resource-based view, focuses attention on how firms develop resources and the associated competitive advantage, thus complementing previous models.

How Multinationals Expand Across Borders

The second set of models focuses on explaining the process by which domestic companies become multinationals (see a review in Cuervo-Cazurra, 2011; Melin, 1992). These include the product lifecycle model, the incremental internationalization model, and the innovation-related model.

An early process model is the product lifecycle model (Vernon, 1966). This takes the concept of the product lifecycle from the marketing literature – in which a product is introduced in the market and then its sales grow, reach maturity, and eventually decline – and applies this idea to explaining how sales and production move across countries from the most to the least advanced economies. Thus, the internationalization process starts with the company in an advanced country introducing a new product to satisfy the needs of sophisticated consumers in advanced economies. As demand in other advanced economies grows, the firm first exports and then produces in the other countries to be more responsive to differing consumer preferences and to counter local competitors. As the product matures, new competitors imitate the innovation and the product becomes standardized, so the company moves production to low-cost countries to reduce production costs and starts selling there. With declining demand, the company stops producing in advanced economies because it is too costly to manufacture there, and serves both advanced and developing countries with imports from low-cost countries. This model, which was developed by abstracting from the experiences of US firms in the 1950s, seems to be a good explanation of the diffusion of innovations across countries, but not necessarily of the expansion of a particular firm across countries (Melin, 1992). Moreover, instead of following this life cycle, nowadays innovations are commonly introduced across multiple countries at the same time, and production is outsourced directly to countries with lower production costs. This is the result of factors such as the disaggregation of value chains across countries, with innovators easily finding manufacturers in lower-cost countries; the creation of innovations in emerging countries that are marketed in emerging and advanced economies; and fast competitive imitation across countries facilitated by information and communication technologies. Hence, although the model generated significant research aiming to validate its arguments, nowadays it is rarely used as an explanation of the internationalization of a particular firm.

The incremental internationalization model (Johanson & Vahlne, 1977), also known as the Uppsala model because it was developed at Uppsala University, has become one of the leading explanations of the internationalization process. Building on behavioral economics (Cyert & March, 1963), it explains the process by which a domestic company expands abroad in search of new markets and becomes a multinational as being driven by managerial knowledge and risk aversion. Managers of a firm consider expanding to other countries to increase sales, using resources and capabilities developed in the home country. Managers have to make two main decisions that shape this expansion. One is the decision on which country to enter. The firm expands sequentially from the home country, first to countries that are similar to the home country, and later to countries that are dissimilar. As managers are risk-averse and know little about foreign markets, they tend to choose countries that are similar to the home country in terms of psychic distance (i.e., differences between countries that limit the flow of information) to reduce the uncertainty and risk of operation and to increase their ability to use existing knowledge and capabilities abroad. Once managers gain direct experience from operating in these countries and expand their knowledge set, they then take the company to countries that are farther away from the home country in psychic distance. The second decision is to select the mode of operation in a particular country, with companies internationalizing gradually within a country by first exporting, then using sales representatives, later using their own sales subsidiaries, and finally establishing production facilities. This sequential process helps managers gain direct knowledge and experience of how to operate in the business and institutional conditions of the host country and also reduces the risk of exposure in the host country by limiting the firm's commitment to a country they do not know well. Once managers gain experience and knowledge from operating in the country, they can take more risks and increase the firm's commitment to the host country.

The incremental internationalization model, which was initially developed using the experience of Scandinavian firms, has been very influential in explaining the expansion of firms and has been subject to extensions as well as critiques. The model was extended to include a network view of the multinational (Johanson & Vahlne, 2003). This proposes that internationalization knowledge can be gained in advance of the firm's foreign expansion from interacting with partners and employees that already have international knowledge, thus providing a broader understanding of knowledge in the model (Forsgren, 2002). Thus, a firm with such a network of sources of knowledge at home may be able to internationalize faster and broader than the original model proposed.

The main criticisms of the incremental internationalization models are directed to the idea that firms follow a sequence of expansion across countries, first entering countries that are closer to home in psychic distance and later those that are farther away, as well as a sequence within a country, entering first via exports and later via foreign direct investment. Thus, for example, the born-global model

(Oviatt & McDougall, 1994), which was developed in international entrepreneurship, was introduced as a challenge to the incremental internationalization model by arguing that small firms in high-tech industries do not expand incrementally. Instead, some of them export to a multitude of countries either at or close to their creation. Changes in the global economy in the form of advances in information and communication technologies and transportation technologies, as well as market liberalization, have enabled newly created firms to start exporting widely (Knight & Cavusgil, 1996). This is especially the case for firms that operate in digital industries whose products can be distributed via the Internet at almost no cost.

A third process model of the multinational is the so-called innovation-related model (Cavusgil, 1980; Czinkota, 1982), referring to the idea of serving foreign markets as akin to an innovation. This model, which was developed in international marketing, explains how a company changes from being exclusively focused on the domestic market to becoming an active exporter as a result of changes in managerial attention and knowledge. Most companies are created to serve the domestic market, as managers tend to have a deeper knowledge of the needs of domestic customers, thus leading their firms to create products and services that serve those needs. However, for some firms their products may become known abroad through exposure at business fairs or word of mouth. Thus, the firm may start receiving requests from customers abroad. In response, the firm may fulfill these sporadic requests without paying much attention to them. However, if the foreign requests increase, managers may start shifting their attention towards fulfilling them, gaining knowledge of how to serve foreign markets in the process. Once managers gain enough experience in serving foreign markets, they alter their attention and the focus of the company towards foreign markets, transforming the firm from a passive to an active exporter and seeking sales in a variety of countries. Although useful for explaining the beginning of the internationalization process via sales, the model seems to be limited regarding its explanatory power as it does not take into account other internationalization methods such as FDI and licensing, and thus could to some extent be considered as the specification of the early stages of the incremental internationalization model.

Although useful for providing explanations and predictions about the development of multinationals and their internationalization process, these traditional models are built on assumptions derived from the study of multinationals from advanced economies. The models tend to assume that the home country is advanced and thus that firms can develop the most innovative products and services to serve the highly sophisticated consumers there. With these innovations in place, the next step is finding other countries in which they can be sold most profitably. The models also assume that there is a well-established institutional arrangement typical of advanced economies that supports firms' development of resources and capabilities and helps firms protect their innovations from unauthorized imitation by competitors. Along these lines, the models also assume that there is a well-established contractual protection system that enables firms to find appropriate suppliers and concentrate on developing and improving their sources of advantage. Thus, most of these models have not paid much attention to how the home country affects the behavior of companies other than as a supportive influence.

However, the supporting environment that characterizes advanced economies – wealthy, demanding consumers that drive innovations, established innovation systems, property rights protections that facilitate the development of innovations, appropriate contract protection norms and institutions, and sophisticated intermediaries – is not universal. Firms in emerging economies suffer from large sections of the population with low levels of income (Prahalad, 2005) and underdeveloped intermediaries and institutions, the so-called institutional voids (Khanna & Palepu, 2010); these challenge the assumptions of traditional models. It is this issue – how the underdevelopment of the conditions of the country of origin affect the internationalization of firms – that the study of emerging market multinationals can help illuminate.

NEW MODELS OF THE MULTINATIONAL: EMERGING MARKET MULTINATIONALS

The study of the global expansion of MultiMexicans is part of a broader theme of analyzing multinationals from emerging markets, which in recent times have become new competitors in the global arena. Some firms, like the Brazilian airplane manufacturer Embraer, the Indian steel maker Tata Steel, and the Chinese telecommunications equipment manufacturer Huawei, have become leaders in their industries. Among the Forbes Global 2000, which lists the largest firms as a combination of revenue, profits, assets, and market value, by 2016 there were 480 firms from emerging markets (Forbes, 2016). Their rise to global leadership has caught the attention of scholars, who have focused on providing a better understanding of how these companies have managed to upgrade their capabilities and challenge established leaders from advanced economies. This attention has resulted not only in the usual research books (e.g., Cuervo-Cazurra & Ramamurti, 2014; Ramamurti & Singh, 2009; Williamson, Ramamurti, Fleury & Fleury, 2013) and articles in academic journals (e.g., see the special issues edited by Aulakh, 2007; Cuervo-Cazurra, 2012; Gammeltoft, Barnard & Madhok, 2010; Luo & Tung, 2007) dissecting the actions taken by these firms. It has also resulted in popular press books (e.g., Guillen & García-Canal, 2012), consulting reports (e.g., the series on the leading emerging market multinationals published by Boston Consulting Group in 2006, 2009, 2011, 2013) and newspaper articles (e.g., Economist, 2008, 2010) describing and celebrating these firms.

One surprise about emerging market multinationals is that they are coming from countries that are underdeveloped and that, according to standard models, should not generate multinationals this early in their development. The investment development path model of foreign direct investment (Dunning, 1981) proposes that the level of inward and outward FDI evolves with the level of development of the country. In underdeveloped countries, there are relatively high levels of inward FDI from foreign firms investing to benefit from the low-cost factor of production and exploit the comparative advantage of the country, and relatively little outward FDI as domestic companies are not internationally competitive because they tend to produce low-tech and unsophisticated products. As the country develops and becomes an emerging economy, the level of inward FDI continues to increase, attracted by the higher sophistication of factors of production at still relatively low costs, while outward FDI starts to increase as domestic companies become increasingly competitive. Once the country has become an advanced economy, the level of inward FDI diminishes because it is relatively expensive to produce there, while the level of outward FDI increases as domestic companies become innovators and seek new markets. Following this logic and given their lower level of development, emerging countries should not be able to support many internationally competitive firms. These firms may be internationalizing merely on the basis of the comparative advantage of their home countries and economies of scale, lacking sophisticated resources and capabilities that would enable them to become global competitors (Rugman, 2010).

Nevertheless, many emerging markets are becoming leading sources of FDI, and some of their firms are achieving regional or even global leadership in their industries. This has surprised many observers and has led to the rapid emergence of literature that is trying to understand the behavior of emerging market multinationals and how they differ from the widely analyzed multinationals from advanced economies (Cuervo-Cazurra & Ramamurti, 2014; Ramamurti & Singh, 2009; Williamson, Ramamurti, Fleury & Fleury, 2013). Much of the literature has focused on describing some of the particular features and unique strategies of emerging market multinationals (e.g., Casanova, 2009; Chattopadhyay, Batra & Ozsomer, 2012; Guillen & García-Canal, 2008; Santiso, 2013). One outcome of this has been studies highlighting the importance of analyzing the influence of the home country on the internationalization of firms (Cuervo-Cazurra & Genc, 2008; Garcia-Canal & Guillen, 2008; Holburn & Zelner, 2010; Luo & Wang, 2012), particularly the role that institutions play in global strategy (Khanna & Palepu, 2010; Peng, Wang & Jiang, 2008; Martin, 2014; Meyer, Estrin, Bhaumik & Peng, 2009).

As a result, we have a Goldilocks debate regarding the novelty of analyzing emerging market multinationals (Cuervo-Cazurra, 2012). Some authors propose that existing models of the multinational can explain emerging market multinationals and thus no new models or ideas are needed (Rugman, 2010). In contrast, other authors propose that new models are needed because these companies are very different in their behavior and drivers of internationalization (Guillen & García-Canal, 2008). A third group of authors proposes that existing models of the multinational can be extended and modified to explain the behavior of multinationals from emerging markets by incorporating some of the distinguishing characteristics of these countries (Ramamurti, 2012).

Models of Emerging Market Multinationals

Some authors have proposed models to explain the particularities in the internationalization of emerging market firms. Most of them are presented as a critique of previous models and highlight some new characteristics of the internationalization of emerging market firms, such as their rapid and wide expansion or their expansion in search of competitive resources. We have four models that address some of these particular features: the LLL model, the springboard model, the "new" model of the multinational, and the nonsequential internationalization model.

The LLL model, or Linkage, Leverage, and Learning model (Mathews, 2006), argues that emerging market multinationals internationalize thanks to a different set of drivers to those identified in the OLI model. Thus, they establish linkages to other companies to acquire advantages externally, have an outward orientation, and focus part of their foreign expansion on the access to strategic assets. Second, they leverage their connections with partners to obtain resources by using networks strategically. And third, they learn, and build their advantages via repetition and continuous improvement.

The springboard model (Luo & Tung, 2007), uses the metaphor of a springboard to explain the internationalization of emerging market firms. These companies are characterized by aggressive, risk-taking acquisitions of critical assets of firms in advanced economies to compensate for their competitive weaknesses. They invest abroad to obtain strategic assets needed to compete more effectively against multinationals from advanced economies, and to avoid home country institutional and market deficiencies.

The so-called new model of the multinational (Guillen & García-Canal, 2008), indicates that emerging market multinationals are internationalizing more quickly and widely than multinationals from advanced economies, despite limitations in their competitive advantage. They achieve this by using strong organizational and political capabilities as well as alliances and acquisitions.

The nonsequential internationalization model (Cuervo-Cazurra, 2011), proposes that emerging market multinationals do not have to follow an incremental internationalization process in which they select countries that are similar to the home country first and countries that are more distant later, as advanced economy firms did. Instead, the firms have two paths. They enter countries that resemble the home country, such as other emerging countries, in which they can apply their knowledge more easily even if the size of the market is not very large. Or they can enter countries that provide better market opportunities, such as advanced economies, even if it is more difficult to use existing knowledge from the home operations.

Implicit Assumptions in the Models of Emerging Market Multinationals

Despite these arguments, the uniqueness of emerging market multinationals and their ability to serve as the basis for new models of the multinational needs to be qualified. The reason is that some of the drivers of the internationalization of emerging market multinationals that some authors claim as unique are not necessarily so, because they also affect the expansion of advanced economy firms (Ramamurti, 2012): global context, industry, and stage of internationalization. First, emerging market multinationals are internationalizing at a time in which communication and transportation technologies and the liberalization of international trade and investment support the internationalization of all firms. Second, many of the emerging market multinationals used to illustrate the research pieces operate in industries that are global in nature and thus their faster and wider internationalization is facilitated by their industry characteristics. Third, many emerging market multinationals are in their early stages of internationalization, and thus their experiences cannot be compared to those of advanced economy multinationals that are already operating globally. Advanced economy firms in their early stages of internationalization in the past faced challenges that are similar to the ones experienced by emerging market multinationals nowadays, such as the lack of globally known brands or few managers with experience serving foreign customers.

What is unique about emerging market multinationals is how the underdevelopment of the home country affects the firm's development of resources and capabilities and subsequent internationalization. For example, the weakness of the home country in supporting the development of advanced capabilities leads many companies to enter advanced economies to purchase capabilities, not only technological but also managerial and organizational (Madhok & Keyhani, 2012). Another example is how the underdevelopment of institutions that support contracts and protect intellectual property rights induce some emerging market multinationals to engage in escape investment, relocating activities abroad to limit the exposure to the home country (Cuervo-Cazurra & Ramamurti, 2014). In some extreme cases, firms even relocate their headquarters to avoid the association with the home country, becoming migrating multinationals (Barnard, 2014).

Most of the attention has been devoted to analyzing multinationals from the so-called BRIC countries (Brazil, Russia, India, and China). These countries, and their firms by association, have received the bulk of attention because they have been considered the up-and-coming economic dynamos of the world (O'Neill, Wilson, Purushothaman & Stupnytska, 2005). Thus, we have several books analyzing multinationals from Brazil (Fleury & Fleury, 2011; Ramsey & Almeida, 2009), Russia (Panibratov, 2012), India (Pradhan, 2008; Sauvant, Pradhan, Chatterjee & Harley, 2010), or China (Alon, Fetscherin & Gugler, 2012; Backaler, 2014; Lacon, 2009; Zeng & Williamson, 2007; Yeung, Xin, Pfoertsch & Liu, 2011). These have provided new and more nuanced understandings of the particular characteristics of these firms in context.

However, the ideas gained from analyzing multinationals from BRIC countries may not be fully applicable to firms from other emerging economies. BRIC countries are the largest emerging countries in terms of population, economic size, and natural resources. This gives their firms the opportunity to grow large and hone their competitive advantages at home before they venture abroad, helping them compete against large multinationals from advanced economies. In contrast, firms operating in small and mid-sized emerging markets may not be able to achieve such advantages at home when their managers decide to invest abroad. Their more limited home markets and lower availability of resources mean that some cannot reach a competitive size at home before they venture abroad, placing them at a relative disadvantage in international markets and requiring them to follow different processes for upgrading capabilities and internationalizing.

MULTIMEXICANS: BETTER UNDERSTANDING CAPABILITIES IN UPGRADING AND INTERNATIONALIZATION

Hence, in this book, we analyze the internationalization of MultiMexicans as a laboratory for identifying novel ways in which firms from smaller and mid-sized emerging countries build up their competitive advantage to international levels and expand globally. And we do so by paying special attention to how the context of operation of the firm affects these processes, analyzing both large and small firms to present a comprehensive understanding of all the issues that these firms face.

One distinguishing characteristic of this book is how we analyze firms in their context. We pay attention to identifying how the conditions of the country influence how firms develop their competitive advantage and expand abroad. In the case of MultiMexicans, the transformation of Mexico in the twentieth century deeply influenced how firms behaved. Mexican firms were sheltered from foreign competition by the import substitution process that was implemented in Mexico from the 1940s to the 1980s, and were quickly exposed to foreign competition during the liberalization of the 1990s (Hoshino, 2001). The 1994 North American Free Trade Agreement opened the door to the entry of many American and Canadian multinationals that were not only much larger, but also had more sophisticated technologies and capabilities. This forced Mexican firms to upgrade their capabilities quickly. Some Mexican firms did so in collaboration with the newcomers, as they became assemblers for foreign firms in the so-called *maquila* parks in the Mexican states bordering the United States. They internationalized indirectly by becoming part of the global value chains of foreign multinationals, initially, later expanding on their own using knowledge gained from the foreign partners on how to compete across borders. Others focused on increasing their scale at home by acquiring local competitors to become the dominant players, and later ventured abroad in search of new markets in which they could grow. And yet others expanded abroad even when they lacked both the size and expertise of foreign markets, taking the plunge and venturing on their own. All these processes were aided by new free trade agreements that made Mexico one of the most open economies in the world, placing additional pressure on domestic firms to become internationally competitive and paving the way for their wide foreign expansion.

Another distinguishing characteristic of this book is the discussion of tradeoffs that firms face in their foreign expansion. For example, in the case of Mexican firms, managers face the choice of expanding into other emerging economies or selecting advanced economies for their foreign ventures. Mexico is positioned next to one of the largest and most demanding advanced markets, the United States. At the same time, it is close to many neighboring countries in Latin America with which it shares cultural and historical ties. Thus, Mexican firms can easily choose to go upmarket and enter the neighboring United States, where they may learn how to serve highly demanding customers that can help them further improve their capabilities. However, this approach is risky, as they face additional challenges from their lower level of marketing sophistication or the negative perceptions of their country of origin. Alternatively, MultiMexicans may choose to move to similar markets in other Latin American countries in which they can benefit from the sale of products to customers that have similar economic and cultural profiles to the ones at home. However, this move may limit their learning and further capability in upgrading.

CONTENTS OF THE BOOK

Hence, in this book, we build on this dual approach – context and tradeoffs – to provide a deep and nuanced discussion of MultiMexicans and draw lessons for managers of other firms in other countries. The book's chapters cover a wide variety of industries and companies to gain a diversity of insights on how firms become multinationals. We use a comparative case study methodology to gain a deeper understanding, selecting two of the leading firms in their sector and comparing their experiences over decades. The last chapter describes this methodology and how we used it in the book.

The second chapter provides an overview of the phenomenon of MultiMexicans. It gives a short introduction to the evolution of the country in recent decades to provide some historical background to those who are not familiar with the development of Mexico. It also aims to dispel some myths about Mexico and its economic backwardness, given its recent and relatively successful development. It then presents an overview of the population of MultiMexicans and a description of their patterns of international expansion, highlighting a few distinguishing characteristics, such as their family ownership and their membership in business groups, that play a specific role in their upgrading and expansion.

The bulk of the book is a series of chapters that study the process of competitiveness upgrading and internationalization of two leading multinationals operating in the same industry. The 21 chapters follow a common structure to facilitate the comparison across industries and the drawing of conclusions. They first provide an overview of the industry and its evolution in Mexico; identify some of the largest foreign and domestic competitors; describe the transformation of two of the leading Mexican firms from domestic to multinational firms; and provide lessons for other managers. The analysis of the case studies is organized into the three broad industry groupings of primary, secondary, and tertiary industries to highlight how MultiMexicans can emerge and be successful in any industry. The section on primary industries includes chapters that compare multinationals in agriculture (Bachoco and SuKarne), mining (Grupo México and Industrias Peñoles), oil (Pemex), and steel (Alto Hornos de México and Industrias CH). The section on secondary industries comprises chapters that analyze firms in food (Bimbo and Gruma), beverages (Grupo Modelo and Cuauhtémoc Moctezuma), footwear (Flexi and Andrea), cement (Cemex and Cementos de Chihuahua), containers and packaging (Vitro and Envases Universales), ceramic tiles (Lamosa and Interceramic), automotive components (Metalsa and Nemak), and appliances (Mabe and MAN Industries). The section on tertiary industries has chapters on retail (Elektra and Coppel), restaurants (El Pollo Loco and Alsea), hotels (Hoteles City Express and Grupo Posadas), entertainment (KidZania and Cinépolis), television (Televisa and TV Azteca), information technology (Binbit and Softtek), telecommunications (América Móvil and Iusacell), consultancy (Sintec and Feher & Feher), and education (Universidad Nacional Autónoma de México and Tecnológico de Monterrey).

The Conclusions chapter summarizes the lessons that can be drawn from the comparison of this variety of firms and industries, and outlines new ideas gained from the comparative analyses. This chapter introduces a framework that explains the process of internationalization of emerging market firms and four upgrading strategies.

The process model presented in the Conclusions chapter proposes that the conditions of the home country influence the characteristics and behavior of managers, firms, and industries, and these, in turn, affect the upgrading of capabilities and subsequent internationalization. This process model results in the following lessons. The first is the contextuality of the processes that enable emerging market firms to upgrade capabilities and internationalize. Two salient conditions of emerging markets, their relative economic underdevelopment and their relative institutional weakness, affect firms directly through the upgrading of capabilities to international levels and internationalization, and indirectly through the interaction among managers, the company, and the industry. To be able to understand how firms in emerging markets can upgrade their capabilities to international levels and what particular patterns of internationalization they follow, we need to understand the conditions of the home country.

The second lesson is the importance of not only the company but also managers and the industry of operation as drivers of the upgrading of capabilities. Much of the research on emerging market multinationals seems to focus on the characteristics of the firm as the main driver of whether it can improve its competitiveness. However, the industry in which the firm operates exercises powerful influences as a driver of upgrading, particularly as the industry deregulates and exposes domestic firms to the rigors of international competition, bringing imports and foreign companies into their home country. At the same time, managers play a crucial role in deciding when and how to upgrade and how to interpret the pressures from outside the firm and changes in the conditions of the home country in their transformation of the competitiveness of the firm.

The third lesson is that competitiveness upgrading is at the base of the internationalization of the firm and serves both as an enabler and a driver. Upgrading is the enabler that helps the firm reach levels of competitiveness high enough to ensure its success abroad. Upgrading is also a driver of some international expansions in which the manager takes the firm abroad to obtain new technologies and connections with customers that can help it compete better at home. Thus, this dual relationship between upgrading and internationalization, in which upgrading is both an enabler and a driver of internationalization, can result in a positive reinforcing loop with upgrading leading to international expansion that in turn results in a higher upgrading and thus more internationalization.

The final lesson is the identification of a set of four strategies that enable emerging market firms to upgrade their competitiveness in support of their internationalization. These four strategies (Improvement, Integration, Inspiration, and Innovation) reflect differences in the locus and focus of capability upgrading. They can be used as guidance for other firms whose managers are considering transforming into multinationals and want to enhance the chances of success at this.

Although this is an academic book, the conclusions presented in each of the chapters and in the concluding chapter of the book can nevertheless be useful for consultants and managers of emerging market multinationals seeking to understand better how they can take companies abroad and make them successful multinationals. As the cases illustrate, the path to success is never a straight one. Rather than take the models discussed in the literature and try to fit them to the conditions of their companies, consultants and managers of emerging market firms may want to consider following the examples of other companies in emerging markets that faced similar home country conditions, such as MultiMexicans, and provide lessons that are more contextually appropriate for their firms. Managers and consultants first need to understand the sources of competitive advantage of the companies at home and then aim to upgrade these to international levels before considering an international expansion. This may not always ensure success abroad, but it will reduce the probability of failure. And when considering how to upgrade the source of advantage, they need to do so in a manner that takes into account not only the conditions of the company but also the conditions of the industry as well as their managerial abilities. Managers are the ones who make the decisions on whether, when, how, why, and where to internationalize their companies and who reap the rewards of successful effort. Even if there are apparent business opportunities in another country, the question is not whether such opportunities exist, but whether these are the right opportunities for the company. This requires preparation and the ability to run a more complex business. In some cases, it may be better not to take the company abroad when the sources of advantage are not transferable to other countries or when the company does not have enough internationally skilled managers and financial resources to support the foreign operation.

REFERENCES

Alon, I., Fetscherin, M. & Gugler, P. 2012. *Chinese International Investments.* New York, NY: Palgrave Macmillan.

AmericaEconomia. 2016. Las 500 mayores empresas de America Latina (The 500 largest firms from Latin America). AmericaEconomia, https://500.americaeconomia.com/

Anderson, E. & Gatignon, H. 1986. Modes of foreign entry: a transaction cost analysis and propositions. *Journal of International Business Studies,* 17: 1–26.

Aulakh, P. S. 2007. Emerging multinationals from developing economies: Motivations, paths and performance. *Journal of International Management,* 13: 235–240.

Backaler, J. 2014. *China Goes West: Everything You Need to Know About Chinese Companies Going Global.* New York, NY: Palgrave Macmillan.

Barnard, H. 2014. Migrating EMNCs and the theory of the multinational, in Cuervo-Cazurra, A. & Ramamurti, R. (Eds.), *Understanding Multinationals from Emerging Markets.* Cambridge: Cambridge University Press.

Barney, J. B. 1991. Firm resources and sustained competitive advantage. *Journal of Management*, 17: 99–120.

BCG. 2006. *The New Global Challengers: How 100 Top Companies from Rapidly Developing Economies Are Changing the World*. Boston, MA: Boston Consulting Group.

BCG. 2009. *The 2009 BCG 100, New Global Challengers: How Companies from Rapidly Developing Economies Are Contending for Global Leadership*. Boston, MA: Boston Consulting Group.

BCG. 2011. *BCG Global Challengers: Companies on the Move: Rising Stars from Rapidly Developing Economies are Reshaping Global Industries*. Boston, MA: Boston Consulting Group.

BCG. 2013. *Introducing the 2013 BCG Global Challengers*. Boston, MA: Boston Consulting Group.

Buckley, P. & Casson, M. 1976. *The Future of the Multinational Enterprise*. London: Macmillan.

Casanova, L. 2009. *Global Latinas: Latin America's Emerging Multinationals*. Fontainebleau, France: INSEAD Business Press.

Cavusgil, S. T. 1980. On the internationalization process of firms. *European Research*, 8: 273–281.

Chattopadhyay, A., Batra, R. & Ozsomer, A. 2012. *The New Emerging Market Multinationals: Four Strategies for Disrupting Markets and Building Brands*. New York, NY: McGraw Hill.

Cuervo-Cazurra A. 2011. Selecting the country in which to start internationalization: The non-sequential internationalization argument. *Journal of World Business*, 46: 426–437.

Cuervo-Cazurra, A. 2011. Internationalization process, in Kellermanns, F. & Mazzola, P. (Eds.), *Handbook of Strategy Process Research*. Northampton, MA: Edward Elgar, pp. 432–451.

Cuervo-Cazurra, A. 2012. How the analysis of developing country multinational companies helps advance theory: Solving the Goldilocks debate. *Global Strategy Journal*, 2: 153–167.

Cuervo-Cazurra, A. & Ramamurti, R. 2014. *Understanding Multinationals from Emerging Markets*. Cambridge: Cambridge University Press.

Cuervo-Cazurra, A. & Genc, M. 2008. Transforming disadvantages into advantages: Developing country MNEs in the least developed countries. *Journal of International Business Studies*, 39(6): 957–979.

Cyert, R. M. & March, J. G. 1963. *A Behavioral Theory of the Firm*. Englewood Cliffs, NJ: Prentice-Hall.

Czinkota, M. R. 1982. *Export Development Strategies: US Promotion Policies.* New York, NY: Praeger.

Dunning, J. 1977. Trade, location of economic activity and the MNE: A search for an eclectic approach, in B. Ohlin, P. O. Hesselborn & P. M. Wijkman (Eds.), *The International Allocation of Economic Activity.* London: Macmillan, pp. 395–418.

Dunning, J. H. 1981. Explaining the international direct investment position of countries: towards a dynamic and development approach. *Weltwirtschaftliches Archiv,* 117: 30–64.

Dunning, J. H. 2009. The key literature on IB activities: 1960–2000, in A. M. Rugman (Ed.), *Oxford Handbook of International Business.* Oxford: Oxford University Press.

Economist. 2008. Emerging-market multinationals: The challengers. *The Economist.* www.economist.com/node/10496684. Accessed February 19, 2013.

Economist. 2010. The emerging markets. *The Economist.* www.economist.com/node/17493411. Accessed September 10, 2013.

Eden, L. & Dai, L. 2010. Rethinking the O in Dunning's OLI/Eclectic Paradigm. *Multinational Business Review,* 18 (2): 13–34.

Fleury, A. & Fleury, M. L. 2011. *Brazilian Multinationals: Competences for Internationalization.* Cambridge: Cambridge University Press.

Forbes. 2006. The World's Biggest Public Companies. www.forbes.com/lists/2006/18/Rank_1.html. Accessed May 17, 2016.

Forbes. 2016. The Global 2000. www.forbes.com/global2000/#6b3cfaf1335d. Accessed May 17, 2016.

Forsgren, M. 2002. The concept of learning in the Uppsala Internationalization Process Model: A critical review. *International Business Review,* 257–277.

Gammeltoft, P., Barnard, H. & Madhok, A. 2010. Emerging multinationals, emerging theory: Macro- and micro-level perspectives. *Journal of International Management,* 16: 95–101.

García-Canal, E. & Guillén, M. F. 2008. Risk and the strategy of foreign location choice in regulated industries. *Strategic Management Journal,* 29(10): 1097–1115.

Grosse, R. E. & Mesquita, L. F. 2007. *Can Latin American Firms Compete?* Oxford: Oxford University Press.

Guillen, M. & García-Canal, E. 2012. *Emerging Markets Rule: Growth Strategies of the New Global Giants.* New York, NY: McGraw Hill.

Hennart, J. F. 1982. *A Theory of Multinational Enterprise.* Ann Arbor, MI: University of Michigan Press.

Hennart, J.-F. 2009a. Down with MNE-centric theories! Market entry and expansion as the bundling of MNE and local assets. *Journal of International Business Studies*, 40 (9): 1432–1454.

Hennart, J.-F. 2009b. Theories of the multinational enterprise, in A. M. Rugman (Ed.), *Oxford Handbook of International Business*. Oxford: Oxford University Press.

Holburn, G. L. F. & Zelner, B. A. 2010. Political capabilities, policy risk and international investment strategy: Evidence from the global electric power industry. *Strategic Management Journal* 31: 1290–1315.

Hoshino, T. 2001. *Industrialization and Private Enterprises in Mexico*. Chiba, Japan: Institute of Developing Economies, Japan External Trade Organization.

Hymer, S. 1976. *The International Operations of National Firms: A Study of Direct Foreign Investment*. Cambridge, MA: MIT Press.

Johanson, J. & Vahlne, J. E. 1977. The internationalization process of the firm: A model of knowledge development and increasing foreign market commitments. *Journal of International Business Studies*, 8: 23–32.

Johanson, J. & Vahlne, J. E. 2003. Business relationship learning and commitment in the internationalization process. *Journal of International Entrepreneurship*, 1: 83–101.

Khanna, T. & Palepu, K. G. 2010. *Winning in Emerging Markets: A Road Map for Strategy and Execution*. Boston, MA: Harvard University Press.

Knight, G. A. & Cavusgil, S. T. 1996. The Born Global firm: A challenge to traditional internationalization theory, in S. T. Cavusgil (Ed.), *Advances in International Marketing*, Vol. 8: 11–26. Greenwich, CT: JAI Press.

Kogut, B. & Zander, U. 1992. Knowledge of the firm, combinative capabilities, and the replication of technology. *Organization Science*, 3: 383–397.

Laçon, J. P. 2009. *Chinese Multinationals*. New Jersey: World Scientific.

Lessard, D. R. & Lucea, R. 2009. Mexican multinationals: Insights from CEMEX, in R. Ramamurti & J. V. Singh (Eds.), *Emerging Multinationals from Emerging Markets*. New York, NY: Cambridge University Press.

Luo, Y. & Tung, R. L. 2007. International expansion of emerging market enterprises: A springboard perspective. *Journal of International Business Studies*, 38: 481–498.

Luo, Y. & Wang, S. L. 2012. Foreign direct investment strategies by developing country multinationals: A diagnostic model for home country effects. *Global Strategy Journal*, 2: 244–261.

Madhok, A. & Keyhani, M. 2012. Acquisitions as entrepreneurship: asymmetries, opportunities, and the internationalization of multinationals from emerging economies. *Global Strategy Journal*, 2(1): 26–40.

Martin, X. 2014. Institutional advantage. *Global Strategy Journal*, 4(1): 55–69.

Mathews, J. A. 2006. Dragon multinationals: New players in 21st century globalization. *Asia Pacific Journal of Management*, 23: 5–27.

Melin, L. 1992. Internationalization as a strategy process. *Strategic Management Journal*, 13(Winter Special Issue): 99–118.

Meyer, K. E., Estrin, S., Bhaumik, S. K. & Peng, M. W. 2009. Institutions, resources, and entry strategies in emerging economies. *Strategic Management Journal*, 30(1): 61–80.

Nonaka, I. 1994. A dynamic theory of organizational knowledge creation. *Organization Science*, 5(1): 14–37.

O'Neill, J., Wilson, D., Purushothaman, R. & Stupnytska, A. 2005. How Solid are the BRICs? Global Economics Paper No: 134 Goldman Sachs. www.goldmansachs .com/our-thinking/archive/archive-pdfs/how-solid.pdf. Accessed April 18, 2018.

Oviatt, B. M. & McDougall, P. P. 1994. Toward a theory of international new ventures. *Journal of International Business Studies*, 25: 45–64.

Panibratov, A. 2012. *Russian Multinationals: From Regional Supremacy to Global Lead*. London: Routledge.

Peng, M. W., Wang, D. Y. L. & Jiang, Y. 2008. An institution-based view of international business strategy: a focus on emerging economies. *Journal of International Business Studies*, 39(5): 920–936.

Penrose, E. T. 1959. *The Theory of the Growth of the Firm*. Oxford: Oxford University Press.

Pradhan, J. P. 2008. *Indian Multinationals in the World Economy: Implications for Development*. New Delhi: Bookwell Publisher.

Prahalad, C. K. 2005. *The Fortune at the Bottom of the Pyramid: Eradicating Poverty through Profits*. Philadelphia, PA: Wharton Business School Press.

Ramamurti, R. 2012. What is really different about emerging market multinationals? *Global Strategy Journal*, 2: 41–47.

Ramamurti, R. & Singh, J. V. (Eds.) 2009. *Emerging Multinationals in Emerging Markets*, Cambridge: Cambridge University Press.

Ramsey, J. & Almeida, A. 2009. *The Rise of Brazilian Multinationals: Making the Leap from Regional Heavyweights to True Multinationals*. Rio de Janeiro: Elsevier.

Rugman, A. 2010. Do we need a new theory to explain emerging market MNEs? in K. P. Sauvant (Ed.), *Foreign Direct Investments from Emerging Markets: The Challenges Ahead*. New York, NY: Palgrave McMillan.

Rugman, A. M. & Verbeke, A. 1992. A note on the transnational solution and the transaction cost theory of multinational strategic management. *Journal of International Business Studies*, 23: 761–771.

Santiso, J. 2013. *The Decade of the Multilatinas*. Cambridge: Cambridge University Press.

Sauvant, K., Pradhan, Jaya P., Chatterjee, A. & Harley, B. 2010. *The Rise of Indian Multinationals: Perspectives on Indian Outward Foreign Direct Investment.* New York, NY: Palgrave Macmillan.

Teece, D. J. 1986. Transaction cost economics and the multinational enterprise: an assessment. *Journal of Economic Behavior and Organization*, 7: 21–45.

Vernon, R. 1966. International investment and international trade in the product cycle. *Quarterly Journal of Economics*, 80: 190–207.

Williamson, P., Ramamurti, R., Fleury, A. & Fleury, M. T. (Eds.) 2013. *The Competitive Advantage of Emerging Market Multinationals.* Cambridge: Cambridge University Press.

World Bank. 2017. Worldwide Governance Indicators. http://info.worldbank.org/governance/wgi/#home. Accessed September 13, 2017.

Yeung, A., Xin, K., Pfoertsch, W. & Liu, S. 2011. *The Globalization of Chinese Companies: Strategies for Conquering International Markets.* New York, NY: John Wiley.

Zaheer, S. 1995. Overcoming the liability of foreignness. *Academy of Management Journal*, 38(2): 341–363.

Zeng, M. & Williamson, P. 2007. *Dragons at Your Door.* Cambridge, MA: Harvard Business Press.

2 MultiMexicans
An Overview

Miguel A. Montoya and Jorge L. Alcaraz[1]

INTRODUCTION

MultiMexicans have increased their participation in foreign markets in recent decades. International changes and new conditions have motivated this growth. Among these conditions can be listed the market's liberalization, relaxation of rules, and the expansion of the global economy. Despite the growing trends, in academic terms, there is an important omission.

This book tries to bridge this gap in understanding how MultiMexicans have been expanding to foreign markets. Moreover, the following chapters reveal what other enterprises can learn from them in eventually expanding their productive activities abroad. Nevertheless, to accurately comprehend what is going on regarding MultiMexicans and how these firms are reaching foreign markets, it is necessary to examine domestic historical conditions and be aware of the characteristics of the firms under scrutiny.

This introductory chapter considers such matters. It examines the nature of the growth process of the Mexican economy since the *Porfiriato* era to recent years. During this time the Mexican economy has experienced all kind of situations, ranging from natural disasters, social, economic, and political problems to periods of growth, wealth, stability, and well-being.

The characteristics under examination at national and firm levels include domestic development and its relationship with the internationalization of domestic enterprises and the national policy addressed to support and promote the internationalization of national enterprises. At the firm level, companies are performing as business

[1]   Corresponding author

groups, and most of the enterprises have a family-owned structure. One more characteristic is the geographic allocation paths and distribution that MultiMexicans are following.

In general, this is the scenario depicted by Mexico and its multinational enterprises. It can give a general idea about the internationalization of Mexican enterprises and will help us to understand the particular processes and paths that different enterprises have followed in their internationalization, as studied in the following chapters.

BACKGROUND

Evolution of the Mexican Economy

During the last part of the nineteenth century and the first decade of the twentieth century, Mexico experienced a period known as *Porfiriato*. This period lasted from 1876 to 1911 and takes its name from the Mexican President in charge, Porfirio Díaz. During this time, Mexico was an authoritarian state with a personal dictatorship. It also established a protectionist commercial policy, consequently decreasing external competence. During the *Porfiriato* there was a significant increase of exports; also, the country received a significant amount of foreign direct investment (Kuntz, 2007). Another important contribution during the term of Díaz was the building of the railroad network connecting the main cities in the country to transport different products between these centers, and also to take merchandise to the ports or to the US border. The majority of the products transported by rail were for domestic consumption (Kuntz, 1995).

Another important feature of this time was the setup of the industrial sector, which began with textile factories, breweries, cigar factories, glass bottles, paper, and basic chemical products, to name a few. At this time some monopolies began to take shape, such as Cervecería Cuauhtémoc (brewery), Vidriera Monterrey (glass bottles), Compañía Industrial Jabonera de la Laguna (one of the world's most important producers of soap), Cemex (cement), Fundidora Monterrey (steel), and United Shoe (shoes and boots). Other important industries were supported by foreign capital, such as the oil, rail, and mining industries. The market of capitals grew as well, and some of the main banks of the period were Banco de Londres y México and the Banco Nacional de México (Banamex) (Haber, 2010).

Notwithstanding the above trends, for the last part of the *Porfiriato*, things started to get worse due to different events. There were strikes in 1906 (Cananea, a mine) and 1907 (Río Blanco, a textile firm), where the workpeople tried to defend their labor rights; the recession in 1907 decreased industrial production; there was a poor harvest in 1909; and in 1910 food prices increased because of droughts. In 1910 the Mexican Revolution took place, mainly driven by the social unconformity regarding political issues and dispossession of land. The *Porfiriato* ended in 1911 when Porfirio Díaz left the country because of the Revolution (Knight, 2010).

The next decade was shaped by civil wars and political, social, and economic instability. Some of the problems from this period, according to Knight (2010), were as follows: (a) the population declined as some people moved to Mexico City and to the USA; (b) the economic impact of the Revolution between 1916 and 1917 yielded the lowest GDP of the time; (c) the government's small budget inhibited investment in important areas; (d) in financial terms, gold and silver changed to fiat money, resulting in inflation in 1916, embezzlement of banks by the revolutionaries and the withdrawal of money by the rich, leading to a collapse of the banks as a consequence; (e) the railroad network and commerce in general were also seriously affected; (f) crop production (corn and beans) decreased during 1917 and 1918; (g) tax increased; (h) mining exports decreased, though they experienced a quick recovery because of the First World War; and furthermore, (i) the Spanish flu also had an awful influence in Mexico between 1918 and 1919.

In spite of all the above, exports did not experience serious problems. This was also the case for henequen and oil: since their production took place near the seashore, they were easier to export. And surprisingly, the industrial sector was not severely damaged; the monopolies and oligopolies remained after the Mexican Revolution (Haber, 1992). The recovery began after 1917, once the new Constitution was enacted.

In the following decade, better conditions were established. During the presidencies of Obregon (1920–4) and Calles (1924–8), the country received important investment from multinational enterprises such as ASARCO, Ford, and Colgate Palmolive (Knight, 2010). Exports increased, but not in all sectors; for instance, there was no increase in the oil sector, which instead turned to Venezuela. The internal market improved along with better conditions for the population, including investement in education and health. Important institutions were created: the *Banco de México* in 1925 and the *Partido Nacional Revolucionario* (PNR) in 1929, which later would become the *Partido Revolucionario Institucional* (PRI). The 1920s brought a modest improvement in the national structure; nevertheless, at the end of this decade, the country suffered the negative effects of the Great Depression (Rosenzweig, 1989).

A remarkable change began in the following period. In the presidencies of Portes (1928–30), Ortiz (1930–2), and Rodriguez (1934–6), Mexico adopted import substitution: a policy that aimed to undertake an internal development enhancing domestic enterprises and the internal market. The creation of institutions continued; examples included *Nacional Financiera* and *Banco Nacional de Comercio Exterior* as well as social institutions like the Confederation of Workers of Mexico, to name just a few (de la Peña & Aguirre, 2006). Some state-owned enterprises were also created: *Comisión Federal de Electricidad, Petróleos de México (Pemex)* and *Ferrocarriles Nacionales de México* (Marichal, 2003).

These last two enterprises, *Pemex* and *Ferrocarriles Nacionales de México*, reflected the new political and economic regime during the Cardenas period (1934–40), the expropriation, which represented a sense of national ideological ownership; a nationalism (Delgado, 2003). All the changes in this decade created the foundations for the development of the Mexican economy in the following years.

Furthermore, these changes played a key part in managing the effects of the Second World War.

During the period of the Second World War, under the presidency of Avila (1940–6), there was an increase in exports (a growth of 170 percent from 1938 to 1945) and the country received considerable amounts of foreign capital (a growth of 106 percent from 1939 to 1945) from investment in more stable countries, compared with those that were suffering the direct consequences of the war. Consequently, national income increased (a growth of 96 percent from 1939 to 1945), as did international reserves (a growth of 763 percent from 1938 to 1945). And this was helpful in establishing the industrialization era. After 1945, when the Second World War was over, imports started to increase and exports to decrease. At this point, a new political regime began: protectionism.

For the following decades, under the presidencies of Aleman (1946–52), Ruiz (1952–8), Lopez M. (1958–64), and Diaz O. (1964–70), Mexico started to achieve great outcomes; this was a period of bonanza in the country. The role of the government was overriding: it conducted investment for infrastructure, health, and education, and encouraged the creation of new enterprises through subsidies, tax exemptions, and credits provided by the development bank. It is important also to mention the political stability and the protection for home industries supplying the domestic market during this period. All these measures drove the country to reach average annual growths of about 6.7 percent of real GDP from 1958 to 1970 and stable inflation of about 2.5 percent (Solís 2000).

The protectionism and its consequent captive market promoted an oligopolistic market, structure, expensive products with low quality, a limited market and growing unprofitability in some enterprises due to controversial relationships between unions and government. Also, the continuous and progressive decrease in exports, as a product of the agriculture industry's deterioration and the increasing gap between savings and investment, drove the country to get into more and more external debt. Finally, two more problems arose: the corruption relating to the protectionism and the uneven distribution of wealth (Cárdenas, 1996).

Nevertheless, things were going to get worse. It is common in the literature to refer to the period between 1970 and 1982 as "la docena trágica" (the tragic dozen years of the presidencies of Echeverria, 1970–6, and Lopez P., 1976–82). During this time, even with the stated problems, Mexico retained the same policy of increasing public spending, funded by the printing of new money and rising wages. In the early 1970s the peso was increasing in value: a situation that worsened with the US dollar's devaluation after the Bretton Woods system concluded and with the increase of oil prices in 1973. Consequently, imports moved up and exports went down, affecting the deficit and, as usual, increasing external debt. The GDP growth rates decreased and inflation went from 6.8 percent in 1972 to 31.2 percent in 1977. The situation was unsustainable and the partial solution was one more devaluation in 1976 (Blanco, 1981).

This last devaluation had an impact, once again, in terms of higher inflation and depressive effects. But then, in 1978, oil reserves were found in the country that, along with increasing oil prices, allowed the country once again to gain access to external funding. The actions taken by the government were, again, public investment (augmented 25.7 percent in 1981) and increase of imports needed to improve and upgrade the oil industry, and, even when oil exports augmented considerably, the government had to take on more external debt (US$10,800 million in 1981). The expansion of public investment was also causing public deficit and, at the same time, indirectly encouraging domestic firm production and with it imports of capital assets (Cárdenas, 2010).

There were no worries or warnings at all; both government and general thinking was that oil prices would continue to grow, and that was good enough to maintain the same pace. However, two unexpected events were about to happen: an increase in interest rates and a decrease in oil prices. These two factors were sufficiently to render the Mexican debt unpayable. A similar situation occurred with enter-prises that had external credit: their debt went too high.

A new forced depreciation occurred in 1982: the exchange rate went from 26.91 to 47 pesos per dollar. But the government was going to take one last desperate action to try to save the situation. Due to the conditions, and considering the continuous withdrawal of money from banks, the government decided to expropriate the banks in Mexico.

The expropriation was a sign of mistrust and risk for other industries, as one effect was that foreign capitals started to leave the country. Regarding imports, a natural reaction was a decrease, but exports suffered as well since oil exports represented up to two thirds of the total. The situation got worse in 1986 when the oil price went down from US$30 per barrel to US$10 per barrel, approximately. During the presidency of de la Madrid (1982–8) the GDP annual growth was close to zero (Mancera, 2009).

To overcome the situation, it was necessary for the International Monetary Fund (IMF) to intervene, and the government had to sign an Intention Letter. In return for this intervention, Mexico was required to conduct programs addressed at reducing inflation and the current account deficit. All the measures and programs developed by the Mexican government had to follow the principles of the Washington Consensus: openness, deregulation, privatization, and – a requirement aimed at developing countries – macroeconomic stabilization (Schettino, 2002).

In terms of openness, Mexico signed up to the General Agreement on Tariffs and Trade (GATT) in 1986. Later, in 1990, during the presidency of Gortari (1988–94), negotiations for a trade agreement with the United States began. Then, in 1992, the North American Free Trade Agreement (NAFTA) was signed, and enacted in 1994 (Arriaga, 1994). Regarding the deregulation, the Mexican Constitution has had several changes making the rules less restrictive, encouraging interna-tional commerce, international movement of capital, and global inte-gration. This is the case with foreign direct investment: changes in the

Constitution have enabled more participation in shares and industries. Concerning privatization, Mexico had many state-owned enterprises that were privatized. Some examples are Telmex, Altos Hornos de México, Aeroméxico, Mexicana, DINA and also the banks that were expropriated.

Then, stemmed by the measures taken and programs conducted, the general economic conditions had a significant recovery. The annual inflation decreased from 159.2 percent in 1987 to 51.2 percent in 1988 and the real GDP increased by 1.4 percent in 1988 and 3.3 percent the year after. In 1989, the public deficit decreased to 5.6 percent. The privatization of banks and negotiations with the USA in relation with a commercial relationship had positive effects on the perception of the country. Then, in 1990 the real GDP grew even more, reaching 4.5 percent (Cárdenas, 2010).

Mexico was doing well; however, since 1992, two situations have attracted attention: inflation and overvaluation of the Mexican peso. Trends in the balance of trade were worsening: its increasing deficit went from US$6,939 million in 1991 to US$15,753 million in 1992, and US$13,481 million in 1993 (American Chamber of Commerce of Mexico, 1995). In addition, the *Zapatista* rebellion (fighting for human rights of indigenous people in Chiapas) in 1994 and the political murders in the same year harmed the image that Mexico was building of being a good place to do business, increasing the distrust from business people. Consequently, serious divestments took place in the country, affecting the international reserves.

The result was a severe depreciation of the Mexican peso in 1994 at the start of the Zedillo presidency (1994–2000). The financial market was driven crazy. There was serious uncertainty that caused an important capital flight, an increase in interest rates, an intense investment in dollars, and the Mexican Stock Market fell, among others. Late in 1994, a floating exchange rate was established in order to balance the market. The outcome was not positive, however; the uncertainty increased and the peso suffered a series of continuous depreciations (Delgado, 2003).

The economy in the country was devastated (the GDP fell in proportion by about 6 to 7 percent in 1994 and inflation grew by about seven times in 1995 as a consequence of the year before), and once again, external intervention was needed to solve the problem. Of course, Mexico had to follow certain rules to get this external assistance, which included fiscal and monetary changes. To close with a flourish, the depreciation of the peso and the strained financial system led to a hard banking crisis. Fortunately, just a couple of years later, there were signs of recovery, in large part due to exports, which were mainly addressed to the USA.

In 2000, and after 74 years in power, the hegemonic party (PRI) left the presidency to transfer power to a party center-right (conservative National Action Party, PAN). However, no important changes occurred in economic or investment attraction policies. The new government of President Vicente Fox (2000–6) did not make any central economic or regulatory changes, despite the shift in ideological climate (Moreno-Brid & Ros, 2009).

At the beginning of the current century, the Mexican economy was doing well, with steady growth, low inflation, a balanced government budget, and a stable peso price. Nevertheless, Mexico had some other problems: high crime and high corruption levels, inequality, non-productivity growth, and monopolies. Education was the weakest among the OECD countries. State income was decreasing because of the noninvestment in Pemex; there was no technology for exploration or refinery modernization. Mexico needed reforms but the president did not have enough representation in the lower house and Congress refused most of his proposals.

When the next president arrived, Felipe Calderon (2006–12), things did not go well. Calderon proposed some other reforms but Congress did not pass them. He also declared a war on drugs, which caused high levels of violence, and did not help the economic situation given investor confidence. In 2008, the crisis that originated in the American banking system hit Mexico's economy. The GDP growth for Mexico in 2008 was 1.4 percent and in 2009 there was a fall of

4.7 percent (IMF). By 2010 and in subsequent years, however, the economy seemed to be making a recovery.

By 2012, President Enrique Peña Nieto arrived (his period will finish in 2018). He had the majority in the Congress, so he could implement the structural reforms that his predecessors could not. Reforms in education, energy, telecommunications, fiscal, and political matters were accepted. These reforms were criticized by some as insufficient. Nevertheless, the effects of these reforms will take time to appear.

Evolution of Mexican Outward FDI

This is what has happened with the evolution of the Mexican economy. Now is the time to check on the historical behavior in terms of outward FDI in Mexico. Even when investments abroad and the participation of multinational enterprises have been growing, compared with developed economies, Mexico is far behind other countries. More even behavior is seen in Mexico, India, Malaysia, and South Africa, which show similar outcomes in terms of OFDI. China and Singapore, along with the developed countries, maintain a significant distance from Mexico. It is important to bear in mind that MNEs are looking for both developing and developed countries (mostly because of location advantages) in which to establish their facilities (Bonaglia, Goldstein & Mathews, 2007).

Among emerging economies in the American Continent, Brazil, Chile, and Mexico are the most important FDI issuers. In Latin America, these three countries are responsible for 75 percent of the whole OFDI (UNCTAD, 2015). The country with the largest OFDI is Brazil, behavior that results in coherent thinking about world trends (countries with bigger economic growth are countries with bigger outward FDI). Mexico is a following country, and although its OFDI is smaller, it has important enterprises at the world level. These enterprises are study cases for both scholars and practitioners.

The evolution of Mexican direct investment abroad, in general terms, during the first two decades after such investment began (with

UCTAD Stat in 1980), formed a steady and almost immovable trend: there were no noticeable investments. Nevertheless, it is interesting to note that an important growth of FDI abroad starts in the early twenty-first century. Over these years, a continuous growth path was clear, with understandable downfalls relating to global crises (2001, 2008, and 2010). Basically, Mexican OFDI is split in both developed and developing countries, and most of the Mexican investment is addressed to developed countries. The next section provides a detailed description of Mexican OFDI by country of destination; see also Table 2.1. Other general behaviors followed by MultiMexicans are addressed as well.

UNDERSTANDING THE INTERNATIONALIZATION OF MEXICAN ENTERPRISE

MultiMexicans share general characteristics that, to a greater or lesser extent, are shaping their internationalization paths. The next section checks these characteristics precisely in order to suitably comprehend the behavior of MultiMexicans in the following chapters. The general scenarios studied here, which are going to provide us with the needed information, are as follows: domestic development, geographical destination, home country measures, business groups, and family business and social ties.

Mexican Multinational Enterprise and Domestic Development

There are studies in which entrepreneurial expansion is seen as a proxy for a country's appropriate economic development. In this sense, the national development can provide some useful insights to understand, to some degree, the internationalization of domestic enterprises. However, applying this to the Mexican case, many doubts arise.

These doubts are because Mexico's development is not congruent with the Mexican enterprises' participation abroad, considering that just a handful of MultiMexicans are among the most important in the whole world, in terms of both foreign assets and transnationality

Table 2.1 *Mexican FDI stock abroad, by geographical destination*

Region/economy	2009	2010	2011	2012
World	84 479	110 014	100 188	131 106
Developed economies	55 933	73 729	60 741	79 555
Europe	12 690	28 939	29 002	35 667
European Union	9 929	28 606	26 858	30 758
Austria	35	11	11	870
Czech Republic	308	..	36	..
France	..	9	9	–1 174
Germany	1 070	246	304	681
Hungary	1 142	1 993	1 929	1 759
Ireland	1 157	..	..	..
Netherlands	2 143	8 430	5 852	13 665
Poland	39	..	39	..
Slovakia	..	..	42	..
Spain	3 123	17 591	18 417	17 457
United Kingdom	913	327	217	–2 498
Other developed Europe	2 762	333	2 144	4 909
Switzerland	2 762	333	2 144	4 909
North America	43 242	44 790	31 740	43 888
Canada	63	132	116	115
United States	43 179	44 658	31 624	43 773
Developing economies	..	34 058	32 694	40 474
Asia	..	–4	67	125
East Asia	..	–4	48	95
China	..	–4	48	95
South Asia	..	..	19	31
India	..	..	19	31
Latin America and the Caribbean	24 360	34 062	32 627	40 349
South America	18 941	24 370	26 090	34 154
Argentina	792	235	388	699
Brazil	13 194	16 186	17 827	22 377
Chile	1 179	1 773	3 008	4 815
Colombia	2 848	4 105	3 747	3 156
Ecuador	441	913	963	1 387

Table 2.1 (*cont.*)

Region/economy	2009	2010	2011	2012
Paraguay	..	..	..	76
Peru	742	802	–172	1 248
Uruguay	..	..	..	38
Venezuela Bolivarian Rep.		–256	356	329
Central America	2 936	3 243	3 391	5 220
Costa Rica	357	177	554	1 046
El Salvador	672	897	675	945
Guatemala	864	930	1 023	1 040
Honduras	397	416	651	1 310
Nicaragua	352	384	344	357
Panama	293	439	145	522
Caribbean	2 483	6 449	3 146	974
Dominican Republic	2 321	2 577	2 310	1 035
Jamaica	162	..	..	–61
Netherlands Antilles	..	3 351	..	..
Puerto Rico	..	512	536	..
Unspecified	4 187	2 228	6 752	11 076

Data in millions of US dollars
Source: UNCTAD FDI/TNC database, based on data from Banco de México.

index. For instance, América Móvil and Cemex are the only two Mexican enterprises to have been part of the world's top 100 non-financial TNCs, in 2012 (UNCTAD, 2013). And concerning the top 100 non-financial TNCs from developing economies and transition economies, 2012, only América Móvil, Cemex, Grupo FEMSA, and Bimbo make the rankings (UNCTAD, 2014).

What is important to point out is that these firms' global participation is not necessarily a reflection of the "excellent Mexican economic development." Thus, it would not be a good decision to conduct an analysis linking Mexican economic development with

MNEs, considering only these enterprises. In fact, it would be better to include, at least, all the most important MultiMexicans.

With this consideration in mind, the idea becomes clearer that enterprise expansion is related to home country economic development. That is, América Móvil, Cemex, Grupo FEMSA, and Bimbo are only a few cases that represent all the MNEs in Mexico. Therefore, only a few enterprises have international impact and, in accordance with the supposition above, this is due to the low economic development that Mexico has had.

It is important to keep in mind that América Móvil has emerged as an enterprise stemmed from Telmex, a state-owned enterprise that was privatized in 1990. The main shareholder of this enterprise is one of the richest men in the world, Carlos Slim Helú, and is also the main shareholder of Carso Global Telecom and Grupo Carso. This could also be a reflection of a poor political system.

In this discussion of deficiencies, it is important to comment that, in the literature of multinational enterprises from emerging markets, one of the reasons why enterprises from these countries want to allocate their investments to other countries is because the home market has limitations for their own growth. Among these limitations are considered institutional deficiencies, deficiencies in political systems, economical limitations, inter alia. In this regard, it wouldn't be surprising to find that one of the drivers for some Mexican enterprises in trying to go abroad is a desire to diminish the risks of conducting business in the home market, such as a poor political system.

There are now two positions to consider: the first one states that there is a direct relationship between domestic development and home enterprises' participation abroad (Dunning & Lundan, 2008); economic development grows, and home enterprises' participation abroad grows as well. The second position is that poor national structural conditions will force home enterprises to find better markets abroad (Luo & Tung, 2007).

There are unquestionably numerous shortcomings in Mexico, and maybe some enterprises are exploring different countries because of this. On the other hand, one way or another, some characteristics in the country have evolved over the years: for instance, growth of the home market, which allows enterprises to grow at a national level, thus improving their inner characteristics and building the needed advantages to go abroad. In this sense, maybe Mexican development has not been so great, meaning that there is only a small number and limited amount of participation of Mexican enterprises abroad. And maybe one proxy that could be reflecting this whole situation is the serious lack of information and records about Mexican firms performing abroad. What is certain is that there is an important field to study regarding the MultiMexicans and the drivers for their internationalization.

Anyway, it is important to mention that the internationalization depends not only on the enterprises; there are several situations that an enterprise should be aware of. The home country's structural evolution is one of them, and it is no small matter; the home environment plays such an important role in the expansion of domestic enterprises that it can even have a direct effect on firms' internationalization behavior (Luo, Xue & Han, 2010).

Mexican Enterprise and Geographical Destination

Regarding classic explanations about MNE behavior, enterprises from developing countries should in theory, precisely because of their level, address their investments to countries with a similar or lower degree of development. However, based on UNCTAD's Bilateral FDI Statistics (2014), Mexican FDI (stock) abroad by geographical destination (see Table 2.1) is following a different path. Specifically, from 2009 to 2012, according to available information, 63.4 percent of Mexican investment has been looking for developed economies (own calculations based on UNCTAD Stats). About 31 percent of the total investment goes to Latin America and the Caribbean, and the remaining percentage to other unspecified countries.

Regarding the investment issued to developed countries by Mexican enterprises, 39 percent goes to Europe, where the main host countries are Spain (21 percent), the Netherlands (11 percent), and Switzerland (3.76 percent). The remaining 61 percent is for North America, where the USA is receiving 60.5 percent of the Mexican investment among developed countries.

In the case of developing countries, almost the whole investment is for Latin America; the Caribbean and Asian countries receive about 3 percent. In Latin America, Brazil is the one attracting most investment, namely 53 percent. After Brazil, percentages decrease considerably: the following country is Colombia, at around 10.5 percent, then Chile at 8 percent. Other countries in the region are receiving lower amounts of investment; however, what is interesting to highlight here is that there are many countries in Latin America where Mexican enterprises are spreading out (Ecuador, Peru, Costa Rica, El Salvador, Guatemala, Dominican Republic, to name a few).

Even when the participation is lower in these countries compared, for instance, with the USA, the relevant issue is that investments are increasing in most of the Latin American countries, which may potentially be a new trend for Mexican investments. This could be showing that enterprises are doing well in these countries, and this might at the same time be a stimulus for other enterprises to invest in those countries.

Table 2.1 also shows that investments in North America are not significantly changing, except in 2011 (which, incidentally, is a downturn). But then, in most Latin America countries, investments are continually increasing. In the case of Mexican investments in countries in the European Union, at aggregate level there seems to be a growing trend; at country level this behavior is not clear from the results. Mexican investors should turn their attention to Latin America for growing opportunities.

Table 2.2 shows the participation of enterprises (foreign assets) by industry, where basically telecommunications is the industry with the biggest contribution (América Móvil: 39.3%). The following industries are the nonmetallic minerals (Cemex, Cementos de Chihuahua: 23.4%), Beverage industry (Grupo FEMSA, Arca: 10.6%),

Table 2.2 *Mexico: Foreign assets of the top 20 multinationals by main industry, 2013*

Industry	Foreign assets (US$ million)	Number of Companies	Companies
Telecommunications	56,000	1	América Móvil
Nonmetallic minerals	33,275	2	Cemex, Cementos Chihuahua
Beverages	15,158	2	Grupo FEMSA, Arca
Mining	14,083	1	Grupo México
Food	9,666	3	Bimbo, Gruma, Alsea
Diversified	5,005	4	Alfa, Xignux, Kuo, Grupo Cars
Chemical & petrochemicals	4,229	1	Mexichem
Oil & gas	1,786	1	Pemex
Steel & metal products	1,609	2	Industrias CH, Altos Hornos de México
Retail trade	721	1	Elektra
Engineering & construction services	697	1	ICA
Auto parts	147	1	San Luis Corp.
Total	**142,376**	**20**	

Source: Basave & Gutiérrez-Haces (2013). Changing Characteristics of Large Mexican Multinationals during Legal Reforms (2015).

and Mining (Grupo México: 9.9%) with similar contributions. The rest of the industries keep falling.

By relating industries to the geographic allocation of Mexican enterprises, several behaviors can be found. For instance, enterprises from the same industry participate in different regions to different extents (nonmetallic minerals). One can also find similar levels of participation in the same region (beverage industry). Perhaps neither

Table 2.3 *Evolution of the Mexican economy*

Year	Event
1876	Porfirio Diaz, Mexico President. Porfiriato begins, and lasts for over 30 years.
1910	Mexican Revolution. Porfiriato ends.
1911–1919	Economy declines because of civil wars.
1917	New Constitution. (The most recent one.)
1925	Banco de Mexico (Central Bank) is created.
1929	Partido Nacional Revolucionario (now Partido Revolucionario Institucional, PRI) is created.
1930	Effects of Great Depression. Mexico begins import substitution policy.
1938	Oil expropriation. Petroleos de Mexico is created.
1939	Exports increase because of Second World War.
1945	Exports decline and "proteccionismo" begins.
1958–1970	Economic stability; 6.7% annual growth.
1970–1982	Economic destabilization. Inflation out of control, devaluation, big debt.
1982	Peso devaluation. Government expropriates the banks in Mexico.
1986	Washington Consensus principles. Mexico signs General Agreement on Tariffs and Trade.
1990	Privatization of some enterprises. Negotiations for a trade agreement with USA begin.
1994	North American Free Trade Agreement (NAFTA) starts. Devaluation of Mexican Peso.
1995	Tequila Crisis.
1996	Economic recovery.
2000	President Vicente Fox arrives. New party in the government (National Action Party, PAN) after 70 years of hegemony.
2006	Felipe Calderon arrives to the Mexican Presidency (he was a PAN member).
2008	Economic crisis because of American banking system.
2009	Economic recovery.
2012	Enrique Peña Nieto is appointed to Mexican Presidency (PRI member).

the particular industry nor the region is enough to clearly identify specific trends. Regarding the region, it ought to be better to check countries instead of regions. Furthermore, these differences suggest that more specific features should also be considered, such as ownership advantages in each single case when trying to identify such behaviors in multinational enterprises.

Most Mexican investment is aimed at developed countries; however, in terms of regions, it is interesting that from the overall Mexican investment abroad, the USA receives about 38 percent, Latin America and the Caribbean 31 percent, and Europe 25 percent. Considering the industry, a clear trend cannot be observed regarding the region of allocation; however, this may be happening because there are just a few multinational enterprises operating in each industry. The diversified industry (see Table 2.2) is the one with the greatest number of multinational companies, and there are only four in this category (Alfa, Xignux, Kuo, and Grupo Carso).

One final point is that if we consider Mexican companies looking for investment from foreign regions in terms of cultural distance, the countries that fulfill this characteristic will be the Latin American and Caribbean ones, and Spain; these countries are currently receiving approximately 44 percent. Let's also keep in mind that at least some of the investment addressed to the USA will certainly be targeted at Mexican migrants and other Latin American people, which is in line with the above statement. Furthermore, linking geographic proximity and institutional proximity with cultural distance could strengthen the point that the USA is the most important destination for Mexican investments abroad.

Home Country Measures and the Mexican Multinational Enterprise

Other aspects that generally seem to have an important impact on enterprise expansion abroad are the policies addressed to promote the internationalization process by home enterprises. These kinds of actions are more frequently found in developed countries.

Nevertheless, developing countries are increasingly becoming aware of the importance of governmental support for home enterprises to boost their expansion to foreign countries through outward FDI. Such measures, developed and implemented by home governments supporting domestic enterprises going abroad strictly in the form of outward FDI, are known as Home Country Measures (HCMs).

In Mexico, the government organization supporting national enterprise participation abroad is ProMéxico. It was established in 2007 as a public trust institution, controlled by the Secretariat of Economy. The main tasks of ProMéxico are to strength the country's image, the attraction of foreign capital, promotion of national exports, and the internationalization of the Mexican enterprise.

In this last case, the support offered by ProMéxico for internationalization through direct investment abroad is addressed either for enterprises that are already internationalized or for enterprises that have not yet internationalized. In the first case, enterprises have access to services like international promotion, advertising, and scheduling meetings with foreign customers. Also, ProMéxico offers legal, technical, and marketing advice, business planning, business trips, and rent of offices abroad, among other services. Basically, these are measures in place for exports in both cases: internationalized and not-yet-internationalized enterprises.

Advice is available for enterprises planning to go abroad, although already internationalized firms can also access this support. These measures include information about foreign markets, matchmaking services, intellectual property advice, viability studies, and networking with foreign governments.

In line with this information, there is one document which points out that the instruments used by ProMéxico for export promotion are also used by Mexican enterprises looking to establish their production activities abroad (CEPAL, 2012). Perhaps it has something to do with the fact that the other document mentions that in Mexico, besides the NAFTA, it has never been a strong policy addressed specifically to support the home enterprise internationalization (CEPAL, 2014).

Commercial agreements are a kind of policy favoring OFDI (Manfra & Fitzmaurice, 2007). In this sense, thinking strictly about NAFTA and considering exports as the stage immediately prior to FDI, it is probable that some Mexican enterprises – having business activities in the USA already – have taken advantage of the NAFTA, at least indirectly, to expand their operations.

The reason why policies addressing OFDI promotion must be created should relate to the fact that home enterprise internationalization will bring important benefits not only for the enterprise itself but also for the home country. These benefits could favor the development of skills, knowledge, incomes, and competitiveness, which at a higher level will favor the country (UNCTAD, 2007). We suggest that the creation of specific policies must embrace a holistic program to ensure that firms and countries get the potential benefits.

Mexican Multinational Enterprises and Business Groups

Alfa, Grupo Carso, Grupo México, and Grupo Televisa share a common characteristic: they are Business "Groups." This is a peculiarity of several MultiMexicans, and probably one of their strengths. It is possible that being part of a Group allows a firm to increase and generate knowledge, better practices, and skills, and not only the generation of these characteristics but also the transference of these intangible assets as well as tangible ones. Furthermore, there is the effect that being part of a business group could have in the internationalization of the affiliated enterprises.

Mexican business groups are not a new phenomenon; there have been business groups in the country for many decades. In 1911, the Garza Sada Group founded Vidriera Monterrey, basically to manufacture glass bottles for Cervecería Cuauhtémoc (incidentally, the group had its beginnings with this brewery). In 1929 the group established two subsidiaries, and a further one in 1936. Then, in 1938, the group was split in two: *Fomento de Industria y Comercio, S.A. (FICSA)* with four enterprises, and *Valores Industriales, S.A. (VISA)* holding twelve firms. Some other firms that this group founded were *Alfa, Seguros Monterrey*, and *Banca Serfín* (Basave, 2001).

During the period of economic expansion and industrialization in Mexico, several firms were established and consolidated, and several business groups were founded as well. Some national groups, identified and privately owned by 1970, included the following (showing the number of subsidiaries in parentheses): Cervecería Cuauhtémoc/Hojalata y Lámina (50), Vidriera Monterrey (32), Fundidora Monterrey (56), Cananea (25), ICA (53), Cremi 29, Grupo Modelo (41), Cementos de Chihuahua (41), TAMSA (38), Saltillo (14), and Cydsa (21) (Cordero, Santin & Tirado, 1981).

Grupo Vitro, for example, is an enterprise with more of a century of history: it started to export in 1935 and in 1985 established a sales subsidiary in the USA. All the experience gathered by Vitro was unquestionably shared and used by the other affiliated companies. In the case of Grupo Simec, this enterprise was acquired by Industrias CH in 2001; by 2006, both enterprises had become the leading special bar quality steel manufacturers in America. Grupo Carso, along with other investors, took part of Telmex's privatization, and afterwards, during 2000, Telmex allowed the creation of América Móvil. Thus, it is easy to see how being part of a business group could bring positive effects.

These business groups are diversified clusters, yet at the same time are part of a holding. Different kinds of enterprise can frequently be found within the same group: for instance, financial or manufacturing enterprises. Talking about financial enterprises that belong to a group, there are many examples; for instance: Grupo Gruma, which holds an important part of Banorte; Elektra, which manages the financial institution named Banco Azteca; Grupo Carso with Banco Inbursa and Casa de Bolsa Inbursa. The fact that a business group holds a financial institution as an affiliated enterprise probably eases the access to funding for other affiliates.

Business groups generate and provide an environment with different advantages needed for internationalization, and affiliates can take advantage of these benefits, letting them compete with other enterprises at home and abroad (Yiu, 2011). A group can develop and provide resources to other inner players, supplying specific and strategic conditions. These resources are not easy to replicate by enterprises outside the group (Zhou, Witteloostuijn & Jianhong, 2013). In spite of this, the literature suggests ambiguity on the part of business groups and influence on members regarding the wide range of potential positive effects (Khana & Rivkin, 2001).

In this vein, it will be highly important to check on the MultiMexicans that are part of a business group and to explore whether there have been any positive effects with respect to these members supporting and boosting their development through the creation of competitive advantages. It is also important to be aware of whether these groups have had any influence on Mexican enterprises going abroad.

Family Business and Social Ties in Mexican Multinational Enterprises

The family-owned structure is quite a common characteristic in Mexican firms. In the early twentieth century, most Mexican firms were family-owned (Marichal & Cerrutti, 1997) – multinational enterprises among them. More recently, most of the enterprises (around 80 percent) in Mexico's stock index are family-owned or owned by an individual, including companies such as Grupo Bimbo, Grupo Elektra, and Industrias Peñoles (Comlay, 2011). It is also important to mention that the Mexican government was the owner of several enterprises which, during privatization, changed to being family-owned (such as Telmex, AHMSA, and TV Azteca).

In Mexican firms, the president of the board holds also the larger part of the shares, about 35 percent of the board members are part of the president's family, 38 percent of them are executive managers, and 57 percent are employees (Castañeda, 2000). With this, given that the family-owned structure is so common and relevant in Mexican enterprises, including multinationals, means that it is important to examine this characteristic to understand the process.

According to Sargent & Ghaddar (2001), given the small number of MultiMexicans representing a considerable percentage of the overall OFDI issued, and the relatively small group of people participating in these activities, it represents an extremely closed elite. Consequently, in this elite it is very common that entrepreneurs with key charges (CEOs, directors, presidents, etc.) are the sons or daughters, brothers or sisters, cousins, or in general, other direct family members of the main shareholders of the enterprise.

Members of the board of directors probably have family ties as well. In this sense, and returning to the extremely close elite, it would be relatively common for people from different key positions in different enterprises or Groups to have personal relationships, thereby indirectly strengthening business ties. Moreover, family ties could represent an important source of advantages enabling enterprises to enhance their results (Arregle, Batjargal, Hitt et al., 2013).

The family-owned structure could mean a source of competitive advantages (Poza, Hanlon & Kishida, 2004). Mexican family-owned enterprises have been shown to have interestingly positive results in terms of performance (Martin & Duran, 2015), demonstrating that the ownership structure to some extent is related to the output of the firm. Moreover, comparing family- and non-family-owned enterprises in Mexico, it is possible to find results where family firms have better economic performance than non-family firms (Espinoza & Espinoza, 2012). In fact, the family business structure could provide specific and better conditions in a firm compared with a non-family business (Aldrich & Cliff, 2012).

It is interesting to see that there are several MultiMexicans owned by families; and also interesting to analyze the social and governmental ties within them. But an aspect that could prove even more important is if such situations have an influence on the expansion of Mexican enterprises abroad, especially considering the huge influence that a small number of companies could have in the whole country. That is, in 2012, the total assets from the top 20 MultiMexicans corresponded to about 11 percent of the GDP in the same year (our own calculation based on information from Basave & Gutiérrez-Haces, 2013, and UNCTAD). It could be possible that these companies keep close relationships with local government and of course with politicians, frequently lobbying to regulate actions or governmental agreements in order to obtain higher and better benefits (Sargent & Ghaddar, 2001).

Since several MultiMexicans are family owned, and the performance of these enterprises is showing good results, the thinking about family enterprises having specific characteristics, providing them with needed elements for internationalization, could be well supported. The relationship between the family enterprise and multinational enterprises is a topic that should be addressed in Mexico; even more when this is a topic that is getting more attention (Pukall & Calabro, 2014).

The following are examples of multinational family-owned enterprises: Cemex (main shareholders are members of the Zambrano family); Grupo FEMSA (Garza Langüera family is the main shareholder); Bimbo (Servitje family); Alfa (Garza Sada family); Grupo Gruma (González Barrera family); Mexichem (Del Valle family); Xingnux (Garza Herrera family); Industrias CH (Vigil González family); and Interceramic (Almeida family).

One last point about family-owned enterprises is that weak institutional conditions in the home country are related to the extent of control of large family-owned enterprises (Fogel, 2006). This could explain why Mexico has a handful of large firms increasing their control with its expansion considering foreign markets. Of course, most of these enterprises are family-owned. In this sense, the family-owned structure could be helpful in offsetting home market constraints and limitations.

All these restrictions and institutional liabilities that enterprises must face in the domestic market are intrinsically creating knowledge and experience which will become a strength and an advantage when dealing in foreign markets (Cuervo-Cazurra & Genc, 2008). Considering this viewpoint alongside institutional weaknesses in the home country, family-owned MultiMexicans are unconsciously developing conditions that will become important advantages for working and performing better in foreign markets.

CONCLUSIONS

The internationalization of Mexican enterprises has been increasing over recent decades. However, what might be more relevant than the mere fact of the OFDI increase by MultiMexicans, is the understanding of this behavior. Examining Mexican history, the evolution and trends of Mexican direct investment abroad, and the geographical allocation of the enterprises, as well as the identification and study of different characteristics of the firms, allows us to figure out and comprehend the behavior exhibited by MultiMexicans.

As suggested, the understanding of this phenomenon has important implications. And its relevance is twofold, both for this chapter and for the following chapters. First of all, understanding the evolution and characteristics of Mexican enterprises reveals important lessons for entrepreneurs in other domestic enterprises, which also have an interest in exploring foreign markets and integrating their productive activities in the global context.

In the same vein, entrepreneurs are recommended to check on the institutional framework and programs that the Mexican government provides, specifically for activities related to internationalization. Another suggestion is to consider the business group structure as a strategy to gain specific advantages and strengthen the capabilities of the firm; this will eventually allow enterprises to expand their domestic activities abroad.

Another suggestion is as follows: the North American market, and specifically the USA, has been of particular interest to Mexican enterprises, as well as to other traditional countries from Latin

America, such as Brazil, Chile, and Colombia. However, the increasing expansion of Mexican investments in some other countries such as Peru, Costa Rica, El Salvador, Guatemala, and the Dominican Republic, could be showing new opportunities for investment.

The second issue concerning the relevance of this chapter, and of course the understanding of Mexican enterprise internationalization, is to set up the scenario for the following chapters. The information so far revised will facilitate the comprehension of the internationalization paths of each of the Mexican enterprises under scrutiny in this book. It will also allow the lessons stemming from these arguments to be internalized, since we already know the context of the MultiMexicans.

REFERENCES

Aldrich, H. & Cliff, J. 2012. The pervasive effects of family on entrepreneurship: Toward a family embeddedness perspective. *Journal of Business Venturing*, 18 (5):573–596.

American Chamber of Commerce of Mexico. 1995. *México: Entorno económico*. México.

Arregle, J.-L., Batjargal, B., Hitt, M. et al. 2013. Family ties in entrepreneurs' social networks and new venture growth. *Entrepreneurship Theory and Practice*:1–32.

Arriaga, V. 1994. El manejo de la relación con Estados Unidos, 1990–1994. *Foro Internacional*, 34(4):572–591.

Basave, J. K. 2001. *Un Siglo de Grupos Empresariales en México*. Mexico: UNAM, Porrúa.

Basave, J. K. & Gutiérrez-Haces, M. T. 2013. Updated features of large Mexican Multinationals, 2012, *Emerging Market Global Players*.

Blanco, J. 1981. *El desarrollo de la crisis en México, 1970–1976, Desarrollo y crisis de la economía mexicana: Ensayos de interpretación histórica*. México: Fondo de Cultura Económica, pp. 297–335.

Bonaglia, F., Goldstein, A. & Mathews, J. A. 2007. Accelerated internationalization by emerging markets' multinationals: The case of the white goods sector. *Journal of World Business*, 42(4):369–383.

Castañeda, G. 2000. Governance of large corporations in Mexico and productivity implications. *Abante, Studies in Business Management*, 3(1):57–89.

CEPAL. 2012. *La inversión extranjera directa en América Latina y el Caribe 2011.* Santiago, Chile: Naciones Unidas.

CEPAL. 2014. *La inversión extranjera directa en América Latina y el Caribe 2013.* Santiago, Chile: Naciones Unidas.

Comlay, E. 2011. Analysis: Family ownership drags on Mexico's equity market, *Reuters.*

Cordero, S., Santin, R. & Tirado, R. 1981. *El poder empresarial en México.* México: Terra Nova.

Cuervo-Cazurra, A. & Genc, M. 2008. Transforming disadvantages into advantages: developing-country MNEs in the least developed countries. *Journal of International Bussines Studies,* 39(6):957–979.

Cárdenas, E. 1996. *La política económica en México, 1950–1994.* México: Colegio de México, Fondo de Cultura Económica.

Cárdenas, E. 2010. *La economía mexicana en el dilatado siglo XX, Historia económica general de México. De la Colonia a nuestros días:* 503–548. México: Color.

de la Peña, S. & Aguirre, T. 2006. *De la Revolución a la Industrialización, Historia Económica de México* Vol. 4. México: UNAM-Océano.

Delgado, G. 2003. *México estructuras política, económica y social.* México: Pearson.

Dunning, J. H. & Lundan, S. M. 2008. *Multinational Enterprises and the Global Economy:* Edward Elgar.

Espinoza, T. & Espinoza, N. 2012. Family business performance: evidence from Mexico. *Cuadernos de Administración,* 25(44):39–61.

Fogel, K. 2006. Oligarchic family control, social economic outcomes, and the quality of government. *Journal of International Business Studies,* 37:603–622.

Haber, S. 1992. *La revolución y la industria manufacturera mexicana, 1920–1925, Historia económica de México.* México: Fondo de Cultura Económica, pp. 415–446.

Haber, S. 2010. *Mercado Interno, Industrialización y Banca, 1890–1929, Historia Económica General de México. De la Colonia a Nuestros Días.* México: Color, pp. 411–436.

Khana, T. & Rivkin, J. 2001. Estimating the performance effects of business groups in emerging markets. *Strategic Managment Journal,* 22:45–74.

Knight, A. 2010. *La revolución mexicana: su dimensión económica, 1900–1930, Historia económica general de México. De la Colonia a nuestros días.* México: Color, pp. 473–499.

Kuntz, S. 1995. *Empresa extranjera y mercado interno: el Ferrocarril Central Mexicano, 1880–1907.* México: El Colegio de México.

Kuntz, S. 2007. *El comercio exterior de México en la era del capitalismo liberal, 1870–1929.* México: El Colegio de México.

Luo, Y. & Tung, R. L. 2007. International expansion of emerging market enterprises: a springboard perspective. *Journal of International Business Studies,* 38(4):481–498.

Luo, Y., Xue, Q. & Han, B. 2010. How emerging market governments promote outward FDI: Experience from China. *Journal of World Business,* 45(1):68–79.

Mancera, M. 2009. Crisis económicas en México, 1976–2008. *Este País,* 214:21–30.

Manfra, P. & Fitzmaurice, P. C. 2007. An economic analysis of foreign direct investment in the globalization process of asia. *Proceedings of the Northeast Business & Economics Association.*

Marichal, C. & Cerrutti, M. 1997. *Historia de las grandes empresas en México, 1850–1930.* México: Fondo de Cultura Económica.

Marichal, C. 2003. Auge y decadencia de las empresas estatales en México, 1930–1980: algunas notas sobre la relación histórica entre empresas estatales y endeudamiento externo. *Historia*(72):12–21.

Martin, J. & Duran, J. 2015. Effects of family ownership, debt and board composition on Mexican firms performance. *International Journal of Financial Studies,* 3:56–74.

Moreno-Brid, J. C. & Ros, J. 2009. *Development and Growth in the Mexican Economy: A Historical Perspective.* New York, NY: Oxford University Press.

Poza, E., Hanlon, S. & Kishida, R. 2004. Does the family business interaction factor represent a resource or a cost? *Family Business Review,* 17(2):99–118.

Pukall, T. & Calabro, A. 2014. The internationalization of family firms: A critical review and integrative model. *Family Business Review,* 27(2):103–125.

Rosenzweig, F. 1989. La evolución económica de México, 1870–1940. *El Trimestre Económico,* 56(1):11–56.

Sargent, J. & Ghaddar, S. 2001. International success of business groups as an indicator of national competitiveness: The Mexican example. *Latin American Business Review,* 2(3):97–121.

Schettino, M. 2002. *México. Problemas sociales, políticos y económicos.* México: Pearson Education.

Solís, L. 2000. *La realidad económica mexicana: Retrovisión y perspectivas.* México: Fondo de Cultura Económica.

UNCTAD. 2007. *World Investment Report 2006. FDI from developing and transition economies: implications for development.* New York, NY and Geneva: United Nations.

UNCTAD. 2013. *World Investment Report 2013. Global Value Chains: Investment and Trade for Development.* New York, NY and Geneva: United Nations.

UNCTAD. 2014. *World Investment Report 2014. Investing in the SDGs: An Action Plan.* New York, NY and Geneva: United Nations.

UNCTAD. 2015. Data Center, *UNCTADStat.*

Yiu, D. 2011. Multinational advantages of Chinese business groups: A theoretical exploration. *Management and Organization Review,* 7(2):249–277.

Zhou, C., Witteloostuijn, A. & Jianhong, Z. 2013. The internationalization of Chinese industries: Overseas acquisition activity in Chinese mining and manufacturing industries. *Asian Business & Management,* 13(2):89–116.

3   MultiMexicans in the Agriculture Industry
SuKarne and Bachoco

Miguel A. López-Lomelí and Joan Llonch Andreu

INTRODUCTION

This chapter analyzes the internationalization process of two successful Mexican Agro firms, SuKarne and Bachoco. Both are among the top Mexican domestic agriculture industry firms based on their annual sales in 2012; SuKarne sold US$2.5 billion and exported US$6.8 million during 2015 (Expok, 2015), and Bachoco sold US$2.63 billion (Bachoco, 2015a).

SuKarne started in the livestock market in 1969, and in 1972 moved to livestock raising and slaughtering, then in the 1980s became an Integrated Meat Production Unit (IMPU), which includes the fattening of livestock. Meat processing was established and later evolved to participate in other important subsectors such as pork, chicken, and fish production and processing, as well as animal hides, earthworm humus, and meat byproducts (SuKarne, 2015).

Bachoco started as a small commercial egg operation and evolved to participate in the production of different categories of chicken products, from live chicken to value-added products, eggs, balanced feed, and live swine, beef, and turkey value-added products, as well as production of vaccines for the poultry industry (Bachoco, 2015b).

Both companies have accomplished their income and profit objectives by supplying competitive products, based in the agriculture industry, which are widely accepted by general consumers due to their value and through their development and connection with other industries such as processed food.

These two companies have used their Mexican models in combination with partnerships with similar international leading companies or through acquisitions to expand internationally. Bachoco operates in Mexico and the USA; SuKarne has plant operations in Mexico and Nicaragua and commercializes its products in three countries: Mexico, USA, and Japan, and exports to 12 countries, including China, Korea, and Canada.

The high-profit results of SuKarne are associated with their business models in beef, pork, chicken, and broad distribution, and their flexibility and capacity to perfectly meet the requirements of customers and consumers in each of their international markets. Bachoco's success is explained by the broadening of its business via a strategic combination of production for different industries – poultry, eggs, animal feed, turkey and beef processing – as well as sales of live swine.

Other domestic companies might draw lessons from these successful expansion models to become multinationals.

THE AGRICULTURE INDUSTRY IN MEXICO

The agriculture industry worldwide includes the production of crops, gardening and horticulture, live animals and animal products, agriculture and animal husbandry services (with the exception of gardening and hunting); the category of crops, gardening, and horticulture includes the production of cereal grains, vegetables, fruits, berries, potatoes, tobacco, mushrooms, flowers, herbs, roots and tubers, beverage crops, spice crops, cotton and other textile plants; gathering of forest mushrooms and truffles; production of seeds for flowers, fruit or vegetables; production of wine grapes and table grapes; production of wine from self-produced grapes; production of edible nuts, and production of olive oil from self-produced olives (Euromonitor, 2013).

The agriculture industry is highly relevant for the economy of the country: in 2012 it contributed 5 percent to Mexico's GDP and employed about 16 percent of the labor force; the value of Mexico's agriculture consumption surpassed Mex$1.1 trillion, with 8 percent annual growth; the category of crops, gardening, and horticulture is the largest, with more than 86 percent of total trade value; the agriculture industry market sales are led by various food processing firms as well hotels and restaurant chains, representing 60 percent of all domestic sales (Euromonitor, 2013).

Mexican agriculture originated in the ancient pre-Colombian era and has developed throughout Mexican history, through the centuries of the Spanish conquest and colonialization, to the independent Mexico of the nineteenth century, including the period known as the Porfiriato (1876–1911), the long term of President Porfirio Díaz, who remained in power thanks to the political and economic stability that his administration brought to the country.

One of the breakthroughs in Mexican agriculture was the start of the Mexican Revolution in 1910, which spread across the countryside to the towns in opposition to the established government of President Diaz after 30 years in power. One of the key causes of this revolution was the ownership of land concentrated in a small group of extremely rich landlords supported by the government, with a highly impoverished agricultural working class. The modern Mexican agriculture infrastructure was redesigned in the post-Revolution period.

The Mexican post-Revolution presidential periods (1911–1940) were characterized by a series of government interventions and the issuance of new policies to regulate the redistribution of the land property and to ensure an appropriate infrastructure for the agriculture industry, supported and protected by the State.

The agricultural economic boom began in 1940 thanks to the accelerated process of Mexico's economic growth, which was superior to the population growth, and the modernization of Mexican industry and the country's infrastructure, which allowed for sustained growth in agricultural production of primary products to satisfy internal food needs and to support international export (Romero, 2002). The evolution of the modern Mexican agriculture industry is shown in Table 3.1.

At the beginning of the 1990s, the Mexican agriculture industry underwent changes that transformed it into a competitive field under the trade liberalization and border openings to free trade between the

Table 3.1 *Evolution of the Mexican agriculture sector in the twentieth and twenty-first centuries*

Year	
1915–1917	President Venustiano Carranza promulgates the law of January 6, declaring null and void all disposals of lands, water, and mountains, as well as buying and selling transactions made after 1876.
1917	The new Mexican Constitution article 17 gives rise to two forms of land ownership: the Ejido (communal land property) and the small property, dissolving the large estates.
1920	Ley de Ejidos
1925	Ley Federal de Irrigación
1926	Ley de Colonización y Ley de Crédito Agrícola
1929	The Ministry of Agriculture creates nine experimental fields with the goal of trying to acclimatize imported seeds and other local varieties to different agricultural areas of the country.
1935	Creation of approximately 800 cooperatives of agricultural production in some of the country's richest natural regions (the Lagunera, Los Mochis, the Yaqui River, Lombardy, and new Italy).
1936	Implementation of the *Agrarian land reform code* under President Cardenas' administration, which changed the agricultural structure of land ownership. Half of the country's cultivated land was given to farmers under the regime of "ejidal possession," which was mainly devoted to crops which were commercialized through the market.
1940	The process of agrarian reform is abruptly interrupted and the government's official economical stimuli given to peasant farming, oriented towards incentivizing the growth of organized agriculture based on conventional business orientation.
1943	The Mexican Government and the Rockefeller Foundation founded the Office of Special Agricultural Studies (OEE).

Table 3.1 (*cont.*)

Year	
1956	Creation of various regional cooperative credit banks aiming to increase and decentralize agricultural financial activities.
1958	The largest volume of government investments in the agricultural sector focused and concentrated in certain states in the north and north-west of the country, where agricultural production for export grew at more than 200%.
1960	Creation of the National Institute of Agricultural Research (INIA), which represented an important step forward of government activities in agricultural research and experimentation, and the formation of technically qualified personnel.
1962	Creation of the International Center of Maize and Wheat Improvement (CIMMYT); institution that links government research programs and disseminates worldwide the advancements in the cultivation of maize and wheat.
1967	Agricultural production reaches a volume growth level equivalent to seven times the Mexican production in 1940. The percentage increases throughout the period were always above the population increases.
1965–1982	This period is associated with the phenomenon of the "agro-industrialization" and "the technification of the livestock production" of the primary sector, which translates to significant growth of crops (oilseeds, horticultural, and tropical) and a boom in livestock (bovine, swine, and poultry).
1982	The Mexican neoliberalism economic model is implemented and gives priority to the inclusion of the Mexican economy into the foreign markets as well as the fulfilment of the international commitments, including all activities in the agricultural sector.
1986–1994	Mexico joins GATT and by 1990/1, most licenses to import agricultural products are abolished. In 1991–4 most

Table 3.1 (*cont.*)

Year	
	agricultural commodities were subject to new fluctuating tariffs of between 0% and 20%.
1990–1999	Agri-food exports grow from Mex$2.9 to 7.0 billion, representing a growth rate average of 10%.
1991–1999	Elimination of agricultural producers' price government protections, elimination of CONASUPO (the National Company for Popular Subsistence) and creation of ASERCA to support producers in commercialization.
1994	Implementation of the North American Free Trade Agreement (NAFTA).
1994–2008	Implementation of PROCAMPO (program of direct support for the countryside) as part of ASERCA.
1995	Alliance for the Countryside (Alianza para el Campo). A set of programs designed to support farmers with productive potential in an open economy. Its major goals are: to increase the producer's income, to improve agriculture balance of trade, to make food production growth twice as much as the population growth, and to ensure the country's food supply.

Source: Adapted from Romero P. (2002) and Yunez-Naude & Barceinas Paredes (2004)

USA, Canada, and Mexico. Given the historical direct participation of the Mexican government in the agriculture industry with different incentives and economic support, in view of the NAFTA implementation, it was necessary to build a structural transition towards the new free trade context prior to the startup of NAFTA. This transition required major measures to reduce the support of the government in this sector, as well as the creation of new agricultural institutions, to help farmers compete mainly in the crops sector in this new liberalized trade scenario (Yunez-Naude & Barceinas Paredes, 2002).

Although the NAFTA impact in Mexico's agriculture industry has been controversial, Mexican farmers faced a severe decline in the purchasing power of corn during the 1990s prior to the NAFTA implementation, which was temporarily interrupted by the devaluation of the peso in December 1994. Studies made ten years after the implementation of NAFTA conclude that Mexican corn prices did not move as expected given a free-trade, competitive environment, in contrast with the behavior prior to the advent of NAFTA in 1994 (Fiess & Lederman, 2004). Therefore, the Mexican economy gradually adapted over the years to cope with the NAFTA competitive trade, as well as the global markets.

Thanks to these developments in the agriculture industry in Mexico, the Mexican agriculture industry currently has a market size of Mex$782,798 million, of which the total value of Mexico's agricultural exports is Mex$253,000 million: a 300 percent increase in six years; the Mexican agriculture industry is one of the most important economic sectors in the Mexican economy, representing 5 percent of the national GDP and 16 percent of employment (Euromonitor, 2013).

The agriculture industry in Mexico is divided into four main categories: agricultural and animal husbandry services; farming of animals; crops, gardening, and horticulture; and hunting (Euromonitor, 2013). Table 3.2 shows the production value by sector, and the forecasts for 2018.

The crops, gardening, and horticulture sector is the most important, representing 86 percent of the total value of the agriculture industry, followed by farming of animals; both together represent more than 90 percent of the industry's value, and the sales of this sector in B2B terms represent 61 percent (Euromonitor, 2013).

Bachoco is the most important company in the Mexican agriculture industry; Table 3.3 shows the relative company production shares.

Selection of SuKarne and Bachoco

During the last three decades, some of the most important Mexican companies related with the agriculture industry expanded their

Table 3.2 *Production by sector and value, 2007–18*

	2007	2008	2009	2010	2011	2012	2013	2014	2015	2016	2017	2018
Agricultural and Animal Husbandry Services	39,454	43,462	42,233	42,001	42,165	42,623	45,240	47,567	49,644	51,995	54,329	56,716
Farming of Animals	62,095	61,835	62,099	63,521	64,103	65,131	70,145	74,585	78,668	83,286	87,999	92,872
Crops, Gardening, and Horticulture	478,150	547,580	582,597	576,897	639,279	674,397	716,679	755,369	790,467	830,032	869,423	909,925
Hunting	575	610	556	580	628	647	697	732	762	796	831	866
Total	580,274	653,488	687,485	682,999	746,175	782,798	832,760	878,253	919,541	966,108	1,012,581	1,060,379

Source: Euromonitor (2013)

Table 3.3 *Industry leaders: company production share in 2010*

	Production share (%)
Industrias Bachoco SA de CV	3.6
Agrícola Cactus SA de CV	2.1
Pilgrim's Pride S de RL de CV	1.2
Proteína Animal SA de CV	0.8
Granjas Carroll de México S de RL de CV	0.4
Other	91.9

Source: Euromonitor (2013)

businesses to international operations: Bachoco, SuKarne, Grupo Minsa, and Grupo Herdez.

SuKarne is a successful 100% Mexican company with vast experience in international joint ventures. Additionally, SuKarne has been recognized as the largest animal protein exporters in Mexico with 74% of the total national exports of beef (Expok, 2015) and both Bachoco and SuKarne are among the top 100 most globalized Mexican companies; in relation to the Agriculture Industry they might be considered among the top 10 (CNN Expansión, 2015), shown in Table 3.4.

SUKARNE

History of SuKarne

The history of SuKarne started with the Vizcarra family's operations in the livestock market in Culiacán, Sinaloa, Mexico, with an investment in the raising and slaughtering of livestock in 1972. Thanks to very successful business performance in the following years, the Vizcarra family inaugurated their first Integrated Meat Production Unit (IMPU) in Culiacan, including the fattening of livestock and meat processing. By 1989 they had expanded to a second IMPU in Mexicali, Baja California. In 1995 the Import/Export operation started

Table 3.4 *International Mexican companies related to the Agriculture industry*

RK 2015	Company	Globalization index 2015	Foreign Sales	% of foreign sales	Countries with operation	Countries
70	Industrias Bachoco	4.2	8,517	20	2	Mexico and the USA
72	SuKarne	4.1	6,250	N/A	2	México and Nicaragua
85	Grupo Minsa	2.5	1,151	N/A	2	Mexico and the USA
94	Grupo Herdez (also in Processed Food)	1.4	839	N/A	10	USA, Canada, Costa Rica, Cuba, El Salvador, Guatemala, Honduras, Nicaragua & Uruguay.

Source: CNN Expansión (2015)

with the United States, and two years later the SuKarne brand was acquired. Darby & Baring became associated with the company, and their third IMPU was opened in Monterrey within this joint venture (SuKarne, 2015).

The year 2000 marked the inauguration of the distribution system with the objective to distribute fresh produce and satisfy the requirements of a broader and diverse set of customers. During this period SuKarne was able to build an extensive network of distribution centers and a broad infrastructure of sales and services, with a fleet of approximately 400 vehicles at their disposal, enabling SuKarne products to be available across 40,000 points of sale, thus covering retail chains, grocery stores, specialty stores, butchers, and restaurants. This became Mexico's largest distribution system for delivery of beef, pork, and chicken; their direct sales represent 36 percent of SuKarne's business (SuKarne, 2015).

In 2004, SuKarne expanded its export operations to Japan thanks to their product quality and their organizational ability in matching specific customer requirements and processing and packaging their products according to their customers' needs. Six years later, in 2010, they expanded export operations to Korea, Angola, and Russia. Currently SuKarne exports to 12 countries: the USA, Japan, Russia, South Korea, Vietnam, Hong Kong, Liberia, Democratic Republic of the Congo, Côte d'Ivoire, Canada, Chile, and China. In 2010 the company expanded further in the pork and chicken meat businesses, and by 2012 their fourth and fifth IMPUs were in operation.

2015 marked SuKarne's international expansion into Nicaragua, with the inauguration of operations and the opening of the sixth IMPU there, along with the opening of commercial offices in the USA and Japan. In 2015 they also relaunched the Mexicali IMPU, becoming one of Mexico's most modern facilities in the industry. The SuKarne Group also expanded into other industries related to their core business of producing and processing meat, such as animal hides, earthworm humus, and compostand meat byproducts.

The highest-profit contributor is their beef business, commercialized in the USA and Japan along with exports to four continents. The success for Grupo SuKarne is based in five pillars:

1. Technology: aiming to achieve the highest quality of product in terms of safety, health and flavor.
2. Continuous Replenishment System (CRS): of supplies of beef, chicken, and pork, efficiently and at highly competitive costs.
3. Holistic integrated operation systems: with centralized strategic processes, allowing continual improvements for cost-effective productivity.
4. Brand presence and awareness: in the domestic market with growing awareness in the international markets.
5. Strong distribution and delivery system: to strategic points of sale of beef, pork, and chicken, both independently and in major retailers.

SuKarne's core strategic action for success, as mentioned by the President and General Director of Grupo Sukarne, Jesús Vizcarra Calderón, was to change the meat commercialization paradigms of the industry by being the first company to sell meat packaged in boxes (versus unpackaged), the first to enter the US market in 1995 – a market that had been neglected by Mexican meat producers – and to find the best markets globally to commercialize every part of the animal: Mexico, Russia, Japan, and the USA have meat preferences for different parts of the nimal (Moreno, 2014). Table 3.5 presents commercial information relating to SuKarne.

The financial performance of SuKarne for the past 15 years cannot be analyzed since the firm does not issue public financial information. SuKarne is not listed on the stock exchange, but is a private capital company.

International Expansion of SuKarne

SuKarne's international expansion was developed through three business strategies: exports, commercialization, and operations. First they focused on exports to the USA, given its strong potential, and later moved forward to export to Japan, and, eventually, to South Korea,

Table 3.5 *SuKarne's commercial information*

Year	Sales (US$ millions)	Livestock Processing
2014	2,400	1,300,000
2012	1,971	1,058,000
2010	1,340	735,000

Source: Chávez (2014) and SuKarne (2015)

Russia, and Angola. Currently they export to 12 countries: the USA, Japan, Russia, South Korea, Vietnam, Hong Kong, Liberia, Republic of the Congo, Côte d'Ivoire, Canada, Chile, and China. Their second move was to start commercialization operations based in the USA and Japan, where they opened commercial offices. Finally, their third move was the opening of their sixth IMPU in Nicaragua, where they found similar conditions to replicate their business model.

The Nicaragua expansion represented an investment of US$115 million, with annual production capacity of 132,000 beef heads; this was possible thanks to an innovative international cooperation in financial coinvestment with private firms such as Rabobank and public institutions such as Bancomext and Bladex, under the coordination of Corporación Interamericana de Inversions – an institution of the Inter-American Development Bank – and with additional support from the Fund for Infrastructure for Central American and Caribbean Countries. Nicaragua's plant will supply both local and international markets (SuKarne, 2015). The timeline of the evolution of SuKarne is presented in Table 3.6.

For over 40 years, SuKarne has led the meat industry in Mexico and worldwide, thanks to its strong focus on achieving the highest standards via the use of innovative processes, and being highly competitive in the domestic and global markets.

Table 3.6 *Evolution of SuKarne*

Year	National	International
1969	The Vizcarra family begins its operations in the livestock market in Culiacan, Mexico.	
1972	Livestock raising and slaughtering begins.	
1986	The first Unidad Integral de Producción de Carne (Integrated Meat Production Unit) (IMPU) is established in Culiacan, which includes the fattening of livestock and meat processing.	
1989	A second Unidad Integral de Producción de Carne (Integrated Meat Production Unit) (IMPU) opens in Mexicali, Mexico.	
1993	El Fondo de Capitalización e Inversión del Serctor Rural (Rural Capital and Investment Fund) partners with the company. Culiacan IMPU Slaughterhouse obtains TIF certificate.	
1995		Import/Export starts with the United States
1997	SuKarne brand is acquired and jointly enters the Third Integral Operation Beef Production Unit in Monterrey. Darby & Baring is associated with the company.	
2000	The first meat distribution routes are established.	
2004		Exports to Japan begin.
2005	A fourth Unidad Integral de Produccion de Carne (Rural Capital and Investment Fund) in Michoacan, Mexico opens.	
2010		Exports to Korea, Angola, Russia, and

Table 3.6 (cont.)

Year	National	International
		other countries begin. Distribution of pork and chicken begins.
2012	A fifth Unidad de Produccion de Ganado (Livestock Production Unit) in the Laguna Region, in north-west Mexico opens.	
2015	The Mexicali plant TIF 120 is reopened as one of the most modern such plants in Mexico. The inauguration of the sixth UGI takes place in Nicaragua.	

Source: SuKarne (2015)

The company has created innovative business processes, restructuring paradigms and revolutionizing the industry, including production and marketing systems, for the benefit of consumers and their value chain. Its business model and operating philosophy has been fundamental to its successful development and steady growth (SuKarne, 2015).

Mexico's national production in 2014 was of 19.7 million tonnes in this sector, with a growth of 11 percent compared with the previous year, and has become the sixth-ranked producer worldwide of beef meat with 1.8 million tonnes a year and exporting one million livestock (Notimex, 2015). SuKarne has become one of the leaders in this sector and started exporting to Egypt in November 2015 (CNN Expansión, 2015a). The company's CEO, Jesús Vizcarra Calderón, expects that during 2016 they will expand exports to more countries, such as Saudi Arabia, United Arab Emirates, Kuwait, Qatar, and Lebanon (Notimex, 2015). The company is focusing on expanding its business model in both global exports and in international commercial and production operations.

BACHOCO

Currently the leader of the Mexican poultry industry, and one of the top ten poultry companies worldwide in producing, processing, and commercializing chicken and eggs, Industrias Bachoco SAB de CV is a holding company. Its major product lines are: chicken, eggs, wine, balanced animal feed, and swine, with additional value-added turkey and beef products; and production of medicines and vaccines for animal consumption (Bachoco, 2015a).

Industrias Bachoco is a vertically integrated company, with operations in México and the USA, more than 25,000 employees, and more than 1,000 facilities, mostly farms, and nine processing plants with a capacity of around 12 million chickens per week and a commercialization network selling to wholesalers, retailers, supermarkets, and food-service operators. Its shares are listed on the Mexican Stock Exchange (Bolsa Mexicana de Valores) and on the New York Stock Exchange (Yahoo Finance, 2015).

Looking at the past 15 years, Bachoco's successful financial performance is evidenced based on their revenue and profit growth. During this period, the group of top executives of Bachoco has shown itself to be highly capable of managing the fluctuations of high peaks in prices of strategic raw materials due to global economic conditions; the fluctuations of supply and demand in poultry (which in some seasons presented over-supply conditions); the Mexican macroeconomic volatility in periods of depreciation of the Mexican peso versus the US dollar; the implementation of NAFTA; and the new circumstances in 2008, when the poultry industry became completely open with a consequent significant reduction in poultry product prices in the USA and the fluctuating purchasing power of consumers as global and domestic economic conditions changed positively or negatively (Bachoco, 2009).

2015 was a positive year for Bachoco: the company established new benchmarks in sales and reached its second highest profit margin (EBITDA) within the last ten years, maintaining a strong financial

Table 3.7 *Grupo Bachoco's financial information*

	BACHOCO			
	2000	2005	2010	2015
Revenue	971.9	1328.7	1957.9	2919
Total Assets	318	547.9	783.2	1441.4
EBITDA	191.1	244.4	250	373
Gross profit	158.6	202	195.1	321.2
Net profit	129.3	164.4	157.1	245.7
Foreign investment	0	0	0	10
Exports	N/A	N/A	N/A	221
Employees	N/A	N/A	23,473	28,281
Countries	1	1	1	2

Data in millions of US dollars

N/A = not available

Source: Self-devised based on Bachoco's public financial information

position with net cash at the end of 2015 of Mex$11,163.1 million. The poultry industry also presented historical growth levels in spite of the critical problem faced by the ban on US products imposed by some countries in relation to the sanitary conditions created by the Avian Influenza outbreak, which affected turkey farms and table eggs. A positive factor was that, in 2015, there was a steady down-trending cost of the main raw materials in US dollars that helped to minimize the effects in purchases by the depreciation of the Mexican peso versus the US dollar (Bachoco, 2016). Grupo Bachoco's financial information is presented in Table 3.7.

History of Bachoco

The antecedents of Industrias Bachoco, SA de CV are Alfonso, Javier, Enrique, and Juan Robinson Bours, who were the second generation of the Dutch immigrant family of Henry Robinson Bours. They lived in

Ciudad Obregon (Bachoco Corporativo, 2015), operated different businesses, such as wheat and sorghum farming, the production of fertilizers, and the sale of automobiles and agricultural machinery. In a difficult economic situation, one of them, Enrique, could not meet his payroll, and his wife provided a surprising and unexpected amount in savings from selling eggs to their neighbors from the family's small farm with chickens (Funding Universe, 2015).

The Robinson brothers decided to focus on egg production and started operations in 1952, naming their company Bachoco (a local Indian name meaning "place where water passes"), initially specializing in brown eggs, which had a price premium in the market. By the mid-1960s, egg production was the main business and the brothers divested their other business to concentrate on this one. They expanded their operations to a plant in Los Mochis and they also opened their first poultry operation, in Culiacan, Sinaloa (Bachoco Corporativo, 2015). Within three years, thanks to their business success, they expanded to open a second poultry processing plant in Celaya, Guanajuato. By the end of 1977 their chicken sales had exceeded their egg sales (Bachoco Corporativo, 2015; Funding Universe, 2015).

Mexico's economic crises of the 1970s also negatively impacted this industry, making it very difficult to survive financially for Mexican chicken and egg producers. An imbalance in pricing versus costs was brought about by the fact that low-quality, low-price imported chicken and eggs were being smuggled from the USA and were destabilizing the markets. Local producers were forced to consolidate in order to achieve economies of scale, while the Government was also focused to adopt measures that allowed chicken products to be maintained affordably for Mexico's low-income consumers (Funding Universe, 2015).

Bachoco faced these market challenges successfully with a careful financial strategy of taking only the debt levels that they could handle, planning their strategy based on the expectation that the industry moved in cycles of high and low prices based on offer and demand (Funding Universe, 2015). Bachoco's response was to hold back production until prices recovered: an approach that allowed them to expand their largest commercialization during the 1980s in the center of Mexico, opening operations in San Luis Potosi and consolidating operations in Mexicali (Bachoco Corporativo, 2015).

The 1990s represented a decade of important decisions for Bachoco and the start of a new era of growth; due to its debt levels, the company made an important reorganization, targeting cost reduction; among many important actions, they transferred their corporate headquarters from Ciudad Obregon to Celaya (Bachoco Corporativo, 2015). This reorganization was an unquestionable success. In 1992 Bachoco reported net sales of Mex$1.05 billion (about US$338.1 million) and net income of Mex$39.4 million (about US$12.7 million) (Funding Universe, 2015).

Bachoco continued with strong results and stable expansion, acquiring a third processing plant in Puebla, which led them to become the second-largest national producer and represented 17 percent of total sales. The strong depreciation of the Mexican peso in December 1994 created an economic environment that gave Bachoco an opportunity to purchase smaller producers, thus achieving 21 percent of the market in 1988. The most important move, though, was their outsourcing of financial resources for future expansion by offering, in 1997, about one-sixth of their outstanding shares on the Mexican and the New York Stock Exchanges (Funding Universe, 2015). The Bachoco historical timeline and international expansion is shown in Table 3.8.

The success of Bachoco can be explained by a strategy aligned to five pillars: (1) diversification in business related to the agriculture industry; (2) technology for processing and packaging; (3) wide distribution; (4) feed branding strategy; and the (5) diversification in other subsectors related to the core business.

Today, Industrias Bachoco is a leader in the poultry industry in Mexico and the sixth largest poultry company in the world (Bachoco,

Table 3.8 *History of Grupo Bachoco*

	Key Events	
Year	Domestic	International
1952	Bachoco is founded as a small table egg operation in the state of Sonora, Mexico.	
1963	Bachoco begins its expansion, establishing operations in Navojoa, Sonora, Los Mochis, and Culiacan, Sinaloa.	
1971	Bachoco initiates its first poultry operation in Culiacan, Sinaloa.	
1974	Bachoco starts operations in the Bajío region, in the State of Guanajuato, located in the center of the country, with the strategy to reinforce its market coverage in Mexico City and the center zone of the country.	
1986	The biggest Bachoco's commercializing center, operation México, opens.	
1987	Bachoco expands its number of facilities, unveiling Operation San Luis Potosí.	
1988	Bachoco keeps growing stronger as Operation Mexicali opens at Baja California.	
1990	Bachoco establishes its headquarters in Celaya, Guanajuato.	
1993	Bachoco begins to extend market coverage through the acquisition of a complex in Puebla, in the south of the country, to strengthen the company's presence and build synergies with Celaya's complex.	
1994	Bachoco acquires a complex located in Jalisco.	
1995	Bachoco enters the Financial markets and completes its initial offering in September 1997. Its securities are listed	Bachoco enters the New York Stock Exchange via American Depositary

Table 3.8 *(cont.)*

| | *Key Events* | |
Year	Domestic	International
	on the Mexican Stock Exchange and trade under the ticker symbol "Bachoco UBL."	Receipts under the ticker symbol "IBA."
1997	At the end of this year, Bachoco acquires the fourth largest poultry processing plant in Mexico and an important producer of animal feed: Grupo Campi, a subsidiary of Grupo Desc with presence in the state of Yucatan and other south-eastern states, continuing with the expansion strategy and reinforcing the national coverage.	
2001	Bachoco reaches an agreement with Avicola Cotaxtla, a broiler producer located in the state of Veracruz, consolidating its presence in this region. At the end of the year Bachoco acquired most of the assets of the table eggs operations of both Avicola Nochistongo and Avicola Simon Bolivar reinforcing this product line and reaching national coverage.	
2005	Bachoco acquires assets of Grupo Sanjor, a private poultry company located in the Yucatan Peninsula.	
2006	Campi brand impulse – Campi brand installed capabilities grow with Veracruz's Fortachón Foods plant acquisition, scoring the highest sales record since its incorporation in 1999.	
2007	Expansion continues: January – Operation Hermosillo starts activities due to Mezquital del Oro company acquisition. February – Complejo Veracruz grand opening.	

Table 3.8 (*cont.*)

	Key Events	
Year	Domestic	International
	March – Operation Noroeste settled in Monterrey, N.L. starts activities.	
	April – One of the most advanced balanced food plants in Mexico starts activities in Aguacalientes.	
2008	Bachoco in Chiapas:	
	January – Bachoco image is updated, abandoning the classic yellow and brown colors on the logo and replacing them with orange and green, colors that reflect the freshness, healthy and natural main aspects of their products.	
	May – The building of five chicken farms kicks off in Chiapas state.	
2009	Bachoco Industries:	
	July – Strengthens its north-east presence with new agreements and asset acquisitions in Monterrey, N.L.	
2013		Bachoco Acquires US Breeding Operation. Bachoco announces that it has reached an agreement to acquire the breeding assets in Arkansas of Morris Hatchery Inc., a US company.

Source: Bachoco Corporativo (2015).

2015c), with an infrastructure that includes more than 1,000 farms, 10 complexes, 64 distribution centers, 25 hatcheries, 10 processing plants, six further processing plants, and 20 feed mills. The business results for 2015 were very positive, and the company is at its best point in history from a financial perspective to make new acquisitions, as stated by financial analysts from the Mexican Stock Exchange (Gallardo, 2015). The cumulative results of their third quarter of 2015 are positive: total sales grew by 12 percent, achieving an EBITDA margin of 14.9 percent: the same margin when compared with the equivalent period of 2014. The company remained in a healthy financial condition with a net cash of Mex$10,303.7 million, and both cash and equivalents increased by 15.5 percent during 2015 (Bachoco, 2015c).

Bachoco Foreign Expansion

As mentioned previously, Bachoco's international expansion is based mainly on expanding into the largest market of the NAFTA region and the largest commercial and financial partner of Mexico: the USA, which in 2013 represented 71 percent of Mexico's exports and 51 percent of its imports (Observatory of Economic Complexity, 2015). As Bachoco was gaining more market share in Mexico and becoming a leader in this industry, it acquired a company in the USA, located in Arkansas, which represented a 25 percent increase in the company's chicken production capacity (Bachoco, 2015b). Bachoco's interest in conquering market share in the USA still continues, as in July of 2015 it announced the acquisition of chicken farms from Morris Hatchery Inc., located in Georgia (CNN Expansión, 2015b). On top of its USA operations, Bachoco exports balanced feed for pork to Cuba.

Among its opportunities for growth, Bachoco stated that it seeks to continue with acquisitions outside Mexico, to increase the export market in both the Mexico and USA operations, and to consolidate and extend its portfolio of products (Bachoco, 2015b).

CONCLUSIONS

From these two successful Mexican companies' internationalization processes, we can draw the following conclusions.

1. Their internationalization strategies were initially to expand their national operations via exports to key global markets: in both cases, initially to the USA and later, in the case of SuKarne, to several foreign key markets/countries for their animal products.
2. Both companies faced a complex challenge in being able to commercialize in the international markets, given that their products are for human consumption: (a) they had to prepare themselves to meet the safety regulations of foreign countries; b) they also had to adapt their products to their requirements of their customers; and c) they additionally had to adapt their products to meet foreign consumers' tastes and preferences. This adaptation represented a deep understanding of these diverse countries' regulations, commercial practices, and, importantly, consumer and customer requirements.
3. An interesting step in internationalization is the strategic move made by SuKarne in establishing commercialization offices and operations in foreign countries to strengthen the sales within those countries, as they did in the USA and Japan.
4. As a second important move to their internationalization processes, both firms followed the exports business with an expansion of their operations, to Nicaragua, in the case of SuKarne, via direct coinvestment and funding with the IDB, and, in the case of Bachoco, to the USA via acquisitions.
5. This represents for both firms the strategic transfers to the new country suggested by Dawson (2007), exporting the business models and organizational culture of the firm, and demonstrates the ability to adapt to the market, evidenced by their capacity to meet foreign regulations and requirements in animal food.
6. Technology played a fundamental role; these two internationalization processes also confirm that firms making business in the agriculture industry reached high competitive levels through state of the art technology and efficiency in processes; first they became leaders in their local markets and then achieved a leading position in the international markets by maintaining high competitiveness based on the technological and efficiency processes performed at global levels.

7. Another important fact is their conservative financial management in maintaining healthy corporate finances. Given their agricultural nature, their pace of expansion is highly sensitive to the changing economic conditions when monetary exchange fluctuations, consumers' purchasing power, and the excesses in supply may make the volume in these markets volatile.

8. The management of both companies focused on growing revenues from their international businesses, and international expansion is among their top priorities, in order to achieve expected higher business results from their international operations in future years.

9. Other animal processing firms from emerging markets can draw from these successful experiences to develop their own internationalization strategies by capitalizing on these principles and adapting them to their own businesses.

REFERENCES

Bachoco. 2009. Annual Report 2008.

Bachoco. 2015a. Annual Report 2014.

Bachoco. 2015b. Corporate presentation.

Bachoco. 2015c. Industrias Bachoco announces third quarter 2015 results Financial reports. Bachoco. 2015.

Bachoco. 2016. Annual Report 2015, https://corporativo.bachoco.com.mx/inversio nistas/informes/#page-inversionistas. Accessed November 15, 2015.

Bachoco Corporativo. 2015. History, https://corporativo.bachoco.com.mx/en/our-company/bachoco-history/ Accessed December 3, 2015.

CNN Expansión. 2015a. La firma Mexicana SuKarne inicia exportaciones a Egipto, www.cnnexpansion.com/negocios/2015/11/09/sukarne-inicia-exportaciones-hacia-egipto. Accessed November 9, 2015.

CNN Expansión. 2015b. Bachoco compra granjas de aves en Estados Unidos, www.cnnexpansion.com/negocios/2015/07/13/bachoco-compra-grajas-de-av es-en-estados-unidos. Accessed December 13, 2015.

CNN Expansión. 2015. Las 100 Mexicanas más Globales 2015, https://expansion .mx/especiales/2015/01/13/las-100-mexicanas-mas-globales-2015. Accessed February 15, 2018.

Chávez, H. 2014. SuKarne revela a qué debe su éxito. ENTREVISTA Efraín Reséndiz Patiño, Director de desarrollo de negocios de SuKarne, www

.elfinanciero.com.mx/economia/sukarne-revela-a-que-debe-su-exito.html, Accessed December 8, 2015.

Dawson, J. A. 2007. Scoping and conceptualising retailer internationalisation. *Journal of Economic Geography*.

Euromonitor. 2013. Agriculture in Mexico, www.euromonitor.com. Accessed December 7, 2015.

Expok. 2015. SuKarne, Empresa mexicana con mayor presencia global y alta RSE: Jesús Vizcarra, www.expoknews.com/sukarne-empresa-mexicana-con-mayor-presencia-global-y-alta-rse-jesus-vizcarra. Accessed October 25, 2015.

Fiess, N. & Lederman, D. 2004. Mexican Corn: The Effects of NAFTA http://siter esources.worldbank.org/INTRANETTRADE/Resources/Pubs/TradeNote18.pdf . Accessed October 12, 2015.

Funding Universe. 2015. Industrias Bachoco, S.A. de C.V. History, www .fundinguniverse.com/company-histories/industrias-bachoco-s-a-de-c-v-history. Accessed September 28, 2015.

Gallardo, E. 2015. Bachoco, robusto para seguir expandiéndose, https://www .eleconomista.com.mx/mercados/Bachoco-robusto-para-seguir-expandiendose-20150503-0046.htmlAccessed October 3, 2015.

Notimex 2015. México es potencia pecuaria en el mundo: Peña Nieto.El Economista, https://www.eleconomista.com.mx/empresas/Mexico-es-potencia-pecuaria-en-el-mundo-Pena-Nieto-20150528-0012.html. Accessed February 4, 2016.

Observatory of Economic Complexity. 2015. Mexico, http://atlas.media.mit.edu/ en/profile/country/mex/#Destinations. Accessed December 13, 2015.

Moreno, M. H. 2014. La historia de una empresa Millonaria. Sukarne, Marketing Negocios, http://marketingnegocioshm.blogspot.mx/2014/10/la-historia-de-una -empresa-millonaria.html. Accessed May 11, 2018.

Romero, P. E. 2002. *Un Siglo de Agricultura en Mexico*. Mexico: UNAM.

SuKarne. 2015. History and Progress, http://sukarne.com/en/page/history. Accessed September 8, 2015.

Yahoo Finance. 2015. Bachoco Company Profile, http://finance.yahoo.com/q/pr?s= IBA+Profile. Accessed September 9, 2015.

Yunez-Naude, A. & Barceinas Paredes, F. 2002. Lessons from NAFTA: The Case of Mexico's Agricultural Sector http://web.worldbank.org/archive/website00894 A/WEB/PDF/YUNEZ_TE.PDF. Accessed December 13, 2015.

Yunez-Naude, A. & Barceinas Paredes, F. 2004. The Agriculture of Mexico After Ten Years of NAFTA Implementation, http://si2.bcentral.cl/public/pdf/docu mentos-trabajo/pdf/dtbc277.pdf. Accessed December 3, 2015.

4 MultiMexicans in the Mining Industry
Grupo México and Industrias Peñoles

L. Arturo Bernal and Isai Guizar

INTRODUCTION

Mexico is a key player in the mining industry worldwide. It is the largest producer of silver and a top-ten producer of multiple other products including lead, zinc, gold, and copper. Grupo México and Industrias Peñoles are two representative Mexican mining companies. In the industry of diversified metals and mining (Forbes, 2015b), Grupo México, with global leadership in copper, is ranked as the eighth largest mining company in the world, while Industrias Peñoles, not far behind, is ranked 31st.

Although both companies started their consolidation at almost the same time, in the 1960s, Grupo México currently has four times the earnings (EBITDA) and total assets of Peñoles, and almost twice the EBITDA margin. An important difference between these two companies is their processes of internationalization. The beginning of Grupo México's internationalization process was related to the acquisition of the US company ASARCO, which already had a minority interest in the Peruvian company, Southern Peru Copper Corporation (SPCC). In addition, it coincides with the succession from father to son of the chairmanship of the board: two years after this succession was the point when Grupo México acquired ASARCO, in 1997, and thus acquired SPCC indirectly. After that acquisition, there was a period of continuous expansion and modernization in the Peruvian mines and, years later, the company replicated that same process in Mexico, together with the acquisition of other mines (see Appendix 1). Besides, there has been interchange of technology between the subsidiaries of Grupo México in Peru and Mexico. In comparison, in Industrias

Peñoles there was also a succession of the chairmanship of the board from father to son. However, the internationalization of Industrias Peñoles to Peru began almost six years after that succession, with a relatively small investment at the outset (see Appendix 2), although, in recent years, this investment has intensified in that country and in Chile.

We start this chapter with an overview of the mining industry, where we analyze the evolution of regulations in Mexico and present an overview of the industrial structure and competitors. In a subsequent section, we explain the cases separately and describe the evolution of each company both locally and internationally, highlighting the key factors that made them multinational companies. Finally, we present some conclusions and lessons.

THE MINING INDUSTRY

The global value of the mining industry has grown at an average annual rate of 14.7 percent since 2004. Despite being severely hit by the global financial crisis, the value of the industry reached a historical high of nearly US$1.5 trillion in 2014. Asia is the main contributor (55 percent), followed by Europe (16.7 percent), Latin America (13.8 percent), North America (10.3 percent), and Africa (4.7 percent). Including iron and steel and the diversified metals and mining industries, there are 84 public multinationals considered "global leading" in the 2014 Forbes list (Forbes, 2015b). The revenue of the top 50 combined exceeds $1.17 trillion. As measured only by profit, the top ten mining companies are in ranked order in Table 4.1.

Latin America is a key player in global production and the volume of reserves of copper, silver, zinc, iron ore, and tin. Brazil, Chile, Colombia, Peru, Mexico, and Argentina contribute nearly 95 percent of the total value of the industry in Latin America. For Chile, Colombia, and Peru, the mineral rents represent over 10 percent of the gross domestic product (GDP). In Mexico, the value of the industry has grown at a steady pace from US$3.67 billion in 2004 to US$14.85 billion in 2014, representing on average 0.9 percent of

Table 4.1 *Financial indicators of Grupo México, Industrias Peñoles, and main competitors*

Company (US$ in million)	Net Sales	Net Profit	EBITDA	Total Assets	Total Equity	EBITDA Margin (%)	5-Yr Sales Growth CAGR(%)
BHP Billiton (Australia)	67,206	15,269	32,359	151,413	85,382	44	6
Rio Tinto (UK)	47,664	9,305	19,996	107,827	54,594	41	2.6
Vale (Brazil)	37,608	1,189	12,493	116,901	56,521	33	13.6
Jiangxi Copper (China)	32,180	442	642	15,355	7,574	2	30.9
Freeport-McMoRan Copper (USA)	21,438	-1,308	8,799	58,795	23,225	18	7.3
Southern Copper (USA)	18,467	1,963	6,803	70,923	21,340	46	9.1
Vedanta Resources (UK)	12,945	-438	4,353	45,374	17,974	37	14.5
Grupo México (Mexico)	**8,174**	**1,326**	**3,014**	**21,562**	**11,904**	**43**	**13.8**
Antofagasta (Chile)	5,290	459	2,245	12,815	8,034	42	12.3
Industrias Peñoles (Mexico)	**4,098**	**-55**	**856**	**2,337**	**3,793**	**21**	**6.5**

US$ in million, except EBITDA Margin and Sales Growth

Source: Bloomberg, 2015.

Mexico's GDP. Mexico is the largest producer of silver in the world, and is a top-ten producer of bismuth, fluorite, wollastonite, celestine, cadmium, sodium sulfate, diatomite, molybdenum, lead, salt, zinc, baryta, graphite, gold, plaster, and copper (BMI Research, 2015).

The current state of the Mexican mining industry and the relative success of its multinational companies is explained not only by its vast endowment of natural resources, but is also tightly linked to some pivotal historical events. Indeed, until 1917, when the Mexican Constitution established that concessions were to be granted only to Mexican citizens (Delgado & Del Pozo, 2002), American and British companies owned most of the investment in the sector. Difficult economic and political conditions, however, forced major amendments in 1930 with a polished mining law that enabled foreign investors to participate in the industry once again. After these amendments, foreign investors reached ownership of 98 percent of the mines working in the country (Urias, 1980).

The fiscal policy, however, was especially robust in the mining industry. By the early 1950s, the effect of sustained increases in tax rates resulted in a severe crisis of investment and production. During the same period, Mexico also experienced the implementation of the economic model of import substitution industrialization (ISI), which promoted policies of centrally planned industrialization. These circumstances surrounded a critical event in the history of the Mexican mining industry: the enactment of the 1961 Mexican law nationalizing mines (Delgado & Del Pozo, 2002). The 1961 law aimed to ensure control by the Mexican Government and Mexican investors over the mining industry, and to foster both the production and domestic consumption of Mexican mining products. This law laid the foundations for the internationalization of Industrias Peñoles and Grupo México.

The ISI model enjoyed relative success in the following years. Until the mid-1970s Mexico experienced sustained economic growth known as the "Mexican miracle." The mining industry played a central role, contributing with significant employment rates and large volumes of investment. This period, however, lasted less than two decades. In the early 1980s, in the midst of a profound economic crisis, Mexico adopted a liberalization economic model, structured by the World Bank and International Monetary Fund. The mining industry stood immune to the liberalization policies; Mexican capital in the mining industry was rather favored by lenient tax policies and by the privatization of reserves in the following years.

Currently, all mining activities are regulated by the Mexican Mining Law, originally enacted in June 1992 and greatly updated in 2014 with a tax reform. Even though all minerals found in the Mexican territory remain state-owned, private parties may exploit these minerals through concessions granted by the federal government. The current regulatory landscape is generally favorable for mining and foreign direct investment. Foreign companies are required to set up local entities to conduct mining activities, but are allowed to fully own the companies.

Mining concessions are granted for an initial term of 50 years, and can be extended upon request to the Ministry of Economy. They can be transferred only to a Mexican individual or an entity organized under the laws of Mexico and qualified to acquire the mining concession.

GRUPO MÉXICO

Grupo México is a holding company with three subsidiaries: a mining division, whose activities are in the mining-metallurgic industry (concerning exploration, exploitation, and benefits of metallic and non-metallic ores); a transportation division (whose main activity is a multimodal freight railroad service); and an infrastructure division (whose activities are engineering and construction services for large-scale projects at the private and public levels). It should be noted that, in order to compare the performance of this company with the other multinational, Industrias Peñoles, this chapter will focus only on the mining division of Grupo México. Significantly, 83 percent of total sales came from this division; the other 16 percent of sales came from the transportation and infrastructure divisions. As shown in Table 4.2, over the last 15 years, Grupo México has been experiencing important growth in key financial areas.

As part of its globalization strategy, the company coordinates its global marketing through its sales offices in Mexico City (Mexico), Lima (Peru), and Tucson (USA). In this regard, export sales are made mainly to the following companies: Amrod Corp. (USA), Cerro Wire & Cable Co. Inc. (USA), Kataman Metals (USA), Prysmian Cables (Italy), Rea Magnet (USA), Coleman Cable (USA), Alan Wire (USA), Silmet S.P.A. (Italy), Irce S.P.A. (Italy), Mitsui & Co., Ltd. (Japan), and Wilhelm Grillo Handelsgesellschaft (Germany), among others. In addition to the sales made by the company abroad, the company conducts exploration processes abroad to locate new deposits and to increase the reserves of its mines in Mexico and Peru. It also has exploration projects in Chile, Argentina, and Ecuador, through concessions obtained in those countries. The company invested US$79.5 million in the exploration process in 2014, US$57.6 million in 2013, and US$62.2 million in 2012 (Grupo México, 2014).

Table 4.2 *Grupo México key financial data*

	2000	2005	2010	2015
Revenue	3,666	5,189	8,140	8,174
Total assets	1,574	2,335	5,417	21,562
EBITDA	957	2,023	2,133	3,014
Gross profit	578	2,243	3,320	3,358
Net profit	259	1,063	1,659	1,326
Foreign investment	2,200	0	224	120
Exports	2,640	N/A	N/A	932.5
Employees	NA	19,143	25,250	30,025
Countries	2	2	2	3

Data in millions of US dollars
N/A = not available
Source: Authors with data from Bloomberg, Expansion and Company's Report

Grupo México began operating in 1942 in the construction industry, through the company Constructora México – the company was named Grupo México until 1994, but in order to facilitate the reading of this chapter, we will refer to the company as Grupo México throughout. Years later, in 1965, American Smelting and Refining Co. (ASARCO), a US mining company created in 1899, with plants in the USA and Mexico, was associated with a group of Mexican investors, led by Bruno Pagliali and Jorge Larrea; the son of the latter is the current Chairman of the Board. ASARCO had previously reorganized its Mexican mines and plants as Compañía Minera ASARCO. This association was due to the changes in the Mexican mining law, which forced foreign companies to sell their shares in such a way that Mexican investors must own 51 percent of the shares. In this case, the Mexican investors acquired 51 percent of the stocks of Compañía Minera ASARCO. Much like the other foreign mining companies with Mexican subsidiaries at that time, the international trade was between parent and subsidiary, so we could say that Grupo México was born as an international company. Appendix 1 summarizes the history of the most important events of the company.

According to the interview with Xavier García de Quevedo[1] in May 2015, this acquisition was carried out by the Mexican investors with funding from New York banks. This was possible because the Mexican investor Jorge Larrea already had a good credit history with those banks, due to past operations of his own construction company. The first decision of Jorge Larrea, as manager of the company, was to mechanize the mines, as mentioned by Mr. García de Quevedo.

In 1974, because of the restrictions on foreign participation in the capital of mining companies in Mexico, the Mexican investors acquired an additional 15 percent stake in the company, so at that point, ASARCO owned 34 percent of the equity. The company then went through a restructuring process. First, Compañía Minera

[1]   Xavier García de Quevedo has served as a member of Grupo México Board of Directors from November 1999 to the present, among other positions in the same company.

ASARCO was renamed Industrial Minera Mexico IMSA, and in 1978 the Larrea family established Mexico Desarrollo Industrial Minero MEDIMSA, in order to control IMSA. A few years later, Grupo Industrial Mineral Mexico GIMMEX was created in order to control MEDIMSA (Grupo México, 2014).

Because of the economic crisis, in 1982 the Government of Mexico was forced to take measures imposed by the World Bank and the International Monetary Fund (Delgado & Del Pozo, 2002). As a part of this process, the Mexican Government started selling their own companies: a total of 96 companies at the beginning of the process (Tanski & French, 2001). In 1988, Grupo México took advantage of this situation and acquired 95 percent of the company Mexicana de Cobre (Mexican copper). An important reason for this acquisition was that, in 1978, this company started exploitation of the La Caridad mine, a mine rich in copper, in association with the Mexican Government. That mine contained a leaching plant, with a production capacity of 22,000 metric tons per year. A total of US$50 million was invested in that mine by the previous owners of the company.

Once Grupo México acquired Mexicana de Cobre, the international experience acquired by ASARCO contributed to the further modernization of the La Caridad mine, because there was an exchange of technology and knowledge with ASARCO through the investigation center in South Lake City, which was verbally confirmed by Mr. García de Quevedo in May 2015. As a result, one year after the acquisition, the company expanded its production capacity by 29 percent. As a part of the same Mexican Government privatization process, in 1990 Grupo México acquired 100 percent of another mine in the Mexican state of Sonora (the Buenvista mine, formerly known as the Cananea Mine) by public auction through their subsidiary, Mexicana de Cobre.

In 1994, there was a change in the board of directors when Jorge Larrea vacated the presidency and his son, German Larrea, became the Chairman of the Board: a position he has retained ever since. Jorge had invited German to be a member of the board of directors in 1981, taking the position of executive vice-president. Regarding his qualifications, according to Bloomberg business (n.d.), German Larrea has a Bachelor's degree in Business Administration from Janus University and a Global Leadership Program certificate from Thunderbird School of Global Management. Before he became chairman of the board of Grupo México, he had founded Grupo Impresa (a printing and publishing company) in 1978 and served as its Chief Executive Officer until 1989.

German Larrea always followed the strategy of his father, but the fact that he also sought the internationalization of the company was confirmed by Mr. García de Quevedo. In 1994, a partnership named Grupo México was created to control MEDIMSA. One of German Larrea's first strategies as Chairman was to diversify into other industries. Consequently, in 1997, in partnership with the American railway company Union Pacific, Grupo México formed a company called Grupo Ferroviario Mexicano GFM, in which Grupo México had a 74 percent stake, with the rest belonging to Union Pacific. In the same year, by public tender, GFM acquired the entire company of Ferrocarril Pacífico (today, Ferrocarril Mexicano), for US$575 million: a railway company whose main operations were in the north and the Pacific of Mexico (Grupo México, 2014). It is important to note that, at that time, the railway owned by Grupo México was carrying only 3 percent of the company's minerals; that is, this acquisition was not made in order to contribute significantly to the corporate mining activities, but rather to the diversification of the business, as was confirmed by Mr. García de Quevedo.

In 1999, even as ASARCO reported financial losses and some environmental problems, Grupo México acquired it for US$2.2 billion through a hostile takeover.[2] To date, Grupo México has retained ASARCO as a wholly owned US operating subsidiary. The main reason for the acquisition of ASARCO was that, at that time, it was the

---

[2] A hostile takeover takes place when the target company resists a merger, and then the acquiring company must decide to pursue the merger by the purchase of the target stock in secret, and at some point makes a *tender offer* (Ross, Westerfield & Jaffe, 2013).

owner of 54.2 percent of the Southern Peru Copper Corporation (SPCC). SPCC is a Peruvian company, created in 1954, which entered into a bilateral agreement with the Peruvian government for the development and exploitation of the following mines and plants: i) the ore body Toquepala, whose operation started in 1960; ii) the mining complex The Cuajone, whose operations started in 1976; and iii) the Ilo copper refinery. It is important to mention that before Grupo México acquired ASARCO, the latter company had its headquarters in New York since 1899, and it had 15 working mines: two in the USA, one in Canada, one in Peru and eleven in Mexico, which together contributed in an important way to the internationalization of ASARCO.

One of the first actions taken by the board of directors after the full acquisition of ASARCO was to restructure it, in order to make it profitable. For example, they got rid of the divisions dealing with the coating of metal parts, and with lime and cement; this was because they were not part of the main business model of Grupo México. With the sale of these two divisions, the company paid bridging credit that was used for the acquisition of ASARCO for US$800 million. In addition, and according to Mr. García de Quevedo, the company relocated its main offices to Arizona. It also adopted a strategy to close units that were not profitable, as can be seen in Appendix 1, so Grupo México decided to close, sell and reduce operations in many US mines and plants. Thus in 2005, ASARCO filed for chapter 11 of the United States Bankruptcy Code,[3] and in 2009 ASARCO emerged from bankruptcy completely debt free and reintegrated in Grupo México. Currently, ASARCO owns the following copper mines: Mission, Ray, and Silver Bell in Arizona; the SX-EW plants: Ray and Silver Bell; a copper smelter in Hayden, Arizona; and a metallurgical complex in Amarillo, Texas (Grupo México, 2014).

By the year 2000, the company had carried out a major restructuring process focused mainly on the internationalization of the

---

[3]   The US Bankruptcy law permits for reorganization. According to this law, the chapter 11 debtor usually proposes a plan of reorganization to keep its business alive and pay creditors over time.

mining division. The main changes were the separation of the railroad division and the creation of a holding company for the mining division. Therefore, Americas Mining Corporation (AMC) was created, with headquarters in Phoenix, Arizona. In particular, its purposes were to hold the capital of the mining subsidiaries, to maintain investments in short-term cash, and to fund mining subsidiaries or receive funds from them. Because of the restructuring, the three mine subsidiaries were: ASARCO in the USA; SPCC in Peru; and Minera Mexico in Mexico (Grupo México, 2014).

In 2002, SPCC started operations in the port of Ilo, Peru. Previously, in 1996, SPCC had been listed on the New York Stock Exchange (NYSE) and on the Lima Stock Exchange (BVL). In order to avail itself of growth opportunities through strategic acquisitions, and given the low prices of copper and other metals, in 2002, Grupo México increased its shareholding in SPCC from 54.2 percent to 75.1 percent through Americas Mining Corporation (Grupo México, 2005). In 2005, SPCC was renamed Southern Copper Corporation (SCC).

In 2003, with the aim of improving cost and efficiency of mineral recovery at the leaching plants, and to eliminate the expensive cartage process using trucks, SPCC started the expansion and modernization of a Leachable Deposits Project at Toquepala in Peru (Grupo México, 2006). In 2005, through SCC, Grupo México acquired Minera Mexico (Mexico Mining) and subsidiaries in an all-stock transaction, through a merger agreement. This transaction made Grupo México the largest mining company in both Mexico and Peru, as well as owner of the largest copper reserves among all public companies and one of the largest mining/metallurgical corporations in the world (Grupo México, 2006).

In 2006, due to a commitment acquired in 1997 with the Peruvian government, SPCC allocated 30.5 percent of that year's total investment to the modernization of the copper smelter in Ilo in Peru. The product of the new smelter would be copper anodes, instead of the blisters that were previously produced. The goal of the project was to maintain the production levels and to use advanced technology to reduce sulfur emissions.

That same year, with the objective of increasing copper cathode production in the Cananea mine (in Mexico), Grupo México started the building of a solvent extraction and electro winning plant. Also, with the aim of allowing the processing of all concentrates produced by its underground mining units, there was an expansion of the 50 percent capacity of the Zinc Electrolyte Plant at the mine in San Luis Potosi, Mexico (Grupo México 2006). In 2007, SPCC ended the project of modernization of foundry processes in the Peruvian plant. Because of this modernization process, the production of blister copper anodes has been replaced, which has enabled cost reductions (Grupo México, 2014).

As a part of the expansion process in Mexico, in 2007 a project called "El Arco" was started in the Mexican state of Baja, California, consisting of an open pit mine with a concentrator with a capacity of 100,000 tons per day, producing copper concentrates with relevant contents of gold. The company also started the construction of a solvent extraction and electro winning plant with an annual production capacity of 35,000 tons of cathodic copper. The investment for this project was approximately US$1.5 billion (Grupo México, 2007). In 2007, Grupo México obtained the mining concessions of the Angangueo mine, which is a polymetallic mine of copper, zinc, lead, and silver. With an estimated investment of US$175 million, Angangueo included a concentrator plant, which had an estimated average annual metal content production of 10,400 tons of copper and 7,000 tons of zinc in the first seven years. The plant began production in the first half of 2015 (Grupo México, 2007, 2008, and 2014).

In 2008, Grupo México acquired a 49 percent stake in the Mexican mine Minera Pilares from the US company Freeport McMoran, which positioned Grupo México as the 100 percent owner of the mine. Pilares is intended to operate as an open pit mine. With this project, the company expects to increase the copper production by 40,000 tons per year, sending ore from the Pilares mine to their concentrator at La Caridad (Grupo México, 2014).

In Peru, construction of the sea terminal for sulfuric acid at Ilo began in 2009 as a complementary project to the modernization of the smelter at Ilo. The sea terminal was built to ship the sulfuric acid produced at the smelter directly. In the same year, construction of the tailing disposal system at Quebrada Honda was begun, with the purpose of increasing the height of the current dam at Quebrada Honda, and to store future tailings from the Toquepala and Cuajone mines. The project has an approximate budgeted cost of US$66 million. The expansion of a Cuajone concentrator was also started, with the purpose of increasing the mining and milling capacity and accelerating and increasing annual copper production by approximately 50,000 tons. In Mexico, expansion of the La Caridad mine began, with an approximate investment of US$230 million, in order to increase the current milling capacity at the concentrator from 90,000 to 120,000 tons per day. With this project, an increase in the annual copper production by 40,000 tons was expected (Grupo México, 2010). From 2010 to 2015, Grupo México has been conducting a process of investment and expansion, locally and abroad, through their subsidiaries in Mexico and Peru. We show that process in Appendix 1.

It is important to mention that in 2014, Grupo México entered an alliance with the Spanish company Magtel, in order to participate in an international tender competition for the Aznalcóllar mine in Seville, Spain. In February 2015, this alliance won the bid. According to an interview with Mr. García de Quevedo, the language, culture, and need for capital in Spain influenced Grupo México's decision (Meza, 2015).

INDUSTRIAS PEÑOLES

Industrias Peñoles is a Mexican company, part of Grupo BAL, a privately held diversified group of independent Mexican companies. The corporate structure of Industrias Peñoles is as follows: Fresnillo plc, Minas Peñoles (Peñoles Mining), Quimica Magna (Magna Chemical), and Infraestructura Peñoles (Peñoles Infrastructure). Industrias Peñoles' mining division is in charge of performing the study, analysis, and development of nonferrous mineral deposits, currently at Mexico, Peru, and Chile, through subsidiaries in each country. This division also explodes minerals with metallic content of gold, silver, zinc, and copper, and oversees the replenishment and increase of reserves. The metals-chemicals division has the task to smelt and refine nonferrous metals and produce high-purity refined metals. Finally, the Fresnillo subsidiary produces silver and gold. At the end of 2014, out of net sales of US$4617.6 million, 81 percent were international sales and the rest were from Mexico. Of the international sales, 89 percent were in the United States, 2.3 percent in Europe, 1.4 percent in South America, and 7 percent in 16 other countries (Industrias Peñoles, 2014). As shown in Table 4.3, in the last 15 years Industrias Peñoles has been experiencing steady growth in the key financial areas such as revenues, total assets, and gross profit, among others.

The mining company Industrias Peñoles started operations in 1887 under the name Compañía Minera Peñoles (Mining Company Peñoles), with the purpose of exploiting three mines in the Mexican state of Durango (Industrias Peñoles, 2014) – the company was named Industrias Peñoles until 1968, but for the sake of simplicity we will continue to refer to the company as Industrias Peñoles throughout this

Table 4.3 *Industrias Peñoles key financial data*

	2000	2005	2010	2015
Revenue	992	1,952	5,090	4,098
Total assets	382	716	1,918	2,337
EBITDA	124	350	1,312	856
Gross profit	12	241	1,094	332
Net profit	–15	156	514	–55
Foreign investment	195	0	108	7
Exports	502.2	1,162.4	3,956.6	3,368.7
Employees	N/A	N/A	8,977	11,555
Countries	2	3	3	3

Data in millions of US dollars
N/A = not available
Source: Authors with data from Bloomberg, Expansion and Company's Report

entire chapter. The first owners of this company were Mexican entrepreneurs. In 1920, the Mexican company Compañía Minerales y Metales (Minerals and Metals Company), a subsidiary of the German company American Metal Co., merged with Peñoles. This merger made Industrias Peñoles a subsidiary of American Metal Co. Even before the birth of Industrias Peñoles, international trade in the mining industry was an exchange between foreign parent companies and their Mexican subsidiaries. Industrias Peñoles was no exception, so it was born as an international company. Before 1920, American Metal Co. had acquired additional properties, including smelters and their rail connections, in other Mexican states.

In 1934, Compañía Metalurgica Peñoles (Metallurgical Company Peñoles) was founded, with the purpose of leasing the smelting and refining plants of the mining company Industrias Peñoles, and gave all contracts to smelt and refine the lead and copper production to the Mexican company, San Francisco Mines of Mexico. The year 1961 was important for the consolidation of Industrias Peñoles because, in preparation for the Mexicanization process,[4] there was a merger between Compañía Minera Peñoles and Compañía Metalurgica Peñoles; as a result, Metalurgica Mexicana Peñoles (Met-Mex Peñoles) was born. After that, American Metal Co. sold its 51 percent interest in Met-Mex Peñoles to two Mexican investors, Jose A. Garcia and Raul Bailleres. The latter had an important role in the consolidation of Industrias Peñoles. Before the acquisition of Industrias Peñoles, Bailleres acquired significant experience as an entrepreneur in both the mining industry and other different sectors. First, he set up the first financial company for mining activities in Mexico, Credito Minero, in 1934. Later, in 1941, he headed a group of Mexican investors to acquire the majority of the brewer, Cervecería Moctezuma (today CM/Heineken). He also directed the financial group that became the main shareholder of one of today's most successful retail firms in Mexico, El Palacio de Hierro, among other companies (ITAM, 2015). Raul Bailleres also had 15 years' experience in

[4]   Mexicanization is the process that forced foreign companies to sell their shares. In the mine sector, Mexican investors must have held 51 percent of the shares.

managing the buying and selling of nearly all the gold, silver, and mercury in the country (Pederson, 1998).

In 1963 Industrias Peñoles opened the chemical plant Quimica del Rey (King Chemistry), a company dedicated to the production and marketing of sodium sulfate, oxide magnesium in varying types and specialties, magnesium sulfate, and ammonium sulfate (Industrias Peñoles, 2014). One year later, Industrias Peñoles acquired 51 percent of Compañía Fresnillo (Fresnillo Company), which at that time owned two Mexican mines: the Fresnillo mine (which produced silver and gold), in the state of Zacatecas, and the Naica mine, in the state of Chihuahua. This latter mine produces lead and zinc concentrates, and today has an installed capacity of 954,000 tons per year of ore milled (Industrias Peñoles, 2014). That same year, Industrias Peñoles also acquired 51 percent of Compañia Zimapan (Zimapan Company), which owned two Mexican mines, El Carrizal and El Monte, both in the Mexican state of Hidalgo (Industrias Peñoles, 2014). Both acquisitions occurred within the context of the aforementioned Mexicanization process. In 1965, American Metal Climax sold its 49 percent stake in Industrias Peñoles for about US$10 million. For that purpose, Industrias Peñoles obtained a US$8 million loan in a US bank (Delgado & Del Pozo, 2002).

In 1967, after the death of the Chairman of the Board, Raul Bailleres, his son, Alberto Bailleres, took over the position and has remained in post to date (Industrias Peñoles, 2014). Before taking that position he had occupied some other positions in other companies in which his father was a main shareholder: for example, in Banco de Comercio (Commerce Bank), where he held the position of branch manager while he was studying economics in a Mexican university. After graduation, he entered Cervecería Montezuma (today CM/ Heineken Mexico), where he occupied many positions until he finally became President of the Board in 1967 (ITAM, 2015). In an interview with the Mexican magazine *CNN*, Bailleres mentioned that he learned discipline at the Culver Military Academy in the United States, which he joined at the age of 15, without knowing English. In that school, he received the Man of the Year award. In addition, he mentioned "that school forged my character, because at that time I suffered the prejudices that exist[ed] in the United States against Mexicans" (Baltazar, 2014).

A year later, in 1968, the company changed its structure, adopting its current name, Industrias Peñoles (Peñoles Industries), and becoming the holding and financial core company, transferring the metallurgical, smelting, and refining operations to the subsidiary, Met-Mex Peñoles. This same year, Peñoles was listed for the first time on the Mexican Stock Exchange and its shares started floating. In 1982, Mexico fell into an economic crisis. The government devalued the local currency, the peso, and some few months later ran out of money, whereupon the country defaulted on its foreign debt. As a result, the peso was devaluated again. Because the mining company Industrias Peñoles was selling most of its products abroad in dollars, and its costs were in devalued pesos, profits were enlarged, which allowed the company to reduce its liabilities. In particular, foreign debt was reduced from US$208 million in 1983 to US$141 million at the end of 1985. Because of its healthy finances, in 1982 the company was in a position to acquire 40 percent of its Met-Mex Peñoles subsidiary from Bethlehem Steel, a US steel producer with headquarters in Pennsylvania (Pederson, 1998).

In 1992 the company started operations in an international marine terminal located in the Mexican state of Tamaulipas, which mainly handles export shipments of bulk chemicals. This terminal has a long-term concession from the federal government to use federal land with sea access. From this terminal, the company sends products to Venezuela, Brazil, and Germany (Industrias Peñoles, 2014; Molina & Araiza, 2011).

In 1994, together with Dowa Mining and Sumitomo Corporation, Industrias Peñoles acquired 51 percent ownership of a Mexican mine, Tizapa, in Mexico State, which is a polymetallic mine producing lead, copper, and zinc concentrates which are exported to Japan. In addition, in that year the company started operations at the La Cienega mine, located in the Mexican state of Durango, which produces zinc and lead concentrates and silver precipitates. In 1996, with the aim of strengthening and integrating its mining and metallurgical sectors, Industrias Peñoles acquired from the American company AMAX, Inc. a minority interest in their subsidiary, Fresnillo (Industrias Peñoles, 2014).

Within the globalization strategy of Industrias Peñoles, one highlight is the alliance with the Chilean copper producer Codelco, established in 1999 in order to exploit the large deposits that it had acquired in the Mexican state of Sonora. In 2000, Industrias Peñoles partnered with Japan's Dowa Mining Co. Ltd. and Sumitomo Corp. to operate the mine Minera Rey de Plata (Silver King Mining) in the Mexican state of Guerrero. Industrias Peñoles had 51 percent ownership of this mine. A year later, the company started operations on the zinc mine Madero, in the Mexican state of Zacatecas, which today has an installed capacity of 2,700,000 tons per year of milled ore (Industrias Peñoles, 2014). Then, in 2003, Industrias Peñoles entered into a 20-year contract with the French company Alston and the US Company Sithe for the construction and operation of a power plant that would ensure the necessary energy for their exploitation and refining process.

As a diversified group, and aiming to shore up market recognition of the value of each of its business segments, in 2004, according to the Mexican newspaper El Siglo de Torreon (2004), Industrias Peñoles made a public tender offer through the Lima Stock Exchange to acquire up to 51 percent of the equity stock of the Peruvian firm Compañía Minera Milpo. As we'll explain later, Industrias Peñoles had been conducting an exploration process in Peru since 1993; however, this operation represented for Industrias Peñoles a further step towards the integration and expansion of its mining activities in Peru. Nevertheless, the Peruvian mining company Milpo rejected the US$108 million offer on the basis that it was insufficient, according to the newspaper Perú 21 (2004a). A few days later, Industrias Peñoles mentioned that it had decided not to make a new offer to acquire Milpo (Perú 21, 2004b).

In order to highlight the market recognition of the value of each of its business segments, in 2008 Industrias Peñoles restructured its mining operations into two groups: i) precious metals, grouped under the Fresnillo plc subsidiary, with three operating mines and related exploration projects; and ii) base metals, under Minas Peñoles, with six operating mines and related exploration projects. This strategy would make the organizational structure of the company more agile and slim (KPMG, 2010). After that, Fresnillo plc was listed on the London Stock Exchange in 2008. In that year, Industrias Peñoles announced that it had carried out the acquisition of a 1.65 percent equity interest in the Canadian miner, Mag Silver Corp, through its wholly owned subsidiary, Minas Peñoles. Mag Silver Corp is a Vancouver-based firm engaged in the acquisition, exploration, and development of mineral properties located in Mexico. Peñoles has been conducting a process of investment and expansion.

An important step in the internationalization process of Industrias Peñoles is the exploration processes abroad. At the end of 2014, Industrias Peñoles led exploration processes in Peru and Chile. In this regard, the company currently has the Peru project Racaycocha, which consists of concessions for 28,000 hectares of fertile land for exploration (Industrias Peñoles, 2014). As can be seen in the contracts held by the Ministerio de Energia y Minas de Peru (2015) (Ministry of Energy and Mines of Peru), the exploration process in Peru is done through contracts between the Peruvian government and the Industrias Peñoles subsidiary in Peru, Peñoles of Peru. By signing this type of agreement, the mining companies have access to tax incentives, such as the return of General Sales Tax (GST) and the promotion tax.[5] In turn, the investor undertakes to carry investments in exploration by an amount, and for a specific

---

[5] According to the Law of the General Sales Tax and Consumer Tax in Peru, in 2015 this devolution tax was 18 percent. On other hand, the regulation of the Municipal Taxation Act defines the tax refund promotion Municipal as 2 percent of the value of transactions subject to GST.

period, for all the mining properties in Peru. For example, in 2003 the concession consisted of an investment by Industrias Peñoles of US$593,900 for 11 months in 23 properties of Peñoles of Peru. In 2005 it was an investment of USD $959,000 for 18 months in 24 properties of Industrias Peñoles in Peru. In 2009, the investment was of US$1.5 million for six years in eight properties of Industrias Peñoles in Peru; in 2010, of US$5.2 million for eight months in two properties; and in 2013, of US$18 million for six months (Ministerio de Energia y Minas de Peru, 2015). Additionally, as part of the expansion of exploration in Peru, in 2014 Industrias Peñoles bought from the Canadian company, Duran Ventures Inc., the project Aguila, a porphyry copper-molybdenum, and a 50 percent stake in the Coro mining concessions, as well as other assets, for US$7 million.[6]

Regarding the reasons for the exploration expansion of Industrias Peñoles in Peru, in an interview with the CEO of Industrias Peñoles, Fernando Alanis Ortega, by the Mexican newspaper *Milenio* (Valdes, 2014), he said that in 2014 the company faced adverse conditions in international markets, when the prices of base metals and precious metals fell from 20 percent to 15 percent. Industrias Peñoles also faced fiscal complications, when the Mexican government increased the mining tax to 7.5 percent, plus an extra 0.5 percent if the company worked in precious metals. In the same interview, the CEO commented that these made the investment in the Peru mines more attractive. In this regard, García (2015) made a comparison of tax burdens in some countries in Latin America, showing that the tax burden mining varies. For example: in Argentina it is between 46 percent and 160 percent; in Mexico it varies from 46 percent to 53 percent on operating profit. In Peru it varies from 42 percent to 52 percent; and finally, Chile is where the lowest tax burden is imposed on mining – the tax is between 38 percent and 49 percent.

---

[6] Duran Ventures is engaged in the acquisition, exploration, and development of porphyry copper, molybdenum, precious metals, and polymetallic deposits in Peru.

As part of the internationalization process, through exploration in Chile, Industrias Peñoles has records dating back to 2007, when it negotiated with the company Anaconda Mining an option to acquire 65 percent of the copper–gold project Inca de Oro. This transaction was for US$22 million. The project was planned to last for forty-eight months, in the area of Copiapo, in the north of Santiago de Chile.[7] Of this investment, US$12 million were used to pay cash to Anaconda Mining, and the rest for exploration expenses (Anaconda Mining, 2007). Nevertheless, Industrias Peñoles decided in 2008 not to continue the project, because it did not meet the investment criteria of Industrias Peñoles (2007, 2008). In 2010, the process of exploration in Chile started again, beginning with selective prospecting to identify opportunities, mainly focused on copper (Industrias Peñoles, 2010); by 2012, the intensive prospecting campaign resulted in a mining concession of 41,000 hectares. As a part of the exploration process in Chile, in 2013 a drilling process was conducted at the Zulema, La Laguna, and Nicole copper prospects (Industrias Peñoles, 2013), and in 2014, geological work began at Llancahue copper prospect (Industrias Peñoles, 2014).

Regarding the reasons for investment in Chile, a study of Wilson & Cervantes (2014) shows that Chile has very significant mineral wealth. In this study, which measures the attractiveness of each country, assuming that all policies are equally good in all countries and regions, Peru is the eighth most attractive country for mining worldwide, and Chile is the most attractive country in Latin America; in terms of this measure of mineral wealth, Chile reached fourth place in worldwide ranking.

COMPARISON AND CONCLUSIONS

From these two companies' internationalization processes, we can draw the following conclusions. First, one of the similarities in the histories of these two companies is that the current Chairmen of the Board are the sons of the former Chairmen of the Board. Also, both studied at

[7] Anaconda Mining is a gold producer with exploration projects in Canada and Chile.

a US school. Industrias Peñoles' chairman, Alberto Bailleres, who – according to the world's billionaires list of Forbes (2015a) – is the third richest man in Mexico and 121st globally, studied at Culver Military Academy at the age of 15, which forged his character (by his own account). Grupo México's chairman, German Larrea, who – according to the world's billionaires list of Forbes (2015a) – is the second richest man in Mexico and 77th globally, earned his bachelor's degree at a US university, Janus University. Before becoming Chairman of the Board, both had other directorial experience or were entrepreneurs: Bailleres was a manager within companies in which his father was a board member, and Larrea founding a printing and publishing company.

Another similarity of these two companies was in terms of Government influence. Changes in Mexican mining law in 1961 decreed that mining could only be undertaken by the state or private companies financed with a majority of national capital. Meanwhile, the US Company ASARCO Incorporated had to sell 51 percent of its interest to a group of Mexican investors. On the other hand, a group of Mexican investors acquired 51 percent interest of today's Industrias Peñoles from the German company, American Metal Co. However, one key difference is that, at that moment, ASARCO owns the Peruvian company Southern Peru Copper Corporation SPCC. Therefore, a few years later when Grupo México acquired ASARCO, it acquired SPCC indirectly.

A major difference in the process to become a multinational company is that, in the case of Grupo México, the process began a couple of years after the succession of the presidency of the board, from father to son, with the purchase of ASARCO. In addition, after this succession, Grupo México conducted a continuous process of expansion and modernization of the mines and plants in Peru, through its subsidiary SPCC, and then this process of expansion and modernization was replicated in Mexico, along with the acquisition of new mines and mining concessions, as shown in Appendix 1. It is important to mention that when Grupo México acquired SPCC indirectly, this company had 50 years' operating experience in Peru, so it had a technological heritage that was shared with the Mexico mines.

Meanwhile, Industrias Peñoles also conducted modernizing processes in its mines and plants in Mexico; however, the process to become a multinational company began with an exploration process in Peru, six years after the succession of the chair of the board, in 1993. For that purpose, Industrias Peñoles created a subsidiary in Peru, Peñoles of Peru. Such investments in Peru were relatively small at the beginning, and have been increasing gradually. They have been more significant recently, in 2013 and 2014, because the tax on mining increased in Mexico. So, given the tax incentives that exist in Peru, and the rich mineral reserves of that country, it has become more attractive to invest there. Both companies also have exploration processes in Chile, as a country rich in minerals with attractive tax incentives for investment in this sector.

An important lesson from these cases is that the indirect acquisition of SPCC by Grupo México included mines that were already being productive, and SPCC had almost 50 years' experience in Peru, which was highlighted with the modernization and expansion of its mines and plants. By contrast, Industrias Peñoles has had to carry out exploration investment through concessions, to detect areas rich in minerals in Peru. Even when it recently detected potential exploitation areas, this internationalization process has made the difference with its competitor, Grupo México.

Finally, it is important to note that Grupo México has diversified its business line to the transportation sector, particularly railways, not in order to transport its own minerals, but to diversify its business. It also supports the infrastructure sector, mainly in oil exploration projects, although these two divisions together represent only 23 percent of total sales. Meanwhile, Industrias Peñoles also has an infrastructure division, but only for the generation of energy for its own mines and plants.

REFERENCES

Anaconda Mining. 2007. Press release dated June 7. Toronto: Anaconda Mining.

Baltazar, E. 2014. *Baillères quería un aula, no un 'Palacio de Hierro'.* CNN Expansión, http://expansion.mx/especiales/2014/10/28/bailleres-queria-dirigir-el-aula-no-un-palacio-de-hierro. Accessed July 20, 2015.

Bloomberg business. n.d. Executive profile of German Larrea. *Bloomberg.* www .bloomberg.com/research/stocks/people/person.asp?personId=1152856&privca pId=879908. Accessed September 18, 2015.

BMI Research 2015. Business Monitor International: Data profile. www .bmiresearch.com. Accessed January 6, 2015.

Delgado, R. & Del Pozo, R. 2002. *Minería, estado y gran capital en Mexico.* Distrito Federal, Mexico: UNAM.

Forbes 2015a. The World's Billionaires ranking 2015. Forbes. www.forbes.com. Accessed October 1, 2015.

Forbes 2015b. The world's biggest public companies: Ranking 2014. Forbes. www .forbes.com. Accessed February 15, 2015.

García, M. 2015. Carga fiscal minera, September 9. El Peruano. www.elperuano .com.pe/noticia-carga-fiscal-minera-32681.aspx Accessed June 25, 2015.

Grupo México. 2014. Annual Reports. BMV. www.bmv.com.mx. Accessed June 27, 2015.

Grupo México. 2010. Annual Reports. BMV. www.bmv.com.mx. Accessed June 25, 2015.

Grupo México. 2008. Annual Reports. BMV. www.bmv.com.mx. Accessed June 16, 2015

Grupo México. 2007. Annual Reports. BMV. www.bmv.com.mx. Accessed June 15, 2015.

Grupo México. 2006. Annual Reports. BMV. www.bmv.com.mx. Accessed June 14, 2015.

Grupo México. 2005. Annual Reports. BMV. www.bmv.com.mx. Accessed June 12, 2015.

Industrias Peñoles. 2014. Annual Reports. BMV. www.bmv.com.mx. Accessed June 10, 2015.

Industrias Peñoles. 2013. Annual Reports. BMV. www.bmv.com.mx. Accessed June 1, 2015

Industrias Peñoles. 2010. Annual Reports. BMV. www.bmv.com.mx. Accessed June 9, 2015

Industrias Peñoles. 2008. Annual Reports. BMV. www.bmv.com.mx. Accessed June 11, 2015

Industrias Peñoles. 2007. Annual Reports. BMV. www.bmv.com.mx. Accessed June 10, 2015.

ITAM. 2015. History and Founders. *ITAM.* www.itam.mx/en/acerca/historia/his toria.php. Accessed April 27, 2015.

KPMG. 2010. Industrias Peñoles: *La minera mexicana da vida a Fresnillo y abre camino en Europa.* Mexico: KPMG.

Meza, O. 2015. *Grupo México inicia la conquista del sector minero en España,* media release, 21 April, Forbes, www.forbes.com.mx/grupo-mexico-inicia-la-conquista-del-sector-minero-en-espana/#gs.JECmKvs. Accessed June 10, 2015.

Molina, J. & Araiza, S. 2011. *Peñoles en la agroindustria empresa orgullosamente mexicana. Revista Mexicana de Agronegocios,* 28: 490–501.

Ministerio de energía y minas de Peru. 2015. Contratos de Inversión en Exploración. *MINEM.* www.minem.gob.pe/_detalle.php?idSector=1&idTitular=189&idMen u=sub154&idCateg=189. Accessed September 15, 2015.

Pederson, J. 1998. *International Directory of Company Histories,* Vol. 22. Detroit, MI: St. James Press.

Perú 21. 2004a. Milpo rechaza oferta lanzada por mexicana Peñoles. http://peru21.pe /noticia/72318/milpo-rechaza-oferta-lanzada-mexicana-penoles. Accessed June 15, 2015.

Perú 21. 2004b. Mexicana Peñoles dice que no hará nueva oferta por Milpo. http:// peru21.pe/noticia/94923/mexicana-penoles-dice-que-no-hara-nueva-oferta-milpo. Accessed June 15, 2015.

Ross, S., Westerfield, R. & Jaffe, J. 2013. *Corporate Finance.* New York, NY: McGraw-Hill.

El Siglo de Torreón. 2004. Da Peñoles paso a etapa expansiva. www .elsiglodetorreon.com.mx/noticia/111565.da-penoles-paso-a-etapa-expansiva .html. Accessed 1 June 2015

Tanski, J. & French, D. 2001. Capital concentration and market power in Mexico's manufacturing industry: Has trade liberalization made a difference? *Journal of Economic Issues,* 35(3): 675–711.

Urias, H. 1980. ¿Quién controla la minería mexicana? *Comercio Exterior,* 30(9): 951–963.

Valdés, L. 2014. *Perú más atractivo que México para invertir en minería.* Milenio Laguna. www.milenio.com/negocios/penoles-mina_de_velardena-fernando_ala nis_ortega-inversion_peru_0_361763870.html. Accessed June 13.

Wilson, A. & Cervantes, M. 2014. *Fraser Institute Annual Survey of Mining Companies.* Vancouver: Fraser Institute.

Table 4.4 *Transformation process of Grupo Mexico*

Company Year of investment	Local Mexico				International				
	Name of company, plant, mine acquired	Amount of investment in US dollars	Type of investment	% property	Destination	Name of company, plant, mine acquired	Amount of transaction in US dollars	Type of investment	% property
1965	Campania Minera Asarco	N/A	Acquisition	51%					
1974	Campania Minera Asarco change name by Industrial Minera Mexico	N/A	Acquisition	15%					
1988	Mexicana de Cobre (miner)	N/A	Acquisition	95%					
1990	Buenavista Mine	N/A	Acquisition	100%					
1997	Ferrocarril Pacifico (railroad)	575 million	Acquisition	74%					
1999					US and Peru	Asarco Incorporated (included the 54.2% of SPCC)	2.2 billion	Acquisition	100%
1999					US	Asarco's Specialty Chemicals Division	503 million	Sale	N/A

Table 4.4 (*cont.*)

Company	Year of investment	Local Mexico				Destination	International			
		Name of company, plant, mine acquired	Amount of investment in US dollars	Type of investment	% property		Name of company, plant, mine acquired	Amount of transaction in US dollars	Type of investment	% property
	2000					US	American Limestone Company	211 million	Sale	N/A
	2001					US	Tennessee Mines Division	N/A	Suspend operation	N/A
	2001					US	Mission and Amarillo mines	N/A	Reduces mine production	N/A
Grupo Mexico	2002					Peru	Southern Peru Copper Corporation SPCC	N/A	Acquisition	75%
	2003					Peru	Leachable Deposits Project, at Toquepala	N/A	Expansion and modernization	N/A
	2005					US	Asarco	N/A	Chapter 11	N/A
	2005	Minera Mexico	N/A	Acquisition	N/A	Peru	Copper smelter of Ilo	N/A	Modernization	N/A
	2005	Ferrosur (Railway)	N/A	Acquisition	N/A					
	2006	Cananea Mine	N/A	Building of a solvent extraction	N/A	Peru	Copper smelter of Ilo	N/A	Modernization	N/A
	2006		N/A		N/A					

Table 4.4 (cont.)

Company		Local Mexico				International				
	Year of investment	Name of company, plant, mine acquired	Amount of investment in US dollars	Type of investment	% property	Destination	Name of company, plant, mine acquired	Amount of transaction in US dollars	Type of investment	% property
	2007	Zinc Electrolyte Plant, Sn Luis Potosi		Capacity expansion						
		El Arco	1.5 billion	Building an open pit mine, a solvent extraction and an electro winning plant	N/A	Peru	Foundry processes	N/A	Modernization	N/A
	2007	Angangueo mine (polymetallic)	175 million	Mining concession	N/A					
	2008	Minera Pilares		Acquisition	49%					
	2009	La Caridad Mine	230 million	Capacity expansion	N/A	Peru	Sea Terminal for Sulfuric Acid at Ilo	N/A	Start building	N/A

Table 4.4 (cont.)

Company	Year of investment	Local Mexico				International				
		Name of company, plant, mine acquired	Amount of investment in US dollars	Type of investment	% property	Destination	Name of company, plant, mine acquired	Amount of transaction in US dollars	Type of investment	% property
	2009					Peru	Tailing Disposal System at Quebrada Honda	66 million	Start building	N/A
	2009					Peru	Cuajone concentrator	N/A	Capacity expansion	N/A
	2010					Peru	Toquepala mine	N/A	Capacity expansion	N/A
Grupo México	2012	Buenavista Mine	38 million	Building of Molybdenum plant		Peru	Tia Maria plant, (electrolyte copper cathodes)	1400 million	Building of electrolyte copper cathodes plant	N/A
	2012	Buenavista Mine	1.3 million	Building of Copper Concentrator						
	2014					Peru	Toquepala mine	289 million	Construction of an in-pit crusher and	N/A

Table 4.4 (cont.)

Company	Year of investment	Local Mexico				International				
		Name of company, plant, mine acquired	Amount of investment in US dollars	Type of investment	% property	Destination	Name of company, plant, mine acquired	Amount of transaction in US dollars	Type of investment	% property
									a conveyor belt system	
	2014					Peru	Cuajone mine	146 million	Technological improvements	N/A
	2014					Peru	Cuajone mine	65 million	Improve slope stability	N/A
	2015					Spain	Aznalcollar mining	N/A	Won a mine concession	N/A

Source: By the authors with information from Section 3 of this chapter

APPENDIX 2

Table 4.5 *Transformation process of Industrias Peñoles*

| Company | Year of investment | Local Mexico | | | | International | | | | |
		Name of company, plant, mine acquired	Amount of investment in US dollars	Type of investment	% property	Destination	Name of company, plant, mine acquired	Amount of transaction in US dollars	Type of investment	% property
Industrias Peñoles	1920	Merge with Compañía Minerales y Metales	N/A	Merge	51%					
	1961	Met-Met Peñoles	N/A	Acquisition	51%					
	1963	Química del Rey (chemical plant)	N/A	Creation	100%					
	1964	Compañía Fresnillo	N/A	Acquisition	51%					
	1964	Compañía Zimapan	N/A	Acquisition	51%					
	1965	Peñoles	10 million	Stake from American Metal Climax	49%					
	1986		N/A	Stake	40%					

Table 4.5 (cont.)

| Company | Year of investment | Local Mexico | | | | International | | | | |
		Name of company, plant, mine acquired	Amount of investment in US dollars	Type of investment	% property	Destination	Name of company, plant, mine acquired	Amount of transaction in US dollars	Type of investment	% property
Met-Met Peñoles	1992	International marine terminal	N/A	Start operations	N/A					
	1993					Peru	Several locations	N/A	Start exploration	N/A
	1994	Aleazin plant (galvanized alloys)	N/A	Start operations	N/A					
	1994	Mine Tizapa	N/A	Acquisition	51%					
	1998	La Herradura mine	77 million	Start operations	N/A					
	1999	Tecnología y Servicios de Agua	N/A	Acquisition	N/A					
	2000	Minera Rey de Plata	N/A	Acquisition	51%					
	2001		N/A		N/A					

Table 4.5 (*cont.*)

Company	Year of investment	Local Mexico				International				
		Name of company, plant, mine acquired	Amount of investment in US dollars	Type of investment	% property	Destination	Name of company, plant, mine acquired	Amount of transaction in US dollars	Type of investment	% property
		Zinc mine Madero		Start operations						
	2002	Azurix Mexico City	N/A	Acquisition of assets	N/A					
	2003	Power plant	N/A	Start building	N/A	Peru	23 different properties	0.593 million	Concession for exploration	N/A
	2005					Peru	24 different properties	0.959 million	Concession for exploration	N/A
	2007					Chile	Inca de Oro (copper-gold project)	22 million	Acquisition	65%
	2008	Mag Silver Corp	N/A	Acquisition	1.65%					
	2009					Peru	8 different properties	1.5 million	Concession for exploration	N/A
	2010	Soledad-Dpolos mine	67.8 million	Acquisition	N/A	Peru	2 properties in Racaycocha	5.2 million	Concession for exploration	N/A

Table 4.5 (cont.)

Company	Year of investment	Local Mexico				International				
		Name of company, plant, mine acquired	Amount of investment in US dollars	Type of investment	% property	Destination	Name of company, plant, mine acquired	Amount of transaction in US dollars	Type of investment	% property
	2010					Chile	(copper molybdenum)	N/A	Concession for exploration	
							Several locations	N/A	Exploration process started again	N/A
	2011	Tiazapa mine	56 million	Expansion	N/A					
	2011	La Ciénaga mine	N/A	Expansion	N/A					
	2011	Saucito mine	N/A	Start operations	N/A					
	2012	Zinc mine Rey de Plata	268 million	Start building	N/A					

Table 4.5 (cont.)

Company	Year of investment	Local Mexico				Destination	International			
		Name of company, plant, mine acquired	Amount of investment in US dollars	Type of investment	% property		Name of company, plant, mine acquired	Amount of transaction in US dollars	Type of investment	% property
Industrias Peñuelos	2012	Plant Quimica del Rey	43 million	Expansion	N/A					
	2012	Gold mine Noche Buena	N/A	Start operations	54%					
	2013					Peru	2 properties in Racaycocha (copper-molybdenum)	18 million	Concession for exploration	N/A
	2014	Mines: Herradura, Soledad-dipolos and Noche Buena	450 million	Acquisition of entire stake that Newmont USA Limited	N/A	Peru	Aguila (porphyry copper-molybdenum)	7 million	Buy the concession for exploration	100%
	2014					Peru	Coro mining	7 million	Buy the concession for exploration	50%
	2015	Subsidiaries related with hydraulic sector	N/A	Sale	N/A					

Source: By the authors with information from Section 3 of this chapter

5 MultiMexicans in the Petroleum Industry
Pemex

Leticia Armenta Fraire and Hugo Javier Fuentes Castro

INTRODUCTION

Petróleos Mexicanos, Pemex, is the government monopoly that has dominated the oil industry in Mexico since 1938. This company develops the entire production chain: exploration, production, industry, logistics, and marketing, and now has six refineries, eight petrochemical complexes and nine gas processing complexes. It is important to note that oil production in Mexico is mostly of the heavy crude type characterized by a lower price with respect to the light type. The discovery of large oilfields in the mid-seventies allowed Pemex to move from being a company focused on meeting domestic demand for hydrocarbons to becoming a major exporter in the international market. Pemex created PMI in order to achieve its internationalization process successfully. The PMI Group was composed of nineteen subsidiaries from 1988 to 2015, located in different countries.

According to our analysis, PMI manages to overcome the constraints that the Mexican legal framework imposes and it has allowed the firm to have the possibility to increase its income even with its low-price oil production. In particular, the investments made by PMI allow for heavy crude production to be processed whilst minimizing the effects on the price of the Mexican mix. Over time, the administrative possibilities of PMI allow Pemex to have the flexibility to take legal, fiscal, and financial advantage of what other countries could offer abroad. However, along with these advantages, which have allowed Pemex a commercial, physical, and geographical presence, PMI has vanished focus along time, losing its main objective for

120

which it was created. The current redesign of the organization of Pemex is affecting the scope of PMI, leading to this organization's return to its origins of trading.

The organization of this chapter is as follows. The first section, entitled "History of Industry," describes the development of the Mexican oil industry. The second section is called "History of PMI" and portrays PMI from its beginnings to date. Once the industrial history has been described, we attempt to understand and interpret the framework on which PMI was created and developed. This framework was developed through the combination and interaction of internal and external factors. The third section discusses the future of PMI as it faces new organizational changes that Pemex is experiencing. The fourth section deals with the question of what we can learn from Pemex's experience. Finally, in the fifth section, we briefly summarize our findings and conclusions.

HISTORY OF THE INDUSTRY

While the history of oil in Mexico as an independent nation began in the nineteenth century, it was in 1901, with the issuance of the first Oil Law, that the arrival of foreign companies and the massive exploitation of oil wells detonated. Thus, foreign companies dominated the Mexican oil industry.

After the boom years and in a context where production came down, 1933 was a key year for two reasons. The first is that the deposits of Poza Rica, Veracruz were discovered, making this new region a revitalizing industry; secondly, the Petroleum Company of Mexico, SA was created (Petromex), which, under a joint investment share between the government and the private sector, established an interventionist profile as the main objective of the new company was to regulate the domestic market of oil and refinement, with the assurance of domestic supply (especially for the needs of government and railways) and the training of Mexican personnel.

And within the period of government of Lázaro Cárdenas, in the years after 1933 there was stress in the job environment, giving rise in

1935 to the creation of the Union of Oil Workers of the Mexican Republic (STPRM) and, in 1937, under a strategy that promoted greater control over the oil industry, the government created an organization that reported directly to the Executive, the General Administration of the National Petroleum (AGPN), which transferred the properties of Petromex.

On March 18, 1938 President Lázaro Cárdenas nationalized the oil industry, with the AGPN provisionally responsible for administering the expropriated property. The nationalization was the last Mexican government's response to job strain and lack of response from businesses to the repeated requests of the Mexican government to improve working conditions. To understand this response, consider that the Cárdenas regime was imbued with the opinion that the government is the engine and regulator of the economy, which assumes that the state plays a strategic role in those sectors that trigger the country's growth, in unison with a corporatist character. Cárdenas was considered to be the person responsible for collecting the Mexican workers into a corporate structure that is subordinated to the government (the Confederation of Workers of Mexico as the focus of the labor movement) – and also peasants (the Mexican Peasant Confederation, which was renamed the National Peasant Confederation, CNC, a little later).

Finally, on June 7 of that year, Pemex and Distribuidora de Petróleos Mexicanos were created in order to reorganize, concentrate, and coordinate the nationalized industry. Pemex is currently still the monopoly that dominates the oil industry in Mexico; hence, talk about the history of Pemex, its foundation and transformation, is a discussion about the evolution of the entire Mexican oil industry.

The productive performance of Pemex has been affected appreciably since the discovery of deposits and the resulting increase in its reserves, starting from 1976 with total hydrocarbon reserves of 6.338 million barrels through 1977 with 11,160 and reaching 72,500 barrels in 1983. This led to Pemex changing from an entity that sought to provide oil to the country and becoming a producing power that

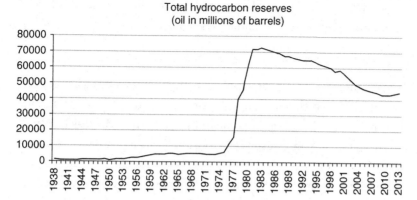

FIGURE 5.1 Total hydrocarbon reserves
Source: Authors, based Pemex. Statistical Yearbook, several years.

could place its production abroad. Figure 5.1 attests to these changes in reserves from 1938 to 2013.

As indicated, the emergence of new oil fields transformed Pemex from an institution focused on satisfying the country's oil needs into an entity capable of offering products abroad. However, all is not so simple, as Mexico produces a high proportion of heavy crude oil of a type whose marketing is complex, given that the transportation and refining of such oil presents special problems compared to light crude. This implies that placement is not simple because it has a lower demand, which, coupled with high production volumes, forces the price down and thus reduces the profitability of the activity.[1] Over the last 15 years, Pemex has exported continuously. Unfortunately, the pace and quality of investment during this period has reversed the decline in its production platform. Due to the brutal fall in

---

[1] Crude oil types that PMI trades are: i) Maya, a heavy and sour crude oil which produces lower yields of gasoline and diesel in simple refineries when compared with lighter crudes; ii) Istmo, a medium and sour crude oil with good gasoline and intermediate distillate yields (diesel and jet fuel/kerosene); iii) Olmeca, the light and sour crude oil that makes good feedstock for lubricants and petrochemicals; iv) Altamira, a heavy crude that has lower gasoline and diesel yields in simple refining schemes compared to lighter crude oils. Source: www.pmi.com.mx/Public/Paginas/Tipoproducto_En.aspx? IdSec=27&IdPag=128

international oil prices and lower production volumes, the result was a reduction of gross profits and losses in 2015.

THE HISTORY OF PMI

Pemex's internationalization process is through its international trading arm, PMI. So the present analysis focuses on the evolution and performance of the group of companies that form PMI; this entity is the group of companies established in the late eighties with the purpose of forming a modern and efficient entity for conducting the international business activities of the company. The firms within this group, with one exception, are neither state-owned nor public, but private and feature Pemex's participation in their equity portfolios. The PMI entity has among its shareholders representatives of Pemex. PMI's mission is "to contribute to maximizing the value of Petróleos Mexicanos through the efficient and competitive operation in international marketing and other activities related to the value chain of Petróleos Mexicanos."[2] The companies forming the group are classified into four types of activity: trade, services (legal, administrative, financial, and commercial), generation of infrastructure or special projects, and the holding company.

The marketing strategy in the early eighties operated through representative offices abroad (mainly in Europe and in different cities in the United States); their main task was to link and monitor the international market, being part of Pemex and therefore subject to the regulations of the state company. This ended up having a serious impact on the responsiveness of the company to the challenges described, as has been already explained.

Thus, from 1988 until today, foreign trade activities have been carried out through several subsidiaries that today constitute the PMI Group with 19 subsidiaries in various countries (Mexico, Spain, the United States, Ireland, Netherlands, and Netherlands Antilles). Concerning the reasons that companies established in one country

---

2   Pemex's web page: www.pemex.com

or another, according to the interview with the official Sergio Guaso Montoya, they focus mainly on the tax benefits that they can provide to the company. The Group is responsible for commercial activities not only relating to crude but also to petroliferous and petrochemical project development, strategic alliances, etc. Around the group, only PMI Comercio Internacional SA de CV is a parastatal firm; the rest are sole proprietorships. They are not state companies as stated in the Statutes of each of these companies.

A fact that should not be overlooked is that, aside from PMI Comercio Internacional SA de CV, the other companies are basically paper; that is, although they are legally constituted, the reason for their existence is more as a platform for activities than as a traditional figure of business.

Considering Table 5.2, in 1988 five companies were created, which would give rise to the PMI Group. Thus, there arose: PMI Services North America, Inc., in Mexico, Pemex International in Spain, PMI Services BV in Holland, PMI Petroleum Holdings Spain, SL in Netherlands Antilles initially (and in 2005 settled in Spain), and

Table 5.1 *Pemex: general data*

	2000	2005	2010	2015
Revenue	448,610	85,293.8	101,506	73,646.7
Total assets	11,370.8	27,603.5	233,777	15,509.3
EBITDA	29,479	51,745.4	50,857.1	31,034.8
Gross profit	26,429.1	46,896.7	43,214.1	−9,748.3
Net profit	−3,654.1	−7,006.4	−3759.8	−44,984.4
Foreign investment	N/A	N/A	N/A	N/A
Exports	15,164.8	38,900.6	46,967.8	21,190.1
Employees	N/A	139,171	147,368	153,085
Countries	5	5	5	7

Data in millions of US dollars
N/A = not available
Source: Authors with data from Bloomberg, Expansion and Company's Report

Table 5.2 *PMI Group*

Trading	Holding companies	Service companies	Projects / Infrastructure companies	
PMI Comercio Internacional, SA de CV. This company trades crude oil and provides commercial, management, and financial services to the PMI Group. Date of Incorporation: May 24, 1989. Nationality: Mexican Type: State-owned company organized as a corporation.	PMI Holdings, BV. Holding company of foreign corporations. Date of Incorporation: March 24, 1988. Nationality: Dutch Type: Private Company	PMI Services, BV. A corporation organized to finance the sale of Pemex's future portfolio. Date of Incorporation: March 31, 1988. Nationality: Dutch Type: Private Company	P.M.I. Campos Maduros Sanma, S. de R.L. A special purpose vehicle for strategic alliances related to the Campos Maduros (Mature Fields) Project. Date of Incorporation: December 7, 2011. Nationality: Mexican Type: Private Company	PMI Midstream del Centro, SA de CV. Development of infrastructure projects related to PMI Group. Date of Incorporation: October 3, 2014. Nationality: Mexican Type: Private Company
PMI Trading Limited. This company commercializes refined	PMI Holdings Petroleos España, SL	Pemex International España, SA	PMI Azufre Industrial, SA de CV	PMI Cinturón Transoceánico Gas Natural, SA de CV

Table 5.2 (cont.)

Trading	Holding companies	Service companies	Projects / Infrastructure companies	
products and petrochemicals, arranges international marine transportation, and performs risk management. Date of Incorporation: May 17, 1991. Nationality: Irish Type: Private Company	Holding Company of foreign corporations. Date of Incorporation: July 7, 1988. Netherlands Antilles. On December 30, 2005, its place of business changed to Spain. Nationality: Spanish Type: Private Company	This company provides market intelligence and management resources to the PMI Group. It holds a corporate seat in Repsol. Date of Incorporation: July 1, 1988. Nationality: Spanish	Development of diverse projects related to sulphur. Date of Incorporation: March 7, 2014. Nationality: Mexican Type: Private Company	Development of infrastructure projects related to PMI Group. Date of Incorporation: October 3, 2014. Nationality: Mexican Type: Private Company
PMI Norteamérica, SA de CV This company is the joint venture partner with Shell Oil Company (Deer Park Oil Company (Deer Park Refining Limited Partnership) at the Deer Park Refinery.	PMI Field Management Resources, SL Holding company of foreign corporations. Date of Incorporation: December 1, 2011. Nationality: Spanish Type: Private Company	PMI Services North America, Inc. Owner of pipelines that transport oil products at the Mexico–US border. Date of Incorporation: May 4, 1988.	Hijos de J. Barreras SA Boat construction. Date of incorporation to the Group: 2013. Nationality: Spanish Type: Private Company	PMI Transoceánico Gas LP, SA de CV Development of infrastructure projects related to PMI Group Date of incorporation: October 3, 2014.

Table 5.2 (cont.)

Trading	Holding companies	Service companies	Projects / Infrastructure companies
Date of Incorporation: January 13, 1993. Nationality: Mexican Type: Private Company		Nationality: United States Type: Private Company	Nationality: Mexican Type: Private Company
Pro-Agroindustria SA de CV Development of projects related to fertilizers. Date of incorporation: December 18, 2013. Nationality: Mexican Type: Private Company	PMI Infraestructura de Desarrollo SA de CV Development of diverse infrastructure projects related to PMI Group. Date of incorporation: November 12, 2013. Nationality: Mexican Type: Private Company	PMI Holdings North America, Inc. This company provides market intelligence and management resources to the PMI Group. Date of Incorporation: July 6, 1992. Nationality: United States Type: Private Company	PMI Servicios Portuarios Transoceánico, SA de CV Development of infrastructure projects related to PMI Group. Date of incorporation: October 3, 2014. Nationality: Mexican Type: Private Company

Table 5.2 (cont.)

Trading	Holding companies	Service companies	Projects / Infrastructure companies
PMI Marine Ltd. This company provides trading operation of crude oil and hydrocarbons for the world market. Date of incoporation: 1993 Nationality: Irish Type: Private company		Pemex Service Europe Ltd. This company provides market intelligence, promotion, and consultancy. Date of incoporation: 1988. Nationality: English Type: Private Company	

Source: Pemex. Statutes of each firm of PMI Group and official website.

Pemex Service Europe Ltd in England, which is not currently operating.

In 1989 PMI Comercio Internacional SA de CV in Mexico was created, the only state company of PMI Group. PMI Trading Limited in Ireland, PMI Holdings North America, Inc., and PMI North America companies – the last two both in the United States – arose in the years 1991, 1992, and 1993. In 1993, it appears that PMI Marine Ltd, incorporated in Ireland but with residing tax in the Netherlands and is currently not operating.

A new group of companies was listed in 2011, 2012, and 2013, namely: PMI Mature Field in Mexico, PMI Field Resources Management in Spain, PMI Holdings BV in the Netherlands, and finally Hijos de J. Barrera SA in Spain. The latest companies to have been created in Mexico are: PMI Sulphur Industrial SA de CV, established on March 7, 2014, and on October 4: PMI Port Services Transoceanic SA de CV, PMI Midstream del Centro SA de CV, PMI Belt Transoceanic Gas Natural SA de CV, and PMI Transoceanic LPG SA de CV.

As already indicated, according to company documents the Mission of PMI is "to contribute to maximizing the value of Pemex through the efficient and competitive operation in international marketing and other activities related to the value of [the] chain of Pemex." The companies forming the Group are classified into four types of activity: trade, service (legal, administrative, financial, and commercial), dedicated to the generation of infrastructure or special projects, and the holdings.

Concerning Table 5.2, companies that are located in the area of trade are: PMI Comercio Internacional SA de CV, PMI Trading Limited, PMI America SA de CV and Pro-Agro SA de CV. Their main task is to export and import hydrocarbons and their derivatives. As mentioned, Marine Ltd PMI is not in operation.

The companies comprising the group of holding institutions are: PMI Holding BV, Petroleum Holding PMI, PMI Field Management

Resources SL, and PMI Infrastructure Development SA CV. Their job is to hire financing options and securities administration.

Companies defined within the scope of services in the group are PMI Services BV, Pemex International Spain SA, PMI Services North America, Inc., and PMI Holdings North America, Inc. Their main activities are intermediation, legal ties, generation of market intelligence services, and management services. Pemex Service Europe Ltd, as already noted, is not currently in operation.

The entities that are grouped under the heading of projects/ infrastructure are Mature Fields SANMA PMI, S de RL de CV, PMI Sulphur Industrial SA de CV, Hijos de J. Barrera SA, PMI Transoceanic Port Services SA de CV, PMI Midstream del Centro SA de CV, PMI Belt Transoceanic Gas Natural SA de CV, and PMI Transoceanic LPG SA de CV. Their vocation is to generate strategic partnerships and shipbuilding.

As mentioned above, the internationalization of Pemex has mainly been through the companies of the PMI Group. The legal framework that defines the organizational structure of Petróleos Mexicanos was used to create the set of companies responsible for the operation of the foreign trade of the parastatal firm. Hence, the corporate governance of PMI Group resembles the corporate design of Pemex.

In this manner, each of the 18 companies that make up the PMI Group currently has a Board of Directors and its own General Director or General Managers. It is noted that from the intensification of international trade in Pemex, as well as the oil discoveries and the model change for Pemex in the nineties, management has become much more complex. A clear sign lies in the different groups of control and surveillance that the Petróleos Mexicanos Law establishes. Considering what we have seen so far, a first reflection is that for Pemex it has been easier to create non-parastatal firms to address with agility international trade operations, than to redesign the administrative bodies; surely, because to reform the Petroleum Act would force them to talk with the Congress to attain a better management design and also a better policy instrument for optimizing control without paralyzing operations. In addition, organizational redesign also involves negotiations with the Union of Petróleos Mexicanos, who maintained a presence on the Board from 1991–2013.

Moreover, control of the operation of companies in the PMI Group, since they are non-parastatal, is achieved on two levels: cross-ownership from the corporate and with the group companies.

The cross-ownership keeps the company in the group of the trading companies. Pemex's shareholding in the capital of PMI Comercio Internacional is 98.33 percent. In the rest of the PMI Group, shareholding, whether direct or indirect, is 100 percent of the share capital. Thus, Pemex maintains 100 percent of PMI Holding BV, PMI Petroleum Holdings Spain, SL, and 48.5 percent of PMI Trading Ltd.

Meanwhile, PMI Holding BV owns 51 percent of J. Barrera SA, 71.7 percent of PMI North America SA de CV, 43.69 percent of PMI Field Resources Management SL, .01 percent of PMI Campo Maduro, and .002 percent of PPQ Productive Chain SL.

In turn, PMI North America SA de CV has 55.55 percent of PMI Services North America, Inc., 100 percent of PMI Holdings North America, Inc., and 51.5 percent of PMI Trading Ltd.

PMI Petroleum Holdings Spain, SL has 28.3 percent of PMI North America SA de CV, 44.45 percent of PMI Services North America, Inc., 100 percent of PMI Services BV, and 100 percent of Pemex International Spain SA.

Pemex exploration had 100 percent of the now extinct PMI Marine Ltd, which in turn had 56.31 percent of PMI Field Management Resources SL, which in turn has 99.99 percent of Mature Fields SANMA PMI, S de RL de CV.

However, the option for the company to keep multiplying entities has generated a certain duplicity in its activities. That is, despite the classification of vocations that the corporation includes in its major lines of business (commercial, holding companies, services, projects, and infrastructure), the statutes of the companies can cover a wide spectrum of activities causing unnecessary repetition to functions, leading to duplication and overlaps. The impression remains that business creation seeks to resolve a circumstantial issue without following a strategic logic. This style of management, that in principle declares itself to pursue the maximization of profits of the state enterprise, ends up creating higher costs of management, operation, and control than if the design were guided by a dedicated business strategy, defined to be comprehensive and inclusive with a minimum of bodies and subsidiaries.

In the eyes of experts, such as the official Sergio Guaso Montoya, the task that PMI has been successful in is trading, which has given support to marketing and distribution. The clearest example is found in the strategy devised for the situation facing Pemex in late 1991. Given the need to open markets for the heavy oil that Pemex produced and the budgetary, institutional, and policy restrictions of the company, the General Director of Pemex authorized PMI Comercio Internacional to develop the Strategic Alliances Project with Shell on the basis of a proposed joint venture in Deer Park refinery owned by Shell, as part of the long-term strategy of the state company.

This company was incorporated on July 6, 1992 in Delaware, in the United States, according to the report of the Board of Directors of Pemex in Session No. 666, on August 18, 1992. The aim of the company was to process crude that was supplied for their partners, returning in refined products to market abroad, in return for a processing fee paid by the partners in equal parts. It was estimated that for the acquisition of 50 percent of the existing assets of the complex, Pemex would have to invest US$180 million and, for modernization, an amount of US$439 million. In total, this would be an investment of US$619 million. The contract would be for a duration of 30 years. The share of the profits generated by the Pemex refinery in Deer Park increased from 2003 to 2006, but thereafter they decreased to represent losses in 2009. After that year, these results are not disclosed separately in Pemex information, but are integrated into the financial statements within a line called "other income," making it difficult to track them. The fact that the companies forming the PMI Group are private and non-parastatal, like Pemex, allows the financial information of the company to remain in the private sphere, and they are not forced to disclose information.

The refinery is located in a place that allows access to storage sites as input supply and distribution of refined products. The objectives of this partnership were to put Maya crude in a refinery with high conversion value, ensure a supply of fuel to the Mexican market, transfer to Pemex knowledge and technology associated with heavy oil conversion projects, as well as to contribute towards the optimization of the National Refining System. After 23 years, it can be seen that only two goals have been achieved: to place heavy oil for processing and to help meet the growing demand for gas in Mexico.

Concerning marketing, the Board of Directors of PMI Comercio Internacional defines the policy to be followed and the formulas of oil prices, which have changed over time and are based on the prices of major crudes and markets where local products are sold, plus an adjustment factor "k," which is reviewed and modified if necessary.

Pemex has continued its marketing line that, even before the advent of PMI Comercio Internacional, all customers in the same geographical region should have the same price, thereby ensuring transparency in the process of assessing each and every one of the shipments of crude PMI Comercio Internacional exports with reference to international benchmarks that reflect market dynamics, thereby fulfilling the requirements of the Regulations of the Federal Law on Public Enterprises.

The approach that has been followed in choosing the production regions in which to sell is to consider those in which greatest added value is generated while processing Mexican products, while the financial strength of customers is analyzed: fundamental conditions to be a client of PMI. If the financial reliability is not fully proven, PMI Comercio Internacional requests additional payment guarantees, such as letters of credit granted by a bank of first order, selected to the satisfaction of the company.

The institutional context that surrounds Pemex and that helps explain the existence of PMI, is summarized in two factors: external and internal. External factors relate to the institutional infrastructure that Pemex is involved in as a government entity and that sets the tone for its production and financial performance. Internal factors are summarized in the way in which Pemex is organized corporately, and set out how the agents who constitute the company respond to the challenges to which increases in production are linked. These factors, and their implications for Pemex and PMI, will now be explained.

External Factors

External factors are related to the institutional infrastructure that Pemex is involved in as a government entity and that sets the tone for its production, accounting, and financial behavior. These external factors are manifested in the institutional inflexibility that the public sector lives with, understanding that the public sector comprises federal government, unions and Congress, and they prevent the placing of their production abroad with benefits for Mexico.

- Federal Government

A challenge that has faced Pemex in a scenario of exponential growth, and the need to market their production under a cost and benefit scheme for the international market, is the procurement regulations of the federal government. A fact that has been the trigger of this problem is that federal law is aimed at the acquisition of commodities: that is to say, generic and basic products without much differentiation among their varieties.

This implies that leaving out all those goods that are not generic or basic and having high differentiation, specifically for the oil industry, would mean talking about goods with high differentiation, whose technological characteristics make them goods with a high level of specificity. A particular feature of the oil industry is the high specificity of the investments required, which is to say that it acquires goods whose potential for alternative use in other markets is very low. In the academic literature, this sort of investment is called *idiosyncratic*.

Thus, the philosophy of government procurement seeks to acquire goods of lower cost, which can be achieved without loss of quality given that, thanks to its non-specificity, it is possible to find a range of very close substitutes. In the case of the acquisition of goods for production or marketing in the oil industry, that is extremely complicated.

Given this restriction, PMI means to Pemex the possibility of having a company that does not conform to the rules for government procurement and therefore can carry out investments with a high level of specificity, attached to the needs and challenges facing a company that has to compete in foreign markets.A second fact affecting Pemex is the impossibility of government agency debt. This limits the ability to acquire goods whose cost is high and thus extend their productive potential. PMI becomes an ideal medium to generate financial horizons that permit the ability to create value to be increased.

• Unions

As noted, external factors can impact the corporate governance of Pemex. Specifically, the union has been influential up to 2014, with representatives on the board and vote counting. Union rules that should influence Pemex involve high recruitment costs, which inhibits flexibility in contracting schemes that would be required to make investments outside the border.

PMI provides degrees of freedom to generate profitable options for the company, without having to limit its productive capacities.

• Congress

The presence of the Congress responds to the desire to inhibit opportunistic behavior by members of Pemex, particularly corruption, and to review projects that endanger the existence and stability of the largest public company in Mexico. This implies a greater level of monitoring and surveillance for Pemex.

In this way, the company increases its costs in decision-making in such vital areas as marketing, distribution, and investment. To clarify this, consider that every project has to be brought before a commission composed of various political parties. This means additional costs in comparison with a private company. One would expect that these deliberations would be subject to agents outside the company, to agendas where various political parties should coordinate, and eventually, political time need not be synchronized with production and trade, which would run the risk of losing opportunities or causing late undertakings.

It may be noted that PMI, as a private entity facing the restrictions described, allows Pemex to lower the costs of decision-making. Negotiation costs are reduced and allow Pemex to have the ability to respond effectively to the opportunities of a company that moves its products abroad.[3]

In summary, we can say that PMI has been a response to the restrictions in the capacity for Pemex, as a public company, to allow limitations, save and reduce costs in decision-making. A clear example of taking advantage of PMI is in refining the heavy crude to sell products without loss of value, also taking advantage of different legal, fiscal, and financial areas offered in the world, to maximize its profit, like any global company.

Domestic Factors

Pemex has changed its form of government over time, mainly because of the size reached by the organization in terms of its increase in production and in exports. There have been four changes: in the years 1971, 1992, 2008, and 2013. The changes in the structure had an impact on the operation of the PMI Group, since organizationally it depends directly on Pemex or any of its agencies, mainly but not exclusively identified, of Pemex Exploration and Production. A key idea is that the changes that will be described are the foundation of PMI, which, although it has allowed the internationalization of Pemex, it has also created a bad growth strategy without a long-run vision and responding to immediate urgencies. As a consequence, different areas within Pemex have duplicity in duties or responsibilities.

---

[3]   These costs are known as *transaction costs*, described by Milgrom & Roberts (1992) as the costs of performing a transaction, or the opportunity costs incurred when a transaction that improves efficiency is undertaken. *Negotiation costs* are the transaction costs related to negotiations between parties. That includes time and resources devoted in negotiation and in improving the negotiating position, as well as losses produced by failure or delays while an efficient agreement is being reached.

Organic Law of Petróleos Mexicanos 1971
As a point of reference let's start with the Organic Law of Petróleos Mexicanos published in the *Official Gazette* on July 6, 1971. The Act states that Pemex will be managed and administered by a Board of Directors and a General Director. The Board of Directors shall consist of 11 members, six of them that represent the State being appointed by the Federal Executive, and the remaining five by the Union of Oil Workers of the Mexican Republic, among its active members who should be plant workers of Petróleos Mexicanos.

The design of government that controls Pemex becomes evident in the Federal Executive control and the series of restrictions to which Pemex, only considering the bureaucratic plot, has been subject. By the nineties a new change was outlined in conception and design of the governance of Pemex.

Organic Law of Petróleos Mexicanos and Subsidiary Entities 1992
The changes made by the Law of 92 for Pemex consolidad a turnaround for the parastatal company. Since its design in the seventies, the company was conceived as an entity whose strength would lie in its vertical integration. Hence, it oversaw various activities in the production of hydrocarbons and their derivatives. However, its administrative operation was undermining the capacity to transform hydrocarbons by failing to maintain adequate rates of investment and technological adjustments that companies in this industry requires. By the nineties, Pemex's trade balance was pronounced in the deficit involving a large weight to the Mexican state. Thus, the company was released from its obligation to provide industrial inputs derived from oil. In this framework, a new form of government for the company was designed.

In the *Official Gazette* on Thursday, July 16, 1992 the "Organic Law of Petróleos Mexicanos and Subsidiary Entities 1992," in which major changes were based on the organization of the state company, was published. Four subsidiary agencies of Pemex were created, namely: Pemex-Exploration and Production, Pemex-Refining, Pemex-Gas and Basic Petrochemicals, and Pemex-Petrochemicals.

A division of activities to be undertaken by the four agencies was specified, separating strategic activities and determining which activities were to be covered by each agency. It was stated that, "The strategic activities that the law instructs Pemex-Exploration and Production, Pemex-Refining and Pemex-Gas and Basic Petrochemicals, can only be done by these organizations." Properly designed activities for "Basic Petrochemicals" were defined implicitly as non-strategic and therefore could be performed by agencies other than the state enterprises. This change meant a shift in the conception of the company: from a state company, whose main role would be to boost the national industry, for which it would provide inputs derived from hydrocarbons, to a State enterprise responsible for providing financial resources to the federation. The 1992 strategy was successful in part whenever thereafter Pemex's trade balance has maintained a surplus position; not the manufacturing industry and in particular the chemical industry petrochemicals. It is important to remember that in 1992, the Strategic Alliances Project with Shell arose in PMI on the basis of a proposed joint venture in Deer Park, a refinery owned by Shell, as part of the long-term strategy of the parastatal entity.

The four agencies were each to have their own board of directors, consisting of four representatives of the State: the three CEOs of the other agencies, and the Council to be chaired by the General Director of Pemex. The eight members of each of the Boards were to be appointed by the Federal Executive. With this design, the administrative burden of the company on a production operation that had barely improved it increased. In this way, there was an increment not only in the costs in delaying decision-making but also in the administrative costs associated with the bureaucratic body of the company.

In this vein the supervision of the decision-making body of the great administrative Pemex was also increased. The supervisory board of each of the decentralized agencies would comprise a Public Commissioner and an alternate appointed by the Secretariat of the

General Controller of the Federation. Petróleos Mexicanos established a supervisory body of the state oil industry to coordinate the activities of the internal control bodies of the subsidiary bodies, which could exert direct control of the same, according to legal provisions.

Organizationally, Pemex grew and multiplied as a result of this change in legislation. The governing body of the company multiplied by four at first, but, as will be seen below, because of the power that was given to the creation and liquidation of many organizations and subsidiaries as deemed necessary, the group of associated companies increased from 1992–2013 by at least six further members.

According to the interview we conducted with the oil expert and official of Pemex, Sergio Guaso, the subsidiary agencies worked with a high level of incoordination, which meant duplication of effort and a lack of overall strategic planning. PMI was no stranger to this lack, where companies doubled goals and lost the central focus to which they were dedicated: marketing. Added to this, when it came to monitoring problems PMI accelerated atomization.

Petróleos Mexicanos Act 2008

The law of 2008 recognizes the need to professionalize the management of Petróleos Mexicanos for the first time. It is shown through the design of their government: a change of perspective regarding the operation of the company; trying to involve production and management criteria.

According to the Law of Petróleos Mexicanos published in the *Official Gazette* on November 28, 2008, the Board of Directors of Petróleos Mexicanos established the organizational and operational structure to better achieve the purpose and activities of the organism. The subsidiary entities of Petróleos Mexicanos would be created by the Head of the Federal Executive. The subsidiary bodies would operate in a coordinated manner, consolidating operations and using financial resources, a general ledger, information, and accountability, as decided by the Board of Directors of Petróleos Mexicanos.

Pemex would be managed and administered by a Board of Directors, and a General Director appointed by the Federal Executive. The Board of Directors of Petróleos Mexicanos was composed of 15 members: six representatives of the State appointed by the Federal Executive, five reps in the Union of Oil Workers, and four professional counselors appointed by the Federal Executive. In order to appoint professional counselors, the President of the Republic would submit their nominations to the Senate.

Each of the subsidiary bodies was managed and administered by a Board of Directors and a General Director, appointed and removed by the Federal Executive. The Boards of Directors were formed by the General Director of Petróleos Mexicanos, reps in the state (designated by the Federal Executive) and at least two professional directors.

The Act established a greater emphasis than in previous laws on the aspect of surveillance. Thus it decreed that internal and external monitoring of Petróleos Mexicanos would be conducted by the Audit and Performance Evaluation Committee (of the Board); a Commissioner (appointed by the Federal Executive); the Internal Control body; the Superior Audit Office (Chamber of Deputies); and the External Auditor. However, in the design adopted, only two of the designated figures were beyond the company and therefore, to the federal government. Bureaucracy grew, justified by the increased vigilance; the board of directors increased significantly, justified by the inclusion of a more professional point of view; but no previous defects were eliminated. As noted, external factors also impacted the organizational structure of Pemex. In this case the increase in agencies monitoring the performance of the company echoed within the organizational architecture of the institution.

These factors had made the PMI as we know it, and will help to understand the shape PMI has taken as a consequence of the internal and external factors' influence.

External factors, through investment rigidities, labor flexibility, poor access to loans, and asset acquisition, created an entity where 20 companies are private and 21 public. This allowed a capacity for rapid investment, borrowing, response to price changes, labor flexibility, and better asset acquisition. Even though domestic factors respond to the growth of the business and financial needs, they do not prevent proper monitoring of PMI's anarchic growth and greater control over their aims.

THE FUTURE OF PMI

As indicated, PMI is not immune to the changes and modifications being experienced by Pemex. The company is currently undergoing an in-depth reorganization in which the subsidiary companies created in 1992 are being combined into two groups. On Tuesday, November 18, 2014, the Pemex Management Council approved the creation of two production companies. The reorganization involved the transformation of the four subsidiaries created in 1992 into two production companies, plus the creation of five subsidiaries with functions not associated with the extraction of hydrocarbons. At the beginning of December 2015, five franchises of Pemex began to operate in Houston, Texas. They are managed by independent entrepreneurs who buy the fuel in the United States, where its cost is lower than that offered in Mexico. It was impossible before, but now the Energy Reform promulgated in December 2013 allows it.

Pemex Exploration and Production thereby became the Subsidiary Production Company (EPS for its initials in Spanish) Exploration and Production, while the Pemex Refining, Pemex Gas and Basic Petrochemicals, and Pemex Petrochemicals units became the Industrial Transformation Subsidiary Production Company. The Exploration and Production EPS will have the Production and Development, and the Exploration management groups.

The five new subsidiary companies created by Pemex became affiliates in 2015 and are in charge of the drilling, logistics, co-generation and services, fertilizers, and ethylene business functions.

The objective of this restructuring is to eliminate the destruction of value as a result of profound incoordination and to eradicate the organizational redundancies in which the legal, human resources, finance, and other areas had fallen. This involves centralizing areas and having a joint and coordinated vision that gives rise to global, not fragmented, views of the market.

In that sense, according to an interview with an expert and official of Pemex, Sergio Guaso, in the light of the new changes, the task for PMI returns to its essential objective of trading, and puts aside activities related to the acquisition of know-how, which showed a high level of ineffectiveness; and finally, it reduces the multiplication of companies.

WHAT CAN WE LEARN FROM THE PEMEX EXPERIENCE?

While the case of Pemex is very particular, given its monopoly characteristic in the domestic market and its state-owned character, its experience makes clear the importance of having a sufficiently flexible and consistent institutional framework to take advantage of market opportunities, but at the same time it has to be strong enough to avoid inefficient and opportunistic behavior. In the absence of this institutional framework, Pemex was forced to create PMI, which, although it allowed the internationalization of the company, involved duplication in the operation and eventually permitted a lack of transparency in the process.

Currently, Pemex's response is to bring back PMI's focus on "trading," seeking to centralize the operation and inhibiting duplication or defining objectives outside the scope of this organism. As already noted, in this case it worked the use of PMI Group as a way to address the external constraints that Pemex faces to place its products on the market, and failed when intended to remedy other shortcomings and limitations such as a lack of innovation, research, or to catch up with best practices. Finally, it should be noted that a challenge will be the ability of Pemex and PMI to break the inertia that has followed their relationship for over 25 years. This involves promoting effective communication, evidencing weaknesses and threats they face while always promoting agreements and solutions that keep in mind the best marketing of Pemex products. They have the ability to prop up companies that are necessary and close those that do not give value.

However, there is a really important challenge to overcome that will allow Pemex to significantly improve its internationalization process, beyond the efforts that are already being made to correct the operation of PMI. The challenge for the government and other entities involved in Pemex's decision process is a framework that provides the maximum flexibility with technical and financial transparency. This actually involves an ad hoc regulation to the characteristics and particular needs of Pemex, and implies making changes in governmental procurement law, and the role of the Congress as well as the petroleum union. These changes may give a new platform for Pemex to overcome major problems that the oil market faces today and those that will be present in the future.

SUMMARY AND FINAL THOUGHTS

The discovery of oil reserves in the mid-seventies made Pemex pass from a company focused on satisfying domestic demand to an important player in the world oil market. PMI opened to Pemex the door to internationalization from 1988. This input revealed a challenge, since Mexico produces a heavy crude oil type, whose marketing is complex because the transportation and refining of such oil presents special complications compared with light crude oil. This means less demand, which, coupled with high production volumes, pushes down the price and therefore the profitability of the activity.

Out of such difficult productive circumstances, PMI managed to overcome institutional inflexibility in the public sector, which imposed a number of problematic external factors on the work. This inflexibility can be seen in four areas:

- The law of federal procurement is focused on the purchase of commodities; i.e. generic and basic products without much differentiation among their varieties. PMI presents to Pemex the possibility of having a company that is not forced to abide by the regulations of government procurement and which therefore can carry out investments with a high level of technological specificity attached to the needs and challenges a company faces when it has to compete in foreign markets.

- Pemex as a state entity cannot borrow, but given that PMI is capable of doing this, it becomes a way to generate financial horizons that allow it to grow its capability to create value.
- PMI provides degrees of freedom to generate profitable options for the company, without having to limit production capacities for trade commitments.
- PMI allows Pemex lower costs for making decisions in a scenario of constant monitoring by the Congress. Negotiation costs are reduced and provide for the ability to respond effectively to the opportunities of a company that puts its products abroad.

However, PMI has not been immune to the organizational changes experienced by Pemex which were denominated in this work as domestic factors. These factors have led to PMI experiencing an anarchic growth of its businesses, responding to the conjunctures and not to a structured long-term vision, while the group companies duplicate tasks among themselves. This in line with what seemed to be a constant in the company: the duplication of areas and activities.

Given the most recent organizational changes, everything indicates that PMI Group will return to its essential task of "trading," which, according to experts, has been successful, but with a long-term view, eliminating duplication and leaving certain tasks aside, such as those related to the acquisition of know-how – which showed a high level of ineffectiveness. Only in one case has the state enterprise established an association for the purpose of acquiring additional technology. This is the case of the association that began with Repsol in 1990; it reached completion in June 2014. Another association involves seeking to resolve issues of the distribution and marketing of petroleum. A clear example is the creation of the Deer Park refinery in Houston, Texas (DPRLP) in 1992 with Shell Oil.

PMI is still necessary because of the persistence of the external factors that have been described. However, Pemex has changed since 2013, following the Energy Reform. Now, private capital can participate in stages as exploration and extraction of oil through different contracts, such as: shared utility, shared production, and licenses. Even if exploration and oil production are considered strategic features by the Mexican State, and they can only be done though assignees (Pemex) and contractors (private firms), this is indeed a very important change.

However, we have seen new strategies in Pemex. At the beginning of December 2015, the company began to operate five franchises in the Mexican operation in Houston, Texas, selling gasoline directly to the American consumer. These are run by independent entrepreneurs who buy fuel in that country, where the cost is less than what is offered in Mexico. This was impossible only a year earlier, but is now feasible thanks to the Energy Reform enacted in December 2013.

REFERENCES

Milgrom, P. R. & Roberts, J. 1992. *Economics, Organization and Management*. Berkeley, CA: Prentice-Hall.

Secretaría de Gobernación. 1971. *Diario Oficial de la Federación*. Ley Orgánica de Pemex, México: Distrito Federal.

Secretaría de Gobernación. 1992. *Diario Oficial de la Federación*. Ley Orgánica de Pemex, México: Distrito Federal.

Secretaría de Gobernación. 1993. *Diario Oficial de la Federación*. Ley Orgánica de Pemex, México: Distrito Federal.

Secretaría de Gobernación. 2008. *Diario Oficial de la Federación*. Ley Orgánica de Pemex, México: Distrito Federal.

Pemex. 1988. *Statistical Yearbook*. Mexico: Distrito Federal.

Pemex. 1990. *Statistical Yearbook*. Mexico: Distrito Federal.

Pemex. 1999. *Statistical Yearbook*. Mexico: Distrito Federal.

Pemex. 2013. *Statistical Yearbook*. Mexico: Distrito Federal.

Pemex. 2015. Pemex Website. www.pemex.com/Paginas/default.aspx. Accessed September 3, 2015.

6 MultiMexicans in the Iron and Steel Industry
Altos Hornos de México and Industrias CH

Jorge L. Alcaraz

INTRODUCTION

The Iron and Steel Industry in Mexico has passed through several changes ranging from global to domestic issues. These changes have shaped this industry along with its enterprises in terms of internationalization. The two Mexican enterprises chosen for this study are Industrias CH and Altos Hornos de México (AHMSA). The two of them are multinational enterprises that nowadays are competing face to face with other multinational enterprises from developing and developed economies. An important issue is how these enterprises have grown so much. This chapter examines the history and evolution of these two enterprises, identifying particular features that have allowed them to establish subsidiaries in foreign markets.

Some of the main key lessons identified, and helpful to take into consideration for other entrepreneurs when thinking about going abroad, are the following: the improvement or creation of networks; strategic alliances; keeping in mind that exports could provide invaluable knowledge and experience about foreign markets; always being clear about the expansion path that the firm is going to follow; and having the ability to adapt.

INDUSTRY

The Mexican Iron and Steel Industry has its very beginnings in the early nineteenth century when the first enterprise was set up to manufacture products made from iron, particularly to meet the demand from mining enterprises (Sánchez, 2009). Nevertheless, most of the information relating to the Steel and Metals Industry in Mexico dates from the early twentieth century, starting with the foundation of Compañía Fundidora de Fierro y Acero de Monterrey, SA (FUMOSA) (Alvarez, González & Rueda, 1988).

After a couple of decades, this industry starts to show important growth. Actually, the development – or, more accurately, the consolidation – was during the 1930s and 1940s. Demand started to grow very rapidly, as did production. It went from 230,000 tons in 1940 (Vernon, 1969) to 3,881,201 tons in 1970 (INEGI, 1981). But the industry didn't have the capacity to fulfill the demand. Besides, there were some restrictions on the importation of steel to Mexico, and the Second World War made heavy demands on the steel market (Alvarez et al., 1988).

In response to the above situation, other enterprises were created. AHMSA was founded in 1942, supported by the Mexican government and the private sector (producing 100,000 tons in 1948); AHMSA was constituted through use of both private and governmental capital. In the same year, another enterprise was created, Hojalata y Lámina SA (HYLSA), all of it through private capital (with an initial productive capacity of 200,000 tons). And one more, Tubos de Acero de México (TAMSA), started operating in 1952, having been established mostly with private capital. Fundidora Monterrey, operating since 1943, started a plan to increase its production capacity, reaching 500,000 tons in 1960 (Rueda, 2001).

Domestic consumption in recent decades increased very rapidly, necessitating a general improvement and increase in production capacity. In light of this, agreement was reached in 1971 to build Siderúrgica Lázaro Cárdenas-Las Truchas (Sicartsa), a state-owned enterprise. But this was not the only action; AHMSA made several important investments and Fundidora Monterrey got huge loans in order to develop its own expansion program.

Nevertheless, the very high oil prices, depreciation of the peso in 1976, inflation, the slowdown in economic development of industrialized countries, increasing preference for steel substitutes (polymers, ceramics, composites, etc.), increasing use of lighter and stronger steel (Díaz del Castillo & Cortés, 2008; Guzmán, 2003; Rueda, 2001), were some of the many major factors that caused crises in the iron and steel industry. The consequence was that the Mexican government had to intervene in order to save Fundidora Monterrey from bankruptcy in 1977. The next year, Sidermex was formed: a holding group with the specific aim to manage activities from the three state-owned enterprises in the iron and steel industry (Fundidora Monterrey, AHMSA, and Sicartsa) (Corrales, 2007).

The industry was about to change. This change was going to be shaped by several events during that period, starting with a devaluation in 1982, market openness, deregulation, privatization, and macroeconomic stabilization (Schettino, 2002). Also, there were various other problems, such as the decreasing of oil prices during the first half of the 1980s, a decrease in demand for domestic steel, devaluation of the peso, issues with unions, production processes becoming obsolete in some enterprises, and the increase of the overall debt in the industry. Things were sufficiently bad that the Mexican government had to absorb the debt of the industry – but it couldn't keep Fundidora Monterrey running, and it was declared bankrupt in 1986 (Villarreal, 1988).

The iron and steel industry had to face its challenges with a deep restructuring, the Industrial Reconversion Program. The aim was to achieve an improvement in the quality of products, a decrease in production costs, an increase in competitiveness and enhanced participation in foreign markets through exports. The main goal was to produce ship steel with sufficient quality to supply the domestic market and also increase steel exports (Soto & Solé, 2001).

After the industrialization model, during the 1990s a new model was started, based on the idea of a free and competitive market. One of the main characteristics of this period was privatization. Sidermex was dissolved and the remaining enterprises of this group, AHMSA and Sicartsa, were destined to be privatized (Corrales, 2007).

The basic challenge still remained, though: enterprises had to increase their productivity and competitiveness, with even more emphasis on the open market and globalization trends. They also had to invest in updates in order to increase their production levels. In fact, production increased, but domestic demand did not increase as much as production: a situation that allowed an increase in exports (Rueda, 2001), assisted to some extent by the devaluation of 1994.

Subsequently, during the privatization period, national production of steel grew; even over the last decade the trend has remained, with a turndown occurring during the crisis at the beginning (2000–2001) and the global financial crisis afterwards (2008–2009), and both situations being overcome a couple of years later. Of course, investments in this industry have been growing as well, several new enterprises have shown up, mergers, acquisitions, and strategic alliances have taken place, strengthening enterprises in this industry (Canacero, 2014). A couple of examples of enterprises entering Mexico are the cases of Arcelor Mittal and Ternium. Sicartsa was acquired by Arcelor Mittal in 2007; Ternium, for its part, acquired Hylsamex in 2005 and a couple of years later it acquired IMSA.

Selection of Enterprises for Study

Regarding the Expansion's report about the 500 most important enterprises in Mexico in 2014, in terms of sales (as shown in Table 6.1), the most relevant enterprises in the metal industry are as follows: AHMSA, DeAcero, Grupo Villacero, and Industrias CH. Other foreign competitors in Mexico are Ternium México (Luxembourg) and Arcelor Mittal (Holland).

Villacero does not produce steel like the other firms, and for this reason is not considered in this study. In terms of production, AHMSA has the better numbers over the last couple of years, even better than foreign enterprises working in the domestic market (Camimex, 2014); DeAcero and Industrias CH also show up among the top enterprises in terms of steel production. Regarding the

Table 6.1 *Sales and steelmakers' production*

Firm	Country	Sales (millions of dollars)								Steelmakers' production in Mexico (thousands of tons)			
		2006	2007	2008	2009	2010	2011	2012	2013	2010	2011	2012	2013
Ternium México[a]	LUX	3,253	3,763	4,342	3,005	4,083	3,820	4,635	4,264	3,381	3,667	3,686	3,722
AHMSA[b]	MX	1,636	1,850	2,413	1,778	2,253	2,759	2,650	2,491	3,690	3,806	3,880	4,156
DeAcero[c]	MX	N/A	N/A	N/A	N/A	2,135	2,537	2,648	2,357	2,266	2,841	2,978	2,589
Grupo Villacero[d]	MX	1,478	1,078	1,494	1,015	1,027	1,569	2,188	2,162	N/A	N/A	N/A	N/A
Industrias CH[e]	MX	1,759	1,857	2,652	1,498	1,832	2,190	2,177	1,868	2,476	2,538	2,475	2,319
ArcelorMittal[f]	HOL	1,695	1,994	3,009	2,444	1,879	2,028	2,076	1,793	3,949	4,065	3,719	4,022
TenarisTamsa[g]	ARG	N/A	N/A	N/A	N/A	N/A	N/A	N/A	N/A	870	872	727	927

N/A: Not Available.

[a] Starts activities in Mexico in 2005.

[b] First investment abroad in 2004.

[c] Opens two warehouses in the USA during 1990s (no specified date on its website).

[d] Grupo Villacero starts marketing and distributing its products in the USA in 1986 through a strategic alliance with S&P Steel Services and Products.

[e] First direct investment abroad in 2005.

[f] Starts activities in Mexico in 2007 with the acquisition of Sicartsa.

[g] TenarisTamsa starts working in Mexico in 2002.

Source: Own elaboration with data from CNN Expansión, Camimex, and Industrias CH financial report.

Globality Index (which considers revenues from abroad and the number of countries where firms have productive activities), Industrias CH is in 38th position, DeAcero is 53rd, and AHMSA is 81st (CNN Expansión, 2015b).

AHMSA is the most important Mexican enterprise in the country in terms of sales in its industry. Comparing AHMSA and Industrias CH in terms of assets, revenues, EBITDA, gross profits, and net profits, the behavior is the same – with the exception of 2015, which apparently was not a good year for AHMSA (see Tables 6.2 and 6.4). In terms of international expansion, both firms have been doing well, and this can be seen from the increase of exports, mainly comparing 2000 with the other three years. The expansion can also be seen in terms of the countries where the firms have operations, referring strictly to direct investment abroad. Considering all of the above, the two enterprises chosen for this research are AHMSA and Industrias CH, also noting that in the case of DeAcero, there is less available information.

ALTOS HORNOS DE MÉXICO (AHMSA)

AHMSA was founded in 1942 with the main aim of satisfying increasing demand. The enterprise was constituted with mixed capital, from the State and privately. AHMSA is located in Monclova, Coahuila (250 kilometers from the US border), and it was established there because of its proximity to raw materials, specifically coal and iron ore fields. Since the very beginning it was established as an integrated steelmaker, including in its productive processes everything from the extraction of raw minerals (mining) to the finished steel products.

For several years AHMSA did pretty well: it experienced amazing growth, made investments to produce its own inputs, and investments to increase its production capacity, and in 1960 it became the bigger steelmaker in Latin America. Notwithstanding this, in the late 1960s the industry started to show inefficiencies due to technological backwardness, corruption, red tape, bad administration, poor planning, and unnecessary hiring of workers (González, 2008), and it was also affected by the oil and steel crisis during the 1970s. These problems led AHMSA to decrease its revenues by about 56 percent during 1971 to 1982 (Romero, 1995).

Despite all this, AHMSA got loans to make investments and increase its production capacity. This led AHMSA into financial problems, with the whole situation being worsened due to the depreciation of the peso in 1976, inflation, the economic recession, and the consequent slowdown of the steel demand (Rueda, 2001). After all of these events, AHMSA ended up in a terrible financial situation and the government had to absorb its debt, integrating AHMSA into the Sidermex holding group in 1978 (Bell, 2005).

AHMSA still needed a plan to improve its conditions of efficiency and productivity (Rojas, 2008). For that aim, AHMSA requested financial assistance from the World Bank. In 1998, the bank conceded the loan with certain prerequisites regarding the modernization plan (González, 2008). However, due to the national downturns during the 1980s the problems in AHMSA kept going on. Finally, AHMSA was privatized in 1991, changing its structural constitution to a family-owned enterprise.

AHMSA was acquired by Grupo Acerero del Norte (GAN). This group was constituted with the specific objective to obtain AHMSA. The roots of the group date back to 1990, when the Autrey and Ancira Elizondo families got the Real del Monte mine, which was helpful when the tender for AHMSA showed up (Corrales, 2006).

According to Corrales (2006), the new owners of AHMSA did not have experience in the steelmaking industry. In fact, they were business people from areas unrelated to steel, such as the pharmaceutical industry, financial sector, and domestic air transportation. Nevertheless, GAN established a set of alliances: with a Dutch enterprise, Hoogovens Technical Services, and with Mission Energy, Co. from the USA (González, 2008).

The Hoogovens enterprise in particular was helpful in the process of modernization (Giacalone, 2004). This program had to be undertaken in 1996. The improvements had to do with both technical areas and administrative terms. The enterprise was doing well; indeed, it acquired important loans from Eximbank, which reflected the financial confidence that other institutions held in AHMSA (Chávez, 1994).

With productive capacity increasing, AHMSA started to broaden its market as well, with the development of a commercial network (DHACSA) with 22 integrated branches spread out along several states of the country. This action was intended to increase the national consumption of steel. Furthermore, another commercial alliance was made with Chaparral Steel in 1994, a US firm that would allow AHMSA to reach the markets of the United States and Canada (González, 2008). Another strategic alliance was with Inland International, a subsidiary of Inland Steel Industries, an enterprise from the USA; both formed Ryerson, a commercial alliance (Mangum, Kim & Tallman, 1996).

Additional important events to highlight in 1994 are the depreciation of the peso and the beginning of the North American Free Trade Agreement (NAFTA). Definitively, both situations had impacts on the iron and steel industry and of course on AHMSA. Fortunately, the modernization process had started in AHMSA several years earlier, and actually a process of increased openness started in this industry with the General Agreement on Tariffs and Trade (GATT) in 1986. So, at the time that NAFTA was launched, the commercial openness actually meant that there was an opportunity to increase participation in other countries.

The outcome of the peso depreciation was to slow down domestic consumption. However, this situation was overcome with an increase of exports. Actually, the modernization process allowed AHMSA to manufacture new and different products with higher value added, replacing imports and increasing exports at the same time (López, 2001).

During the following years, AHMSA repeatedly obtained loans from different financial institutions and restructured its debt a couple of times, but then, from 1996 onwards, AHMSA's situation started to worsen: high debt rates; international economic conditions started to worsen (with the important influence of the Asian crisis); steel demand fell; certain production costs increased; an excess of steel in the market started to present a problem and as a consequence the price of the steel fell further. To counteract the situation, AHMSA sold some assets to get liquidity and be able to pay interest (López, 2001). However, it was not enough, and in 1999 it was declared in cessation of payments (Vargas & Simon, 2005).

The cessation of payments was one condition that allowed AHMSA to keep on going, but some other actions taken were also to try to decrease production prices, conducting different investments with the aim of increased productivity and quality, and to enhance the firm in an integral way. Also, commercial and strategic alliances had been helpful for AHMSA, but not all of them had thrived. In fact, in order to solve its financial issues, AHMSA had several options to ally with national and international firms, but none of them could be brought to fruition.

As if this were not enough, in 2004 the Ministry of Finance and Public Credit issued arrest warrants against the managers of AHMSA (Alonso Ancira and Xavier Autrey, among others) due to tax fraud. During that same year, Xavier Autrey was caught, but in the following year, all charges were lifted against him and the rest of the accused (Barajas & Fuentes, 2005).

Fortunately, not all news was bad. In particular, the internationalization of AHMSA with the subsidiary that was set up in Israel was now performing foreign direct investment and not only exports. This happened when Alonso Ancira was living in Tel Aviv, avoiding the warrant referred to in the previous paragraph. Basically, on one particular day he saw a chance to do business, conducted some research, and after a short time was negotiating with the Israeli government, founding AHMSA Steel Israel Ltd in 2004. This subsidiary works like a holding company, managing other firms in Israel. Such is the case with Arava Mines (copper mines), owning 100 percent of the shares, and Acqwise, a company related to wastewater treatment (Anderson, 2008). This latter company is a coinvestment with an

Israeli enterprise, with AHMSA holding 50.1 percent of the shares (AHMSA, 2015).

Things started to get better later in the decade. In 2006 AHMSA started a new investment program supported by its own funding, specifically addressed to maximize enterprise efficiency and profitability, bringing with it an increase in production of 40 percent. A downturn in steel demand caused by the financial crises in this period influenced sales, both in the domestic and foreign markets; however, actions implemented by AHMSA, like the savings and efficiency program, helped the firm to overcome the global problem.

Other important activity included the new investment abroad made by AHMSA in 2008, establishing a sales office in the USA (AHMSA, 2012). With this investment, AHMSA has been increasing its exports over the following years. This new subsidiary represents the firm's interest in continuing to expand its participation in foreign markets, and AHMSA is achieving increased exports with this direct investment abroad.

Another relevant event arose out of AHMSA's Fenix project in 2013. Thanks to this project, the firm opened its most important facilities, allowing it to increase its production and giving it the chance to satisfy the steel demand (Sánchez, 2015). Without any doubt, further great news is that it should soon be possible to lift the payments secession that was enacted 15 years ago (CNN Expansión, 2015a).

The last five years have looked good for AHMSA. The recovery of international markets and improved demand for steel are good signals, and for any eventuality in those trends, AHMSA has the ability to easily increase exports if the domestic market shrinks, and vice versa. The financials in Table 6.2 show how AHMSA has been doing in recent decades.

Some additional investments conducted by AHMSA, but not directly related to its main productive activities, are as follows. Mexicans & Americans Trading Together, Inc. (MATT Biz) is

Table 6.2 *AHMSA's financial information*

	AHMSA			
	2000	2005	2010	2015
Revenue	1,326.5	2,225.4	2,641.5	2,595.1
Total assets	3,596.6	3,539.1	4,549.7	3,608.7
EBITDA	273.6	547	241.7	14.5
Gross profit	126.1	328.5	170.5	−255.7
Net profit	118.7	218.6	51.2	−272
Foreign investment	N/A	N/A	N/A	N/A
Exports	88.9	240.1	218.2	292.6
Employees	17,264	14,098	19,795	26,800
Countries	1	2	3	4

Data in millions of US dollars. N/A: Not Available
Source: Authors' own elaboration with data from Bloomberg, Expansion and Company's Report.

a nonprofit company and AHMSA's subsidiary, established in 2006. This organization looks to promote bilateral participation between the USA and Mexico in areas related to culture and the economy. With this initiative, the group is also looking to increase its presence in the USA. AHMSA, through MATT Biz, has also been investing, from 2006 to the present, in MeetMe, Inc. (formerly Quepasa Corporation), a US enterprise owner of one of the most important websites for the Hispanic community (AHMSA, 2015).

Two more investments are worth mentioning. The first one follows the same mechanism as MATT Biz: AHMSA has been investing, from 2011 to date, in Boom Financial, Inc. (formerly m-Via, Inc.), an enterprise related to money transfer via cellular. In one more investment abroad, AHMSA acquired 80 percent of Moonen Yachts Holding BV, a Dutch enterprise in the business of boat-building (AHMSA, 2015). See the complete evolution of AHMSA in Table 6.3 for more details.

Table 6.3 *AHMSA timeline*

	Local	International
1991	AHMSA was privatized, acquired by Grupo Acerero del Norte (GAN) Modernization program kick-off	Alliance with Hoogovens Technical Services (Dutch) and with Mission Energy, Co (USA)
1992	GAN gets MICARE, a steam coal producer	
1993	Commercial Network (DHACSA). 22 branches spread out along several States of the country Is listed on the Mexican Stock Market	
1994		Commercial alliance with Inland International, a subsidiary of Inland Steel Industries an enterprise from the USA. Commercial alliance Chaparral Steel, a US firm which will allow AHMSA to reach the markets of the United States and Canada
1996		Listed on the New York Stock Market
1999	It was declared in cessation of payments	Suspended from the Mexican Stock Market
2000	Millennium Business Award for Environmental Achievement	Unlisted from the New York Stock Market
2004	Arrest warrants against the managers for tax fraud	Xavier Autrey is caught in Menorca, Spain Alonso Ancira founds AHMSA Steel Israel, in Tel Aviv

Table 6.3 (*cont.*)

	Local	International
2005	All charges related to the tax fraud were lifted	Arava mines, subsidy of AHMSA Steel Israel, starts to work. Wholly owned enterprise AHMSA invests in Aqwise, Israeli enterprise related with water waste treatment (50.1% of shares)
2006	Proyecto Fenix is launched, investment aimed to improve efficiency and production; the most important investment since that in the 1990s	It is founded the firm Mexicans & Americans Trading Together, Inc (MATT Biz) in the USA. A nonprofit company that looks to promote bi-lateral participation between the USA and Mexico and the increase of its presence in the USA. First investment in MeetMe Inc., formerly Quepasa Corporation, a US enterprise owner of one of the most important web sites for the Hispanic community
2008		AHMSA stablishes a sales office in San Antonio, Texas (USA).
2011		AHMSA is investing through MATT Biz, since 2011 to date, on Boom Financial, Inc. (formerly m-Via, Inc.); enterprise related with money transfer via cellular.
2013	AHMSA acquired through its subsidiary MIMOSA 81% of AGRO, enterprise involved with the production, distribution, and sales of fertilizers and petrochemicals	

Table 6.3 (*cont.*)

	Local	International
2014		AHMSA acquired 80% of Moonen Yachts Holding BV, a Dutch enterprise in the business of boat building

Source: Own elaboration.

AHMSA Internationalization

Considering the internationalization process in AHMSA, it has been not precisely a progressive evolution, and specifically the entry into other countries through direct investment abroad. Basically, AHMSA went first to a very "different" region, instead of expanding to a more close and known location. It established a wholly owned subsidiary in Israel (Arave Mines, a copper mine), and is also the main shareholder of an enterprise related to wastewater treatment in the same country. Both enterprises were established before attempting to get into the US market.

AHMSA is an integrated steelmaker; some of its subsidiaries are mines, so it is logical to focus on the same core business, and by and large steelmaking enterprises need water treatment facilities. But why expand into Israel, with its different culture, language, and so on? In fact, during the time when Mr. Alonso Ancira Elizondo was a fugitive, accused of tax fraud in Mexico, he went to live in Israel, thanks to a colleague who was working at his enterprise. Suddenly, he simply saw a chance to do important business, and the result is already there to be seen: he turned that chance into AHMSA Steel Israel and Arava Mines.

What is important to highlight here is that both Alonso Ancira and Xavier Autrey are entrepreneurs: they have this background and, as such, are always looking to do business. In this sense, it is quite relevant in such a study as this to take into consideration the "entrepreneurship" variable and how it can affect the internationalization trends of enterprises. Maybe the shrewdness exhibited by Alonso Ancira is what has kept AHMSA alive over so many years, and is what will give it an advantage in the future.

A further subject is the subsidiary that AHMSA started in 2008 in the USA, specifically in San Antonio, Texas. This subsidiary, AHMSA International, is acting as a springboard for AHMSA to increase its share of the US market. The situation in the USA is a great deal for AHMSA because, so far, it has not needed to invest in a new brand factory. Thus, in terms of the internationalization process, this strategy could be an interesting option for other enterprises: considering a "springboard strategy" in order to optimize their entry and increase their participation in foreign markets.

The entry of AHMSA to the USA with such a smooth move (a sales office) could be a signal that this firm is reshaping its internationalization path. Also, it is very peculiar that just a couple of years after AHMSA's entry into Israel, it settled a subsidiary in the USA. It suggests that AHMSA might have developed and built specific capabilities and advantages to enable it to make explosive moves abroad, internationalizing the firm.

INDUSTRIAS CH

Industrias CH was founded in 1934 (with private capital) under the name of Herramientas México, SA (Tlalnepantla Archivo Histórico, 2015), and after a while it changed its name to Campos Hermanos SA. It started in Coyoacán as a small and humble facility; the owners at the very beginning were just two brothers, and later two others got into the family business. The firm grew following the demand trends of the time, moving the plant to Tlalnepantla in 1941. In the early 1960s, it started to produce special bar quality (a type of steel, also known as engineering steel or engineered special bar quality). The firm grew amazingly while supplying the domestic market, and it also exported to countries in Central America (Díaz del Castillo & Cortés, 2008).

In the case of this firm, and unlike the other enterprise studied previously, no substantial historical information is available, even given the firm's impressive growth over recent decades and considering that it has made an important contribution to the industrialization of Mexico. The available information is simply scarce, and the evolution of the enterprise is very unclear due to the lack of records. Despite this situation, some useful information could be gleaned from annual reports, the enterprise website, and news.

It was in 1991 when the firm was sold and acquired by new owners, adopting the current name, Industrias CH, along with the new administration, which still remains in place. Just like the previous holder, the new owner is a family: the family Vigil González. This new administration has prior experience in the industry: the main shareholder and the current Chairman of the Board of Directors, Rufino Vigil González, was the Chief Executive Officer of a steel-related products corporation since 1973. Before that, from 1971 to 1973, he worked as a manager in a construction corporation, and from 1988 to 1999 he was a member of the Board of Directors of a Mexican investment bank (Reuters, 2015).

The new management established a new course for the firm. The strategy is clear and has been on the owners' minds since they bought the enterprise: enhance the manufacturing processes' efficiency and diversify the business with higher added value products, acquiring enterprises related to the steel industry, within Mexico and abroad.

After two years, and thanks to the good results so far earned by Industrias CH, it was possible to conduct the first acquisition. In 1993 it bought Procarsa SA de CV and then, in 1997, Compañía Mexicana de Perfiles y Tubos, SA de CV, diversifying and expanding its share market with more and different products. In 1999 it merged with Grupo Ruvi SA de CV, and with it acquired the enterprise Siderúrgica del Golfo SA de CV (owned by Grupo Ruvi), consequently receiving an increase in both sales and production.

It is important to say that the factors affecting the industry at world level, as well as at domestic level, have also had an impact on this enterprise. Notwithstanding this, Industrias CH has always enjoyed a robust structure, right from its strategy to its finances. This strength has allowed it to pay for acquisitions without going into debt, and it even used to pay its suppliers in cash, sometimes in advance. Basically, the absence of debt in Industria CH has been a key factor in bearing up imbalances in the iron and steel industry.

In 2001, Industrias CH acquired an 82.5 percent share of Grupo Simec, which owned four other steelmakers in several states of the country. Afterwards, through Simec, in 2004 it acquired Grupo Sidenor Mexico. The acquisition of Grupo Simec has proved to be a highly important strategy in the growth of Industrias CH, as it has shown itself to be the main subsidiary of Industrias CH, reflecting the largest part of the net sales of the group. Both Simec and Industrias CH are listed on the Mexican Stock Exchange, and Grupo Simec is also listed on the American Stock Exchange.

All the acquisitions so far had been Mexican enterprises, but the next year the firm started to go abroad, following the same strategy of acquisitions; and Simec showed itself again to be a great deal, since the acquisitions were made through it. In 2005, Republic Engineered Products Inc. (now known as Republic Steel) was acquired, along with seven subsidiaries in the US (four in Ohio, one in New York, one in Indiana, and one in Tennessee) and one in Canada (Ontario). By this stage, Industrias CH and Simec had become the most important special-bar-quality steelmakers in Mexico and in the USA.

In subsequent years, Industrias CH has continued acquiring enterprises through Simec both at home (Corporación Aceros DM and some others belonging to Grupo San in 2008) and abroad (in 2011, Bluff City, with two factories in the US: one in Ohio and the other one in Tennessee). This last acquisition, Bluff City (BCS Industries), is once again a key acquisition in the US: this firm will add value to Industrias CH's products, since BCS has facilities for heat treatment and cold drawing.

Furthermore, Industrias CH conducted an investment program, looking to increase its production capacity in two of its enterprises in Mexico (San Luis Potosí in 2012 and Tamaulipas in 2013). And, during 2014, a couple of projects were approved, one of them to produce special bar quality steel and the other, helical pipes.

In 2010, Industrias CH started an investment program in Brazil, with the main aim being to supply the domestic market in that country; the subsidiary was scheduled to start production in 2015. This transaction represents a greenfield: an investment that implies a higher risk and greater engagement in comparison with other acquisitions, and is the most difficult to conduct in terms of internationalization.

There were two more acquisitions in 2010. Industrias CH bought Lipa Capital and Ilia Capital. Both enterprises were important because they held intellectual property of particular interest to Industrias CH. This fact reflects both the relevance that new technology has for Industrias CH, and the strategy of the firm, since new technology increases the added value of its products.

As can be seen, this steelmaker has been growing since its very inception. The financial information in Table 6.4 shows this trend for the last 20 years. The growth, expansion, and internationalization process in the case of Industrias CH has been a very active, aggressive, constant, and permanent program of investments in both domestic and foreign markets.

This enterprise has always been conducting acquisitions, initially inside the country and then, after a while, abroad. But not only that, Industrias CH has entered Brazil – a country not too far from Mexico in terms of cultural distance – with a totally new investment looking to serve the domestic market; a situation which is interesting in terms of its internationalization path (for a summary of transactions, see Table 6.5).

Industrias CH's Internationalization

In terms of internationalization, the domestic growth of Industrias CH represents an important source of knowledge and experience that

Table 6.4 *Industrias CH financial information*

	Industrias CH			
	2000	2005	2010	2015
Revenue	167.5	1,489.7	2,146.7	1,847.6
Total assets	515.7	1,832.4	2,637.9	2,521.2
EBITDA	53	216.8	214	229.3
Gross profit	48.8	175.8	123.9	148
Net profit	35.6	119	82.4	28.2
Foreign investment	NA	60	500	NA
Exports	53	216.8	214	229.3
Employees	N/A	N/A	N/A	N/A
Countries	1	3	4	4

Data in millions of US dollars. N/A: Not Available
Source: Own elaboration with data from Bloomberg, Expansion and Company's Report.

other enterprises can take into consideration and learn from, assuming their own domestic activities are also relevant. As Industrias CH found, its strategic diversification in Mexico turned into a series of specific advantages at the very moment it took the decision to expand abroad.

The acquisitions conducted by Industrias CH in the USA and Canada were also strategic in a couple of ways. First, facilities in the north-east of the USA are near to both inputs and customers. Additionally, Bluff City adds value to the steelmaking process with heat treatments. Second, the facilities acquired in the south-west of the USA are basically on the border with Mexico, and additionally, in that area but on the Mexican side, Industrias CH owns a steelmaker.

These facilities assure the availability of resources and low-cost transportation. Thus, a lesson for potential international newcomers is to develop a thorough expansion plan, considering several inter-linked strategies that could maximize the acquisition of advantages.

Table 6.5 *Industrias CH timeline*

	Local	International
1991	Industrias CH is acquired by the new owner, the family Vigil González Establishment of the new strategy: enhance the manufacturing process's efficiency and diversification with higher value-added products, acquiring enterprises related to the steel industry, inside Mexico and abroad	
1993	Acquisition of Procarsa SA de CV, a steel pipes producer	
1997	Acquisition of Compañía Mexicana de Perfiles y Tubos SA de CV, Steel pipes and tubular shapes producer	
1999	Merger with Grupo Ruvi SA de CV and Siderúrgica del Golfo SA de CV (owned by the former company). Enterpise manufacturer of merchant and structural shapes	
2001	Acquisition of 82.5% of Grupo Simec SAB de CV. This firm produces special bar quality steels, merchant and structural shapes and rebars. This enterprise owned four subsidiaries in Mexico, which were acquired as well	
2004	Industrias CH – through Simec – acquired Grupo Sidenor Mexico (two firms). Main	

Table 6.5 (*cont.*)

	Local	International
	production of Sidenor is special bar quality steel, merchant shapes and rebar	
2005		Acquisition of Republic Engineered Products Inc. (Republic Steel nowadays). This is a US firm with seven subsidiaries in this country (four in Ohio, one in New York, one in Indiana, and one in Tennessee) and one in Canada (Ontario). The enterprise produces special bar quality steel
2008	Acquisition of Aceros DM and Grupo San. Both firms are important producers of rebar in Mexico	
2010		Starts building a brand-new enterprise in Brazil, a greenfield: the name of the firm is GV do Brasil Industria e Comercio de Aco LTDA, and its main products are merchant steel
		Acquisition of Lipa Capital, a company holding particular intellectual property of interest to Industrias CH
		Acquisition of Ilia Capital, a company holding particular intellectual property of interest to Industrias CH
2011		Acquisition of Bluff City Steel, a firm in the US with two

Table 6.5 (*cont.*)

	Local	International
		subsidiaries, one in Ohio and the other in Tennessee. These are facilities for heat treatment and cold drawing
2012	Investment program on its subsidiary from San Luis Potosí, with the aim to increase its production capacity	
2013	Investment in a new subsidiary in the North of the country (Tamaulipas)	
2014	Investments in several firms in Mexico (Jalisco, Tlaxcala, San Luis Potosí, etc.)	Investments in its subsidiaries in the USA and Brazil

Source: Own elaboration.

Such strategies not only allow companies to exploit these foreign markets but also gain more advantages there.

As well as setting up new enterprises, acquisitions provide knowledge. The merging of such strategies is probably what resulted in the greenfield conducted by Industrias CH in Brazil. This implies that enterprises could gain advantages by the development of particular actions; however, considering that the interaction of different situations could further boost the creation and acquisition of advantages that result in more complex processes like the greenfield, there is enormous potential relevance for enterprises in always continuing to implement new strategies, as they bring with them new advantages.

In the research and development field, during 2010, Industrias CH acquired two enterprises: owners of intellectual property. This demonstrates that enterprises should invest in research and development either for the creation or the acquisition of new technology, since this is also considered another important issue in terms of internationalization.

CONCLUSIONS

AHMSA and Industrias CH are a couple of steelmakers that have experienced all kinds of situations, from the best periods of economic growth in Mexico to awful situations generated by international conditions linked with the worst national downfalls. In spite of these and other factors, both enterprises have entered international markets, not merely with exports but with foreign subsidiaries as well. This final section integrates two parts, one of them gathering some relevant similarities between these two enterprises and the other showing the lessons to be learned from these firms.

Similarities

It is broadly accepted that exports can act like the anteroom to outward foreign direct investment (OFDI). Focusing on the new administrations (from the early 1990s onwards), both firms have dealt with exports since the very beginning. Of course, working in this area helped the enterprises to become familiar with the international market. Exporting gave them knowledge and experience of foreign markets, diminishing the perception of risk in the long run and increasing each firm's confidence to enter foreign markets.

Regarding the location, the particular distributions of both enterprises in Mexico had meaningful advantages concerning the North American market. The two enterprises have subsidiaries in north Mexican states neighboring the USA. This proximity to the foreign market means low costs in both labor and transportation compared with other competitors.

Concerning structural organization, both enterprises were acquired in the same year (1991) and both by families. In both cases, members of the family occupy key positions in the respective enterprises, are members of the board, and also hold shares. Maybe this situation is a cultural issue that has a positive impact on the performance of these two enterprises. Actually, there is academic literature regarding Mexican enterprises, suggesting a positive correlation between family ownership and performance of enterprises (Arregle, Batjargal, Hitt et al., 2013); and family bonds could also be a source of features impacting on firms' improvement (Martin & Duran, 2015). Notwithstanding this kind of structural organization, family ownership could be a reflection of a weak and unreliable institutional system; that is, the family-owned structure could be helpful in overcoming negative conditions in the home country.

In terms of business groups, in theoretical and empirical terms, enterprises are not always benefited by their integration into business groups. In the case of the two enterprises studied in this chapter, however, the effects seem to be positive. The main enterprises of AHMSA and Industrias CH both seem to gain positive effects from conforming to business groups. And this is not surprising, considering that business groups generate a propitious environment where affiliates can gain advantages for internationalization (Yiu, 2011).

Another factor that is making a difference in both enterprises is their financial situation. On the one hand, AHMSA has always experienced problems, whilst at the other extreme Industrias CH has always been healthy in financial terms. Both enterprises have been investing in their own firms, growing and improving their performances, one with debt and the other without it. AHMSA's behavior had been consistently too aggressive and high-risk until one day the situation was no longer sustainable. However, this fearless attitude is perhaps what allowed this firm to keep working after all the problems that it had experienced.

In relation to their financial situation, both enterprises are listed on the Mexican Stock Exchange, but only Industrias CH is trading, since AHMSA was declared in secession of payments. Being in the stock exchange could mean an advantage for the internationalization process. Enterprises could get external debt-free funding and there is no need for either the owners or the firm to undercapitalize — and this does not necessarily imply lower shares and loss of control for the owner.

When trading on the stock exchange, enterprises have a duty to share all their information – which means that enterprises have to act as transparently as possible. The implications go further, since enterprises also need to improve their administrative processes and have tight control over all the processes, making the enterprise perform in the best way possible.

In terms of entrepreneurship, both Alonso Ancira and Rufino Vigil have been listed several times by important magazines as being among the most outstanding entrepreneurs in Mexico. Maybe it is worth taking a look at what characteristics they have in common that have allowed them to get into foreign markets through direct investment abroad, and perhaps try to consciously repeat their actions, or at least try to emulate their competence.

Lessons

Several lessons can be learned from these enterprises. For instance, political, commercial, and industrial conditions do not remain the same over time; there are always going to be changes. Some of the conditions that AHMSA and Industrias CH have had to overcome are changes in the regulatory and political frameworks: in particular, new environmental standards. In commercial terms, new products and different consumer trends must be accommodated, and also new competition. Economic cycles at international, national, and industry levels are important as well.

Enterprises need to be very flexible in order to adapt their activities, their processes, and in general their participation to new conditions. The ability to adapt to change will become a strength and an advantage when an enterprise decides to expand abroad, since global activity frequently changes as well. Both AHMSA and Industrias CH had to adapt their own realities several times during their lives, and now their capacity to bear up and take advantage of changes is remarkable.

Naturally, a precondition for internationalization is to have the specific advantages that are going to allow the enterprise to compete and preserve those advantages. Exports is an important area that allows managers to know how foreign markets behave regarding their products. But not only that, exposure to foreign markets provides the knowledge and comprehension of that particular and distinct market abroad, along with an understanding of different cultures, different institutional conditions, behaviors, and attitudes, and experience of dealing with multiple currencies, and even seemingly insignificant things like dealing with different time zones.

The evolutionary process of the enterprise is also a source of advantages. In this sense, managers need to keep their minds clear about what they really want in the medium and long run, because the actions implemented have to be in the interests of those ambitions. In the case of Industrias CH, for instance, its growth process is based on the acquisition of enterprises, and clearly this will have built important advantages into this firm that have permitted it to buy other enterprises in other countries. Most importantly, Industrias CH has stated this means of expansion and diversification as its strategy.

Another important topic is the continuous investment in updates. Enterprises need to consider and establish a program for updates in order to produce better conditions in terms of know-how, administrative and technical process, and development of human resources, to name a few. Both AHMSA and Industrias CH have been investing in their own facilities, upgrading processes and general productive conditions. Industrias CH has even been looking for added value in foreign markets. Perhaps, in an intensive capital industry like iron and steel, continuous investment is a mandatory requirement for survival. However, the lesson here, and generically for all industries, is to take care about investment in updates and the advantages that they could bring to the firm.

In terms of domestic and international production, it is always going to be harder to act alone. Both networks and strategic alliances could ease the process, and can be considered like advantages for enterprises that are also in a position to determine their own process of internationalization. Another related point here is the matter of business groups, given the viewpoint that they could act as sources of advantages for insiders and enterprises affiliated with these groups that are going to have advantages that they wouldn't enjoy otherwise.

Healthy finances are also a very important point to have in consideration. Healthy finances can be a determinant for the expansion, and managers need to be aware of this matter. In the case of Industrias CH, it has never had this problem, and has been expanding its activities abroad without any financial difficulties. However, in the case of AHMSA, a large part of its life has involved financial burdens, and its finances have definitively had a negative effect on it.

Also related – and this is one of the main topics and restrictions when there is an interest in going abroad – is the availability of capital. Being realistic, this is a serious and very common problem. However, a possible solution could be trading on the stock market. This can demand several important changes in a firm, but it can also represent access to external funding without getting loans and without the need to undercapitalize.

Furthermore, being listed on the stock market can strengthen a brand, easing its entering to foreign markets or strengthening it abroad. Something along these lines has been the case for Industrias CH – or, more precisely, Grupo Simec. Let's remember that Industrias CH acquired some enterprises in the USA through Grupo Simec, and this group is listed on the New York Stock Exchange. This is another strategic move of Industrias CH with its subsidiary. Maybe other enterprises could consider this strategy when considering going abroad.

One more key lesson to check here is the consideration that, in the case of both Industrias CH and AHMSA, their entering foreign markets has been undertaken in singular moments. Basically, they conducted their investments when the industry was experiencing positive moments. Industrias CH's investments abroad took place during 2005, 2010, and 2011; and in the case of AHMSA, during 2006 and 2008. In these years, the national production and domestic demand experienced good times. Maybe it is not a coincidence, but either way, managers should pay heed to this situation.

An interesting topic to have in consideration is the entrepreneurship in internationalization. In both cases under study here, the main owners have been businessmen, and as businessmen they may have specific talents that allow them both to identify business opportunities and also to undertake whatever is necessary to reach their goals. Perhaps managers should be aware of these skills in order to identify them for their conscious use, or if necessary, to try to develop them.

Finally, family-owned enterprises are an important sector of enterprises in developing countries. Actually, as mentioned above, there are several MultiMexicans with a family structure. The point here is that there is evidence suggesting that this structure causes positive effects on enterprises. This structure also allows institutional liabilities to be overcome. Perhaps other family-owned enterprises could be aware of this situation and start to consider the family-owned structure as a source of resources providing specific advantages to the firm.

REFERENCES

AHMSA. 2012. Reporte Anual 2011. Monclova.

AHMSA. 2015. Reporte Anual 2014. Monclova.

Alvarez, L., González, M. L. & Rueda, I. 1988. Actualidad de la industria siderúrgica en México productividad y organización del trabajo para la exportación. *Problemas del Desarrollo*, 19(73): 7–42.

Anderson, B. 2008. La caída y el ascenso de Alonso Ancira; Expansión; www.cnnexpansion.com/negocios/2008/09/17/la-caida-y-el-ascenso-de-alonso-ancira; Accessed March 9, 2015.

Arregle, J.-L., Batjargal, B., Hitt, M. et al. 2013. Family ties in entrepreneurs' social networks and new venture growth. *Entrepreneurship Theory and Practice*: 1–32.

Barajas, A. & Fuentes, V. 2015. ...Y perdonan castigo a AHMSA; Reforma; http://vlex.com/vid/perdonan-castigo-ahmsa-193833063; February 15, 2015.

Bell, L. 2005. *Globalization, Regional Development and Local Response: The Impact of Economic Restructuring in Coahuila, Mexico*. Amsterdam: Dutch University Press.

Camimex. 2014. *Informe Anual 2014 de la Cámara Minera de México*. México.

Canacero. 2014. *Perfil de la Industria Siderúrgica en México 2014–2013*. México.

Chávez, S. 1994. Notas sobre la historia de AHMSA, 1941–1992, in I. Rueda (ed.), *Tras las Huellas de la Privatización. El Caso de Altos Hornos de México*: 60–102. México: Siglo XXI Editores.

CNN Expansión. 2015a. Juez acepta pedido de AHMSA para levantar suspensión de pago; CNNExpansión; www.cnnexpansion.com/negocios/192015/01/08/juez-acepta-pedido-de-ahmsa-para-levantar-suspension-de-pago; Accessed April 6, 2015.

CNN Expansión. 2015b. 100 Mexicanas globales. *CNN Expansión* (1157): 88–89.

Corrales, S. 2006. Impactos regionales de la modernización en Altos Hornos de México. *Problemas de Desarrollo. Revista Latinoamericana de Economía*, 37(145): 105–134.

Corrales, S. 2007. Alianzas, fusiones y adquisiciones en la Industria Siderúrgica. *Economía y Sociedad*, XII(20): 93–107.

Díaz del Castillo, F. & Cortés, E. 2008. *La industria del acero en México, los 100 años, Tercer Congreso Científico Tecnológico*: 1–11. Ciudad de México.

Giacalone, R. 2004. *La Regionalización del Acero en América Latina. El Caso del Consorcio Amazonia*. Buenos Aires: Biblos.

González, G. 2008. *El Estado y la globalización en la industria siderúrgica mexicana*. México: Casa Juan Pablos.

Guzmán, A. 2003. Las fuentes del crecimiento en la siderurgia mexicana. Innovación, productividad y competitividad. *Estudios Sociológicos*, XXI(2): 477–479.

INEGI. 1981. *La Industria Siderúrgica en México*. México: INEGI.

López, C. 2001. AHMSA: Estrategia de modernización integral 1992–1998, in I. Rueda and N. Simón (eds.), *De la Privatización a la Crisis: El Caso de Altos Hornos de México*: 119–153. México: Porrúa.

Mangum, G., Kim, S.-Y. & Tallman, S. 1996. *Transnational Marriages in the Steel Industry: Experience and Lessons for Global Business*. Westport, CT: Quorum Books.

Martin, J. & Duran, J. 2015. Effects of family ownership, debt and board composition on Mexican firms performance. *International Journal of Financial Studies*, 3: 56–74.

Reuters. 2015. Grupo Simec SAB de CV; Reuters; www.reuters.com/finance/stocks/officerProfile?symbol=SIMECB.MX&officerId=457944; Accessed April 4, 2015.

Rojas, G. 2008. Contrastes regionales en el norte: Principales cambios en las estructuras económicas de Monclova y Ciudad Acuña en las décadas recientes. *Frontera Norte*, 20(39): 101–130.

Romero, S. 1995. *Una proyección a futuro, El Desarrollo de una Industria Básica, Altos Hornos de México 1942–1988.* Monclova: Arte y Cultura Monclova.

Rueda, I. 2001. Evolución de la industria siderúrgica en México, in I. Rueda & N. Simón (eds.), *De la privatización a la crisis. El caso de Altos Hornos de México*: 89–116. México: Porrúa.

Schettino, M. 2002. *México. Problemas sociales, políticos y económicos.* México: Pearson Education.

Soto, M. d. R. & Solé, F. 2001. El cambio tecnológico en la industria siderúrgica mexicana. *El Cotidiano*, 18(109): 97–106.

Sánchez, A. 2015. AHMSA, la ganadora del boom siderúrgico en 2014; El Financiero; www.elfinanciero.com.mx/empresas/ahmsa-la-ganadora-del-boom-siderurgico-en-2014.html; Accessed March 12, 2015.

Sánchez, G. 2009. Los orígenes de la industria siderúrgica mexicana. Continuidades y cambios tecnológicos en el siglo XIX. Tzintzun. *Revista de Estudios Históricos* (50): 11–60.

Tlalnepantla Archivo Histórico. 2015. La Industrialización; Tlalnepantla; www.tlalnepantla.gob.mx/archivohistorico/2industrializacion.asp; Accessed April 3, 2015.

Vargas, F. & Simon, N. 2005. Efectos de la apertura comercial en la rentabilidad y generación de EVA en las empresas siderúrgicas mexicanas. Los casos de AHMSA e HYLSA. *Hitos de Ciencias Económico Administrativas*, 11(31): 105–120.

Vernon, R. 1969. *El Dilema del Desarrollo Económico de México.* México: Diana.

Villarreal, R. 1988. La reconversión en la industria siderúrgica paraestatal de México. *Comercio Exterior*, 38(3): 191–201.

Yiu, D. 2011. Multinational advantages of Chinese business groups: A theoretical exploration. *Management and Organization Review*, 7(2): 249–277.

7 MultiMexicans in the Food Industry

Bimbo and Gruma

Jorge E. Gómez and Miguel A. López-Lomelí

INTRODUCTION

This chapter analyzes the internationalization process of two success-ful Mexican Food manufacturers and distributors, Bimbo and Gruma/ Maseca ("Gruma"), both of them among the top Mexican domestic food manufacturers based on their annual sales in 2014. Bimbo sold Mex$187.05 billion (Bimbo, 2000) and Gruma sold Mex$49.9 billion (Gruma, 2016a) in that year. Additionally Bimbo and Gruma are ranked among the top 10 most global Mexican companies (CNN Expansión, 2016a; El Informador, 2016).

Each group has achieved its income and profit objectives through the development of a highly competitive multinational company, offer-ing high-value products of leading brands to target consumers, excep-tional manufacturing processes, and continuous innovation, achieving high productivity and efficiency, state-of-the-art distribution and com-mercialization with disciplined financial management, while behaving in a sustainable and socially responsible manner.

These two companies have achieved success by using their original Mexican models to expand internationally to countries with diverse economic characteristics worldwide. Bimbo operates in 22 countries in America, Europe, and Asia and possesses 163 plants and 52,000+ distribution routes (Bimbo, 2015a, 2016a). Gruma operates in 112 countries across the globe and possesses 79 production plants in America, Europe, Asia, and Oceania (Gruma, 2016b).

The high profits of Bimbo are associated with the assiduous pursuit of the entrepreneurial vision of the company's founders through an outstanding and continually strengthened distribution system, along with superior products resulting from the company's focus on innovation, R&D, and marketing efforts (Bimbo, 2015a). Gruma's results are associated with their value creation and marketplace innovation, high productivity, and efficiency through use of advanced technologies, and strong distribution system and disciplined financial management and structure (Gruma, 2016a).

Other domestic food companies might draw lessons from these successful expansion models to become multinationals, especially when aiming to export and adapt their business models to other countries that present similar or diverse opportunities for success (Gruma, 2016a).

THE FOOD INDUSTRY

Food is considered to be any substance that is consumed to provide nutritional support to the human organism, and encompasses all types of bio agents, such as vitamins, minerals, carbohydrates, fats, and proteins, that support the growth of the body. Due to the evolution of the culture of consumption and consumer demand, food has developed into a new format known as packaged food (PRNewswire, 2015).

The food and beverage industry commercializes products which satisfy the universal and essential human needs of eating and drinking for life and well-being, thus the relevance and importance of this industry is based not only on the essential nature of the products being commercialized but also on economic value, the capacity for growth as the population grows, and the potential for new business opportunities as consumers demand new and healthier foods and beverages. This is an industry with a vast supply chain that extends from agriculture and animal production to the processing of food and beverages to commercialization in a local or global manner (Pfitzer & Krishnaswamy, 2007).

The relevance of this category is evidenced by the amount of revenue that it produces: by the year 2020, the food industry's business is estimated to reach revenues of US$3.03 trillion, with a compound annual growth rate (CAGR) of 4.5 percent from 2015 to 2020 (Food Processing, 2016).

The food industry is dynamic, with continued evolution and change as all the parties – suppliers, manufacturers, and retailers – aim to satisfy the wide and evolving needs and desires of consumers. Through advanced marketing, the food and beverage firms look to understand the consumers' new preferences, purchase decisions, and demands for variety, affordability, safety, and quality, taking advantage of the data and knowledge of retailers who share this invaluable commercial information with their suppliers. On top of that, the food industry must also adapt to the evolution of the retail formats worldwide (USDA, 2016). The Food Retail Industry is a business that comprises all types of food products (packaged and unpackaged) and beverages (alcoholic and non-alcoholic) and includes the retail sales of all these products (MarketLine, 2015).

Both the food and retail industries are characterized by being highly globalized and dynamic, moving at the pace that consumers' needs and desires dictate while serving multiple cultures, habits, and preferences.

As already mentioned, the food and beverage companies compete in a global, highly dynamic market, which is a challenge for the firms' corporate operating structures that must be innovative, adaptable, and responsive to changing consumer preferences and demands in order to be competitive (Food Engineering, 2015). The fast pace of change in consumers' expectations regarding quality, food safety, and breakthrough products is evidenced by the innovation strategies implemented by Nestlé with the creation of its division of Nestlé Health Science, focused on nutritional therapy to change the course of health for consumers, patients, and health-care institutions, and with its division of Nestlé Skin Health, focused on developing specialized solutions for the health of skin, hair, and nails to be used throughout consumers' lives (Nestlé, 2015).

Table 7.1 *Mexico food retail industry value, 2010–14*

Year	2010	2011	2012	2013	2014
US$billion	145.7	144.5	149.0	156.1	176.9
Mex $billion	1,937.7	1,922.7	1,982.2	2,076.7	2,352.8
€ billion	109.7	108.9	112.3	117.6	133.3
% growth		−0.80%	3.1%	4.8%	13.3%
CAGR: 2010–14				5.0%	

Source: MarketLine (2015)

THE FOOD INDUSTRY IN MEXICO

The Mexican Food Retail Industry

The Mexican food retail industry represents sales of US$176.9 billion in 2014, with a compound annual growth rate (CAGR) of 5 percent in the period of 2010–14. For reference, the industry grew by 3.5 percent CAGR in the USA and 1.5 percent in Canada, respectively, during the same timeframe, reaching values of US$1,007.3 billion and US$95.7 billion in 2014 (MarketLine, 2015).

In terms of spending, the average amount spent per household on food and beverages was equivalent to 23 percent of their total income, while in India the equivalent figure was 45 percent and in the Russian Federation it was 36 percent in 2010 (World Bank, 2016). This fluctuation among countries is influenced by the relation in costs versus total income per household; additionally, the growth of this industry in Mexico is mainly due to the growth of modern retailers, overall population, population in urban areas and in income (Ornelas, 2015). Table 7.1 shows the Mexico food retail industry value during this period.

Packaged Food

The performance of the packaged food industry is influenced by factors that moderate consumption, such as government taxes and regulations, exchange rates, inflation rates, competition among store formats, consumer trends, and seasonality, among other factors.

Packaged Food Trends in Mexico

A good example of the factors that influence the performance of this category is the Mexican Government's new regulation, implemented in 2014: a special tax was imposed on products classified as highly calorific (from 275 calories per 100g up), whereby Mex$1.00 per liter was imposed on sugar-sweetened beverages, aiming to prevent diabetes among the Mexican population (Passport, 2016). This affected not only the sales of soft drinks but sales in other categories as consumers decided to reduce the quantity and frequency of purchases in order to save some money and still purchase soft drinks at a higher price; Mexico is an important market for soft drink producers since it is one of the leading consumers of carbonated drinks, ranking fourth in the world (Mexican consumers drink nearly 137 liters per capita according to WorldAtlas, 2016).

Among the categories affected by these government regulations we find confectionery, pastries, ice cream, cakes, and sweet and savory snack products. This triggered a health and wellness trend among consumers, who evaluated their food product choices based on budget constraints or health concerns. One of the actions taken by manufacturers in response to this challenge was downsizing: by offering smaller versions of products, unit prices could be maintained so that consumers could still afford them. Additionally, the junk food tax triggered consumers to look for smart substitutes in snacks and breakfast foods. Sociodemographic dynamics in the Mexican market, such as middle class population growth, expansion of urban areas, and increased women in the workforce, positively impacted consumption of ready-to-eat food, especially salads and salad dressings, and extra convenience food, such as instant noodle cups and shelf-stable soups, which increased sales in 2015 (Passport, 2016). Table 7.2 shows the top Mexican Food and Beverage Companies.

Selection of Bimbo and Gruma

In terms of global operation, Bimbo and Gruma are two companies in the Mexican food industry that rank in the top 100 most global

Table 7.2 *Top Mexican food and beverage companies*

#	Company	Country	Sales (M-MXP)	Operational profit	Gross Profit
1	Fomento Económico Mexicano (FEMSA)	MX	311,589	33,735	23,276
2	Bimbo	MX	219,186	14,121	5,915
3	Coca-Cola FEMSA	MX	151,914	22,645	10,329
4	Sigma Alimentos	MX	93,568	10,904	6,310
5	Arca Continental	MX	76,454	12,754	7,659
6	Grupo Modelo	BEL	62,153	31,869	N/A
7	PepsiCo de México	USA	58,419	N/A	N/A
8	Gruma	MX	58,279	7,368	1,085
9	Grupo Lala	MX	48,183	5,640	3,950
10	Cuauhtémoc Moctezuma – Heineken	NL	47,000	N/A	N/A

Source: CNN Expansión (2016b)

Mexican companies: Bimbo is at number 3 and Gruma at number 10 in the rankings based on their international income, their number of international employees, and the number of countries where the firms have production facilities (CNN Expansión, 2016a).

Additionally, Bimbo was ranked number 10 and Gruma number 51 in the rankings of the most important 500 Mexican companies in 2016 (CNN Expansión, 2016b). By many important measures, Bimbo has been recognized as the firm with the most important conversion to renewable energy in the food industry, and for its commitment to reducing the ecological footprint of its transportation and distribution operations by the Ministry of the Environment and Natural Resources (Bimbo, 2016b). Gruma has also been recognized for two consecutive years with the "World Finance 100" Award by *World Finance Magazine*, which compiles a list of 100 individuals and companies based purely on excellence in their field (World Finance, 2016), and in 2013 – again for two consecutive years – Gruma Mexico was recognized by the Great Place to Work Institute as the best company to work for in Mexico (Gruma, 2016b). Based on these significant facts, both companies are considered to be among the leading Mexican firms in the food industry expanding to international markets.

BIMBO

History of Bimbo

Bimbo's origin is essentially as a bakery. Don Lorenzo Servitje, who worked in his father's bakery since the age of 16, took over the business when his father passed away while he was studying at university, and in 1945 he started *Panificación Bimbo*, a company to produce and commercialize loaves of bread on a massive scale in association with Jaime Jorba, an excellent sales and commercialization professional, Jaime Sendra, uncle of Lorenzo Servitje and professional in the bakery industry, Alfonso Velasco, a recognized baking technician who was trained in the USA, and José T. Mata, an imports–exports expert and previous partner of Servitje (Bimbo, 2016a).

With their initial success, two years later Bimbo as a company was founded as Bimbo SA and commercialized large and small loaves of bread, as well as rye and toasted bread, all of them wrapped – which was an innovation back then. In 1947, in addition to the launch of the pancake line, an important innovation that was to become one of Bimbo's greatest strengths was implemented: the distribution fleet that made Bimbo products available and fresh everywhere in Mexico (Bimbo, 2016a).

Continuous expansion directed by Jaime Jorba led Bimbo to continually launch new products and product lines, such as the sweet bread line, buns, pound cakes (large, medium, and small sizes), Bombonete, Negrito, and Gansito, which was launched individually wrapped into the market in 1958; all these launches took place along with a continuous expansion of the distribution routes in parallel, and by 1960 Bimbo SA's operations expanded to Guadalajara and Monterrey, and other commercial geographical areas (Bimbo, 2016a).

Over the last 15 years, Bimbo's revenue has practically increased four times compared with 2000. This steady growth is the result of a management strategy to focus on strategically significant investments, such as the opening of new production plants; in innovation and technology to implement state-of-the-art production processes to achieve superior quality and efficiency; and in strategic acquisitions in the food products sector, among them the Mexican firms Lara, Coronado Pastelerías El Globo, La Corona, Mrs. Baird's, Sara Lee, Four-S Baking, and Pacific Pride; the overseas firms Bimar Foods (USA), Park Lane (Germany), Sara Lee (Spain and Portugal), Fargo (Argentina), Lagos del Sur (Chile), and Jin Hong Wei (China); and by establishing new strategic partnerships such as Day Hoff (USA), Arcor (Argentina), Licorp (Peru), and Noel (Colombia). It is important also to underline the effort made by Bimbo's international management team during this period to improve the financial performance of Bimbo Bakeries USA. Inc. (BBU) and Organización Latinoamérica (OLA), and focus on profitability in Europe and Asia (Bimbo, 2000, 2005, 2010, 2015a). Table 7.3 shows general information about Bimbo.

Bimbo has experienced an important and smooth transition in its top management with no negative consequences for the operations and direction of the firm; as of mid-2013 Daniel Servitje Montul became Chairman of the Board of Directors, taking over from his uncle, Roberto Servitje, who has vast experience in the Bimbo firm since 1945, leading the company following his brother Lorenzo Servitje since 1979 as CEO and later Chairman of the Board of Directors (Bimbo, 2016a; CNN Expansión, 2013). In recent years, in addition to the strategic areas mentioned earlier, Bimbo has placed a heavy focus on developing strong new product introductions that leverage its cross-border capabilities (Artesano, Villaggio, and Nature's Harvest breads), together with a greater emphasis on sustainability through focusing on the four pillars of Well-being, the Planet, Community, and Associates, and the integration and restructuring of acquired companies (Bimbo, 2015b). Recently, Bimbo has announced

Table 7.3 *Bimbo: general data*

	2000	2005	2010	2015
Revenue	3,329.4	5,152.8	9,281.2	13,839.8
Total assets	2,556	3,491.4	8,021.3	11,587.4
EBITDA	493.1	613.2	1,197.9	1,367.5
Gross profit	343.9	441.9	902.5	891.6
Net profit	193.5	259.8	427.4	326.5
Foreign investment	N/A	N/A	450	N/A
Exports	861.2	N/A	N/A	2,603.3
Employees	63,371	70,645	102,000	125,416
Countries	11	16	19	21

Source: Authors with data from Bloomberg, Expansion and Company's Report. Data in millions of US dollars. N/A = not available

its 2020 Vision: "In 2020 we transform the baking industry and expand our global leadership to better serve more consumers" (Bimbo, 2015b, p. 9).

In terms of contribution by region in net sales, North America represents 53 percent, Mexico 34 percent, the rest of Latin America 10 percent, and Europe 3 percent. The highest contributor in terms of gross earnings (EBITDA, Earnings Before Interest, Taxes, Depreciation, and Amortization) is Mexico with 58 percent, followed by North America with 41 percent.

Bimbo's results are mainly driven by increased volume in Mexico due to better consumption, innovative product introductions such as Levissimo snacks and Lime Chips, along with the cross-market product launches of Artesano and Nature's Harvest breads. In the US market the results are due to the consolidation of prior acquisitions, positive exchange rates, category growth of the sweet baked goods, snacks, and breakfast products, plus successful product launches of Sara Lee Artesano and Thomas' Swirl Breads. In Canada, results were driven by the introduction of Campagnard; in Latin America due to volume growth in Brazil; and in the majority of the countries in Central America, by positive currency exchange rates and growth of premium breads and tortillas (Bimbo, 2015b).

Bimbo's operations over the last year achieved double-digit growth in: net sales, operating income, adjusted EBITDA, and net income, based on 163 manufacturing facilities with more than 52,000 distribution routes reaching 2.5 million points of sale, more than 10,000 products commercialized under 100 brands and 127,000 employees worldwide.

International Expansion of Bimbo

Bimbo first focused on the United States by beginning to export there; five years later they looked at Central American countries and made an important investment there, opening a manufacturing plant in Guatemala, then one year later moved to Argentina and founded a Latin American corporate structure with a vison to expand in this region. 1998 marked the start of a new and important period of international expansion through strategic acquisitions with the acquisition of *Mrs. Baird's*, a bakery company in the USA, followed by many others in the following years.

Bimbo's internalization process continued through a combination of the opening of manufacturing and commercial facilities, acquisitions, and alliances following a "diversification approach" generally characterized by expansion to diverse and distant geographical areas and by the fact that the organizations that were acquired and integrated into the firm had different knowledge bases (Torres & Jasso, 2005).

The international growth of Bimbo is based on the same Mexican business model principles, the core aim being to offer "fresh bread and pastries everywhere all the time" with diverse product lines and a distribution network that allow the bread to be present at every point of sale for consumers of all socioeconomic levels (SELs). The evolution of Bimbo is presented in Table 7.4.

Table 7.4 *Evolution of Bimbo*

Year	Local	Global
1943	The idea to create a baking company is born. The name Bimbo appears for the first time.	
1945	The company Bimbo, SA is created. The Bimbo Bear Cub becomes the company's logo. The first products launched into the market are: cellophane wrapped large and small white loafs of bread, rye bread, and toasted bread.	
1947	Initial structuring of the Vehicles Department. The pound cakes line is launched into the market.	
1948	At the beginning of this year, there were already nine Bimbo products in the market: White bread (large & small), Toasted, Rye, Sweet, Buns, Pound Cakes (large, medium, & small sizes).	
1949	The first depot outside Mexico City is inaugurated in the city of Puebla.	
1950	The "38" makes its appearance: a vehicle decorated with loudspeakers, a record player and microphones to announce the product in small towns and rural settlements.	
1952	The production of the Donas del Osito (Bear Cub's doughnuts) starts, as well as a	

Table 7.4 (cont.)

Year	Local	Global
	new buns line: Bimbollos, Medias Noches & Colchones.	
1954	Bimbo starts its Social Responsibilities activities by earmarking a percentage of profits to open and maintain a school. Keik is born as a brand dedicated to making cupcakes in three different flavors: strawberry, orange, and chocolate. Its name is changed to Marinela in 1957.	
1955	On its tenth anniversary, Bimbo had: 700 associates, 140 vehicles.	
1956	Start-up of the Bimbo Occidente plant (in Guadalajara). Don Roberto Servitje was its first General Manager.	
1957	Bombonete, Negrito, and Gansito – sprinkled with minced pecan – were launched into the market.	
1958	The individual packaged Gansito – a chocolate-coated cake filled with cream and strawberry jam and sprinkled with chocolate chips – is launched into the market.	
1960	Inauguration of the Bimbo del Norte plant in the city of Monterrey, Nuevo León.	

Table 7.4 (cont.)

Year	Local	Global
1963	The first administrative restructuring takes place. The Corporate Structure is created with offices on Ejército Nacional Avenue in Mexico City.	
1964	Bimbo acquires the rights for the Sunbeam brand in Mexico from Quality Bakers of America.	
1967	The Super Submarinos Marinela are launched into the market in three different flavors: strawberry, vanilla, and chocolate.	
1971	Barcel starts its operations with the acquisition of a small chocolate plant in Mexico City.	
1972	Bimbo installs the largest bakery in Latin America and one of the ten largest in the world in Azcapotzalco, Mexico City.	
1973	Bimbo makes incursions in the jams and marmalades market. The Carmel line meets Marinela's raw materials supply needs.	
1974	The brand Suandy is born devoted to produce Rosca de Panqué (around pound cake), Biscotel, Pastisetas, and Chocolate Cake.	

Table 7.4 (*cont.*)

Year	Local	Global
	The Tía Rosa sweet bread appears with Banderillas, Doraditas, and Orejas.	
1975	Conchas Bimbo start to be produced. Barcel launches Palomitas Barcel (popcorn): candied, salty, and with chili pepper.	
1976	Tortillinas Tía Rosa are launched into the market.	
1978	Ricolino is created as the leading brand of Bimbo for candies and chocolates. Bubulubu is born.	
1979	Don Roberto Servitje is appointed Director General of Bimbo. Bimbo is comprised of: 3 Enterprises, 12 Plants, 15,000 Associates, and its capital increased over 60,000 times.	
1980	Bimbo starts trading 15% of its shares on the Mexican Stock Exchange (BMV).	
1984		Bimbo starts its expansion by exporting to the USA.
1986	A new organizational structure is created, from which a single industrial group emerges.	
1989		Bimbo Central America is created with the construction of a plant in Guatemala inaugurated in 1990.

Table 7.4 (cont.)

Year	Local	Global
1990	Corn tortillas are launched into the market under the Milpa Real brand and the Lonchibon brand products. Barcel launches Chips.	
1991		Inauguration of Bimbo Argentina and the Latin American Region Corporate structure.
1993	Inauguration of the new Bimbo Corporate Office Building in Santa Fe, Mexico City.	
1995	Bimbo acquires Coronado, a company devoted to making candied goat milk-based products.	The Ideal plant in Chile and the Bimbo Argentina plant start operations.
1997	Daniel Servitje is appointed CEO of Bimbo.	
1998		Bimbo acquires the American bakery "Mrs. Baird's".
2001		Bimbo acquires Plus Vita and Pullman in Brazil.
2002		Bimbo acquired the West region baking business of George Weston Limited – owner of the Oroweat brand – in the United States.
2004		Bimbo joins Joyco, manufacturer of Duvalín, Bocadín, and Lunetas.
2005	Bimbo acquires Chocolates La Corona and the El Globo bakery.	

Table 7.4 (*cont.*)

Year	Local	Global
2006		Bimbo acquires the bakery Panrico in Beijing, initiating its presence in the Asian market.
2008		Bimbo buys the Nutrella bakery in Brazil.
2009		Bimbo acquires George Weston Foods Ltd in the United States.
2010	Bimbo acquires Dulces Vero in México.	
2011		Bimbo becomes the largest baking company in the world with the acquisition of Sara Lee North American Fresh Bakery, Fargo in Argentina, and Bimbo Iberia in Spain and Portugal.
2012	Bimbo completes the largest and most important renewable energy conversion by a company in the global food industry. Parque Eolico with the opening of Piedra Larga wind farm, Bimbo supplies green electricity to almost all its facilities in Mexico.	
2013	The First Ecologic Sales Center from the largest worldwide bakery company is launched to reduce the environmental impact of its operations, easing the effects of climate change. The Ecologic Sales Center will be powered from the energy produced in the Piedra Larga Windfarm. Its electric vehicles	

Table 7.4 (*cont.*)

Year	Local	Global
	are powered by the wind generated in this windfarm. This effort positions Bimbo as a modern and innovative company, firmly committed to protecting the environment.	
2014		Bimbo acquires Canada Bread to promote its global growth strategy in Canada and the United Kingdom, reaffirming itself as the world's largest baking company. In the same year, the company acquired Supan in Ecuador, strengthening its presence in Latin America.

Source: Bimbo (2016a)

Bimbo's Foreign Entry Strategies

In 2013, one of the founders and Chairman of Board of Bimbo, Don Roberto Servitje, retired and Daniel Servitje became the third CEO of Bimbo, a position held previously by his father Lorenzo Servitje and his uncle, who took over in 1979. Daniel Servitje is also a member of the board of directors of Grupo Financiero Banamex, SA de CV, Coca-Cola FEMSA, SAB de CV, Board of Walmart Mexico Providers, Mexican Institute for Competitiveness, BC, The Consumer Goods Forum Latin America, and Conservation Council (The Nature Conservancy). He takes this responsibility at a time when Bimbo has been evolving over 70 years into becoming the largest baking company in the world, providing high quality, good taste, and fresh breads, buns, cookies, snack cakes, English muffins, bagels, pre-packaged foods, tortillas, salty snacks, and confectionary products, in a committed mission to nourish, delight, and serve the world (Bimbo, 2015b, 2016a).

GRUMA

Gruma is a Mexican company that has become the leader in corn and flour tortilla production and commercialization worldwide, and has also achieved a leading position as a producer and commercializer of wheat flour and related products, such as bases for flatbreads, pizza, and wraps, and other food products such as rice, snacks, pasta, condiments, and palm hearts. The company has achieved important business growth worldwide, expanding its operations to America, Europe, Asia, and Oceania with a strong presence in 112 countries, owns 79 production facilities, and has a successful portfolio of global brands (Maseca and Mission) and multiple local brands (Guerrero in the USA, and Tortiricas and Tosty in Costa Rica). Innovation and technology are key pillars in its successful business model and have allowed Gruma to commercialize its products and services to satisfy a diversity of consumers with different lifestyles, cultures, and needs, as well as managing to satisfy the business needs of its customers worldwide. Gruma is committed to social responsibility, fostering the development of the communities where it conducts its business, operating with environmentally friendly facilities, creating new jobs, and offering high-value products to customers and end-consumers (Gruma, 2016b).

The Mexican Corn Tortilla

The Corn Tortilla is highly appreciated as a daily food in Mexican households of all socioeconomic classes. It is eaten every day all year long, both on its own, like traditional bread, and in a wide variety of combinations, including its fundamental role in the preparation of tacos with all the other Mexican food filling options; the tortilla is a cultural icon of Mexico, including the Tequila and the Mariachi bands (Mexico Desconocido, 2001).

Evidence has been found that corn was prepared for human consumption more than ten thousand years ago; it is described in historic documents by the first Spanish conquerors and colonizers during the 1520s in reference to one of the mostly appreciated and eaten foods by the Mexican Indian civilizations such as the Aztecs, the Tlaxcaltecas, and the rest of the tribes. Tlaxcala means "place of the corn tortillas" (Sabrosía, 2014).

The tortillas are prepared from a dough of corn and cooked individually, their size being between 12 and 18 cm in diameter and 1 to 2 mm thick; tortillas can be found in white, yellow, red, and blue colors, depending on the type of corn used, and they are consumed at breakfast, lunch, and dinner. The tortilla is rich in fiber and carbohydrates, minerals (calcium and phosphorus), and vitamin B3, thus providing a good source of energy. A wide variety of Mexican dishes are prepared with corn tortillas, such as tacos, quesadillas, chilaquiles, enchiladas, tostadas, and tortilla soup (Sabrosía, 2014).

The importance of tortilla consumption in Mexico is evidenced by the number of tortillas that are consumed per person in a year. In 2014 the consumption of corn tortilla was between 7.3 and 9.4 million tons, with an average consumption per person of 90 kilograms of tortillas a year (Excelsior, 2014). Interestingly, in the United States, due to the growth of the Hispanic community as well as the penetration of their typical foods into the Anglo-Saxon American population, customers in the USA spent US$2,900 million on tortillas during 2013, i.e., 38 percent more than on bread intended for hamburgers or hot dogs, according to a study by the firm Packaged Facts (Mundo Ejecutivo Express, 2016).

Gruma has experienced steady financial and commercial growth in the past 15 years, demonstrated by their financial results, commercial expansion, and increasing number of employees. Gruma's revenue has practically doubled since 2000. This steady growth is the result of a management strategy to focus on building on Gruma's strengths, capitalizing on acquired skills and competitive advantages, and concentrating on strategies for continuous value creation for the core businesses. By achieving strong financial results, the company is focusing on using additional resources to expand its business globally via strategic acquisitions, and on manufacturing investments by capitalizing on profitable growth opportunities in Mexico, the United States, Europe, and Asia – especially in the Iberian Peninsula, Southern France, Italy, Portugal, Malta, Russia, and Malaysia. Here, the company has focused on increasing its production capacity and on technological modernization aligned with the company's commitment to protect the global environment in order to grow the business more efficiently and profitably (Gruma, 2014). Gruma's general information is presented in Table 7.5.

Gruma, like Bimbo, experienced an important and smooth transition in its top management as of 2012 when Juan Gonzalez Moreno became Chairman of the Board of Directors, taking over from his father, Don Roberto González Barrera; Juan Antonio González Moreno is Chairman of the Board and Chief Executive Officer of Gruma and Gimsa, and also has deep experience in the operations of the company, having held many strategic positions such as Chief

Table 7.5 *Gruma: general data*

	2000	2005	2010	2015
Revenue	1,925	2,450.1	3,662.4	3,679.8
Total assets	2,282.8	2,524.5	3,151.8	2,573.3
EBITDA	155.1	249.2	281.4	566.1
Gross profit	86	143.6	162.4	465.2
Net profit	24.6	108.9	34.2	48.1
Foreign investment	N/A	N/A	7	15
Exports	1,237.8	1,665.3	2,431.4	2,689.1
Employees	16,513	18,765	N/A	N/A
Countries	7	8	11	11

Source: Authors with data from Bloomberg, Expansion and Company's Report. Data in millions of US dollars. N/A = not available

Executive Officer of Special Projects of Gruma Corporation, President of Azteca Milling, Vice President of Central and Eastern Regions of Mission Foods, President and Vice President of Sales of Azteca Milling, and Chief Executive Officer of Gruma Asia & Oceania, among others (Morningstar, 2016).

In recent years, Gruma has placed a strong priority and focus on strategies to optimize its product portfolio, distribution fleets, expansion into the most profitable products, optimization of marketing, advertisement and administrative costs, and in investment projects for value creation. Along with a solid strategic refocusing in its core businesses and divesting non-strategic businesses such as the wheat flour operations in Mexico, this has resulted in stronger finances and a clear and flexible structure. Gruma now stands as one of the largest manufacturing companies of corn flour and tortillas in the world (Gruma, 2014).

The success of Gruma is accounted for by a core strategy aligned to five pillars: (1) solid corporate strategic direction and organizational development; (2) innovation; (3) marketing; (4) sustainability and technology; and (5) multi-market, multi-category, and multi-target consumers (Gruma, 2014, 2016a, 2016b).

Today, Gruma's infrastructure includes approximately 18,000 employees and 79 plants, and a presence in over 100 countries through its global and regional brands, with operations in the United States, Mexico, Central America, Europe, Asia, and Oceania. The company's headquarters are located in Monterrey Nuevo Léon, Mexico.

History of Gruma

The entrepreneurship and vision of the founder, Mr. Roberto Gonzalez Barrera, allowed him to foresee that the Mexican market of tortillas needed a new process to produce more tortillas and in a faster way to take advantage of the business opportunities that the consumption of tortillas among the Mexican population offered. He realized that tortillas were mainly cooked in an old fashioned way with rustic artefacts. Working along with his father, Mr. Roberto M. Gonzalez

Gutierrez, who was an engineer, they devised a way to prepare and preserve the dough for the preparation of tortillas (Gruma, 2016b).

They developed an innovative dried product, a flour of "nixtamal" – the basis of the tortilla dough – which just needed water to be added to prepare the dough for cooking the tortillas. The same principle applied to the hot cake flour. This new product of "tortilla flour" could be preserved for extended periods, to be used on demand. Furthermore, it enabled a simplified tortilla manufacturing process. This innovative product represented a technological breakthrough in the industry of tortilla production, and completely revolutionized the process of producing tortillas in Mexico (Gruma, 2016b).

By 1949, Don Roberto González Barrera and his father Don Roberto M. González Gutiérrez founded their first manufacturing plant, Gruma "Molinos Azteca" in Cerralvo, New Leon, Mexico, with a production capacity of 150 tons per month of the new product. In the 1950s the new company focused first on developing a "nixtamalized" corn flour of superior quality, and in improvements to the manufacturing process aiming to create higher quality tortillas with the best flavor, texture, and color. Their leading brand, Maseca®, which is derived from "Masa + Seca" (dry + dough), was launched on the market. A second plant, built in Acaponeta, Nayarit, was opened while the company faced two commercial challenges: first, achieving a level of efficient and uniform manufacturing production; and secondly, commercially introducing the new product Maseca with their potential customers, the tortilla small retailers, selling the benefits of this new corn flour as the raw material for the preparation of tortillas as well as raising awareness with final consumers that these new tortillas were as good as traditionally prepared ones (Gruma, 2016b).

During the 1960s the company focused on efficiency in its manufacturing facilities by using a group of researchers to increase profitability in the production processes as well as developing next-generation technology for manufacturing. This period was also characterized by expansion in Mexico and opening seven new corn flour mills (Gruma, 2016b).

Internationalization of Gruma

The 1970s represent the beginning of the internalization period of the company, since the firm started up operations in Costa Rica in 1973, producing and commercializing and mass distributing packaged tortillas. This international expansion to Costa Rica was a learning point for Gruma, which allowed it to develop high-speed machines and incorporate Soy protein to nutritionally improve the tortillas. The proven-formula tortillas could be manufactured, packaged, preserved, and distributed without losing their properties, and the creation of a solid distribution network serving a large number of distribution routes made obvious sense. Today, Costa Rica remains the headquarters for Gruma's R&D processes (Gruma, 2016b).

In the mid-1970s the company entered the United States through the acquisition of the Mission Foods plant in California. This entry into the world's most developed market was also a key business learning point for successful future expansions. The focus on R&D of the best manufacturing machinery and technology for corn tortilla production allowed Gruma to develop another important business in parallel: for the production and commercialization of machinery to produce corn tortillas, Gruma founded TecnoMaiz, SA DE CV, which develops, manufactures, and markets all types of corn tortilla production, from machines that produce 50 tortillas per minute for small Mexican neighborhood tortilla shops to production lines with a capacity to produce 600 tortillas per minute. This machinery is now recognized as the best quality brand of tortilla making equipment (Gruma, 2016b).

In the 1980s Gruma strongly focused on becoming an international company, and as part of its international program, the firm acquired ten plants in the United States as well as the "Guerrero" brand, which is a leading brand among Hispanics, and with the investment in the construction of the first corn flour mill in Texas, the firm created "Azteca Milling," a subsidiary that would quickly became a successful profit contributor and facilitate significant growth in the tortilla flour sales in the United States (Gruma, 2016b).

The 1990s represented a period of international and financial focus. The world's largest tortilla mega-plant was opened in Los Angeles, California, with a daily production of 14 million units. In Central America, the operations of the firm were expanded into Guatemala, El Salvador, Honduras, and Nicaragua. The company also expanded into the South American market with the acquisition of the second largest player in Venezuela, Molinos Nacionales (Monaca). A new daily production record of 25 million tortillas was achieved in the USA by building an even newer mega-plant in Los Angeles, California (Gruma, 2016b).

To strengthen the company's investment capacity, on the financial front two important steps were taken: the firm's initial public offering of Gruma shares on the Mexican Stock Exchange in 1994 and, four years later, the listing of Gruma's shares on the New York Stock Exchange with the symbol GMK (Gruma, 2016b).

The 2000s represented a second wave of aggressive international expansion, beginning with the first tortilla manufacturing facility in Coventry, England. The UK was the bridge to move into Europe, followed by a start of sales in eastern European countries. In the European market the company identified a great business opportunity in producing flatbreads as well as wraps. More acquisitions followed: a wheat tortilla factory in Holland and a corn flour mill in Italy, the Pride Valley Foods company in England, the Rositas Investments company – producer of wheat flour tortillas and corn chips – and a new plant to manufacture wheat flour tortillas and corn taco shells in Australia, and a plant specializing in flatbreads (pita, pizza dough, naan, and wheat-flour tortillas) in Malaysia (Gruma, 2016b).

Additionally, the company entered China by building a wheat flour tortilla plant in Shanghai, recognizing the great market potential represented there. Next-generation plants with state-of-the-art technology were also built in Melbourne, Australia and Panorama, California, United States. Some of their facilities in Mexico were also expanded, enabling them to diversify the product portfolio in their local and global markets, thereby satisfying consumer demands with a wide diversity of tastes and preferences and serving a large consumer base seeking both healthier foods and care for the environment (Gruma, 2016b).

As of 2010, the last few years have been characterized by an emphasis on sustainability and environmental care, aiming to operate manufacturing and administrative facilities that use the best technology to allow efficient use of energy, water, and waste, as well as reducing pollutant emissions. This new focus led Gruma to be recognized and certified "LEED Gold" (Leadership in Energy and Environmental Design, leadership in design energy and environmental), an award bestowed by the US Government; currently the California production facilities are Gruma's worldwide benchmark. New acquisitions allowed expansion to new international markets, including grits and corn flour manufacturing in Cherkassy, Ukraine, to satisfy the product requirements of the Eastern European region and some countries in North Africa. The acquisition of strategic assets of the Albuquerque Tortilla Company and the Casa de Oro Foods tortilla plant in the USA, a leading plant producing tortillas of corn and wheat in Russia, and the snacks brand *Solntse* in Mexico, have further expanded the company's reach, as has the purchase of a mill with the most advanced milling technology for grits – an important raw material in the production of beer, cereals, and snacks – in Turkey. Gruma is also now the leading company in the production and marketing of corn and wheat tortilla, fried food, and salsas, along with Mexico Foods España in Spain, aiming to strengthen its presence in central Europe (the Iberian Peninsula, the south of France, Italy, Portugal, and Malta) (Gruma, 2016b).

On the marketing front, the Mission brand was successfully introduced in the modern retail channel in Singapore and Malaysia. Two strategic financial steps were taken: the purchase for US $450 million of shares of ARCHER DANIELS MIDLAND and refinancing credit for US$400 million; this step eliminated the financial risks of short-term debt and provided significant savings in interest rates. This period also represented a transition in the top management of Gruma: the death of the Founder and Chairman, Roberto González Barrera, translates into the second generation taking over, with Juan Gonzalez Moreno being appointed Chairman of Board by the shareholders and starting the construction of a production facility in Russia (Gruma, 2016b). Gruma's evolution and expansion are presented in Table 7.6.

Gruma's Foreign Entry Strategies

In 2012, the Founder and Chairman of Board of Gruma (as well as of the Banorte-Ixe banking group), Don Roberto González Barrera died and his son Lic. Juan Gonzalez Moreno was appointed Chairman of Board by the shareholders. Juan Gonzalez Moreno inherited his father's personal talent, entrepreneurial characteristics, and business acumen, and with a deep knowledge and vision for the business, focused on making it more innovative, market-oriented, sustainable, and environmentally friendly to succeed in facing the dynamics of the twenty-first-century global marketplace.

In 2016 Gruma is one of the largest manufacturers of corn flour and tortillas worldwide, commercializing leading brands present in over 100 countries through its global brands Maseca® and Mission®, together with the regional brands, Guerrero® in the United States; Tortiricas® and Tosty® in Costa Rica, and with operations in the United States, Mexico, Central America, Europe, Asia, Australia, and Oceania. Gruma has 18,000 employees and 79 plants, achieving net sales of US $3.4 million, 70 percent of which come from international operations outside of Mexico, led by the new vision of the second family generation and Chairman of the Board, Juan Gonzalez Moreno (Gruma, 2016a, 2016b).

CONCLUSIONS

From these two successful Mexican companies' internationalization processes we can draw the following conclusions.

Table 7.6 *Evolution of Gruma*

Year	Mexico	International
1949	Gruma was founded in Cerralvo, Nuevo Leon, Mexico. Molinos Azteca, the first "nixtamal" corn flour production plant, began operating in Cerralvo, Nuevo Leon, with 45 employees who worked over three shifts to manufacture about 150 tons of products per month.	
1950s	Maseca was born, its name deriving from the concepts of "Masa + Seca" (dry + dough). The 1950s was a decade of experimentation and was crucial in achieving a product that was acceptable to customers, who wanted to have a tortilla with optimal color, texture, and flavor.	
1960s	Gruma opened seven new corn flour mills. This was a period of expansion for Gruma nationwide during which the use of corn flour in Mexico began to become a reality. Maseca began to position itself as a synonym for quality, but also as a	

Table 7.6 (*cont.*)

Year	Mexico	International
	staple food in the Mexican diet.	
1970s		In 1973, the company began operations in Costa Rica with the production and marketing of packaged tortillas, and put great effort ino mass distribution.
		In the mid-1970s, Gruma arrived in the United States and purchased the Mission Foods plant in California.
		At the same time, a new business was growing and with proprietary technology, Gruma's affiliate, TECNOMAIZ, SA de CV, was founded.
1980s	Gruma is considered an international company.	As part of its expansion strategy into the international market, Gruma acquired ten plants in the United States.
		Gruma built the first corn flour mill in Edinburg, Texas, which created Azteca Milling, a subsidiary that would quickly produce profits and would represent significant growth in flour sales for the tortilla industry in the United States.
		In the United States Gruma also acquired *Guerrero*, a brand with strong roots in southern California, which is now much beloved by Mexicans in the USA.

Table 7.6 (*cont.*)

Year	Mexico	International
1990s		In 1990 Gruma built its tortilla mega-plant on Olympic Boulevard in Los Angeles, California. It is now the world's largest plant with a capacity of 14 million units per day. The production level achieved by Gruma enabled the company to strengthen its presence in Central America by expanding operations into Guatemala, El Salvador, Honduras, and Nicaragua.
	In 1994 Gruma made its initial public offering of shares on the Mexican Stock Exchange.	In 1995 Gruma built a plant in Rancho Cucamonga in Los Angeles, California, which surpassed the Olympic plant's production when it achieved a record-breaking production of 25 million tortillas per day. In 1998, Gruma's shares were listed on the New York Stock Exchange under the ticker symbol GMK.
2000		The United Kingdom became the beachhead for entrance to the European market. In 2000 Gruma opened its first tortilla facility in Coventry, England. With this decision, the Mexican company became a local producer instead of an importer.
2004		Gruma acquired a wheat tortilla factory in Holland and a corn flour mill in Ceggia, near Venice, Italy.
2006		After an exhaustive analysis, Gruma entered the Asian market

Table 7.6 (cont.)

Year	Mexico	International
		by building a wheat flour tortilla plant in Shanghai, China.
		Gruma purchased the Pride Valley Foods company in Seaham, England.
		In Oceania, Gruma bought the Rositas Investments company.
2007		Gruma acquired a new plant in Melbourne, Australia: OZ-Mex, a manufacturer of wheat flour tortillas and corn taco shells.
2008		Gruma built next-generation plants equipped with cutting-edge technology to diversify its product portfolio and care for the environment in Melbourne, Australia and Panorama, California, United States.
2009	Gruma celebrated 60 years of existence.	
2010		Gruma Corp., a subsidiary of Gruma SAB de CV in the United States, opened its California plant, designed to meet the highest specifications in terms of sustainability and environmental care – so its construction has been certified "LEED Gold" (Leadership in Energy and Environmental Design, leadership in design energy and environmental), an award bestowed by the US Government. Gruma purchased a grits and corn flour manufacturing plant with an

Table 7.6 (cont.)

Year	Mexico	International
		installed capacity of 65,000 tons of product per year in Cherkassy, Ukraine.
2011		Gruma strengthened its presence in the US by acquiring the assets of the Albuquerque Tortilla Company for 100 million pesos. In Russia, Gruma acquired a leading plant producing tortillas of corn and wheat and snacks, Solntse Mexico, for US$7 million. Gruma acquired the plant of tortillas Casa de Oro Foods in the United States for US$20 million. Gruma bought a corn mill in Turkey for $15.5 billion, to produce Semolina in Turkey. It is important to point out that the new mill in Turkey is equipped with the most advanced milling technology for grits, a product used in the manufacturing of beer, cereals, and snacks. Gruma launched the Mission brand in the self-service channel in Singapore and Malaysia.
2012	Mr. Roberto González Barrera passes away. The Shareholders of Gruma appoint Lic. Juan Gonzalez Moreno as Chairman of Board. Gruma purchases shares of Archer Daniels Midland,	

Table 7.6 (*cont.*)

Year	Mexico	International
	benefitting all its shareholders. The company closed the operation worth US$450 million.	
2013	For the second consecutive year, Gruma is recognized by Great Place to Work as the best company to work for in Mexico. The company also deserved its "Credibility and Respect" award.	In Washington, United States, Juan González Moreno, Chairman of the Board and Chief Executive Officer of Gruma, receives a "Good Neighbor–2013" award granted by the United States Chamber of Commerce.
		In Lumpur, Malaysia, Gruma produced the largest wrap in history, which reached a length of 248 meters. The development involved more than 1,500 Malaysian consumers.
		Gruma refinanced credit for US$400 million and improved costs and its debt profile. The company obtained two syndicated loans: one for $220 million and another for $2,300 million. Loans are for a term of five years with an average life of 4.2 years and start from write-downs in December 2014, in both cases.
2014	During the month of May, Juan González Moreno is honored as Entrepreneur of the Year by the Association of Mexican Companies in the United States.	On June 11, Gruma announces the purchase of Mexicofoods España, the leading company in the production and marketing of corn and wheat tortilla, fried food, and salsas.

Table 7.6 (cont.)

Year	Mexico	International
	Gruma sells its operations of wheat flour in Mexico to Grupo Trimex.	Juan González Moreno places the first stone of the new Gruma factory in Moscow.

Source: Gruma (2016)

1. Their internationalization strategies were a combination of investments and strategic acquisitions that enabled them to export their business models to countries with a vast diversity of economic conditions compared with the Mexican economy. They both learned from their initial entry into the USA to expand into other developed countries such as the European Union, Australia, and Oceania; additionally, both expanded into China after careful analysis of these countries' socioeconomic conditions and commercial and financial regulations, taking into account specific business strategies particular to that expanding economy, and used the successful business model of Mexico to expand into the emerging markets worldwide.

2. In the marketing field, these two Mexican food companies are an important demonstration of the "Glocalization Efforts" (a combination of standardization and adaptation): both firms focused in product R&D and consumer research to successfully develop Glocal product and marketing strategies to satisfy a wide variety of consumer tastes and cultural eating differences in a wide diversity of the international markets as well as concentrating in the market penetration of core products/brands such as loaves of bread and corn tortillas in multiple markets. Both companies had been successful in connecting with their target mid–low-class consumer segments and appealing to them in a new environment against local competition.

3. The management of both companies have focused in the last decade on becoming one of the largest global food companies and expecting higher sales from their international businesses, with one of their top priorities being to become more competitive based on their global capacities to optimize costs and drive profits.

4. Technological advancement is another of the top priorities of both companies: the vision of the management is to prioritize investment in state-of-the-art technological advances through innovation and R&D, aiming to make each company one of the most sustainable environmental and socially responsible companies in the world.

5. Other food firms from emerging markets can draw from these successful experiences to develop their own internationalization strategies by capitalizing on these principles and adapting them to their own businesses.

REFERENCES

Bimbo. 2000. Annual Report, www.mzweb.com.br/grupobimbo/web/conteu do_en.asp?tipo=30049&id=0&idioma=1&conta=44&submenu=&im g=&ano=2010. Accessed July 14, 2016.

Bimbo. 2005. Annual Report, www.mzweb.com.br/grupobimbo/web/conteu do_en.asp?tipo=30049&id=0&idioma=1&conta=44&submenu=&im g=&ano=2010. Accessed July 1, 2016.

Bimbo. 2010. Annual Report, www.mzweb.com.br/grupobimbo/web/conteu do_en.asp?tipo=30049&id=0&idioma=1&conta=44&submenu=&im g=&ano=2010. Accessed July 3, 2016.

Bimbo. 2015a. Annual Report Summary, www.grupobimbo.com/en/investors.ht ml . Accessed June 27, 2016.

Bimbo. 2015b. Integrated Annual Report, www.grupobimbo.com/en/investors.ht ml. Accessed July 4, 2016.

Bimbo. 2016a. Bimbo Web Page, www.grupobimbo.com/en/our-group/in-the-worl d.html. Accessed July 4, 2016.

Bimbo. 2016b. Bimbo Web Page – Green Press Releases, www.grupobimbo.com/en/ press-room/press-releases/1101/1111/grupo-bimbo-the-most-important-conver sion-to-renewable-energy-in-the-food-industry.html. Accessed July 4, 2016.

CNN Expansión. 2013. Roberto Servitje se retira de Bimbo, http://expansion.mx/ negocios/2013/04/09/roberto-servitje-se-retira-de-bimbo. Accessed July 8, 2016.

CNN Expansión. 2016a. Las 100 Mexicanas más Globales 2016, www.grupobimbo .com/es/sala-de-prensa/noticias/2016/las-100-mexicanas-mas-globales-2016.ht ml. Accessed July 12, 2016.

CNN Expansión. 2016b. Las 500 empresas mas importantes de México, http:// expansion.mx/rankings/interactivo-las-500/2015. Accessed July 12, 2016.

El Informador. 2016. Gruma, de Juan González Moreno, en top 10 de empresas globales, www.informador.com.mx/economia/2016/667099/6/gruma-de-juan-g onzalez-moreno-en-top-10-de-empresas-globales.htm. Accessed July 26, 2016.

Excelsior. 2014. Consume cada mexicano 90 kilos de tortillas al año, www.excel sior.com.mx/nacional/2014/09/19/982604. Accessed July 27, 2016.

Food Engineering. 2015. The World's Top 100 Food & Beverage Companies, www .foodengineeringmag.com. Accessed June 30, 2016.

Food Processing. 2016. Global Packaged Food Market by 2020 Will Be a $3.03-Trillion Industry, www.foodprocessing.com/industrynews/2015/global-pack aged-food-market-by-2020-will-be-a-3-03-trillion-industry/. Accessed June 30, 2016.

Gruma. 2014. Annual Report, www.gruma.com/media/613627/ar_gruma_2014 .pdf. Accessed June 15, 2016.

Gruma. 2016a. Company overview, www.gruma.com/media/649173/gruma-jan16 .pdf. Accessed June 14, 2016.

Gruma. 2016b. Gruma Website, www.gruma.com/en.aspx. Accessed June 13, 2016.

MarketLine. 2015. Food Retail in Mexico, http://marketline.com/. Accessed June 1, 2016.

Mexico Desconocido. 2001. La tortilla, sol de Maíz, www.mexicodesconocido.com .mx/la-tortilla-sol-de-maiz.html. Accessed June 1, 2016.

Morningstar. 2016. Juan Antonio Gonzalez Moreno, Chief Executive Officer and Chairman of the Board of Gruma and GIMSA, http://insiders.morningstar.com/tr ading/executive-profile.action?PersonId=PS00003VJP&flag=Director&insider=Ju an_Moreno&t=0P00000JEMM&region=usa&culture=en-US&cur=. Accessed July 27, 2016.

Mundo Ejecutivo Express. 2016. Consumo de tortilla en EU apuntala éxito de Gruma, http://mundoejecutivoexpress.mx/negocios/2016/03/17/consumo-tor tilla-eu-apuntala-exito-gruma. Accessed June 31, 2016.

Nestlé. 2015. Annual Report, www.nestle.com/asset-library/documents/library/docu ments/annual_reports/2015-annual-review-en.pdf. Accessed June 1, 2016.

Ornelas, S. L. 2015. Inside Mexico's Processed Food Industry. *MEXICONOW*, www.mexicofoodsummit.com/docs/processed_food.pdf. Accessed June 2, 2016.

Passport. 2016. Packaged Food in Mexico. *Euromonitor International*, www.euro monitor.com/. Accessed June 4, 2016.

Pfitzer, M. & Krishnaswamy, R. 2007. The Role of the Food & Beverage Sector in Expanding Economic Opportunity, https://utzcertified.be/attachments/article/ 308/0806_report_20_eo_food__beverage_final.pdf. Accessed May 30, 2016.

PRNewswire. 2015. World Packaged Food – Market Opportunities and Forecasts, 2014–2020. *PRNewswire*, www.prnewswire.com/news-releases/world-pack aged-food–market-opportunities-and-forecasts-2014–2020–300132434.html. Accessed May 15, 2016.

Sabrosía. 2014. La historia de las clásicas tortillas de maíz, www.sabrosia.com/20 14/09/la-tortilla-de-maiz/. Accessed May 15, 2016.

Torres, A. & Jasso, J. 2005. Cross border acquisitions and mergers: Learning processes of Mexican corporative groups. *Innovation*, 7(2–3): 240–255.

USDA. 2016. Global Food Industry, www.ers.usda.gov/topics/international-mar kets-trade/global-food-markets/global-food-industry.aspx. Accessed May 15, 2016.

World Bank. 2016. Mexico – Share of Spending by Sector – Total Consumption, by Consumption Segment, http://datatopics.worldbank.org/consumption/country/ Mexico. Accessed May 14, 2016.

World Finance. 2016. World Finance 100, www.worldfinance100.com. Accessed May 10, 2016.

WorldAtlas. 2016. Countries With the Highest Levels of Soft Drink Consumption, www.worldatlas.com/articles/countries-with-the-highest-levels-of-soft-drink-c onsumption.html. Accessed May 18, 2016.

8 From Family Firms to MultiMexicans in the Beer Industry

Grupo Modelo and Cuauhtémoc Moctezuma

Edgar Rogelio Ramírez-Solís and Verónica Ilián Baños-Monroy

INTRODUCTION

Mexico is not just the land of tequila anymore; it is a new key player in the global beer market. The objective of this chapter is to present an overview of the history and current situation of the beer industry in Mexico. We will also offer some advice gleaned from lessons learned for any firm from an emerging market looking for internationalization. In the first section, we begin this overview with a notice about a concession to brew European-type beer in Mexico during the sixteenth century.

We will review how a country in which beer was barely known in the nineteenth century became today's number-one exporter globally. Mexico also has the seventh largest beer market in the world in terms of volume and value. Due to the distinctive features of Mexican-market beer, we have decided to include the beer industry as part of the list of MultiMexicans even though the major players are no longer Mexican firms.

The brewery industry in Mexico has come a long way since its origins in the late 1800s with the first small factories located in Mexico City; this is the main topic of the first section. We will learn how 72 beer producers established in 1899 were forced to close due to fierce competition in under 50 years, and how only two players bought the rest of breweries. We include an analysis of these two companies

(Grupo Modelo and Cuauhtémoc Moctezuma) because they grew in importance as Mexican companies over almost a century, and only in very recent years were both firms purchased by multinational companies. We will review how these two companies nowadays dominate both domestic and imported brands with a very varied portfolio, and with leading brands in very specific regions and nationwide; these companies also benefit from strongly positioned brands in consumers' minds and from long-term presence in Mexico. We will finish the chapter with conclusions about the development of this duopoly, and how and why these Mexican companies were willing to be bought by multinationals. For convenience and the least confusion, we will refer to "Grupo Modelo" throughout this chapter, although in fact the company only adopted this name as recently as 1991, having previously been known as Cervecería Modelo.

HISTORY OF MEXICAN BEER INDUSTRY

From the Sixteenth to the Nineteenth Century

Brewing in Mexico has a long tradition. The first official concession to brew European-style beer was granted to Alfonso de Herrero in 1543 or 1544. In the years just before Mexico's independence (1810), beer consumption was established in Mexico. However, it was not until the late nineteenth century that "modern" brewing was born (Reyna & Kramer, 2013).

In the late 1880s there were already two major breweries, one in Mexico City (founded in 1860) and one in Toluca (1865). Cervecería Toluca y México was a family business founded by a German, Santiago Graff (Márquez, 1992).

From the mid-nineteenth century to the early twentieth century, a large number of breweries were opened in various regions of the country. Some of these included: Cervecería Cruz Blanca in Mexico City, founded by Emil Dercher in 1869 (which produced the first lager); the San Diego Brewery, founded by Carlos Fredenbaen in 1860; the Cervecería Sonora, founded by George Gruning, Dr. Albert

Table 8.1 *Major breweries in Mexico, 1860–1900*

Company	Foundation year	Place (City and Mexican state)
Cervecería San Diego (disappeared in 1989)	1860	Mexico City, State of Mexico
Cervecería Toluca y México (was bought by Grupo Modelo in 1935)	1865	Toluca, State of Mexico
Cervecería Alsaciana (disappeared; unknown date)	1881	
Fábrica de Cerveza y Hielo Monterrey	1886	Monterrey, Nuevo León
Cervecería Sonora (was bought by Cervecería Moctezuma in 1982; in 1985 Moctezuma was merged with Cervecería Cuauhtémoc)	1887	Hermosillo, Sonora
Cervecería Piazzini (sold one year later to Francisco Sada; was the origin of Cuauhtemoc Moctezuma)	1889	
Cervecería Cuauhtemoc	1890	
Cervecería La Estrella (sold in 1954 to Grupo Modelo)	1890	Guadalajara, Jalisco
Cervecería Guillermo Hasse (in 1896 changed its name to Cervecería Moctezuma)	1894	Orizaba, Veracruz
Compañía Cervecera de Chihuahua (was bought by Cervecería Cuauhtémoc in 1965)	1896	Chihuahua, Chihuahua
La Gran Cervecería Yucateca (two years later, changed its name to Cervecería Yucateca; was bought by Grupo Modelo in 1979)	1898	Mérida, Yucatán
Compañía Cervecera Porfirio Díaz (disappeared; unknown date)	1898	Cuernavaca, Morelos
Cervecería Central (disappeared; unknown date)	1899	
Cervecería del Pacífico (was bought by Grupo Modelo in 1954)	1900	Mazatlán, Sinaloa

Source: Compiled by the authors based on information from Recio, 2004; Márquez, 1992; Reyna & Kramer, 2013; and Pérez, Guzmán & Mayo, 2012.

Hoeffer, and Jacob Schuele in 1896 (Recio, 2004), and others established between 1860 and 1900 (see Table 8.1).

The establishment of a railroad system in Mexico at the end of the nineteenth century allowed the importation of machinery and malt from the United States, but it also forced Mexican breweries to compete against US beer, which began to be distributed in the country. By 1890, the first substantial, industrial brewing facility in the country was built in Monterrey by Cervecería Cuauhtémoc (Pérez, Guzmán & Mayo, 2012).

In 1899, five companies (out of a total of 72 beer producers) dominated the Mexican market: Compañía Cervecera de Chihuahua, Compañía Cervecera de Toluca y México, Cervecería Cuauhtémoc, Cervecería Sonora, and Cervecería Moctezuma; they owned 74.61 percent of the Mexican market. Just one year later, in 1900, there were only 29 breweries in Mexico (Reyna & Kramer, 2013).

The Twentieth and Twenty-First Centuries

The existing breweries during the nineteenth century and the first two decades of the twentieth century had the following characteristics. First, foreigners or immigrants played important roles in launching these early breweries. They contributed greatly to the development of the Mexican beer brewing industry by transferring advanced technologies from Europe and the United States. Second, these firms were local producers in the sense that each one of them catered primarily to the local market in its vicinity.

Between 1910 and 1920, imports of beer increased because of problems in distribution, due to the Mexican Revolution. However, at the end of the armed conflict, imports dropped dramatically due to the start of Prohibition in 1919 in the United States, and also because in early 1921, Cervecería Cuauhtémoc restarted its total production, after seven years, when the railway operation occurred (Cerutti, 2000).

By 1918, there were 36 beer producers in Mexico, and by the twentieth century only two producers remained. Prohibition in the United States during the 1920s helped the Mexican beer industry, with Americans crossing the border to drink, especially in Tijuana. This spurred breweries along the border, such as Mexicali Brewery and the Aztec Brewing Company, both in Baja California (Recio, 2004).

In 1924, beer production in Mexico was a little over 52,000 liters per year. By 1925, despite the strong preference still for "pulque" and "mezcal" in the center of the country, Mexico was producing over 53,750 liters of beer per year (INEGI, 2014a). To promote their product further, European immigrant beer brewers campaigned against native drinks such as "pulque"; they claimed such drinks were produced by unsanitary methods and promoted beer as "rigorously hygienic and modern." The strategy proved successful, with "pulque" now generally looked down upon and imbibed by relatively few people (Reyna & Kramer, 2013).

By 1927, there were 30 breweries but only five of them controlled 77 percent of Mexican production; this situation allowed the big companies to buy out the small ones until only two of them remained. In 1927, all companies together produced over 71,500 liters of beer per year. The oldest brewery firm in Mexico, Compañía Cervecera de Toluca y México, failed to report profits to its shareholders and was finally purchased by Grupo Modelo in 1935 (Recio, 2004); in the same year, Mexican beer production dropped to just under 42,500 liters (INEGI, 2014a).

The Mexican beer industry is vertically integrated. Cervecería Cuauhtémoc's internal production system began with the production of beer bottles in 1899, and its rivals also embarked on the internalization of raw material production. Grupo Modelo started producing malt in 1929, beer bottles in 1935, and cardboard in 1954, all in Mexico City. It also established a carton-producing subsidiary in 1959, and a bottle-manufacturing subsidiary in 1968, both in the state of Mexico. Cervecería Moctezuma established its own malt-producing subsidiary in 1957 and completed systems for the internal production of beer bottles and cardboard by 1962 (Hoshino, 2001).

During the second half of the 1950s, Cervecería Moctezuma began to expand aggressively; it started in 1957 with the takeover of Cervecería del Norte, located in Monterrey. In the early 1970s, Cervecería Moctezuma built a brewery in Guadalajara, giving each of the big three companies a brewery in the country's second largest city. As the three largest beer-brewing companies expanded their production networks across the country by penetrating each other's sphere of influence, smaller firms disappeared one after another (ibid.).

As is shown in Table 8.2, the clear majority of beer production in Mexico was for domestic consumption, until the last decades of the twentieth century; and, today, the country has become the leading beer exporter worldwide.

After 1955, the beer industry was approaching a state of oligopolistic control by Cervecería Cuauhtémoc, Cervecería Moctezuma, and Cervecería Modelo, which together accounted for 86.8 percent of the total production. Among the big three, Cervecería Cuauhtémoc enjoyed the largest share, with the breweries acquired after 1929 contributing half of the company's production, indicating that corporate takeovers were instrumental in boosting its market share. At the time, both Grupo Modelo and Cervecería Moctezuma had only one brewing plant each, in Mexico City and the state of Veracruz, respectively, but their shares of production were high at 30.8 percent and 22.7 percent, respectively. The two companies could attain large production volumes because they were located in densely populated areas where large markets were readily available. The rest of the breweries were small in size with individual production shares of less than 3 percent at most (Hoshino, 2001).

When Cervecería Cuauhtémoc acquired Cervecería Moctezuma in 1985, Grupo Modelo lost its top ranking in sales. This action left only two big players in beer industry: Cervecería Cuauhtémoc Moctezuma and Grupo Modelo.

During the twenty-first century, Mexico reached its peak in the internationalization of its beer industry. In 2003, Mexico displaced the Netherlands as the worldwide exporter in beer sales, selling 1.39 million tons, with sales, primarily to the USA, continuing to increase.

Table 8.2 *Beer production, domestic sales, and per capita consumption in Mexico*

Year	Production (liters)	Sales in Mexico (liters)	Per capita consumption
1930	72,065	71,644	4.3
1935	82,513	81,517	4.5
1940	179,198	176,087	9.0
1945	340,843	317,558	14.1
1950	494,898	493,302	19.1
1955	658,942	682,696	22.7
1960	852,058	823,104	24.0
1965	1,098,448	1,085,891	26.0
1970	1,460,037	1,433,697	29.0
1975	1,986,514	1,937,286	34.0
1980	2,733,320	2,600,102	38.6
1985	2,914,721	N/A	N/A
1990	3,873,405	N/A	N/A
1995	4,420,483	4,453,619	47.5
2000	5,985,123	6,004,134	59.9
2005	7,202,954	7,266,495	68.2
2010	7,991,604	7,991,594	69.9
2013	8,436,671	8,464,533	71.5

Source: Authors, from information of INEGI, 2014a

Grupo Modelo and Cervecería Cuauhtémoc Moctezuma send more than 80 percent of their exports to the USA.

The beer sector employs 55,000 people directly and around 2.5 million indirectly, and makes up 4 percent of tax collection (Cerveceros de México, 2015). Mexico is also the leading supplier of beer to the United States, Australia, Chile, Guatemala, Argentina, and New Zealand; it is the third supplier to Canada and the fourth to China and Japan (El Economista, 2015).

Mexico is the world's sixth-largest beer producer and sixth-largest beer consumer. Mexico's beer market will grow by 2.6 percent annually through 2020, according to Heineken's Mexican head of operations (Forbes, 2014).

In the next two sections, we will focus on Grupo Modelo and Cervecería Cuauhtémoc Moctezuma; they invested, in 2015, about US\$3 billion in Mexico, which will enable the company to move from a production of 9,000 to 12,450 million hectoliters, meaning an increase of 40 percent compared to 2014 (El Economista, 2015).

GRUPO MODELO

Grupo Modelo, the largest beer manufacturer in Mexico, operates eight breweries with a total annual installed capacity of 71.5 million hectoliters of beer (Euromonitor, 2014); it is also the twelfth largest beer producer in the world and the most profitable brewery in Latin America. Grupo Modelo is a holding company; it is vertically integrated, beginning with its overseeing of the selection of seeds and germination of hops, and including brewing and bottling plants and distribution by trucks and ships. Grupo Modelo operates through two business divisions: domestic and export. The beer brands brewed and distributed by the group include Corona Extra, Modelo Especial, Victoria, Pacifico, and Negra Modelo, among others. Grupo Modelo also exports seven brands and has a presence in more than 180 countries (AB InBev, 2014).

According to the latest financial data, Grupo Modelo had a weaker performance between 2011 and 2014, due to the competitors in the central region of Mexico, where it has a larger market share, while in the northern region, which has a smaller but growing presence, it experienced stronger performance (CNN Expansión, 2015).

However, we can observe the big picture in Table 8.3: how revenue has been growing since 2000 up to 2015 due to the international expansion of the Corona brand.

History

Braulio Iriarte founded Grupo Modelo in 1925 in Mexico City, with the help of Mexican President Plutarco Elias Calles. Grupo Modelo

Table 8.3 *Grupo Modelo: general data*

	2000	2005	2010	2015
Revenue	3,666.6	5,189.4	8,139.5	8,174.5
Total assets	1,574.1	2,335	5,417.4	5,185.8
EBITDA	956.7	2,617.2	4,008.9	3,586.8
Gross profit	577.7	2,243	3,320.9	2,694.6
Net profit	258.7	1,063.4	1,659.4	1,194.8
Foreign investment	N/A	84	N/A	N/A
Exports	2,640.4	N/A	N/A	932.5
Employees	44,040	47,593	36,707	32,934
Countries	2	2	3	3

Data in millions of USD dollars. N/A = not available
Source: Authors with data from Bloomberg, Expansion and Company's Report

soon came under the control of Pablo Díez Fernández, who became its general director in 1930 and its majority stockholder in 1936. Born in Spain in 1884, Díez Fernández immigrated to Mexico at the age of 21 with money he borrowed from the Dominican fathers under whom he had studied. He first worked as an accountant for a bakery and established the first mechanized bakery in Mexico (Culturebeer, 2015).

Díez Fernández kept Grupo Modelo a private company that financed its expansion into producing malt, bottles, bottle caps, corks, and cartons through its own earnings rather than borrowing. He also acquired the regional breweries Victoria (1935), Estrella (1954), and Pacífico (1954). Grupo Modelo spent heavily on advertising during the late 1940s and early 1950s – much more so than did its rivals. By 1956, it was the leading brewery, passing Cervecería Cuauhtémoc and Cervecería Moctezuma, with 31.6 percent of total beer production in Mexico. Grupo Modelo established plants in Ciudad Obregón (1960), Guadalajara (1964), and Torreón (1966) and created a national distribution network (Funding Universe, 2015a).

In 1961, Grupo Modelo established a subsidiary company, Cervecería Modelo de Noroeste, in the state of Sonora, and another subsidiary, Cervecería Modelo de Guadalajara, in Guadalajara. Subsequently, in 1966, Grupo Modelo established a subsidiary, Cervecería Modelo de Torreón, in Coahuila. This expansion pushed Grupo Modelo's influence into Cervecería Cuauhtémoc's territory, and into areas previously untouched by the big three (Cervecería Cuauhtémoc, Grupo Modelo, and Cervecería Moctezuma), namely, the northern area along the Pacific Coast and the Yucatán Peninsula.

Antonio Fernández Rodríguez, also Spanish born, succeeded Díez Fernández as CEO of the firm in 1971. Under his leadership, Grupo Modelo's share of the Mexican market grew from 39 percent in 1977 to 45 percent in 1985 (Culturebeer, 2015).

The international expansion of the Grupo Modelo products began late; it was not until 1976 that the company began exporting Corona to the USA. Antonio Fernández, the new CEO, set his sights on the American market by adopting a US-style bottle for Corona; but the brand ran into trouble because a Puerto Rican company held the trademark for a beer of the same name. The legal issue was not settled until 1985. In 1977, Grupo Modelo held only one percent of the market abroad for Mexican beers. Ironically, Corona's sales in the United States did not grow until it readopted the traditional clear bottle, with its long neck and brand name in raised letters painted on the glass. Grupo Modelo also repositioned the beer in the US marketplace by ending discounting, in order to upgrade its image, and it conceded to importers the right to make promotional objects such as T-shirts and key chains with the Corona label (Funding Universe, 2015a).

In 1979, Grupo Modelo acquired Cervecería Yucateca with its famous brands in Mexico: Montejo and León. Grupo Modelo also began construction of its brewery in Oaxaca, the Compañía Cervecera del Trópico, which started operating in 1984. Also in 1979, the barley and malt company, Cebadas y Maltas, was founded in Tlaxcala (Grupo Modelo, 2015).

Table 8.4 *Grupo Modelo timeline: important events*

Year	Domestic Event	International Event
1925	Starts operations	
1928	Sales of the Modelo and Corona brands reach 8 million bottles	
1933		First sporadic exports of Corona to the USA
1935	Grupo Modelo acquires Compañía Cervecera de Toluca y México	
1954	Grupo Modelo acquires the Cervecería del Pacífico in Mazatlán, Sinaloa, and Cervecería La Estrella in Guadalajara, Jal.	
1960	Modelo acquires Cervecería Modelo del Noroeste in Sonora	
1967	Cervecería Modelo de Torreón, Coahuila is founded	
1976		Corona starts being formally exported to the USA
1979	Construction of a new brewery in Oaxaca. Cebadas y Maltas is founded in Tlaxcala.	
1981	Inamex de Cerveza y Malta is created in Texcoco, Estado de México	
1985	Grupo Modelo acquires all rights to the name "Corona"	First beer exports to Japan, Australia, New Zealand, and other countries in Europe
1986		Corona becomes the second most popular imported beer brand in the USA
1989		Starts exporting to Europe and New Zealand
1990		Corona starts being exported to Hong Kong,

Table 8.4 (*cont.*)

Year	Domestic Event	International Event
		Singapore, Greece, Netherlands, Germany, and Belgium
1997	The brewery in Zacatecas, Compañía Cervecera de Zacatecas, begins operations	Corona beer becomes the number one imported premium brand in the US market
2003		First manufacturing facility in Idaho, USA
2007		Joint venture with Constellation Brands to form Crown Imports LLC
2010	Opening of a new brewery in Coahuila	
2013		Acquisition of Grupo Modelo by Ab Inveb

Source: Authors based on secondary research

Barton Beers, Ltd., Modelo's Chicago-based importer for the 24 states west of the Mississippi, was largely credited with spurring Corona's growth in the United States by targeting students, some of whom had sampled the brew on spring break at the Mexican resorts of Cancún and Cabo San Lucas. Barton's television commercials featured attractive young people chilling out with bottles of Corona on sun-drenched tropical beaches fringed with palm trees. Often served in bars and restaurants with a wedge of lime, Corona appealed to the exotic, while its light flavor, similar to US beers, offered a comforting taste of familiarity. Meanwhile, Corona's other US-based importer, Gambrinus Co. of San Antonio, was targeting millions of Mexicans with Spanish-language commercials linking the beer to evocative sounds and images intended to inspire nostalgia for the mother country (Chicago Tribune, 2007).

It was Carlos Alvarez, an independent beer importer in San Antonio, Texas, and the person chiefly responsible for bringing Corona to the USA, who guessed that Californians and Texans would remember Corona from visits south of the border. The trick was simply to make it look like the same beer sold in Mexico. Before 1981, when Corona was sold in stubby brown bottles designed specifically for the export market, Corona was a sleeper, found in tiny quantities in a few Southwestern states. No more than 100,000 cases crossed the border: hardly a splash in the big US market. Starting with a few select chili parlors in trendy Austin, Alvarez slowly rolled out Corona in the new bottle and label in Texas, Southern California, and Arizona. By 1983, Grupo Modelo was shipping more than 100,000 cases a month. In 1986, American beer drinkers put away more than 14 million cases of Corona, up from 1.8 million cases in 1984 and 5.5 million cases in 1985. Though Corona's tall, clear bottles weren't even available yet in major East Coast markets like New York and Philadelphia in 1987, the brand was already number two on the imported beer charts, above Molson's, which is available nationwide (Cassel, 1987).

Corona was ranked behind only Heineken among imports. Sales soared again in 1987, to 22 million cases. Then Corona hit a snag, attributed to a bizarre rumor that the brew was contaminated by urine. In addition, Gambrinus reportedly created resentment in northeastern markets by signing agreements with disreputable distributors who jacked up prices and provided shoddy service. In 1992, Corona regained its second ranking north of the border, with 15 million cases sold. Moreover, the beach-party advertising was working in other parts of the world, including Australia and New Zealand, where Corona was the top imported beer, and Japan, where it ranked second (Funding Universe, 2015a).

During the 1980s, Corona Extra became the fastest growing imported beer in the history of the USA, and from the mid-eighties the business world began to talk about the "Corona phenomenon." Later on, production on Corona Light began, to be exported exclusively to the US market. In 1985, Grupo Modelo began its expansion into other markets. It entered first Canada and Japan, and later Australia and New Zealand. In 1989, it began to export to Europe and then, later, Grupo Modelo reached Russia, Africa, and Latin America (Grupo Modelo, 2015).

In 1981, a new facility called "Inamex de Cerveza y Malta" was created in Estado de México. During 1985, Grupo Modelo started beer exports to Japan, Australia, New Zealand and other countries in Europe; one year later, Corona became the second most popular imported beer brand in the USA (Grupo Modelo, 2015).

Results in Mexico itself were not as good, even though Corona was the top beer in the USA. Grupo Modelo's sales in its home country dropped in 1982 and 1983 because of the nation's economic crisis, and the 1981 level of consumption was not surpassed until 1987. In 1984, the company opened its own plant in the state of Tlaxcala for producing barley malt. A decade later, this complex included 63 grain silos and was turning out 100,000 tons of malt per year. In 1991, Grupo Modelo's sales volume forged ahead of Cervecería Cuauhtémoc Moctezuma (Funding Universe, 2015a).

Internationalization

In 1985, Grupo Modelo began its expansion into other markets. It entered first Canada and Japan, and later Australia and New Zealand. In 1989, it began to export to Europe and later Russia, Africa, and Latin America. In 1990, Corona reached countries such as Hong Kong, Singapore, and Greece, besides other countries with a strong beer tradition such as the Netherlands, Germany, and Belgium (Grupo Modelo, 2015).

Cervecería Modelo changed its name to Grupo Modelo in 1991 and went public in 1994, offering 13 percent of its shares on Mexico City's stock exchange. Because the company had virtually no debt and was earning large quantities of dollars and other hard currencies, its shares rose even during the severe recession that gripped Mexico following the sudden and devastating depreciation of the peso in December 1994. During 1997, operations began at the brewery in

Zacatecas, Compañía Cervecera de Zacatecas – the largest in Latin America (Grupo Modelo, 2015).

With the advent of the NAFTA Area in 1994 and eventual elimination of trade barriers, including tariffs, Grupo Modelo decided to protect itself from an invasion of US beers into the Mexican market by forming a partnership with Anheuser-Busch. It sold a 17.7 percent stake in the company (and a similar share of its unlisted operating subsidiary, Diblo) in 1993 to Anheuser-Busch for $447 million. Grupo Modelo remained the exclusive distributor of Anheuser-Busch's products in Mexico, a position it had secured in 1989. Four Modelo beers, including Corona, continued to be imported and distributed in the United States by Barton Beers and Gambrinus, rather than Anheuser-Busch. The two enterprises agreed not to open breweries or bottling plants in each other's home country. Anheuser-Busch received an option to raise its stake in Modelo and Diblo to 50 percent within four years. In 1996, Grupo Modelo had 644 distribution agencies and subagencies, all centrally administered except for 183 affiliates. (ibid.).

Carlos Fernández González, a great-nephew of the founder, succeeded his uncle as general director of the firm in 1997, at the age of just 31. Quality control was being based on Japanese and US "just in time" methods. In 1998, the stock increased by 24 percent in price even though all shares on Mexico City's stock exchange fell by an average of 24 percent during that year (Funding Universe, 2015a).

Also in 1997, Grupo Modelo accounted for 55 percent of all beer sales in Mexico and produced 35 million hectoliters. Corona Extra itself held 32.5 percent of the national market. During the year, Corona overtook Heineken to become the leading imported beer in the United States. Grupo Modelo held 80 percent of the export market for Mexican beers and was distributing its brands in 143 countries (Grupo Modelo, 2015).

Also in 1997, Grupo Modelo was operating 33 companies, which owned approximately 1,394 facilities, including one factory each for producing metal cans, plastic caps, glass bottles, and cardboard boxes, and a number of convenience stores. Net sales came to Mex$15.52 billion (US$1.93 billion) and consolidated net profit to Mex$2.36 billion (US$293.5 million) in 1997 (ibid.).

Anheuser-Busch appeared to fare poorly under the partnership with Grupo Modelo, because in the late 1990s Budweiser and Bud Light were selling well only in tourist areas of Mexico. Nevertheless, the US firm exercised its option by raising its equity holding in Grupo Modelo to 37 percent in 1995 and 50.2 percent in 1997, bringing its total investment to about US$1.6 billion. The sale price was in dispute, however, since the pact called for it to be 19 times earnings. With Grupo Modelo's stock trading at 38 times earnings in early 1998, its shareholders demanded more money, insisting that the valuation of Diblo's earnings should include profits from nonconsolidated subsidiaries as well as companies in which Diblo held majority control. The matter was referred to international arbitration, which, in September 1998, ruled in favor of Anheuser-Busch (Funding Universe, 2015a).

Although Anheuser-Busch won this round, the company was angered by Grupo Modelo's decision in 1996 to renew its alliances with importers Barton Beers and Gambrinus for another ten years. In 1998, Anheuser-Busch was marketing what a Wall Street Journal article called "Corona clones" in southern Florida and Virginia, with at least one of the three beers scheduled for national distribution. Wholesalers were said to suspect that the introduction of these beverages had resulted from the giant US brewer's failure to win distribution rights for Corona. Regardless of this troubled and rumor-laden partnership, Grupo Modelo remained the top Latin America beer maker, and its Corona Extra product remained a leading import in the United States.

In the late 1990s Carlos Fernández also established a new relationship with August Busch IV, CEO of Anheuser-Busch, because his father, August Busch III, had left a damaged image with his Mexican partners. In those years, the American brewery decided to sell itself to Belgium's InBev (Kesmodel, 2008). Since then the former American brewery has been known as AB InBev.

In the USA, Grupo Modelo imports and markets its brands through its joint venture known as Crown Imports. In that country, three of the Grupo Modelo brands are among the top five imported beer brands, and it is the only company to have its six export brands among the top 20. Further, Modelo Especial is the third most popular imported brand in the USA, Corona Light is the fifth (besides being the first among the imported light beers), Pacífico is the fifteenth, and Negra Modelo the nineteenth (Grupo Modelo, 2015).

By 2003, Grupo Modelo had started the construction of its first plant outside Mexico in Idaho Falls, USA, intending to produce malted barley to be used in beer production; the facility was never intended to produce beer. Construction of this factory started in October 2002 and was completed in June 2005 (Miller, 2010). Grupo Modelo invested US$84 million in the plant. In April 2010, Grupo Modelo and Cargill formed a joint venture named Integrow Malt in order to operate the Idaho Falls plant and supply malt and barley (Food Processing Technology, 2015).

In 2007, the joint venture between Grupo Modelo and Constellation Brands to form Crown Imports LLC was announced. The joint venture imports to the United States the Corona Extra, Corona Light, Negra Modelo, Modelo Especial, and Pacifico brands owned by Grupo Modelo, in addition to Tsingtao from China and St. Pauli Girl from Germany. This marked the first time since the 1978 introduction of Grupo Modelo brands into the USA that they have been imported and marketed by a single entity (Constellation Brands, 2007). In 2010, the construction of the new brewery in the state of Coahuila was finished – the most modern in the world according to the company (Grupo Modelo, 2015).

In 2011, Grupo Modelo increased its beer production by 6 percent to 39.09 million hectoliters. Grupo Modelo, through its own convenience store banner Extra, sells soft drinks, wine, liquor, food, and its in-house beer brands. In 2013, Grupo Modelo was employing nearly 33,000 people directly and 180,000 indirectly (Grupo Modelo, 2014).

Since June 2013, AB InBev – a company based in Leuven, Belgium – has owned Grupo Modelo; therefore, they added Corona as their newest global brand (AB InBev, 2014). The purchase was valued at US$20.1 billion, giving AB InBev a 95 percent ownership stake in Grupo Modelo. This acquisition had been in preparation since 2012; however, it was delayed by an antitrust suit in the USA, where Grupo Modelo's Corona brand and AB InBev's Budweiser and Bud Light brands are amongst the top-selling beers. In order to alleviate these issues, it was established that Grupo Modelo's brands would be distributed by Constellation Brands Inc. in the USA and by AB InBev in all other countries (Euromonitor, 2014).

The acquisition allows Grupo Modelo to expand its brands into additional countries. Therefore, this action was a win–win purchase for both companies, allowing them to take advantage of each other's channel distributions and the prestige of their major brands. With this action, AB InBev would produce about 400 million hectoliters of beer a year: 75 percent more than world beer manufacturer number two, SABMiller (Reuters, 2012).

In 2015, Constellation Brands, which markets Grupo Modelo brands in the United States, invested US$2,275 million in Mexico: US$1,650 million earmarked for the expansion of its facility in Coahuila and US$625 million for its packaging company Industria Vidriera de Coahuila. Grupo Modelo also invested US$350 million in Yucatan for the construction of both an aluminum packaging plant and a new brewery (El Economista, 2015).

CERVECERÍA CUAUHTÉMOC MOCTEZUMA

Cervecería Cuauhtémoc Moctezuma is the second largest beer manufacturer in Mexico, under the brand names Superior, XX Lager, Tecate, Tecate Light, Indio, Heineken, Sol, Bohemia, and Carta Blanca. In 2014, it was exporting these beverages to 63 countries and producing beer and food cans, crown caps, glass bottles, labels and wrappers, cardboard boxes, soft-drink cases, refrigerators, and vending machines. This company has six production facilities in Mexico. In

Table 8.5 *Cervecería Cuauhtémoc Moctezuma: general data*

	2000	2005	2010	2015
Revenue	N/A	N/A	N/A	2,490.3
Total assets	N/A	N/A	N/A	14,718.9
EBITDA	N/A	N/A	N/A	850.9
Gross profit	N/A	N/A	N/A	425.1
Net profit	N/A	N/A	N/A	652.5
Foreign investment	N/A	N/A	N/A	N/A
Exports	N/A	N/A	N/A	N/A
Employees	N/A	N/A	N/A	30,996
Countries	2	2	3	3

Data in millions of US dollars; N/A = not available
Source: Authors with data from Bloomberg, Expansion and
Company's Report

2015, Heineken Mexico was employing more than 16,000 people directly (Heineken, 2015).

Although the performance continues to grow over the years, Cervecería Cuauhtémoc Moctezuma still holds second place in sales after Grupo Modelo. Heineken, the new owner, decided to focus on producing more premium beers, which means less volume but at a higher price.

HISTORY

Cervecería Cuauhtémoc was founded in 1890 by Isaac Garza Garza, his brother-in-law Francisco Sada Muguerza, Jose Muguerza, and Jose Maria Schneider. In 1894 Francisco Sada, another kinsman of the Mexican founding families, joined the company as its general manager. Schneider sold his shares in the company in 1897, and thereafter it developed as a family-controlled business (Hoshino, 2001).

In the beginning, this brewery produced 1,500 bottles of beer per day. Cervecería Cuauhtémoc produced its first beer barrel in 1893 and made its mark in this period by winning first prize in the Chicago and Paris world fairs; this was the first recognition of a Mexican beer. A subsidiary, Cervecería Central, was opened in 1901 to supply Mexico City and the surrounding states (FEMSA, 2015).

In 1903, Cervecería Cuauhtémoc produced 80,000 bottles of beer a day and 100,000 barrels a year, and in 1909 it was producing 300,000 of each and employing 1,500 workers. By then the enterprise had expanded vertically. Bottle caps had begun to come into wider use in the United States following their invention there in 1892, and Cervecería Cuauhtémoc was among the earlier companies in the world to start using them (Hoshino, 2001).

No company had more than one production base until 1929, when Cervecería Cuauhtémoc purchased Cervezas La Central in Mexico City (Hoshino, 2001). In 1930, Cervecería Cuauhtémoc transformed the way beer is stored by replacing wood barrels with metal cylinders. This prevented carbon gas leaks and enabled pasteurization, to supply an improved product (FEMSA, 2015).

Cervecería Cuauhtémoc successfully adjusted to the Depression conditions of the 1930s. Beer shipments, after sinking to 14.4 million liters in 1932, reached 24.3 million in 1934 – when the company was producing about 40 percent of the beer in Mexico – and 54.7 million in 1940 (Funding Universe, 2015b).

Internationalization

We can trace the internationalization process of Cervecería Cuauhtémoc since its brand Tecate was an independent brewery. Alberto Aldrete founded the Tecate brewery (in the town of the same name in Baja California) in 1944 and relied on exports to the USA, but later began to sell in other parts of Mexico. In 1954, Cervecería Cuauhtémoc Moctezuma acquired the Tecate brewery (El Financiero, 2014).

As of 1955, Cervecería Cuauhtémoc had malt-producing plants in Monterrey, Mexico City, and the state of Baja California. At early stages of Cervecería Cuauhtémoc's internal production of malt, it

Table 8.6 *Cervecería Cuauhtémoc Moctezuma timeline: important events*

Year	Domestic Event	International Event
1890	Started operations	
1893	The first draft beer under the Cuauhtémoc brand was launched	Carta Blanca won the Gold Medal award in Chicago and Paris World Fairs. These were the first international recognition of a Mexican beer
1903	First brewery to replace corks with metal caps	
1905	Bohemia brand is launched	
1930	Started replacing wood barrels with metal cylinders to store beer	
1944		First sporadic exports of Tecate to the USA
1954	Acquisition of Tecate brand	
1969	Construction of a streamlined brewery at Toluca, State of Mexico	
1985	Merge with Cervecería Moctezuma	
1991		Started exporting to European market with the Sol brand, and more than 55 countries
2004		Repurchased 30 percent of the Cervecería Cuauhtémoc Moctezuma stock owned by John Labatt Limited. Heineken USA undertook the promotion, sales, and distribution of Tecate, XX, Sol, Carta Blanca, and Bohemia. Agreement with the Coors Brewing Company whereby Cervecería

Table 8.6 (*cont.*)

Year	Domestic Event	International Event
		Cuauhtémoc Moctezuma became the exclusive seller of Coors Light in Mexico
2006		Acquisition of the Brazilian brewing company Kaiser
2010		Trading 100 percent of Cervecería Cuauhtémoc Moctezuma stock shares for 20 percent of the Heineken stock shares

Source: Authors based on secondary research

used imported barley, the raw material for malt production. However, the company took steps to encourage local farmers to grow barley suited for beer production by guaranteeing the purchase of their crops and by distributing imported seeds of high-yielding varieties. Consequently, by the 1950s it was able to procure barley locally. To procure this barley, the company's beer sales agents began to double as intermediaries to purchase barley.

Also in 1955, Cervecería Cuauhtémoc took up more than 50 percent of the market in the northeastern states of Nuevo León, Tamaulipas, and Coahuila. Grupo Modelo dominated the central part of the country, which included Mexico City, the states of Mexico, Guanajuato, and Querétaro; while Cervecería Moctezuma was the strongest in the states of Veracruz, Tlaxcala, Puebla, and Hidalgo close to the Gulf of Mexico. It is possible to say that Cervecería Cuauhtémoc had the northeastern part of the country under its sphere of influence, Grupo Modelo the central part, and Cervecería Moctezuma the states near the Gulf of Mexico. The total population of the three states within Cervecería Cuauhtémoc's sphere of influence was much smaller than that in the spheres of influence of its two rivals. In other words, it was imperative for Cervecería Cuauhtémoc to secure production bases in other locales in order to keep growing. It thus advanced first into Mexico City, which was part of Grupo Modelo's sphere of influence, and then into the state of Veracruz, which constituted Cervecería Moctezuma's sphere of influence. There were areas not under the influence of any of the big three, notably the northern area along the Pacific Coast (the states of Sinaloa and Baja California Sur) and the Yucatan Peninsula (the states of Yucatan and Campeche). The former area was the territory of Cervecería del Pacifico, which controlled 50.2 percent of that regional market, while the latter was dominated by Cervecería Yucateca with an 81.3 percent share of the market (Hoshino, 2001). Later, however, these two areas were incorporated into the spheres of influence of the big three.

In 1965, Cervecería Cuauhtémoc took over Cervecería Juárez located in the state of Chihuahua, and toward the end of the 1960s, it established in the state of Mexico a new brewery equipped with the most advanced technologies (ibid.).

Also in 1965, Cervecería Cuauhtémoc acquired the Compañía Cervecera de Chihuahua, with its brands Chihuahua and Cruz Blanca; those brands disappeared during the 1980s because of confusion between the names Carta Blanca and Cruz Blanca. The latter beer was exported to the USA with little success. In Mexico, Cervecería Cuauhtémoc also sold Chihuahua but with a different label (O. Canizales, personal communication, May 20, 2015).

Cervecería Cuauhtémoc decided to open an office to market its brands in the USA, even though sales were very low, and they decided to close their office and go with local distributors. "During 1960s and 1970s, Cervecería Cuauhtémoc exported Carta Blanca, with very low sales because its strategy was giving a premium treatment to the brand, using different bottle, but the US market was expecting something that seems more like the idea of a Mexican beer. That explain the success of Corona, when Grupo Modelo use the same packaging and bottle than in Mexico; the US market was expecting more austere package" (ibid.).

Cervecería Cuauhtémoc has energetically sought to improve not only the technology for beer production but also that for manufacturing containers and packages. During the 1920s, wooden boxes were replaced by cardboard boxes, and the package size was reduced from 60 bottles per box to 25. The reduced size and weight of a unit package went a long way toward making transportation faster and safer, and toward reducing costs and storage space. In 1953, it started using brown bottles to prevent a change in the quality of the beer, and in 1954 it started producing canned beer for the first time in Mexico. The company started using a six-bottle carton in 1960. The company was the first to use plastic cases in 1971, and refrigerator tanks in the early 1980s (Hoshino, 2001).

In 1980, Cervecería Cuauhtémoc exported 0.2 million hectoliters, which represented approximately 1 percent of the beer production of the firm that year. In 1996, the company exported 1.2 million hectoliters, which represented 5.9 percent of its total production that year. The export effort of the firm during the 1980s and 1990s can be better understood if we consider two facts: the volume of exports grew by more than 29 times in a span of just 16 years; and in 1980 most of the exports were destined for the USA (Vera-Cruz, 2002). Their volume and the number of export countries continued to grow in the following years, despite some episodes of economic crises in Mexico during the 1980s and 1990s.

In 1985, Cervecería Cuauhtémoc acquired Cervecería Moctezuma SA, a rival brewery, in bankruptcy court. The transaction gave to Cervecería Cuauhtémoc at least 50 percent of the national beer market, although the federal government was a partner in the acquisition. This added to Cervecería Cuauhtémoc's portfolio the renowned brands XX Lager, Superior, Sol, and Noche Buena (FEMSA, 2015). Since 1985, the brewery has been known as Cervecería Cuauhtémoc Moctezuma (Cervecería Cuauhtémoc Moctezuma).

In 1991, when Cervecería Cuauhtémoc Moctezuma opened in Navojoa, Sonora, "one of the most modern breweries in the world," according to them, they also began to export to European markets with the Sol brand, and positioned their products in more than 55 countries (ibid.).

The start of exports prompted the company to establish agreements and strategic alliances with international partners, particularly with major corporations, with considerable economic weight in the NAFTA market. In July 1994, Cervecería Cuauhtémoc Moctezuma signed an agreement with John Labatt Canada whereby it acquired 22 percent shares of Cervecería Cuauhtémoc Moctezuma. Before the partnership with John Labatt, FEMSA (the holding group which owned Cervecería Cuauhtémoc Moctezuma at the time) sought a strategic partner to help Cervecería Cuauhtémoc Moctezuma to restructure its marketing strategies. So, FEMSA sold 8 percent of the shares to Phillip Morris Company, matrix of Miller Brewing Company, the second largest brewery in the USA; this had successfully introduced innovative sales strategies in the US beer market. However, the alliance of FEMSA and Phillip Morris proved to be of little importance after the alliance with John Labatt (Vera-Cruz, 2002).

In 1994, Tecate reached its 50th birthday as the best-selling imported beer in the United States. In a partnership with the Canadian John Labatt Limited brewery they acquired 30 percent of FEMSA shares and signed an agreement with Labatt to associate their respective companies in the United States (FEMSA, 2015).

In 1996, Cervecería Cuauhtémoc Moctezuma was exporting to over 60 countries. In the same year, Cervecería Cuauhtémoc Moctezuma sold 91.3 percent of its total beer sales volume in the Mexican market. In 2001, the company exported beer brands to more than 70 countries worldwide, with the USA being the most important market. Tecate beer was the fourth largest import brand in the USA in 2004. Total export sales represented 8.7 percent of Cervecería Cuauhtémoc Moctezuma's total beer sales volume (FEMSA, 2005).

In 2004, FEMSA repurchased 30 percent of the Cervecería Cuauhtémoc Moctezuma stock owned by John Labatt Limited, which allowed them to control imports, marketing, and distribution of their brands in the USA. An agreement was announced with the Coors Brewing Company, whereby FEMSA became the exclusive seller of Coors Light in Mexico for 10 years (FEMSA, 2015).

On January 1, 2005, Heineken USA replaced Labatt USA as the exclusive importer, marketer, and distributor of FEMSA Beer brands in the USA (FEMSA, 2005).

It was in 2006 when Cervecería Cuauhtémoc Moctezuma made the first international acquisition in its history when it purchased Brazilian brewer Kaiser (Cervejarias Kaiser) from the Molson Coors Brewing Company. Cervecería Cuauhtémoc Moctezuma or FEMSA Beer acquired ownership of 68 percent of the equity of Kaiser for US $68 million, using cash in hand. Molson Coors retains 15 percent ownership, and Heineken maintained its existing 17 percent stake (FEMSA, 2006).

On December 31, 2009, Cervecería Cuauhtémoc Moctezuma was classified as the tenth largest brewing company in the world, in terms of volume of sales, and in Mexico Cervecería Cuauhtémoc Moctezuma was the second largest beer producer, also in terms of sales volume. In 2009, approximately 66.4 percent of the FEMSA Beer sales volume came from Mexico, with 24.8 percent from Brazil and 8.8 percent from exports. By December 31, 2009, Cervecería Cuauhtémoc Moctezuma had sold 40,548 million hectoliters of beer and produced and/or distributed 21 brands of beer under 14 different presentations, resulting in a portfolio of 111 different products in Mexico (FEMSA, 2010).

On April 30, 2010, FEMSA announced the closure of the transaction by which FEMSA agreed to exchange 100 percent of its beer operations for a financial participation of 20 percent in the Heineken Group. Since then, FEMSA has had a minor participation in the Heineken Group, one of the leading brewers in the world. The economic participation of 20 percent in the Heineken Group was made up of 43,018,320 shares of Heineken Holding NV and 43,009,699 shares of Heineken NV, in addition to 29,172,504 additional shares to be delivered by an instrument of delivery of assigned actions (ibid.).

By May 31, 2011, 13,147,233 shares had been given through the instrument of delivery of assigned actions. For the period of eight months from May 1 to December 31, 2010, FEMSA has recognized an income by participation of Mex$3,319 million of its economic participation in the Heineken Group (FEMSA, 2010). Heineken took control over FEMSA Beer in an all-stock deal valued at US$7.7 billion. Heineken secured an operation with 43 percent of the Mexican beer market and a 9 percent share in Brazil. The United States is the most profitable beer market, according to Heineken. Brazil is second and Mexico is fourth (Reuters, 2010).

Cervecería Cuauhtémoc Moctezuma announced in March 2015 the construction of a new plant in Chihuahua with an investment of US$490 million (El Economista, 2015).

CONCLUSIONS

As we discuss in this chapter, Grupo Modelo and Cervecería Cuauhtémoc Moctezuma are a *de facto* duopoly in the Mexican beer market. The history that led to this duopoly has left vestiges on the industry's present structure. One is the geographical distribution of beer breweries. These are distributed across the whole country, as well as being located in the three major urban centers of Mexico: Mexico City, Monterrey, and Guadalajara. Both members of the duopoly have their breweries distributed widely across the country, although Cervecería Cuauhtémoc Moctezuma's plants are relatively more concentrated in the northern part of the country while Grupo Modelo's are found more in the southern part. Taking into consideration transportation costs, it would be possible, and economically rational, for the two companies to locate their plants in the north or south and divide the market between them into their respective spheres of influence. The market had been divided in this manner until the 1950s. The present geographical distribution of breweries is a result of the harsh competition between the two companies, which induced each company to penetrate its rival's sphere of influence.

Another vestige left by the industry's history is that both Cervecería Cuauhtémoc Moctezuma and Grupo Modelo maintain vertically integrated production systems, internally undertaking all operations from the production of raw materials to the distribution of the final products. The internalized production of malt is a practice common among beer producers around the world. What is peculiar to the procurement of raw materials for beer production in Mexico is that materials other than malt, namely containers, bottle caps, labels, packaging materials, etc., are produced internally. For Cervecería Cuauhtémoc Moctezuma these materials are supplied by affiliated business enterprises, while Grupo Modelo has three subsidiary firms manufacturing labels and cartons, one producing glass bottles, and two others making bottle caps.

Throughout the history of Mexico's beer industry, Cervecería Cuauhtémoc Moctezuma has always been the driving force behind the industry's transformation into an oligopoly. The company has been able to play such a leadership role because of its level of innovation, which it has displayed in the introduction of new technologies, in embarking on the internalized production of raw materials, in expanding its distribution network, and in its aggressive advertising campaigns. It has vigorously pursued these undertakings because they have served as effective means of ensuring Cervecería Cuauhtémoc Moctezuma's growth. The success of these ventures has largely been dictated by the characteristics of the Mexican beer producing industry and the course of industrialization in Mexico.

The Beer market worldwide has changed. Multinational corporations (MNCs) from small or medium-sized countries, such as Heineke (Netherlands), Carlsberg (Denmark), Ab InBev (Belgium), and SABMiller (South Africa), have adopted successful merger and acquisition (M&A) strategies. Some important players from large countries, such as Anheuser-Busch and Miller in the USA, and Cervecería Cuauhtémoc Moctezuma and Grupo Modelo in Mexico, have become takeover targets.

We discussed in this chapter how, in a relatively short period, Mexico became the most important exporter of the world – so why did Mexico lose the ownership of its two major breweries? First, big MNCs aimed to gain footholds in those regions of the world where beer consumption was rising fast, such as Mexico and Brazil. Second, large brewery groups aimed to increase their initial positions in foreign markets to become dominant players in order to reap the maximum benefits of integrating nationally confined activities, such as management, distribution, and production.

Therefore, instead of focusing on small takeover targets, already acquired by the big players in many markets, the focus since the beginning of the twenty-first century has been on the acquisition of large MNCs such as Grupo Modelo and Cervecería Cuauhtémoc Moctezuma. M&A activity has driven most international growth in the industry. As in many industries, organic growth through Greenfield investments, which played a role in the early days of the beer industry's internationalization, has very little importance today.

Even now that both companies are no longer Mexican, it is still important to recognize that they started operations in Mexico and that the raw material is still Mexican. In addition, there are thousands of Mexican employees involved in the brewing manufacturing process. At this point it is fair to say that, due to this amazing product, Mexico is known everywhere because of the positioning of its beer. Maybe many people around the world are unfamiliar with the country and its geographical location, but for sure, they will have – at least once in their lives – tasted or watched a commercial about a Mexican beer.

As outlined in other chapters of this book, similar industries are taking advantage of the image of Mexico even though Mexico is facing high rates of violence related to its ongoing battle against drug traffickers. Nevertheless, this is only a partial glimpse of what has been happening in Mexico, and this incomplete story has created a misleading brand narrative that damages Mexico's tourism industry, threatens foreign investment, and reduces its relationship with the USA to a security arrangement.

To revitalize Mexico's brand, leaders in government, business, and civil society must unite around a coherent and more positive new narrative. Mexico as a brand has a powerful and attractive presence in highly developed countries. Smaller companies looking to export their products to these markets can exploit this opportunity.

REFERENCES

AB InBev. 2014. Annual Report 2013. *AB InBev*. www.ab-inbev.com/content/da m/universaltemplate/abinbev/pdf/media/annual-report/ABI_AR13_EN_Full .pdf. Accessed April 23, 2015.

Cassel, A. 1987. Mexico Finds Beer a Successful Export. *Philly*. http://articles .philly.com/1987–03-15/business/26223455_1_corona-extra-beer-drinkers-bot tle. Accessed May 13, 2015.

Cerutti, M. 2000. *Propietarios, empresarios y empresas en el norte de México*. México: Siglo XXI.

Cerveceros de México 2015. Nosotros. *Cerveceros de México*. www.cervecerosde mexico.org.mx/. Accessed June 18, 2015.

Chicago Tribune. 2007. Beer Sales a Crowning Glory. *Chicago Tribune*. http://art icles.chicagotribune.com/2007–11-11/business/0711100013_1_corona-extra-ga mbrinus-barton-beers. Accessed April 13, 2015.

CNN Expansión. 2015. Grupo Modelo pierde mercado en México. *CNN Expansión*. www.cnnexpansion.com/negocios/2015/06/01/grupo-modelo-le-hace-falta-ver-mas-box. Accessed June 10, 2015.

Constellation Brand. 2007. Grupo Modelo, Constellation Brands Beer Import Joint Venture, Crown Imports LLC, Operational. *CBrands*. www.cbrands.com/news-media/grupo-modelo-constellation-brands-beer-import-joint-venture-crown-im ports-llc-operational. Accessed May 9, 2015.

Culturebeer. 2015. Una Compañía Cervecera Mexicana fundada por un español. *Culture Beer*. www.culturebeer.com/sitio/sec_contenidosview.php?sec_id=62. Accessed April 9, 2015.

El Economista. 2015. Industria cervecera sigue los pasos de la automotriz: SE. *El Economista*. http://eleconomista.com.mx/industrias/2015/06/17/industria-cer vecera-sigue-pasos-automotriz-se. Accessed June 17, 2015.

El Financiero. 2014. Tecate celebra 70 años con la mira puesta en la conquista de EU. *El Financiero*. www.elfinanciero.com.mx/monterrey/tecate-celebra-70-ano s.html. Accessed May 22, 2015.

Euromonitor. 2014. Beer in Mexico. USA: *Euromonitor*. http://search.proquest.com/ docview/1563700029?accountid=11643. Accessed March 12, 2015.

Food Processing Technology. 2010. Grupo Modelo Brewery, Coahuila, Mexico. *Food Processing Technology.* www.foodprocessing-technology.com/projects/grupo-brewery/. Accessed June 4, 2016.

Food Processing Technology. 2015. Grupo Modelo Barley Malting Facility, USA. *Food Processing Technology.* www.foodprocessingtechnology.com/projects/grupo/. Accessed April 14, 2015.

Forbes. 2016a. Industria cervecera, un mercado a prueba de crisis. *Forbes.* www.forbes.com.mx/industria-cervecera-un-mercado-a-prueba-de-crisis/. Accessed June 6, 2016.

Forbes. 2016b. Grupo Modelo: guía para conquistar al mundo a través de una Corona. *Forbes.* www.forbes.com.mx/grupo-modelo-guia-para-conquistar-al-mundo-a-traves-de-una-corona/. Accessed June 6, 2016.

Forbes. 2014. Latin America to Drive Volume and Margin Expansion for Anheuser-Busch InBev. *Forbes.* www.forbes.com/sites/greatspeculations/2014/09/05/latin-america-to-drive-volume-and-margin-expansion-for-anheuser-busch-inbev/. Accessed April 10, 2015.

FEMSA. 2010. Annual Report. *FEMSA.* http://ir.femsa.com/mx/reports.cfm. Accessed April 10, 2015.

FEMSA. 2005. FEMSA global offering. *SEC.* www.sec.gov/Archives/edgar/data/1061736/000119312505115614/d424b1.htm. Accessed April 20, 2015.

FEMSA. 2006. Femsa Acquires Controlling Stake in Brazilian Brewer Kaiser. *FEMSA.* http://ir.femsa.com/releasedetail.cfm?releaseid=185460. Accessed April 10, 2015.

FEMSA. 2015. About us. *FEMSA.* www.femsa.com/en/node. Accessed April 1, 2015.

Funding Universe. 2015a. History of Grupo Modelo. *Funding Universe.* www.fundinguniverse.com/company-histories/search/?q=modelo. Accessed March 24, 2015.

Funding Universe. 2015b. Valores Industriales S.A. History. *Funding Universe.* www.fundinguniverse.com/company-histories/valores-industriales-s-a-history/. Accessed April 20, 2015.

Grupo Modelo. 2014. Informe anual. *Grupo Modelo.* www.gmodelo.com.mx/download/informe_anual/Reporte_Anual_2013_Grupo_Modelo.pdf Accessed April 11, 2015.

Grupo Modelo. 2015. We are and History. *Grupo Modelo.* www.grupomodelo.com.mx/. Accessed March 26, 2015.

Heineken. 2015. About us. Official Website. www.theheinekencompany.com. Accessed April 28, 2015.

Hoshino, T. 2001. Industrialization and Private Enterprises in Mexico. 2: Oligopolistic Competition and Enterprise Innovation: Cuauhtémoc in the Beer Brewing Industry. *I.D.E.Occasional Papers Series*, (36):24–45.

INEGI. 2014a. Estadísticas históricas de México. *INEGI*. www.inegi.org.mx/prod_serv/contenidos/espanol/bvinegi/productos/nueva_estruc/HyM2014/12%20%20Industrias%20manufactureras.pdf. Accessed April 26, 2015.

INEGI. 2014b. Encuesta Anual de la Industria Manufacturera (EAIM). *INEGI*. www.inegi.org.mx/. Accessed April 11, 2015.

Kesmodel, D. 2008. Anheuser-Busch: The Incredible Secret Story of the Fish that Got Away. *Wall Street Journal*, July 16. http://blogs.wsj.com/deals/2008/07/16/anheuser-busch-the-incredible-secret-story-of-the-fish-that-got-away. Accessed August 11, 2008.

Marketline. 2015. *Industry Profile: Beer in Mexico*. London: Marketline.

Márquez Colín, G. 1992. *Concentración y estrategias de crecimiento industrial en México, 1900–1940*. México, DF: Centro de Estudios Económicos, El Colegio de México.

Miller, J. 2010. This Bud's for You, Thanks to Mormons. *The Washington Times*. www.washingtontimes.com/news/2010/sep/9/this-buds-for-you-thanks-to-mormons/?page=all. Accessed September 9, 2015.

Pérez-Sánchez, B., Guzmán-Sala, A. & Mayo-Castro A. 2012. Evolución histórica de la Cervecería Cuauhtémoc: un grupo económico de capital nacional. *Hitos de Ciencias Económico Administrativas*. 18(52): 119–136.

Recio, G. 2004. *El nacimiento de la industria cervecera en México, 1880–1910*. Working paper. San Diego, CA: Center for US-Mexican Studies. University of California.

Reuters. 2010. Heineken buys FEMSA beers. *Reuters*. www.reuters.com/article/2010/01/11/us-heineken-femsa-idUSTRE60A16L20100111. Accessed April 15, 2015.

Reuters. 2012. AB InBev buys out Corona maker Modelo for $20 billion. *Reuters*. www.reuters.com/article/2012/06/29/us-modelo-abinbev-idUSBRE85S0B420120629. Accessed June 6, 2015.

Reyna, M. del C. & Kramer, J. P. 2013. *Apuntes para la Historia de la Cerveza en México*. México, DF: INAH.

Vera-Cruz, A. O. 2002. Apertura económica, exportaciones y procesos de aprendizaje: el caso de la Cervecería Cuauhtémoc-Moctezuma. *Análisis Económico*, 17(35): 203–232.

9 MultiMexicans in Footwear
Flexi and Andrea

Francisco J. Valderrey and Adriana Sánchez

Footwear is a key industry in many countries, mainly due to the large number of people employed throughout its production process in addition to those involved in its commercialization. Consequently, production has historically shifted from country to country, across continents, to wherever unskilled workers would accept lower wages. After all, basic manufacturing skills are easy to learn or transfer from one place to another. An abundance of raw materials is a second key factor, and the combination of both gives a competitive edge; this is exemplified by the rise of the current leading player, China.[1] The industry is mature and stable, with global retail sales estimated by Euromonitor at US$375 billion for the year 2013, and with more than 21 billion pairs of shoes manufactured every year.[2]

Shoemaking is important to Mexico and crucial to the local manufacturers based around the city of León, in the State of Guanajuato. Historically, the town has centered its economic activities on the production of leather and shoes. Although thousands of artisans and small shops are still in business, reduced numbers of companies have surfaced over the years, creating large enterprises, with a few multinational companies in the making. Two of those, Grupo Flexi (also known by its registered trademark, "Flexi") and Fábricas de Calzado Andrea SA de CV (also known by its registered trademark, "Andrea"), overshadow their competitors and are extending their activities overseas. Both are among the largest manufacturers of shoes nationwide, but their strategies, managerial skills, company values, and business trajectories show different paths towards becoming global.

[1] Zhang & Yuanyuan, 2011.   [2]   APICCAPS, 2013.

In this chapter, we show how both companies followed different routes in striving for success within Mexican borders and beyond. Flexi and Andrea offer a view of the internationalization of companies in a market without a clear leader; therefore, we have an example of *MultiLatinas* different from the most renowned cases of Pemex, Cemex, Bimbo, or industrial groups, thus presenting the opportunity to analyze how smaller enterprises may become multinational corporations. In fact, contrary to the popular image of a multinational company as a large corporation with facilities in many countries, the commonly accepted definition also includes enterprises of smaller size, as long as they have some added value operations in foreign markets.[3]

Although both organizations are part of the same industry and belong to the same local cluster, they present some important differences. Flexi is more focused on the manufacturing process and is one of the largest shoemakers in Mexico; its road to internationalization has been slow and at first reactive to conditions in global markets. Andrea, on the other hand, has shown more rapid growth leveraged on marketing strategies. This is a sales-driven organization with manufacturing capacity that has targeted the sophisticated US market as the first step to internationalization. Flexi relies on product quality and full control of its operations, while Andrea proves to be a more agile organization. The former is a valid example of the many companies following a well-thought-out plan for international expansion, with reduced exposure to the hazards of global competition. The latter presents a more appealing illustration to new ventures that are willing to address demanding consumers at once, even without previous experience abroad. Both routes have similarities but yield different results.

Ultimately, the lesson to be learned may apply to the many enterprises in similar industries in developing economies: going international is a hard choice, but it may also be the decision that could set

---

[3]   Cuervo-Cazurra, 2010.

a company apart from its competitors. In the cases of Flexi and Andrea, the internationalization process brought organizational changes, improved manufacturing capabilities, and, above all, changed managerial vision, making clear the importance of being constantly alert in order to remain competitive in global markets.

FOOTWEAR: A GLOBAL INDUSTRY

Footwear is among the most important global consumer industries, as well as one of the more peculiar. Understanding the industry requires an examination of its value chain and the threats and opportunities imposed by globalization. Therefore, in this section, we present the main factors that make footwear a unique and globalized industry.

A Look at the Industry

At first glance, the footwear industry may appear to be the simple manufacturing and selling of shoes, but there are many other sectors associated with those activities. The industry is dynamic and has overcome profound changes over the last few decades in technology, machinery, input materials, and distribution. Shoemaking is already a global process, with changes in the buying experience as well.[4]

The value chain for the footwear industry is also becoming more complex and geographically dispersed,[5] with global competitors sourcing in different countries of Asia, manufacturing in Mexico, and marketing their products in Europe, as done by Nike, Crocs, and many other leading brands. Innovation has shaken the selection of the basic raw materials, as well as the entire manufacturing and marketing processes; furthermore, the diversity of products requires different industrial processes and creates a dependency upon new business models.[6]

The industry faces important challenges due to rapid changes in demand, strong competition on the supply side, and a high degree

[4]   Cardinali & Gigliotti, 2012.
[5]   Federación de Industrias del Calzado Español, 2012.
[6]   European Commission, 2006.

of globalization. Footwear is fashion-influenced and, consequently, product life cycles are shorter and the risk of being left out of the consumer preference is always present. Fragmentation of suppliers is evident, while the need for improvements in technology, strategic intelligence, and agile supply chains imposes higher capital investments on large corporations; those are gaining leverage on the distribution channels, but without reaching a full leadership position. Retailers, on the other hand, continue widening their range of operations, favoring their own brands while new business models are created. Although the changes described are common to many industries, in the specific case of footwear the importance is amplified by the impact on employment, protectionism, and the extension of the whole global chain into an increasing number of countries.

The International Perspective

Over the years, the dominant position of developed countries has shifted to China, India, Vietnam, Brazil, and other emerging economies, including Mexico. The population is a key factor in determining the size of the consumer market, but disposable income creates an important distortion. American consumers, for instance, purchase a total number of pairs each year that is similar to the number purchased in heavily populated countries such China or India. Trade flows show Europe to be the continent importing the largest number of pairs, followed by North America. In fact, many consumers in wealthy markets consider shoes as fashion items, with per capita expenditures in the hundreds of dollars in some countries. This is the point of convergence between footwear and the fashion and apparel industry, which is a much larger industry with a market size of US$1.7 trillion and 75 million people employed during 2012, when combining both industries, according to the World Trade Organization's (WTO) statistical data.[7]

---

[7]   APICCAPS. 2013.

The footwear industry involves complicated dynamics of international trade. Repeatedly, nations make their debut on the global rankings, while production sites and markets change or even reverse the logistics of the flow of raw materials and finished products. Bitter rivals may suddenly become each other's suppliers or customers, and e-business dissolves national borders. Another key element of this industry is the dependency on a few raw materials, mainly leather, which reaches approximately one-half of the aggregate cost of materials.

THE MEXICAN FOOTWEAR INDUSTRY

Mexican shoemakers are becoming more integrated into the global footwear industry, but the Mexican industry has some distinctive insights. It is important to consider the roots of shoemaking activities in the country, the present outlook, the importance of geographical concentration of producers, and the nature of the main competitors. The information from this section will cover those points.

Historical Evolution

In the early eighties, due to the import substitution program that lasted from 1940 to 1984, the makers of many products could easily obtain a captive share in Mexico, and sometimes even a monopolistic position. The absence of competitors paved the road for shoemakers; paradise lasted for many years until the nation joined the international commercial arena.[8] In fact, between 1985 and 1994 the nation started a unilateral commercial liberalization program; by 1986 it joined the GATT and a new flow of imports had an impact on the local footwear industry. By 1994, when the North American Free Trade Agreement (NAFTA) allowed free trade of most manufactured merchandise among Mexico, Canada, and the USA, the local industry was suddenly facing much larger competitors, superior in marketing, technology, and operations expertise. Pressed by many nations, by September 2001

[8]   Kerber, 2002.

the country had to vote in favor of the admission of The People's Republic of China into the WTO. Mexican manufacturers from different industries were troubled by the thought of competing at arm's length with Chinese companies.[9] Trade associations attempted to stop unfair competition, but without visible results, while the government had little interest in protecting a decaying industry, particularly not at the expense of a commercial dispute with the Asian nation.

Although global players continue to challenge Mexican shoemakers, the local footwear industry has overcome the challenge of having to share its market with foreign competition. Production by the year 2013 reached 244 million pairs, and the country ranked once again among the top ten exporters worldwide.[10] Furthermore, its contribution to employment, total GDP, and manufacturing added value remained constant between 2008 and 2012, as shown in Table 9.1.

Present Outlook

A brief analysis of the local footwear industry shows a fragmented industry, strong competition among dominant retail groups and a few major manufacturers, and reduced buying power from consumers.[11] Large manufacturers have the upper hand on the supply side, even though they are negligible in number (probably around 2 percent of the total industrial base), as compared with the thousands of small and medium enterprises (SMEs), out of the estimated 7,398 shoe-manufacturing units.[12] The little regulation also favors atomization of production, since entry and exit barriers are minimal; labor legislation and environmental protection are two issues of concern, but laws are either not too stringent or not properly enforced, especially in the case of smaller companies. Those enterprises also benefit from the lack of brand recognition, although at the expense of downward pressure on pricing.[13]

Even though few companies are export-oriented, total sales abroad reached approximately 26 million pairs in 2012, with revenues

---

9   Ibid.   10   Prospecta, 2014.   11   Euromonitor, 2014.
12   INEGI, 2012.   13   Euromonitor, 2014.

Table 9.1 *Mexican shoe industry, 2008–12*

Shoe Industry Mexico	2008	2009	2010	2011	2012
Production (Mex $ million)	12,889	12,548	13,449	13,192	13,558
% Annual growth	−4.45%	−2.65%	7.19%	−1.92%	2.77%
% Total GDP	0.11%	0.11%	0.11%	0.10%	0.1%
Trade balance, US$ million	−291	−203	−254	−306	−293
Exports, US$ million	260	259	329	411	520
Imports, US$ million	552	461	583	718	813
% Total exports	0.09%	0.11%	0.11%	0.12%	0.14%
% Manufacturing exports	0.11%	0.14%	0.13%	0.15%	0.17%
Manufacturing employment	47,470	45,589	47,955	47,550	48,389
% Manufacturing employment	1.46%	1.54%	1.56%	1.5%	1.5%

Source: Adapted from Mexico's Ministry of Economy (Secretaría de Economía, 2013).

of US$520 million. In spite of these positive figures, there is a trade deficit in this industry, with imports of 68 million pairs to satisfy the demand for less expensive products from a growing population. Vietnam is the leading exporter to Mexico, with 33 percent of total value, followed by China and Indonesia, with 17 percent each. Mexican shoes, though, have a significantly higher added value than less expensive shoes imported from Asia. A breakdown of Mexican exports per country indicates an overwhelming concentration in the US market, roughly 80 percent of value and quantity.[14]

Geographical Concentration

The industry in Mexico presents a high degree of geographical concentration, with approximately 68 percent of production located in

[14]   Ibid.

the state of Guanajuato, 18 percent in the state of Jalisco, and 13 percent near Mexico City and the neighboring State of Mexico. The reason behind such concentration is explained by a historical presence in some locations of skilled artisans and suppliers specializing in their own lines of products, such as men's and children's shoes in León, women's shoes in Jalisco, and athletic shoes around Mexico City.[15]

León, known as the capital city of the footwear industry, is the most important urban area in the state of Guanajuato and ranks fifth in population in the country, with more than 1.5 million people, a number of thriving industries, and a large number of family-owned businesses. Its inhabitants have made their living making shoes over many decades and entrepreneurs have been there since early times when merchants and artisans from northern Mexico established themselves within the boundaries of modern León.

There are different factors at the root of the footwear industry in León but, arguably, "the four pillars" are the clustering of activities, direct commercialization of the products, entrepreneurial skills, and trade associations. The first factor is very evident, as demonstrated by a myriad of tanneries, or *tenerías*, and small shoe-making shops, or *picas*, usually with fewer than ten employees. Although work is done with little machinery, in aggregate those small shops supply many thousands of shoes daily. The second factor, direct selling of shoes, is almost as old as the manufacturing of the product and has been present in León for many years, especially at the *tianguis* or informal markets. The third pillar is the entrepreneurial culture, which seems to be inherited by people from León. Companies are constantly created by those who learn how to use the tools of the trade. Finally, trade associations are paramount to the industry's success, especially as they are capable of securing the support of government entities at the local and federal level. Cámara de la Industria del Calzado del Estado de Guanajuato (CICEG), a trade organization with more than

---

[15]   Martínez, 2006.

one thousand members, is leading those efforts, especially by being the organizer of SAPICA, a trade show that attracts hundreds of qualified buyers from around the globe by exhibiting the local offering. The main supporting entities are ProMéxico, the federal entity devoted to foster trade, foreign investment, and the internationalization of Mexican enterprises; and the Coordinadora del Fomento al Comercio Exterior (COFOCE), a governmental organization for the promotion of trade in the State of Guanajuato. The above-mentioned four pillars could be considered the cornerstones of the industry's success in León, but other factors are helping the city, such as a frenzy of logistical activities at Guanajuato Puerto Interior, an inland port that serves the shoe industry by providing logistics support to exporters, and the role of universities, among others.

Competitors

In terms of market share, three Mexican companies hold similar percentages: Andrea at 9 percent, Emyco at 8 percent, and Flexi at 7 percent, while the rest of the competitors have minimal representation. Figure 9.1 provides a picture of the main competitors by National Brand Owner (NBO).

Andrea started as a little shop in 1973 and later ventured into selling through leaflets. After seven years, it built a plant in León and spread all over the nation.[16] Andrea has been adding new product lines and is becoming the industry leader.[17] Emyco started in 1926, and during the sixties and seventies signed licensing agreements to produce international brands, also selling those in the national market. From this collaborative experience with American companies, Emyco obtained state-of-the-art technology and gained a quality image associated with the Hush Puppies and Florsheim brands.[18] Ever since, Emyco has been one of the leading manufacturers, with a yearly production of more than four million pairs, owning over 100 stores throughout the country.[19]

[16]   Euromonitor, 2014.   [17]   www.andrea.com/mx.   [18]   Kandell, 2010.
[19]   www.emyco.com.mx.

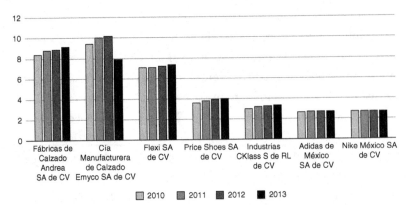

FIGURE 9.1   National Brand Owner (NBO) company shares of footwear by percentage value, 2010–13
Note: Adapted from Euromonitor International, 2014.

Flexi is a family-owned group that started in León in 1935 and expanded vertically during the seventies. The company produces over thirteen million pairs a year, and is also the leading exporter, with a large number of its own stores both locally and in different foreign markets.[20] No other competitor is of a similar size, but there are other important local players. C-Klass and Prices Shoes, both based in the Guadalajara area, are rivals to Andrea in selling through catalogs, while Grupo Cuadra has gained international recognition in the exotic leather segment. Cuadra started operations in León in 1991 and after two years was able to export boots; soon after, the group started its own network of high fashion stores around the country and is presently expanding into the USA.[21]

FLEXI AND ANDREA

As previously stated, León is home to a concentration of leading shoe makers in Mexico. Two of those, Flexi and Andrea, are especially important because of their size, impact on employment, technology use, and marketing efforts, among other factors. In this section, we

[20]   www.flexi.com.mx.   [21]   www.cuadra.com.mx.

present an overview of the history of both companies, as well as their internationalization process.

The Rise of Flexi

In 1935, Mr. Roberto Plasencia Gutiérrez ("Don Roberto") started his own shop, as was often done in León, and many years later, during the sixties, it became Flexi, a shoe-making company with modern serial production. By 1973 Flexi started to export shoes under its own brand name,[22] and by 1988 its private brand, Flexi Country, gained popularity in the local market and also became an international success. The firm employs approximately 4,600 people at four different plants, with a direct presence in foreign markets and a strong reputation for quality.

Leadership has not been an issue over the years; the founder of Flexi was successfully replaced by his own son, also known as Don Roberto (Plasencia Saldaña). The first Don Roberto was the founding father, but the next one was remarkable as well. By 1963, the son took full responsibility for consolidating the organization as a business group. By 2015, a third Don Roberto (Plasencia Torres) was taking over the leadership of the company, backed by a great deal of experience in marketing and sales within the organization.

Although the personalities of the leaders were of great importance to Flexi, the fact is that the organization followed a clear path; at the core of the business model there is a value proposition for quality and comfort, backed by Flexi's leadership in product design and manufacturing according to high-quality standards and advanced technology.[23] The Flexi brand was born in 1965, but it was probably the launch of the Flexi Country brand in 1988 that demonstrated to Don Roberto that good quality alone was not sufficient to reach broader markets. The company was betting on promotion and communication with the client, and nowadays it also shares information with the customer base through its own website and popular social

[22]   www.flexi.com.mx.   [23]   Morales & Rendón, 2014.

networking services, while it conveys information to the market through advertising in printed and digital media. Flexi is capable of reaching customers in sophisticated markets such as the USA, Japan, Canada, and the European Union, as well as countries in Latin America and Asia, using its own network of 326 stores and international distributors, either directly or through its e-commerce system.[24] Over 4,000 major clients, including a few department stores, support wholesales all across the local market and abroad.[25] Table 9.2 shows a timeline with important landmarks in the history of the company.

Key activities for Flexi are related to the production and distribution of shoes, a process where innovation and manufacturing techniques based upon quality control systems are of utmost importance. In the whole process of reaching customers, Flexi relies on key partners, mainly foreign suppliers of raw materials and a network of thirteen local companies that carry out *maquiladora* production, as well as outsourcing from four companies in Vietnam.[26] At the bottom of the structure, there is a system for tracking new fashion trends, improving quality standards, and administrating its own store chain, as well as managing marketing, logistics, and corporate social responsibility programs.[27] This structure is funded by the revenues generated from the sale of more than 13 million pairs a year through its own store chain, exports, and wholesales through authorized distributors.[28] Flexi is a privately held company and therefore does not report financial data or information about its foreign export activities or sales from subsidiaries.

Flexi: Going International

Flexi went through several different stages throughout its internationalization process, as described by the import/export director and the international sales director and summarized in the next paragraphs.[29] The process started in 1985 when many Mexican companies were

---

24   De la Rosa, 2013.   25   Vázquez, 2014.   26   Rábago, 2008.
27   Palacios, 2013.   28   Vázquez, 2014.   29   Rábago, 2008 and Horta, 2015.

Table 9.2 *The road to success for Flexi*

Year	Domestic Market	International Impact
1935	Founded by Don Roberto Plasencia Gutiérrez	
1945	Structuring of operations	
1963	Serial production is introduced	
1965	Flexi brand is born	
1969	Vertical integration with "Pieles y Curtidos Cosmos," a leather supplier	
1970	Central Leather Supplier Plant	
1973		International expansion through *maquiladora* production of Nike, Clarks, and Rockport
1988		Flexi Country brand, a success abroad
2000	First concept stores inspired by nature	
2001		Brand Positioning in International Markets Plan Expansion in Costa Rica, Guatemala, Honduras, and El Salvador, between 2002 and 2008
2002		
2004	National expansion: 30 new stores in Mexico	
2005		Partnership with a boot company to sell indirectly in the US market
2008	Intense growth and introduction of advanced operation systems (JDA software collaboration) ISO 9001–2008	
2009		First distribution center for export markets
2010	ISO 9001–2008	

Table 9.2 (*cont.*)

Year	Domestic Market	International Impact
2012		First three stores in Texas, USA
2013		Three more stores in the USA and online store in the USA
2014		Loyalty program outside Mexico
		24 international stores in Mexico (total)
2015	302 stores in Mexico (total)	24 international stores in Mexico (total)

Note: Data from Euromonitor 2014 and corporate data from Flexi.

approached by global brands to outsource their production. The lack of opportunities in the national market was a driving force for Flexi, as well as many other enterprises, to look for opportunities elsewhere. Nevertheless, production specifically for export markets started after 1994, when NAFTA favored the import of better raw materials at reduced prices and the export of finished products processed under the PITEX program, an export promotion tool designed to favor direct investment in Mexico through fiscal concessions to local and foreign companies producing for export markets. A sour end to the maquiladora boom came as the Mexican shoe industry started to lose international competitiveness and could no longer face Chinese and Asian manufacturers. During those years, the country was lagging behind in technology and product quality, while input prices continued to rise. Worsening conditions were difficult to ignore, but few people were as outspoken as Don Roberto Plasencia, who gave a warning to the local shoe industry. According to his view: "in a world of global competition, it is difficult to sleep quietly. What happens in any corner of the world has an impact in distant places. I see this as an opportunity: yes, we need to be cautious, but we also need to be confident in our own strength."[30]

---

[30]   Recollection of a comment by Don Roberto mentioned by Mr. Alejandro Vega, former sales director at Flexi and former CICEG CEO, during an interview, March 17, 2015.

That was the appropriate timing for the enterprise to devise its own international strategy, relying on the Flexi brand. By 2001, the organization had created "Brand Positioning in International Markets Plan," a document that would set the compass for international expansion. The plan was flexible enough to privilege domestic sales while looking for opportunities in new markets. Following this plan, Flexi ventured into Central American countries such as Costa Rica (seven stores), Guatemala (six stores), Honduras (three stores), and El Salvador (two stores); Costa Rica has been the market with the strongest presence, and the entry into each country did not follow a straight timeline. The second major move was to enter the US market through a strategic alliance with a Mexican catalog sales company specializing in cowboy boots. Although it was a positive experience, Flexi tried afterward to concentrate on marketing its own brand through its own sales channels. On a third stage, Flexi reached a number of spread-out markets, such as Canada, countries in the Middle East, and Japan. The opening in 2009 of a distribution center near the local airport provided a backbone for exports and international distribution; in fact, the center allows for an inventory of two million pairs and is technologically advanced.

Flexi's success has made previous roadmaps to international expansion obsolete. The brand is present in major international trade shows, which allows for better international recognition. While the organization contemplates a further advance in Europe and Asia, its presence in Central American countries keeps growing steadily. Flexi is the leading brand in Costa Rica, while Panama, Nicaragua, and Peru are the immediate targets for wholesaling. The US market, though, has proven to be the new frontier. After a good response to a virtual shoe shop, Flexi opened its first three retail stores and has opened three more under its own brand and property. The stores are located in shopping malls in Texas and Oklahoma.

The expansion will continue: management has found an ideal formula, blending a pleasant shopping experience through the

Internet while offering physical stores that reassure the customer about the design and quality of the product. Although future plans for the USA have not been disclosed, Flexi is positioning its brand in such a competitive market. In only two years, the company has more than doubled the number of stores in Guatemala, Costa Rica, El Salvador, and the USA, reaching 24 stores overall outside Mexico. There is a mixed approach to ownership of the stores: in the USA, the stores are fully owned by Flexi, whereas in other countries the organization looks for partners with expertise in the local market.[31]

The Rise of Andrea

Andrea started operations in 1973 in Mexico City, as a large shop. Roberto Ruiz is the CEO, but his public appearances are infrequent at best, and it is hard to find a directory of the company or the organizational chart. Very early on, he came out with the idea of selling shoes directly through leaflets and catalogs; sales increased exponentially and consequently, Andrea needed a large plant to satisfy demand. In 1980, management chose to build the new facilities at the León cluster; this was a major turning point in the history of Andrea that led to its becoming a strong shoe-making company.

The direct selling system continued in parallel with the new manufacturing activities, and by 1990 Andrea started geographical expansion through the opening of its own chain of stores, first in Mexico and then in the USA. In 2005, the company expanded its product lines with the Mia brand of lingerie. One year later, Andrea created new brand names for men's shoes, such as Forastero, created specifically for the American market. In 2007, the company launched a new line of beauty products for women and a line of blue jeans. Table 9.3 shows a timeline with important landmarks in the history of the company.

[31]   Horta, 2015.

Table 9.3 *The road to success for Andrea*

Year	Domestic Market	International Impact
1973	Production starts in Mexico City	
1976	From sales to local shoe stores to leaflet sales	
1980	First plant in León and corporate offices	
1990	Sales spread nationwide with stores in nine towns	
1993	First shoe catalog using celebrities and more fashionable products	
1998	New distribution center provides higher capacity for national sales expansion	
2001	Product line expansion into lingerie with the Mia brand	First outlet in Chula Vista, California
2005	New line expansion with IU cosmetics and beauty care products and Andrea Jeans	Ferrato and Forastero brands designed for the American market
2006		
2007		
2011	E-commerce with HotSALE	
2013	*Credipag*, proprietary credit system	17 international stores
2015	Special product launch for the 40th anniversary	Exports to Brazil, Colombia, Guatemala, Argentina, and Spain
	145 stores in Mexico	

Note: Information from Andrea web page and additional sources.

Over the last 40 years, Andrea has built an unusual organization. It is hard to define its true nature: the core business is still footwear, but the firm is targeting different segments with a growing array of products, especially in apparel and fashion. The many thousands of sales associates (more than 180,000) make Andrea a major player in direct marketing in its home country, with the potential to compete with different product offerings. Direct marketing has granted many people a very desirable value proposition, which is to start their own business with the potential to sell products from a diversity of product lines. The system, called "Estrellas Andrea" (or in English, Andrea Stars), is complex and looks to provide a number of increasing benefits to loyal associates and forge a feeling of partnership with them. They create "a network of friends, family, and acquaintances through samples of products, where profits are given by the sales volume of each person."[32] Andrea Stars purchase catalogs at marginal prices, which they use, in turn, to show available products to their customers. They can purchase those products with discounts that range from 20 to 30 percent, with additional bonuses that range from 3 to 15 percent, once they reached pre-established quotas. They pick up the product at the nearest point of sale, deliver it to the customer, and secure payment. In addition to the sales network, there is a distribution chain with 145 stores in Mexico and 17 in the USA, all supported by telemarketing and customer care programs.

The exceptional growth of Andrea is based on offering products of acceptable quality, affordable price, and deferred small payments, while its promotional strategies make it easier for the sales force to reach the customer base. Billboards and printed advertising in magazines and its own catalogs have made Andrea a well-recognized brand. In 2013, the firm dropped the use of celebrities in favor of using normal models, with an increase in mass media publicity.[33] Andrea has seen a strong growth in sales value, reaching Mex$13.6 billion (equivalent to US$1 billion) in 2013, Mex$12.2 billion during 2012, and Mex$11 billion for the year 2011. Revenues come from different sources, mainly women's footwear, men's footwear, women's underwear, and children's footwear.

Although Andrea made changes in its product offerings, the most relevant strategic moves involve production strategies and retail

[32]   SoyEntrepeneur, 2009.   [33]   Euromonitor, 2014.

operations, along with bold actions to increase brand recognition and geographical extension. Production, in fact, is based on outsourcing from 35 factories in León, Guadalajara, and Mexico City, with some imports from Asia.[34] Another area of importance to management is social media; in fact, an analysis of the corporate Facebook page over the first three months of the year 2014 showed satisfaction among users, with few complaints and widespread agreement with the content generated by Andrea, especially those messages with images and little text.[35]

Retail is the key to further growth; customers have access to the company's own brands as well as to additional leading brands at the many different points of sale. Stores give support to direct marketing activities and changes are expected in the immediate future, such as an Internet-based selling platform that presumably will be the backbone for further expansion in local and international markets in a more distant future. The company is venturing into e-commerce by offering products directly through its own web page and by participating in nationwide coordinated events in Mexico such as the Hot Sale, a four-day online shopping event that attempts to replicate Cyber Monday.[36]

The organization has also been successful in financial terms, and it generates different revenue streams. A large percentage of sales are in cash or on short-term financing, which gives the company the potential to invest in new outlets, and Andrea Stars' purchases for their own personal use add more cash to the main selling activities. Andrea has developed its own proprietary payment system called *Credipag*, which offers sales associates the ability to receive immediate payments through debit or credit cards, with the option of deferring payments with no interest charges for up to three months and easy financing for up to six months. No other competitors have a similar system, which clearly gives Andrea a competitive edge in a segment of the market where many customers have limited access to

---

[34]   Ibid.   [35]   Arroyo, 2014.   [36]   www.hotsale.com.mx.

credit or even basic banking services. Andrea is a privately held company and therefore it does not report financial data or information about its foreign export activities or sales from subsidiaries.

Andrea: Going International

Most probably, the internationalization of Andrea came as a part of its expansion frenzy in Mexico. The growing number of outlets, the increasing number of Andrea Stars, and their ties to compatriots on the other side of the border paved the road to the US market. At first, sales were made through the so-called *paisanos*, first-generation Mexican residents in the neighboring country; Andrea was appealing to the Hispanic community, where the brand was identified as fully Mexican. In fact, as of today, the corporate websites for American consumers address potential buyers and distributors in Spanish, without an English version. Only specific instructions for Andrea Stars and directions for locating stores are translated into English; even the name Estrellas Andrea is used, instead of the easy translation into Andrea Stars. The major difference, though, lies in the technology supporting sales in the American market: Andrea Stars have access through the Digital Ordering Kiosk, the Internet Ordering Systems, and the Automatic Telephone Ordering System. The return policy is also more generous.

In 2001, Andrea opened an outlet in Chula Vista, California; by 2014, there were 17 fully owned stores in the USA, covering the states of Arizona, Colorado, Georgia, Illinois, Nevada, and Texas. California has the strongest presence, and the cities serviced by Andrea range from small ones, such as Santa Clara, to large metropolitan areas, such as Greater Los Angeles or Chicago. The common denominator, though, is the presence of large Hispanic populations. In addition to the points of sale, Andrea operates its own logistic systems with eight warehouses distributed on both sides of the border.

Andrea operates in the USA through different companies, such as Andrea West USA LLC in the city of San Diego, California, and Andrea Apparels, which also acts as a distributor of Mexican footwear brands and provides logistics support for other direct marketing organizations.[37] Nowadays the organization is looking at different markets, such as Asia, where it analyzes the possibilities of extending its direct-selling model to China.[38]

LESSONS FOR INTERNATIONAL MANAGERS

In this section, we compare the internationalization processes of Flexi and Andrea, sharing the lessons that both enterprises may offer to managers in developing countries. Those lessons are intended for business people planning to expand into foreign countries, mainly in Latin America. In fact, many companies in the region need to deal with non-supportive governments, fierce competition with firms of similar size, and well-established foreign brands. Nevertheless, the lessons may also be valuable for enterprises worldwide, especially those trying to reach consumers in highly competitive markets such as the USA.

Two Ways to Reach International Markets

The internationalization processes of Flexi and Andrea cannot be separated from the rise of the local shoe industry in León; in fact, it would be hard to understand the success of either organization if it did not fall under the umbrella of the local cluster. Although shoe companies had been exporting for decades, only a slow process of adjusting to foreign competition, developing skills, and building their business models allowed both companies to emerge with the new breed of Mexican MultiLatinas. The context was as critical as ever: during the eighties, a flock of foreign purchasing agents visited León. They were astonished by the low costs and the skills of artisans; eventually, they started the *maquiladora* process, which in turn allowed shoemakers to grow and look at international opportunities.[39]

The time was ripe for Andrea and Flexi to go international since they had already built the muscle for serving foreign markets. As we can see in Table 9.4, both organizations have some similarities. They

---

[37]   www.andrea.com.mx.   [38]   El Economista, 2013.

[39]   Interview with Mr. Francisco Allard, assistant director, Department of Economic Development of the State of Guanajuato, March 18, 2015.

Table 9.4 *Flexi and Andrea: comparison inside and outside Mexico*

Features	Inside Mexico			Internationalization	Outside Mexico	
	Flexi	Andrea			Flexi	Andrea
Experience in local market	Since 1935	Since 1973		Experience (first exports)	1988	2003
Employees	4,600	3,000		Markets served	Multimarket: Costa Rica (7)*, US (6), Guatemala (6), Honduras (3), El Salvador (2)	Single market: USA (17)
Market share	7%	9%				
Distribution channels	Department stores, independent distributors, own store chain	Sales associates and own store chain		Distribution	Own store chain, web platform, authorized distributors	Own store chain and sales associates, eight distribution centers in the USA
Outlets	302	145		Outlets	24	17
Promotional strategies	Outdoor advertising, printed media, points of sale, web platform	Outdoor advertising, printed media, personal promotion, web platform		Trade shows	Very active	Only purchasing and sourcing activities
Brand (perception)	High quality, fair price	Average quality, slightly overpriced		Commercial missions	Active	Seldom

Table 9.4 (cont.)

Features	Inside Mexico		Internationalization	Outside Mexico	
	Flexi	Andrea		Flexi	Andrea
Innovation strategies	Product, design, and quality	Marketing and finance	Online platform	Same for Mexico and USA, in English, local stores information, communication, and content	Web page slightly different from Mexico, mainly in Spanish
Online platform	Sales, product information, and social media	Customer service and specific sales promotions, social media			Sophisticated ordering systems: digital ordering kiosk, Internet ordering system, and automatic telephone ordering system
Ownership	Family owned	Partners			
Product offering	Footwear, men's and women's, and limited supply of accessories	Footwear, men's, women's, children's, bags, clothing, beauty products, and cosmetics		Central America: same as Mexico, except for local store information and contact	
Payments	Cash and credit card for customers and trade credit to distributors	Direct credit to sales associates and proprietary payment system			

Note: Information from Andrea web page and additional sources.

* the number in parenthesis indicates the total number of stores per country, 2014.

employ a relatively similar number of people, taking into consideration that Andrea Stars are not employees, and almost match each other's market share. In addition, both organizations use some of the same promotional strategies and focus their business on shoe making and the marketing of their own products. The differences, though, are evident in terms of the relationship with the customer base: Flexi meets the customer in 302 outlets spread nationwide, while Andrea offers only half that number of points of sale. Flexi brings the customer a high-quality product at a fair price, while Andrea offers average quality at a relatively higher price, which includes generous commissions to the sales associates that are technically treated as discounts on the final price of the products.

The differences are even more important in terms of international vision. While Flexi ventured first into markets of lesser importance, Andrea went straight ahead into the American market. Flexi worked patiently, building a network of stores exclusively promoting its own brand, whereas Andrea made changes to the product offering, adjusting to consumer tastes in the Hispanic market. Flexi tried different formulas, such as partnerships or alliances in the US, until it decided to proceed with direct ownership of the outlets; Andrea, on the other hand, never agreed to share control of the operation.

Flexi shows the benefits of sticking to a brand name, controlling every step of the operation, and cautiously following a roadmap from the easier markets to the hardest market. Andrea's example, on the other hand, shows a way to achieve international success for those companies with more aggressive marketing strategies. This is a sales-driven organization, like many others that become successful in a short time, with a different business model, making products more appealing to local customers in different markets. Flexi offers uncompromised quality, while Andrea gets closer to the customer, turning sales associates into buyers and later on into business partners. In both cases, management runs a tight ship and leadership is transferred through generations. Business plans are carefully followed, although

Andrea seems to be more capable of making major turns, such as in the case of entering foreign markets. Andrea, indeed, shows how to generate incremental business through networking, splitting profits with thousands of associates, and reaching out to specific demographic groups such as the Mexican migrant population in the USA; customers are Spanish-speaking people already established on the other side of the border, independent of their legal status.

Andrea and Flexi, both in national and foreign markets, do not relinquish control of their operations. Flexi has a reputation for strict quality control during the manufacturing process, while Andrea focuses more on controlling the sales process, even in minute detail. Both companies ventured into other markets after local success. Flexi has been open to the world for many years, actively participating in trade shows and commercial missions, with permanent representation in local institutions fostering exports. Andrea, on the other hand, sends its own purchasing representatives to major footwear events. They do not exhibit products; they strike deals, mainly for input materials.

As previously stated, both organizations reached the US market following different paths: Flexi ventured in after many years of experience in fragmented markets, while Andrea entered the same country without relevant international experience. Much of the information for this chapter was collected through interviews, but the reasoning behind Andrea's decision to go international remains unclear. Apparently, it was not a deliberate strategy, but happened naturally, mirroring the flow of people, products, and ideas between the bordering countries. Flexi, on the other hand, designed a plan for internationalization; in fact, it had to back up on a number of occasions because of macroeconomic factors, financial obstacles, or a partner's decisions. In the end, the organization learned the lessons and changed course. Changes in leadership had a profound impact in Flexi, but not in Andrea. Both companies had their own landmarks tied to changes in production, marketing strategies, and technology improvements.

MultiLatinas Entering the American Market

The experience offered by the two Mexican shoe companies could be of value to enterprises of other nationalities expanding from their home ground, in particular to the American market. The US market is one that few Mexican companies dare to enter with a direct presence. On the positive side, the Hispanic market accounts for 16.9 percent of the US population. It is a $1.5 trillion market, considering only disposable income, which is more than the GDP of the vast majority of the countries in the world.[40] It is also a peculiar market where Spanish is spoken along with English or vice versa, which means that companies with the required language and cultural capabilities have a natural advantage. Their commercial message may reach the *nostalgia* market in second- or third-generation Mexican American families that have much larger purchasing power. On the negative side, the market has plenty of restrictions, rules, and regulations to abide by that only costly legal specialists can handle properly. Insurance is a must, and the legal system is completely different from Mexico's, as are the distribution channels, sales territories, and financial or fiscal issues.[41] Those are perilous waters for naïve exporters or investors, but Andrea had no hesitations and was determined to extend its commercial success against all odds. Flexi followed suit, but only once it felt prepared.

Organizations from different parts of the world might be tempted, as in the case of Flexi, to proceed cautiously through minor neighboring markets until ready to face major competitors in the US. Although this is a preferred path for many companies, it might not be in tune with modern times. In fact, managers looking to become global players will have to face the difficulties associated with serving sophisticated buyers immediately, leaving aside tortuous itineraries through minor markets. The opportunities are not limited to Mexican

40   Nielsen, 2012.
41   Interview with Mr. Miguel Muñoz, partner at Muñoz-López & Associates, PLLC, March 25, 2015.

enterprises, as globalization favors the marketing of products or services from every corner of the planet.

Another important lesson for international managers relates to the double-edged sword of dealing with Asian countries, mainly China. On the one hand, sourcing from those countries reduces manufacturing costs; on the other hand, it is the easiest way to open the door to foreign competition. Mexican shoemakers tried to stay away from those competitors, focusing their efforts on demanding trade barriers from their government. In the specific cases of China and Vietnam, the result of such strategies had doubtful results; to some, those barriers kept the Mexican shoe industry alive for a number of years, while others point to a different reality, namely, the overwhelming presence of Chinese and Vietnamese shoes in the local market.

CONCLUSIONS

In the previous section, we presented some suggestions that may be valuable for international business people. Those lessons may apply to different situations, although the recommendations were intended for decision-makers in developing markets, especially in Latin America. There is much more to learn from Flexi and Andrea; both organizations reacted to: a) a similar environment, Mexico; b) the same industry, shoe manufacturing; and c) the same local competitive environment, the city of Leon. The main decisions, though, were dependent upon the use of technology, funding for the operation and expansion projects, the commitment to innovation, and organizational decision making. Those differences were more difficult to perceive while Flexi and Andrea were conducting business within the same market. In fact, they never became fierce competitors, as each company was addressing its own customer base. Indeed, the divergence became notorious when both organizations ventured into foreign markets. That was the point in time when the differences in their fundamental values and strategies showed two distinct enterprises. Flexi follows a more conservative approach to doing business while offering fair value to the customer. Andrea, on the other hand, is constantly seeking new ways to please the consumer, with a more appealing proposal at the expense of quality.

Flexi and Andrea are not ordinary organizations, but there are many other companies in Mexico with the potential to venture into foreign countries, especially in the shoe industry. Those companies will have to decide upon the entry mode to other markets. Some will consider Central America as the first step to internationalization; after all, those territories are unappealing to most of the largest MNEs, there are no language or cultural barriers, purchasing power is relatively similar, and the geographical proximity has a positive impact. That was the roadmap followed by Flexi. Andrea, instead, was looking at the American market at the outset of its intentions of selling abroad.

Entering the American market was a matter of choice for Flexi and Andrea, but presumably, Mexican companies going international in the future will face no similar dilemma. By the year 2050, the Hispanic market in the USA will reach 128.8 million people – more than the entire population of Japan – with immense disposable income. Much wealth is already being transferred from Mexico to the northern side of the border, which means increasing investments and business opportunities. Startup companies are already multiplying in Mexico, looking at opportunities in Silicon Valley or the most sophisticated segments in the USA. Andrea may offer a great example to those ventures, with the hint of innovative business models. The lesson may apply, as well, to enterprises in other developing countries, and the same reasoning is valid when looking at other developed markets.

Are Mexican companies at a disadvantage when going overseas? The issue has been a subject of debate and there are many different answers. The label "Hecho en México," or "Made in Mexico," may have a good or bad impact depending on the product promoted. Some people may be reluctant to fly on an airplane fully assembled in Mexico, but the label works positively in some industries. In reality, the national automotive industry is in the top rankings for quality and safety, while the incipient aerospace industry is attracting many manufacturers. In the shoe industry opinions vary widely, although the fact is that Mexican shoes lack international recognition.[42] Few brands are even known to foreign consumers, but a positive effect can be seen in Latin American nations. In some of those, especially in Central America, the country is perceived as an industrial giant, even technologically advanced.[43] Is the perception of Made in Mexico changing after the success of Flexi or Andrea? Most probably the effect is negligible. However, as implied by the comments about the potential of the US market, the "Hecho en México" label can be beneficial to brands well positioned in the home country. Andrea, in fact, spends very little in advertising north of the border, since prospects are already familiar with its name. Flexi addresses the customer base in the USA by focusing on quality, and not so much by looking at the nostalgia market.

Although Flexi and Andrea followed different paths of internationalization, both companies reveal paths to success in a foreign land. Their efforts are showing new alternatives to other shoemakers while offering valuable lessons to organizations looking for opportunities abroad. Managers at the many companies wishing to compete globally may find reassurance about their projects when looking at how both enterprises were capable of surmounting obstacles in their home country, competing with well-positioned brands, and establishing their own facilities in a highly competitive market. In the end, Flexi and Andrea tell us the same story: facing competition away from home is harsh, but going international may create the divide that sets successful organizations apart.

REFERENCES

Andrea Apparels. About Andrea Apparels. *Andrea Apparels*. www.andreaapparels .com/about-us. Accessed February 21, 2015.

---

[42] Interview with Mr. Miguel Esquer, consultant and former director at Prospecta, March 3, 2015.

[43] Interview with Mr. Francisco Allard, assistant director at Department of Economic Development of the State of Guanajuato, March 18, 2015.

APICCAPS. 2013. *World Footwear Yearbook*. Porto, Portugal: Portuguese Footwear, Components and Leather Goods Manufacturer's Association.

Arroyo, J. M., 2014. Las Relaciones Públicas en la comunicación digital de Calzado Andrea. *Revista Ktarsis, Universidad de La Salle Bajío*. http://bajio.delasalle.edu .mx/delasalle/revistas/ktarsis/num%2012/alumnos_a_lasrelaciones.php. Accessed February 21, 2015.

Cardinali, S. & Gigliotti, M. 2012. The internationalization of retailers and manufacturers in the footwear industry: different approaches in different countries. *International Journal of Management Cases*. 60: 59–72.

Cuadra. 2015. Homepage. *Grupo Cuadra*. www.cuadra.com.mx. Accessed March 14, 2015.

Cuervo-Cazurra, A. 2010. Multilatinas. *Universia Business Review*, 25: 138–154.

De la Rosa, G. 2013. Flexi y Coqueta "calzan" en e-commerce. *CNN Expansión*, July 24. www.cnnexpansion.com/negocios/2013/07/24/tienda-online-recibe-10-mdd-de-inversion. Accessed November 28, 2014.

El Economista. 2013. Definen ganador. *El Economista*. December 11. http://ele conomista.com.mx/foro-economico/2013/12/11/definen-ganador. Accessed November 21, 2014.

Emyco. 2015. *Emyco*. www.emyco.com.mx. Accessed March 14, 2015.

Euromonitor. 2014. *Apparel and Footwear in Mexico*. Euromonitor International, www.euromonitor.com./ Accessed March 29 2015.

European Commission. 2006. ICT and e-Business in the Footwear Industry. *E-Business Watch*. http://aei.pitt.edu/54204/1/2006-2007.pdf. Accessed March 14, 2015.

Fábricas de Calzado Andrea. 2015. Nuestra historia. *Andrea*. www.andrea.com/ mx/historia. Accessed March 14, 2015.

Fallas, C. 2014. Zapatería Flexi continúa expansión y abre séptimo establecimiento en Costa Rica. *El Financiero*, November 13. www.elfinancierocr.com/negocios/Flexi-abre-setimo-establecimiento-pais_0_628137184.html. Accessed March 14, 2015.

Federación de Industrias del Calzado Español (FICE). 2012. Estudio de Prospectiva sobre Escenarios Futuros para la Industria del Calzado a Medio y Largo Plazo. *Federación de Industrias del Calzado Español (FICE)*. Madrid, Spain.

Flexi. 2017 Historia. *Flexi*. www.flexi.com.mx. Accessed March 14, 2015.

Horta, F. 2015. Van a Conquista de EU. *Periódico A.M.* February 18. www.am.com.mx /leon/valoragregado/van-a-conquista-de-eu-181565.html. Accessed May 18, 2015.

HotSale. 2015. ¿Qué es HotSale? *HotSale*. www.hotsale.com.mx/que-es-hot-sale .html. Accessed March 14, 2015.

ICB Structure. 2015. Industry Classification Benchmark. *ICB*. www.icbenchmark .com/Site/ICB_Structure. Accessed February 10, 2015.

Instituto Nacional de Estadística y Geografía (INEGI). 2012. *Estadísticas a propósito de la industria del calzado.* INEGI http://www.inegi.org.mx/. Accessed February 10, 2015.

Instituto Valenciano de la Exportación (IVEX). 2009. Sector Calzado en México. *Instituto Valenciano de la Exportación (IVEX).* Valencia, Spain.

Kandell, J. 2010. Mexican Shoemaker Relies on Sex Appeal, Not Bank Credit. *Institutional Investor Global Finance Market News, Analysis, and Research.* March 16. www.institutionalinvestor.com/Article/2446502/Mexican-Shoem aker-Relies-on-Sex-Appeal-Not-Bank-Credit.html#.WKpDKPkrLIU. Accessed November 14, 2015.

Kerber, V. 2002. China y El Calzado Mexicano. *Comercio Exterior* 52 (10): 900–906.

Martínez, A. 2006. *Capacidades competitivas en la industria del calzado en León: Dos trayectorias de aprendizaje tecnológico.* México: Plaza y Valdés Editores.

Morales, A. & Rendón, A. 2014. Comportamiento tecnológico de grandes empresas de capital privado nacional en la industria del calzado. *Universidad Autónoma Metropolitana- Xochimilco.*

Nielsen, 2012. *The Hispanic Market Imperative.* Quarter 2, 2012.

Palacios, J. 2013. Modelos de Negocios: Flexi. *Periódico AM.,* December 7. www .am.com.mx/opinion/leon/modelos-de-negocio-flexi-5537.html. Accessed November 14, 2014.

PROSPECTA. 2014. Visión 2030: Una industria en transformación. *IMEBA,* 166.

Rábago, M. 2008. Flexi: hemos dejado muy en alto al sector del calzado de México en los mercados internacionales. *Empresa exterior.com,* February 4. http://empresaex terior.com/not/13908/flexi-hemos-dejado-muy-en-alto-al-sector-del-calzado-de-mexico-en-los-mercados-internacionales-. Accessed November 14, 2014.

Secretaría de Economía de México. 2013. Industria del Calzado. *Secretaría de Economía de México.* www.gob.mx/se/. Accessed March 14, 2015.

SoyEntrepeneur. 2009. ¿Cómo funciona el modelo de ventas por catálogo? *SoyEntrepeneur,* www.soyentrepreneur.com/como-funciona-el-modelo-de-ventas-por-catalogo.html. Accessed November 14, 2014.

Vázquez, L. 2014. Flexi da pasos firmes en municipios del norte de Guanajuato. *El Financiero,* February 10, www.elfinanciero.com.mx/empresas/flexi-da-pasos-firmes-en-municipios-del-norte-de-guanajuato.html. Accessed November 14, 2014.

Zhang, J. & Yuanyuan, D. 2011. Analysis on the International Competitiveness of Chinese Footwear Industry, 2011, in *Information Management, Innovation Management and Industrial Engineering (ICIII), 2011 International Conference on* (Vol. 3, pp. 258–261). IEEE.

10 MultiMexicans in the Cement Industry

Cemex and Grupo Cementos de Chihuahua

Mario Adrián Flores Castro and Lucía Rodríguez-Aceves[1]

INTRODUCTION

Since the early twentieth century, the use of cement has become a popular and strategic element in the economic growth of every country. In Mexico, the first factories were set up in the early twentieth century and since then, major structural changes in the country's economy have radically altered the structure and functioning of the cement industry. In this sense, evolution of the production level, capacity, and consumption statistics were influenced by fluctuations in domestic construction activities, plant modernizations, economic conditions, new regulations, and the level of cement imports.

The cement industry has particular key elements such as high transportation costs relative to production costs, low labor intensity, and is highly capital intensive, as well as energy intensive, besides the ecological impact if basic conditions are not considered when the raw products are extracted. Consequently, competition generally occurs at a regional level and only a few multinational companies have the capacity to own and operate plants in or near markets they want to attend. Particularities of the industry force companies to develop peculiar strategies in order to generate above-average profits. As an example, merging and acquisitions is one of the main internationalization strategies, but tactic strategies differ greatly among companies.

[1] **Acknowledgements**
We sincerely thank Don Federico Terrazas and Rogelio Zambrano, who kindly shared their time and experience with us.

This chapter discusses the peculiarities of the cement industry in Mexico in terms of recent performance and the domestic market structure. In addition, it also examines and compares two MultiMexicans in order to identify similar patterns in their internationalization processes. On the one hand, some scholars consider Cemex the most remarkable corporate success story emerging from Latin America, with an outstanding international expansion and a highly efficient operation and management system – "The Cemex Way." On the other hand, Grupo Cementos de Chihuahua is the fourth in size in the Mexican industry, well managed and organized, with a robust growth plan and an important presence in Mexico and the United States. In this chapter, we also share some experiences extracted from interviews with presidents of both companies.

The findings reveal different strategies, ambitions, opportunities, challenges, and management styles that could be useful for other companies that have in mind to expand overseas – as an example, choosing the right markets to enter by analyzing in detail the conditions of the local and global economy, and having in mind that crises are opportunities. Besides, establishing rules and discipline when deciding to expand locally and overseas, as well as acting in the short term, expecting results in the medium, are only some of the lessons learned from the cases studied.

CEMENT INDUSTRY

The Global Industry

It is one of the leading sectors in the building materials industry, where Portland cement is the most common type produced. The cement industry is highly capital-intensive with significant economies of scale effects. The sector's asset intensity, combined with capital requirements and high-cost distribution networks, impose high barriers to entry and exit.[2] Since the high cost of land transportation reduces the competitiveness of a cement plant to

[2]   Casanova, 2009.

around 500 km radius,[3] it is estimated that 90 percent of world cement demand is covered by local manufacturers.[4]

Historically, global cement consumption grew more quickly than new capacity was added during the late 1980s. This reversed in the 1990s, resulting in significant overcapacity, particularly in Asia. In 2002–6, the rate of growth in cement consumption exceeded the additional new capacity. However, in the last few years, demand has grown more slowly than capacity. In fact, total worldwide cement production in 2016 reached 4.2 billion tons (hereinafter, bt),[5] which represents a 21.1 percent climb compared to production in 2010 (3.3 bt). In contrast, according to the 2016 Research's Global Cement Forecast Report,[6] global cement consumption was expected to reach 4.0 bt in 2016 and 4.2 bt by 2020, representing an increase of only 4.7 percent.

In terms of geographic distribution in the cement industry, the importance of the developing world growth is clearly evident. In particular, it accounted for 59 percent of global cement consumption in 1985, increased to 90 percent in 2010, and is expected to comprise 93 percent of demand in 2025. From those countries, China's consumption on its own increased from 19 percent of the global cement consumption in 1985 to 57 percent in 2010.

According to the Global Cement Directory 2016,[7] the largest companies in the building materials universe in 2016, measured by its capacity and number of plants, are: the recently merged LafargeHolcim, the Chinese Anhui Conch and CNBM (Sinoma), the German HeidelbergCement and, in fifth place, the Mexican Cemex. It is noteworthy that the rank position is the result of the collapse of demand in key markets that occurred in 2008.

The cement sector remains highly fragmented. While the big global players enjoy strong market positions, pricing power, and control of trading networks, their market shares are still small.[8] Today, the multinational cement companies already own more than

3   Lafarge, 2008.   4   Lucea & Donald, 2010.   5   Statista, 2016.
6   AggNet, 2016.   7   Saunders, 2015.   8   Casanova, 2009.

70 percent of the cement capacity in developed countries. They also own over 80 percent of the capacity in Latin America.

The Mexican Industry

Cement is essential for construction, and for this reason both sectors in Mexico are strongly related. According to The National Institute of Statistics and Geography (hereinafter, INEGI),[9] the correlation between cement production in tons with the physical volume index in the construction sector is 0.73. Aligned with the global industry, the main type of cement produced in Mexico is Portland with over 90 percent of production.

In the rank of global cement consumers by volume, Mexico places 14th on the list with 35 million metric tons (mmt), behind Vietnam. Regarding volume of cement production, Mexico (35.4 mmt) places 15th on the list, behind Japan, South Korea, Egypt, and Thailand, but ahead of Germany, Indonesia, France, Canada, the UK, and Spain.[10]

Historically, cement was first authorized for use by the Mexican construction industry in 1902.[11] Four years later, the first cement plant was constructed in Mexico. From the time of its introduction through the early 1940s, Mexico's cement industry evolved at a moderate pace. In 1944, spending on public infrastructure in Mexico increased significantly and since that year have had a sustained growth. Nevertheless, by 1995, the financial crisis that affected the Mexican economy along with the application of anti-dumping duties imposed by the United States on cement imported from Mexico, seriously affected the sector. At the end of the decade, the Mexican economy recovered. Table 10.1 shows the cement production in Mexico in millions of metric tons from 1990 to 2015.

In 2011, six companies participated in the Mexican cement industry: Cemex (49% share of domestic market), Holcim-Apasco (21%), Cooperativa Cruz Azul (16%), and Corporación Moctezuma (10%). The remaining 4% was split between Grupo Cementos de

---

[9] INEGI, 2011. [10] CW Group, 2016. [11] Orta, 2005.

Table 10.1 *Mexican cement market data (production, 1990–2015)*

Year	Production (mt)	Year	Production** (mt)	Imports (mt)	Exports (mt)	Consumption (mt)	Consumption per capita (kg)
1990	23.8	2001	30.8	0.1	2.3	28.9	291
1991	25.1	2002	31.5	0.1	1.7	30.1	298
1992	26.9	2003	31.8	0.1	1.2	30.7	299
1993	27.1	2004	35	0.1	1.9	31.4	301
1994	29.7	2005	40.1	0.1	3.3	32.8	315
1995	23.9	2006	40.9	0.1	3	35.5	339
1996	25.4	2007	43.4	0.1	2.5	36.6	346
1997	27.5	2008	42.3	0	2.3	35.8	329
1998	27.7	2009	40.9	0	1.1	36.4	329
1999	29.4	2010	38.5	0.1	0.9	34.5	307
2000	31.7	2011	35.9	0.1	1	35	308
		2012	36.3	0.1	1.2	35.2	307
		2013	34.3	0.1	1.5	32.9	283
		2014	36.6	N/A	N/A	35.2	294
		2015	39.6	N/A	N/A	N/A	N/A

Note: **Excludes exported clinker. mt = million tons.
Sources: Created by the authors based on data from the National Cement Chamber[12] and INEGI.[13]

12   CANACEM, 2017.   13   INEGI, 2011.

Table 10.2 *Main competitors in the Mexican cement industry*

Company	Cement plants (mt)	Production capacity (mt)
Cemex	15	29.3
LafargeHolcim-Apasco	7	12.9
Cementos y Concretos Nacionales (Cruz Azul)	4	8.3
Cemento Moctezuma	3	5.1
Grupo Cementos de Chihuahua	3	4
Cementos Fortaleza (Elementia)	3	0.6
Total	33	57.5

Data in million metric tons per annum
Source: Created by the authors based on data from the National Cement Chamber[15] and The Global Cement Directory 2017.[16]

Chihuahua and Lafarge. Surprisingly, the Mexican cement industry had not had a new competitor for 70 years, until 2012, when Cementos Fortaleza was founded. The new competitor is well supported by two prominent partners, Carlos Slim and Antonio del Valle Ruiz, both members of the Forbes list of billionaires.

With the new entrant in the market and the merger of Lafarge with Holcim-Apasco, in 2016 the six companies dominating the domestic market were: Cemex (40%), LafargeHolcim (22%), Cruz Azul (16%), Moctezuma (13%), Grupo Cementos de Chihuahua (25%), and Cementos Fortaleza (Elementia) (4%).[14] Table 10.2 shows the number of cement plants as well as the annual cement production capacity of the six big players in the domestic market. It is worth mentioning that, except for Cemex, the five companies in the market tend to be concentrated in particular regions. For example, LafargeHolcim is mainly located in the center and south of the

[14]   Perilli, 2017.   [15]   CANACEM, 2017.   [16]   Saunders, 2015.

country, Moctezuma has two plants in central Mexico, and Grupo Cementos de Chihuahua has three plants in northern Mexico.

Regarding Mexican cement market data, Table 10.1 shows production, imports, exports, consumption, and consumption per capita from 2001 to 2015. It highlights the growth in production and exports from 2004 to 2008, followed by the contraction caused by the 2009 financial crisis, as well as the slow recovery initiated in 2011.

In Mexico, approximately 80 percent of the cement sales are retail. Therefore, an efficient distribution network is key to success. According to INEGI,[17] in 2011, about 20 percent of production was sold in bulk to large construction companies focused on developing infrastructure. The remaining 80 percent of production was sold in 50 kg bags, used either by formal residential construction firms (50 percent of the total) or in informal (do-it-yourself) projects (32 percent of all purchases). Regarding the Mexican cement exports, from 2001 to 2010, exports were mainly to United States, Guatemala, Belize, Brazil, and Argentina.

CASES

On the one hand, Cemex is a global leader in the building materials industry with over 100 years of experience and presence in more than 50 countries. On the other hand, Grupo Cementos de Chihuahua is a leading supplier of cement, aggregates, concrete, and construction-related services in Mexico and the United States. Both companies are Mexican, have strong operations in the home country and have expanded internationally to increase their market scope. In addition, acquisitions have undeniably been an important instrument of the companies' internationalization strategy in order to grow and compete against national and international competitors. Cemex is the leading company in Mexico in terms of its capacity and market share; Grupo Cementos de Chihuahua is ranked in fourth place. In order to contextualize the size and the growth of both companies,

17   INEGI, 2011.

as well as their relevance in the Mexican market, Table 10.4 and Table 10.5 show the evolution of the main financial indicators.

In the following section, we describe in detail the domestic and international expansion of Cemex, highlighting some of the strategic decisions made by the executives of the company.

Cemex Domestic and International Expansion

Cementos Mexicanos SA (Cemex) was founded in 1930 as a result of merging two companies, Cementos Hidalgo, founded in 1906, and Cementos Portland Monterrey, founded in 1920. However, for practical purposes, it is considered that Cemex was founded in 1906. In 1948, Cemex's annual production capacity reached 124,000 tons, a nearly fourfold increase from 1906. The Monterrey-based company remained a local player until the 1960s, when it began expanding and vertically integrating cement and concrete production throughout Mexico, and with it gaining a national presence. Specifically, from 1966 to 1984, Cemex expanded throughout the Mexican territory, acquiring Cementos Maya's plant in Merida (in 1969), the Cementos Portland del Bajío plant (in 1976), as well as Cementos Guadalajara (also in 1976). Also, Cemex opened new plants in Valles, Torreon, Ensenada, among other cities, with important technological advances resulting in cost savings and increasing production capacity. The company was listed on Mexico's stock exchange in 1976.[18]

In 1980, further growth was facilitated by the Mexican government's import-substitution policies – in particular, the "Programme for the promotion of the cement industry," which encouraged national players to fulfill the needs of the Mexican market and restricted foreign competition. With limited growth opportunities abroad, Cemex started to diversify.[19] In the 1980s, it became a large-scale conglomerate with assets in engineering, hotels, mining, and petrochemicals. In 1982, a severe economic

---

[18]   Reference for Business, 2005.   [19]   Hoeber, 2008.

crisis in Mexico forced the government to liberalize the economy to attract foreign investment, after decades of protecting domestic firms.

In 1985, Lorenzo Zambrano was appointed CEO. He was the founder's grandson and an engineering graduate with a Stanford MBA. He had spent his teenage years at the Missouri Military Academy, Missouri, and later earned an industrial engineering degree from the Tecnológico de Monterrey, Mexico's version of MIT, according to Forbes writer Claire Poole. In 1985, for the first time, Cemex's annual sales exceeded 6.7 million tons of cement and clinker, and of that output, the company exported 574 thousand tons.[20] Table 10.3 shows a timeline of Cemex's domestic expansion.

In 1986, the company entered a joint venture with Houston-based producer Southdown Inc. in the southern United States. The two operating companies, Southwestern Sunbelt Cement and Texas Sunbelt Cement, ground imported clinker and marketed the cement output. A similar venture was established with Heidelberg Cement, Danish Aalborg Cement, and American Lehigh, which eventually became the market leader in white cement throughout the United States.[21]

Facing threats from foreign rivals, Cemex first consolidated its domestic position through the takeover of two leading Mexican cement manufacturers. In 1987, it acquired Cementos Anáhuac and a 49 percent stake in Control Administrativo Mexicano, which in turn held 93 percent of northern producer Cementos de Chihuahua. Also, in 1989 it acquired Cementos Tolteca. The motivations for such acquisitions were various. First, Anáhuac was targeted because of its large-scale cement plants and its significant exports to the United States, while in Tolteca Cemex acquired Mexico's most-established cement brand and assets in the southern United States. The state in Cementos de Chihuahua allowed Cemex to expand its reach into a region that had formerly been dominated by this single player.

[20]   Cemex, 2017.   [21]   Hoeber, 2008.

Table 10.3 *Timeline of Cemex's domestic expansion*

Year	Local	International
1906	Cementos Mexicanos SA (Cemex) was founded in 1930 as a result of the merging of two companies, Cementos Hidalgo, founded in 1906, and Cementos Portland Monterrey, founded in 1920.	
1948	Cemex's annual production capacity reached 124,000 tons, a nearly fourfold increase from 1906.	
1969	Cemex initiated its domestic expansion and vertical integration strategy. It acquired Cemento's Maya plant in Merida. The company also opened new plants in Valles, Torreon, Ensenada, among other cities.	
1976	Cemex acquired Cementos Portland del Bajío's plant and Cementos Guadalajara. In this year, the company was listed on Mexico's stock exchange.	
1980	The Mexican government launched the "Programme for the promotion of the cement industry," which encouraged national players to fulfill the needs of the Mexican market and restricted foreign competition. Cemex started to diversify and became a large-	

Table 10.3 (*cont.*)

Year	Local	International
	scale conglomerate with assets in engineering, hotels, mining, and petrochemicals.	
1982	After a severe economic crisis, the Mexican government was forced to liberalize the economy. Cemex saw this as an opportunity.	
1985	Cemex's annual sales exceeded 6.7 million tons of cement and clinker. 574 thousand tons were exported, mainly to the USA. Lorenzo Zambrano was appointed CEO of the company. Zambrano initiated a divestment of all the non-cement holdings and concentrated on geographic diversification.	
1986		The company started a joint venture with the American company Southdown.
1987	To consolidate its domestic position, Cemex acquired Cementos Anahuac and a 49% stake in "Control Administrativo Mexicano," which later became Grupo Cementos de Chihuahua. Cementos Anahuac had large-scale cement plants and significant exports to the USA.	Cemex started a joint venture with Heidelberger, Aalborg, Lehigh, another American company.
1989	Cemex acquired Cementos Tolteca. This company was acquired because it was the most	Cemex acquired Houston Shell and Concrete, Gulf Coast Portland Cement, Houston

Table 10.3 (*cont.*)

Year	Local	International
	well-established cement brand and had assets in the southern USA. Cemex controlled around 60% of Mexico's cement market and became one of the ten largest cement companies in the world.	Concrete Products, and Aggregate Transportation, all American companies. In the same year, Cemex acquired Sunbelt (JV w/Southdown), which had a presence in Spain.
1992		Cemex subsidiary Sunbelt purchased Pharris Sand & Gavel, based in the Bahamas. In this year, Cemex also entered into the European market, acquiring La Valenciana and Sanson, Spain's two largest cement companies.
1993		Cemex acquired the company Concern located in Trinidad.
1994		Cemex entered into Latin America, acquiring Venezuela's largest cement maker, Vencemos. The company entered Panama by acquiring Cemento Bayano and also purchased a minority in Trinity cement.
1995		Cemex acquired Cementos Nacionales, the largest player in the Dominican Republic and Haiti.
1996		Cemex acquired control of two of Colombia's leading cement manufacturers, Cementos Diamante and Cementos Samper. Cemex became the

Table 10.3 (*cont.*)

Year	Local	International
		third-largest cement producer in the world.
1997		A major opportunity arose with the Asian economic crisis of 1997–8 and Cemex became a buyer in that region. The first acquisition was in the Philippines, for about 40% stakes of Rizal Cement.
1998		Cemex bought an additional 40% of stakes of Rizal Cement and 14% of Semen Gresik in Indonesia.
1999		Cemex acquired additional stakes of Semen Gresik. Indonesia was a low-cost production country, was strategically located for cement exports and had significant growth potential.
2000		Cemex acquired a 90% stake in the Assiut Cement Company. The strategy changed from exporting to Egypt to buying production capacity in a growing market.
2001		Cemex became the second largest cement producer in the United States with the acquisition of Southdown. This was the result of a segmentation by region, rather than by countries. Cemex also acquired Saraburi cement in Thailand,

Table 10.3 (*cont.*)

Year	Local	International
		Grinding Mill in Bangladesh, Pastroello Travaux Routiers in France, and Wangan in Japan.
2002		Cemex acquired Puerto Rican Cement Co. in Puerto Rico.
2003		Cemex acquired Dixon-Marquette Cement in USA.
2005		Cemex acquired Britain's RMC Corporation, the world's largest Concrete company.
2007		Cemex acquired the Australian firm Rinker, at a cost of US$14,000 million.
2010		Cemex overcame the most complex financial crisis in recent history by adapting its operations worldwide to the new market dynamics.
2012		Cemex listed its South and Central American operations on the Colombian Stock Exchange.
2016		Cemex celebrated 110 years of building a better future.

Source: Own elaboration, but based on Hoeber[22] and complemented with Cemex timeline history located on the company's website.[23]

Thanks to these transactions, Cemex controlled roughly 60 percent of Mexico's cement market and became one of the ten largest cement companies in the world.

In the early nineties, the Mexican President Carlos Salinas de Gortari initiated public programs for infrastructure modernization, increasing the demand for cement, as well as increasing the

[22]   Cemex, 2017.   [23]   Hoeber, 2008.

government-set price for cement. Gradually, an increase from $46 per ton to $72 per ton was allowed. The production costs of about $30 per ton at Cemex's Mexican plants were the lowest in North America.[24] Having a great situation in Mexico, the expansion of Cemex occurred in different phases, each focusing on a particular market or area with distinct characteristics. By internationalizing, Cemex hoped to lessen its dependence on the Mexican market, leverage more stable cash flows, build scale and scope, and thus establish itself as a global player in the cement sector. Countries in geographic proximity, and those of similar culture and language, were natural markets for Cemex, but the key consideration was market characteristics. Cemex was particularly interested in markets with high growth potential.[25]

In 1992, with a loan from Citicorp, Cemex initiated its international expansion into the European market with the acquisition of Valenciana and Sanson, Spain's two largest cement companies. Beyond creating a solid position in Europe, the deal brought financing advantages as Cemex was able to raise cheaper funds through the Spanish unit. Consequently, Valenciana became the umbrella holding company for all future international acquisitions.

In the early nineties, US firms began to reduce investment in the cement sector and diversify into other businesses. This created opportunities for foreign cement makers for two reasons. First, shortages opened the US market to imported cement. Second, US assets in the sector were now on the market. In 1992, Cemex subsidiary Sunbelt purchased Pharris Sand & Gravel, while in 1994, Cemex paid competitor Lafarge US$100 million for the Balcones cement plant. This Texas plant could have helped Cemex bypass some anti-dumping regulations. Cemex also benefited from the passage of the North American Free Trade Agreement (NAFTA), which went into effect in 1994.

During the peso crisis in 1994–5, many Mexican companies went into liquidation, but due to its strong export capabilities and

[24]   Reference for Business, 2005.   [25]   Lucea & Donald, 2010.

international operations, Cemex survived. In fact, Cemex experienced a big drop in domestic sales. Specifically, sales in the formal segment dropped by as much as 50 percent whereas in the informal/self-construction segment they dropped by only 10 to 20 percent. In that situation, Cemex made an estimate and calculated that the do-it-yourself segment accounted for almost 40 percent of cement consumption in Mexico and had a market potential of US$500–600 million annually. Realizing the potential of this segment, Cemex expanded its presence in the retail channel by setting up 2020 kiosks of *Construramas* (i.e. small stores to sell building materials) to establish closer relationships with the informal segment.

Cemex started its expansion throughout Latin America, where it met fierce competition from Lafarge and Holcim. In 1994, the company acquired Venezuela's largest cement maker, Corporación Venezolana de Cementos (Vencemos). Cemex entered Panama in the same year by acquiring Cemento Bayano. The following year, it bought Cementos Nacionales, the largest player in the Dominican Republic and Haiti. In 1996, Cemex acquired control of two of Colombia's leading cement manufacturers, Cementos Diamante and Cementos Samper, for about US$700 million. With that transaction, Cemex became the third-largest cement producer in the world. After various companies' acquisitions in Chile, Costa Rica, Puerto Rico, and Nicaragua, Cemex became a so-called "MultiLatina." Table 10.3 also shows a timeline of Cemex's international expansion.

A major opportunity surfaced with the Asian economic crisis of 1997–8, which had a negative impact on the construction sector. When local firms began selling off noncore assets in building materials and governments started divesting their stakes in cement operations, Cemex was a buyer again, as valuations began to fall. Cemex acquired Rizal Cement Company in Philippines and Semen Gresik Group in Indonesia. Indonesia was a low-cost production country, was strategically located for cement exports, and had significant growth potential, and was therefore quite important to Cemex's development and growth in Asia.

In 1998, the company launched an innovative experiment called "Patrimonio Hoy," which means "an inheritance or legacy," and enabled very poor people to pay for services and building materials and upgrade their homes. This program blended the pursuit of profit and social responsiveness at Cemex. The program had various key objectives, for example, positioning the company as a responsible corporate citizen that is committed to society, generating business that represents competitive advantages, and building social capital.[26]

At the end of the 90s, Cemex decided to refine its market segmentation. Instead of analyzing countries as the strategic level of analysis, it changed to regions inside the countries.[27] Not surprisingly, in 2001 Cemex became the second-largest cement producer in the United States with the acquisition of Southdown for US$2,500 million.

In 2005, the company paid US$5,800 million to acquire Britain's RMC Corporation, the world's largest concrete business. In 2007, Cemex acquired the Australian firm Rinker, at a cost of US$14,000 million. In sum, Cemex expanded to South America, Central America, North America, the Caribbean, Asia, Africa, and Oceania with the same formula, acquiring the most important cement companies and merging operations.

The 2008 crisis affected Cemex substantially. The main causes were the three recent acquisitions to which it had committed its financial situation (Southdown, Britain's RMC Corporation and Rinker). The money for the acquisitions was achieved from short-term bank loans, and part of the company's strategy was to sell some of its plants to pay their debts. From its purchases in Spain, the company borrowed heavily and the degree of indebtedness of Cemex reached its limits with the purchase of Southdown. Cemex's liquidity was supported by a significant generation of free cash flow as well as the availability of bank credit lines and access to diverse funding sources. In 2007, the world economic crisis came and everything

---

[26]   Sharma, Mohan & Singh, 2003.   [27]   Lucea & Donald, 2010.

changed: sales decreased, Cemex's debt lost its investment grade, and banks applied pressure to collect their debts. In fact, in 2009, net sales decreased by 28 percent and EBITDA decreased by 35 percent, and free cash flow after capital expenditures for maintenance was reduced by 53 percent.

In response to the crisis, in August 2009, Cemex signed a financing agreement with its major creditors, which provided a payment schedule ending in February 2014. At the end of September 2009, Cemex accounted a debt of $US21,000 million.[28] In October of the same year, the company sold Rinker to its competitor Holcim for US$1,700 million as a means of reducing its debt. In addition, Cemex implemented a program to reduce costs by US$900 million and decreased by US$1,500 million capital investment in maintenance and expansion. Additionally, Cemex recapitalized the company by issuing shares, mainly to limit capital expenditures through 2013.

After the crisis, Cemex's strategy was to focus on the core business of cement, ready-mix concrete, and aggregates. Thus, the company sold all its noncore assets. Furthermore, Cemex has undertaken various initiatives with respect to cost-cutting in recent years. For example, Cemex decreased its global headcount by approximately 28.5 percent, from 61,545 employees in 2007 to 44,000 employees in 2011. With respect to capacity, in 2009 Cemex suspended operations in 27 cement kilns, and closed 300 ready-mix concrete plants and nearly 50 aggregates sites. Reduction in the plant capacity allowed Cemex to align itself with market demands, which decreased significantly after the global economic recession in 2008. Reduced capacity also helped the company to avoid additional costs arising from unused resources. Table 10.4, shows some data highlighting the financial evolution of the company from 2000 to 2015.

---

[28]   CNN Expansión, 2009.

Table 10.4 *Cemex financial data evolution, 2000–15*

	2000	2005	2010	2015
Revenue	5,719.4	16,292.4	14,072	14,253.8
Total assets	15,758.5	29,216	40,878.7	31,475
EBITDA	2,180.4	3,805.1	2,364.1	2,468.6
Gross profit	1,682.8	2,644.4	850.5	1,497.7
Net profit	1,016.8	2,245.7	−1068	75.8
Foreign investment	N/A	N/A	N/A	N/A
Exports	2,999.1	14,800.9	8,686.8	10,805.4
Employees	N/A	N/A	N/A	57,000
Countries	11	15	17	19

Note: data in millions of US dollars; N/A means not available data.
Source: Own elaboration based on data from Cemex annual reports[29]

In the next section, the main strategies followed by Cemex in order to become one of the world leaders in the concrete and cement industry are described.

Cemex Strategy and Business Model

Cemex traditionally focused on high-margin product cement and had further exposure to ready-mix concrete, especially in the Mexican market, where it had acquired several concrete companies during its domestic expansion. Aggregates were not a major contributor to Cemex's revenues. The company focused increasingly on the overall chain value and considered strengthening the downstream business in order to become a "building materials solution provider" rather than a supplier of isolated products.

Cemex's competitive advantages are continued innovation, a high level of commitment to customer service and satisfaction, proven post-merger integration expertise, digital evolution (efficient production, distribution, and delivery processes through sophisticated

[29]   Cemex, 2015; 2008.

information systems), and the ability to identify high-growth market opportunities in developing economies.[30] Regarding this last competitive advantage, over the years, Cemex gained significant experience in emerging markets, relevant insights about market dynamics and customer profiles, as well as a strong brand recognition. In addition, over time, Cemex developed a state-of-the-art takeover approach and showed the necessary discipline in making acquisitions. As Lorenzo Zambrano stated: "Since 1992, we have made 15 significant acquisitions. We have learned a lot from each of those transactions, as well as from the transactions we did not do. We have learned how to identify potential value and network synergies in an acquisition opportunity. We have learned how to integrate new acquisitions with increasing speed and efficiently. We have learned how to recover our financial flexibility quickly after the transaction is completed."[31]

The business model has changed over time due to the new competitive arena. The company's strategy emphasized improving profitability through efficient operations. Cemex also shifted from selling products to selling complete solutions.[32] The business model is based on a single global identity (acquired companies are almost always renamed "Cemex"), common organizational structures and operating processes, a common IT platform, centralized back office functions, and a strong emphasis on operational best practices, business process gap analysis, benchmarking, and performance measurement.[33] Reporting lines are adjusted depending on the function (e.g., back office functions). Therefore, the Cemex subsidiaries focus on making and selling cement, while centralized functions are tightly controlled by the parent company in Mexico. Operationally, Cemex is known for its deployment of technology and information systems as management and product-delivery tools to keep its cost structure competitive and leverage organizational knowledge. This approach has gained fame as "the Cemex

[30] Cemex, 2015. [31] Zambrano, 2004.
[32] Sharma, Mohan & Singh, 2003. [33] Casanova, 2009.

Way," which elevates organizational structures to the status of corporate strategy.[34]

The logic behind Cemex's selection criteria in acquiring companies in different markets is two-pronged.[35] The first aspect is the selection of countries experiencing strong population growth. In cases where potential acquiring companies had access to marine terminals, estimates of potential growth were made at a regional level and not only at the country level. A second selection criterion lay in the ability to acquire most, if not all, of the shares of the company of interest. Because Cemex's strategy was to implement far-reaching organizational changes in acquired companies, it was crucial to carry out such changes without delay. Logically, this was easier if absolute power over the new company could be brought to bear. Consequently, Cemex's presence is mainly in developing countries.

Grupo Cementos de Chihuahua Domestic and International Expansion

Grupo Cementos de Chihuahua is a leading supplier of cement, aggregates, concrete, and construction-related services in Mexico and the United States. In order to provide a better contextualization of the relevance of the company in the Mexican economy, Table 10.5 shows Grupo Cementos de Chihuahua financial data for 2010 and 2015.

In Mexico Grupo Cementos de Chihuahua mainly operates in Chihuahua State, with three cement plants located in Juárez, Salamayuca, and Chihuahua. Grupo Cementos de Chihuahua also operates 32 concrete plants, 230 concrete-mix trucks, six concrete block plants, six aggregate plants, a gypsum plant, and two precast concrete plants.

In the United States, it participates successfully in the cement and concrete market. It operates three cement plants with an annual production capacity of 2.17 million tons, located in Tijeras (New Mexico), Rapid City (South Dakota), and Pueblo (Colorado). Grupo

---

[34]   Casanova, 2009.   [35]   Lucea & Donald, 2010.

Table 10.5 *Grupo Cementos de Chihuahua financial data, 2010–15*

	2000	2005	2010	2015
Revenue	N/A	N/A	543,098	755,121
Total assets	N/A	N/A	1,917,418	1,371,576
EBITDA	N/A	N/A	37,128.1	68,377.1
Gross profit	N/A	N/A	44,719.8	10,5514
Net profit	N/A	N/A	6,598.8	57,686.8
Foreign investment	N/A	N/A	N/A	N/A
Exports	N/A	N/A	N/A	N/A
Employees	N/A	N/A	2,558	2,694
Countries	3	3	3	3

Note: data in millions of US dollars; N/A means not available.
Source: Own elaboration based on data from Company's Report[36]

Cementos de Chihuahua also owns 21 distribution centers located in Texas, New Mexico, Colorado, South Dakota, North Dakota, Wyoming, Minnesota, Iowa, Kansas, and Montana. In addition, Grupo Cementos de Chihuahua is one of the leaders in producing mix-concrete in South Dakota, Minnesota, Iowa, Missouri, Oklahoma, and Arkansas. In total, it operates 84 mix-concrete plants and owns 427 concrete-mix trucks and 236 trucks for cement and aggregate transportation.[37]

Regarding the history of the company, Grupo Cementos de Chihuahua was founded in 1941 in Chihuahua, Mexico by a mining businessman. In the beginning, the company had difficulties mainly caused by lack of knowledge. In order to assure a successful start, it was necessary to involve a group of investors from Chihuahua headed by Don Eloy Vallina, as well as forming a partnership with an American cement company called Market Cement Corporation. In 1943, cement-making operations began with a capacity of 60,000 metric tons (wet process). The company has been owned by the

[36]   Grupo Cementos de Chihuahua, 2016.
[37]   Grupo Cementos de Chihuahua, 2016.

renowned Terrazas family, which by the early twentieth century controlled fifty haciendas and ranches throughout the state. Also, the
Terrazas family had a long tradition of becoming important actors in
the politics of the Chihuahua state. When the company started, the
market was relatively small but the growth was constant, so in 1952
the plant expanded its capacity to 170,000 metric tons.

In response to the growing demand, in 1962 a Concrete Division
was created with the name Concretos Premezclados de Chihuahua SA
de CV and in 1972 a new plant in Ciudad Juárez began operations. This
plant was successfully working when the CEO of the company identified an opportunity to export cement to El Paso, because in that city
the local cement plant was old and had higher costs, and the geographic location was a clear competitive advantage for Grupo
Cementos de Chihuahua. Consequently, in 1982, the plant in
Ciudad Juarez increased its production capacity to 630,000 metric
tons. The American cement companies reacted and pressed the
American government for legal protection, in terms of new taxes to
cement imports. Grupo Cementos de Chihuahua exports struggled
but continued growing, and a partnership was even started with
Cemex. In 1992, Grupo Cementos de Chihuahua became the name
of the company. In the same year, Grupo Cementos de Chihuahua
started operations in the Mexican Stock Exchange positioning the
company in a higher scale. Therefore, a new plant was built in
Salamayuca, near Ciudad Juárez, aiming to increase exports to the
United States. As was expected, the American legal protection
intensified.

International expansion was initiated in 1994, triggered in part
by the New Orleans flood, because in that moment the United States
required large amounts of cement so the legal protection was left in
standby. Grupo Cementos de Chihuahua knew that the tax elimination was temporary and took the decision to enter the American
market. In the same year, the company acquired a cement plant in
Tijeras New Mexico, near Albuquerque, owned by Holcim.
In that year, the American economy was in trouble and the plant

worked at 50 percent of its capacity, but after the landscape changed for the better, the plant worked at its full 100 percent capacity. It is noteworthy that Grupo Cementos de Chihuahua proved its efficiency at learning and complying with regulatory aspects of the United States in order to succeed in this market.

In 1997, a new aggregates plant began operating in Juárez, Chihuahua, with an installed annual capacity of 1,800,000 tons. Nevertheless, the company identified a new opportunity to keep growing in the American market and in March 2001 acquired Dakota Cement's assets and working capital located in South Dakota. The state government owned the cement plant and the deal closed after building a close relationship with the state governor. With the acquisition, Grupo Cementos de Chihuahua total production capacity increased to 3.3 million metric tons. From that point until now, Grupo Cementos de Chihuahua has focused only on Chihuahua, which is one particular market in the northwest of the country, perhaps because of the intensified competence in the regions dominated by Cemex.

Around 2003, Grupo Cementos de Chihuahua became a member of the Portland Cement Association in the United States. The association continuously shares relevant information about the market and the cement industry with its members. After a close analysis, the company forecast an opportunity in the center of the country because in the short term the cement demand would greatly exceed the offer. Thus, a five-year project was initiated which required the construction of a cement plant in El Paso, Colorado. In 2008, the plant began operating, and it was the most modern and efficient in the United States.

In 2005, Grupo Cementos de Chihuahua entered Bolivia through a partnership with a businessman in that country. Grupo Cementos de Chihuahua acquired a minority stake of 48 percent of the company owned by the partner. The company had great financial results and the growth plans were clear. Cement production in Bolivia was low cost, mainly because of the gas surplus. Nevertheless, the

Bolivian government expropriated one of the plants, and Grupo Cementos de Chihuahua abandoned its operations in that country. "Yes, the Bolivian government expropriated one of our plants and did not pay us back. In that moment, we were worried and decided to leave Bolivia. We were expecting that the situation was going to be wors-[e] ... we lament the situation because the Bolivian economy is good," recalled Don Federico Terrazas, Ex-CEO of Grupo Cementos de Chihuahua.[38]

Table 10.6 shows a timeline with the key events in the history of Grupo Cementos de Chihuahua and summarizes the fact that the company has expanded to several states in North America, as well as to South America, allowing a diversification in sales and income sources.[39]

In 2008, Grupo Cementos de Chihuahua had a new plant in the United States that required a significant investment (US$350 million) and was partially financed by debt. In the same year, the financial crisis greatly affected the global economy and the United States was no exception. In 2007, demand for cement in the United States was for around 120 million tons, and in 2008 was dramatically reduced to only 65 million tons. The crisis had a substantial impact on Grupo Cementos de Chihuahua operations: the plants in Mexico and overseas had to work at 50 percent of their capacity, thus failing to break even. "Those years required authentic sacrifices to keep the company running," noted Don Federico Terrazas, Ex-CEO of Grupo Cementos de Chihuahua.

Grupo Cementos de Chihuahua, under the leadership of CEO Don Federico Terrazas, saw opportunities during this crisis. The company sought to become more efficient and lower its costs. In fact, one of the main raw materials to produce cement is gas as a fuel, and the cost of a million BTUs increased from US$4 to $10 in the years of the financial crisis. Thus, Grupo Cementos de Chihuahua

---

[38]   Interview with Don Federico Terrazas, Grupo Cementos de Chihuahua founder and ex-CEO, conducted by the authors on January 25, 2015.

[39]   Grupo Cementos de Chihuahua, 2016.

Table 10.6 *Grupo Cementos de Chihuahua (GCC) timeline events*

Year	Local	International
1941	GCC was founded in Chihuahua, Mexico by a mining businessman. The beginning of the company was complicated mainly due to the lack of knowledge regarding the industry.	
1943	A group of investors and a partnership with an American cement company led GCC to start operations with a capacity of 60,000 metric tons.	
1952	The first plant in Chihuahua expanded its capacity to 170,000 metric tons in response to market demand.	
1962	GCC created a Concrete division with the name Cementos Premezclados de Chihuahua.	
1972	GCC opened a new plant in Ciudad Juárez in order to serve the market near the border with the USA. The local cement plant was very old and had higher costs.	
1982	The plant in Ciudad Juárez increased its production capacity to 630,000 metric tons. A considerable amount of the sales were exports to USA.	
1992	GCC adopts its current name and is listed on the stock market. In the same year, a new	

Table 10.6 (cont.)

Year	Local	International
	plant was built in Salamayuca, near Ciudad Juárez, also to increase exports to the USA.	
1991		GCC launched its US division with the purchase of a cement manufacturing facility in Tijeras, Nuevo Mexico. Besides, the company purchased a distribution terminal in Albuquerque and in El Paso. The company was decided to enter the US market and the international expansion was triggered in part by the New Orleans flood because in that moment USA required huge amounts of cement and the legal protection was left in standby.
1994		GCC purchased a distribution terminal in Albuquerque and in El Paso. The company acquired a cement plant in Tijeras, New Mexico owned by Holcim. The company decided to enter the US market.
1997	A new aggregates plant began operations in Juárez, Chihuahua, with an installed annual capacity of 1,800,000 tons.	
2001		GCC acquired Dakota Cement in Rapid City, South Dakota. The company identified a new opportunity to keep growing in the American market.
2003		GCC became a member of the Portland Cement Association in

Table 10.6 (*cont.*)

Year Local	International
	the United States. Based on relevant information, the company initiated a project that lasted five years and ended with the construction of a cement plant in El Paso, Colorado.
2005	GCC acquires a minority stake (48%) in a cement plant in Bolivia. The cement production in Bolivia had low costs mainly because of the gas surplus. Nevertheless, the Bolivian government expropriated one of the plants and GCC abandoned its operations in the country.
2008	GCC launched a state-of-the-art plant in Pueblo, Colorado.

Source: Own elaboration based on company reports and the interview with Don Federico Terrazas.

bought a charcoal mine, as it provided a cheaper source of fuel that reduced costs to US$3.50 or $4.

More recently, in the fourth quarter of 2013, Grupo Cementos de Chihuahua announced that sales rose 10.3 percent compared with the fourth quarter of 2012 with double-digit increases of cement sales volume in the United States, and of concrete, block, and aggregates in Mexico. 32.2 percent were sales in Mexico and 67.8 percent in the United States. At the end of March 2014, Grupo Cementos de Chihuahua had 2,687 employees. According to Don Federico Terrazas, the company is expected to continue growing. "We are happy because we are now selling 85 million tons [which] is good. We expect to end 2015 selling 90 million tons. We are planning an expansion in the Dakota plant because we [foresee] that in 2019 the American economy in the construction sector will grow considerabl[y]." Don Federico Terrazas, Ex-CEO of Grupo Cementos de Chihuahua.

Grupo Cementos de Chihuahua Strategy and Business Model

In the USA, from Denver, CO to Minot, ND, Amarillo, TX to Great Bend, KS, Glendive, MT to Elida, NM, Grupo Cementos de Chihuahua's strategic locations allow the company to reach a level of operational efficiency unlike most in the cement manufacturing and distributing business. Grupo Cementos de Chihuahua produces its own raw materials and delivers finished products on site. Therefore, the company has developed a trifecta of efficiency in manufacturing, logistics, and marketing. In addition, the company has access to the highest quality raw materials available because it owns a sizable limestone quarry in Pueblo, Colorado. This is one of its most important competitive advantages in comparison with the local competitors. "Due to the basic fact that it does not make economic sense to ship cement much more than 350 miles by rail or 180 miles by truck, the vertical geography of our plants helps support our operations from as far north as the Canadian border and as far south as Mexico," noted Steve Ambrose, VP of Sales, Marketing and Logistics for Grupo Cementos de Chihuahua's US operations.[40] "The quality of our limestone at Pueblo is some of the highest in the industry and the plant doesn't generate any waste because of the quality of the raw materials," said Gina Nance, plant manager of the Pueblo site.[41]

Grupo Cementos de Chihuahua has been an innovation-driven company since its inception. Therefore, technology is present in the production processes as a key resource to increase fuel and energy efficiency. Consequently, the company produces cement at lower costs than the rest of its competitors. "We're the second newest plant of this kind in the US with the most up-to-date technology in the industry ... most plants across the US have been in operation for

---

[40]   Shaw, 2014.   [41]   Shaw, 2014.

30 years or more. Our operation is more fuel- and energy-efficient," explained Gina Nance, plant manager of the Pueblo site.

Grupo Cementos de Chihuahua strongly focuses on its customer-first service. The company works with its clients to make sure demands are met, even if that means specific mix requirements. Grupo Cementos de Chihuahua's goal is to retain long-term customers but also to reach new ones, and that is written in their strategic vision. "We've been very focused on the customer since the start ... what really sets us apart is that we really care about and listen to our customers ... Grupo Cementos de Chihuahua's North American president and global CEO meet with customers regularly," said Steve Ambrose, Vice President of Sales, Marketing and Logistics for Grupo Cementos de Chihuahua's US operations.

COMPARISON AND CONCLUSIONS

In this section, we highlight the most important elements deriving from relevant insights regarding the international expansion of both cases described. In terms of similarities, both companies started operations in Mexico, had an expansion stage within the Mexican territory, and later identified and seized business opportunities abroad. In addition, both companies have operations in the USA, taking advantage of the border with one of the most demanding markets in the world. Besides cement production, Cemex and Grupo Cementos de Chihuahua have other operations that complement their value proposition, such as ready-mix concrete retailing, cement distribution, aggregates, cement block production and other activities related to the core business. Moreover, both invested in Latin American countries with socialist regimes, such as Bolivia and Venezuela, and experienced bad results due to local policy changes. Furthermore, both companies adapted and implemented best practices, developed within their facilities in the Mexican territory, into facilities overseas. Finally, Cemex and Grupo Cementos de Chihuahua now have new leaders: Rogelio Zambrano as President of Cemex and Federico

Terrazas Junior at Grupo Cementos de Chihuahua. Both graduated from the Tecnológico de Monterrey.

In terms of differences between Cemex and Grupo Cementos de Chihuahua, an important one is the relative size of the operations. Cemex is much bigger than Grupo Cementos de Chihuahua, as is evident in the sales and production volumes. In the same vein, Cemex has a presence in most of the Mexican territory whereas Grupo Cementos de Chihuahua is established only in the north part of Mexico. In international markets, Grupo Cementos de Chihuahua only has operations in the USA, while Cemex participates in more than 50 countries, and most commonly in emerging markets. Moreover, although both companies have innovations and successful strategies implemented in the way they produce and operate, Cemex has world-class innovations such as "The Cemex Way," the "Shift" platform, and other best practices shared between their facilities in different countries. Finally, Cemex's internationalization strategy was aggressive and mainly focused on acquiring companies that could adopt their operating systems. Grupo Cementos de Chihuahua was more conservative, searching for opportunities and when necessary building plants and facilities from nothing. After considering similarities and differences, we identified some lessons that are worth sharing.

On the one hand, Grupo Cementos de Chihuahua is focused only on the USA outside Mexico. This approach helped the company to be concentrated, specializing in one market and consequently having important scale efficiencies that resulted in profits. In addition, Grupo Cementos de Chihuahua identified strategic opportunities to reduce costs, as was the case of the acquisition of the coal mine in the USA, as well as maintaining an important part of its operations in Mexico. One of the strengths of Grupo Cementos de Chihuahua was the management of its debt, always taking care not to exceed the limits and the risks, and having the necessary available cash for its expansions. Along with the financials, another element of the success is operating efficiency, based on good relationships with the employees and the replication of best practices to other plants and facilities. Furthermore, the use of appropriate information has allowed the company to make intelligent decisions that had a positive impact in the medium and long term. Finally, Grupo Cementos de Chihuahua has responded appropriately to difficult situations, as was the case with the acquisition of a plant near the promised Walmart headquarters, which in the end was never installed.

On the other hand, Cemex has operations in several countries, which implies bigger challenges. In particular, Cemex has been facing several challenges around the world, entering new markets and buying and selling companies. For example, in Venezuela, Hugo Chavez (the former Venezuelan president) expropriated cement companies. Cemex sued the Venezuelan government to recover the value of its assets. The Venezuelan government refused to pay back the value, but Cemex – along with its competitor, Holcim – pushed and forced the government's hand, and obtained part of the value of its assets in a bonus from the Venezuelan state-owned oil and natural gas company (PDVSA). Cemex and Holcim finally sold the bonus to recover part of their investments. Another experience was the acquisition of Rinker in Australia, one of the biggest business deals in the company's history. The 2009 world economic crisis and the financial situation of Cemex forced the company to sell Rinker. Nowadays, Cemex needs to reduce debts in order to maintain its position as a leader in the global cement market. We want to highlight that in each deal, Cemex has developed and acquired knowledge that has been useful for the next merger or acquisition, and such knowledge and expertise represents one of its main strengths. Nowadays, Grupo Cementos de Chihuahua is achieving better financial results than Cemex because it is mainly focused on a part of the USA cement market – which, incidentally, is recovering at a constant pace. After the bad experience with the Bolivian government, which also expropriated some Grupo Cementos de Chihuahua assets in that country, the company decided to be more careful in its international expansion. According to Don

Federico, Cemex is not searching for any new investments in Latin America or other regions in the short term.

It is well known that the cement and concrete industry is strongly related to the economic development in any given region, and intrinsically correlated with the construction industry. In consequence, the performance of cement companies greatly depends on the economic performance at a local, regional, and global level. For this reason, one of the main insights in both cases is that companies must be prepared for both good and bad times. Having a diverse portfolio in terms of geographical and product scope, as well as healthy finances and efficient operations, are key aspects for survival in a competitive market when an economic crisis occurs. In addition, Don Federico and Rogelio agreed that good things come after crises: for example, innovation and efficiencies. In both cases, after numerous economic crises, new processes have been developed in order to become more efficient and reduce costs, and in the end, the companies became stronger.

Finally, we consider that one important enabler in the international expansion of both companies is the academic education of the leaders and their families. In fact, well-educated families played an important role in the evolution of both companies. For example, Don Federico's father and a couple of uncles studied at prestigious universities in the USA. In addition, both Rogelio Zambrano and Don Federico are alumni of one of the most well recognized universities in Mexico, Tecnológico de Monterrey. In both cases, the leaders are recognized businesspeople with clear values of honesty, punctuality, responsibility, and commitment with high quality education. Don Federico is a member of the board of directors of the Tecnológico de Monterrey and Rogelio Zambrano was a faculty member of the same institution for more than 20 years.[42] In the same vein, both Rogelio Zambrano and Don Federico Terrazas are examples of hard-working and visionary executives who are willing to learn from the dynamism

[42]   Interview with Don Rogelio Zambrano, Cemex CEO, conducted by the authors on May 11, 2015.

of the market in order to adapt and take advantage of what is coming. Hearing about how great leaders have faced challenges and opportunities with the international operations of these two Mexican companies was really a wonderful opportunity to learn how a multinational company can have success in global markets.

REFERENCES

AggNet. 2016. World Cement Demand Revised Downward. April, 12. *AggNet.* www.agg-net.com/news/2016-world-cement-demand-revised-down ward. Accessed February 24, 2017.

CANACEM, 2017. National Cement Chamber. http://canacem.org.mx/home-2/. Accessed February 20, 2017.

Casanova, L. 2009. From MultiLatinas to Global Latinas: The New Latin American Multinationals (Compilation Case Studies). *Interamerican Development Bank, Washington DC.* www.iadb.org/en/research-and-data/research-data,1612.html. Accessed May 22, 2015.

Cemex. 2017. Cemex website. www.cemex.com/AboutUs/CompanyProfile.aspx# sthash.fO4k2WfH.dpuf. Accessed 20 November, 2016.

Cemex. 2015. Building a Better Future. Annual Report, Cemex. www.cemex.com /CEMEX_AR2015/index.html. Accessed July 13, 2016.

Cemex. 2008. Tough Times Call for Tough Actions. Annual Report, Cemex. www .cemex.com/InvestorCenter/files/2008/CEMEX_ar2008.pdf. Accessed July 15, 2015.

CNN Expansion. 2009. Cemex vende operaciones en Australia. October, 1st. *CNN Expansión.* www.cnnexpansion.com/negocios/2009/10/01/CEMEX-vende-operaciones-en-australia. Accessed July 25, 2016.

CW Group. 2016. Global Cement Volume Forecast Report. *CW Research.* October 2016.

Grupo Cementos de Chihuahua. 2016. Grupo Cementos de Chihuahua website. www.gcc.com/opencms/opencms/es/quienes_somos/historia/?Level=1&url=/ es/quienes_somos/index.html. Accessed July 25, 2015.

Hoeber, H. 2008. Cemex. Building a Global Latina, in M. Hitt, R. D. Ireland & R. Hoskisson, (eds.), *Strategic Management Cases: Competitiveness* and Globalization. Cengage Learning.

INEGI. 2011. Mexico at a Glance. *INEGI.* www.inegi.org.mx/prod_serv/conte nidos/espanol/bvinegi/productos/integracion/pais/mexvista/2011/mex atg_2011.pdf. Accessed July 25, 2015.

Lafarge. 2008. Annual Report, *Lafarge*. www.lafarge.com/sites/default/files/atom s/files/03162009-publications_finance-annual_report_2008-uk.pdf.   Accessed August 21, 2015.

Lessard, D. & Lucea, R. 2009. Mexican Multinationals; Insights from Cemex, in R. Ramamurti & J. V. Singh (eds.), *Emerging Multinationals from Emerging Markets*: 280–311. Cambridge: Cambridge University Press.

Lucea, R. & Donald, D. 2010. ¿Cómo mantienen su ventaja competitiva las multinacionales de economías emergentes? El caso de Cemex. *Universia Business Review*, 25:76–97.

Orta, A. 2005. Mexico's Cement Industry Market Overview. *Global Cement*. www .globalcement.com/news/itemlist/tag/Mexico. Accessed August 13, 2015.

Perilli. 2017. The Other Side of the Wall. *Global Cement*. January, 18. www .globalcement.com/news/item/5692-the-other-side-of-the-wall.   Accessed February 24, 2017.

Reference for Business. 2005. Cemex SA de CV – Company Profile, Information, Business Description, History, Background Information on Cemex SA de CV. *Reference for Business*. www.referenceforbusiness.com/history2/44/CEMEX-S-A-de-C-V.html. Accessed April 25, 2016.

Saunders, A. 2015. Preview: The Top 100 Global Cement Companies and Global Per Capita Capacity Trends. December, 1st. *Global Cement*. www .globalcement.com/magazine/articles/964-preview-the-top-100-global-cement-companies-and-global-per-capita-capacity-trends. Accessed February 25, 2017.

Sharma, A., Mohan, S. & Singh, S. 2003. Case Analysis Series. Cemex: Innovation in Housing for the Poor. *Michigan Business School*. www.bus.umich.edu/Fac ultyResearch/ResearchCenters/ProgramsPartnerships/IT-Champions/CEMEX .pdf. Accessed August 15, 2015.

Shaw, M. 2014. Grupo Cementos de Chihuahua of America. *US Builders Review*. www.usbuildersreview.com/case-studies/gcc-america-state-art-processes-perfecting-cement-production-supply-chain.   Accessed July 24, 2015.

Statista. 2016. World Cement Production 2010–2016. *Statista*. www.statista.com /statistics/219343/cement-production-worldwide/. Accessed February 20, 2017.

Zambrano. 2004. Remarks of Lorenzo Zambrano, Annual Analyst and Investor Meeting. July 1st. www.cemex.com/MediaCenter/Files/LHZ-transcript.pdf. Accessed April 19, 2016.

11 MultiMexicans in the Ceramic Tile Industry
Lamosa and Interceramic

Daniel Lemus-Delgado

INTRODUCTION

This chapter discusses the process of internationalization of two leading companies in the Mexican market. The first one is Grupo Lamosa, which is the leading company in this market. The second firm is Interceramic, the third largest company in the country by market share. These companies were selected not only because of their size and importance in the market, but because of the strong ties they present outwards due to the geographical location in which they originally arose. In addition, in both cases, the fabrication of ceramic tiles is their primary manufacturing activity. The experiences of Lamosa and Interceramic present a good opportunity to learn how, in the process of internationalization, the identity of the companies matters.

Indeed, both companies have a location close to the border, one in the State of Nuevo León and the other in the State of Chihuahua. From this perspective, this chapter proposes that a key element for understanding the internationalization processes of the MultiMexicans is located in the geographical factor that contributes to the formation of a distinct identity. Thus, this chapter suggests that in the internationalization phenomenon of the Mexican companies it is important also to consider the identity of the border's entrepreneur, which is framed in a specific historical and social context.

Therefore, this chapter proposes that the geographical factor, framed in a particular social context, can be considered in two dimensions. The first dimension is like a physical space. The second dimension is like an ideational space. Evidently, as physical space, the geography of a region provides proximity to international markets, as well as access to certain resources that generate comparative advantages with other companies in other areas. As an ideational space, geography favors the construction of an identity distinct from a community. In this case, the region as a mental space, favors the imaginary construction of a particular type of entrepreneur. This collective imagination pushes the idea of innovation and internationalization as a part of the identity of the Northern businessman. Specifically, this chapter proposes that Lamosa and Interceramic share a huge tradition of internationalization that has its roots in the identity of one type of businessman.

Beyond these identity narratives and whether they correspond to reality or not, it is a fact that the construction of these identities has driven the internationalization process of some Mexican companies located in the north of the country. Both Lamosa and Interceramic are in this group of companies. This chapter analyzes these two companies as cases of the way in which the identity and the region constitute essential pieces that explain the internationalization process of some MultiMexicans.

CERAMIC TILE INDUSTRY HISTORY, TRENDS, AND PROSPECTS IN MEXICO

Mexico has a strong tradition in the production of ceramics and ceramic tiles as a construction element. In fact, this material has been used as a decorative element since the end of the sixteenth century, when it was introduced by the Spanish (Soler, 2003). Consequently, some urban centers, particularly the city of Puebla, stood out for the exquisite workmanship of these materials since the year 1580, which allowed this city to become an important Viceroyalty center of production during the eighteenth century (Macías, 2011). The manufacture of ceramic tiles was made in artisanal workshops through union associations. The unions were corporate organizations with established ordinances that regulated the artisanal production and maintained standards of quality (Seijas, 2014).

Despite the importance as an ornamental element of the main buildings of colonial Mexico, and the first decades of independent living, it wasn't until the twentieth century that the industrial production of ceramic tiles was carried out for the first time. Ladrillos Monterrey, antecedent of Lamosa, was the pioneering company of this activity, and in 1932 began the industrial production of this product. In its origins, the production of ceramic tiles was a complement to the primary activity of this company, which was brick manufacture for the construction of new Government buildings, as well as new factories that were set up in different cities of the country (Viscaya, 2006).

During the 1940s Mexico began one important industrial takeoff derived from both exogenous and endogenous factors. The post-revolutionary Government promoted the policy of import substitution in order to strengthen the country's industrialization project (Hansen, 2004). Therefore, previously established industries, such as the breweries, cement, glass, and brick works, got a substantial push. This impulse allowed their expansion to reach a national dimension as well as to have the capacity for technology transfer from industrialized countries. These measures led to the development of an industry protected by the State and a business community dedicated to capital accumulation. However, these companies lacked the long-term strategies that would allow them to arise beyond a national market, since they were operating under regressive production schemes (Hernández, 2004).

Those industries located at the border advanced their development by the internal dynamic of the US market, as shown in the paradigmatic case of the industry established at the city of Monterrey. While this phenomenon was not entirely new, since it had been experienced previously in different periods of the nineteenth century and the first half of the twentieth century, the post-war boom that significantly influenced US citizens' ability to purchase and the growth of the middle class in this country, facilitated the industrial consolidation of the northern industrial groups of Mexico (Saragoza 1990). The ceramic tile industry was no exception to this trend.

Favorable conditions in Mexico for the development of the ceramic tile industry lasted from the 1940s until the first half of the 1970s, when the so-called "Mexican miracle" came abruptly to an end. The industry experienced difficult times due to continuous devaluations, the Mexican market's contraction, the debts in dollars that some of these companies had accrued, and the presence of an economic policy that left aside the protectionism that the Mexican industry used to emphasize (Cardenas, 2012). The change of a protectionist policy to one based on the attraction of Foreign Direct Investment (FDI), international trade liberalization, and the promotion of exports eventually forced firms to modernize in order to survive in a highly competitive environment (Ruíz & Moreno-Brid, 2006).

Those companies that succeeded in moving from business models based on a protectionist context to one of a free market found themselves in privileged situations to accelerate their economic growth through free trade agreements, particularly the North American Free Trade Agreement, which allowed these companies to venture into a vast market. Paradoxically, at the same time, this expanded the polarization of the Mexican economy (Dussel 2003).

Mexico is one of the primary producers of ceramic tiles worldwide. For example, in 2013, Mexico occupied tenth position worldwide as a manufacturing country of ceramic tiles. In that year, Mexico produced 1.9% of the total world production, with an output of 228 million square meters. That same year, the main world producers were China with 9.6% of the total world production; Brazil, with 7.3%; India, with 6.3%; Iran, with 4.2%; Spain, with 3.5%; Indonesia, with 3.3%; Italy, with 3%; Turkey, with 2.9%; and Vietnam with 2.5% (Stock, 2014).

China led the list of the main consumers of ceramic tile in 2013, its market representing 39.4% of the size of the market worldwide, with a consumption of 4,556 million square meters. The list of top ten consumers is complemented by Brazil (837 million sq. m.), India (748 million sq. m.), Indonesia (360 million sq. m.), Iran (350 million sq. m.), Vietnam (251 million sq. m.), Saudi Arabia (235 million sq. m.),

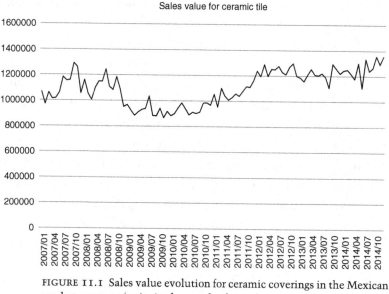

Sales value for ceramic tile

FIGURE 11.1 Sales value evolution for ceramic coverings in the Mexican market, 2007–14 (units in thousands of pesos)
Source: Authors, based on INEGI

Russia (231 million sq. m.), the United States (230 million sq. m.), and Turkey (226 million sq. m.) (Stock, 2014).

For the Mexican ceramic tile industry, market behavior in the United States is significant because this country is the primary export market for Mexican products. Thus, it is important to heed the growth of this market (Stock, 2014). In addition, the United States is the main importer of this product. In 2014, it imported 350 million sq. m. The other nine major importers worldwide that year were Saudi Arabia, Iraq, France, Nigeria, Germany, Russia, Thailand, South Korea, and the United Arab Emirates (Stock, 2014).

The production performance has had ups and downs, as shown in Figure 11.1. As well as in other industrial sectors in Mexico, the macroeconomic trends in the country and the recent structural reforms allow the growth of this industry to be projected, which, leveraged from the domestic market, can consolidate its internationalization activities. However, adverse local conditions, such as an insecure climate and corruption, affect the chances of better economic performance.

In terms of the Mexican internal conditions, two trends are favorable for the future expansion of these enterprises. The first factor derives from the housing deficit and demographic profile of the Mexican population. In this sense, the Federal Government estimated that the country's housing deficit, which is defined as the houses that are inappropriate or will be needed due to overcrowding, exceeds 15 million units. This condition will boost domestic demand for ceramic tiles and bathroom accessories. A second favorable factor is the energy reform adopted in Mexico in 2014. Insofar as the production and distribution of the natural gas network increases, we can expect a stable, consistent, and cheaper gas supply, which will increase the profitability of sector companies (Prognosis, 2014).

The performance of the residential construction in Mexico is strongly linked with the market for ceramic tiles. In the 2008–13 period, the residential construction sector in Mexico faced several obstacles that affected its performance. In 2014, however, some indicators of private residential construction revealed a sector recovery. Thus, during 2014, private development in Mexico presented an improvement compared with the previous year (Banco de Mexico, 2015).

However, at the same time, the ceramic tile manufacturing industry faces a scenario that could limit the ability of companies to maintain and increase their profit margins, to raise their productivity through technological innovation or to expand their market through acquisitions and mergers. These elements include low growth and stagnation of the construction industry in Mexico and the increase in lower price ceramic tile imports, particularly from Asia (Prognosis, 2014).

Therefore, company mergers can be expected in the near future or sales of some of their business units, with the capitalization intention to strategically reorient their priorities, focus on a market segment, and more successfully face an environment that is expected to grow in the coming years but will be extremely competitive. Thus, for example, Lamosa decided to sell its toilet and bathroom furniture business unit to the multinational Colombian company Corona by the end of 2014, which includes two plants that generate 3.5 million pieces per year as well as the export and marketing operations in the United States (Herrera, 2014).

Two representative cases of the ceramic tile industry in Mexico have been chosen. Grupo Lamosa is the most important company in this sector. This company has deep historical roots. By contrast, Interceramic is more recent. However, the two companies share a similar geographic context and the identity is a key factor to explain their export activities. When we analyze the internationalization of companies in Mexico, these two companies will demonstrate how regional differences are important in these phenomena. Also, Lamosa is the biggest company in Mexico in this sector and Interceramic is the third.[1]

LAMOSA

Grupo Lamosa's origins date back to the year 1890, when the Americans William W. Price, John R. Price, and David Isaac Jones established Compañía Fabricante de Ladrillos de Monterrey (Brick Manufacturer Company of Monterrey). With an initial investment of 75 thousand pesos, the company began to work a year later, with 75 workers and with an annual production projection of 20 million bricks a year (Rojas, 2009). Originally, Ladrillera Monterrey had three types

---

[1]   The second largest Mexican company in ceramic tile is Vitromex, a part of Grupo Industrial Saltillo (GISSA). The company was founded by Don Isidro Lopez Zertuche in Saltillo, Coahuila, where it began operations in 1928 as a producer and distributor of kitchen products. In the early 1960s he started production of ceramic tiles. Subsequently, the company formally ventured into the automotive smelting industry in 1964. GISSA's growth and structure from 2000 has been achieved through a series of strategic investments and reorganizations, which include plant expansion, acquisitions, partnerships, divestment of business segments and other strategies for the expansion, diversification, and profitability of their products and markets. GISSA is a Mexican company that manufactures and markets products in three business sectors: auto parts, construction, and home (Bolsa Mexicana de Valores, 2015). Since the ceramic tile industry is not the company's core business, Vitromex was not considered for this study.

of customers. Firstly, the City Hall, which replaced the city's center cobbled streets with brick streets. A second group of customers was Monterrey's factories which began to settle in the last decade of the nineteenth century. Thus, Ladrillera Monterrey supplied to factories such as Cervecería Cuauhtémoc, Vidriera Monterrey, and Fundidora de Hierro y Acero de Monterrey. The third group was formed by the demand for the construction of houses both for workers and for the city's first residences and in other parts of the country, mainly the city of Mexico and the port of Tampico (Rojas, 2009: 121–122). Since its inception, Ladrillera Monterrey exported its bricks to the State of Texas, mainly the city of San Antonio, as well as the island of Cuba (Rojas, 2009).

The hard years of the Mexican Revolution limited the factory's growth possibilities. The company faced harsh challenges that culminated in its restructuring and its acquisition by new partners. In 1929 Ladrillera Monterrey, SA (Lamosa) was established; its major investors were Bernardo Elosúa, Viviano L. Valdez, and Canuto Hinojosa, which generated a new momentum for the company (Rojas, 2009). Despite the difficulties derived from the great depression and the economic instability of the post-revolutionary period, the company came through thanks in part to the benefit derived from its production technology, particularly from the Fate Root Heath brand brick-making machine, and the replacement of firewood with natural gas imported from the South of Texas. The use of gas allowed more uniform products to be made, as well as reductions in costs and the attenuation of the workers' physical work, which significantly raised the company's productivity (Rojas, 2009).

An important step in the company's consolidation occurred in 1933, when investors Elosúa and Valdes identified a new market for expansion, incorporating the manufacture of ceramic tiles as a new line of business. In this way, a decade later, ceramic tiles constituted one of Lamosa's basic products. In 1957, Lamosa created the brand Crest and became one of the first manufacturers in Mexico to produce cement-based ceramic adhesives. In addition, during the 1960s,

Lamosa began the production of toilets and bathroom furniture products through its subsidiary Sanitarios Azteca, SA. The last years of the 60s brought new technological advances that were quickly adopted by Lamosa, which helped to increase its production of ceramic tiles in a meaningful way. During the 1980s, Lamosa began to automate its main processes to produce ceramic tiles and was one of the first producers of ceramic tile in Mexico that introduced kilns. The 1990s were defined by a change in the organizational structure and corporate governance of Lamosa, which strengthened its presence as a leading producer of ceramic tiles in Mexico. In November 2007, with the acquisition of Porcelanite for US$825 million, the Porcelanite–Lamosa business became one of the largest producers of ceramic tiles in the world, with a production capacity exceeding 120 million square meters (Lamosa, 2014).

Today, Grupo Lamosa's operations are organized into three divisions. The first, Ceramics, includes the business of ceramic tiles, toilets, and bathroom furniture. The sales of this division accounted for 75 percent of the total of the company's consolidated sales in 2013. The reasons that Lamosa has consolidated as the most important maker of ceramic tiles in Mexico include being a leader in the market of adhesives, with more than 50 percent of market share. It has also taken on a diversification strategy with its products, presenting an approach to address different socio-economic segments and participate in the launch of innovative lines.

The 20 percent of the total consolidated sales derived from products that are exported to 15 countries in South America, as well as the United States and Canada. In the United States, Lamosa competes with some of the largest producers of ceramic tiles in other countries, as well as other types of floor coatings, such as carpets, wooden floors, and laminates. At the same time, Lamosa is the leader in the Mexican ceramic tile sales market. This division has nine centers of production established in six states of Mexico (Lamosa, 2014).

The Ceramics division has been mainly responsible for prompting the internationalization of the company, particularly due to the export of toilets for the North American market. The local toilet and bathroom furniture industry is best positioned to benefit from exports due to its strategic location, low-cost production, and high-quality products with good performance, compared to European and Asian competitors. Sales in this sector experienced higher growth for the company, increasing by 18 percent in 2013, in comparison with the previous year.

The second division consists of the Adhesives sector, which includes adhesives and specialized construction materials; it operates 13 plants, one of which is in the city of Guatemala. The adhesives division generated consolidated sales of Mex$2,377 million in 2013, which accounted for 25 percent of Lamosa's consolidated sales. This division is mainly engaged in the manufacture and distribution of adhesives and nozzles for the installation of ceramic and natural tiles in floors and walls, as well as stucco and waterproofing coatings (Lamosa, 2014).

Lamosa's third division is Real Estate. This division was established at the beginning of the 1980s with the intention of developing land that was once used in the activities of the Ceramics division, either to establish factories in those areas or to ensure removal of necessary inputs to the ceramic tile production processes. Subsequently, the Real Estate division was dedicated to the sale of urban and commercial areas in the city. This division has participated in the development and sale of residential and commercial projects within the metropolitan area of Monterrey. Although it has recently decreased its operations significantly, it eventually carries out the sale of properties that are part of the company's real estate inventory. During 2013 this division recorded sales to a value of Mex$47 million (Lamosa, 2014).

The Ceramics division has Mexico's largest distributor network. The international network of distributors adds up to 200, which have established 2,000 points of sale in Mexico, the United

Table 11.1 *Lamosa's main financial information, 2000–15*

	2000	2005	2010	2015
Revenue	296	347	694.6	671.6
Total assets	342	522.4	1,242.6	915.7
EBITDA	57.8	84.1	142.6	135.4
Gross profit	102.8	138.4	257.6	273.2
Net profit	21.6	46.9	39.8	44.3
Foreign investment	N/A	N/A	N/A	N/A
Exports	25.6	56.3	96.5	69.3
Employees	N/A	N/A	N/A	4,700
Countries	N/A	N/A	N/A	18

Data in millions of US dollars
N/A = not available
Source: Authors with data from Bloomberg, Expansion and
Company's Report

States, Canada, and 15 countries in Central and South America. The Adhesives division covers more than 5,000 points of sale. Lamosa's most important market is in Mexico, which accounts for 80 percent of its sales. Together, the employees of Grupo Lamosa amounted to 5,521 people (Lamosa, 2014).

As shown in Table 11.1, the company has experienced significant growth in revenues in recent years. This growth is reflected in other indicators of the company. Although exports declined in 2015 compared with 2010, the future is optimistic for two reasons. First, the internal market will continue to grow in the coming years by the evolution of the demographic pyramid in Mexico. Second, the economic recovery in the United States after the 2008 crisis, because this country is the main destination of Mexican ceramic tile industry exports.

INTERCERAMIC

Interceramic is a company dedicated to the production and marketing of glazed ceramic tiles. It manufactures and distributes ceramic and complementary products such as adhesives and nozzles for ceramic tile installation, bathroom and kitchen furniture, and natural stones.

Interceramic's history, in comparison to Grupo Lamosa, is more recent. In fact, the company was founded in the city of Chihuahua in 1978 and began operations a year later (Interceramic, 2014). However, as in the case of Lamosa, this company was a brick factory that was founded in 1959 (Alba, 2000). This factory, owned mainly by the Almeida family, was called Ladrillera Industrial. Interceramic was constituted from Ladrillera Industrial's capital and other Almeida family companies. These companies included Inmobiliaria Chihuahuense, Bodegas Modernas, Inmuebles Aldama, Impulsora Independencia, and Fomento Portales y Promotora Norteña (Alba, 2000).

The origin of Ladrillera Industrial fits in the projection of Chihuahua as an industrial hub derived from the new post-revolutionary economic elite brought together by Eloy Vallina S. Garcia, a businessman of Asturian origin. Vallina's initiative in 1933 founded Banco Comercial Mexicano, which years later would reach a national projection. This bank became the lever for the state's industrial development, thanks to the capital it provided, as well as to the network of entrepreneurs who formed around this project important companies such as Cementos Chihuahua, Aceros Chihuahua, Celulosa Chihuahua, and Plywood Ponderosa de Mexico. In this context, Ladrillera Industrial arose. Eloy Vallina S. Garcia, who had only 12.5 percent of the capital, served as the first company's President (Alba, 2000).

The transformation of this company from brick to tile manufacture was the result of a trip to Italy by its founder, Óscar Almeida Chabre. There, he discovered the possibilities of expansion in the Mexican market of ceramic tiles as a decorative element in construction, so he decided to establish the new company. Once in Mexico, the project was established and the first two ovens and an entire factory were bought to make very hard floors (MexMedia, 2012). Originally, the company was founded as Sociedad Anónima de Capital Variable (an equivalent of a limited liability company) and in 1987 it became a public company (Interceramic, 2014).

Since its inception, the company adopted technology to differentiate itself from its competitors. Its first production plant used an Italian single-fired production process, thus becoming the first manufacturer in North America to adopt this technology. "We were the first producer in all of North America that brought this new technology for floors in 1977 and 1978; production started in May '79," said Victor Almeida, a descendant of the company's founder, in an interview (MexMedia, 2012). Since its introduction, this technology has shown that it allows shorter cooking time and less use of energy, thus allowing the manufacture of high-quality products at lower costs (Puertas, 1971).

Ten years after its foundation, the company opened a second manufacturing plant that originally operated under a scheme of a joint venture with the American company Armstrong World Industries, Inc. (Interceramic, 2014). Currently, Interceramic distributes and sells its products in Mexico, the United States, Panama, and Guatemala. In addition, it participates in the Chinese market through a joint venture with one of the leading producers of ceramics in that country, Guangdong Kito Ceramics Co., Ltd. The distribution and marketing of its products in Mexico is done through 257 stores (Interceramic, 2014).

As shown in Table 11.2, in comparison with Lamosa, Interceramic is a company that is undiversified in exports; but this situation has not prevented its profits from growing. Although exports have not reached the highest figure from 2005, they are stable.

In the United States, Interceramic has different distribution channels which are: i) the network of 14 stores called "Interceramic Tile & Stone Gallery," ii) a network of more than 50 independent distributors who distribute their products in locations not covered by their own stores, iii) two stores of "Interceramic Marble Collection," distributor of marble, granite, and other products of natural stone, and iv) "Lowe's" stores, which sell Interceramic products in the more than 1,500 points of sale that this wholesaler currently has in the country. In Central America, there are two stores in the countries of Panama and Guatemala, markets in which Interceramic

Table 11.2 *Interceramic: general data*

	2000	2005	2010	2015
Revenue	N/A	409	442	542
Total assets	N/A	401	349.5	420
EBITDA	2.5	53.6	43.6	42.4
Gross profit	N/A	30.44	20.46	30.7
Net profit	N/A	28.7	6.9	8.1
Foreign investment	N/A	0	20.6	0
Exports	121.1	175.5	154.4	163.3
Employees	N/A	N/A	3,900	4,500
Countries	2	2	3	3

Data in millions of US dollars

N/A = not available

Source: Authors with data from Bloomberg, Expansion and
Company's Report

started operations in early 2008. In China, there is a significant number of local businessmen who are exclusive distributors of "ICC," the
brand name that distributes their products in that country
(Interceramic, 2014).

During the internationalization process of Interceramic,
a significant variation compared with other multinational
Mexican companies has been the transformation of its operations
in China. The reason Interceramic has sought to expand into that
market is due both to the level of construction in China and the
lack of innovation in product distribution and marketing. As such,
Interceramic began an ambitious project of franchises in that country that started with 22 stores in 2011. The General Director and
President of the Board of Directors, Victor Almeida, considers it
essential to benefit from the Mexican experience. "Through ICC,
Interceramic China, has created a national franchise system in that
country, which is very similar to that operated in Mexico, and in
the city of Foshan, we already have a three thousand square meter

Table 11.3 *Main domestic and international events of Lamosa and Interceramic*

Lamosa		Interceramic	
Year	Event	Year	Event
1890	The company was established as Compañía Ladrillera de Monterrey	1959	A brick factory was established as antecedent of Interceramic
1929	Restructuring of the company	1978	The company was founded in the city of Chihuahua
1932	Replacement of firewood with natural gas imported from the South of Texas was an important technological innovation	1979	Interceramic implements an Italian single-fired production process, thus becoming the first manufacturer in North America to adopt this technology
1933	Manufacturing of ceramic tiles begins as a new line of business	1980	Interceramic opens its first plant in the USA, in Tulsa, Oklahoma
1957	First manufacturer of cement-based ceramic adhesives	1989	Interceramic opens a second manufacturing plant that originally operated as a joint venture with Armstrong World Industries, Inc.
1963	The company began the production of toilets and bathroom furniture	1997	Interceramic opens a 240,000 square foot warehouse facility and training center
1984	First incursions in the Real Estate business	2008	Interceramic sells in Panama and Guatemala
1995	Ladrillera Monterrey changes its name to Grupo Lamosa, SA de CV	2010	The company announces Interceramic China and expands its business in Asia in 2010 through a joint venture with Guangdong Kito Ceramics Co., Ltd
1998	Lamosa continues its expansion, incorporating Adhesivos de Jalisco		

Table 11.3 (*cont.*)

Lamosa		Interceramic	
Year	Event	Year	Event
1999	Opening of a new adhesive plant, Hidalgo, Mexico		
2002	Acquisition of Industrias Niasa, to expand its Adhesives Business		
2004	Opening of a new wall tile plant to enhance the company's market share in the luxury segment		
2007	Acquisition of Porcelanite, to become one of the largest producers of ceramic tiles in the world		
2015	Grupo Lamosa sells its sanitary ware business to the Colombian company Corona to focus on its Ceramic Tile and Adhesives businesses in Mexico and abroad		
2016	Grupo Lamosa buys Ceramica San Lorenzo, strengthening its presence in South America. The acquisition allows the company to increase its ceramic tile production capacity by 40%, through plants and distribution centers in Argentina, Chile, Colombia, and Peru.		

Source: Elaboration of author with sources of the companies

ceramic center, half of the space for display," (Vanguardia, 2010). Previously in China, Interceramic had been in their market for six years through an outsourcing system, producing floors and tiles, supplying ceramic floor tiles, mosaic glass, and natural stone to be sold in Mexico and the United States. But, in the words of its General Director, "seeing the local market, which is the second largest economy worldwide, and seeing the level of construction, which is truly impressive, and observing there are very little marketing and very little perception of the product, we decided to launch there this same innovative model we have in Mexico," (Vanguardia, 2010).

CONCLUSIONS

To understand the internationalization processes of Mexican companies, an important element to consider is the geographical environment. The regions are essential components in the process of internationalization and innovation (Scott, 1998). This is the case of the two companies selected for this case study: Lamosa and Interceramic. The origin of these companies is in two border states of Mexico: Nuevo Leon and Chihuahua. Similarly, many other companies in the north of Mexico, including the first generation of the more powerful industries like Cemex, Cervecería Cuauhtémoc Fundidora de Fierro y Acero Monterrey, Lamosa, and Interceramic, have built a strong practice of internationalization, since they were established, as an element of their identity.

Indeed, these businessmen regard themselves as different from the rest of the business community of other Mexican regions. A collective imaginary has been generated about businessmen who come from the north as being people from the borders, characterized by the entrepreneurial spirit and Government autonomy to do business, or even to do it in spite of the Government. This entrepreneurial community, in the collective imagination, supposedly found in the challenges of internationalization a way of differentiating itself from other business groups in Mexico. This is an entrepreneur with a discernable regional culture that constitutes business elite in the region to finally be part of the elite of elites nationwide (Hernández, 2004).

Business groups from the north of Mexico have created a common speech to legitimize the existence of its members as actors in a continued economic growth and as architects of the local modernity. As Rivére (1998) has cautioned, two elements stand out of this discourse: the anticenter purpose of Mexico City and the adversity discourse, which by strengthening their will places these companies in the most competitive field. Historically, they have fostered a regionalism that in their own eyes makes them seem as pioneers, innovators: aggressive and competitive (Vázquez, 2004). In this sense, internationalization is part of a broader universe, which combines competitiveness, innovation, and differentiation, in which regional identity plays a fundamental role.

While it is true that both companies were not founded in the same period, their proximity to the US market was an incentive to start the internationalization processes early in the life of each company. The two companies began as brick factories and evolved into the development of higher added value products and innovation in production processes, both for the design of products and distribution channels. In particular, the distribution channels have had a substantive role in the companies' search to expand their markets. The two companies have opened their outlets directly in different models of customer service for their products, as well as to establish meaningful partnerships abroad with large wholesalers that facilitate the placement of their products.

In this logic of creating value from innovation, internationalization is inscribed. Through the experiences of internationalization in the US market, we have explored their presence and participation in other markets. Like other Mexican companies that have been analyzed in the chapters of this book, it can be said that the *natural* area of internationalization is Latin America, derived not only from the geographic proximity of some countries, but above all from a cultural and linguistic closeness that favors interaction in these countries.

However, this proximity to Latin America has not limited the possibilities for other markets. In fact, the size of revenues shows for both companies that to enter the US proved relevant, not only due to its geographical proximity but also because it is the main importer globally of this type of decorative element. The case of Interceramic is particularly significant, as it has sought a presence in China, given the growing demand in the Chinese market. Here, the novelty of Interceramic's presence in China has been taking the franchise model developed in Mexico to China where the store's display is a fundamental component for sales.

The internationalization problems faced by companies are linked to the macroeconomic environment. Like other sectors and other multinationals from emerging economies, the larger the link is to the exterior, the more the fluctuations of international markets affect their operation and profit. The case is particularly significant when it comes to the hiring of debt in dollars, whose fluctuation negatively affects the performance of the companies.

However, in both cases a continuous domestic demand is the main engine of both companies. The landscape of the construction industry in Mexico looks positive for the next few years, in spite of Mexico's reduced and non-encouraging growth when compared with the expectations generated by the economic reforms and the proximity to the US market. In this sense, the size of the Mexican market and its growth projection for the next decade have increased the importance of national activities for both companies. This is so, even when there is a stiff national competition in the ceramic tile market, as well as the arrival of foreign products, mainly Chinese and Brazilian, as well as Spanish and Italian.

The experience of these companies shows that the possibility of access to capital and to make major investments have been an essential element for their internationalization. The two companies traded on the Mexican Stock Exchange (Bolsa Mexicana de Valores) as an option for their financing. With this legal status, companies have resorted to heavy loans with the intention of consolidating their productive activities. An example of this situation is the purchase of Porcelanite by Lamosa to expand its presence in the Mexican market and thus leverage its internationalization. These opportunities for accessing resources generate different options to venture into the international market and compete in a growing but highly segmented industry.

It is in this segmentation that the small and medium enterprises can transfer some of the significant experiences which can be used to obtain an important differentiation for their development and consolidation. Specifically, these experiences can be reduced to three major elements. First, find a regional vocation from the internal dynamics of each region. Second, find in innovation the key to differentiation; innovation may include processes, products, and distribution channels. Third, consider internationalization as a complement to the activities of the national market. Both the experience of Lamosa and Interceramic prove that only with a solid national base can the internationalization activities be guaranteed as a complement. The construction industry's expectations in Mexico will allow continuous growth and consolidation in the domestic market and, as a complement, the international markets.

Lastly, it is noteworthy that a complementary element that explains the motivations for the internationalization processes of these companies is a cultural factor derived from the creation of a distinct and differentiated identity for northern Mexican businessmen. This identity is framed not only in a geographical but also in a cultural context. The internationalization of these companies can be explained from the social-historical context that formed a distinctive identity of Monterrey's business groups. Gauss (2010) noticed that, similar to Colombia's *antioquians* and Brazil's *paulistanos*, the business groups from the north of Mexico advanced on their company's vision by means of establishing an identity for themselves. This process is not specific to Latin America since, for example, when Chinese entrepreneurs need to adapt to new economic environments, they increase through representation and discourse the exaltation and updating of socio-cultural, territorial, and spatial identity traits that may contribute to maintaining their international competitiveness (Paix, 1998).

In the case of northern Mexican entrepreneurs, this identity drew on their particular vision of economic development and industrial growth that had its roots in distinctive regional relations. The owners of the business groups formed powerful networks that integrated industrial production shaped vertically and horizontally, building on ties of kinship, marriage, and joint investment. These networks allowed the identity of the northern Mexican entrepreneur to be rewritten as an individual willing to challenge the corporate and State development of the industry-based economic model. In this way, they proclaimed themselves as guarantors of growth from a private origin and, therefore, advocates of what they considered should be the Mexican economy.

REFERENCES

Abshire, R. 2009. *Garland: A Contemporary History*. San Antonio: Garland Chamber of Commerce.

Alba, C. 2000. *Historia regional de Chihuahua: Perfil socioeconómico*. México, D.F.: LIMUSA, CONALEP y SEP.

Banco de México. 2015. Reporte sobre las economías regionales. Octubre-Diciembre 2014. *Banxico*. www.banxico.org.mx/publicaciones-y-discursos/pub licaciones/informes-periodicos/reportes-sobre-las-economias-regionales/%7BF E0349BD-B3E7-40D0-2CB1-4F41F319933F%7D.pdf. Accessed April 2, 2015.

Bolsa Mexicana de Valores. 2015. Empresas emisoras: Lamosa. *BMV*. www.bmv .com.mx/. Accessed March 29, 2015.

Cárdenas, E. 2012. De la economía mexicana en el dilatado siglo XX, 1929–2010, in Sandra Kuntz (Ed.), *Historia Mínima de la Economía Mexicana, 1519–2010*: 232–302. México, D.F.: El Colegio de México.

Dussel, E. 2003. La polarización de la economía mexicana: aspectos económicos y regionales, in John Bailey (Ed.), *Impactos del TLC en México y Estados Unidos: efectos subregionales del comercio y la integración económica*: 41–68. México, D.F.: FLACSO-Miguel Ángel Porrúa.

Hansen, R. 2004. *La política del desarrollo mexicano.* México, D.F.: Siglo Veintiuno Editores.

Hernández, M. 2004. *La cultura empresarial en México.* México, D.F.: Universidad Autónoma de Aguascalientes.

Hernández, I. 2013. Sector report: Ceramics sector Mexico. *UK Trade and Investment.* www.google.com.mx/url?sa=t&rct=j&q=&esrc=s&source=web& cd=1&ved=0CBwQFjAA&url=https%3A%2F%2Fs3.amazonaws.com%2FSta gingContentBucket%2Fpdf%2F20100917104751.pdf&ei=ok06VZbgIYSEsAW cw4GABQ&usg=AFQjCNE5j1MecdB2y49ZcuE6kKSM1YpuPw&bvm=b v.91427555,d.b2. Accessed November 3, 2014.

Herrera, E. 2014. Grupo Lamosa vende su negocio de sanitarios. Corona, una empresa colombiana, adquirió el 100% de sus acciones. *Milenio.* www.milenio .com/monterrey/Grupo_Lamosa_vende_negocios_sanitarios-Lamosa_sanitar ios-Lamosa_Corona_0_430157015.html. Accessed January 17, 2015.

Gauss, S. M. 2010. *Made in Mexico: Regions, Nation, and the State in the Rise of Mexican Industrialism, 1920s-1940s.* University Park, PA: Pennsylvania State University.

Interceramic. 2014. Informe anual 2013. *Interceramic.* www.interceramicusa.com/ uploads/investors/Bmv2013.pdf. Accessed December 12, 2014.

Lamosa. 2014. Informe anual 2013. *Lamosa.* www.lamosa.com/docs/annualre ports/Lamosa-AnnualReport_2013sp.pdf. Accessed December 8, 2014.

Macías, G. 2011. Religión y cultura: elementos potenciales del desarrollo económico, el caso de Tepeaca de Negrete en Puebla, in Rogelio Martínez (Coordinador), *Turismo espiritual: una alternativa para el desarrollo de las poblaciones:* 50–58. Guadalajara: Universidad de Guadalajara y COECYTJAL.

MexMedia Group. 2012. Victor Almeida: Empresario del año. *Empresarios AEM.* www.empresariosaem.com/2012/11/victor-almeida-empresario-del-ano/. Accessed March 29, 2015.

Paix, C. 1998. Identidad espacial y redes de empresarios en la recomposición de los espacios asiáticos. El caso de Taiwán y Sinagpur, in Carlos Alba, Iván Bizberg & Helén Rivére (Eds.), *Las regiones ante la globalización:* 347–387. México, D.F.: El Colegio de México.

Prognosis. 2014. Lamosa: Preparada para reanudar el crecimiento. *BMV.* www.bmv .com.mx/indcobr/indcobr_567673_1.pdf. Accessed January, 29 2015.

Puertas, F. 1971. Monococción y cocción rápida para la fabricación de pavimentos cerámicos. *Boletín de la sociedad española de cerámica y vidrio,* 17 (2): 63–71. http://boletines.secv.es/upload/197716063.pdf. Accessed November 20, 2014.

Rivére, H. 1998. Elaboración de una nueva configuración regional, simbólica y real, por parte de los empresarios locales del Norte de México, in Carlos Alba,

Iván Bizberg & Helén Rivére (Eds.), *Las Regiones ante la globalización*: 23–43. México, D.F.: El Colegio de México.

Rojas, J. 2009. *El Patrimonio histórico industrial de Nuevo León: Las fábricas pioneras*, vol. 1. Monterrey: CECYTE-CAEIP.

Ruíz, P. & Moreno-Brid, J. 2006. Efectos macroeconómicos de la apertura y el TLCAN, in Monica C. Gambrill (Ed.), *Diez años del TLCAN en México*: 19–33. México, D.F.: UNAM-CISAN.

Saragoza, A. 1990. *The Monterrey Elite and the Mexican State, 1880–1940*. Austin, TX: University of Texas Press.

Scott, A. 1998. Fundamentos geográficos del comportamiento industrial, in Carlos Alba, Iván Bizberg & Helén Rivére (Eds.), *Las regiones ante la globalización*: 23–43. México, D.F.: El Colegio de México.

Seijas, T. 2014. *Asian Slaves in Colonial Mexico: From Chinos to Indians*. New York, NY: Cambridge University Press.

Soler, M. 2003. The Use of Spanish Ceramics in Architecture, in Robin Gavin, Donna Pierce & Alfonso Pleguezuelo (Eds.), *The Story of Spanish and Mexican Mayólica*: 77–102. Santa Fe, NM: International Folk Art Foundation.

Stock, D. 2014. World Production and Consumption of Ceramic Tile. *Infotile*. www .infotile.com/pdfFile/Product/ProductFile/212201414050.pdf. Accessed October 24, 2014.

Vanguardia. 2010. Intentarán recubrir el mundo: Tiene Interceramic la mira en China. *Vanguardia*. www.vanguardia.com.mx/intentaranrecubrir%60elmundo tieneintercseramicachina%60enlamira-605915.html. Accessed February 22, 2015.

Vázquez, M. 2004. Grupos económicos en el Norte de México. *Problemas de desarrollo: Revista Latinoamérica de Economía*, 35(137): 96–115.

Vizcaya, I. 2006. *Los orígenes de la industrialización de Monterrey: una historia económica y social desde la caída del Segundo Imperio hasta el fin de la Revolución (1867–1920)*. Monterrey, N.L.: Fondo Editorial de Nuevo León-ITESM.

12 MultiMexicans in the Containers and Packaging Industry

Vitro and Envases Universales

Jose F. Moreno

INTRODUCTION

This chapter describes the history and current situation of two MultiMexicans in the containers and packaging industry. The two companies are: Vitro (producer of glass containers), and Envases Universales (producer of metal containers). They started as family businesses, and they found the key to success in their own sector. This key allows them to expand their business not only in Mexico, but also out of their home country. As with other businesses in Mexico, Vitro and Envases Universales have suffered economic shocks, radical technology changes in their sector, and internal problems created by the normal business cycle. This chapter is divided in the following sections: an introduction to the containers and packaging industry in Mexico; a history and current situation report about these multinationals; and a conclusion that summarizes the lessons learned from these two successful corporations.

THE CONTAINERS AND PACKAGING INDUSTRY IN MEXICO

The use and production of containers and packaging is an activity as old as bartering and trading. Mankind has always been looking for better ways to transport and protect products. The use of baskets, bowls, and bags created with different materials is part of human history. This activity has grown enough to be considered one of the most important industries in the materials sector. The containers and packaging industry is always in constant development, looking for the lightest, most flexible, and most resilient packaging for products.

The containers and packaging industry within the materials sector includes manufacturers of metal, wood, glass, or plastic containers, and manufacturers of paper and cardboard containers and packaging. The global market for this industry comprises products manufactured for packaging purposes that are used by numerous end users including the food, beverage, healthcare, toiletries, and personal care sectors, and other industrial product manufacturing companies.

Just in 2014, the growth of this industry in Mexico was 4 percent, which is approximately equivalent to US$14,500 million (Enfasis Packaging, 2014). The production of this industry represents 1.7 percent of the Mexican GDP, which makes it a fundamental activity in the materials sector of this country. It is very interesting to notice that plastic containers have grown exponentially, followed by metal and glass containers. The latest Research and Markets report mentions an expected growth of 6.87 percent in the global containers and packaging market, over the period 2014–19 (PR Newswire, 2014). These numbers confirm that this industry has been growing strongly and consistently, and it is expected to continue in the same trend.

The containers and packaging industry is very versatile in terms of application. Its global market can be segmented into the following: food packaging, beverage packaging, healthcare products packaging, industrial packaging, and others, including personal and homecare products packaging. In Mexico, food and beverage packaging alone represents 55 percent of the whole containers and packaging market (Notimex, 2015).

As with other production industries in Mexico, the containers and packaging industry is in constant change due to new trends and challenges that are created by markets and consumers (locally and internationally). The main challenges for MultiMexicans in this industry are: (1) the fast evolution of packaging products, and the main competition against plastic products; (2) containers and packages are one of the main sources of pollution in the world (Losada, 2000), which requires these companies to dedicate a big part of their budgets to help the environment; and (3) Mexican companies have problems selling their products in foreign markets because the lack of education among company owners about containers and packaging norms and regulation in foreign countries (Castillo Zavala, Trejo Gil & Muñoz Brandi, 2013).

It is no surprise that food and beverage packaging is the most important branch of this industry. In the last two decades, one of the main factors driving the growth of the containers and packaging industry has been the increase in consumer preference for processed and packaged foods. Migration to urban centers, growth of the middle class, and common dual-income working households have caused a lack of time to cook at home (Lingle, 2014). Therefore, there has been an increase in purchase of grocery items, including frozen and chilled foods from retail stores. This consumer adjustment is a global trend, but its impact is more visible in developing countries such as India, China, and South America.

As endorsement of this global trend, the largest and most relevant multinational companies of the containers and packaging industry in Mexico are in the segment of food and beverage packaging production. Plastic and metal are the most common materials used to produce food containers, while glass is for beverage containers. This chapter studies two MultiMexicans that are heavily dedicated to the transformation of raw materials into food and beverage packaging products. As in other industries, after NAFTA, international firms acquired several Mexican container companies. However, Vitro and Envases Universales not only kept their Mexican origins but also became product leaders and multinational corporations.

The first MultiMexican presented in this chapter is Vitro, which is considered the leader in glass production in Mexico and one of the most important corporations around the world. The second multinational presented is Envases Universales Group, which is a leading manufacturer of rigid packaging solutions and is focused on the manufacture of steel and aluminum cans and plastic packaging for beverages, food, and other products. Although the two companies are not in direct competition due to their focus on dissimilar production materials (Vitro specializes in glass and Envases Universales specializes in aluminum and plastics), this chapter shows that these companies' performance is affected not only by the same global trends and market conditions, but also by traditions and culture strongly related to the way "family business" is done in Mexico.

VITRO

Vitro, SAB de CV (BMV: VITROA) is the leading producer of glass in Mexico, with over 100 years of experience in the containers and packaging industry. It was founded in 1909 in Monterrey, Mexico. Until 2014, this corporation had subsidiaries in Bolivia, Brazil, Colombia, Costa Rica, Guatemala, Panama, and the USA. Their products are sold in 34 countries between the Americas, Europe, and Asia. Table 12.1 provides the financials and Table 12.2 summarizes the history of the firm.

Table 12.1 *Financials of Vitro, 2000–15*

	Vitro 2000	2005	2010	2015
Revenue	2,961.7	2,218.1	1,591.1	892
Total assets	3,355.2	2,834.4	2,496.1	2,294.5
EBITDA	571.3	304.7	228.7	191.4
Gross profit	359	148.3	116.3	142.5
Net profit	35.8	4.4	–94.9	1,490.2
Foreign investment	N/A	N/A	N/A	N/A
Exports	789.2	648.9	N/A	261.1
Employees	N/A	N/A	N/A	N/A
Countries	4	6	8	8

Data in millions of US dollars
N/A = not available
Source: Authors with data from Bloomberg, Expansion and Company's Report

Table 12.2 *Timeline of Vitro, 1909–2011*

	Key Events	
Year	Domestic	International
1909	On December 6th Vidriera Monterrey is founded for the purpose of satisfying the demand for glass containers from the beer industry in Mexico.	
1918	Vidriera Monterrey begins to generate profit shortly after it became necessary to expand its small installations and increase production.	
1923	The installations are expanded and reach a capacity of 150 thousand glass bottles daily in order to supply glass containers to other liquor, medicine, and food industries.	
1934	A new subsidiary is established: Vidriera Mexico, SA in Mexico's capital city to supply the growing demand for glass containers in central Mexico.	
1935		The company begins to export glass bottles, crystal products, and flat glass to Guatemala, El Salvador, Honduras, Nicaragua, Costa Rica, and Panama.
1936	One of the first three corporate companies is established in Monterrey, Fomento de Industria y Comercio (FIC), to administer the company's operating units.	

Table 12.2 (*cont.*)

	Key Events	
Year	Domestic	International
1944	Vidriera los Reyes, in the state of Mexico, is founded in order to supply glass containers to meet the internal and international market demands.	
1950		FAMA begins to export machinery, glass container conveyers, and molds to Uruguay, Australia, and West Germany.
1951	In order to meet glass container demand in the central and western part of Mexico, Vidriera Guadalajara is incorporated into the corporation.	
1956	Float glass undertakes the acquisition of the first float glass furnace in Mexico and Latin America.	
1964		Associating itself with an important beer and soft drink bottler in Central America, the company strengthens its regional position by establishing manufacturing plants in Costa Rica and Guatemala.
1968	Vidrio Plano de México SA brings on line its first float glass line with the help and technical assistance of Pilkington Brothers Limited.	
1976	FIC becomes a publicly traded company by issuing shares and	

Table 12.2 (*cont.*)

	Key Events	
Year	Domestic	International
	registering on the Mexican Stock Exchange.	
1979	FIC changes its name to Vitro SA. Vitro Flex SA is formed to manufacture automotive glass.	
1985		The beginnings of what is known today as Vitro Packaging is created, with its headquarters in Plano, Texas, north of Dallas, to distribute glass containers in the USA.
1991	Vitro Flotado SA concludes the construction of its second furnace in García, Nuevo León to meet the national and international market demands.	
1992		Vitro acquires ACI America (today Vitro America), increasing its presence in the flat glass market in the USA with more than 200 points of sale in the country.
1995		Vitro acquires Vidrio Lux, the largest glass container manufacturer in Bolivia.
1996		Vitro acquires 51 percent of Vidrios Templados Colombianos (Vitemco) to create Vitro Colombia, a facility dedicated to process laminated and tempered glass for the automotive industry as well as the construction industry.

Table 12.2 *(cont.)*

	Key Events	
Year	Domestic	International
1998	Vitro SA changes its name to Vitro SA de CV.	
2001		Vitro Cristal glass is created after acquiring 60 percent of the shares of Cristalglass Vidrio Aislante SA, a holding company of the Spanish group Cristalglass, covering the architectural market in Europe.
2002	Vitro and AFG Industries establish a strategic alliance to produce float glass in Mexicali, Northern Baja California.	Vitro Chaves, a business unit in Portugal also servicing the architectural market, joins the regional effort.
2006	The company takes total control of Vitro Flex upon the conclusion of Vitro's strategic alliance with Visteon, and acquires 100 percent of the shares.	Vitro, together with its partners in Central America, acquires most of the shares of the market leader in Panama that is focused on the manufacture of glass containers.
2007	Vitro acquires all the shares of the Mexican company then called Vitro AFG, located in Mexicali. Vitro Cristalglass, Vitro's subsidiary in Europe, brings on line its new furnace with the capacity to temper and thermally harden large-dimension glass laminate. The first furnace of Vitro Cosmos is fired up, a plant located in the Industrial Valley of Toluca, for the manufacture of glass containers for cosmetics,	

Table 12.2 (cont.)

	Key Events	
Year	Domestic	International
	fragrances, toiletries, and pharmaceutical products.	
2008	Vitro Cristalglass brings on line its new production line for laminated and safety glass by increasing its flat glass conversion capacity.	
2015		Vitro sells the whole division of glass bottles as part of its financial restructuring, and keeps the division of glass for construction, auto parts, and other glass containers.

Source: Vitro's website (www.vitro.com/en/our-company/history)

Vitro has two main types of business: glass containers and flat glass. Between these two business types, this company provides solutions for multiple markets, including food, beverage, wine, cosmetics, pharmaceutical, automotive, and construction. This company is also a provider of raw material, machinery, and equipment for industrial use. Canales Santos (2002) explains that one of the main reasons for Vitro's success is its constant investment in research and development. Innovation in machinery and equipment that facilitates the production and processing of glass has pushed Vitro up, separating it from its competitors.

Like other corporations, Vitro has experienced periods of expansion and recession. However, these periods have not always been caused by the economic and industrial cycle, but also by changes in administration and vision inside the company. Although Vitro is a multinational corporation, it could still be considered a family business. Since Vitro's foundation, the Sada family has been an important component of its leadership. Roberto Sada Garcia founded and led Vitro for several decades. Since its creation, Vitro was focused on the production of glass bottles to fulfill the requirements of Cervecería Cuauhtémoc (later FEMSA) that was led by relatives from the Garza Sada branch of the family. The business of both companies (FEMSA and Vitro) grew not only in Mexico, but also in North America and Latin America. During Roberto Sada's leadership, Vitro began the period of internationalization doing business and acquiring subsidiaries in Central and South America. Vitro also exported machinery to produce glass bottles to Europe and Asia. This is an example of how Vitro was focused not only on production, but also on innovation.

In 1972, Adrian Sada Trevino (son of Roberto Sada Garcia) took control of Vitro and made it a public company as part of the strategy to consolidate it as one of the most important companies in Mexico. During Sada Trevino's leadership, innovation in equipment and diversification in new markets were cornerstones in the growth of Vitro. Developing new glass products would help Vitro to reduce its dependence on the single business of glass bottles. In 1991, Adrian Sada Gonzalez and Fernando Sada Gonzalez (sons of Sada Trevino) were assigned as President of Board of Directors and CEO, respectively. While Sada Gonzalez's brothers were in control of Vitro, a lot of international acquisitions were made in businesses related to the industry of glass. These acquisitions were mainly in South America and the United States. However, this disproportionate expansion would require a huge amount of cash flow that Vitro didn't have. For that reason, during the privatization of the Mexican banking system in 1992, Sada's family bought Banco Serfin (acquired in 2000 by Grupo Financiero Santander).[1] For several years, Adrian Sada Gonzalez was the head of both Vitro and Serfin.

A major problem arose for Vitro when, in 1995, once Carlos Salinas de Gortari had vacated the presidential chair, a currency crisis

---

[1] Similarly, the Garza Sada Family acquired Bancomer to support the growth of FEMSA.

couldn't be avoided and the Mexican peso experienced huge devaluation. This event left Vitro with vast amounts of debt that could be paid only by selling several parts of the company. Since then, Vitro has survived various cuts to its previous expansion, up to the most recent sale to Owens-Illinois in 2015. Now, with Adrian Sada Cueva (son of Adrian Sada Gonzalez) as the CEO, Vitro is looking to surge again, now focusing its efforts in different markets from the ones in which the company originated in 1902.

It is important to note the expansion of Vitro's presence around the world during the period analyzed. Also, it can be observed that Vitro has been decreasing in revenue and size during the same period. However, its profit is currently reversing the negative trend after a difficult period caused partially by external factors, such as the USA, and also caused by internal factors, such as leadership transition and a high level of debt.

Currently, Vitro is in the process of completing a restructuring of its debts, leaving it with a more clear and positive vision of its future. In 2015, Adrian Sada Cueva announced that Vitro had sold its food and beverages packaging business to Owens-Illinois, which included five factories in Mexico, the operation in Bolivia, and distribution of products in the USA (Herrera, 2015). After this deal, Vitro is focusing most of its business on being a supplier of glass to the automotive, construction, and cosmetics industries. It is important to mention that Vitro's 2015 first quarterly sales were US$289 million just in food and beverage packaging alone.[2] This amount represents 70 percent of Vitro's total sales.

ENVASES UNIVERSALES DE MEXICO

Mr. Isaias Zapata Guerra and his son, Isaías Zapata Oscoz, founded this company in 1993 under the name of Zapata Envases SA de CV. It was created to satisfy packaging needs in the food, paint, and chemical markets. In 1997, Zapata Envases expanded its product line by adding

[2]   These sales are from the first quarter of 2015.

PET packages specifically for the beverage market. In 2004, Zapata Envases merged with Envases Universales de México SA de CV, creating the Envases Universales Group. There are no financials available on the firm. Table 12.3 provides the summary of the history of the firm.

Currently, the Envases Universales Group comprises 45 plants, five distribution centers, and three sales offices. The group possesses strategically distributed locations in Mexico, Guatemala, Colombia, the USA, Scandinavia, China, and Korea. In 2007, Envases Universales and Rexam created a joint venture in Guatemala to create a facility that is dedicated to making 12 oz. beverage cans. This facility has received several quality awards (PR Newswire, 2015). Quality and innovation have been the two keys to success for Envases Universales, and the company dedicates a large amount of resources to test its packages in state-of-the-art testing labs. As part of the innovations, Envases Universales produces food and beverage packages that are also attractive to the final consumer. Envases Universales has its own design department that works very closely with its clients, in order to advise and support food and beverage producers in making their products eye-catching.

In addition to quality and innovation, location and production capacity are important concerns for Envases Universales. They promise to deliver to their clients a high-quality package on time. For that reason, their plants are located close to their main clients. Mazatlan's plant is an example of this strategy because it supplies packaging services to local tuna fish and vegetable producers. Also, their flexible production lines allow them to produce whatever their clients require in a very short time.

All this success in Envases Universales is linked to the experience and knowledge of the Zapata family. The Zapata family has been doing business in the containers and packaging industry since 1926. Mr. Cayo Zapata Molinero, who founded what is now Grupo Zapata, introduced the metal cap for glass bottles known as the "tapon corona." Grupo Zapata grew and expanded not only in Mexico, but also in

Table 12.3 *Timeline of Envases Universales, 1993–2015*

	Key Events	
Year	Domestic	International
1993	Mr. Isaías Zapata Guerra and his son Isaías Zapata Oscoz founded the company Zapata Envases SA de CV, now called Envases Universales de México, SAPI de CV. This company was established on a 104,000 square meter site in the town of Cuautitlán in the State of Mexico.	
1994	Zapata Envases SA de CV started operating in May 1994, manufacturing plastic containers for the chemical and food industries in Cuautitlán, in the State of Mexico.	
1995	The manufacturing of metal containers for packaging of food products started both at the plant located in Cuautitlán, State of Mexico, as well as at the plant located in Mazatlán, Sinaloa. At the Sinaloa plant, the main production line produces cans for seafood products.	
1998	The expansion of a new industrial group started with the construction of a plant dedicated to the production of PET bottles for the carbonated drinks and water bottling industry.	
2001	The second plant of the PET division was built in December	

Table 12.3 (*cont.*)

	Key Events	
Year	Domestic	International
	2001, located in the city of Apizaco in the State of Tlaxcala next to the facilities of one of the company's main clients. The third plant of the PET division was built in Mazatlán, Sinaloa. This operation was subsequently discontinued at this location.	
2003	The company Envases Universales de México SA de CV was acquired from a group of banks. This company was dedicated to the production of aluminum cans for the carbonated drink, juice, and beer industry, located in the town of El Salto, Jalisco.	
2004	Decided by the Board of Directors, the company Zapata Envases SA de CV merged with the company Envases Universales de México SA de CV, the latter persisting and subsequently modifying its trade name to Envases Universales de México SAPI de CV. With this, the integration of the Industrial Group and the three divisions – Food and General Line, PET, and Aluminum Division – took place.	

Table 12.3 (*cont.*)

	Key Events	
Year	Domestic	International
2004	Also in 2004, the plant for 208-liter drum production and the plant for the production of 19-liter water jugs was built on neighboring land in the same town of Cuautitlán, in the State of Mexico. The tin division from FEMSA was acquired, the company called Compañía Mexicana de Latas, SA de CV, dedicated to the production of metallic containers for the packaging of seafood products, located in Ensenada, Baja California, was subsequently transferred to Mazatlán, Sinaloa.	
2005	The company called Empaques Sewell SA de CV was acquired from the Pepsi Cola system, a company dedicated to the manufacture and sale of PET preforms and bottles.	
2006		The expansion of the group abroad starts with the opening in Guatemala of the company Envases Universales de Centroamérica SA, which would produce and sell aluminum cans for the carbonated drinks, juice, and beer industries. That same year, by decision of the Board of

Table 12.3 (cont.)

	Key Events	
Year	Domestic	International
2007		Directors, the company Empaques Sewell SA de CV and Compañía Mexicana de Latas SA de CV merged into the company Envases Universales de México, SAPI de CV, the latter persisting. A business in participation with the international manufacturer Rexam is formalized in Guatemala, creating a joint venture through the company called Envases Universales de Centroamérica Rexam SA.
2008	The group of companies led by the company called Industrias Innopack SA de CV, located in the town of Salto, Jalisco, was acquired. The group was dedicated to the manufacture and sale of PET preforms and bottles for the carbonated drinks and water bottling industry. This group was the second largest in Mexico in the manufacture of this type of products. With this acquisition, Envases Universales de México SAPI de CV placed itself as one of the two main PET bottle and preform manufacturers in Mexico. Industrias Innopack, SA de CV, had 14 plants geographically distributed in the towns where the main carbonated drink and water bottling companies were located. From that 14 plants acquired, 10 are located in Mexico and 4 in Colombia.	
2011		The Danish company Glud & Marstrand was acquired, one of the main metal container manufacturers in Europe, dedicated to the production of containers for the packaging of food products such as meat,

Table 12.3 (*cont.*)

	Key Events	
Year	Domestic	International
		milk, seafood, cookies, etc. Currently the group has 5,367 employees, with 40 plants and five distribution centers located in Mexico, Guatemala, Colombia, the United States, Denmark, Sweden, South Korea, and China, and from these countries it serves approximately 1,500 clients.
2013		An increasing number of Russian enterprises have chosen to cooperate with Glud & Marstrand. To improve their service and the accessibility to this clientele, a sales office was opened in Moscow.
2015		Envases Universales de Mexico is proud to announce that through one of its subsidiaries and jointly with Rexam, it has completed the acquisition of Envases del Istmo SA (Endelis), a company engaged in manufacturing beverage cans in Colon, Panama. As part of the transaction, a long-term supply agreement has been signed for aluminum cans and ends with SABMiller and Florida Ice & Farm Company SA (FIFCO), from whose subsidiaries the Endelis shares were purchased.

Source: Envases Universales' website (www.envasesuniversales.com/es/node/2498#node/2507|case=2507)

Latin America and Europe. However, in 1990, Grupo Zapata was divided due to some internal problems that also caused some family divisions.

Then, taking the experience and support from some members of their family, Mr. Isaias Zapata Guerra and his son, Mr. Isaias Zapata Oscoz, founded Zapata Envases, which would merge with Envases Universales in 2004. This merger caused a change in their trading name to the current name of Envases Universales de Mexico, erasing with it the obvious connection that existed between Zapata Envases and Grupo Zapata.

Envases Universales began its process of international expansion in 2006 when it opened Envases Universales of Centroamerica in Guatemala. It continues to expand its business in Central America. More recently, in 2011, a Danish company called Glud&Marstrand was acquired, but Envases Universales' directors decided strategically to retain the name of Glud&Marstrand to represent the company in all its current business in Europe.

A final contributor to the success of Envases Universales as a young multinational is the fine work that its financial department has done over the years. Before the merger with Envases Universales, Zapata Envases used debt as a main source of capital, allocating bonds and other types of liabilities in the equity market. This financial strategy has also been fruitful after the merger. Just recently, Standard & Poor's increased their corporate credit rate from MXA– to MXA (Standard & Poor's, 2014). This credit rate confirms Envases Universales' healthy financial situation, even given all its recent expansion and acquisitions. Because of being a private corporation, most data is not available. However, the international expansion is shown based on the number of countries where Envases Universales has current operations.

CONCLUSIONS

Despite the current challenging business environment, Mexico is home to successful containers and packaging production companies that have learned not only to survive but also to lead and expand a whole productive sector. The Asociacion Mexicana de Envases y Embalaje mentioned in its most recent report (AMEE, 2015) that the whole industry is currently using 90 percent of its production capacity, which means that companies in this business need to find novel ways to expand their businesses soon. Companies in this industry, such as Vitro and Envases Universales, are clear examples of how hard work, innovation, and quality will create growth and international expansion in this sector.

It is important to mention that in order to create success in a multinational packaging corporation, quality and innovation are required in all areas of the business: production, sales, research, financials, and management. Most of the companies in this sector are considered capital intensive, and their production processes require state-of-the-art technology. However, in the case of MultiMexicans, an additional area should always be studied carefully because it can make the difference between success and failure: the family relationships inside the business.

Both multinationals discussed in this chapter, Vitro and Envases Universales, have gone through the process of internationalization and expansion. However, their paths to becoming multinational corporations are so different that it is very interesting to study and compare them. Vitro began its internationalization a long time ago, in 1935, while Envases Universales has been considered a multinational since 2006. Both companies began their international expansion by doing business abroad in Central America.

Morales Fajardo (2013), referring also to Basave (2000), explains that some of the main motivations for MultiMexicans to invest and do business in Latin America are: consolidation in markets previously known by exports; diversification of risk; integration of production chains; and taking advantage of investment opportunities that allow them to control specific markets. Vitro and Envases Universales are examples of these globalization strategies.

Also, both companies began their internationalization by exporting their products to several countries, especially in the Americas. Once generating sales in foreign markets, Vitro and Envases Universales began the acquisition of competitors already established in those countries where they had decided to expand. In the case of Vitro, its expansion was gradual but broad, and took several decades, while Envases Universales's expansion has been narrower, but with very strategic phases focusing only in markets they knew well.

It is important to mention that both companies have founded their expansion on their high-quality products and services. However, the main reason for their success overseas cannot only be based on this factor, but also on other internal, and unique, factors that allow them to create opportunities to grow out of their home country. In the case of Vitro, its innovation in the whole glass production process has been a relevant cause of development, while for Envases Universales, its vision and financial health have helped to generate growth.

Mexico is full of cases of family businesses. However, MultiMexicans that could still be called family business are included. The two companies mentioned in this chapter showed that is difficult to create success in business and keep strong family relations at the same time. In the case of Vitro, we see how connections and relations are not the main source of its success, but the innovation in glass production and the creation of human capital; or in the case of Envases Universales, where business knowledge passed from generation to generation, this was not enough to create expansion overseas, but the quality of services and products offered was the primary factor. Next, a brief profile and history of these two companies was presented to help the reader to understand the current situation and challenges of these multinationals.

REFERENCES

Asociacion Mexicana de Envases y Embalaje (AMEE). 2015. Anuario Estadístico 2015. Chapters 3 and 6. pp. 21–50.

Basave, K. J. 2000. *Empresas Mexicanas ante la globalización*. México: Porrua.

Canales Santos, E. 2002. Historia Parcial de Vitro. *Ingenierías*. Enero-Marzo 2002, Vol. V, No. 14. pp. 25–29.

Castillo Zavala, A., Trejo Gil, C. O. & Muñoz Brandi, V. M. 2013. *Envase y Embalaje: A Través de la Historia*. Observatorio de la Economía Latinoamericana, No. 185. México.

Enfasis Packaging. 2014. La Industria de envase y embalaje en México. *Enfasis Packaging*. February 2014. www.packaging.enfasis.com/articulos/68958-la-industria-envase-y-embalaje-mexico. Accessed July 23, 2016.

Herrera, E. 2015. *Venta de Vitro la hace mas solida, afirma Sada Cueva*. Monterrey. *Milenio*. May 2015. www.milenio.com/monterrey/venta_vitro-Owens-Illinois_vitro_0_517748253.html. Accessed July 23, 2016.

Lingle, R. 2014. A closer look at the global food container market. *Packaging Digest*. March 2014. www.packagingdigest.com/food-packaging/closer-look-global-food-container-market. Accessed July 24, 2016.

Losada, A. 2000. *Envase y Embalaje, Historia, Tecnología y Ecología*. Designio. México.

Morales Fajardo, M. E. 2013. *La internacionalización de las empresas mexicanas en América Latina. Memorias de la 13a Reunión Nacional de Ciencias Empresariales: "Escenario Internacional, Ventajas y Desventajas para México y las empresas."* Oaxaca: Universidad Tecnológica de la Mixteca.

Notimex. 2015. México produce 10 millones de toneladas de envase y embalaje al año. *Terra*. January 2015. http://noticias.terra.com.mx/mexico/estados/mexico-produce-10-millones-de-toneladas-de-envase-y-embalaje-al-ano,134e672782fca410VgnCLD200000b1bf46d0RCRD.html. Accessed July 22, 2016.

PR Newswire. 2014. Global Container and Packaging Market 2015–2019: Key Vendors are Amcor, Ball, Crows Holdings, International Paper and Rock-Tenn. *PR Newswire*. December 2014. www.prnewswire.com/news-releases/global-container-and-packaging-market-2015-2019-key-vendors-are-amcor-ball-crows-holdings-international-paper-and-rock-tenn-300009009.html. Accessed July 22, 2016.

PR Newswire. 2015. Rexam's Joint Venture with Envases Universales in Guatemala Receives International Recognition for Operational Excellence. Chicago, IL. *PR Newswire*. May 2015. www.prnewswire.com/news-releases/rexams-joint-venture-with-envases-universales-in-guatemala-receives-inter national-recognition-for-operational-excellence-300084845.html. Accessed July 23, 2016.

Standard & Poor's. 2014. Standard & Poor's sube calificaciones de Envases Universales. *Standard & Poor's*. May 2014. www.standardandpoors.com/rat ings/articles/es/la/?articleType=HTML&assetID=1245367724190. Accessed July 24, 2016.

13 MultiMexicans in Automotive Components
Metalsa and Nemak

Laura Zapata and Andreas M. Hartmann

INTRODUCTION

This chapter discusses the development of Metalsa and Nemak, two Mexican suppliers of automotive components that have worked their way up to prominence in the international arena, with operations in the Americas, Europe, and Asia. The chapter starts with a general description of the institutional context under which the automotive industry has developed in Mexico. We then present the growth paths, both at the national and the international levels, and the technological development of Metalsa and Nemak. The chapter concludes with a comparison of both companies' paths to internationalization.

The development of the automotive sector in Mexico and the expansion of its presence overseas is the result of a series of events and transformations triggered by Mexican governmental policies and international commercial agreements. NAFTA has played a significant role in the Mexican automotive sector. A gradual deregulation of the sector that started in 1994 and was completed in 2004 has brought business opportunities for foreign companies, forcing both domestic and foreign companies producing in Mexico to improve their quality and reduce production costs in order to maintain and/or increase their business operations.

The automotive components industry in Mexico has moved from a process of mere assembly and little productive integration to a phase of adopting new technologies and creating its own technological developments that impact production processes and allow greater vertical integration. Efficiency and specialization have become crucial for automotive suppliers to maintain domestic market share and expand their presence overseas. The examples of Metalsa and Nemak show that in order to grow from a minor domestic player to a competitor in the global market, firms need a strategy for sourcing and developing technology and strong financial underpinnings. The global competitiveness of both companies has its foundation in the upgrading of their productive capabilities, namely through the association with or acquisition of foreign companies, incorporation of Total Quality Management models and methodologies, and adaptation to customer needs, including highly sophisticated custom-designed components. In that sense, the Mexican plants of both companies provide standardized processes while the foreign plants either focus on production or specialize in the manufacture of technologically advanced products. Financial support from the holding companies has also been a key ingredient for Metalsa and Nemak for achieving their international goals.

THE AUTOMOTIVE INDUSTRY IN MEXICO

Government policies have played an important role in the development of Mexico's automotive sector. The import substitution policy that started in 1962 helped establish a local production base, because for around three decades, OEMs that wanted to sell cars in Mexico were required to produce a substantial part of their offer inside the country. Under this regime, some foreign companies (e.g., Mercedes-Benz, Peugeot) withdrew from Mexico, while others strengthened their local manufacturing base, although with a reduced range of cars (e.g., Ford, General Motors). This policy was gradually abandoned during the 1980s, leading to the establishment of new manufacturing plants in the country such as the Ford-Mazda JV in Hermosillo, Sonora. At the beginning of the 1990s, Mexican vehicle production was given a tremendous boost when NAFTA allowed free export of Mexico-assembled cars to the USA and Canada. In this way, "Mexico became increasingly integrated into the North American [automotive] production system" (Humphrey & Memedovic, 2003). The current openness for foreign investments based on free-trade agreements with over 40 countries (Miranda, 2007) has helped create a highly developed supplier infrastructure in the country. Several foreign-based OEMs also maintain R&D centers in Mexico for partial design and testing activities. In fact, over 80% of the passenger cars assembled in Mexico are destined for exportation (Covarrubias, 2014). In summary, Vicencio (2007) points out six phases in the evolution of the automotive industry in Mexico:

1. Birth of the industry and start of operations (1925–60): Low production costs, low transportation costs, and low salaries were the main reasons why American automotive companies started operations in Mexico. Ford installed assembly lines in 1925, followed by General Motors in 1935, and Chrysler three years later.

2. Growth based on import substitution (1961–76): During this period, the substitution policy, which supported domestic automotive firms by limiting foreign vehicles imported for sales, allowed the operation of new international players in this industry: Nissan (1961), Volkswagen (1964), and new production plants for Ford, General Motors, and Chrysler. Between 1965 and 1970, the industry grew by 40 percent.

3. Focus on international competitiveness through trade protection and export promotion (1977–89): In 1972, a second presidential decree was published promoting an increase in exports by 30 percent. This change pushed automotive companies to increase competitiveness and modernize their infrastructure.

4. Trade liberalization (1990–93): A decree for automotive industry modernization and promotion was launched. Contrary to the 1962 decree, this new policy authorized imports of new vehicles if there was a surplus trade balance for the industry. In 1993, 20 percent of vehicles sold were imported.

5. NAFTA and gradual liberalization of the automotive industry (1994–2002): Since the signing of NAFTA in 1994, the automotive industry has been increasingly active in the region, increasing its competitiveness, integrating its production structure, and investing in technological development.

6. Modern approach to strengthening the competitiveness and development of the internal market (2003–present): In December 2003, the Mexican government enacted a decree to support the competitiveness of the

automotive industry and foster the development of the domestic car market by promoting the domestic and international expansion of Mexican automotive firms. New supplier companies and automaker firms, such as Toyota and KIA, started operations.

Over the last two decades, automobile production in Mexico has increased dramatically: in 1997, the combined production of passenger vehicles and trucks was only 1,359,542 units. In 2013, total production attained 3,054,849 units, with 1,771,987 cars and 1,282,862 commercial vehicles (OICA, 2017). Table 13.1 shows the development with its generally ascending tendency and its cyclical ups and downs,

Table 13.1 *Automotive production in Mexico, 1997–2013*

Year	Cars	Commercial Vehicles	Total
1997	N/A	N/A	1,359,542
1998	N/A	N/A	1,452,847
1999	993,772	556,153	1,549,925
2000	1,279,089	656,438	1,935,527
2001	1,000,715	840,293	1,841,008
2002	960,097	844,573	1,804,670
2003	774,048	801,399	1,575,447
2004	903,313	673,846	1,577,159
2005	846,048	838,190	1,684,238
2006	1,097,619	947,899	2,045,518
2007	1,209,097	886,148	2,095,245
2008	1,217,458	950,486	2,167,944
2009	942,876	618,176	1,561,052
2010	1,386,148	956,134	2,342,282
2011	1,657,080	1,023,970	2,681,050
2012	1,810,007	1,191,807	3,001,814
2013	1,771,987	1,282,862	3,054,849
2014	1,915,709	1,452,301	3,368,010
2015	1,968,954	1,597,415	3,565,469

Source: Own elaboration with data from OICA (2017); only total numbers were available for 1997–8

especially the severe crisis that struck the US market in 2009. In 2015, Mexico ranked ninth among the car manufacturing countries of the world, hosting assembly plants for passenger cars engineered by OEMs based in Germany (Volkswagen), Japan (Honda, Mazda, Nissan, Toyota), and the USA (Chrysler [which was also partially used for assembly by the Italian-based parent, Fiat], Ford, General Motors) (Statista, 2017). Since 2016, three other plants – two German-based (Audi, BMW) and one Korean-based (KIA) – have been opened. In the utility vehicle sector, there are assembly plants for trucks designed in China (Giant), Germany (Daimler, MAN), Japan (Hino, Isuzu), Sweden (Scania, Volvo), and the USA (Freightliner, International, Kenworth), as well as for Brazilian-designed buses (Marcopolo). Of all the foreign direct investment that Mexico received in 2015, 19.9 percent belonged to the auto and auto parts industry (Secretaría de Economía & Proméxico, 2017). In contrast, there are only two small sports car manufacturers (Mastretta and Vuhl) and one mid-sized bus and truck manufacturer (Dina) selling authentically Mexican-designed vehicles, all of which rely heavily on parts originally designed for foreign brands.

The overwhelming presence of foreign vehicle manufacturers in Mexico is based on a unique set of factors. On the positive side, the available infrastructure and availability of sufficiently trained labor allows the manufacturers to run assembly operations effectively while enjoying considerable cost advantages, chiefly based on low wages (Covarrubias, 2014). On the negative side, we need to mention market size and technology level: even with a population of 127 million (World Bank, 2017), only 1.6 million new vehicles were sold domestically in 2016 (AMDA, 2017). The country does not have the technological competencies to launch a major home-grown OEM in the automotive sector, as "Mexico's ratio of BERD [business enterprises' expenditure in R&D] to GDP is well below the OECD median" (OECD, 2014).

However, the OEMs and their assembly plants only add about 25 percent of the value of a car (Maxton & Wormald, 2004). A great range of parts and subassemblies, such as fully instrumented dash-boards, wire harnesses, passenger seats, gearboxes, etc., are typically brought in from the so-called "tier one" suppliers, which in turn rely on tier two and tier three suppliers. In 2012, there were over one thousand automotive suppliers operating in Mexico (Secretaría de Economía, 2012). When setting up a new assembly plant, foreign OEMs usually prefer to invite their most important tier-one suppliers to build production facilities near the new location, enabling them to install just-in-time production systems with low inventory and high flexibility for the OEM. In Mexico, examples of such inter-firm pro-duction systems can be found in Hermosillo (Ford), Puebla (Volkswagen), and Toluca (Chrysler–Fiat), among others. The opportunities for local firms to capture a part of these global value chains have been rather limited (Álvarez, 2002), since 89 out of the world's 100 most important automotive suppliers have operations in Mexico (Covarrubias, 2014). While newly established inter-firm production arrangements are set up in the way of closed systems that lock out other suppliers, older plants and changes in buyer–supplier relationships over time open opportunities for other firms to become part of the automotive value chain.

This chapter presents the cases of the two notable exceptions from the industry structures described above: the home-grown Mexican automotive supply companies Metalsa and Nemak. In 2016, Nemak was ranked 9th and Metalsa was ranked 17th among the most internationalized Mexico-based firms, well ahead of other domestic industry participants – with the possible exception of Katcon, a privately-held company that does not publish any financial data (cf. Table 13.2). Both Metalsa and Nemak originated from the country's metalworking center, Monterrey, which has benefitted the firms not only technologically but also by their proximity to the US border, providing an international outlook and contacts with for-eign partners. In fact, we will show that the business models of both firms have included international elements since their inception. The objective of this chapter is to retrace the internationalization

Table 13.2 *Auto part manufacturers among Mexico's 100 most globalized firms*

2016 Rank	Company Name	2015 Globality Index	2014 Foreign Sales (in Mex$ millions)	Number of Countries Where Company Operates	2014 Employees Overseas
9	Nemak	12.2	53,496	15	10,000
17	Metalsa	7.1	20,000	15	7,000
34	Katcon	3.4	6,000	12	600
66	Rassini	1.5	5,567	3	1,100
75	Grupo Bocar	1.4	N/A	4	500
79	Grupo Gonher	1.2	N/A	3	750
81	Kuo Automotriz	1.1	2,700	3	700

Source: Expansión, 2016

paths of these two firms and to show how they have ascended to prominent positions in their respective global niches, overcoming the limitations of their home country's institutional setup.

The following sections concentrate on the growth of Mexico's top two automotive suppliers, Metalsa and Nemak, and how their technological development has led them to a long and fruitful process of internationalization.

METALSA

Metalsa was founded in 1956 by Guillermo Zambrano, and in 2007 it joined Grupo Proeza as a new business unit, while remaining owned, controlled, and operated by the Zambrano family. Grupo Proeza, a diversified Mexican group with headquarters in Monterrey, Mexico, consists of three strategic business units: Citrofrut produces citrus and other tropical juices, Zánitas provides health care services, and Metalsa produces automotive parts. Metalsa manufactures structural components for the light and commercial vehicle markets. Products include light duty frames, space frames, suspension modules, body structures, safety systems, hinges, transmission modules, and fuel tanks for passenger cars and light trucks as well as chassis frames, side rails, and cross members for heavy trucks and buses.

Metalsa is the second largest supplier of light vehicle Body on Frame (BOF) chassis in North America, with a market share of approximately 40 percent, and the largest supplier in South America, where it holds a market share of approximately 50 percent (Fitch, 2013). Even though Metalsa has a broad international presence, over one third of its production goes to the Mexican market; the NAFTA region represents 62 percent of its sales.

In November 1956, the company Manufacturas Metálicas Monterrey was founded by several local investors, headed by Guillermo Zambrano Gutiérrez. The objective was to meet the demand for public lighting buttresses, which at the time were imported from the United States to Mexico City. A presidential decree that promoted import substitution and export promotion turned out to be key to boosting Metalsa's original business.

Initially, the small factory had 60 employees working with a bending press and several small presses and guillotines. "Thinking about governmental policies, we realized that in every presidential period many jobs were suspended, especially at the beginning; we'd need to make other things," says Guillermo Zambrano. "We started to manufacture structural shapes and lines fitting electrical conduction, being a product more stable and durable" (Metalsa, 2014).

Years later, Guillermo Zambrano visited several supplier plants for the automotive industry in the United States. He was convinced that Mexico faced a great future with economic and demographic growth and he shared his idea to produce automotive parts in Mexico. In May 1960, an association contract was signed with A. O. Smith, which held 40 percent of the venture, while the remaining 60 percent belonged to the Mexican shareholders. This association remains in place today and laid the foundations for Metalsa's internationalization process, which has included the acquisition and construction of manufacturing plants abroad and the acquisition of technological centers that have been a great lever for innovation, total quality management methodologies, and the technological development of productive processes.

Taking advantage of Mexican governmental decrees intended to foster the automotive industry, in 1974 Metalsa expanded its international agreements with different US-based automotive OEMs to produce some parts in Mexico, such as the chassis for the Chrysler pick-up truck D-100. During the 1980s, Metalsa introduced a Total Quality Management system and a company philosophy that focuses on people as a mind force instead of a mere labor force, starting with the implementation of statistical process control. These internal changes provided Metalsa with efficiency in processes, quality in products to face economic crises, and – years later – technological innovation.

Japanese-style Total Quality Management was introduced by Metalsa in 1991. This philosophy was well aligned with Metalsa's business strategy and allowed it to implement a new way of operating. In 1993, the Quality as Way of Life model (QWL) consolidated the quality management program started at the beginning of the 1980s. In 1999, this system was replicated throughout the organization, offering the opportunity to standardize all operations. QWL became the platform for developing control mechanisms and the transfer of best practices in all of Metalsa's administrative and manufacturing activities. Relying on the same mindset, the Metalsa Operation System (MOS) was designed as a complement to QWL in order to consolidate the evaluation of different World Quality Awards criteria. Both approaches have been critical in Metalsa's international expansion (Taboada, 2002). Nowadays, the Metalsa Model aligns strategy and execution, where organizational strategies lead the direction through development tools such as Metalsa Operation System and Total Personal Quality Metalsa, assuring the execution of its strategies.

The beginning of the twenty-first century has offered Metalsa an opportunity for exponential growth of its operations worldwide. Through the acquisition of Tower Automotive's commercial vehicle business in 2000, Metalsa expanded its operations in the United States and obtained a trading platform for entering new markets, including Europe and South America, directly and with greater force. To assure the long-term success and continued stability and health of Metalsa, as well as the generation of value for all of its stakeholders, in 2007 Grupo Proeza acquired 100 percent ownership of Metalsa. This decision was crucial for Metalsa's international expansion and was based on a clear vision of being one of the best suppliers worldwide of components for light and commercial vehicles.

In 2008, Metalsa expanded its international presence by opening offices in Yokohama, Japan, and Pune, India, and starting the construction of a facility in Jamshedpur, India, which began operations in 2010 by producing beams for Tata and Mahandra-Navistar trucks. The facility produces customized class 5, 6, 7, and 8 side rails for medium and heavy trucks and possesses high-tech manufacturing capabilities such as roll-forming, plasma cutting, CNC hydraulic piercing, offset bending, and powder coating to satisfy local and export markets. Even though the economic crisis of 2009 led to a drop of 40 percent in sales, it was not an obstacle for Metalsa to continue its international strategy.

The economic crisis of 2009 and the financial support of Grupo Proeza presented Metalsa with the great opportunity to acquire Dana Holding Corporation's structural products business in 2010. The acquisition included plants in Argentina, Australia, Brazil, the United States, Venezuela, and a joint venture in the United Kingdom, thereby expanding Metalsa's manufacturing footprint to support business in new regions. It also brought a long-term commitment to innovation, quality, and customer service to the global structural components market for light and commercial vehicles. In 2010, Metalsa's sales reached US$1.197 billion, an increase of 330 percent over 2009. One important aspect of the Dana acquisition was the challenges faced by Metalsa that provided it with lessons for its future international expansion. One of the challenges was a lack of prior understanding of stakeholders; for instance, unions play a relevant role in productive processes, and state governments may provide incentives if the foreign firm accomplishes several requirements, such as compensation packages. Another challenge was the integration of both organizational cultures in order to benefit from qualified labor and automated processes. Despite these initial difficulties, the combination of two organizations with strong cultural values and innovative capabilities in different regions created a global competitor with superior performance in the challenging automotive industry (Trailer, 2010). A business model focused on excellence and efficiency has been the pillar of Metalsa's rapid international expansion over the last five years. After the Dana Holding acquisition, Metalsa started operations in India (2009), Japan (2009), Russia (2012), and Thailand (2013). In 2010, the Jamshedpur plant in India took up the production of beams for Tata and Mahandra-Navistar Truck. With this addition, Metalsa had five manufacturing facilities around the world dedicated to the production of side rails and chassis frames for commercial vehicles. In 2012, Metalsa started the construction of a plant in Thailand to produce beams for Volvo trucks. In 2013, Metalsa acquired ISE Automotive, with operations in China, Hungary, Turkey, and South Africa, as well as two research centers. Approximately 2,500 ISE employees joined the Metalsa organization, expanding the Metalsa team to more than 11,000 employees in nearly every major automotive market worldwide. These acquisitions and greenfield investments are of strategic value for Metalsa's long-term business plan, leveraging its global commitment to innovation, quality, and customer service to reach its Vision 2020: "To be the best global choice of automotive structures, offering our customers innovative solutions focused on product and process technologies, safe and sustainable, exceeding the quality and service at a competitive cost" (Metalsa, 2014).

As shown in Table 13.3, Metalsa has experienced significant international expansion aligned with an increase in international agreements between Mexico and the rest of the world, governmental support for the automotive industry, and its efficiency-oriented business model.

Metalsa's production indicators reflect its strong business position in the BOF light vehicle segment and in structural parts for commercial vehicles, along with a geographic diversification of operations, long-term relationships with customers, and a solid financial profile. The company's ratings are limited by industry cyclicality and the concentration on three main clients (Toyota, Ford, and Chrysler), as well as operations concentrated in the North America region in the light vehicles segment (Fitch, 2013).

Over the last five years, Metalsa has doubled its sales from US$1,197 million in 2010 to over US$2,440 million in 2014. This number reflects its continuous improvement and global presence. The integration process has led to a combined workforce of more than 13,000 employees in nearly every major automotive market worldwide (Metalsa, 2014). The Metalsa Operation System (MOS) facilitates the transfer of best practices across the organization. MOS is a repository of knowledge and includes processes, practices, and indicators to which all plants have access (Metalsa, 2014). This system has helped Metalsa to become a truly multinational organization and assures the total satisfaction of its 34 customers, which is reflected in several awards, such as the 2010 Business Development Award from VW Argentina and the 2010 and 2011 Quality Certificate of Achievement from Toyota (Metalsa, 2014).

NEMAK

Nemak, officially known as Tenedora Nemak SA de CV, is a Mexico-based automotive supplier with worldwide activities. Unlike other major firms in the industry (e.g., Delphi, Magna, etc.), Nemak has maintained an exclusive focus on a single type of automotive component, namely aluminum cylinder heads and engine blocks, where it

Table 13.3 *Key events in Metalsa's internationalization process*

	Key Events	
Year	Domestic	International
1956	Foundation in Monterrey, Mexico.	
1960		Association with A. O. Smith to export automotive parts to the United States.
1974		Starts exporting automotive parts for Chrysler pickup D-100, United States.
1980	Metalsa introduces Total Quality Management philosophy.	
1993	Quality as Way of Life model (QWL) consolidates quality in operations; Metalsa Operation System controls and supports transfer of best practices for administrative and operations activities around the world.	
1995		75 percent of total sales are for exports to United States.
1995	Exports sales amount to US$80 million, 100 percent more than 1994.	Investment of US$5 million in a plant for assembling Mercedes-Benz automotive parts in Brazil.
1997		Strategic alliance with Tower Automotive. Tower Automotive purchases 20–40 percent of Metalsa's shares and Metalsa obtains access to Tower's technology, allowing an expansion of the product range for the Mexican firm.
2000		Metalsa acquires the commercial vehicles business

Table 13.3 (*cont.*)

	Key Events	
Year	Domestic	International
		from Tower Automotive with a manufacturing facility in Roanoke, VA.
		This operation generates an annual income of US$18 to 72 million. It also gives Metalsa an increase in its participation in the North American market from 10 to 55 percent.
2006	Metalsa starts operations of a new plant in Saltillo, Mexico.	
2006		Metalsa starts operations of a Technical Center in Detroit, MI, USA.
2007	Proeza acquires 100 percent ownership of Metalsa.	
2008		Metalsa opens offices in Yokohama, Japan and Pune, India, and starts the construction of a facility in Jamshedpur, India.
2010		Metalsa assumes control of Dana Holding Corporation with headquarters in Maumee, Ohio. The US$150 million transaction includes 10 Dana manufacturing facilities that produce structural components for chassis and body structures in light and commercial vehicles, with accompanying administrative, technical, and sales centers in Argentina,

Table 13.3 (cont.)

	Key Events	
Year	Domestic	International
2010		Australia, Brazil, the United States, Venezuela, and a joint venture in the United Kingdom. Metalsa starts operations of its plant in India which produces beams for Tata and Mahandra-Navistar trucks. The facility produces customized class 5, 6, 7, and 8 side rails for medium and heavy trucks, and possesses high-tech manufacturing capabilities such as roll-forming, plasma cutting, CNC hydraulic piercing, offset bending, and powder coating to serve local and export markets.
2012		Opening of an office in Russia. Start of the construction of a plant in Thailand.
2013		Acquisition of ISE Automotive from Nordwind Capital: a total of eight plants, four in Germany, one plant in each of the following countries: China, Hungary, Turkey, and South Africa, and two engineering centers in Germany and Hungary.
2014		Metalsa starts operations of its own plant in Thailand to produce beams for Volvo trucks. Sale of the Venezuelan plant, from which Metalsa's Brazilian customers were supplied.

has risen to the position of a global market leader. Additionally, Nemak manufactures transmission components and other die-cast aluminum parts for the automotive industry. From its relatively humble beginnings in 1979, the company grew to annual sales of US$54 million in 1992; from there to the year 2006, the compound annual growth rate was 26 percent (Valtierra, 2013). After reaching annual worldwide sales figures of over US$3 billion in 2007, Nemak kept growing vigorously, and in 2013 attained sales of US$4.391 billion and an EBITDA of US$611 million, with 88 percent of sales taking place outside of Mexico. With an estimated 2013 world market for aluminum powertrain elements worth US$19.9 billion, Nemak thus had a market share of approximately 22 percent (Targeted News Service, 2012). At the end of 2011, Nemak had a 60 percent market share in cylinder heads and 45 percent in engine blocks within the NAFTA area (Ramírez, 2012). In 2013, the company had approximately 20,000 employees and operated 35 production facilities in 15 countries around the world (Nemak, 2014b), being cited as 52nd among the world's automotive suppliers and the only one among the world's top 100 to be based in Mexico (Automotive News, 2016).

Nemak has always been an incorporated company, although before 2015, the entirety of its shares was held conjointly by Alfa (93.24 percent) and Ford Motor Co. (6.76 percent). In July 2015, the Nemak stock was finally listed on the Mexican Stock Exchange (Milenio, 2015). Independently of these changes in minority ownership, Nemak is part of and controlled by the diversified conglomerate Alfa, which goes back to the so-called Grupo Monterrey, a family-owned and family-managed industrial group based in Northeastern Mexico. When Alfa was split off in 1974, it was composed of a steel mill, a cardboard factory, and some mining operations. Over the years, Alfa's leadership has managed its portfolio of businesses very actively, acquiring and divesting within a broad range of businesses. Its first international venture was a co-investment in a steelmaking facility in Venezuela in 1998. After a severe crisis that started in 2000, the main business of steel was finally sold off to cover debts and to invest in other businesses, such as Nemak. As of 2014, Alfa was active in petrochemicals (Alpek), aluminum automotive parts (Nemak), refrigerated food (Sigma), telecom services (Alestra), and oil exploration (Newpek). Alfa had production units in 23 countries, employed 68,000 people, and attained worldwide sales of US$15.9 billion (Alfa, 2015).

On a global level, the Mexico-based Tenedora Nemak acts as a holding company for its foreign subsidiaries (Nemak, 2014b). Manuel Rivera stood at Nemak's helm for twenty years, from 1993 to 2013, a stability in leadership that probably contributed to the 39-fold sales growth the company achieved over the same period (Graña, 2013). His successor, Armando Tamez, had also been working for Nemak for 28 years before being appointed as CEO (Just Auto Global News, 2012).

Beginnings and Development of Technological Capacities

Nemak started operations in 1979 as a joint venture between the Monterrey-based Grupo Alfa and Ford Motor Co., which originally held 80 percent and 20 percent of Nemak's shares, respectively. Ford wanted to outsource the production of high-tech aluminum components, an activity in which it did not possess a specific advantage. Even in its 2014 Annual Report, Ford kept listing Nemak as an "unconsolidated joint venture," which confirms its continued importance for the auto maker. The technology level inherited by Nemak was thus not particularly developed, with inefficiencies and quality problems. For this reason, Nemak went looking for technological assistance and in 1982 concluded an agreement with Italy-based Teksid to provide technological assistance in exchange for a 5 percent royalty on Nemak's sales. This collaboration was deepened when, in 1989, Teksid – a subsidiary of Italy-based automaker Fiat – acquired 20 percent of Nemak's shares from Alfa, which was left with a 60 percent ownership. In 1990, Nemak started to work its way out of the technological dependency by creating its own R&D department and improving its understanding of its core processes to reduce rejection rates (Pozas, 1999). By 1992, the technological dependence on Teksid had decreased, so royalties were reduced to 3 percent of Nemak's sales. The fine-tuning of the aluminum casting process helped Nemak become self-sufficient to the point that in 1996, it could go beyond the recipes provided by Teksid, stopping royalty payments altogether (Valtierra, 2013) and repurchasing its shares (Marsh, 2000). The improved control of the production process was made evident in the production of aluminum powertrain components, where scrap rates went down from over 2 percent in the 1980s to under 0.3 percent in 1997 (Valtierra, 2013). Concurrently, Nemak started working with university research centers in Northeast Mexico; this kind of collaboration was later extended to other universities in Canada, the USA, and Germany. In the course of this industry–university cooperation, a large number of technology-oriented Masters and PhD theses have been written about specific aspects of aluminum alloys and casting processes (Valtierra, 2013). These efforts correspond with the industry trend to use smaller engines working at higher temperatures, which increases demands for material specifications (Sedgwick, 2011).

Today, Nemak uses different aluminum casting techniques in its facilities around the world, including advanced techniques such as robots and 3D laser inspection (Anonymous, 2008). Nemak has the capacity to co-develop with its customers over 100 products per year. Around 400 employees are dedicated to R&D. Nemak has registered over 70 patents and trademarks and received several quality awards, such as Ford's Q1 Award; General Motors' Quality, Service, Technology and Price ("QSTP") Award; DaimlerChrysler's Supplier of the Year and Gold Awards; Porsche AG's Supplier Award; and Volkswagen Group's Product Quality Award (Nemak, 2014c). To maintain quality standards, Nemak has invested in personnel training (El Norte, 2008; Targeted News Service, 2012) and seeks to keep rotation low (Gibbs, 2007). Technology transfer between plants has become a strategic issue, such as for the future plant in Mexico that will use the state-of-the-art High Pressure Die Casting technology currently used in Nemak's Polish plant (Nemak, 2014b).

Nemak's Domestic and International Growth

Before going international, Nemak expanded its Mexican facilities, building new plants in 1996 and 1998. Since the year 2000, Nemak has pursued a path of international growth, including both acquisitions and greenfield investments (cf. Table 13.4). The first step was a transfer of a going concern from its US-based parent Ford Motor Co., which passed on to Nemak two of its plants located in Canada. In 2003, Nemak started a strategy of actively looking for investment opportunities in Europe (Sánchez, 2003). Its first achievement was obtaining a contract to manufacture cylinder heads for Opel, the European branch of General Motors. Nemak decided to build a new plant in the Czech Republic, which would supply Opel factories in Germany from a location that was relatively close but that benefited from a lower labor cost. Once established in Europe, Nemak saw an

Table 13.4 *Nemak's main financial information, 2000–15*

	2000	2005	2010	2015
Revenue	N/A	1,369.7	2,882.6	4,476.2
Total assets	N/A	1,258.9	3,040	4,180.2
EBITDA	N/A	149.1	355.9	779.1
Gross profit	N/A	98.3	154.1	480.8
Net profit	N/A	66.6	51	320
Foreign investment	N/A	80	300	80
Exports	N/A	1,139.3	NA	1,690
Employees	N/A	6,194	13,808	20,287
Countries	2	4	11	13

Data in millions of US dollars

N/A = not available

Source: Authors with data from Bloomberg, Expansion and Company Reports

opportunity to widen its client portfolio by acquiring German-based Rautenbach. This move not only put Nemak in a working relationship with several European OEMs, but also included the acquisition of the technology and image of a top-of-the range supplier to high-performance car manufacturers such as BMW and Porsche. Additionally, Nemak's executives saw it as a way to start working with Korean and Asian manufacturers, using Europe as a springboard (Sánchez, 2005).

Back home in Mexico, Grupo Industrial Saltillo lost its Norwegian partner in 2006 and was forced to sell its aluminum casting plant to rival Nemak, which was then able to fortify its leading position in its growing home market. As the outsourcing trend in the global auto industry continued, Italy-based Fiat sold its Teksid cylinder head plants to an investment group, which resold most of them to Nemak in 2007, adding going concerns in Argentina, Brazil, China, Mexico, Poland, and the USA. The fact that just seven years after freeing itself from technological dependency, Nemak would overtake plants that used to belong to its former technology provider shows an amazing speed of learning. With the acquisition of Norsk Hydro's casting units in 2007, Nemak became the largest supplier of aluminum cylinder heads and engine blocks in the world (Anonymous, 2007) and fortified its position in three European countries: Austria, Germany, and Hungary, while a small Swedish facility would be closed subsequently. In 2012, Nemak expanded its core business into the production of aluminum transmission parts by acquiring the US-based company J. L. French Automotive Castings, which included three plants in the USA and one in Spain. After completing this series of acquisitions, Nemak returned to making greenfield investments in BRIC countries. Its parent, Ford Motor Co., commissioned it to build two cylinder head plants: one in India (2012) and a second one in China (2015). Additionally, Nemak started operating a new facility in Russia in 2015, which is a key supplier for Volkswagen's new factory in Ulyanovsk.

Because of these internationalization moves, in 2013, 60 percent of Nemak's sales were generated in North America, 32 percent in Europe, and the rest in South America and Asia (Nemak, 2014b). In Asia, the company has made greenfield investments in India and China and is working with both Japanese and South Korean clients, showing its impetus to become a truly global company. However, access to major clients in Japan is difficult as long as they keep production parts either in-house or within their respective *keiretsus*. In 2013, Ford Motor Co. accounted for at least 34 percent of Nemak's worldwide sales (25 percent for Ford North America, 8 percent for Ford Europe, 1 percent for Ford South America, plus an unspecified number for Ford's JVs in China). Only seven global clients (General Motors, Ford, Chrysler, Volkswagen Group, BMW, Hyundai, and Daimler) generated 93 percent of Nemak's sales volume in 2013 (Nemak, 2014b). In the last three years, Nemak's revenues have gradually increased from US$3.9 billion in 2012, to US$4.6 billion in 2014 (Nemak, 2014c).

As shown in Table 13.4, Nemak has experienced significant growth in revenues in recent years. Similar to Metalsa, Nemak's international expansion has been fostered by governmental policies and corporate financial support (see Table 13.5).

CONCLUSIONS

The internationalization processes that Metalsa and Nemak have followed show three main criteria as prerequisites: membership in an industrial group, technological development based on partnerships with or acquisitions of foreign firms (external knowledge), and a narrow specialization in one type of product.

Within such capital-intensive industries, membership in a diversified conglomerate offers strong financial support. Since 2007, Metalsa has been a member of Grupo Proeza; this ownership has been essential for Metalsa's internationalization process. Grupo Proeza is a diversified group consisting of three strategic business

Table 13.5 *Key events in Nemak's internationalization process*

	Key Events	
Year	Domestic	International
1979	Nemak starts operation as a JV between Grupo Alfa and Ford Motor Co. in García, Mexico.	
1982		Starts technology supplier contract with Teksid-Fiat with 5 percent of royalty on sales.
1990	Creation of Nemak's own R&D department.	
1996		Ends technology supplier contract with Teksid-Fiat.
2000		Acquisition of two aluminum casting plants from Ford Motor Co. in Windsor, Canada (one plant closed down in 2009) in exchange for 5 percent of Nemak's shares.
2003		Greenfield investment of US$200 million in Plzen, Czech Republic to produce for Opel (GM).
2005		Acquisition of German-based Rautenbach-Guss Wernigerode GmbH, Rautenbach-Aluminium -Technologie GmbH, Rautenbach Slovakia, s.r.o. in Wernigerode, Germany; Žiar, Slovakia for 80 million USD having Volkswagen, Skoda, Audi, Daimler-Chrysler, BMW, Porsche, Peugeot Citroën, and Ssang Yong as main customers.
2006	Acquisition of Castech SA de CV (had been jointly owned by	

Table 13.5 (*cont.*)

	Key Events	
Year	Domestic	International
	Grupo Industrial Saltillo, Mexico, and Norsk Hydro, Norway) for 136 million USD.	
2007		Acquisition of Teksid plants from TK Aluminum Ltd., previously owned by Italian-based Fiat for US$496.8 million and an 11.5 percent interest in Nemak. Plants are located in Frontera, Mexico; Dickson, TN, USA; Betim, Brazil; Nanjing, China; Bielsko-Biala, Poland; and San Agustín, Argentina.
2007		Acquisition of Hydro Aluminum ASA from Norwegian-based Norsk Hydro (Norway) for US$546 million with plants in Linz, Austria; Dillingen, Germany; Györ, Hungary, and Charlottenberg, Sweden (closed later on).
2012		Acquisition of US-based J. L. French Automotive Casting, Inc. with an estimate investment of US$350–400 million, with plants in Sheboygan, WI, USA; Glasgow, KY, USA; Benton Harbor, MI, USA; San Andrés de Etxebarria, Spain.
2012		Greenfield investment of US$16 million in Chennai, India to produce mainly for Ford Motor Co.

Table 13.5 (*cont.*)

	Key Events	
Year	Domestic	International
2014		Greenfield investment of US$42 million in Chongqing, China with Changan Ford as main customer.
2015		Greenfield investment of US$80 million in Ulyanovsk, Russia to produce for Volkswagen.

units: Metalsa, Citrofrut (which produces citrus and tropical juices), and Zánitas (which provides health care services).

Nemak is a member of Alfa, which ranked seventh among Mexico's firms in 2013 (CNN Expansión, 2014). Its parent, Alfa, used the proceeds from the sale of the Hylsa steel company to acquire some of Nemak's international competitors (Sánchez, 2007). Currently, Alfa also controls businesses in telecom and IT services (Alestra), petrochemicals (Alpek), natural gas and oil (Newpek), and refrigerated food (Sigma).

Another similarity between Metalsa and Nemak is how they upgraded their technology bases, namely through association with or acquisition of foreign companies. Metalsa's acquisition of Dana Holding (2010) and ISE Automotive (2013) provided the firm with technology centers and engineering locations strategically located near the OEMs to fully support product development by personnel experienced in manufacturing and new technology development. Meanwhile, Nemak worked in association with Italy-based Teksid to obtain continued technological assistance. The acquisition of aluminum foundries from Rautenbach and Norsk Hydro provided Nemak with a whole range of different casting techniques.

Specialization in the production of a specific type of automotive component has been essential for international expansion. Metalsa manufactures structural components for the light and commercial vehicle markets. Its product portfolio flexibility enables it to participate in strategic areas of the automotive industry. In 2014, light vehicle chassis represented 56 percent of total sales, followed by body structural components (17 percent) and side rail cross-members for commercial vehicles (15 percent). Nemak's specialization has allowed it to be at the center of an ongoing technological change in the automotive industry, which requires downsized engines with stricter material specifications and lighter engine parts.

Both Metalsa and Nemak started their journeys in the automotive sector with the support of US-based partners, and initially produced mainly for US-based clients, so the international outlook was there from the beginning. After consolidating operations at home, both firms used first acquisitions and then greenfield investments to expand their activities abroad. Both companies' internalization processes were boosted by major acquisitions of competitors that already operated in several countries: Metalsa acquired Dana Holding (in 2010) with locations in six European and South American countries and ISE Automotive (in 2013) with plants in Europe, Asia, and Africa. Between 2005 and 2013, Nemak acquired four different firms that were already present in the Americas, Europe, and China. Today, both companies' major focus for further expansion lies in emerging markets, with new investments in Russia, India, and China.

The growth of the auto industry and its component suppliers has been accompanied by an evolution in production processes that are supported by computer-aided manufacturing and process automation systems. Together with comprehensive quality assurance systems, the corresponding organizational capabilities have become qualifying conditions for all tier-one suppliers. Companies that did show the managerial foresight and financial means to invest in such capabilities were thus able to strengthen their positions, while others have been acquired or had to close. In the case of the Mexican auto industry, the government only offered favorable market conditions for its few national champions without supporting them through major public R&D investments, so foreign input has been crucial. On the other hand, the suppliers' connections to foreign companies proved to be important stepping stones in their international expansion paths.

From a macroeconomic perspective, the enactment of NAFTA opened a unique window of opportunity for all automotive suppliers that could demonstrate their technological readiness. For both Metalsa and Nemak, however, Mexico has been more than an export platform; they created or seized many opportunities to become truly global players and continue to expand in growing emerging markets, including their own. From a strategic point of view, excellence in performance and strong relationships with customers allows these MultiLatinas to understand and even anticipate market needs, in order to defend their positions as world-class competitors.

REFERENCES

Alfa. 2015. Alfa Company Homepage. *Alfa*. www.alfa.com.mx. Accessed May 4, 2015.

Álvarez, M. de L. 2002. Cambios en la industria automotriz frente a la globalización: El sector de autopartes en México. *Contaduría y Administración*, 206: 29–49.

AMDA. 2017. Cifras 2016, venta de vehículos ligeros. Diciembre 2016. www.amda .mx/index.php?option=com_content&view=category&layout=blog&id=197&Itemid=595. Accessed February 20, 2017.

Anonymous. 2007. Apr. nemak becomes largest global producer of engine castings. *Modern Casting*, 97(4), 10–16.

Anonymous. 2008. Apr. core competence, and much more. *Foundry Management & Technology*, 136(4), 48–53.

Anonymous. 2009. Nemak completes announced closure of sssex plant. *Modern Casting*, 99(3), 19.

Automotive News. 2016. Top 100 global OEM parts suppliers. *Automotive News*, June 20. www.autonews.com/assets/PDF/CA105764617.PDF. Accessed February 22, 2017.

CNN Expansión. 2014. Las 500 empresas más importantes de México. *CNN Expansión*. www.cnnexpansion.com/rankings/2014/las-500-empresas-mas-importantes-de-mexico-2014. Accessed April 26, 2015.

Covarrubias, A. 2014. *Explosión de la industria automotriz en México: De sus encadenamientos actuales a su potencial transformador*. Mexico City: Fundación Friedrich Ebert en México.

El Norte. 2008. Se unen Conalep y Nemak para impulsar carreras profesionales técnicas. *El Norte*, February 15. http://biblioteca.itesm.mx. Accessed January 1, 2015.

Expansión. 2016. Las 100 mexicanas más globales. *Expansión*, January 29. http://expansion.mx/expansion/2016/01/25/las-100-mexicanas-globales. Accessed February 20, 2017.

Fitch. 2013. Fitch Rates Metalsa's Proposed Unsecured Notes BBB-(exp) Professional Services Close-Up. http://biblioteca.itesm.mx. Accessed on November 29, 2014.

Ford Motor Co. 2015. 2014 Annual Report. *Ford Company Homepage*. http://corporate.ford.com/homepage.html. Accessed May 4, 2015.

Gibbs, S. 2007. Nemak accelerates on the global track. *Modern Casting*, 97(5), 33–37.

Graña, J. 2013. Capitanes. *Mural*, February 1. http://biblioteca.itesm.mx. Accessed January 1, 2015.

Humphrey, J. & Memedovic, O. 2003. *The Global Automotive Industry Value Chain: What Prospects for Upgrading by Developing Countries*. Vienna: United Nations Industrial Development Organization.

Just Auto Global News. 2012. Mexico: Manuel Rivera to retire as CEO of Nemak. *Just Auto Global News*, December 5. www.just-auto.com/companies/nemak-tenedora-nemak-sa-de-cv_cid129. Accessed January 1, 2015.

Kuo. (s.d.) *Kuo Company Homepage*. www.kuo.com.mx/contenido.php. Accessed December 31, 2014.

Marsh, P. 2000. The art of being good in parts. *Financial Times*, Mar 1. http://biblioteca.itesm.mx. Accessed February 14, 2015.

Maxton, G. P. & Wormald, J. 2004. *Time For a Model Change: Re-Engineering the Global Automotive Industry*. Cambridge, UK: Cambridge University Press.

Metalsa. 2014. *Metalsa Company Homepage*. www.metalsa.com. Accessed November 29, 2014.

Milenio. 2015. Nemak debuta en BMV. *Milenio*, July 1. www.milenio.com/negocios/Nemak_mercado_valores-Nemak_BMV-debuta_Nemak_BMV_0_546545427.html. Accessed July 1, 2015.

Miranda, A. V. 2007. La industria automotriz en México: Antecedentes, situación actual y perspectivas. *Contaduría y Administración*, 221, 211–248.

Nemak. 2014a. Nemak to invest US$125 million in new HPDC plant in Mexico. *Nemak*. www.nemak.com/#aboutus. Accessed May 4, 2015.

Nemak. 2014b. Annual Report 2013. *Nemak.* www.nemak.com/docs/InfoFina-20 13.pdf. Accessed December 28, 2014.

Nemak. 2014c. Annual Report 2014. *Nemak.* www.nemak.com/docs/InfoFina-20 13.pdf. Accessed September 15, 2015.

OECD. 2014. OECD Science, Technology, and Industry Outlook 2014. *OECD Publishing.* www.oecd-ilibrary.org/science-and-technology/oecd-science-technology-and-industry-outlook-2014_sti_outlook-2014-en. Accessed April 26, 2015.

OICA. 2017. Production Statistics. *OICA.* www.oica.net/category/production-statistics. Accessed February 20, 2017.

Pozas, M. 1999. *Mexican Firms in the Global Economy.* Doctoral dissertation. Baltimore, MD: Doctoral Dissertation, Johns Hopkins University.

Ramírez, M. 2012. Gana Nemak mercado del TLCAN. *El Norte*, May 7. http://biblioteca.itesm.mx. Accessed January 1, 2015.

Rassini Homepage. 2014. *Historia.* www.rassini.com/historia.html. Accessed January 1, 2015.

Rugman, A. M. & Verbeke, A. 2004. A perspective on regional and global strategies of multinational enterprises. *Journal of International Business Studies*, 35, 3–18.

Sánchez, C. 2003. Busca Nemak más contratos. *El Norte*, October 8. http://biblioteca.itesm.mx. Accessed May 4, 2015.

Sánchez, C. 2005. Compra Nemak planta alemana. *Reforma*, February 1. http://biblioteca.itesm.mx. Accessed February 14, 2015.

Sánchez, C. 2007. Revoluciona Alfa área de autopartes. *El Norte*, March 16. http://biblioteca.itesm.mx. Accessed January 1, 2015.

Sánchez, C. 2009. Adquirirá Metalsa planta de chasises. *Reforma*. December 17. http://bibliotecadigital.itesm.mx. Accessed November 29, 2014.

Secretaría de Economía. 2012. *Industria automotriz – Monografía.* www.economia.gob.mx/files/comunidad_negocios/industria_comercio/Monografia_Industria_Automotriz_MARZO_2012.pdf. Accessed October 26, 2014.

Secretaría de Economía & Proméxico. 2017. Sector Automotriz. *Proméxico.* http://mim.promexico.gob.mx/swb/mim/Perfil_del_sector_auto. Accessed February 20, 2017.

Sedgwick, D. 2011. Fewer Cylinders Mean Winners and Losers Among Suppliers. *Automotive News.* http://biblioteca.itesm.mx. Accessed January 1, 2015.

Statista. 2017. Passenger Car Production in Selected Countries in 2015, by Country (in million units). www.statista.com/statistics/226032/light-vehicle-producing-countries/. Accessed February 20, 2017.

Taboada Garza, A. A. 2002. Comparación de Premios de Calidad Mundiales y Evaluación al Modelo Calidad como Forma de Vida de Metalsa. Master's thesis.

Tecnológico de Monterrey. http://biblioteca.itesm.mx. Accessed November 29, 2014.

Targeted News Service. 2012. WAT Grant Initiates Successful Partnership Between LTC and Nemak. *Targeted News Service*, August 20. http://biblioteca.itesm.mx. Accessed January 1, 2015.

Trailer-Body Builders. 2010. Metalsa Completes Purchase of Dana's Structural Components Business. *Trailer/Body Builders*, March 9. http://bibliotecadigital .itesm.mx. Accessed November 29, 2014.

Valtierra, S. 2013. Innovación y tecnología en la industria y su relación con la vinculación académica. *Academia de Ingeniería, A.C.* www.ai.org.mx/ai/ima ges/sitio/201310/ingresos/svg/presentacion_academia_de_ingenieria_dr_salva dor_valtierra_vf.pdf Accessed October 26, 2014.

Vicencio, A. 2007. La industria automotriz en México. Antecedentes, situación actual y perspectivas. *Contaduría y Administración*, 221, 211–248.

World Bank. 2017. Mexico. http://data.worldbank.org/country/mexico. Accessed February 20, 2017.

14 MultiMexicans in the Domestic Appliance Sector
Mabe and Man Industries

Hugo Javier Fuentes Castro, Leticia Armenta Fraire, and Alfonso Brown del Rivero

INTRODUCTION

The cases we present here are those of two companies, both of which were started in the middle of the twentieth century and which, throughout their history, have been involved in the industrial evolution of Mexico, from the impulse generated by a policy based on the import-substitution model, founded on an economy closed to external markets for reasons of local-economy protection, until today, where motivation has turned towards exports and industrial transformation. The story of Mabe is the story of the most important Mexican enterprise in the domestic appliance industry. Man Industries, a smaller firm with a correspondingly slower international trajectory, is illustrative of the road followed by other Mexican enterprises in their process of expansion into foreign markets.

Although the history of each of the companies has its own peculiarities, they have in common that both Mabe and Man Industries have been able to take advantage of the conditions that the environment provides to them, and, at the same time, they had seen opportunities to improve themselves during difficult times. One fact, discovered in this work, is that the expansion of Mabe benefited the expansion of Man Industries; because Mabe has positioned Mexican household appliances with a high reputation for quality in foreign markets.

This chapter is composed of six sections. The first two, "The Industry at Global Level" and "The Domestic Appliance Industry in Mexico," give a brief description of the domestic appliance industry at

385

international and Mexican levels, respectively. The following two sections, "Mabe: A Particularly Successful Case" and "Man Industries, Mexico," describe the stories of the two companies and feed the "Lessons for International Managers" section, where they point out and reflect the lessons that leave the entrepreneur competing or wanting to compete in international markets. In the last section, final remarks are made.

THE INDUSTRY AT GLOBAL LEVEL

The domestic appliance industry is made up of two broad areas: large appliances and small appliances. The first are those which are used in a stationary manner, such as air conditioners, water heaters, freezers, washing machines, and refrigerators. The smaller appliances are those which can be moved and held easily, such as vacuum cleaners, mixers, coffee machines, and portable heaters, amongst others.

Worldwide production of domestic appliances is distributed geographically in the following manner: 46.8 percent of production is based in Asia, which has three of the world's major producers: China, Japan, and South Korea. North America, including Mexico, is responsible for 22.1 percent of global production, with the European Union at 20.6 percent, Latin America at 2.5 percent, and the rest of the world at 8 percent. The five principal producers of domestic appliances in order of importance are China, the United States, Japan, Germany, and South Korea.

According to estimates from ProMéxico, in 2014 Mexican exports rose to fifth place globally, displacing the USA. Domestic appliances produced in Mexico are principally exported to the United States (86 percent), with the remainder being distributed between Canada (4 percent), Colombia (2 percent), Chile (1 percent), Peru (1 percent), and others (6 percent).

In 2014, the region with the greatest consumption of domestic appliances was the Asia Pacific region at 40.2 percent (specifically China), followed by North America, including Mexico, at 24.7 percent, the European Union at 4.1 percent; Latin America at 3.2 percent,

and the rest of the world at 7.8 percent. Some of the principal manu-
facturers of domestic appliances are: LG Home Appliances, Whirlpool,
Electrolux, BSH Bosch und Siemens, Haier Group Company, Arçelik,
GE Appliances, Miele, Samsung Home Appliances, and Mabe.

Mabe is the third-largest domestic appliance manufacturer, in
terms of importance, in Latin America. It has 15 manufacturing centers worldwide, eight of which are in Mexico. The company makes
and sells kitchens, refrigerators, washing machines, and driers. The
company exports to over 70 countries, principally the USA, as a result
of its partnership with General Electric. Its headquarters are located in
Mexico City, and in 2012 it had 19,751 employees and sales of US
$3,462 million.

THE DOMESTIC APPLIANCE INDUSTRY IN MEXICO

According to information from the Manufacturing Industry Monthly
Opinion Survey (EMIM) issued by the National Institute of Statistics
and Geography (INEGI) – see Table 14.1 – the value of domestic
appliance manufacture in 2014 was Mex$47.04 million, of which
Mex$2.2 million was from the small appliance sector and Mex

Table 14.1 *Domestic appliance production in Mexico*

Year	Manufacture of small domestic appliances	Manufacture of white goods	Total production value
2007	5,939,074.26	47,916,251.45	53,855,325.71
2008	3,901,833.29	42,235,365.40	46,137,198.69
2009	1,642,928.51	40,935,862.24	42,578,790.75
2010	2,316,786.34	45,694,992.33	48,011,778.66
2011	1,910,164.55	44,887,036.61	46,797,201.16
2012	2,039,731.12	44,716,659.07	46,756,390.19
2013	2,110,084.67	42,634,557.68	44,744,642.34
2014	2,123,098.36	43,241,400.69	45,364,499.06

Source: authors using data from INEGI, EMIM

Table 14.2 *People employed in the domestic appliance industry in Mexico*

Year	People Employed
2007	684,917
2008	636,952
2009	557,700
2010	638,471
2011	622,838
2012	626,406
2013	604,739
2014	627,333

Source: authors using data from INEGI, EMIM

$44.84 million from the white goods sector (95.32 percent). In the first months of 2015 the sector had sales of Mex$8.24 million.

Domestic appliance manufacture in Mexico has decreased in recent years because of the financial crisis, particularly as the main export market is the USA, which suffered a significant contraction. According to the Manufacturing Industry Monthly Opinion Survey (EMIM), the value of production showed a fall in 2008 and 2009. This was offset in 2010 by growth. Unfortunately, however, there was another significant fall from 2011 to 2013, where production value decreased to levels even lower than previously, although in 2014 there was a small recovery. Additionally, employment in the industry in 2007 (see Table 14.2) was higher than in the period 2007–2014, with nearly 685,000 people employed. This level shrank to 558,000 in 2009 but recovered in 2010 to 638,500. In 2014 there were 627,300 people employed in the sector.

ProMéxico considers that the real Annual Growth Rate (AGR) forecast for the domestic appliance manufacturing industry at world level for the period 2014 to 2020 is 4.1 percent. For the Mexican industry, this figure is estimated to be 4.2 percent.

According to information from the National Statistical Directory of Economic Units of the National Statistical and Geographical Institute (INEGI), there are 279 manufacturing entities in the domestic appliance industry in Mexico, divided in the following way:

Mexico City (49), Mexico State (38), Jalisco (36), Nuevo León (26), Queretaro (21), Tamaulipas (15), Puebla (14), Chihuahua (14), Coahuila (11), Baja California (8), Guanajuato (9), San Luis Potosí (6), Chiapas (5), Yucatan (5), Michoacan (4), Durango (3), Guerrero (3), Hidalgo (2), Morelos (2), Tlaxcala (2), Veracruz (2), Sinaloa (1), Sonora (1), Tabasco (1), and Zacatecas (1).

The development of the domestic appliance industry in the above states is extremely important. The industry has experienced strong growth which has followed on from growth in income and the formation of a middle class in the country. The industry is concentrated principally in states with a large industrial production sector, and this is particularly true in the case of Mexico City, Mexico State, Jalisco, Nuevo León, and Querétaro, which together have 68.27 percent of all manufacturing plants in Mexico.

An example of the positive impact of the growth of the domestic appliance industry at regional level is demonstrated in Queretaro, where production generates US$1,000 million annually, according to data from the state Sustainable Development Directory. "This sector is responsible for between 4 and 5 percent of GDP at state level. It can justifiably be referred to as the most fully integrated manufacturing chain that exists in Queretaro; that is to say, "from the smallest screw to the simplest injection-moulded plastic component to the finished refrigerator," according to Marcelo López Sánchez, head of the Directory (Metalmecánica, 2014).

Another important example is that of Nuevo León, the state in which domestic appliance production was worth US$3,188 million in 2012. "The state was notable for 54.6 percent of national production, with a value of US$5836 million," indicated Joan de Haene Godefroy, Nuevo León Domestic Appliance Cluster executive. Additionally,

Nuevo León is the main exporter of domestic appliances in Mexico, with a value of US$1,692 million, representing 53 percent of net income.[1]

States with slightly lower industry participation are: Tamaulipas, Puebla, Chihuahua, and Coahuila, which together account for almost 20 percent of plants involved in the sector. It is worth noting that at national level the industry employed 52,278 people in 2014, rising to 52,985 at the beginning of 2015, according to INEGI and quoting statistics from the National Statistical Directory of Economic Units (EMIM). The country has maintained a commercial surplus, exporting 84 percent of production to the USA, followed by Canada and Colombia. Last year Mexico exported a total of Mex$96.2 million worth of domestic appliances. In fact, Mexico is Latin America's principal exporter. According to a report compiled for ProMéxico, in 2013 the country was the principal exporter of fridges and freezers with separate exterior doors, and the second most important exporter of washing machines with a capacity of 10 kg or more.

It is worth noting that foreign direct investment (IED) in the period 2002 to 2013 was in the region of US$1,800 million, with the USA and South Korea being the major investors. As previously mentioned, Mexico has an important domestic appliance industry and is the most important exporter in Latin America and sixth most important globally, above industry leaders such as South Korea, Turkey, and France.

The country has important domestic companies (Mabe and Koblenz, among others) and foreign businesses (for example, Whirlpool, LG, and Samsung) which have not only invested in manufacturing plants but also in research and development centers. In addition, other, smaller enterprises have also made significant contributions to the industry and expanded their operations to other countries; one example being Man Industries.

---

[1]   Ibid.

The biggest export market for Mexico is North America. According to the Global Trade Atlas, the United States and Canada represent 88.5 percent of total Mexican domestic appliance exports. The size of the Mexican domestic appliance industry and its geographical location next to the United States makes the USA Mexico's most important export market. Low wage costs and the free trade zone at the border have made Mexico an important manufacturing base for multinational companies seeking access to the US market.

The supply chain in Mexico has improved over time thanks to the improved national integration of domestic appliance enterprises, in exactly the same way as the automobile industry aided the development of the automobile parts and plastics industries. Particularly notable has been an increasingly highly qualified and specialized workforce which has translated into increased productivity and a strengthening of the Mexican manufacturing industry. In previous years, items for assembly had to be imported into Mexico where they were put together and then returned to their country of origin. The situation, however, has changed, and an increasing amount of manufacturing operations throughout the whole industry are being carried out in Mexico. New technologies are being adopted and created in Mexican design and manufacturing centers.

Principal Domestic Appliance Producers in Mexico

Mabe, a leader in the Mexican market, is the third most important provider of domestic appliances in Latin America. The design company manufactures and distributes products under the brand names of General Electric, Easy, IEM, and Mabe.

Commercial and manufacturing operations are located in Canada, Mexico, Central America, Brazil, Argentina, Colombia, Venezuela, Ecuador, Peru, and Chile. It has fifteen manufacturing plants worldwide; eight are in Mexico and the others in Latin America and Canada, with a technology center in the city of Queretaro. It exports to over 70 countries and is the principal exporter of white goods to the United States, thanks to its regional alliance with General Electric. In 2012, the journal *Expansion* placed Mabe at position number 47 on the list of Mexico's largest companies, registering sales of US$3,462 million as well as having 19,751 employees.

In Mexico, after Mabe, Whirlpool is the second most important in terms of domestic appliance sales. From 2002 to 2012, Whirlpool doubled its manufacturing business in Mexico. The company has four plants, two manufacturing refrigerators and washing machines in Apodaca, Nuevo León; one manufacturing ovens, compact refrigerators, and washing machines in Celaya, Guanajuato; and the other producing refrigerators in Ramos Arizpe, Coahuila. In addition, the company has distribution centers in Apodaca, Merida, Culiacan, Guadalajara, Celaya, and Mexico State. It is important to recognize that Whirlpool Mexico is one of the ten most important subsidiaries in terms of financial yields of the Whirlpool Corporation; 60 percent of all domestic appliances that Whirlpool manufactures in Mexico are exported to the United States, Europe, and Latin America, with the remaining 40 percent being for domestic consumption.

Koblenz is a Mexican business with over 50 years in the market which designs, manufactures, and markets vacuum cleaners, hydrowashers, floor cleaners, ovens, washing machines, and refrigerators, among others. The company has two plants, located in Cuautitlan Izcalli and Vallejo, and employs over 2000 people, including a research and development team. In 2012 it posted sales of US$50 million and sold 70 percent of its production in Mexico. The remaining 30 percent of production is exported to over 27 countries, principally in Europe, North America, South America, and the Middle East.

Man Industries, Mexico, was founded in 1949 and produces and sells small domestic appliances such as liquidizers and fans, as well as having service and parts centers. Its operations are divided into the following: the Dycoman Line (saucepans and irons), and fans, liquidizers and Confort heaters. Man Industries produces items for brands such as Black & Decker, Citlali, Elgin, Coromex, Roca, Cimermex, Volvo, Record, Turmix, and Starmix as well as its own line of products. Its products are exported to Spain, Germany, Austria, Italy, Guatemala, El Salvador, Honduras, Costa Rica, the Dominican Republic, and the USA. It has 700 employees.

Gestar Electrodomésticos is a producer of domestic appliances located in Puebla. It manufactures products such as irons, liquidizers, mixers, extractors, ovens, and fans.

Termicel was founded in 1979 and concentrates on the production of electrical harnesses for domestic appliances and apparatus including refrigerators, lighting, and automobiles, among others. Operations are divided between the manufacture of electrical harnesses, injection products, processes, and materials.

Tisamatic provides grey cast-iron products to producers of brand-name items in the automotive and domestic appliance industries. The company principally manufactures parts used in the assembly of refrigerator compressors. Some of its clients are Mabe, Whirlpool, and GE. Its production plant is located in San Luis Potosi. Eighty percent of the parts made by Tisamatic for both the automotive and domestic appliance sectors are exported worldwide. Tisamatic exports 5 percent of its production directly to the USA, with just 15 percent remaining in the country for domestic consumption.

Some recent developments which have been made by enterprises in this sector will now be outlined. At the end of the year 2000, international companies, such as Sweden's AB Electrolux and South Korea's LG Electronics, were also manufacturing in Mexico with the intention of entering the US market. In this same period, Samsung constructed a refrigerator and air conditioner manufacturing plant in Queretaro, and Whirlpool invested over US$320 million in Mexico with the aim of increasing its production of refrigerators, washing machines, and cookers.

In 2005, Electrolux opened a US$100 million plant in Juarez capable of producing 1 million refrigerators annually, while also adding washingmachines to their product range.

MABE: A PARTICULARLY SUCCESSFUL CASE[2]

Mabe, a leading enterprise in the Latin American market, is an important example for Mexican companies that wish to become more globalized. Mabe has always been a company that has dealt successfully with the multiple changes in the structure of the domestic economy, from the beginning of the drive towards industrialization to the more recent multiple economic crises. In the same way, Mabe has adapted to the change implied in the crossing of national frontiers, but even more than this the business has kept expanding while simultaneously changing processes and innovating. An explanation of the development of Mabe, as well as its current situation, will follow.

Mabe was started by two entrepreneurs, Egon Mabardi and Francisco Berrondo, in Mexico City in 1946. The name of the company was an amalgamation of the surnames of the two founders and production was focused on the manufacture of bases for fluorescent lamps and built-in furniture. From the 1950s onwards the company began to develop a reputation for innovation and growth, diversifying production into gas ovens and refrigerators.

Continuing this tendency of continuous change and challenge, in the 1970s Mabe entered the export market, becoming Mexico's principal exporter of domestic appliances. By the end of that decade it had a presence in South America, Central America, and the Caribbean. This is particularly noteworthy because, during this time, Mexico experienced a period of growth and stability, which encouraged the growth of enterprises in a market closed to foreign competition and one which therefore was ripe for exploitation by Mexican industry. Without doubt, Mabe knows how to take advantage of these opportunities to develop and grow, and in addition it has the confidence to make decisions that show its maturity as a company without becoming complacent and losing sight of its business ambitions.

---

[2]   Financial information was requested from Mabe and Man Industries, but it was not provided. On the other hand, neither company is publicly traded.

One example of the creative spirit within Mabe was seen in 1964 with a completely new innovation: lining the interior of refrigerators with plastic. This marked a trend in the industry and positioned the brand at the vanguard of innovation in the domestic appliance industry.

Unfortunately, the company was not immune to the crises experienced by the country in the 1970s and 80s. This was a time of continuous currency devaluation, rapidly expanding external debt, lack of investment, and plummeting sales. The period from 1982–85 was particularly difficult for the company when it was joined by a 32-year-old engineer, Luis Berrondo, signifying a generational change in management. At that time Mabe had two manufacturing facilities and experienced strikes, as well as adjustments and changes to the workforce, particularly redundancies. According to Luis Berrondo,[3] there came a time when, given the severity of the crisis the company was experiencing, strike action was actually a relief for the company as it could not sustain the continued accumulation of inventory.

In 1985 the decision was made to either sell the enterprise or find a technical partner who could make the changes necessary to open new doors. Three possible partners were proposed: Whirlpool, Phillips, and General Electric (GE). The decision was finally made to partner with the latter, which was headed by Jack Welch, a management expert who worked tirelessly throughout the 80s to make GE a dynamic and competitive concern.

This brand framework therefore came into being, although it was not initially defined in terms of association, until in 1986 GE proposed that Mabe should commence production of cookers for the US market. This led to the San Luis Potosi plant eventually becoming the biggest producer of gas cookers worldwide. Finally, in 1987 GE and Mabe formed a partnership which can be seen as textbook example of "synergy," defined as two entities that complement and empower each other. One partner, Jack Welch, headed a growing and visionary

---

[3] We are very grateful for the interview granted to us by Luis Berrondo, president and director of Mabe, for the purposes of this research.

enterprise and was famed for his determination to make GE either a leader in every market in which it had a presence or to leave that market. On the other hand, Mabe was an enterprise with a cheap and specialized workforce which also had ambition, an able director and a pressing need to widen its market.

In the same year and at the same time as the association with GE, the situation of Mabe's competitors in Mexico was becoming critical. Firms such as Acros, IEM, and the Saltillo Group, with brands such as Easy and CINSA, experienced a significant drop in sales as a result of the crisis. Mabe gave these enterprises a further lease of life by purchasing them, meaning that, by the end of the 80s, it controlled 50 percent of the Mexican market.

Paradoxically, just five years after confronting a severe crisis, Mabe was positioned as the leader in the Mexican market and, along with GE, was planning how to penetrate the largest market in the world: the USA. In 1990, over 66 percent of the cookers and refrigerators sold in the USA were produced by Mabe in Mexico, and 95 percent of GE domestic appliance sales were produced by Mabe. This marked a deep and significant change in understanding that was fundamental to the globalization process at Mabe over the subsequent years. This understanding can be divided into four categories: the first is how to work under conditions of severe economic crisis. The second is the acquisition of enterprises as a form of expansion, understood as brand-acquisition positioning rather than imposition of the purchasing brand. In third place is the generation of the organizational restructuring necessary to permit the integration of the new enterprises in such a way as to streamline coordination, eliminate duplication, and propel sales. Finally, in fourth place is the creation of alliances with the aim of opening markets and accessing new technologies.

The 90s was a decade of expansion into international markets and the application of the knowledge outlined above. According to Luis Berrondo, in 1992, while on a GE training course on globalization, it occurred to him to look for new markets in Latin America – an idea which became more concrete in subsequent years. In 1993 Mabe created an alliance with Ceteco, a Dutch Company, which opened the door to the Venezuelan market and which permitted them to have contact with other countries in the region by way of the Regina brand. In Colombia Mabe acquired the Polarix Company, which dedicated half of its production to the domestic market under the Centrales name. The other 50 percent of production was exported to Venezuela, Ecuador, Peru, Chile, and other Central American countries.

In 1994 Mabe decided to create a technical and organizational platform in order to cement its international presence and pause before passing from being a company focused on – according to Luis Berrondo – the production of domestic appliances to a company capable of designing them. This was how the Mabe Technical and Project Center (CTyP) in Queretaro came into being, with the later establishment of the Mabe–Sanyo plant, specializing in compressors, being set up in San Luis Potosi (Mexico). It is important to note that Mabe has generated tools such as Quality Function Deployment (QFD), which permits the translating of client requirements into technical parameters. Without doubt, this has become an important instrument for fulfilling the specifications and regulations of each market and assisting in brand differentiation.

It must not be forgotten that with 1994 came the implementation of the North American Free Trade Agreement (NAFTA), initiating an economic policy which promoted commerce and market liberalization. According to Luis Berrondo, the previous knowledge gained by the company as a result of its strategy of internationalization facilitated the exploitation of opportunities offered by the new treaty.

In 1995 Mabe set up an operation in Colombia in which it began to produce domestic appliances under the Mabe, GE, and Centrales brands. It also entered the Ecuadorian market by purchasing the Durex Brand, which also had operations in Peru. In 1996 Mabe entered the Peruvian market and in 1998 it acquired the Venezuelan companies Condesa and Admiral at the same time as Madosa and the Dutch company Ceteco merged. This same year, Mabe became part of Fagor in Argentina, with a 50 percent share purchase of the Kronen brand. Together with Fagor it acquired two plants previously owned by Maclean, in Ahedo and San Luis, which produced the brands Patrick-Fagor and Saccol. Finally, it purchased the Inresa brand in Peru, which gave it access to the low-income market sector in the Andean nation.

Between 1998 and 2002 Mabe closed its Venezuelan operations, taking advantage of the production capacity that it had in neighboring countries. This meant effectively that almost all Mabe products were imported from different production plants located in Mexico, Colombia, and Ecuador, although it still retained one cooker assembly plant in Guacara. By the year 2014 Mabe had raised its level of participation in the Venezuelan market to between 28 and 30 percent (El estímulo, 2014).

In 1999 Mabe founded the Quantum plant in Celaya (Mexico) with the aim of producing refrigerators for export. The units produced at this plant come under the Side by Side and Top Mount brands.

During the first decade of the new millennium Mabe continued to grow. In 2003 the company initiated a strategic expansion plan in the biggest market in Latin America: Brazil. It acquired CCE Refrigeration and took control of GE Dako and thus created Mabe Brazil (Domestic Appliances), with plants in the interior of Sao Paolo in Campinhas, Itu, and Hortolandia. Also in 2003, Mabe consolidated its acquisition of Kronen Argentina with the shareholder participation of its partner Fagor, while simultaneously taking ownership of the Patrick-Fagor and Saccol brands. These operations consolidated the position of Mabe Argentina and are clear proof of the capacity of the company to assume risks at moments in which the "Country of the Pampas" was undergoing a severe crisis, particularly in the domestic appliance industry (El Cronista, 2003).[4]

---

4   Although the consumption of domestic appliances did recover in this year, 70 percent of home appliances sold at this time in the Argentine market were manufactured outside the country, mainly in Brazil. According to the national chambers of commerce, the cost of assembling a domestic appliance in Brazil was 20 percent

In 2005 Mabe opened in Montreal, in the Canadian province of Quebec, as a result of acquiring the Canadian firm Camco, at that time the largest Canadian manufacturer of domestic appliances. In 2006 it entered the Russian market through an alliance with Fagor Spain, owner of the De Dietrich and Mabe brands. In 2007 it purchased the Costa Rican Enterprise Atlas Eléctrica, owner of the Atlas and Cetron brands. This heralded a change in the Central American globalization strategy, which until that time had been based solely on distribution and not production, as Mabe had been doing in South America.

The year 2008 saw the acquisition in Brazil by Mabe of the subsidiary company BSH Continental, which had previously been owned by the German enterprise BSH Bosch und Siemens Hausgeräte GMBH, and acted as a distributor for the Bosch and Continental brands. In a similar fashion, Mabe entered the Chilean market through the purchase of GE Appliances Chile, with which it sought to increase its market participation level of 10 percent and continue its distribution of GE products.

In 2010, continuing its line of innovation, Mabe developed materials that inhibited the production of bacteria in food containers. This innovation was the result of an alliance with the Advanced Studies and Research Center (Cinvestav) in Queretaro, and was assisted by the Queretaro State Science and Technology Council.

The second decade of the new millennium brought with it the black cloud which had begun with the 2008 crisis and which subsequently spread across the globe. As a result, there was a significant fall in global economic activity, the effects of which can still be felt today. In 2012 Mabe began the gradual cessation of its manufacturing operation in Montreal, finally closing the plant in 2014 and transferring operations to Ramos Arizpe, with the subsequent creation of 1000 jobs. Thus, driers and dishwashers were produced in Mexico for the first time in the company's history, the new products being destined for export to the American continent and other world markets, notably that of Europe.

lower than the cost of doing so in Argentina, meaning a considerable competitive disadvantage for the latter.

It is important to note that in 2009 Mabe was required to cut 150 job, in its Canadian plant following the loss of an important contract for the manufacture of washing machines. One of the principal factors behind the eventual closure of the Montreal facility was the strength of the Canadian dollar and the knock-on effect that this had on labor costs.

For its part in 2013 Mabe Brazil filed for bankruptcy protection in the municipality of Hortolandia, São Paolo. As a part of the process the company closed its plant based in the Itu locality of the same state to concentrate production in Campinhas.

In January 2014 Mabe inaugurated a plant manufacturing stove extractor hoods, San Luis Potosi, as part of the agreement it had with the Italian company Faber North America, part of the Franke group. Today Mabe has plants in Mexico, Costa Rica, Ecuador, Colombia, Brazil, and Argentina and undertakes commercial operations as well as sales and service operations all over the American continent. Table 14.3 presents an outline of Mabe's operations in chronological order.

The future holds new challenges and, at the same time, opportunities. GE, Mabe's partner for over 25 years, announced in September 2014 the sale of its third-largest company (in terms of income) of the seven businesses that make up the conglomerate: its domestic appliance arm (Hansegard, 2014). The purchaser was the Electrolux Company, who, wanting to gain market share in America, paid US $3,300 million for the business. With the purchase Electrolux saw the opportunity to invigorate its growth in the region, which had stalled in comparison with the growth experienced in Europe.

As a further part of the agreement, Electrolux would buy 48.4 percent of the shares of Mabe; however, the competition authorities in the USA prevented the transaction. Finally, GE sold its stake in Mabe to the Chinese company Haier. In the opinion of Luis Berrondo, "this brings many business opportunities to produce more products in Mexico."[5]

---

[5]   Anderson, 2016.

Table 14.3 *History of Mabe*

Year	Domestic Market	International Markets
1946	Founded by Don Egon Mabardi and Don Francisco Berrondo. Started production of fluorescent lamps and built-in furniture	
1950	Diversification of operations. Started production of gas stoves and refrigerators	
1960		Main Mexican exporter of electric appliances. Mabe products were exported to Central America, the Caribbean, and South America
1986		A new factory started operations in San Luis Potosi, with production mainly destined for export. It was the world's largest gas stove production plant
1987	Acquires IEM, Easy, and CINSA. Acquired over 50 percent of market share by the end of the decade	Started a joint venture with General Electric in order to enter the United States market. Alliance with Ceteco, a Dutch company, allowed entrance to the Venezuelan market
1994	The MABE Technology and Projects Center was set up in Querétaro A Mabe-Sanyo Joint Venture opened in San Luis Potosí	Started operations in Colombia where produced and distributed electric appliances under GE, Mabe, and Centrales brands
1995		Bought Durex brand in Ecuador, which also had operations in Peru
1996		Started operations of Mabe Peru

Table 14.3 (*cont.*)

Year	Domestic Market	International Markets
1998		Bought Condesa and Admiral in Venezuela. In Argentina started a 50 percent joint venture with Fagor to produce under the brand Kronen
2003		Bought CCE refrigeration in Brazil and took control of Mabe Brazil, with plants in Sao Paulo and Hortolandia
2005		Took full control of Kronen in Argentina, and Mabe Argentina was created
2006		Acquired the Canadian firm Camco in Montreal, Province of Quebec
2007		Entered Russian market through an alliance with Fagor Spain Purchased the Costa Rican company Atlas Electrica
2008		Entered Chilean market, taking advantage of the Brazil experience
2009		Became a subsidiary of German BSH Bosch und Siemens Hausgeräte GMBH, distributor of Bosch, Continental, and BSH Continental brands in Brazil
2012		Started progressively closing Montreal plant programmed to close permanently in 2014. Operations transferred to Ramos Arizpe and 1000 new jobs created
2013		Mabe Brazil asks for bankruptcy protection from Municipality of Hortolandia,

Table 14.3 (*cont.*)

Year	Domestic Market	International Markets
		Sao Paulo. As part of the same process, Itu plant was closed and production concentrated in Campinhas
2014		In January a new plant making extractor hoods for cookers was opened in San Luis Potosi, as part of alliance with the Italian company Faber North America, a subsidiary of the Franke Group
2015		
2016		Electrolux bought the electric appliances division of GE and with that 48.8 percent of Mabe shares
		Mabe has factories in Mexico, Costa Rica, Ecuador, Colombia, Brazil, and Argentina
		Develops commercial operations throughout the American Continent
		GE sells 48.4 percent of its stake in Mabe to Chinese company Haier

Source: author

MAN INDUSTRIES, MEXICO

Man Industries[6] was founded in 1949 by Don Luis Pérez, a Spanish immigrant who brought looping machines to Mexico that were used to overlock female stockings, which at that time were knitted. In time

---

[6] We are very grateful for the interview granted to us by Oscar Pardo, Marketing Director of Man Industries, for the purposes of this research.

Dupont developed nylon pantyhose and Don Luis' business decreased because of the outdated technology used. Thus, he decided to reposition his business towards the production of motors. In 1955 the company began to produce electric drills, taking advantage of the nascent growth of Mexican industry. He began to produce motors for one of the most important drill manufacturers in the North American market at that time, Skill. This allowed Man Industries to develop its production capacity, and later, at the beginning of the 1970s, it began to produce motors for liquidizers. At the beginning, motors were produced for both General Electric and Black & Decker liquidizers.

With time, Don Luis came to realize that the Mexican market was in the process of expansion and that he could produce and sell liquidizers under his own brand name. Fans were subsequently added to the list of products, and with these two items began a process of brand consolidation and development in the domestic market. These two products therefore have been the production focus of the company for almost all of the last 40 years.

From 1995 onwards, and still being managed by Don Luis, the commercial management of the company was overhauled and new export markets were sought in the face of the difficult situation being faced by the Mexican economy at that time. Initially the company sent representatives to trade fairs in Chicago on its own account, with no assistance from the Mexican government, and with the intention of contacting buyers from other Latin American markets and taking advantage of their presence at the exhibition. In addition, Don Luis also had good contacts in Spain, Italy, and Germany. Export to these three countries, as well as to other Central American nations such as El Salvador and Guatemala, was facilitated by the fact that the Mexican products were certified.

These exports were maintained over the course of several years although in a sporadic fashion; they did not represent a priority for the company until 2012, when, under the management of Pilar Pérez, the most aggressive internationalization process in the history of Man Industries was begun, being based on the capacity and know-how acquired over the years by the company which permitted them to compete on a large scale in other markets. In August 2014 Oscar Pardo was named Marketing Director of the company with the objective of further developing the export market potential and winning greater market share.

One year after having initiated this plan, very satisfactory results were observable: export activity had been consolidated and was a more stable area for the company, which was now marketing products all over Central America and the Caribbean, including in Cuba, Colombia, and Peru. Export activity was also being initiated in some African countries (Nigeria, Senegal, Morocco, Tunisia, Ghana, and Togo) as well as the Dominican Republic. In this new period the help of ProMéxico was particularly important in locating potential buyers and entering negotiations with them, especially in East Africa and the Middle East; this was due principally to ProMéxico-organized commercial missions to these countries, which helped significantly in building relationships between Mexican businesses and those abroad. It is worth mentioning that these countries represent very attractive opportunities for business. For example, Nigeria is a country with over 165 million inhabitants with great potential for economic growth due to its oil wealth. The market for domestic appliances in Nigeria – particularly of the kind produced by Man Industries – is beginning to expand.

Business contacts with Eastern European countries have been established in a similar fashion. In these markets, Man Industries can compete effectively due to the fact that Mexico has already experienced this process of expansion of the middle class and an improving quality of life for many. In addition, the small domestic appliance industry segment in which Man Industries is established in Mexico is beginning to show signs of maturity, which highlights the importance to the company of entering international markets as part of using its knowledge and manufacturing capacity more efficiently at the same time as reinforcing its competitive capacity.

The company is also entering new markets, such as those for irons and pressure-cookers. "It is a very competitive market, and I would say even more than European or Korean brands, those from China are more competitive. We are practically the only Mexican company that still produces domestic appliances from scratch and which is not part of or dependent on a multinational corporation; we are a company which is 100% Mexican."

In this process of incursion into international markets, Man Industries has benefited from the experience and presence of Mexican products and companies in international markets, particularly domestic appliance companies such as Mabe. Mexican manufacturing is prestigious and recognized for its high quality: "the Mexican (consumers) know that we produce a line of products which are really good; they are durable and in some cases, go on forever." This has helped the expansion of Man Industries into international markets and increases the likelihood of investment in the medium term, in Mexico or abroad, that will permit the company to further take advantage of and consolidate its presence in these markets.

Man Industries employs approximately 700 people and provides work indirectly for more than 2,000 more due to the fact that 95 percent of its suppliers are Mexican. Its operations are divided into the following: the Dycoman product line (pressure cookers and irons), fans, liquidizers, and the Confort line of heaters. It has produced items for the following brands: Black & Decker, Citlali, Elgin, Coromex, Roca, Cimermex, Volvo, Record, Turmix and Starmix, in addition to its own label. Table 14.4 presents an outline of Man Industries' operations in chronological order.

LESSONS FOR INTERNATIONAL MANAGERS

The cases analyzed in this chapter can provide valuable information for other businesses that are involved in the process of internationalization. The story of Mabe is that of a Mexican enterprise that has become a leader in the international market for domestic appliances. How can Mabe be defined, and what is the source of its success? For its

Table 14.4 *History of Man*

Year	Domestic Market	International Markets
1949	Casa Man founded by Don Luis Pérez	
1954	Started production of blenders, the first to be produced completely in Mexico	
1959	Started production of engines for General Electric, parts for Kenmore, and parts and mechanical transmissions for GE washing machines	
1961	Industrias Man de México SA de CV was created and started production of the 410 blender model in pastel colors, signifying great success for the company Started production of drills for Skill and Rockwell	
1969	Started production of electric motors for General Electric fans, blenders for diverse brands such as Elgin, Record, and Turmix, and a special blender for the Federal Electricity Commission during the period of rural electrification	
1971		Exports to Venezuela commenced
1980	Man Industries established its leadership in the production and distribution of blenders and fans	

Table 14.4 (*cont.*)

Year	Domestic Market	International Markets
1990		A new export plan was implemented and Man Industries reached alliances with distributors in Spain, Germany, Guatemala, El Salvador, Honduras, Costa Rica, the Dominican Republic, Cuba, Venezuela, Chile, Peru, and the United States Man Industries participated in International Trade Fairs such as those in Chicago and Germany
2015	A new line of irons and pressure cookers was launched. The company consolidated its position as leader in the production and commercialization of blenders and fans in the domestic market	

Source: Authors, using data provided by the company.

President, Luis Berrondo, Mabe can be described as a "flexible" enterprise. Flexibility is understood here as its ability to adapt; in fact, Luis Berrondo considers that "the key word is adaptation." This capacity is based on practices such as knowing how to read the market environment, taking advantage of circumstances, being confident in your capacity to produce under changing circumstances, and being supported by an open-minded and hard-working team. This ability to adapt is found in different aspects that define one's personality.

Mabe is a business that understands how to capitalize on the advantages of an industrial model based on substituting imports and that had sufficient vision to take advantage of the commercial opening provided by the entry of Mexico into the General Agreement on Tariffs and Trade in 1986, and subsequently the game-changing NAFTA agreement (TLCAN) in 1994. In fact Rafael L. Nava y Uribe indicated that the company participated in an advisory capacity in the consultation groups organized by the Secretary for the Economy together with leading industries with the aim of designing and nego-tiating commercial treaties.[7]

Both enterprises have weathered economic crises. As can be seen, the crisis that Mexico experienced in the 80s was a learning experience, and one which subsequently enabled Mexican businesses to withstand and even grow in extremely difficult circumstances. This experience helped Mabe make economic decisions in countries like Argentina and Brazil. In the words of Luis Berrondo, a fundamental principle is "grow or sell." In Table 14.5 data is presented data about the evolution of both companies.

As part of its expansion strategy, Mabe has acquired established businesses and, as has been shown, will continue brand commerciali-zation. In other words, Mabe understands that its brand benefits from having a presence in any given country or region. For example, the acquisition of the Inresa brand permitted the company to enter the low-income market segment in Peru. In this way, it has learned how to set up distribution networks in the countries in which it operates. Central American operations are coordinated from Colombia and Mexico, and those in Chile and Venezuela are controlled from Ecuador.

Mabe has learned how to generate the organizational framework necessary that permits the union or integration of those businesses that it acquires in a way that favors coordination, eliminates duplica-tion and exploits the strengths of each business entity. Mabe has also combined a group of financial and fiscal specialists in each country, which has allowed it to translate the reality of each country into the

---

[7] We would like to thank Rafael L. Nava y Uribe, the Director of Institutional Relations at Mabe, for his kind assistance in the realization of this study.

organizational language of Mabe as a group, with the aim of facilitating management and coordination. Another thing that should also be mentioned is that Mabe has a policy of always appointing managers who were born in the country of operation. The reasoning behind this is to always have someone in charge who is familiar with the local market as well as the culture of the organization and understands the likes and dislikes of local consumers.

Both Mabe and Man Industries have been associated with industry leaders recognized for their competitive edge, whether in the field of producing wholly or partly-finished products or developing their capacities for innovation and location to penetrate foreign markets. In the case of Mabe, this company has been particularly adept at developing partnerships with the aim of opening markets and/or generating technology. Examples of this capability are Mabe's relationship with General Electric and its alliances with Sanyo, the Research and Advanced Studies Center (Cinvestav – Querétaro branch), Faber North America, the Electronic Products Research Center (CIDES), and the High-Technology Research Center (CCAT). It is particularly important to note the fundamental importance of the alliance with General Electric, without which it would have been impossible to understand the resurgence of the enterprise in the middle of the 1980s and its subsequent growth in the United States and other markets.

The alliance with Haier without doubt marked a new step for the Mexican Enterprise which was, according to Luis Berrondo, a key asset for their manufacturing base. This is borne out by the plants that Mabe has in Mexico, Costa Rica, Ecuador, Colombia, Brazil, and Argentina and the commercial service and distribution operations on the American continent.

Mabe continues to manufacture and have sole rights to use the GE Appliances brands in Central and Latin America, and will try to broaden its production and export capacity to the US market. Luis Berrondo indicated in January 2016 that "this change can mean a growth in the next three years of the order of 15 to 20 percent." In addition, this opens the possibility for Mabe to access the Asian and European markets in a broader way, where Haier is very strong (Anderson, 2016).

Both companies have learned how to differentiate their brand, how to focus on a particular market niche in accordance with the socioeconomic level of consumers, how to differentiate products in accordance with preferences, use, and customs of different countries, how to be innovative with the use of alternative materials, and how to develop new products and satisfy regulations. This was possible in part due to the alliances previously described in the case of Mabe as well as, significantly, the metamorphosis it underwent with the creation of the Mabe Technology and Project Center (CTyP) in Queretaro. This center represented, in the words of Luis Berrondo, the possibility of making Mabe not only a production company but also a design enterprise, and he considers the concentration of design in this center a significant achievement which has enhanced and enriched the company.

Among examples of these achievements could be found the following: i) none of the components produced utilizes cadmium or lead, both highly toxic materials. This has enabled a technology which is in accordance with the strictest specifications and, in fact, the ecological specifications of both Mabe and GE are even more rigid than those established in the USA. Another example of this evolution in technology and the desire to be at the forefront is Teon, a ceramic nanotechnology, which contains silicon oxide, giving Mabe cookers greater protection and resistance to high temperatures without being damaged. ii) The capacity to respond to the washing or cooking requirements of different markets. In Costa Rica, cookers are electric. In Ecuador, induction cooktops are sold as a result of government regulation. In Argentina, as in Europe, washing machines are front-loading, although in Mexico both front- and top-loading designs are equally common. Also in Mexico, it is common to find an integrated stove-top comal (griddle); Mabe therefore iii) offers a range of different products with different technological characteristics. The refrigerator can be electric or gas, with either high or normal capacity. In the same way, driers can be loaded from the front or the top or be integrated and it is important to note that electrical voltage varies from country to country. iv) Mabe offers different types of consumers a product priced according to their income level. Consumers with few resources acquire their domestic appliances piecemeal, while those of the highest socioeconomic level have bespoke kitchens and laundries.

Both companies have benefited from high-quality Mexican workmanship and its recognition in the market. Without doubt, this has been an important factor in the development trajectory of both companies, which has allowed them to offer competitive products. In the case of Man Industries, the company has benefited from the reputation and market position of Mexican products in other countries. International expansion of businesses in the sector, such as Mabe, has had a positive effect on other, smaller companies such as Man Industries as foreign consumers identify Mexican products with quality and their high level of competition. As a summary, Table 14.5 shows different aspects that describe the profiles of Mabe and Man Industries within and outside the Mexican market.

CONCLUSIONS

Flexibility and capacity for adaptation have been key for both the companies studied in this chapter. In order to accommodate environmental conditions, both Mabe and Man Industries have capitalized on the advantages of an industrial model based on the substitution of imports and had the vision to go forward and take advantage of the opportunities for commerce initiated by Mexico in the mid-1980s. MABE has always had a tendency to expand, overcome, and adapt during times of economic difficulty. Enabling this has been a solid work team and a labor force capable of adapting to environmental changes.

The same characteristics are observable in the case of Man Industries, a company which has had to adapt to market conditions at different times in its history, creating partnerships with more

Table 14.5 *Mabe and Man: comparison inside and outside Mexico*

Features	Inside Mexico		Internationalization	Outside Mexico	
	Mabe	Man		Mabe	Man
Experience in Local Market	Since 1946	Since 1949	Experience (first exports)	1960	1971
Employees	23,000	700	Markets Served	More than 70 countries, including the United States, Canada, Central America, Colombia, Peru, Ecuador, Brazil, Argentina, and Chile	Central America, Dominican Republic, Cuba, Spain, Germany, and Italy
Distribution Channels	Department stores	Department stores	Distribution	Department stores	Authorized Distributors
Distribution Channels	Department stores, own stores, and Internet.	Department stores	Manufacturing plants	15	1

Table 14.5 (cont.)

Features	Inside Mexico		Internationalization	Outside Mexico	
	Mabe	Man		Mabe	Man
Brand (Perception)	High quality, fair price	Fair quality, fair price	Trade Shows	Very active	Seldom
Innovation Strategies	Product, design, and quality	Design	Commercial Missions	Active	Seldom
Online Platform	Sales, product information, and social media	Company and product information, and service centers, Web page in Spanish.	Online Platform	Same for Mexico and USA, in English, local stores information, communication, and content	Web page in Spanish
Ownership	Partners	Family owned			
Product Offering	Refrigerators, ovens, stoves, washing machines	Blenders, fans, irons, and pressure cookers			

Source: Information from Mabe and Home appliances Man web pages and additional sources.

established companies who can provide them with parts or produce finished products. All of this has helped create a base from which to penetrate international markets in search of consumers who have similar characteristics to their Mexican counterparts in the small domestic appliance industry.

In the domestic appliance industry Mabe competes with global enterprises such as: Whirlpool, Electrolux, Samsung, and LG, as well as local companies which can be divided into large, medium, and small concerns. In this environment Mabe has plotted different courses: partnerships with firms and institutions, acquisition of local market-leader companies in new markets that Mabe wished to enter, brand differentiation, focusing on market niches according to socio-economic level, offering products on the market according to the profile of a particular region, and launching items with innovation and potential characterized by the use of new materials, a practice which has been successful and which the company sums up as: "It's not about innovation for innovation's sake; it's about producing useful and convenient technology that can fulfil the needs of the clients and end-users."

In summary, the success of Man Industries and Mabe, a leader in Latin America in the domestic appliance industry, is based on flexibility and the capacity to adapt to the economic circumstances of the market. Now, more than ever, this capability will be fundamental in confronting the new challenges that will appear; in the first case, penetrating new markets and establishing partnerships, and in the second, identifying new partners and continuing growth.

The international expansion of successful enterprises such as Mabe generates positive effects for smaller companies such as Man Industries as consumers from other countries associate Mexican products with quality and competitiveness. In this sense, successful companies generate positive externalities for smaller companies, which helps them penetrate new markets.

REFERENCES

Anderson, B. 2016 ¿Qué le traerán los chinos a Mabe? *Milenio* January 18. www.m
ilenio.com/firmas/barbara_anderson/traeran-chinos-Mabe_18_667313301.html.
Accessed February 20, 2016.

Bloomberg Business. Controladora Mabe SA de CV. *Bloomberg L.P.* www.bloom
berg.com/research/stocks/private/snapshot.asp?privcapId=23419045. Accessed
February 18, 2017.

CNN Expansión. 2014. Mabe inaugura planta en San Luis Potosí. *CNN
Expansión*, January 17. http://expansion.mx/negocios/2014/01/17/mabe-inau
gura-planta-en-san-luis-posoti. Accessed February 18, 2017.

Cooney, P. 2008. Dos décadas de Neoliberalismo en México: resultados y retos.
Novos Cadernos NAEA, 11(2): 15–42. www.periodicos.ufpa.br/index.php/ncn/
article/viewFile/ 270/437. Accessed July 18, 2016.

Cordera, R. & Orive, A. 1981. *Desarrollo y Crisis de la Economía Mexicana.*
México: FCE.

El Cronista. 2003. Fagor vende 50% de McLean y se va del país. *El Cronista*,
November 12. www.cronista.com/impresageneral/Fagor-vende-50-de-McLean-y-
se-va-del-pais- 20031113–0045.html. Accessed February 20, 2016.

El estímulo. 2014. Mabe Venezuela aumentó su participación de mercado. *El
estímulo*, December 16. http://elestimulo.com/elinteres/mabe-venezuela-aume
nto-su-participacion-de-mercado/. Accessed February 20, 2016.

Hansegard, J. 2014. Electrolux comprará el negocio de electrodomésticos de GE. *The
Wall Street Journal*. September 8. http://lat.wsj.com/news/articles/S
B10001424052970203708204580141830828714608?tesla=y&mg=reno64-wsj&url=
http://online.wsj.com/article/SB10001424052970203708204580141830828714608
.html. Accessed February 20, 2016.

Man Industries. Nosotros. *Industrias Man.* www.industriasman.mx/nosotros.ht
ml. Accessed July 18, 2016.

Mabe. *Mabe.* www.mabe.com.mx/Default.aspx. Accessed August 17, 2016.

Metalmecanica. 2014. Pronósticos para la industria metalmecánica mexicana en
2014. *Metal Mecanica*, January. www.metalmecanica.com/temas/Pronosticos-
para-la-industria-metalmecanica-mexicana-en-2014+7095737?pagina=4.
Accessed July 18, 2016.

Metalmecanica. 2014. Panorama de la industria de electrodomésticos en México.
Metal Mecanica, October. www.metalmecanica.com/temas/Panorama-de-la-in
dustria-de-electrodomesticos-en-Mexico+100434. Accessed August 17, 2016.

Morales, R. 2014. Electrolux compra 48.4% de Mabe. *El Economista*, September 8. http://eleconomista.com.mx/industria-global/2014/09/08/electrolux-compra-4 84-mabe. Accessed February 20, 2016.

Portal Invest in Celaya. 2011. Sectores e Industrias. Electrodomésticos. *DLMP.* w ww.dlmp.org/invest/espanol/index.php?option=com_content&view=arti cle&id=86:electrodomesticos&catid=77:comun&Itemid=488. Accessed June 15, 2016.

ProMexico. 2013. *Industria de Electrodomésticos 2013*. Mexico. ProMexico.

ProMexico. 2014. *Industria de Electrodomésticos 2014*. Mexico. ProMexico.

ProMexico. 2015. Electronics and Electrical Appliances Industries, Dynamism and Growth. *Negocios*, 9: 11–15.

Quiminet. 2012. Mabe cerrará fábrica lo que implicará la pérdida de casi 700 puestos de trabajo. *Quiminet*, February 6. www.quiminet.com/noticias/mabe-cierra-pla nta-2672539.htm. Accessed February 20, 2016.

The Business Year. 2013. Keep it Cool. Interview to Luis Berrondo, CEO of Mabe. *The Business Year.* www.thebusinessyear.com/mexico-2013/keep-it-cool/inter view. Accessed January 19, 2016.

15 MultiMexicans in the Retail Industry
Elektra and Coppel

Miguel A. Montoya, Maria E. Vázquez, and Miguel A. López-Lomelí

INTRODUCTION

This chapter analyzes the internationalization process of two success-ful Mexican retailers, Elektra and Coppel. Both are among the top Mexican domestic retailers based on their annual sales in 2013: Coppel sold Mex$73.5 billion (Euromonitor, 2014a) and Elektra sold Mex$20.2 billion (Euromonitor, 2014b).

Both groups have accomplished income and profit objectives using a credit program model that targets the middle and base of the pyramid socioeconomic consumer segments in need of credit to pur-chase household appliances, clothing, and electronics, as well as addi-tional banking and financial services in Mexico.

These two companies have used their Mexican models to expand successfully internationally to countries with similar eco-nomic characteristics. Elektra operates in seven countries (Mexico, the United States, El Salvador, Guatemala, Honduras, Panama, and Peru) and Coppel operates in two countries (Brazil and Argentina).

The high-profit results of Elektra are associated with the finan-cial business via credit and banking services and their product mix. Coppel's success is explained by the strategic combination of a broader market segment (C, D, and E consumers), credit system, merchandise mix, geographic store coverage, and branding strategy. Other domestic companies might draw lessons from these successful expansion mod-els to become multinationals, especially when aiming to export their

418

business model to other countries that offer similar conditions to allow them to succeed.

THE EVOLUTION OF RETAIL

Retail is one of the largest sectors in many national economies, making a substantial contribution to the world economy and employment. It frequently represents the second-largest sector in a country's economy, contributing around 13–17 percent to employment, 25–30 percent to business activity, and 8–17 percent to GDP (Wrigley & Lowe, 2010). The industry represents US$13.5 trillion in global revenue and is expected to maintain a 4.5 percent growth for the period 2015–20 (Euromonitor, 2015).

The arrival of the department store in the middle of the nineteenth century marks the start of the evolution of modern shopping practices. This new format allowed consumers and shoppers to purchase, in a one-stop shopping location, a large variety and mixture of goods. Department stores incorporated additional entertainment and hospitality activities as part of the shopping experience, and achieved immediate success with customers. Based on this, other retailers also started to develop a new customer experience, creating an attractive and pleasing environment where shopping was more than just a transaction (Roth, 2013).

Grocery retailers also evolved from the small general store format to the new concept of the supermarket, then to the modern hypermarket, in a matter of a few decades. In recent decades, the retail industry has quickly and intensively modernized thanks to the proliferation of distribution and shopping channels, technological advances, and globalization of markets (KPMG, 2015).

The industry is highly globalized, with large retailers operating in an average of 10.2 countries and international operations that represent an average of 33 percent of total sales (Deloitte, 2014).

The core of the internationalization process involves four major strategic transfers, which are required if the retailer is to succeed in the new market: (1) culture and business model of the firm; (2) capability to adapt to the market; (3) operational retailing practices; and (4) consumer values and expectations (Dawson, 2007). Research has demonstrated that retail internationalization does not follow the normal path laid out in generic strategy models. It is typically a disjointed, fragmented process with periods of expansion and success mixed with disruption and discontinuity, often products of opportunistic incidents and fortune (Burt, Davies, McAuley & Sparks, 2005).

THE MEXICAN RETAIL INDUSTRY

The origins of modern Mexican retail go back to the post-Independence period when European and American immigrant dealers introduced new retailing practices. In the mid-nineteenth century the store Almacén de Novedades appeared as an antecedent of the department store, but it was not until the period known as the Porfiriato (1876–1911) that, thanks to the political and economic stability achieved by President Porfirio Díaz, the first department stores such as Las Fábricas de Francia, El Palacio de Hierro, and the Gran Almacén were established (Casa Palacio, 2015; Deutsch & Bunker, 2010; Palacio de Hierro, 2015).

The post-World War II decades were the period of the arrival and consolidation of supermarkets and convenience store chains, facilitated by the Mexican economic environment. The government's development of urban areas, urban employment, roads, and communications encouraged migration from the countryside to the cities. This urban growth translated to changes in the urban population habits of consumption, triggering greater competition in the retail industry among the self-service stores, which increased their market share taken from the traditional forms of retail such as traditional municipal markets, weekly street markets (tianguis), and traditional (family run) stores. The historical evolution of the Mexican retail industry is presented in Table 15.1.

During the 1990s, the Mexican retail industry underwent changes that transformed it into a highly competitive field,

Table 15.1 *Timeline: history of retail in Mexico*

Year	Historical development of key retailers
Mid-1800s	Almacén de Novedades appears as an antecedent of the department store
1847	Las Fábricas de Francia is founded by J. B. Ebrard
1872	El Puerto de Liverpool is founded by J. B. Ebrard, importing goods from Liverpool, UK
1891	El Palacio de Hierro is founded by J. Tron y Cía
1936	El Puerto de Liverpool relaunches the department store format with superb new facilities
1941	Coppel is founded by the Coppel family
1947	Sumesa opens its doors in Monterrey, Nuevo León
1947	Caltmax opens its doors in Tijuana, Baja California
1947	Almacenes Blanco is founded in Mexico, DF
1947	The first major department store of Sears is inaugurated in Mexico City
1948	Merco opens its doors in Coahuila, Nuevo León, Tamaulipas, and Zacatecas
1950	Elektra is founded
1955	Farmacias Benavides (national drug chain) is founded in Monterrey, Nuevo León
1958	Jerónimo, Plácido, and Manuel Arango found Aurrerá, a grocery retailer
1962	Ángel Losada Gómez opens its first chain store, Gigante Mixcoac, located in Mexico City
1962	The first combination of grocery and general store opens in Mexico City under the name Comercial Mexicana
1963	Superama opens its doors in Mexico, DF
1968	The opening of the first great Soriana shopping center in the city of Torreon, Coahuila, is the event marking the formal beginning of what is now known as the Soriana Organization
1970	Juan Manuel Ley opens the first supermarket of LEY in Culiacan
1970	Chedraui's first supermarket is inaugurated in the city of Xalapa, Veracruz
1970	Suburbia's first department store opens
1970	FAMSA opens a store in Monterrey

Table 15.1 (*cont.*)

Year	Historical development of key retailers
1977	OXXO is founded by FEMSA Comercio in Monterrey, Nuevo León
1988	7-Eleven opens its doors in Mexico, DF
1989	Farmacias Guadalajara (national drug chain) is founded in Guadalajara, Jalisco
1991	Aurrerá (CIFRA) and Wal-mart Mexican joint venture Sam's opens in Mexico City as a new strategic format; Wal-Mart acquires 100 percent of Aurrerá in 1997
1991	Farmacias del Ahorro (national drug chain) starts operations in Chiapas
1992	Price Club opens in Mexico City
1993	Price Club and Costco joint venture: in 1997 it changes its name to Costco Wholesale
1997	H-E-B expands its business across the border into Mexico with a new store in Monterrey

Source: Authors

especially in the supermarkets sector (GAIN-Report, 2010). One major change involved the entry into the market of large international retailers. During this time, important international players entered the Mexican market through alliances like Comercial Mexicana and Costco (1991), CIFRA and Walmart (1991), Gigante and Fleming (1992), Carrefur and Gigante (1994), Kmart and Liverpool (1994), and Auchan and Comercial Mexicana (1995) in an effort to capture market potential and market growth. By 1999, seven of the 20 largest retailers in the world were located in Mexico (Bocanegra, 2008).

Wal-Mart is now the leader of the Mexican retail industry due to an implementation of a strategy of economies of scale and efficiency which forced all other players to follow it into a pricing war (Porter, 1996). Wal-Mart's dominance through the strategy to operate with low operational costs and high efficiency, a strategy that Mexican retailers cannot profitably meet, forced other players to define and develop different strategies that allowed them to compete successfully, including increased cost controls and innovation (Di Gregorio, Thomas & de Castilla, 2008).

Thanks to these developments in the retail industry, currently the Mexican market has a size of US$229,801 million, with a per capita consumption of US$1,934.60 (US per capita consumption is US$9,089), and expected growth rate of 2.2 percent for 2014–19. The Mexican retail industry is one of the most important economic sectors in the Mexican economy, representing 14 percent of the national GDP, 49.9 percent of the economic units, and 30.5 percent of employment (INEGI, 2010).

The retail industry in Mexico can be divided into two main categories: grocery and non-grocery retailing. Grocery retailing represents 55 percent of total retail sales (Euromonitor, 2014c). When analyzing the development of all the types of retailers (grocery and non-grocery), Coppel and Elektra are among the most important. Table 15.2 shows the store-based retailing company shares.

Selection of Elektra and Coppel

During the last three decades, some Mexican retailers expanded their businesses into international operations: OXXO (part of Grupo FEMSA), Coppel, Chedrahui, Elektra, and FAMSA. In terms of their global operations, Coppel and Elektra are both ranked in the top 100 most global Mexican companies: Elektra is number 36 and Coppel is at 97 in the rankings based on the number of international offices and the degree of internationalization (CNN Expansión, 2015b).

Additionally, Coppel has been recognized as one of the 50 fastest growing retailers based on revenue growth over a five-year period of maintained aggressive growth (Deloitte, 2015). Based on these

Table 15.2 *Store-based retailing company shares: percentage value, 2010–14*

% retail value rsp, excl sales tax	2010	2011	2012	2013	2014	Origin	Int. Oper.
Wal-Mart de México	9.7	10.3	10.8	10.6	10.7	USA	Yes
FEMSA Comercio	2.6	2.8	3.1	3.4	3.6	Mexico	Yes
Organización Soriana	4	3.8	3.7	3.6	3.4	Mexico	No
Coppel	**1.9**	**2.1**	**2.3**	**2.5**	**2.8**	**Mexico**	**Yes**
El Puerto de Liverpool	1.9	1.9	1.9	2.1	2.2	Mexico	No
Grupo Comercial Chedraui	1.8	1.7	1.8	1.8	1.8	Mexico	Yes
Controladora Comercial Mexicana	1.7	1.6	1.6	1.6	1.6	Mexico	No
Farmacias Similares	1.2	1.2	1.2	1.3	1.4	Mexico	No
Home Depot México	0.9	0.9	1	1.2	1.2	USA	Yes
Grupo Sanborns	1.3	1.2	1.2	1.2	1.2	Mexico	No
Casa Ley	0.9	1	1	1.1	1.1	Mexico	No
Corporativo Fragua	0.9	0.9	1	1	1.1	Mexico	No
Grupo Palacio de Hierro	0.6	0.9	1	1	1	Mexico	No
Elektra	**0.7**	**0.7**	**0.6**	**0.5**	**0.5**	**Mexico**	**Yes**
Central Detallista	0.6	0.6	0.6	0.6	0.5	Mexico	No
Danone de México	0.4	0.4	0.4	0.5	0.5	France	Yes
Grupo Famsa	0.5	0.5	0.4	0.5	0.5	Mexico	Yes
7-Eleven México	0.4	0.4	0.4	0.4	0.4	Mexico	No
Herbalife Internacional de México	0.3	0.3	0.4	0.4	0.4	Mexico	Yes
Farmacias Benavides	0.4	0.4	0.4	0.4	0.4	UK	No
Others	67.6	66.3	65	64.4	63.8		
Total	100	100	100	100	100		

Source: Euromonitor (2014c)

relevant facts, both companies are considered among the leading Mexican retailers expanding into international markets. Currently, Elektra operates 1,032 stores and Coppel 1,075 (Elektra, 2013).

ELEKTRA

History of Elektra

The antecedent of Elektra was the furniture factory that Benjamin Salinas opened with his brother-in-law, Joel Rocha, in 1906 in Monterrey, Nuevo León. Established in the 1920s, their first furniture store was called Salinas & Rocha, and their sales model consisted of giving credit to shoppers with weekly payments that became an added value in their business, allowing customers of lower socioeconomic levels to acquire these goods.

In 1950 the family ventured into the business of manufacturing radios and televisions, and in 1959 the first Elektra store opened with a business model of selling goods with a credit program directly door to door. The business had opened 12 Elektra stores in Monterrey by 1968, and from 1976 to 1989 the credit program was suspended due to the national economic situation.

In 1987 Ricardo Salinas was appointed the new CEO of Elektra in the middle of a serious Mexican economic crisis in which he faced the possibility of bankruptcy of the business. To survive against these conditions he had to undertake a major restructuring of Elektra's operations.

As shown in Table 15.3, in the past 15 years the revenue has steadily been growing due to a combination of commercial expansion, product mix, and customer satisfaction. The negative net profit results in 2015 are due to a negative fluctuation in financial instruments versus their previous year's value owned by Elektra, and does not imply cash flow (Elektra, 2015a).

Thanks to the successful restructuring and business model of Elektra, the shareholders were led by Ricardo Salinas into new businesses which resulted in the creation of two groups of businesses known as Grupo Elektra and Grupo Salinas, making Grupo Salinas one of the most important business groups in Mexico.

The highest profit contributor is their financial business, which is the key success for Elektra. Every Elektra store has a bank inside it:

Table 15.3 *Elektra: financial data*

	2000	2005	2010	2015
Revenue	1557.7	2835.6	2649.4	4792.6
Total assets	1506	4776.4	9711.5	11518.2
EBITDA	239.3	475.8	536.8	489.2
Gross profit	665.5	1357.2	1828.1	2694.8
Net profit	118.7	273.4	36.7	–325
Foreign investment	N/A	N/A	0.13	N/A
Exports	N/A	N/A	N/A	N/A
Employees	18,541	24,328	37,500	84,333
Countries	5	4	7	9

Data in million US$

N/A = not available

Source: Authors with data from Bloomberg, Expansion and Company's Reports

Banco Azteca offers credit to enable Elektra's clients to buy in the store. Elektra stores offer electronics, appliances, furniture, motorcycles, tires, cell phones, and computers.

Elektra works mainly with seven strategic suppliers, which provide 62 percent of the total supplies of the company. In Mexico, Elektra has 11 distribution points and 1,200 sales centers. Banco Azteca offices are located within the stores, and there are 1,032 Elektra stores in Mexico and 2,372 independent bank offices (Elektra, 2015b).

International Expansion of Elektra

Elektra first focused on Latin America for its strong growth potential and started simultaneous commercial operations in 50 stores in four Latin American countries: Guatemala, El Salvador, Honduras, and the Dominican Republic (now closed) in 1997, since these countries are culturally, economically, and socially similar to Mexico. The stores used the same logo, sold the same products, had similar credit policies, and provided financial services and the money transfer services of Western Union.

Later, Elektra expanded to Peru, Panama, Argentina (now closed), and Brazil. The Latin American growth of Elektra is based on the same Mexican business model: to offer credit for the consumption in the store via a bank focused on the middle of the pyramid, they realized that people not only need to buy credit, but also save in their bank. The transformation of Elektra is presented in Table 15.4.

As part of its expansion into Latin America, in 2005 the company began to franchise its brand Elektra. By 2010 it had 795 stores in Mexico. Between 1997 and 2010 the company expanded its operations in Latin America to 50 stores in Peru, 47 in Guatemala, 23 in Honduras, 12 in Panama, 13 in Argentina, and seven in Brazil.

Elektra Foreign Entry Strategies

Argentina: Despite the fact that Elektra's business model did not exactly suit the country's socioeconomic characteristics, due to its large middle class, the group thought that the country had huge growth potential. Elektra entered with an investment of 60 million dollars and the simultaneous opening of 35 stores, and commercial operations and insurance services began in 2007. Unfortunately, adverse political and macroeconomic environments influenced the development of the business. Foreign currency controls, import and export restrictions, control on capital flows, high inflation, and a nonpayment culture made Elektra's business impractical. Additionally, Elektra could not open its Banco Azteca due to financial regulations in this country. Since Argentinian regulations did not allow the operation of the two business axes (Finance and Retail), along with the crisis factors and the economic slowdown, Elektra decided to close operations in Argentina in 2013.

Brazil: The expansion into this country was intended to happen via an acquisition. However, Elektra entered the Brazilian market with a

Table 15.4 *Transformation of Elektra*

Year	Local transformation	International transformation
1906	Foundation and first store, Salinas & Rocha	
1950	Elektra is founded	
1976	As a result of the peso devaluation, Elektra changes its credit sales strategy to cash only	
1989	Elektra reinstates credit sales	
1993	Elektra's first public offering on the Mexican stock market	
1994		Elektra list its shares in the form of GDS on the NY Stock Exchange
1996		Contract with Western Union services for electronic money transfers
1997		Opening of stores in Guatemala, El Salvador, Honduras, and the Dominican Republic
1998		Elektra starts selling in Peru
1999	Elektra acquires 94.3% share of S&R	
2001	Acquisition of the Curacao store chain	
2002	Mexico's government grants a license to operate a bank (Banco Azteca); Banco Azteca starts operations in 800 locations (inside the stores of Elektra and S&R)	Elektra closes operations in El Salvador
2003	Elektra asks for a license to the SHCP to expand its	

Table 15.4 (*cont.*)

Year	Local transformation	International transformation
	banking services (insurance and retirement funds)	
2004	Seguros Azteca starts operations in Mexico	Elektra obtains a license to operate in Panama (financial services)
2005		GDS program ends with the NYSE Commercial Operations in Panama start with a franchise agreement Insurance business get Guatemala, Honduras, Panama, and Peru
2006	Comisión Nacional de Seguros y Fianzas (Mx) licenses Seguros Azteca (insurance)	Approval from the Monetary Board to operate Banco Azteca in Guatemala
2007		Authorization by the Honduras government to operate Banco Azteca Banco Azteca starts operations in Guatemala Starts commercial operations in Argentina
2008	Elektra Mexico introduces the FAW cars from China	Operations begin in Brazil through Elektra store format Banco Azteca begins operations in Peru and Brazil
2009	Elektra cancels FAW operation	Banco Azteca begins operations in El Salvador
2010	Banco Azteca starts Presta Prenda (pledge)	
2011		Microcredits start in Peru and Brazil

Table 15.4 (cont.)

Year	Local transformation	International transformation
2012	Opens Punto Casa de Bolsa (stock subsidiary)	Elektra acquires Advance America (nonbank short-term loans in the United States); Elektra starts microcredit in Guatemala and El Salvador
2013		Elektra ends operations in Argentina Starts Prestaprenda in Guatemala
2014	Elektra acquires Blockbuster Mexico	
2015		Elektra ends operations in Brazil

Source: Elektra (2014)

direct investment in 2008: 10 stores and bank branches opened at the same time in the northeast region, and microfinance services started operations in 2011. The Brazilian market is seen as a key strategy within the expansion of Elektra, given its potential.

Dominican Republic: Elektra entered via store openings in 1997 with the advantage that there was no other business model that allowed the population to acquire products with the credit program offered by Elektra. However, the Group's management complained of smuggling that was overlooked by the government, which prevented them from working on an equal footing. Due to the lack of profitability, the stores closed in 2002.

El Salvador: With a market potential for financial services for the middle of the pyramid, Elektra entered El Salvador with an investment of 12 million dollars. Despite the advantage of Elektra's credit model matching El Salvador's middle-of-the-pyramid socioeconomic consumers' needs, due to lack of profitability the stores ceased operating in

2002. However, Banco Azteca returned, investing in the simultaneous opening of 29 branches throughout the country in 2009, and the microfinance business started in 2012.

Honduras: Elektra entered Honduras, the second poorest country in Latin America, with store openings following the same expansion process as in Guatemala: first the store, offering all the services; next, the insurance service; and finally, the bank in 2007, initially opening 46 branches through direct investment.

Guatemala: After initial store openings, Elektra continued promoting its banking products in Guatemala in 2005. It initially offered insurance services and, two years later, Banco Azteca arrived, simultaneously opening 75 points of sale; additional microfinance services entered in 2012. The business model followed the Mexican model of combined store and bank. The entry of Wal-Mart, however, forced Elektra to open 60 bank branches in one day.

Panama: Given Panama's status as a dollarized economy and the second worst country for income distribution among the social classes in Latin America, Elektra identified an opportunity to provide financial services for the middle of the pyramid and entered the country with a franchise program.

Peru: Due to its great economic development, Elektra viewed Peru as a great opportunity for business, entering with the opening of 10 stores and one distribution center with a total investment of 6.5 million dollars. The insurance business started in 2005, while the bank operations started three years later, focusing on unattended market segments; this guaranteed high potential profits for Elektra in Peru. The microfinance business started in 2011.

Although Elektra's expansion has been focused on Latin America, the group is open to other business opportunities; an example of this is the expansion to the USA through the acquisition of Advance America, Blockbuster, and Total Play in Mexico.

Expansion to the United States had different characteristics to those of the rest of the continent. Elektra acquired Advance America (AA) to access the market segment of 49 percent of US households who have no more than US$2,000 for an emergency. The average loan is US$385 and lasts 18.1 days. Elektra entered with a business model without retail credit because the company is convinced that the United States is a mature and competitive market in which Elektra is not certain to fit.

The attractiveness of the business lies in the financial opportunities of small or large loans (credit card or loft loans). The target consumer segment is the bottom of the pyramid and a little higher for US standards of living. It is important to note that, in order to obtain a loan, a person must be a resident or a citizen. These are payday loans: borrowers must (i) have a checkbook, (ii) have a salary, and (iii) be a formal resident or citizen. In the United States, Elektra does not necessarily seek to replicate the Mexican store credit model; since in the United States the credit cards represent a strong competitor for these consumer segments.

Elektra has learned from the management of the acquired company that their Hispanic customers are no different from the typical mix of the US population, so there is no cultural affinity when approaching potential customers in this population segment.

Elektra has become the leader in financial services and specialized commerce in Latin America. The company focuses on the middle of the pyramid by extending credit in more than 6,000 sales centers in eight countries. Capital expenditure in recent years has been focused on expanding and maintaining the sales centers. Revenues from international operations represent 26 percent (Elektra, 2014).

In 2015, Ricardo Salinas decided that it was the right moment to institutionalize the governance of Elektra and Grupo Salinas by delegating the responsibility for the business decisions and strategic direction to the General Managers and Staff of each business branch of both groups (CNN Expansión, 2015a).

COPPEL

Coppel is considered the largest department store in Mexico, above Liverpool (1936) and Palacio de Hierro (1891) – two companies that were established before Coppel entered the market. Its strategy is to target low-income consumers (representing around 50 percent of Mexico's population) with a merchandise mix that includes home appliances, electronics, furniture, apparel, and footwear. Sales are the result of supplying easy credit options, secured by weekly payments, to those consumers who are unable to obtain credit in any bank or financial institution, and not requiring any personal guarantee to acquire it.

As shown in Table 15.5, Coppel has maintained a steady financial and commercial growth over the past 15 years, as demonstrated by its financial results, commercial expansion, and growing number of employees. These results make it one of the most profitable retailers in Latin America.

The success of Coppel could be explained by a strategy aligned to five pillars: (1) selection of market segment; (2) geographic expansion and an increasing number of stores; (3) merchandise mix; (4) branding strategy; and (5) credit system (Ugarte, 2012).

Today, Coppel has an infrastructure that includes 1204 stores with over 1.7 million square meters of effective sales area; 130 distribution centers; 18 warehouses; more than 8,500 vehicles; and more than 90,000 employees.

History of Coppel

Coppel started operations in 1939 when Luis Coppel Rivas and his son, Enrique Coppel Tamayo, opened a store called "El Regalo." At that time, the first international operation started as Coppel was sourcing merchandise in the United States, traveling to Dallas to buy goods, and branching out into foodstuffs, bicycles, furniture, and electronics. Coppel's business model then was based on extending credit to his customers, who were often poor and unable to get credit anywhere else, secured by weekly payments (Reference for Business, 2015).

In 1970, Coppel began selling clothing, TV sets, and household appliances under a revolving credit scheme, thereby introducing an innovation to the market. Additionally, Coppel added perfume, shoes, and tennis clothing to the assortment at the stores (Coppel, 2013).

In 1985, Enrique Coppel Luken, a grandson of the founder, became the chief executive and chairman of the board of the firm. Taking over a local company with a dozen stores, Coppel Luken began a national expansion, ending in 1990 with 23 stores and an international sourcing operation in Calexico, California with a warehouse and a team of international buyers. By 2002, Coppel started its growth at a rate of 40 stores every year, entering cities such as Guadalajara, Monterrey, Puebla, and Tijuana (Cuadros, 2012).

In 2002, with 189 Coppel stores in 24 Mexican states, the company bought the Calzados Canadá footwear chain. With this acquisition, they added 149 stores located in almost all parts of the country, and a factory able to turn out four million pairs of shoes per day. The Canadá stores were remodeled and continued operation under the name Tiendas Coppel-Canadá (Reference for Business, 2015).

Table 15.5 *Coppel: general data*

	2000	2005	2010	2015
Revenue	589	1800	3293	5759
Total assets	585	1820.4	3288.9	5853.1
EBITDA	129.5	205.7	460	1237.1
Gross profit	209	778	1495	2598
Net profit	71.7	94.1	308.8	900.2
Foreign investment	N/A	N/A	N/A	N/A
Exports	N/A	N/A	N/A	N/A
Employees	8,441	21,320	60,845	84,331
Countries	1	1	3	4

Data in million US$
N/A = not available
Source: Authors with data from Bloomberg, Expansion and Company's Reports

Coppel continued its growth during the beginning of the twenty-first century, opening stores in Mexico City and the southern part of Mexico. This expansion was financed by the International Finance Corporation, the private credit arm of the World Bank, which extended the company a US$30 million loan in 2002, expressing its interest in financing profitable private long-term projects in Mexico with a strong social impact. The IFC granted Coppel a new 10-year loan of US$35 million in 2005 (IFC, 2005). By 2009, Coppel had reached 786 stores (Coppel, 2013).

In 2006, Afore Coppel, a pension funds management, began operations using the existing customer base as its potential market. The opportunity to serve a market of 20 million Mexicans without financial services, and 50 million who needed loans to buy merchandise because they were living on less than Mex$600 a month, was very important for Coppel, but in order to gain the scale to do that, the company needed an alliance with a bank – or its own bank. After a relatively unsuccessful alliance with Banca Afirme, S.A. Coppel decided to open operations of BanCoppel in 2007 (Coppel, 2013). Coppel's historical timeline is shown in Table 15.6.

Coppel Foreign Entry Strategies

In 2008, Enrique Coppel Tamayo died and Agustin Coppel Luken took the leadership of the retailer so that Enrique Coppel Luken concentrated on the retailer's international expansion plans and their recently acquired financial interests in Afore Coppel; with this objective in mind, in 2010, Coppel opened two stores in Curitiba, Brazil and four stores in Buenos Aires, Argentina, via direct investment, approaching international expansion with a progressive perspective in mind, as explained by Agustin Coppel:

> In the past six years we have been analyzing these markets, [and have] prepared the teams, obtained the points of sales and started operations and growth. It is an important and long investment

process; we want to consolidate what we have before expanding into other countries.

(Ugarte, 2012)

In 2013, Coppel had 1062 stores in Mexico, 14 stores in Brazil, and 14 stores in Argentina. This operation generated a revenue of US $62 billion for Mexico and US$159 million as the result of international operations representing only 0.1 percent of Coppel's revenue (Coppel, 2013). By the end of 2014, Coppel had 1144 stores, giving them a 2.8 percent share of the Mexican retail market, ahead of competitors like Liverpool (2.2 percent), Elektra (0.5 percent), and Grupo FAMSA. Additionally, they led mixed retailers by 29 percent, and variety stores with a 62 percent share (Euromonitor, 2014c). In 2015, one strategic move in terms of product offering was the agreement to commercialize exclusively in Coppel the Jennifer Lopez brand apparel and household product line (Rizo & García, 2015).

CONCLUSIONS

There are five relevant points for managers and academics to draw from the internationalization processes of these two Mexican companies:

1. In spite of the standardization/adaptation debate in international business expansion, their internationalization strategy was split into two areas: business model and marketing strategy to consumers. Regarding the business model, they opted for standardization versus the option of adaptation to new local markets. To succeed in this standardization approach, the critical step was to select countries with similar economic and consumption conditions, representing a good opportunity to operate with the same business model that had allowed them to succeed in the Mexican economy, thus aiming to minimize critical domestic and foreign internationalization barriers, both economic and commercial (Evans, Bridson, Byrom & Medway, 2008). The selection of expansion opportunities was based on a careful analysis of these countries' socioeconomic conditions and their commercial and financial regulations,

Table 15.6 *Coppel history*

Year	Domestic	International
1941	Mr. Luis Coppel Rivas and his son, Enrique Coppel Tamayo founded the business with one gift store named "El regalo" (The Gift)	
1971	Coppel started to sell apparel	
1991	Coppel Corporation was founded in Calexico, California, as a warehouse with international buyers	
1993	Coppel started its growth at a rate of 40 stores every year	
2002	Coppel acquired a big shoe store (Calzados Canadá) with 160 stores	
2006	Afore Coppel, a pension funds management, began operations	
2007	BanCoppel, a bank supported by Coppel, began operations	
2008	Coppel had 501 stores and 266 shoe stores	
2009	Coppel finished the year with 816 total stores	
2010		Lojas Coppel opened three stores in Curitiba, Brazil Coppel opened four stores in Buenos Aires, Argentina Coppel started consolidating operations and sourcing offices in Shenzhen, China
2011		Coppel started consolidating operations in Shanghai and Ningbo, China

Table 15.6 (cont.)

Year	Domestic	International
2012		Lojas Coppel has eight stores; Coppel has 11 stores in Buenos Aires, Argentina
2013		Coppel has 1071 stores in Mexico, 14 stores in Argentina and 14 Lojas Coppel stores in Brazil
2015	Acquisition of 51 Viana's stores with operations around the country	

Source: Coppel (2013)

as well as an understanding of mid-/low-class consumers, to minimize the barriers to foreign expansion.

2. Research in retail internationalization has determined that the consumer is one of the most critical elements in the success of the retailers' internationalization process, since consumers' acceptance of a new retail outlet defines their success in the new market (Rudienė & Stašys, 2015). Therefore, these two success cases of Mexican retailers represent important evidence for the marketing field concerning (a) the adaptation of a marketing strategy to a new country while maintaining the standardized business model of the home country; and (b) developing branding and marketing strategies to successfully connect with new target mid-/low-class consumer segments and appealing to them in a new environment against local retail competition.

3. Both firms followed an internationalization process that included the strategic transfers to the new country suggested by Dawson (2007); exported their culture and business models and the organizational culture of the firm; demonstrated the capability to adapt to the market, evidenced by their country entry strategies as well as Elektra's entry into the loan business for low-income consumers in the United States; operated their international businesses via exporting their operational retailing practices;

and successfully established a marketing strategy that met the foreign countries' consumer values and expectations.

4. These two internationalization processes also confirm what research in this field has demonstrated, namely the fact that retail internationalization does not follow the normal path laid out in generic strategy models. Both Mexican retailers followed their own business models and did not pretend to follow other leading international retailers' expansion models (Burt, Davies, McAuley & Sparks, 2005). This additionally confirms the fact that internationalization in retail presents periods of expansion and success, mixed with disruption and discontinuity, as evidenced by the closing of operations and in some cases the "closing and coming back" of Elektra.

5. Income growth continues to be one of the key motivators of retail internationalization (Evans, Bridson, Byrom & Medway, 2008); the management of both companies have expectations of higher revenues from their international businesses, which confirms that they both coincide in the need to build "economies of scale" as one of their top priorities, to achieve expected higher business results from their international operations (information provided to authors).

Other retail firms from emerging markets can draw from these successful experiences to develop their own internationalization strategies by capitalizing on these principles, adapting them to their own particular businesses.

REFERENCES

Bocanegra, C. O. 2008. Para entender el comercio minorista en México a partir de los noventa. *Revista Nicolaita de Estudios Económicos*, 3(2): 89–104.

Burt, S., Davies, K., McAuley, A. & Sparks, L. 2005. Retail internationalisation: from formats to implants. *European Management Journal*, 23(2): 195–202.

Casa Palacio 2015. La Historia-Cronología, www.casapalacio.com.mx/corporativo. Accessed November 3, 2015.

CNN Expansión 2015a. ¿Ricardo Salinas cambió?, www.cnnexpansion.com/nego cios/2015/10/29/ricardo-salinas-cambio. Accessed November 3, 2015.

CNN Expansión 2015b. Las 100 Mexicanas más Globales 2015, www.cnnexpan sion.com/tablas/2015/01/20/las-100-empresas-mexicanas-mas-globales. Accessed November 1, 2015.

Coppel 2013. Brief overview of Coppel as potential partner to enter to Mexican market. *Coppel*, 1(2013): 1–19.

Cuadros, A. 2012. Mexico's Coppel brothers emerge with $16 billion fortune, www .bloomberg.com/news/articles/2012-11-15/mexico-s-coppel-brothers-emerge-wi th-16-billion-fortune. Accessed November 14, 2015.

Dawson, J. A. 2007. Scoping and conceptualising retailer internationalisation. *Journal of Economic Geography*, 7(4): 373–397.

Deloitte 2014. Global Powers of Retailing, www2.deloitte.com/content/dam/Del oitte/global/Documents/Consumer-Business/dttl-CB-GPR14STORES.pdf. Accessed November 18, 2015.

Deloitte 2015. Global Powers of Retailing, www2.deloitte.com/content/dam/Del oitte/global/Documents/Consumer-Business/gx-cb-global-powers-of-retailing.p df. Accessed November 17, 2015.

Deutsch, T. & Bunker, S. B. 2010. Transatlantic retailing: the Franco-Mexican business model of fin-de-siècle department stores in Mexico City. *Journal of Historical Research in Marketing*, 2(1): 41–60.

Di Gregorio, D., Thomas, D. E. & de Castilla, F. G. 2008. Competition between emerging market and multinational firms: Wal-Mart and Mexican retailers. *International Journal of Management*, 25(3): 532.

Elektra 2013. *Annual Report 2013*, http://quote.morningstar.com/stock-filing/An nual-Report/2013/12/31/t.aspx?t=XMCE:XEKT&ft=&d=ce7447796efce98332a8 bf4e521d13e3. Accessed December 4, 2015.

Elektra 2014. *Annual Report 2014*, www.grupoelektra.com.mx/Documents/ES/D ownloads/Grupo-Elektra-Informe-Anual-2014.pdf. Accessed December 4, 2015.

Elektra 2015a. *Annual Report 2015*, http://quicktake.morningstar.com/stocknet/ secdocuments.aspx?symbol=xekt&country=esp. Accessed May 5, 2016.

Elektra 2015b. Grupo Elektra Presentation. www.grupoelektra.com.mx/Documen ts/ES/Downloads/2Q15EngEKT.pdf.

Euromonitor 2014a. Coppel local company profile, www.euromonitor.com. Accessed November 20, 2015.

Euromonitor 2014b. Elektra local company profile, www.euromonitor.com. Accessed November 20, 2015.

Euromonitor 2014c. Mixed retailers in Mexico, www.euromonitor.com. Accessed December 1, 2015.

Euromonitor 2015. Retailing in 2016: new insights and system refresher, www.eu romonitor.com. Accessed December 3, 2015.

Evans, J., Bridson, K., Byrom, J. & Medway, D. 2008. Revisiting retail internationalisation: drivers, impediments and business strategy. *International Journal of Retail & Distribution Management*, 36(4): 260–280.

GAIN-REPORT 2010. Mexico Retail Sector Report 2010. Retrieved from https://
gain.fas.usda.gov/Recent%20GAIN%20Publications/Retail%20Foods_Mexico
%20ATO_Mexico_2-23-2011.pdf. Accessed May 11, 2018.

IFC 2005. IFC's second financing to Coppel in Mexico, http://ifcext.ifc.org/ifcext/
pressroom/ifcpressroom.nsf/1f70cd9a07d692d685256ee1001cdd37/f92a455eb
f925b6d852570420054f3da?OpenDocument. Accessed November 14, 2015.

INEGI 2010. Censo de Población y Vivienda 2010, www.censo2010.org.mx.
Accessed December 1, 2015.

KPMG 2015. Evolution of retailing; reinventing the customer experience. KPMG
web page Industry: Consumer Markets, Retail, www.kpmg.com/cn/en/issuesan
dinsights/articlespublications/pages/evolution-retailing-o-200912.aspx.
Accessed December 14, 2015.

Palacio de Hierro 2015. Nuestra Historia El Palacio de Hierro, www.soytotalmente
palacio.com/historia. Accessed November 3, 2015.

Porter, M. 1996. What is strategy? *Harvard Business Review*, 74(6): 61–78.

Reference for Business 2015. Coppel, S.A. de C.V. – Company Profile, Information,
Business Description, History, Background Information on Coppel, S.A. de C.V.,
www.referenceforbusiness.com/history2/17/Coppel-S-A-de-C-V.html. Accessed
December 4, 2015.

Rizo, A. & García, G. 2015. Coppel y J-Lo. Los reyes del barrio. *Expansión*, 46(1164):
76–82.

Roth, D. 2013. *The History of Retail in 100 Objects*, www.retail100objects.com.
Accessed December 2, 2015.

Rudienė, E. & Stašys, R. 2015. The identification of the retail internationalization
elements effected upon consumers. *Regional Formation and Development
Studies*, 16(2): 66–77.

Ugarte, J. 2012. Coppel va por las 1,000 tiendas, www.cnnexpansion.com/negocios/
2012/04/16/coppel-va-por-las-1000-tiendas. Accessed December 11, 2015.

Wrigley, N. & Lowe, M. 2010. The globalization of trade in retail services, www
.coursehero.com/file/10747622/46329746/. Accessed November 30, 2015.

16 MultiMexicans in the Restaurant Industry
El Pollo Loco[1] and Alsea

Edgar Muñiz Ávila, Lucía Rodríguez-Aceves,
and José Manuel Saiz-Álvarez

INTRODUCTION

The Mexican restaurant industry has mainly evolved under the influence of contextual factors, such as global food price increases, Mexico's fiscal reforms, the negative perception of the country as an unsafe tourist destination, as well as by the strong influence of the US market in Mexico with the introduction of food chains. This chapter discusses some particular aspects of the Mexican restaurant industry, and provides analytic information related to the economic sector, recent business performance of firms in Mexico, and the domestic market structure.

The restaurant industry in Mexico is mostly characterized by a large number of micro-enterprises and small and medium enterprises (SMEs), commonly informal and created as self-employment. Moreover, Mexico's geographic location is peculiar and places entrepreneurs and business men and women in a dilemma when considering entry into international and neighboring markets, mainly the USA and Latin America, and the Caribbean. Furthermore, within the Mexican restaurant industry, a cultural aspect relating to the predominance of family firms is also peculiar, and has a strong influence on the management style and on the companies' decision-making process.

In this particular context, some MultiMexicans in the food industry have emerged and succeeded. For this reason, the chapter also examines and compares two companies to identify similarities

[1] We sincerely thank the Ochoa family, founders and owners of El Pollo Loco, all of whom kindly agreed to share their time and experience.

and patterns in their internationalization processes. First, El Pollo Loco, three decades after its foundation, is known as the first Mexican franchise company in the food industry to cross the Mexican frontiers. Second, Alsea, founded in 1998, is today the leading food service company in Mexico, manages 1,816 corporate units and has a presence in five countries. This chapter is rich in insights derived from interviews with key actors in both companies, as well as with an in-depth review of secondary data from a variety of sources.

Findings relate to the fact that both companies are family firms, their histories and trajectory differ substantially regarding their age and size, as well as their consolidation and internationalization strategies. However, both El Pollo Loco and Alsea experienced exponential growth at the beginning of their operations. The former exploited a novel product and a secret recipe as a competitive advantage. The latter secured a twofold strategic alliance and an agreement to exploit property rights in Mexico, when the franchising industry was still in its infancy.

This chapter's contribution is to report the lessons learned from both cases, regarding their consolidation and internationalization processes. Examples of those experiences include: (1) acting in good faith and without contracts is not to be recommended, even if a close friendship exists; (2) having an experienced executive team, with an academic formation in management and strategy, increases the chances of successfully negotiating exclusivity rights; and (3) a proper understanding of the specificities of market segments of interest is as important as the quality and novelty of the product or service to be offered.

AN OVERVIEW OF THE MEXICAN FOOD SERVICE INDUSTRY

In New Spain, the food service industry began in the sixteenth century. Mexico was the first country in Latin America that initiated and regulated public accommodation and a food service business. In December 1525 the first food service market was installed in

Mexico City with sales of wine, meat, and other necessities.[2] In 1785, the first café started operating at the corner of Tacuba and Monte de Piedad. In the nineteenth century, inns were reformed and adopted the French buzzword "restaurant" to restore (from French, *restaurer*) the energies of their customers. In 1906 the first Sanborns Café was opened. In 1936 the chef Guillermo Kaiser, from Germany, founded the *Bellingshausen*. In 1940, Mr. José Inés Loredo founded the Tampico Club and the Arroyo restaurant, and in 1964, *VIPs* and *El Portón* began operating. Such options attracted clients mainly from the middle and upper classes. For low-income citizens, *fondas* and *taquerías* emerged and were commonly visited. In particular, *fondas* are small independent restaurants that are popular among middle- and low-income consumers who do not eat at home, while *taquerías* are focused on selling one of the most traditional dishes in Mexico, the *taco*.

Complementary to these family food businesses, franchise activities began to develop in Mexico around the mid-1980s (Cuevas, Bellon & Pelayo, 2011), probably promoted by the abrogation of the control and registration of technology transfer and use and exploitation of brands and patents law in 1985.[3] This encouraged the establishment of foreign companies in the Mexican market. In 1990, the legal definition of the term "franchise" appeared in the industrial property law (Calderón & Ayup, 2008). Since then, the franchise industry in Mexico has been growing continuously, with an annual increase of 10 percent on average (US Commercial Service, 2009), bringing prosperity to the food and beverages sector.

Added to franchises and traditional family businesses, in 2015, according to the National Restaurant Chamber (CANIRAC), and the last census from The National Institute of Statistics and Geography (INEGI), 515,059 economic units were dedicated to preparing food and beverages in Mexico, employing 1.5 million people in direct jobs, and 3.5 million in indirect ones. The sector represents 1.5 percent of the

---

[2]   INAES is the National Institute for Social Economy in Mexico. See www.inaes.gob.mx/doctos/pdf

[3]   SEGOB is the Interior ministry that publishes the *Official Gazette*. http://dof.gob.mx

Gross Domestic Product (hereinafter, GDP), and 13 percent of the tourism sector. Surprisingly, over the 15 years from 1999 to 2014, the average growth rate was 4.5 percent (INEGI, 2014).

The market value of full-service restaurants grew to Mex$28 million in 2012, with VIPs, Sanborns, Toks, and Yum being the leading brands. But the great jump happened in 2013 when the market value surged to Mex$164 billion. It is noteworthy that this remarkable growth was made in just one year. It is expected that the average per capita consumption will grow by 4.5 percent in Compound Annual Growth Rate (hereinafter, CAGR) terms over the five years from 2014 to 2019, while total food consumption is expected to grow by 5.6 percent in CAGR terms over the same period. In Table 16.1 the year-to-year food service industry growth is shown.

Regarding the composition of the Mexican restaurant market, this economic sector is divided into five categories, as follows: (1) *Fine Dining/Full-Service* restaurants, which refers to higher-priced establishments targeting middle- to high-end consumers; (2) *Casual Dining* restaurants, meaning affordable, family-friendly dining outlets; (3) *Fast Food*, such as, for example, McDonald's and Burger King; (4) *Quick and Casual* restaurants, which include coffee shops and target middle-income consumers; and, finally, (5) *Independent* restaurants, such as street/mobile outlets (kiosks, stalls, etc.). Table 16.1 shows the market sizes for each of these categories, and makes plain that *full-service* restaurants have a significantly higher share compared with the rest.[4]

The sector is highly fragmented, as full-service restaurants in Mexico serve a wide range of consumers. However, the majority of outlets are independent family-owned *fondas* and *taquerías*. Restaurants that belong to the "organized" restaurant segment are chains (e.g., franchises) and large establishments, which only represent around 5 percent of all the restaurants in Mexico, and generate 6 percent of all sales value in the sector. In this sense, from the 428,000

---

[4]   CANIRAC is the National Restaurant Chamber; see www.canirac.org.mx.

Table 16.1 *Market size–Mexico food service / *Year-to-year food service industry growth comparison*

Category	Consumer Food service	Home Delivery/ Takeaway	Cafés/Bars	Full-Service Restaurants	Fast Food	Street Stalls/ Kiosks	Pizza Consumer Food service	Mexico	World
		Market size–Food service in Mexico						Year-to-year food service industry growth comparison	
2005	47,334	716	4,499	25,400	5,798	10,921	1,350	N/D	N/D
2006	46,905	747	4,726	24,475	6,069	9,889	1,335	3%	2.2%
2007	47,523	783	4,854	25,549	6,371	9,967	1,365	2.8%	2.3%
2008	46,487	789	4,949	24,998	6,353	9,398	1,358	-1%	-1%
2009	41,365	733	4,618	21,647	5,928	8,439	1,237	-8%	-1%
2010	41,077	722	4,589	21,385	6,075	8,307	1,215	-1.5%	1%
2011E	42,603	743	4,763	22,273	6,326	8,498	1,254	2%	1.2%
2012E	44,362	771	4,961	23,284	6,622	8,724	1,300	4%	1.8%
2013E	46,338	804	5,184	24,387	6,979	8,985	1,354	4.5%	2%

Table 16.1 (cont.)

Category	Consumer Food service	Home Delivery/ Takeaway	Cafés/Bars	Full-Service Restaurants	Fast Food	Street Stalls/ Kiosks	Pizza Consumer Food service	Year-to-year food service industry growth comparison	
								Mexico	World
2014E	48,636	843	5,448	25,668	7,401	9,277	1,416	5%	2.6%
2015E	51,352	887	5,764	27,165	7,905	9,631	1,490	5.6%	2.8%
2016	N/D	N/D	N/D	N/D	N/D	N/D	N/D	5.9%	3%

Note: E stands for Expected.
Source: Euromonitor (2016)[5]

Market size–Food service in Mexico

---

5   Euromonitor 2016. http://0-www.portal.euromonitor.com.millenium.itesm.mx/portal/analysis/tab

establishments dedicated to food sales in Mexico, 75 percent are medium and small independent restaurants.[6]

A study performed by Feher & Feher regarding 200 franchising companies showed that 2,613 new units were opened in 2014 in the domestic market.[7] These units generated 19,180 new direct jobs, mainly in Mexico City and the Metropolitan Area, Puebla, Querétaro, and Nuevo León. Furthermore, 74 percent of the companies consider the franchising sector as stable (FranquiciasHoy, 2014). For such reasons, leading foreign companies consider Mexico to be a good place to invest, by entering through franchises or through joint ventures with strong Mexican operators such as Alsea or the Mexican Restaurants Corporation (CMR). Table 16.2 shows the main companies operating restaurants and competing in the domestic market, as well as sales for 2014, brands, number of outlets, and the first year they started operating in Mexico.

The importance of franchises in the Mexican restaurant industry is highlighted in Table 16.2. In fact, franchises were 4 percent of consumer food service, and had about 13 percent of value sales in 2013. Therefore, franchising is now one of the most used strategies in the food service industry, with an expected accumulated annual growth of 25 percent in sales from 2012 to 2017 (Euromonitor, 2016).

In short, and as previously stated, the food service industry in Mexico is booming and it is increasingly representative of the economy. Its fragmentation and informality have not allowed many companies to internationalize and compete globally. But the cases of Alsea and El Pollo Loco are exceptions to this rule, so they are worthy of analysis in order, perhaps, to imitate their successful business strategies as applied in Mexico and overseas.

CASES

The cases we are going to describe are Alsea[8] and El Pollo Loco,[9] both Mexican companies with a peculiar internationalization strategy.

---

[6]   Salcido, 2014.   [7]   FranquiciasHoy, 2014.   [8]   Alsea, 2015.
[9]   El Pollo Loco, 2015.

Table 16.2 *Main restaurant chains*

Company Name	Sales (Mex $ million)	Outlet Name	Number of Outlets	Type	First unit in Mexico (year)
		Domino's Pizza	610	Pizza	1989
		Starbucks Coffee	507	Coffee Shop	2002
		Burger King	447	Fast Food	2002
		Chili's	51	Casual Dining	1999*/2005
		Italiannis	72	Full Service	2012
ALSEA	15,719	PF Changs	22	Full Service	2008
		California Pizza Kitchen	21	Pizza	2007
		Pei Wei	0	Casual Dining	2012
		VIPs	255	Restaurant	1964*/2014
		El Portón	81	Restaurant	1964*/2014
		Wings	14	Full Service	1968
		La Destilería	5	Mexican Food & Bar	2006
Corporación Mexicana de Restaurantes	2,133	Fonda Mexicana	4	Mexican Food	1991
		Chili's	59	Casual Dining	1992
		Olive Garden	8	European FSR	2012

Table 16.2 (cont.)

Company Name	Sales (Mex $ million)	Outlet Name	Number of Outlets	Type	First unit in Mexico (year)
		Red Lobster	3	Casual Dining	2013
		Capital Grille	1	Fine Dining	2013
Grupo Sanborns	40,514	Sanborns	165	Full Service	1946
		Sanborn's Café	28	Restaurant	1903
Premium Restaurant	3,628,660	Pizza Hut	178	Pizza	1993
Brands/Yum International		KFC	328	Fried Chicken	1992
Grupo Gigante	–	Toks	125	Full Service	1971
		Panda Express	22	Restaurant/Asian Fast Food	2011
		Beer Factory	7	Casual Dining	1997
		Garabatos	13	Full Service Restaurant	1988
Grupo Garabatos	–	Casa del Pastor	4	Taquería – Quick and Casual	2001

Note: *Year of the first unit operating in Mexico/Year in which Alsea first operated a unit.
Source: Own elaboration with information from companies' websites, Euromonitor, and industry contacts.

On the one hand, Alsea is a leading restaurant operator in Mexico and Latin America. It manages more than 2700 units and has a multi-brand portfolio, including the operation of Domino's Pizza, Starbucks, Burger King, Chili's, California Pizza Kitchen, P. F. Chang's, Pei Wei, Italianni's, and The Cheesecake Factory.

On the other hand, El Pollo Loco is the first Mexican franchise company in the food industry to cross the Mexican border. Besides, El Pollo Loco's internationalization process was innovative because the founder, short of financial resources but possessing a lot of creativity, developed a new concept that, 40 years after its creation, is still authentic, valid, and solid.

Alsea

Alsea is a multinational company that operates 2,784 units around the world, representing 15 brands located in six countries. Alsea's brands that are leaders in their respective segment are Domino's Pizza, with a 58 percent market share, and a total sales contribution of 18 percent for the company. Starbucks has a market share of 41 percent, as does Burger King, but their contributions in sales differ by 2 percent, being of 29 percent for Starbucks and 27 percent for Burger King. Other trademarks (The Cheesecake Factory, P. F. Changs, California Pizza Kitchen, Italiannis, Chilis, VIPs, and El Porton) are 50 percent of the market share, and contribute 26 percent of the total sales of Alsea (see Table 16.3).[10] One of the key factors of success in the multinational is that Alsea's business model includes backing for all of its business units through a shared service and a support center that provides assistance to all of the administrative and development processes, as well as helping the supply chain.[11] Table 16.3 shows the main brands owned or operated by Alsea and the units per country, as well as the format of the food service concepts.

---

[10]   El Financiero, 2015.   [11]   Oxford Business Group, 2015.

Table 16.3 *Alsea's brands and units per country, 2014*

Brands	Units	Brands	Units
Domino's Pizza	640	Chili's Grill & Bar	42
Mexico	596	California Pizza Kitchen	20
Colombia	44	P. F. Chang's China Bistro	21
Burger King	561	Mexico	16
Mexico	433	Argentina	1
Argentina	77	Chile	1
Chile	35	Colombia	1
Colombia	16	Brazil	2
Quick Service Restaurants	**1,201**	Pei Wei Asian Dinner	2
Starbucks	583	Italianni's	63
Mexico	443	The Cheesecake Factory	1
Argentina	76	**Casual Dining**	**149**
Chile	62	VIPs Mexico	260
Colombia	2	El Portón Mexico	84
Coffee	583	**Family Dining**	**344**
Shops			
		Total Alsea units	2,277
		Corporate	1,826
		Sub-franchises	461

Source: Alsea's Annual Report 2014.

According to CNN Expansión and the ranking of the 500 Greatest Companies in Mexico in 2015, Alsea is in position 108. Furthermore, in 2013, in its ranking of the 100 Mexican companies with a global presence, CNN Expansión positioned Alsea in 62nd place with a global index of 4.5. In Table 16.4 the evolution of Alsea's financial data and long-term statistics regarding net sales and revenues, total assets, and passives are shown, as well as the number of units and collaborators from 1997 until 2014. The company's growth is impressive, as in under 20 years the number of collaborators has increased almost 30 times, net sales have increased 42 times, and net revenues ten times. Growth mainly due to an aggressive expansion

Table 16.4 *Alsea's long-term financial data, 1997–2014*

Year	Net Sales*	Net Revenue*	Total Assets*	Passive with Cost*	Number of Units	Collaborators
1997	536	69	518	28	197	2,013
1998	1,057	86	901	274	265	3,835
1999	1,736	161	1,349	194	335	5,655
2000	2,529	115	1,664	299	409	6,834
2001	2,681	30	1,533	210	425	6,893
2002	2,764	138	1,651	170	463	6,950
2003	2,871	117	1,709	142	472	7,336
2004	3,589	169	2,134	95	626	10,483
2005	4,665	285	3,365	798	728	13,629
2006	6,026	228	4,040	610	865	16,797
2007	6,985	489	5,295	1,033	989	19,200
2008	7,787	139	6,510	1,790	1,135	21,024
2009	8,587	106	5,808	1,302	1,171	19,981
2010	8,948	159	6,110	1,597	1,206	22,127
2011	10,699	230	9,374	4,056	1,283	23,212
2012	13,520	402	9,798	4,969	1,421	27,619
2013	15,697	663	12,435	5,043	1,862	32,362
2014	22,787	624	29,337	11,239	2,784	60,051

*Mex$ (in million)
Source: Own elaboration with data obtained from the Company annual reports.

strategy, allowing a 14-times proliferation in the number of units from 197 in 1997 to 2,784 in 2014.[12]

Alsea's History and International Expansion

Alsea's history goes back to 1989, when Cosme Torrado and his brothers brought Domino's Pizza to Mexico, because it required an investment per store that was consistent with their investment capabilities at the time. A change in the franchise policies of Domino's

[12]   Alsea, 2016.

Pizza International opened the doors for the Torrado family to acquire the master franchise in Mexico, and in December 1990 they signed the rights to exploit the franchise in Mexico until 2025.

In 1992, the first "Distribuidora e Importadora (DIA)" distribution center in Mexico was created. DIA is part of the supply chain of Alsea, and is in charge of distributing all the elements needed by the different Alsea brands to operate. From 1999, when Alsea's initial public offering on the Mexican Stock Exchange was launched, the company started its process of aggressive expansion through the acquisition of different prestigious and global brands, as well as an increasing number of units in the domestic market. As evidence of the success of Alsea's expansion strategy, in 2002, the first Starbucks in Mexico was opened and Burger King was included in the portfolio. Brands like Starbucks are powerful to the consumers and the consumption trend is global. Therefore, Alsea has focused on identifying and negotiating brands with a high certainty of success. "From every ten restaurants, only one survives after the second year of existence. It is an industry where it is difficult to create a concept. This is the main reason why we have chosen brands that proved to be successful in different markets. It is very difficult to find," says Fabian Gosselin, Alsea's CEO.[13]

In January 2004, Alsea became the main shareholder in West Alimentos, which was the franchising company for Burger King Corporation in Mexico. In March 2004, Alsea signed an agreement with AFC Enterprises to operate the brand Popeyes Chicken & Seafood in Mexico, and in June 2004 the first store was opened. It was important for the company to introduce new brands in the same sector, but in different segments, in order to avoid cannibalization between their units. As an example, in 2005, the company entered the Casual Dining segment with the acquisition of nine Chili's restaurants in six states throughout Mexico. In particular, Alsea acquired 60 percent of Aldi Group's shares, which was the

[13]   Comunidad de negocios, 2013.

franchiser of Chili's Grill & Bar for the central region of the country, including Mexico City and the states of Morelos, Puebla, Hidalgo, and Querétaro. Table 16.5 shows a timeline with the main events in the history of Alsea's growth and international expansion.

Alsea's internationalization continued, and in 2006 it purchased the rights to exploit the brand Burger King in Argentina and in Chile. Nevertheless, the Torrado brothers suffered the hardship of closing down Domino's Pizza shops in Argentina.[14] Their operation failed to work out because they were ignorant of the local public's special characteristics. "Argentina is a country that has a very strong tradition in pizza. Here, the mass [of customers] is more limited, and Domino's, which was offering thick pizza, failed. We are going to study the Argentine market, but it will be very hard for us to bring that brand back to the country," stated Cosme Torrado, Founder of Alsea.

In 2008, operations in Colombia started with the purchase of Domino's Pizza and Burger King. In the same year, Alsea acquired the brand California Pizza Kitchen in Mexico. In 2009, the company signed the contract to operate P. F. Chang's in Mexico, which was the brand's first unit outside the United States. In 2010, Alsea opened the 1,000th corporate unit in its portfolio. In the same year, Fabian Gosselin became the CEO of the company. One of Gosselin's correct decisions was to continue with important elements in the organization of the company. The main motivation for this was the world economic crisis, which had weakened the operations of the company over a couple of years.

In 2012, Alsea introduced Pei Wei to Mexico, an Asian food chain owned by P. F. Changs, under the concept of "fast casual" dining. From the outset it was declared as a pilot test of the concept, and it started with three units in Mexico City. 2013 was a year full of important operations for the group. In September, Alsea reached an agreement with Walmart Mexico to acquire VIPs restaurants in a transaction valued at US$617 million. VIPs is one of the most iconic

---

[14]   Knowledge Wharton, 2006.

Table 16.5 *Alsea's timeline*

Year	Local	International
1989	Cosme Torrado and his bothers bring Domino's Pizza to México. The first unit is opened	
1990	Alsea becomes master franchisee of Domino's Pizza in Mexico	
1992	First distribution center in operation (DIA)	
1998		Domino's Pizza decreases its growth in Mexico. Naturally, Alsea opened its frontiers entering into Brazil with the brand
1999	Alsea's IPO	
2002	Alsea signs a joint venture with Starbucks coffee and starts operations with Burger King in Mexico	
2004	Alsea celebrates the opening of the first 500 units.	
2005	Casual dining operations start with Chili's Grill & Bar	
2006		Alsea acquires the units of Burger King in Argentina and Chile. Also signs an alliance with Starbucks Coffee to develop the brand in Brazil
2007		Alsea signs an agreement with Starbucks Coffee to develop the brand in Argentina and Chile
2008	Alsea acquires the brand California Pizza Kitchen in Mexico	Alsea opens units of Domino's Pizza and Burger King in Colombia
2009	California Pizza Kitchen (CPK) and P. F. Chang's Bistro begin operations in Mexico	

Table 16.5 (cont.)

Year	Local	International
2010	Alsea celebrates the opening of the first 1000 units. Fabian Gosselin becomes Alsea's CEO.	
2012	Acquisition of Italianni's/Burger King Master Franchise in Mexico First Pei Wei operating in Mexico	
2013	Alsea reaches an agreement with Walmart Mexico to acquire VIPs restaurants in a transaction valued at $617 m The group acquires a 100% share of the operation of Starbucks in Mexico	Alsea acquires a 100% share of the operation of Starbucks in Argentina and Chile, and signs the agreement to develop and operate the same brand in Colombia
2014	Acquisition of Starbucks' remaining stakes in Mexico Alsea initiated the closing of the three units of Pei Wei in Mexico City	Acquisition of minority stake in Grupo Axo Acquisition of Starbucks' remaining stake in Chile and Argentina Acquisition of Grupo Zena in Spain
2015	Alsea creates two business units, Alsea Mexico and Alsea International. The new organizational structure aims to improve operating margins and profitability metrics	

Source: Own elaboration with data obtained from Alsea's reports (3Q 2014) as well as secondary sources.[15]

[15]   Alsea website: www.alsea.net/uploads/pdf/en/alsea_investor_relations_presentatio n_3Q14.pdf.

and well-regarded consumer brands in Mexico, with a nationwide presence of 362 restaurants. VIPs' sales in 2012 generated revenues of $466 million.[16] In the same year, Alsea acquired 100 percent of the operations of Starbucks in Mexico, Argentina, and Chile, and signed the agreement to develop and operate the same brand in Colombia. Alsea also obtained the exclusive rights to operate P. F. Chang's in Brazil and acquired the master franchise to operate the Cheesecake Factory in Latin America.

For Alsea, the selection of brands in its portfolio has been a key aspect of its business. In fact, the company has considered different market segments in order to avoid cannibalization among its brands, and until 2014 owned ten brands in total. The variety in its portfolio is also related to the type of service provided, from full-service restaurants to fast food and coffee shops.

Alsea constantly searches for opportunities in other industries, perhaps pushed by the expertise obtained regarding the franchise sector or because it has already gained knowledge about the market segment (e.g. the middle- and high-end). For example, in 2014 Alsea acquired a 25 percent minority stake in Axo, a company specializing in fashion clothing and luxury items such as Tommy Hilfiger, Coach, and Guess, among 14 brands. Axo has around 2,200 points of sale and 116 retail stores in Mexico. In addition, in October of the same year the company reported the finalization of the acquisition of 71.76 percent of Grupo Zena in Spain. Grupo Zena has been operating in Spain for 40 years, with an extremely experienced management team that has obtained solid results and a successful growth strategy. "The acquisition of Grupo Zena is an unequaled opportunity for growth and consolidation of our business model. It increases the Company's geographic diversification, which will enable us to create long-term value for all of our shareholders," said Fabian Gosselini, Alsea's CEO.

---

[16]   Alsea, 2016.

This is an opportunity for Alsea to enter the Spanish market through the leading multi-brand restaurant operator, thus Grupo Zena will become its expansion platform outside Latin America, strengthening the geographic diversification strategy established by the company to generate new avenues of growth, to improve its margins and operating flow, and to increase the profitability of the business.

In 2015, Alsea closed the three units of Pei Wei since they did not meet the objectives of profitability and synergy. In volume, the three units represented less than 1 percent of the sales of the company. "Once we accomplished what was established in the contract with P. F. Changs, and due to the low results compared with the expected, Alsea decided to close the three Pei Wei units ... Always looking for the synergies and the profitability for our stakeholders," noted Selene González, Corporate Communications Manager, Alsea.[17]

In the same year, derived from the growth of the company in Mexico and overseas, and aiming to maximize the potential of the group, a new organizational structure was implemented. In particular, the group created two business units, Alsea Mexico and Alsea International, in order to be more focused on the operations.[18] Federico Tejado is the new CEO for Alsea Mexico and Fabián Gosselin is in charge of Alsea International. The new business units, Management and Finance areas, as well as Human Resources and Strategic Planning, will report to Alberto Torrado, Chairman of the Board of Directors. "This new organizational structure will enable us to ensure closeness and focus on our operations, with the aim of achieving a steady recovery of our operating margins and profitability metrics," noted Alberto Torrado, Executive President of Alsea.

Alsea has some challenges ahead of it. The diversification of new products (e.g., clothes and accessories), the participation in new continents, the size of the operations, as well as the fact that the novelty of concepts used usually tends to decrease the interest of customers, and rivals are strengthened as time passes by.

[17] CNN Expansión, 2015a.   [18] CNN Expansión, 2015b.

Nevertheless, the group has a capable executive team that has taken it to the place where it is now, and it is expected that the challenges will be successfully confronted.

El Pollo Loco

El Pollo Loco, the company that created the concept of "grilled chicken" in the world, was founded in January 1975 by Juan Francisco "Pancho" Ochoa in Guasave, Sinaloa, Mexico. To the residents of Guasave, Ochoa's style of cooking was not novel, but it was enormously popular. Using a recipe he learned from his mother, Ochoa marinated his chicken in a combination of herbs, spices, and citrus juices before flame-grilling it. The result became a local favorite, fueling the rapid growth of the El Pollo Loco concept. By the end of the decade – four years after the first chicken stand opened – Ochoa and his family and friends had established 92 restaurants in 20 Mexican cities, making full use of the opportunity before them. El Pollo Loco demonstrated enviable strength as a dining concept, encouraging Ochoa to make a bold geographic leap into the United States. The history of the company is grounded on five main characters: Pancho, who is the founder and creator of the concept, and his four brothers, José, Jorge, Jaime, and Jesús.

Unlike Alsea, El Pollo Loco México is not a public company. Therefore, it was not possible to obtain financial data to present the evolution of the company numerically. Nevertheless, in the following lines the history of the company is described, highlighting important events that substantially affected the progress of the firm.

El Pollo Loco's History and International Expansion

On January 6th, 1975, Mr. Francisco Ochoa and his wife opened the first El Pollo Loco, which was a small place adapted to sell grilled chicken, having previously been managed as a shoe store by Mr. Francisco. The success of the first restaurant soon encouraged Mr. Francisco to invite his brothers to learn about the business and to work with him. That was the beginning of the growth of the company in the domestic market. The second subsidiary was opened in San Luis Potosí by his brother Jaime Ochoa in 1977, in response to the market that enjoyed grilled chicken in the local carnival and wanted to have the product available after the event finished. At that time, the concept was widely accepted because it was new, tasty, and affordable by a variety of segments. In consequence, in one month that subsidiary sold 15,000 chickens. The rapid growth of the business inhibited the chances to plan and design a strategy. Furthermore, the success of the business was partially dependent on other factors, such as hard work, for example: "I think that a person's achievements are the result from his hard work. Even if you have luck, faith, and a destination path, it is very difficult to reach your dreams if you do not work hard," says Francisco Ochoa, El Pollo Loco founder.

Afterwards, new subsidiaries were opened in Sonora, Michoacán, Guadalajara, Tampico, Saltillo, Monterrey, Distrito Federal, Mexicali, and Tlaquepaque – all of them with considerable success, and mostly operated by Pancho Ochoa's brothers, sisters, and cousins, as well as by friends. As Mr. José Ochoa commented, there was no formalized franchise structure; instead, the Ochoa family wanted to help their close relatives and allowed them to use the brand and recipe. It is noteworthy that the rapid growth was due to family values and brothers' union. After five years, in 1980 the Ochoa family had 92 units operating in Mexico located in a variety of cities. Table 16.6 shows a timeline of the history of El Pollo Loco and the main events.

Mr. Francisco Ochoa had friends in Los Angeles, because he had worked in that city when he was young, just like millions of immigrants that looked for opportunities in the United States. That was the main motivation for selecting the location for the first subsidiary overseas. The first El Pollo Loco in Los Angeles was opened on December 8th, 1980 on Alvarado Street, with the support of four investors: Hugo Martínez, who owned 20 percent, Humberto Gálvez with 40 percent, and Jaime and Pancho Ochoa with the rest.

Table 16.6 *Timeline of El Pollo Loco Mexico*

Year	Local	International
1975	El Pollo Loco is founded in Guasave Sinaloa.	
1975–1980	Domestic expansion to an operation of 92 restaurants across the country (San Luis Potosí, Saltillo, Torreon, Nuevo Laredo, Reynosa, Morelia, Guadalajara, Mexico D.F., among many others).	
1980		Opening of the first subsidiary in Los Angeles. The success was unexpected, with long lines waiting.
1980–1983		Opening of 12 restaurants/ expansion in the United States. All the new units were located in California and franchised to American businesspeople.
1983–1986		The Denny and Ochoa families opened 25 subsidiaries in Japan, the Philippines, Singapore, and Malaysia. Francisco Ochoa was present at the openings of all the stores.
1987		Palenque concept creation in USA. Francisco Ochoa was a serial entrepreneur and after the legal situation with El Pollo Loco USA, he decided to innovate and launched a new Mexican food concept.

Table 16.6 (*cont.*)

Year	Local	International
1996	International brand selling and agreement to develop 17 franchises and the rest of Mexican territory.	
2004		Litigation for the El Pollo Loco brand ownership. The Ochoa family noticed that El Pollo Loco USA registered the name of the Mexican brand at the intellectual property office; therefore, they decided to start a legal fight.
2004–2014	Over 40 restaurants in Mexico, family owned/ aggressive expansion in the territory; creation of family groups	Expansion of Palenque concept in USA. Creation of Pollo Palenque, Palenque Grill, and Puerto Palenque.

Source: Own elaboration with data obtained from El Pollo Loco website and interviews with Ochoa family.

The initial success fueled aggressive expansion, much as it had five years earlier in northern Mexico. "When we opened the restaurant in Los Angeles, there was a huge waiting line to buy a grilled chicken. Probably it was like two blocks from the restaurant ... We had to [do] something about it in order to retain the customers ... we came out with the idea to give them free sodas, newspapers and popsicles ... At the end of the day, the waiting line was still there ... to those still in the line we gave them coupons to be exchange[d] the next day for a free grilled chicken," recalled Mr. Pancho Ochoa.

In 1982, the operation of El Pollo Loco Mexico attracted the attention of the Ochoa family. At the same time, one of the partners who was the owner of 40 percent of the company in the United States, and the president of these operations, deliberately initiated a financial mismanagement. In the middle of 1983, the Ochoa family noticed the deplorable financial situation of El Pollo Loco International. At that point, Humberto Gálvez had sold the operation of El Pollo Loco in Japan, as well as more than 50 new franchises. Nevertheless, there was no sign of the money obtained. The Ochoa family asked for legal advice in Mexico and in the United States, and created and initiated a strategy to successfully terminate Humberto Galvez's participation in the partnership.

At the same time, there were three different businesses: 1) El Pollo Loco International, the owner of the restaurants in the USA; 2) El Pollo Loco Franchise, the franchiser in the USA; and 3) El Pollo Loco Overseas, for the rest of the world. Despite the success of the business, the financial situation was critical. The franchisees requested their original investments due to the negligence of the previous management. Moreover, the subsidiaries in the United States were in debt for more than US$2 million. The situation pushed the Ochoa family to sell the brand El Pollo Loco and the assets in the United States to Denny's group, an American restaurant chain. Denny's also absorbed El Pollo Loco's debts and obtained the rights to exploit the brand globally, with the exception of the Mexican territory. Specifically, the operator acquired Ochoa's twelve restaurants in Los Angeles for US$11.3 million. It is noteworthy that an agreement was signed to jointly develop subsidiaries with a global scope in the following five years. This agreement also included clauses stating that both El Pollo Loco Mexico and El Pollo Loco United States could use new procedures, recipes, or developed technologies promoted by either of the two parties. Finally, the agreement stated that neither El Pollo Loco Mexico nor El Pollo Loco United States could compete with a similar concept in the next five years. At that moment, the history of the company changed substantially.

Later on, Denny's and the Ochoa family opened 25 subsidiaries in Japan, as well as in the Philippines, Singapore, and Malaysia.

The family received 25 percent of the initial payment and one-third of the royalties for each new franchise. At that moment, Mr. Pancho acted as a consultant, supervising the recipe of the marinade, and some of the operational processes at different locations.

El Pollo Loco was performing admirably by the mid-1990s, but the company had recorded only negligible physical growth since the start of the decade. The chain had increased from 12 units to 200 units between 1983 and 1991. During the next five years, only 16 further units were added to the chain. The parent company's executives declared their intention in 1996 to make El Pollo Loco a 600-unit chain by the end of the decade.

Recently, in the United States, the company became El Pollo Loco Holdings, Inc. The corporation's activities are conducted principally through an indirect subsidiary, El Pollo Loco, Inc., which develops, franchises, licenses, and operates quick-service restaurants under the name El Pollo Loco and operates under one business segment. On June 25, 2014, the "Company" operated 168 and franchised 233 El Pollo Loco restaurants.

In 1984, Don Pancho and his family moved to Monterrey. At that time, 92 restaurants operated in Mexico and the family was working hard to consolidate and modernize the brand El Pollo Loco in the country. In 1985, the first restaurant with drive-through and soda refill was opened. In 1989, Pancho Ochoa became the President of El Pollo Loco Mexico, and initiated the unification process with respect to the franchisees' contracts and royalties, as well as the sales and distribution of the marinade. The majority of the franchisees in Mexico came from family and friends, and some of them did not accept the new conditions that, for example, required investments to improve the restaurants. As a consequence, the chain reduced the number of units to around 40: the units owned by the family and 25 franchisees.

In 1987, the company was swept up in corporate maneuverings when TW Services, Inc., one of the largest restaurant companies in the world, acquired Denny's and El Pollo Loco. From 1983 to the end of the decade, El Pollo Loco – under the control of Denny's and TW Services – grew to be a nearly 200-unit restaurant chain. The growth was impressive, but it was achieved almost entirely in California. Under TW Services' control, an attempt to greatly broaden the chain's geographic presence had scored only moderate success in Arizona, Nevada, and Texas. Elsewhere, the efforts to export the concept failed, leading to the closure of units in Florida, Hawaii, and as far away as Japan, by the beginning of the 1990s.

In 1992, the Ochoa family entered a partnership with César Balsa and Jorge Cossío to develop El Pollo Loco in Mexico City and Cancun, opening new units and positioning the brand. In addition, under the partnership, an investment to develop TGI Fridays started, but achieved no success due to the economic crisis of 1995. As a result, only one restaurant in Mexico D.F. was left. Because of the crises, Mr. Pancho – as well as the majority of Mexicans – had financial problems, and had to sell assets in order to pay his debts. They had to start again, and the family searched for a strong partner in order to develop the domestic market. At that time, Ray Perry was the CEO of El Pollo Loco United States, and a new partnership started. In the same year, Denny's sold El Pollo Loco United States to a bigger company called American Securities Capital Partners. From that moment, the good relationship between the Ochoa family and El Pollo Loco United States came to an end.

In 1996, the American company bought the foreign development rights for the El Pollo Loco concept from the Ochoa family and signed an agreement to develop 17 franchisees and the rest of the Mexican territory, with the exception of Nuevo León, Coahuila and the cities of Nuevo Laredo and Gómez Palacios. Nevertheless, the American company did not fulfill its obligations, and the agreement to develop El Pollo Loco in Mexican territory was terminated. Afterwards, the Ochoa family had a further problem: the American company sued them for ownership of the brand. Nevertheless, after a few years of litigation, a Federal court in Laredo, Texas found that the El Pollo Loco Mexico brand legally belonged to the Ochoa family.

Francisco Ochoa held a meeting in Nuevo Laredo with Steve Carley, new President of the group American Securities Capital Partners, in order to reach an agreement to develop the Ochoa Territory (Nuevo Leon, Coahuila, Nuevo Laredo, and Gómez Palacios) and the rest of Mexico. There were two further meetings in Nuevo León and California, respectively. In August 2003, the representatives of American Securities presented a Business Plan to develop the Mexican territory, beginning with Tijuana BC, but the representatives of American Securities wanted a ridiculous amount of money to be paid by the brands. American Securities questioned the Ochoa family's contribution to the project and Don Francisco Ochoa responded about the trademark, but the Americans said that they were the owners of the El Pollo Loco trademark in Mexico, so a legal fight began for the possession of the brands as American Securities maintained that the agreement made in 1996, in collaboration between El Pollo Loco USA and El Pollo Loco SA de CV, allowed them the right and title to the brand of El Pollo Loco in Mexico. In 2004, when the Ochoa family reviewed the ownership of the brand at IMPI, they were surprised that the rights of the brand were indeed on behalf of the American group, which had acted upon the 1996 agreement.

On March 28, 2004 a trial for the possession of the brand El Pollo Loco in Mexico began in Laredo, Texas. Finally, on October 31, 2007 the Judge of the Federal Court of Laredo, Texas, ruled in favor of the Ochoa family.

Nowadays, El Pollo Loco Mexico has more than 40 restaurants in Mexico. In the chain, four brothers and 17 cousins are involved. It is noteworthy that the extended Ochoa family is now working on a succession plan that will allow the institutionalization and professionalization of the whole company. One of the aspects is the division of regions in the Mexican territory, and the rights to exploit each of them by the families represented.

To improve efficiency and reduce costs, technology has been a constant in the Ochoa family's business. For example, they started using coal to grill the chicken, and nowadays they combine gas and other technological devices that also give their products a better presentation. Regarding the price and quality, one of the aims of El Pollo Loco is that the product must be affordable and standardized. For that reason, even though the raw materials are subject to increases in price, the restaurants maintain the prices and also the supply of all the chicken sides. Logistics is another important element. In particular, the Ochoa family implemented "The Comisariato," consisting of a distribution center that is in charge of buying raw materials, preparing the chicken sides, and delivering them to the restaurants. "The Comisariato" takes advantage of economies of scale, reduces the costs of logistics, and increases control in the use of raw materials.

In addition to the previous comments, some of the key factors in the success and rapid growth of El Pollo Loco have been marketing, technology, price, quality, and logistics. Regarding marketing, Mr. José Ochoa registered the brand, logo, and jingle of El Pollo Loco, and Mr. Jorge Ochoa designed advertisements and promotions.

Mr. Jesús Ochoa is the person who maintains order and brings structure to the family. Mr. José Ochoa is the negotiator, who dominates the norms, rules, processes and, in the right moments, who contributed the most to solving the legal issues. Furthermore, the new generation of the Ochoa family is involved in the operation of the company, and is pushing forward to improve the efficiency and productivity of the restaurants. For example, the creation of the marketing department centralizes the spending on advertising, promotions, and discounts, as well as developing market positioning strategies. Another example is the creation of a distribution center that prepares and supplies a variety of ingredients to different restaurants, as sauces and chicken. The distribution center permits economies of scale when purchasing, reducing logistics expenses, and promoting operational controls. Finally, according to the Ochoa family, the secret of El Pollo Loco Mexico's success has been the quality of its products, affordable prices, and reinvestment of profits. "We truly believe that the quality of our products ... the chicken and food complements like the sauces ... it's been essential for the success of El Pollo Loco.

The customer is always right, so we have to listen to them in order to build loyalty," said Mr. José Ochoa.

The main challenges for the future are to consolidate the group, to maintain product quality in all the restaurants and the distribution center, to introduce new products, and to solve the process of family succession. Today, after three decades, it is known as the first Mexican franchise company in the food industry to have crossed the Mexican frontiers.

The company is facing a variety of additional challenges that must be addressed. One of them is the fact that the restaurants are divided into groups, according to the ownership of the Ochoa brothers. In other words, restaurants owned by Mr. José Ochoa represent one group, those owned by Mr. Francisco Ochoa represent another group, and so on. Consequently, problems relating to economies of scale, lack of standardization in operations and administrative processes, misunderstandings about shared suppliers, and issues related to human resource selection and recruitment, are constant. Furthermore, each group has a different growth rate and, sometimes, different product offers. Overall leadership and a common business plan to develop the Mexican territory is also missing, but it is what is expected as a result of the succession process.

Mr. Pancho Ochoa may be considered a serial entrepreneurial. He is also the founder of the Texas-based Mexican fast-food chains, Taco Palenque, Pollo Palenque, and Palenque Grill. In 1987, Mr. Pancho bought a piece of land in Laredo, Texas and in July of that year, he opened a restaurant that offered authentic Mexican food with recipes from Sinaloa. In 2014, Taco Palenque had 18 restaurants all over Texas, and the brand had a remarkable presence in the region. In total, and as a result of the Palenque concept, nowadays Mr. Pancho Ochoa, his son Charles, and his wife and daughter, as well as Juan Francisco Jr., own 20 business units around Texas.

COMPARISON AND CONCLUSIONS

Similarities and Differences in the Internationalization Process

In our attempt to get deep insights into the internationalization process of Mexican companies in the food service industry, we have established that some of the main differences are related to corporate governance and organizational structure. Alsea has a Board of Directors, and El Pollo Loco is run by a family council. Besides, Alsea is organized in divisions according to brands, and the locations of their operations, in Mexico or overseas. El Pollo Loco is organized by family groups, geographically distributed in regions across the country. Both business models and expansion strategies differ substantially, as Alsea expanded organically and aggressively, acquiring new brands and rights to exploit them across markets, while, in contrast, El Pollo Loco offered a unique product and the growth responded to demand.

In the same vein, we found some similarities between both cases. First, both companies started operations on a small scale and grew rapidly. Second, the speed of internationalization in both cases was relatively high. El Pollo Loco opened its first subsidiary in the United States within five years of starting operations, and Alsea tried to introduce the first Domino's in Brazil after nine years. Third, family is an important factor in both companies, from their foundations to date: the Torrado brothers in the case of Alsea, and the Ochoa family with El Pollo Loco. Finally, the internationalization process started in both cases with a cooperative strategy, but in the case of Alsea was motivated by market saturation, and in El Pollo Loco by excitement to explore new frontiers.

Enablers, Barriers, and Peculiar Aspects of the Internationalization Process

Aside from similarities and differences, we also identified enablers, barriers, and peculiar aspects for each case. Both companies had to suffer a market-based validation process of their business models before being successful. Alsea identified the opportunity to bring to Mexico a franchise model with the vision to replicate and adapt a new business model. Nevertheless, the company also needed to test the concept with a pilot unit, and once the company proved the success of the first group, an organic expansion of the firm was initiated. Some of the reasons why Alsea became succesful are described in the following paragraphs.

First, Alsea avoided cannibalization. The selection of 11 brands that it owns or represents do not compete among themselves for the same market segments. Second, Alsea's expansion and accelerated growth have been guided by three paths: an organic, aggressive expansion, the growth of Alsea's new brands, and the acquisition of new licenses or brands to develop. Such expansion included a geographical expansion to exploit other markets. Third, Alsea maintains its commitments to the brands, complying with the agreements in each of the contracts. Fourth, Alsea is focused on a growing middle-class client sector that aspires to have new experiences and good service. Fifth, the group has been able to attend all kinds of market segments. Sixth, Alsea has learned, during the expansion process, what its customers want, which trends will be developed in the future using testing brands and concepts in different countries. Once the knowledge and expertise are acquired, Alsea replicates the processes in different markets and diversifies. Seventh, Alsea has changed its organizational structure in order to become more efficient to increase its profitability margins.

On the other hand, El Pollo Loco improved product performance, marketing, and commercialization strategies, as well as operational processes. Using a trial and error method, managers established 11 stores in the country and they certainly contributed to a better understanding of the most profitable models and markets. Some enablers were that Mr. Francisco Ochoa lived for a while in Los Angeles, California, so he had the business expertise after the rapid expansion in Mexico and established his cooperative strategy with

Denny's that allowed El Pollo Loco to explore new markets in the Philippines, Malaysia, Japan, and Singapore. Finally, and more importantly, El Pollo Loco offered a novel and high-quality product that was tasty and affordable. The barriers for El Pollo Loco were the lack of knowledge regarding the American regulations to establish a business, as well as some market characteristics. Also, the language was a factor that impacted the process, with the lack of a trustworthy and professional network in Los Angeles.

One peculiar aspect of El Pollo Loco's internationalization was the market selection. It could have been expected to explore the Latin American markets, because of the language, cultural, and historical closeness to Mexico, but the company instead selected a developed economy. Another aspect is the simplicity of the product offered: grilled chicken. It became so popular, and without any substantial adaptation, that the product had great acceptance in the United States, Japan, Malaysia, and other markets.

Lessons Learned

Finally, some lessons learned that may be useful for companies within the food service industry, or even working in other sectors, may be the following. First, focusing on the company's expertise is essential. For example, even if Alsea had never developed a brand on its own, it mastered the process of replicating and executing. Such a process allowed the company to enter other countries and be successful there.

Second, managerial skills and market vision are fundamental in selecting the right brands or businesses to invest in, as well as in identifying both the correct markets and the appropriate time to enter them. Once the market in the new country is well understood, diversification may follow. Managerial skills should be composed of expertise, but also must be reinforced by academic training.

Third, to define a vision and to execute it well are processes that have the same level of importance; therefore, assigning adequate resources in terms of human capital that can be focused on a company's own activities is vital. Fourth, innovation in terms of internal processes, methods, organizational structures, as well as novelty business models, products or services, should be in the mind of decision-makers in every company aiming to be internationalized.

Fifth, any company interested in going overseas must learn how to deal with regulations and cultural issues that change in different contexts. Commonly, know-how may come from partners in the host country. Consequently, long-term relations, abilities to negotiate, key performance indicators, monitoring, and control processes, as well as written agreements and contracts, are key for reducing the risks derived from entering new markets. Finally, the founders' personality and vision should permeate through the whole company. Possessing entrepreneurial and managerial abilities, as well as having at one's disposal hard-working human resources, may be the necessary beginnings of generating a multinational company.

REFERENCES

Alsea. 2015. Alsea webpage. www.alsea.net. Accessed February 20, 2015.

Alsea. 2016. Annual Report 2015. www.alsea.net/uploads/pdf/en/alsea_conclude s_process_adquiring_zena.pdf. Accessed July 25, 2016.

Calderón-Monge, M. E. & Ayup-González, J. 2008. The brand management with market orientation: Overview's franchisees. *Estudios Gerenciales*, 24(108), 61–77.

CNN Expansión 2015. Mexicanos "le hacen fuchi" a Pei Wei y cierra restaurantes. *CNN Expansión*, February, 13. www.cnnexpansion.com/negocios/2015/02/13/ mexicanos-le-hacen-fuchi-a-pei-wei-y-cierra-sus-puertas. Accessed March 21, 2015.

CNN Expansión. 2015. Alsea divide sus operaciones en dos unidades de negocio. *CNN Expansión*, April 13. www.cnnexpansion.com/negocios/2015/04/13/alsea-divide-sus-operaciones-para-potenciar-su-crecimiento. Accessed February 14, 2015.

Comunidad de negocios. 2013. Fabián Gosselin: "En la Argentina todavía hay mucho para hacer a largo plazo", May 12. www.lanacion.com.ar/1581243-fabian-gosselin-en-la-argentina-todavia-hay-mucho-para-hacer-a-largo-plazo. Accessed March 22, 2015.

Cuevas, C. Y., Bellon, L. A. & Pelayo, J. 2011. *Los retos y oportunidades para mejorar el desarrollo del modelo de franquicia en México*. Paper presented at the V Congreso de la Red Internacional de Investigadores en Competitividad.

Euromonitor. 2016. Full-service Restaurants in Mexico. Consumer food service. *Euromonitor*. http://0-www.portal.euromonitor.com.millenium.itesm.mx/portal/analysis/tab. Accessed May 10, 2016.

El Pollo Loco. 2015. El Pollo Loco website. www.elpolloloco.com.mx. Accessed May 24, 2015.

El Financiero. 2015. Grandes bocados. *El Financiero*. www.elfinanciero.com.mx/pages/marcas-de-alsea-tienen-el-liderazgo.html. Accessed June 19, 2015.

FranquiciasHoy. 2014. El sector franquicias de México se expandirá con fuerza en 2014. *FranquiciasHoy*, March 15. www.franquiciashoy.com/recursos/notifranquicias/mar-2014/el-sector-franquicias-de-mexico-se-expandira-con-fuerza-en-2014. Accessed April 13, 2015.

INEGI. 2014. Censos económicos. Mexico D.F. National Institute of Statistics and Geography. www.inegi.org.mx. Accessed November 1, 2015.

Knowledge Wharton. 2006. After Meteoric Growth in Mexico, ALSEA, a Specialist in Franchising, Seeks its Future in the Southern Cone Countries, June 28. http://knowledge.wharton.upenn.edu/article/after-meteoric-growth-in-mexico-alsea-a-specialist-in-franchising-seeks-its-future-in-the-southern-cone-countries/. Accessed December 26, 2015.

Oxford Business Group. 2015. Alsea: Food and beverages. *Oxford Business Group* www.oxfordbusinessgroup.com/analysis/alsea-food-and-beverages. Accessed June 10, 2015.

Salcido, V. 2014. Food Service – Hotel Restaurant Institutional. Restaurant Sector in Mexico 2014. *GAIN report*. MX0347. USDA Foreign Agricultural Service. http://gain.fas.usda.gov. Accessed April 12, 2015.

US Commercial Service. 2009. CS Mexico Market Report. Franchise Services Sector in Mexico. *United States of America. Department of Commerce*. www.franchise.org. Accessed Jun 10, 2015.

17 MultiMexicans in the Hospitality Industry

Hoteles City Express and Grupo Posadas

Eileen Daspro and Raúl Montalvo

INTRODUCTION

The Hospitality Industry and Tourism in Mexico

The importance of tourism as an economic activity in Mexico cannot be overstated. Officially, tourism has been the third most important source of income for Mexico, with an equally important potential in terms of broader economic development in the country, given its impact on employment generation and infrastructure investment. In 2012, Mexico received 23 million tourist arrivals, experiencing a slight decline of 1.23 percent in comparison with the previous year; nevertheless, there was an increase of 7.17 percent in the inflow of international tourism receipts, reaching US$12,720 billion. In 2014, Mexico rose again to the list of the top ten destinations worldwide, in tenth position, with more than 29 million tourist arrivals after experiencing an impressive growth of 20.5 percent with respect to the previous year, allowing it to move up five places (UNWTO, 2015).

The lodging industry has benefited significantly from the strong performance of tourism in Mexico. Lodging revenue from foreign tourists alone increased by 13 percent in 2014, and by 9 percent in 2015; similar growth was experienced among domestic tourists in Mexico. The total value of the lodging industry in 2015 was Mex $265.8 billion and is expected to rise at 5 percent CAG through 2020, reaching Mex$340.1 billion. It is expected that the growth of domestic and foreign hotel chains in the tourism industry will continue in future years as a result of the prevailing deficit in the hotel market with high quality standards.

Driving this growth in the Mexican lodging industry is Grupo Posadas, whose value grew by 5 percent in 2015 with vibrant sales among its hotel brands, Fiesta Inn, One Hotels, and Fiesta Americana. The last, a luxury hotel brand, is the second most important in the country (after Corporación Milenium), and enjoys a 3.5 percent market share in a very fragmented Mexican lodging industry. Hoteles City Express, a mid-market hotel category, is also an industry leader, ninth in terms of market share in Mexico. It too experienced steady sales growth in 2015. By targeting business travelers and guaranteeing standardized service quality across locations in key Mexican business corridors, Hoteles City Express has been able to grow its business by focusing on underserved segments. Both Grupo Posadas and Hoteles City Express have prospered in the hyper-competitive Mexican lodging industry, not only because of their growth in the Mexican market but because of their ambitious strategic plans for continued expansion abroad (Euromonitor, 2016).

As of 2011, there were 58 known hotel chains, located and operating mostly in developed tourist destinations in Mexico, managed by 46 different tourism operating companies. Hotel chains amounted to 325 hotels, representing 20 percent of the accommodation units that existed at the time. Fifty-seven out of the 69, i.e. 82 percent of the establishments of "Special Class" (special category) and "Gran Turismo" (grand tourism) categories, were part of a national or international hotel chain, while in the five-star category, the proportion decreased to 74 percent of establishments; for four-star establishments it fell to 31 percent, and to just 1.3 percent of three-star hotels. Nationally, the hotels exceeded 355,000 rooms, of which 43 percent were three-star or superior. The level of concentration experienced by the industry would be less complicated if the companies could agree on joint strategies, operating policies, and targeted investment (Olguin, 2011).

Table 17.1 shows data concerning the numbers of rooms of the main hotel chains in Mexico in 2013. An important issue in

Table 17.1 *Numbers of rooms of the main hotel chains in Mexico*

Hotel chain	Number of hotels (units)	Number of rooms	Brands
Posadas	106*	18,825	Live Aqua, Fiesta Americana Grand, Fiesta Americana, Fiesta Inn, Hoteles One, and The Explorean
City Express	73	8,091	City Express, City Junior, and City Suites
Grupo Real Turismo	38	8,000+	Camino Real, Quinta Real, and Real Inn
Starwood Hotels	24	5,000+	St. Regis, W, Sheraton, Westin, Luxury Collection, Four Points by Sheraton, and Le Meridien
AMResort	22	7,500	Zoetry, Secrets, Dreams, Now, and Sunscape
Hyatt Hotels Corporation	4	1,546	Hyatt Regency

*At the time of writing there are more than 130 hotels.
Source: El Economista (2013)

the hotel industry in Mexico is the classification of hotels. In the early 1990s, the Ministry of Tourism decided that hoteliers could freely determine the category of their facilities, which triggered a plethora of stars being plastered on hotel façades. This was in part a consequence of the lack of official recognition of accreditation with international organizations. Moreover, under that system, owners or operators chose between the existing categories they judged the most appropriate for their establishments, and they could even create new ones. It was at this point when concepts such as "Gran Turismo" and "Special Class" emerged as ways of defining and differentiating categories above the traditional five-star rating, which was considered the highest class at the time (Reyes, 2011).

HOTELES CITY EXPRESS SAB DE CV

Hoteles City Express SAB de CV is the leading hotel chain in Mexico in the business traveler segment, with 96 operational hotels in Mexico and Latin America as of December 15, 2014. It is the third largest hotel group in Mexico after IHG and Grupo Posadas; however, it is considered the leader in the limited services segment where it competes with brands like One, Ibis, Misión Express, and Real Inn. Hoteles City Express provides affordable, modern, functional lodging solutions with limited service offerings for Mexican business travelers. It opened its first hotel in Saltillo, Coahuila, in 2002. Its CEO, Luis Eduardo Barrios Sanchez, has more than 25 years of hotel industry experience, having occupied the position of Director General at Grupo Posadas from 1994–9 and Finance Director at the same company from 1986–93 where he was responsible for the international expansion of Grupo Posadas's hotels in Brazil and Argentina through the acquisition of local chains.

Hoteles City Express was founded in 2002 with the aim of reaching a strategic market niche in Mexico: the value-oriented business traveler. Its initial value proposition was to bring better service and comfort to business travelers throughout the country. Traditionally, business executives in Mexico stayed in upscale hotels, but after 2000, Mexican companies felt increasingly obliged to cut costs and economize, and business travelers were forced to look for more affordable lodging options. Hoteles City Express has distinguished itself from its competitors by specializing in the highly fragmented and unattended segment of national business travelers who had been mostly ignored by the large, upscale, national, and international hotel chains like IHG (InterContinental, Crowne Plaza) and Grupo Posadas (Fiesta Americana, LiveAqua, One). It successfully identified a niche opportunity in the hotel industry and created a unique value-oriented service offering, combining high-quality hotel standards and an affordable price, which at the time of its inception was uncommon in the Mexican hotel industry. By 2013, Hoteles City

Express had grown into the third largest hotel chain in Mexico with 90 hotels, ranked third behind IHG with 133 hotel units and Grupo Posadas with 124 hotels (City Express, 2015).

According to Javier Arce, Director of Development at Hoteles City Express, the business traveler segment was ignored until 2003. Travelers whose jobs demanded that they make one or two overnight business trips per week in the same week had been mostly unserved. According to Arce, "[t]he five-star segment dominated the industry for a long time, and later the four-star segment. However, there still was a clear need for a service offering that could offer the hotel guest a branded, standardized lodging offering with consistent, quality service, and a clean comfortable room, bathroom, kitchen, etc. regardless of location in the country" (Jiménez, 2014). This gap in the Mexican hotel industry would grow in size with the growth of manufacturing, export, logistics, and agricultural sectoral development in Mexico post-NAFTA, and Hoteles City Express quickly seized the opportunity that emerged.

As of December 2014, with over 96 hotels throughout Mexico, Costa Rica, and Colombia, Hoteles City Express was considered the fastest-growing hotel chain in Latin America and the market leader in Mexico in affordable hotels for business travelers. Hoteles City Express had developed and operated different hotel brands occupying unique niches within the business traveler segment. By 2014, 76 percent of their hotel units were Hoteles City Express brand, 15 percent were City Express Junior, 7 percent City Express Suites, and 4 percent City Express Plus (City Express, 2015). Their different hotel brands offered only those services that business travelers required to rest or work comfortably in a modern, affordable hotel. In their words, they offered "Justo lo que necesitas" ("Only what is needed"). For example, in Mexico, the majority of its hotels are operated under the City Express and City Express Plus brands, which are aimed at business travelers seeking comfortable, affordable lodging. These limited additional services included free continental breakfast, wireless Wi-Fi access, and a business center on site.

Moreover, the City Suites brand is focused on inexpensive, extended-stay lodging alternatives with greater amenities such as kitchen appliances. Here, guests enjoy furnished apartments with hotel-type services. City Junior, another hotel segment run by the company, is even more economical than City Express, and targets sales and administrative professionals who travel frequently for work-related purposes and thus require budget-friendly lodging options.

Despite their affordable rates, all of the company's brands meet strict international quality control standards in both the hotels' physical installations as well as their service delivery. For example, all of the hotels have electronic locks, fire alarm systems, air conditioning, heating, and wireless Internet. This formula of affordable price combined with quality lodging offerings has enabled Hoteles City Express to achieve a high level of hotel occupancy and growth from 2003 to the present.

According to its 2014 Report for Investors, Hoteles City Express has achieved its remarkably rapid national and international expansion by identifying key strategic locations in dynamic business corridors throughout the country, where economic activity is poised for greatest future growth. These include: a) the energy and petro-chemical corridor in and around Veracruz, Campeche, Tampico, and Coatzacoalcos; b) the industrial and manufacturing corridor of Monterrey, Apodaca, Reynosa, and Nuevo Laredo; c) the maquila-dora and export logistics corridor in Northwest Mexico, including Tijuana, Mexicali, Nogales, Ciudad Juárez, and Matamoros; d) the mining corridor in Laguna, including Durango and Cananea; and e) the agricultural export corridor of western Mexico, including Los Mochis, Cuilicán, etc. In sum, Hoteles City Express aimed at creating lodging offerings for business travelers emanating from Mexico City in every major industrial or commercial center in the rest of Mexico.

Hoteles City Express has strategically identified for future site development industrial and commercial corridors relating to proposed economic reforms or recent or proposed commercial openings. These include the recent opening of the natural gas and petrochemical sector to private investment in Western Mexico, sustained growth in Mexico's dynamic automotive and automotive part industry in the advent of NAFTA, recent increases in investment in communication and transportation infrastructure, and the resurgence in maquiladora manufacture activities at the northwestern Mexico border, as overall levels of violence in the region have subsided.

According to Arce, the success of Hoteles City Express is owed also to the standardization of its processes, similar to those of the automotive industry in Mexico, whose own exponential growth directly benefited the expansion of Hoteles City Express. Arce noted that every hotel was always made with the same materials to the same quality, using the same interiors and furnishings, and thus guests would find consistent hotel offerings under the Hoteles City Express brand whether they were in Cali or Mexico City. According to Arce, this is their primary source of competitive advantage: "When you make a reservation in Hoteles City, there are no surprises" (Jiménez, 2014).

Arce attributes Hoteles City Express's sustained growth and expansion in Mexico and Latin America to three key sources of advantage. The first is that Hoteles City Express successfully identified and purchased land in strategic locations at competitive prices: not an easy feat in many of the well-developed urban centers where it has recently begun operations. The second key factor, according to Arce, is the ability of its management to obtain permits and licenses quickly when they are needed to build and operate: a factor that he attributed directly to the company's excellent relations with local government authorities and its position of transparent commitment to high ethical standards wherever it does business. In addition, Arce has recognized the potential obstacle that unions and labor demands could have played for construction growth in the region. Arce attributed the success in avoiding such obstacles to the company's willingness to work with the unions and to use astute negotiation skills to move forward in alignment with union demands.

International Expansion

The company currently operates 96 hotels, 98 percent of which are in Mexico, with 1 percent in Costa Rica and 1 percent in Colombia. They have increased the hotel chain's presence through a variety of means, including sole proprietorship in 35 percent of cases, coinvestment in 28 percent, franchising in 24 percent, and leasing in 13 percent. As of December 2014, its international expansion has been limited to a Hoteles City Express in San José, Costa Rica (2012), and another in Cali, Colombia (2013), and the purchase of land in both Peru and Chile for future hotel construction. In fact, the hotel chain was recently recognized in the World Economic Forum as one of the 16 Latin American businesses with the greatest dynamism and growth in the region. Specifically, in the next five years, Hoteles City Express plans to operate 15–20 hotels outside Mexico. These international markets are both geographically close and culturally similar, as well as representing important partners of Mexico in the 2011 Pacific Alliance. This Latin American trade block includes Mexico, Peru, Chile, and Colombia, and together accounts for 37 percent of Latin American GDP and over 225 million consumers (Alianza del Pacífico, 2018). Its aim is to strengthen the integration and exchange of goods, services, capital, and people among member countries. Hoteles City Express' internationalization trajectory is summarized in Table 17.2.

This will enable Hoteles City Express to diversify its product offerings and attend to the regional needs of Latin American travelers, which have grown in recent years. Although Barrios has publicly committed to expansion throughout the region, for now the hotel chain will focus on those destinations where there is a clear market opportunity and where their successful experiences in Mexico can easily be duplicated. According to Arce, Chile is a clear future target, both for its membership in the Alliance and for its 6–7 percent annual GDP growth rates. Currently, 34 percent of City Express hotels are wholly owned and 24 percent have been set up with a joint venture partner. While they are not closed to international expansion through

Table 17.2 *Hoteles City Express internationalization process*

	Key events in internationalization process of Hoteles City Express	
Date	Domestic	International
2002	City Express founded	
2002	City Express first hotel opens	
2004	City Express Suites opens	
2008	City Express Suites Junior opens	
2010	City Express San Luis Potosi obtains LEEDs green building certification	
2013		Opening of City Express in San José, Costa Rica, and Cali, Colombia through acquisition of local hotel chains
2014	City Express sells 1,000,000 shares of company stock on the Mexican stock exchange to raise funding for expansion	Ongoing development of City Express hotel operations in Bogotá, Medellín, Colombia and Santiago, Chile
2015	100 hotels in operation in Mexico. Presence in 29/32 states of Mexico.	City Express announces futures plans to expand to Texas, USA

Source: Hoteles City Express (2015)

foreign direct investment, their aim is to expand internationally through franchising and international joint venture to grow their presence overseas quickly. Arce also mentioned Ecuador and Panama as additional high potential sites for future Hoteles City Express development. They have also opened hotels in Mexico that form part of the strategic Pacific corridor, including Manzanillo and Lázaro Cárdenas. Central America has also been mentioned, but Arce warned that this would only be pursued if the franchise's high operating standards could clearly be guaranteed there, too.

Hoteles City Express has already sought financing on the Mexican stock market, being highly sought after, raising Mex$130 million in capital destined to fund new hotel construction and investment. Its stock dividends have been double-digit in the last two years and its net profits have grown 200 percent a year, closing at Mex$2.5 million at the end of the second quarter 2014. Stock capitalization and bank financing have enabled the company to open 15 new hotels per year. Key indicators of Hoteles City Express' financial performance in recent years are summarized in Table 17.3.

According to Javier Arce, Hoteles City Express will have grown by 22 percent in 2014 and by 20 percent in 2015. They expect to maintain that rapid pace of national and international expansion in the future, refocusing new hotel development on Central and South America in future years where, according to Arce, they are "convinced there is no clear, strong competitor."

Table 17.3 *Hoteles City Express: general data*

	2005	2010	2015
Revenue	N/A	N/A	103.8
Total assets	N/A	N/A	655.4
EBITDA	N/A	N/A	36.2
Gross profit	N/A	N/A	20.8
Net profit	N/A	N/A	13.2
Foreign investment	N/A	N/A	N/A
Exports	N/A	N/A	N/A
Employees	N/A	N/A	2,869
Countries	1	2	4

Data in US$ million
N/A = not available
City Express began operations in 2002
Source: Authors with data from Bloomberg, Expansion and Company's Report

GRUPO POSADAS

Grupo Posadas is a public company listed on the Mexican Stock Exchange, which has undertaken an aggressive growth plan in recent years. As a part of this plan, they have opened one hotel per month, and an additional 100 hotels are projected to be operating within the next five years. It currently operates more than 130 hotels and over 20,000 rooms within its seven brands, taking advantage of centralized management and economies of scale. The geographical coverage of Grupo Posadas, with its different brands in 55 cities all around Mexico, allows the company to make agreements with large-, micro-, and medium-sized companies (Grupo Posadas, 2013, 2014). See Table 17.4 for further information regarding the number of hotels, rooms, and brands of Grupo Posadas.

In 1982, Posadas de México was founded as the result of a merger between Fiesta Americana Hotels and Posadas de México – at which time the latter had a total of 13 operating hotels. Ten years later, Grupo Posadas began operations in the Mexican Stock Exchange. The following year, the hotel chain undertook important changes to accommodate the growing market of business travelers. Despite this growth, it was not until 1998 that the expansion of Grupo Posadas to South America began.

In 1989, Gaston Azcárraga Andrade inherited the presidency of Grupo Posadas, founded by his father, Gaston Azcárraga Tamayo in 1967. In 2005, Gaston Azcárraga Andrade, together with a group of investors including Angel Losada Moreno, President and CEO of Grupo Gigante (a former retail supermarket chain), acquired Mexicana de Aviación (the first Mexican international airline) for US$165 million. In August 2010, the financial situation of the airline became unsustainable due to the high labor and operation costs, and on August 27, the company and its subsidiaries stopped operating and were declared bankrupt. Mr. Azcárraga Andrade had been under investigation and was facing an arrest warrant (CNN Expansión, 2014a). Since then, his brother José Carlos Azcárraga Andrade has overseen the hotel group.

Grupo Posadas is considered Mexico's largest hotel company, opening a hotel almost every month, and with plans to open 100 more hotels. In 2017 alone, it operated over 150 hotels. In 2014, for example, they opened 22 hotels, which represented a new record in this sector in the country (CNN Expansión, 2014b). Nevertheless, since 2012 they have also sold some hotels to increase their liquidity and in some cases, in spite of having sold the hotels, they continue to run them (Ugarte, 2013b).

Grupo Posadas is a stock corporation with variable capital; the administration of the company is run by a Management Board and a General Director. The Board of Directors is responsible for establishing general strategies for conducting the business of the company and its subsidiaries (Grupo Posadas, 2013).

Table 17.4 shows financial results for Grupo Posadas from 2000 to 2015. The company's strategic plan has focused on continued growth and sustained financial health, needed to continue expanding their offerings by both building new hotels and launching new concepts to the market. It is important to keep in mind the matter of exchange rate volatility and its impact on the company's finances.

Table 17.4 *Grupo Posadas: general data*

	2000	2005	2010	2015
Revenue	368.4	470.9	529.9	435.8
Total assets	955.3	1116.7	1095.3	799.7
EBITDA	96.6	113.6	80.9	86
Gross profit	71.9	75.3	45.4	59.8
Net profit	27.6	34.9	1.9	−29.7
Foreign investment	N/A	N/A	N/A	N/A
Exports	64.2	54	N/A	N/A
Employees	N/A	N/A	N/A	N/A
Countries	5	5	5	5

N/A = not available
Source: Grupo Posadas (2015)

Grupo Posadas has seven brands, which are: (1) Live Aqua, which was founded in 2004 and is the first lifestyle brand of the group (in these hotels, the experience is everything); (2) Fiesta Americana Grand, founded in 1998 and created for those who seek luxury combined with excellent service; (3) Fiesta Americana, a five-star hotel chain which could be considered the flagship brand of the group; (4) The Explorean, a hotel which represents an adventurous experience, since it is located in the middle of the Mayan rainforest; (5) Fiesta Inn, the business-class concept of the company designed to fulfill all the needs of business travelers, a growing niche in the country: at the time of writing, the group owns 62 hotels of this type; (6) One, founded in 2006, a three-star concept, created for people who only care about having a clean bed and a place to spend the night; and finally, (7) Gamma. Since there are 1,500 four- and five-star hotels, of which 41 percent do not belong to a particular brand, Grupo Posadas decided to launch a concept called Gamma Fiesta Inn, since they consider that 615 of these hotels possess franchise potential (Grupo Posadas, 2013).

The main competitors for the Fiesta Americana hotels are other international and Mexican hotel chains such as Camino Real, InterContinental, Crowne Plaza, Marriott, Sheraton, Weston, Hilton, and Hyatt. The main competitors for Fiesta Inn hotels are independent local operators and Mexican and international chains such as Holiday Inn, Hoteles City Express, Holiday Inn Express, Best Western, Mission, Hampton Inn, and NH hotels (Bolsa Mexicana de Valores, 2014).

In terms of total number of rooms (including hotels owned, leased, and operated), of the Top Ten in Mexico, the combined brands of Grupo Posadas have a market share of approximately 27 percent. When considering just the five-star hotels of the Fiesta Americana brand, the market share is 22 percent. In the four-star category, Fiesta Inn has 26 percent of the market, and in the "low price" three-star category, the One hotels have 55 percent of the market share. In these three categories, Grupo Posadas is considered the market leader (Bolsa Mexicana de Valores, 2014).

International Expansion

Being the largest hotel company in Mexico, and a consolidated and well-known brand, requires Grupo Posadas always to be planning its next move. Although it is not the company's first international expansion, in the coming five years they are planning to develop – with an investment of US$450 million and in a partnership with Bighorn Capital Inc. – up to ten upscale hotels under the Live Aqua boutique hotel brand. The locations of the properties are planned to be gateway cities such as Chicago, Los Angeles, Miami, Houston, and Washington, DC, which are attractive since they all have a significant number of Hispanic visitors and large Hispanic populations (Karmin, 2015). In fact, this is not their first operation in the US market, since they previously operated more than 200 rooms in Laredo, Texas.

It is interesting to analyze, in this new investment, the partnership of three big players. One partner, Grupo Posadas is a big, consolidated company with 45 years of history in the hospitality sector, and the second partner, Bighorn Capital is an investor with a lot of experience in real estate. The third partner is Début Hotel Group, with five different lifestyle hotel brands in major cities like Hollywood, New York City, and Miami. The latter is both experienced in the US market, and renowned for its innovative design and total guest experience (Karmin, 2015).

Inevitably, there is an evolution process where decisions have to be made and from which lessons are learned. The new international expansion for the company, with a new concept and in a new market, comes almost three years after Grupo Posadas sold all of its 29 hotels in South America to Accor, the French hotel giant and leading global hotel operator (Valadez, 2015).

In South America in 2008, Grupo Posadas was operating ten hotels in Brazil, two hotels in Argentina and one hotel in Chile, despite the operational challenges that these markets represented (Grupo Posadas, 2013). One of the main strategies of the group has been to improve profitability by getting rid of assets that represent a heavy financial burden and to look for important partnerships in terms of the operation of some of their hotels. In summary, the Group strives for efficiencies that permit consolidation in the domestic market in Mexico, and to expand internationally to markets with huge potential, such as the USA. The main idea was to have a diversified brand and a strategic location portfolio to improve the likelihood of obtaining sustainable growth in the coming years and competing in an industry where threats to profitability include highly seasonal demand, diverse market segments, exposure to fluctuations in the global and local economic environment, and ups and downs in the real estate sector, to mention just a few potential challenges. Table 17.5 summarizes the growth of Grupo Posadas in both domestic and international markets.

Commitment to social responsibility remains an important part of the company's strategy, along with corporate efforts to consolidate and continue the growth of all the categories that are part of the group, keep developing and attracting customers through loyalty programs (which represent an important percentage of total room occupancy), and continue strategic alliances with companies such as AVIS, VISA, and American Express, and with other loyalty programs such as Mexican airline Aeroméxico's Club Premier (Grupo Posadas, 2015b).

LESSONS

The national and international success of Hoteles City Express and Grupo Posadas can be attributed to several factors. First, the tourism industry has grown continually for decades as global incomes rise, representing 10 percent of global GDP in 2014 (UNWTO, 2015). As the industry grows and matures, industry players must seek out untapped market niches and diversify their product portfolios to hedge against risk and market fluctuations. The tourism industry's favorable growth trend is expected to continue, with projected growth in tourism volume anticipated to be 3.4 percent per year across the globe – an international trend that benefits equally both Hoteles City Express and Grupo Posadas, and posits significant challenges as competition within the industry is anticipated to grow. As tourism volume and

Table 17.5 *The growth and internationalization process of Grupo Posadas*

	Key Events	
Year	Domestic	International
1967	Gastón Azcárraga Tamayo founds Posadas under the name Promotora Mexicana de Hoteles	
1982	Fiesta Americana hotels and Posadas de Mexico merge and Grupo Posadas is founded	
1988		Grupo Posadas with the Fiesta Inn brand starts operating in Laredo, Texas
1989	Gastón Azcárraga Andrade inherits the presidency of Grupo Posadas	
1992	Grupo Posadas is listed on the Mexican Stock Exchange	
1998	Fiesta Americana Grand brand starts operating	Grupo Posadas expands to South America, starting in Brazil, Argentina, and Chile
2004	Live Aqua brand starts operating	
2005	Grupo Posadas acquires the Mexican airline Mexicana de Aviación	
2005–2006	One brand starts operating	
2010	Mexicana de Aviación is declared bankrupt	
2010	José Carlos Azcárraga Andrade becomes President of Grupo Posadas	
2015		Grupo Posadas signs a license agreement to operate five Live Aqua hotels in the United States in the next six years. The plan includes the following cities: Chicago, Los Angeles, Miami, Houston, and Washington, DC.

Source: Grupo Posadas (2015a)

competition increases, leading industry players, such as Hoteles City Express and Grupo Posadas, will need to develop more diverse product offerings, catering for the unique needs of both existing and untapped new customer segments. In the case of Hoteles City Express, one new segment has proved to be the national and regional business traveler, whose presence increased following the North American Free Trade Agreement (NAFTA) and the subsequent growth of key economic sectors in Mexico, such as the maquiladoras in the Mexican–US border region, and the agricultural export belt in the north-west of Mexico. Hoteles City Express created for these customers a value-oriented service offering which did not compromise on high quality hotel standards or service. The potential growth of business tourism will undoubtedly continue to rise as economic integration, trade, and investment in North America intensifies as NAFTA matures and the implementation of the Trans-Pacifíc Partnership trade agreement, to which Mexico, the United States, Canada, Peru, and Chile are members, becomes an even closer reality.

Similarly, as international tourism grows, Grupo Posadas will be well suited to take advantage of this favorable trend and must diversify its hotel product portfolio throughout the region both in the luxury segment and in the business segment. For both hotel chains, international expansion will depend on the companies successfully identifying, securing, and paying for strategic real estate locations, whether they cater for traditional vacationers or business travelers.

The pace of expansion of both Hoteles City Express and Grupo Posadas can also be attributed in great part to the significant efficiencies both companies achieved through economies of scale in their operations across the region – a key driver to success in the Mexican lodging industry. Financing their expensive and ambitious expansion plans has also been made possible by selling off unprofitable assets, as demonstrated by Grupo Posadas, and by both companies' decision to go public and raise needed financing on the Mexican stock exchange to fund their ambitious growth plans. Moreover, both Hoteles City

Express and Grupo Posadas have demonstrated flexibility in determining their preferred international modes of entry into foreign markets, employing not only greenfield investments but also global franchising and international joint ventures, depending upon the financing required, the cultural similarity of the market to Mexico, and the presence of a suitable partner. Their careful analysis of the unique situational context of the markets in which they develop new properties, and to adapt to those characteristics, is an important explanatory variable in their success at home and abroad.

REFERENCES

Alianza del Pacífico. 2018. ¿Qué es la Alianza? https://alianzapacifico.net/que-es-la-alianza/. Accessed May 14, 2018.

Bolsa Mexicana de Valores. 2014. *Bolsa Mexicana de Valores webpage*. Informe annual 2013. www.bmv.com.mx/Digital/fina/POSADAS/2013/posadas_infoanua_2013.pdf. Accessed January 5, 2015.

City Express. 2015. City Express hoteles presentación corporativa. *City Express Company Web Page*. www.cityexpress.com/media/7547/presentación-corporativa.pdf. Accessed June 1, 2015.

CNN Expansión. 2012. City express se internacionaliza. *CNN Expansión*. www.cnnexpansion.com/negocios/2012/01/13/city-express-se-internacionaliza. Accessed June 15, 2015.

CNN Expansión. 2014a. Los empleados de mexicana meten amparo. *CNN Expansión*. www.cnnexpansion.com/negocios/2014/04/09/empleados-de-mexicana-meten-amparo. Accessed January 5, 2015.

CNN Expansión. 2014b. Grupo Posadas abrirá 49 hoteles en 2016. *CNN Expansión*. www.cnnexpansion.com/negocios/2014/12/01/grupo-posadas-abrira-49-hoteles-en-2016. Accessed January 5, 2015.

Euromonitor. 2016. *Lodging in Mexico*. Accessed February 15th, 2017.

Lortia, A. 2013. Segmento de lujo atrae más inversión hotelera. *El Economista*. https://www.eleconomista.com.mx/empresas/Segmento-de-lujo-atrae-mas-inversion-hotelera-20130522-0154.html Accessed September 12, 2015.

Grupo Posadas. 2013. *Grupo Posadas webpage*. www.posadas.com/es/empresa. Accessed May 14, 2018.

Grupo Posadas. 2014. *Grupo Posadas webpage, informe anual 2014*. www.posadas.com www.posadas.com/es/empresa. Accessed January 5, 2015.

Grupo Posadas. 2015a. Operative & Financial Results: First Quarter 2015. *Grupo Posadas*. http://cms.posadas.com/posadas/Brands/Posadas/Region/Mexico/Hot els/Finanzas/Catalogs/Media/Informe_Anual/Reporte_Anual/Espanol/Reporte_ Anual_2014.pdf. Accessed September 12, 2015.

Grupo Posadas. 2015b. Informe Anual 2014. *Grupo Posadas*. http://cms.posadas .com/posadas/Brands/Posadas/Region/Mexico/Hotels/Finanzas/Catalogs/Med ia/Reportes_trimestrales/Ingles/Quarters_2014/1Q15.pdf. Accessed September 12, 2015.

Jiménez, I. 2014. La estrategia detrás del éxito de Hoteles City Express. *Forbes*. www .forbes.com.mx/la-estrategia-detras-del-exito-de-hoteles-city-express. Accessed May 30, 2015.

Karmin, C. 2015. Grupo Posadas plans US expansion. *The Wall Street Journal*. www .wsj.com/articles/grupo-posadas-plans-u-s-expansion-1435266099. Accessed November 30, 2015.

Olguin, C. 2011. Especializarse o morir. *CNN Expansión*. www.cnnexpansion.co m/expansion/2011/09/14/especializarse-o-morir. Accessed November 1, 2014.

Reyes, J. L. 2011. Clasificación hotelera lluvia de estrellas o fiesta de disfraces. *CNN Expansión*. www.cnnexpansion.com/expansion/2011/09/14/clasificacin-hote lera-xlluvia-de-estrellas-o-fiesta-de-disfraces. Accessed November 15, 2014.

Ugarte, J. 2012. City Express "hospedará" a Latinoamérica. *CNN Expansión*. http:// expansion.mx/negocios/192012/02/15/city-express-hospedara-latinoamérica. Accessed May 14, 2018.

Ugarte, J. 2013a. City Express buscará 3200 mdp en bolsa. *CNN Expansión*. www .cnnexpansion.com/negocios/2013/05/30/city-express-va-por-3219-mdp-a-la-bo lsa. Accessed November 30, 2015.

Ugarte, J. 2013b. Posadas hospeda mejores finanzas. *CNN Expansión*. www.cnnex pansion.com/negocios/2013/01/30/posadas-hospeda-mejores-finanzas. Accessed January 5, 2015.

UNWTO. 2015. *UNWTO Tourism Highlights 2015*. https://wedocs.unep.org/bit stream/handle/20.500.11822/19525/UNWTO2015.pdf?sequence=1&isAllowe d=y. Accessed May 14, 2018.

Valadez, R. 2015. Retoma Grupo Posadas expansión internacional. *Milenio*. www .milenio.com/negocios/Grupo_Posadas_0_543545747.html. Accessed November 30, 2015.

18 MultiMexicans in the Entertainment Industry

KidZania and Cinépolis

Raúl Montalvo and Eileen Daspro

INTRODUCTION

THE MEXICAN ENTERTAINMENT INDUSTRY

The Mexican entertainment industry includes a range of business categories, including amusement parks and movie theaters. It has grown significantly in size and value in recent decades due to a growth in population, increased urbanization, and the rise in disposable income in Mexico. This chapter reviews the successful international trajectory of two of this industry's leaders in Mexico: KidZania in the Mexican entertainment industry and Cinépolis in the Mexican movie theater industry. The two companies' experiences reveal important explanatory drivers behind their success, which include: the global mindset of their founder, the creation of a highly unique service offering, and careful attention to execution and intellectual property protection overseas through the careful selection of international franchisees.

Amusement Parks and Entertainment Services

The industry segment concerning amusement parks and entertainment services includes amusement parks, ballrooms, discotheques, and circus productions. It experienced rapid growth in Mexico, increasing in value by 44 percent from 2006 to 2012 with an estimated value of Mex$30 billion in 2012. In part, this rapid increase was fueled by a 1 percent annual population growth in Mexico during the same period and a 37 percent increase in per capita disposable income. Moreover, a 2 percent increase in urbanization from 2006 to 2012 spurred demand for entertainment services. This growing demand was dominated by households that represented 97 percent of the industry's consumers, half of which were under the age of 29 (Euromonitor, 2013a).

In 2012, the industry segment was composed of 6,894 companies with micro companies (fewer than nine employees) dominating the industry with 89 percent of total market share. The industry is highly fragmented; the two leading companies, La Feria de Chapultepec and Six Flags, generated only 9 percent of the total entertainment services volume in Mexico in 2010. La Feria de Chapultepec is an outdoor fair located in Mexico, with more than 50 rides and games as well as fast food, sweets, and snacks. It is visited by more than 1.5 million visitors a year, and accounted for 7 percent of the volume of Mexican amusement parks and entertainment services sales in 2010. Six Flags Mexico, the second most important player in the Mexican industry, accounted for 2 percent of total service production in 2010 and received 2.2 million visitors in 2011. Six Flags is a traditional amusement park with roller coasters, children's rides and games, and live entertainment and food. In addition, Parque Plaza Sésamo in Monterrey received 900,000 visitors in 2012. It offers roller coasters, carnival rides, and family dining. It is the third most important company in the Mexican entertainment industry. Together, these three players were ranked by the Themed Entertainment Association as the second, third, and fifth most important theme parks in Latin America in 2012, based on visitor attendance that year (AECOM, 2013).

KidZania, the fourth most important actor in the Mexican entertainment industry, is an entertainment services business focused on children, whereby visitors "play the role of adults" in over 50 adult professions in a real child-sized city, with buildings, shops, and cinemas as well as vehicles and pedestrians moving along its streets. According to André Fabre, KidZania's Director of Operations in Mexico, KidZania's unique focus on formative "educational entertainment," or "edutainment," that is both values-driven and educational, captured an important national and global tendency in the industry.

Other popular amusement and entertainment parks in Mexico include the amusement park Selva Mágica in Guadalajara as well as Xcaret Eco Theme Park in The Mayan Riviera. Some smaller entertainment and educational services have existed in Mexico that focus specifically on children, and on educational forms of entertainment. Their focus is mostly local and/or regional. These include Granja las Américas in Mexico City, which is a family entertainment facility focused on environmental conservation. Live interaction with farm animals is the main attraction, along with workshops to manufacture everyday household food items such as tortillas, milk, and bread. Similar educational theme parks include Parque Fundidor in Monterrey, Nuevo León, and Parque Explora in León Guanajuato.

Future prospects for the amusement park and entertainment industry in Mexico are very promising. The value of the entertainment services industry in Mexico is expected to grow by 43 percent from 2013 to 2018 as per capita disposable incomes rise by an estimated 35 percent, population size grows by 5 percent, and urbanization increases by an estimated 7 percent during the forecasted period.

Movie Theaters

The industry segment of movie theaters includes motion picture or videotape projection in cinemas, both open-air and in other projection facilities. It also includes the activities of cine-clubs. The country enjoys a world-class cinema infrastructure and has the fifth highest movie attendance rate in the world: 196 million in 2012. In fact, the movie theater industry in Mexico is considered one of the most solid and attractive industries in Mexico given its continuous growth and profitability over the last decade (Euromonitor, 2013b). From 2006 to 2012 alone, this industry experienced a growth of 71 percent, reaching a total value of Mex$12.7 billion in 2012. This is particularly remarkable given that the global economic crisis took place during this same time period. Approximately 90 percent of the demand comes from households and the remaining from businesses. Most of the segment's growth comes from movie theater attendance, spurred by increases in technological developments and the move to 100 percent digital projections, as well as equally innovative offerings in terms of the sound, projection, experience, movie theater design, and a growing diversity of both local and global film offerings.

The movie theater industry in Mexico is highly concentrated in a duopoly with two major chains: Cinépolis and Cinemex, the latter of which bought Cinemark Mexico from Cinemark Holdings USA in 2013. These two companies together account for 98 percent of the market share in Mexico. In fact, the level of concentration increased through mergers and acquisitions between 2006 and 2012, when the total number of companies in the industry declined by 12 (Euromonitor, 2013b).

As of 2012, there were a total of 5,044 movie theater screens in the country. The number-one player is privately owned Operadora Cinépolis SA de CV, owner of the Cinépolis brand, the fourth-largest cinema chain in terms of number of screens worldwide. As of September 2012, it operated 3,000 screens, with 571,583 seats and a staff of 19,787 in Mexico alone, and the number has kept growing. The theater chain projects not only films, but live and pre-recorded concerts and sporting events as well. Cinépolis has successfully introduced innovative concepts to the movie theaters market, including the first concept of a luxury cinema: Cinépolis VIP and Macro XE and 4DX screens. It has also innovated in the design of its movie halls with stadium seating, double-armrest, and in-theater food and drink service.

The second largest player is Grupo Cinemex SA de CV, a subsidiary of Entretenimiento De Mexico SA De CV, which operates 38 theaters in Mexico and a total of 422 screens.

Prospects for future growth of the Mexican movie industry are very optimistic. The Mexican movie theater industry is expected to experience a Compound Annual Growth Rate of 8 percent between 2012 and 2018, in a country with a forecasted population growth rate of 6 percent and a 48 percent increase in the annual disposable income for the same period. Interestingly, one can observe a high correlation between the movie theaters' turn-over of local producers and the nominal GDP. The number of visitors will continue to grow, as will the value of the industry due to industry innovations, such as movies on demand via the Internet (Euromonitor, 2013b).

KidZania and Cinépolis: Global Players in the Mexican Entertainment Industry

Each year, *Expansión* magazine ranks 100 of the most global Mexican companies. Each company is assigned a global index score based on three weighted criteria: 1) total sales revenue from overseas operations (80 percent), 2) number of countries where the company operates factories or offices overseas (10 percent) and 3) the percentage of total company revenue obtained from operations outside Mexico (10 percent). In the 2015 ranking, two private Mexican entertainment companies stood out: KidZania and Cinépolis. KidZania was ranked number 16. It is one of the three companies in the recreation, sport, and leisure category to be included in the top 100 global rankings, the others being Cinépolis, the Morelia, Michoacán-based movie theater chain, which was ranked 74, and CIE, the event and concert organizer and operator of Centro Banamex in Mexico City, which earned the lowest industry ranking on the index, of 85.

In the case of KidZania, the company enjoys a very strong, diverse global presence, with 50 percent of its revenues being obtained from its overseas franchises in more than 22 countries, including Japan, Chile, Malaysia, Indonesia, Turkey, Dubai, and Egypt among others, with eyes on opening multiple operations in the United States in 2016. Its most recent park opening was in London in June 2015. In the case of Cinépolis, the Morelia-based movie theater chain started in 1971; the exact percentage of revenue from overseas sales is not public information, but it operates in 12 countries worldwide, which include complexes in Mexico, Central and South America, India, and the United States.

KIDZANIA

KidZania, a wholly owned and privately held Mexican corporation, was founded in 1996 by its current President, Xavier López Ancona, an "accidental" Mexican entrepreneur from a large Mexican family with an educational profile that prepared him for international success. His first international experience was a year in high school: he studied in Tulsa, Oklahoma as a teenager. He then returned to Mexico and studied for his BA in Business Administration at Universidad Anahuac in Mexico City. Later, he would return to the United States to study for his MBA at the prestigious Kellogg School of Business at Northwestern University. One day, while working as VP of Risk Capital at GE in Mexico City, an old Northwestern classmate came to visit Xavier, suggesting that he quit his job and they start a business together. His former colleague refused to take no for an answer, showing him videos of a day care center concept from the USA with a unique twist: children kept themselves entertained, playing adult roles such as doctor, store clerk, etc. The idea seemed simple: build a kid-sized city where children could both have fun and be entertained. López Ancona continued to work at GE Capital in Mexico City for the next few months while developing the business model in his spare time. Eventually he asked for a six-month sabbatical to work on his business idea full time and ultimately never returned to GE Capital. KidZania has been born.

KidZania's first edutainment facility was named Ciudad de los Niños, in its initial Mexico City location, and was an interactive indoor entertainment and educational center where children could experience the world of adults in a smaller-scale replica of a real, functioning city complete with working businesses, public services, etc. It was opened on September 1, 1999 in a mall in Santa Fe, a growing Mexican city suburb. Its success in its first year of operation in the Mexican City location exceeded initial expectations, with over 10 million visitors to date (KidZania, 2017). Since its opening, two additional locations have been opened in Mexico, in the northern city of Monterrey in 2006 and in Cuicuilco in 2012, a southern Mexico City neighborhood.

Learning and play were the inspiration for KidZania's unique business concept: "edutainment." KidZania successfully identified the pastime of children "playing" adult roles as universal and requiring no special technology or instructions for kids to perform. KidZania offered children between the ages of 1 and 14 the opportunity to play adult roles: doctor, firefighter, police officer, or veterinarian. The business model integrated two businesses in one: that of a family entertainment and educational center and a powerful corporate communications and marketing tool.

The latter business concept was developed in the KidZania Mexican complexes through the offering of interactive activities designed in conjunction with local industrial partners such as Bimbo bakeries and Cemex cement and concrete products. In each of its global locations, KidZania has identified and worked closely with local business sponsors of the different workshops or role play activities in each facility. The presence of locally known and well-recognized brands in each KidZania workshop adds a sense of realism to the activities in which the children participate. These same industry partners plan, finance, and supervise the design and construction of each workshop and pay fees to KidZania for their ongoing operations in the city. From an early age, the local business sponsors can establish an interactive, trusting, emotional relationship with the many visitors of KidZania, which include the child attendees (between ages 1 and 14), their parents (between 20 and 40 years), as well as grandparents, teachers, older siblings, etc.

Over the years, KidZania has clearly identified three different market segments it hoped to target with its year-round indoor edutainment concept: (1) young families with children between the ages of 1 and 14 who visit mostly on weekends, during holidays, or for birthday parties; (2) school groups and summer camps that visit during the week; and (3) adults who utilize the facilities after normal business hours for institutional or corporate events. By targeting three different market segments, KidZania has achieved a consistent flow of visitors to its facilities, regardless of the season or day of the week: a distinct competitive advantage over traditional outdoor seasonal amusement parks, whose attendance is concentrated on the weekends and/or in certain seasons, weather permitting.

There were two primary revenue sources. Approximately 60 percent of the company's total revenue emanates from sales generated within the edutainment facility – entrance tickets, birthday party facility rentals, purchase of food and beverages, and the sale of KidZania merchandise and souvenirs. The other 40 percent of corporate revenues is derived from innovative sponsorship contracts with the hundreds of global business sponsors that pay KidZania for ongoing permits to operate their businesses on a smaller, more limited scale within the model country of KidZania. Future company growth in the medium term could also be derived from new revenue sources including interactive web page usage fees, greater merchandising of their trademarked merchandise and possibly feature films. These multiple revenue streams have enabled the company to grow rapidly and consistently on an international scale. In fact, Lopez Ancona has confirmed the company's plan to open 80 more global locations in coming years at an expansion rate of 4–5 new centers per year. Unfortunately, financial figures are not available, as KidZania is a privately run company.

Once admitted to the country facility of KidZania, children receive their stamped passport, a security bracelet and a check for 50 Kidzos, the official currency of KidZania. The more tasks and work-related activities the kids perform during their KidZania stay, e.g., painting a house, delivering mail, announcing the evening news, etc., the more Kidzos the children can earn – and subsequently save in a KidZania bank for use in future visits or to spend on merchandise and/or services in KidZania.

According to KidZania, this combination of reality with entertainment represents a unique, authentic, and powerful learning experience for children about the world in which they live and their role in it. They learn about work, professions, basic finance, and basic concepts of civic and community participation. In addition, they develop valuable social skills such as independence, cooperation, and decision making.

All KidZania facilities have a parents' lounge, equipped with modern comfortable furnishings, free Internet, television, magazines, etc. Parents may rest, engage in conversation, get work done, study, etc., or even go shopping in the mall, while their child is learning and having fun. This is made possible thanks to the advanced security system that tracks children and makes it impossible for them to leave the establishment without a parent. In crowded, hot, polluted emerging market cities like Mexico City, Kuala Lumpur, or Mumbai, this represents an important additional or extra space, after home and school to relax, unwind, or socialize.

Indeed, the KidZania business model has proven successful, both nationally and abroad. Since its founding in 1996, 25 million people have visited KidZania in one of its 14 country locations, and currently 6,500 people are directly employed by the company. Each year, each park receives between 500,000 and 800,000 visitors, according to Hernán Barbieri, KidZania's Director General. In 2014 alone, 10 million visitors attended KidZania, or 30,000 per day in all of the KidZania global cities.

Its national and international success is unparalleled and has been recognized for its outstanding business success around the globe. As of 2015, KidZania CEO López Ancona affirmed that 50 percent of all the company's revenue was generated from international sales outside Mexico. In 2010, KidZania earned Mexico's national export prize in the franchise business category. On five different occasions, The Association of Mexican Franchises recognized KidZania as the "Best Mexican Franchise Overseas," most recently in 2013. Moreover, on six different occasions, KidZania has been recognized by Retail and Leisure International with the prestigious "Global Leisure Operator Award" for its innovative business model, vision, service excellence, and commitment to sustainability. The same organization has twice awarded KidZania the "Highly Commented and Innovative Retail Leisure Concept Award," most recently in 2014.

KidZania: International Trajectory

KidZania's expansion has not been limited to the Mexican market with its current company-owned Mexican locations in Santa Fé, Mexico City (1999), Monterrey (2006), and Cuiculco, Mexico City (2012). In 2006 it began its global expansion trajectory by opening a KidZania franchise in Tokyo, and it has since created a rapid, diverse global footprint in a relatively short period. According to KidZania COO Andrés Fabré, KidZania Tokyo was a strategic site choice in the Asian region, and would represent a flagship presence of the KidZania brand in Asia in a city of great economic and cultural importance. Future smaller complexes in the region would be developed later, once the brand had gained regional recognition. Other regional flagships include Dubai in the Middle East, and soon-to-be-opened London in Western Europe. By the close of 2014, KidZania had opened international franchise locations around the globe in 14 other countries, including: Tokyo, Japan (2006); Jakarta, Indonesia (2007); Koshien, Japan (2009); Lisbon, Portugal (2009); Dubai, United Arab Emirates (2010); Seoul, South Korea (2010); Kuala Lumpur, Malaysia (2012); Santiago, Chile (2012); Bangkok, Thailand (2013); Mumbai, India (2013); Kuwait (2013); Cairo Egypt (2013); Istanbul, Turkey (2014); with forthcoming locations in Sao Paolo, Brazil (2014); London (2015); Saudi Arabia (2015); and the Philippines (2015). A summary of the internationalization trajectory of KidZania is shown in Table 18.1.

KidZania also has plans underway to open new franchises in Singapore, Russia, and Qatar as well as in multiple cities across the United States, including New York, Los Angeles, and Chicago. In addition, it is currently negotiating deals with possible partners in Germany, France, and Australia for future international operation locations. In total, KidZania company owned and franchised edutainment centers employ 6,500 people globally and have received over 10 million visitors.

According to Andres Fabré, KidZania COO, the company's motivations for internationalization emanated from the model itself.

Table 18.1 *The growth and internationalization process of KidZania*

	Key Events for KidZania	
Year	Domestic	International
1996	KidZania founded by Xavier López Ancona	
1999	Ciudad de los Niños opens in Santa Fé, Mexico	
2006	KidZania opens in Monterrey, Mexico	KidZania franchise opens in Tokyo, Japan
2007		KidZania franchise opens in Jakarta, Indonesia
2009		KidZania franchise opens in Koshien, Japan and Lisbon, Portugal
2010		KidZania franchise opens in Dubai, United Arab Emirates; Seoul, South Korea
2012	KidZania opens in Cuiculco, Mexico	KidZania franchise opens in Kuala Lumpur, Malaysia; Santiago, Chile
2013		KidZania franchise opens in Bangkok, Thailand; Munbai, India; Cairo, Egypt
2014		KidZania franchise opens in Istanbul, Turkey; Sao Paolo, Brazil
2015		KidZania franchise opens in London, UK; Jeddah, Saudi Arabia; and Manila, Philippines

Source: KidZania (2015)

The unique "edutainment" concept had clear global appeal, as the desire to "play the role of adults" was universally common. Moreover, the economic and demographic requirements needed to sustain a KidZania franchise would only allow for perhaps four complexes in total in Mexico; internationalization was inevitable.

KidZania's international expansion has been rapid and aggressive, enjoying important first mover advantages in key markets in both emerging and developed markets worldwide. According to Cammie Dunaway, Global Marketing Officer and President of KidZania USA, market selection criteria have been based mostly on demographic conditions, similar to those present in the first center location in Mexico City. According to COO Andres Fabré, these conditions exist in a total of 75 locations around the world, many of which have already been developed as KidZania franchise locations or are currently being evaluated for future development. Specifically, KidZania seeks out cities with a high density of kids aged from 4 to 14 years, with at least 700,000 or more children within 1–1.5 hours' travel distance from the proposed location. In addition, they consider geographical circumstances, such as extreme hot or cold weather, since their indoor year-round edutainment facility is particularly attractive in locations with less than desirable weather. They are often located in upscale, commercial malls, so access to prime, commercial real estate is also a key consideration (Delo, 2013).

KidZania's rapid, successful international expansion has been achieved through global franchising. In the global franchising model, KidZania grants to an individual or company (the franchisee) the right to run the business, selling its service utilizing the franchisor's business format and trademark. Important advantages associated with this growth strategy include diversification risk, access to cheap labor in other countries, and, most importantly, the potential to increase quickly its physical presence and brand awareness overseas with limited investments. In addition, KidZania earns annual royalties from the operations of its global franchisees. The model's success requires the development of solid, ongoing relationships with its overseas franchisees. KidZania COO Andres Fabré identified the need for highly qualified, ethical franchisees overseas, whose drive, leadership, and "know-how, know-who and knowledge of the system" would prove critical for successful global expansion. Ideally, the franchisee would also be a financially solid, independent company with a full-time Chief Executive Officer and a dedicated team of professionals committed to the business's success. Franchisees with professional experience in media, entertainment, or hospitality businesses were particularly well suited to the task.

KidZania expected its global franchisees to secure the location, adapt the center design to local preferences and regulations, maintain all construction documents, and identify and seek the collaboration of local industry partners. In addition, the international franchisees would build the entertainment center, and hire and train a staff of up to 400 local employees in the KidZania business model. Similarly, KidZania global franchisees were responsible for marketing the edutainment center locally and regionally, and operating it in accordance with Sante Fe procedures and guidelines while growing the brand and sales within their defined territory. Meanwhile, the KidZania concept behind each global franchise remained the same: children's universal desire to play the role of adults, with only the execution being adapted to be locally relevant. For example, in Mexico the children work in a tortilla factory, while in Japan they prepare sushi. The corporate sponsors of the product and service workshops are overwhelmingly local, familiar to the children and their parents.

Global franchisee relations are carefully developed and sustained and have been key to the company's rapid global expansion and successful global brand presence. Global franchise locations are visited and audited by headquarters staff. All of the top 27 global franchise site managers return annually to the KidZania headquarters in Mexico City for ongoing training in KidZania standards and procedures. Headquarters carefully monitors preservation of the original business concept, yet at the same time has in place a well-articulated authorization process whereby local franchisees may request permission to realize adaptations to the business model. In practice, franchisees overseas have faced widely varying regulatory and cultural environments in which to operate. Significant elements of their business model – from human resources and employee management to the marketing of their services to the day-to-day execution – might be impacted. For example, Fabré noted that while Mexican parents are not allowed to accompany the children while participating in the workshops, in South Korea, for cultural reasons, parents both want and expect to accompany their children at all times.

An important explanatory variable behind their global success was K.I.A., or KidZania Intelligence Agency. Its primary objective had been to monitor and ensure that all KidZania centers achieve their maximum performance, through the provision of ongoing consultation and advice which enables franchisees to achieve the consistency and quality required to implement the international franchise model. Specifically, K.I.A. provided analysis and data to the executives of each center so that they could make more informed business decisions about the running of their local center through suggestions, action plans, and know-how that would guarantee the sustainability of each business. The K.I.A. team verified that the knowledge gained by global franchisees in their training was being effectively applied in practice. Each year they evaluated the centers with a seal called "ISOK," a symbol of excellence and the success of a KidZania center.

In addition, KidZania invested heavily in employee development to guarantee KidZania's operational excellence. To achieve this aim, KidZania University was founded in 2007 to transmit knowledge generated in KidZania Santa Fe to the global franchisee teams responsible for opening, operating, and delivering service excellence in the edutainment centers overseas. Its mission set forth: (1) to offer the best possible role play experiences for visitors; (2) to provide a more effective means of interactive communication among global franchise partners; (3) to promote a work environment that allows for the development and growth of the work team; (4) to provide the best tools to support the industry partners; (5) to achieve sustainable returns for the shareholders; (6) to offer the highest level of commitment and participation for the improvement of the communities; and (7) to support solutions to care for the environment.

KidZania University began by offering its first global franchise training course. Initially there were 69 general, strategic, and operations courses. Course content was enriched over time and became increasingly more specialized to prepare each of the 23 key people from the global franchise teams to develop the KidZania business model in their countries of origin. Moreover, KidZania University collected and communicated in a clear and unified manner the general know-how needed to start and run a KidZania center, while developing in its students the abilities and attitudes that its corporate philosophy espoused.

Andrés Fabré, Chief Operating Officer at KidZania, attributes the company's international success to ten key factors which include: (1) *Impeccable execution and service excellence.* Fabré notes that both represent the pillars of the company's successful international expansion. (2) *Learn from previous experience.* KidZania has researched and learned about previous business models that have been internationally successful, and they analyzed these previous experiences to gain important lessons. (3) *Always seek out experts and consultants.* Fabré notes, "One must understand that there is always someone better than you who can help you. Coaches, local managers, business consultants can all be of help in achieving international success." (4) *Be certain that your brand is internationally recognized.* Fabré added that the company's name was changed from "Ciudad de los Niños" to KidZania. The company needed a brand with international appeal that could be pronounced in many languages, and that was unique wherever it was established. (5) *Overcapitalize.* Fabré wants the business to have sufficient capital, with some extra financing to fund the rapid international expansion, even if that mean taking on debt. (6) *Register the company's intellectual property in as many markets as possible from the outset.* According to Fabré, KidZania did this in both markets which they knew they would enter as well as the ones they identified as having potential, in order to lock in the protection of their global trademarks. He noted that in China alone, there are over 30 copy-cats of their business concept (Kidzmania, Kidmundo, etc.), and new ones appear daily. He noted that the role playing concept per se is not open for patent protection, but that they place a strong emphasis on excellence in execution to differentiate their business concepts globally. (7) *Look for accelerated growth.* Fabré also identified the importance of first mover advantage: "It is important to be the first player; if you grow slowly, the competition and the imitators will impact your business. Rapid growth ensures your place in the market and makes you less susceptible to copying." (8) *Conduct feasibility studies.* "Every time we think of entering a new market, the first thing we do is conduct a feasibility study to understand if the market is suitable for our business, the approximate number of visitors, etc. We can now predict with sufficient certainty whether a market is profitable or not." (9) *Make decisions objectively, and be ready for both positive and negative responses.* The decisions should be made solely based on numbers and facts, not on hunches or impulses. (10) *Mode of entry.* KidZania chose franchising to expand internationally rapidly. To do so, they carefully evaluate and select a partner with sufficient capital, with local market know-how, with knowledge of the local culture and with valuable contacts with the potential commercial sponsors with which they will develop a key relationship. Given the hefty initial investment fee of US$15–35 million needed to open a KidZania, international franchisee partners have provided the necessary financing to maintain a rapid global expansion rate. This entry mode differs from those in Mexico, where the establishments are owned and run by KidZania corporate. Moreover, in the all-important US market, KidZania has opted to enter via an international joint venture, and has spent months analyzing and identifying the right US partner to introduce the edutainment business in the US market.

CINÉPOLIS

The company's origins date back to 1971 in Morelia, Mexico where Enrique Ramírez Miguel founded the company under the original name of Cinematográfica Cadena de Oro, SA. Between 1972 and 1973 the concept of Cinemas Gemelos (Twin Screens) started. In 1994, the Cinépolis brand was created along with the introduction of multiplex theaters. In 1999, the Cinépolis VIP concept was launched, consisting of more exclusive theater offerings with bigger and more comfortable seats and food service inside the theater. By 2008, the company had introduced Extreme Cinemas, which were characterized by the experience of realistic sound and moving seats. In 2011, Cinépolis began its international expansion with the introduction of the VIP concept into the US market.

Forty years after its foundation, Cinépolis is Mexico's undisputed top national and global player in the movie theater industry. Since the concept of Cinépolis was created, the company has experienced a compound annual growth rate of 18 percent. This success is undeniably attributable to the remarkable leadership of Alejandro Ramirez Magaña, whose father, Enrique Ramírez Villalón, invited him in 2003 to choose between continuing his work as an international economist – who studied at Harvard and Oxford and with experience working at the OECD, the World Bank, the Mexican government, etc. – and returning to run the family's movie theater business. In 2004, Alejandro Ramirez Magaña became General Director of Cinépolis and on January 1, 2006 he became the company's CEO (CNN Expansión, 2013b).

Under Ramirez Magaña's administration, Cinépolis has experienced remarkable, continuous growth, an elusive feat for most third-generation family businesses, especially during years of economic crisis. From 2012–14 alone, the sales of the company grew from Mex$10,000 million to Mex$15,000 million. His outstanding achievements in the movie theater industry were recognized in 2013 when he received the Global Achievement in Exhibition Award by CinemaCon (CNN Expansión, 2014). This award was granted to him for the cultural practices and working environment of the company and his achievements in revolutionizing the industry globally with service innovations such as the premium and luxury theater concepts.

Cinépolis is not only a leader in the Mexican theater industry; in fact, it is the largest movie theater operation in Latin America and the fourth largest worldwide behind Regal Entertainment Group, AMC

Theaters and, Cinemark. As of 2015, Cinépolis maintained a theater presence in 12 countries and 187 cities in total, of which 98 cities were located in Mexico, nine in Central America, 47 in South America, 27 in Asia, and two in the USA (Cinépolis, 2015). The total audience in 2014 alone was 157.7 million people in Mexico and 44.1 million in the other locations such as India, the USA, Central and South America. Unfortunately, financial figures for Cinépolis are not available because it is a privately run company.

Through its business philosophy of continuous innovation, top-notch service, social corporate responsibility, understanding the consumers and monitoring its competitors, amongst others, Cinépolis has become a leading global player in the movie theater industry.

The Market at Home

Mexico is the fifth country globally in terms of visits to the movie theater per year – just behind India, the USA, China, and France, and number 14 in terms of income from ticket sales to attend the movie theater. The market share of Cinépolis in Mexico is 65.46 percent, with a presence in 98 cities, and showing an increasing growth in recent years. In 1971 it started with three screens and today in Mexico alone – its largest market – it has 2,908 screens and is still growing. Just in Mexico, Cinépolis is expected to open 1,500 more screens over the coming five years.

The main competitor for Cinépolis in México is Cinemex, with a market share in Mexico of 30.94 percent, which at the end of 2013 acquired 31 theaters owned by Cinemark. Today, Cinépolis is already 100 percent digital and can receive satellite signals, considerably lowering distribution costs; Cinemex has yet to overcome this hurdle (El Economista, 2014). The competition in this industry is still mainly dominated by Cinépolis in the three largest cities in Mexico, with a local market share of 55.95 percent in Mexico City, 86.68 percent in Guadalajara, and 57.28 percent in Monterrey.

By the end of 2014, Cinépolis owned and operated more than 3,800 screens in 455 cinema complexes located in Mexico, Central and South America, the USA, and India. As of 2015, Cinépolis operates in Mexico (2,908 screens), Chile (143 screens), Costa Rica (29 screens), El Salvador (24 screens), Guatemala (46 screens), Honduras (10 screens), Panama (32 screens), Colombia (43 screens), Peru (36 screens), Brazil (302 screens), India (181 screens), and the USA (93 screens).

The Company

In a very dynamic market, threatened by Internet movie streaming, illegal pirated movies, and the merger trend, Cinépolis has shown resounding resilience. Cinépolis has responded to such threats as the merger of Cinemex and MM Cinemas with constant innovation. These include, but are not limited to, the introduction of the multiplex cinema concept and the stadium-type theaters which allow for better film viewing among moviegoers.

An important differentiator of Cinépolis is that it has managed to create new theater offerings for different market segments, thereby growing its industry's potential, not only at home in Mexico, but overseas as well. An example of this is the Cinépolis VIP brand in Mexico, which has been very successful, and Cinépolis Luxury brand in the USA. In both cases, a premium theater concept was designed and opened in an upscale location, only after an extensive analysis of the market. In the case of the USA, the Cinépolis luxury theaters are located in the states of California and Florida.

Innovation as a Differentiator

Cinépolis has been an industry innovator in Mexico and abroad since its inception. For example, Cinépolis has carefully employed the use of technology not only to attract more customers but also to serve them from the very beginning. For example, Mexican ticket buyers may purchase tickets either online or with their smartphone. They have also maintained a very active social media presence. By 2015, there were 7.7 million fans on Facebook, 2.8 million followers on Twitter, and 1.4 million fans on Google+. Since 2013, Cinépolis Klic was launched in Mexico as a video-on-demand platform where people pay for the movie they choose and watch at home, increasing its presence in the market. Cinépolis was also one of the first theaters to introduce a customer loyalty program. They have broadened their theater content offerings beyond films alone to include sporting events, such as soccer matches, and concerts. In addition, in a business where around 55 percent of the income comes from selling tickets and around 35 percent from selling food and advertising, Cinépolis innovated on all revenue-generating fronts.

Cinépolis is characterized by its diverse portfolio of movie theaters, which allows the company to target a broad and segmented audience, with different needs and preferences, looking for a particular entertainment experience, atmosphere, size of the screen, type of sound, etc.

Cinépolis currently offers the following movie theater concepts: (1) Traditional movie theaters: their seating design is stadium-type, which allows for better viewing; (2) VIP premium: this theater concept offers more comfortable and bigger, leather, reclining seats, as well as food service inside the theater with a menu that includes not only soft drinks but alcoholic beverage choices such as whiskey, beer, etc.; (3) Macro XE: the characteristics of this theater concept are a bigger 4K screen of 170 square meters, a digital 7.1-channel surround system and 3D; (4) IMAX: the characteristics of this theater concept are a 4K big screen that offers twice the resolution of traditional digital projection thanks to IMAX technology; (5) 4DX: this theater concept, in addition to motion seating, offers some realistic special effects such as fog, water spray, and wind effects, amongst others; (6) Sala Junior: this unique theater concept is characterized by a playground inside the theater, with traditional seats and puff-style seats.

The company has also been committed to supporting a comprehensive corporate approach of social responsibility. Some of their programs are: (1) Del Amor Nace la Vista, which helps people with low incomes to have cataract eye surgery; (2) Vamos todos a Cinépolis, where more than 3.1 million kids in poverty in Mexico and Latin America have been taken to the movies for the first time; (3) Hazlo en Cortometraje and Festival Internacional de Cine en Derechos Humanos "DH Fest," where young filmmakers compete in human rights-themed film productions; (4) Ruta Cinépolis, where travelling movie caravans project films in low-income regions in Mexico; (5) Festival Internacional de Cine de Morelia, founded in 2003, which today is regarded as one of the most important film festivals in Mexico and Latin America.

Due to all of these initiatives, the company has been recognized with several corporate social responsibility awards, such as the gold medal in the Eagle Awards and in the Effie Awards Mexico, (Cinépolis, 2015).

Cinépolis: Its International Trajectory

Cinépolis's internationalization trajectory has been rapid and has been accompanied by continuous growth. The sequence of its domestic growth and internationalization path is summarized in Table 18.2.

Cinépolis's first internationalization project was supposed to be in Ecuador more than 15 years ago, but the opportunity was never consolidated and the project was abandoned early on. The internationalization strategy was redefined, and locations thereafter were carefully selected based on criteria such as the availability and development of well-located real estate and the tax and legal framework in the host country. In some cases, agencies were hired in order to conduct a complete analysis of the market and to decide on whether the investment was worth pursuing. Another important decision was to have local country managers who could understand and adapt the business model to the local markets. As expected, the outcomes and circumstances were not always the same across markets; while in some countries Cinépolis was the market leader, in others it had to compete with cinema chains that were both movie distributors and competitors, as in the case of Colombia.

Table 18.2 *The growth and internationalization process of Cinépolis*

Year	Key Events for Cinépolis	
	Domestic	International
1971	Enrique Ramírez Miguel founds the company with the name Cinematográfica Cadena de Oro	
1972–73		The company introduces the concept of Cinemas Gemelos (one movie theater with two screens)
1994	The Cinépolis brand is created	
1999	The concept of Cinépolis VIP is launched	
1999		Cinépolis starts operations in Guatemala
2003		Cinépolis starts operations in Costa Rica
2004	Alejandro Ramírez Magaña, grandson of the founder, becomes CEO of Cinépolis	
2005		Cinépolis starts operations in El Salvador
2005		Cinépolis starts operations in Panama
2008	The concept of Extreme Cinemas is introduced	
2008		Cinépolis starts operations in Colombia
2010		Cinépolis starts operations in Brazil
2010		Cinépolis starts operations in Peru
2010		Cinépolis starts operations in Honduras

Table 18.2 (cont.)

	Key Events for Cinépolis	
Year	Domestic	International
2011		Cinépolis introduces the concept of VIP to the US market
2014		Cinépolis starts operations in Chile through the acquisition of the local Cine Hoyts
2014		Cinépolis starts operations in India after acquiring Fun Cinemas from Essel Group
2015		The company operates in 12 countries

Source: Cinépolis (2015)

Nevertheless, Cinépolis's international trajectory changed with the purchase of Cine Hoyts in Chile, where nearly overnight they experienced remarkable success. The combination of a well-positioned brand, well-located and -equipped theaters with good technology revealed that acquisitions could, under some circumstances, be a very good strategy for Cinépolis's global expansion. Their success in Chile was reinforced by the fact that Chile was a country with one of the highest levels of income per capita in the region and with a stable economy and business environment (El Financiero, 2014).

In the case of India, where the entrance was also through an acquisition, there were some circumstances favoring the expansion of Cinépolis in the country. On the one hand, there was a boom in real estate together with the presence of a growing middle and upper-middle class. Also, India experienced the highest global level of ticket sale volume with 2.7 billion tickets in 2013 – more than twice the number of people in the USA, the market in second place. Moreover, India is the number-one producer of films by quantity in the world. In 2012 alone, around 1,602 films were produced in India, in comparison with 745 in China and 476 in the USA (Forbes, 2014).

For Arturo López, General Director of Investments and Growth of the group, acquisitions can be seen as a good growth strategy for the company. At the moment, the company is evaluating further acquisitions in Latin America, Asia, and Europe (El Financiero, 2015a). It has recently been announced that the company acquired the second largest movie theater chain in Spain, called Yelmo Cines, adding to its portfolio 414 more screens in 20 cities around the country (El Financiero, 2015c). A summary of Cinépolis's international expansion strategy by mode of entry can be found in Table 18.2.

Since the signing of the Trans-Pacific Partnership (TPP), of which Mexico is a member, Alejandro Ramírez, CEO of Cinépolis, has mentioned his interest in entering countries such as Indonesia and the Philippines. In addition, a strategy will be to focus on emerging markets where there is a growing middle class and where the share of entertainment in the consumers' expenditure is beginning to grow. For example, between 2004 and 2014, the percentage of global households visiting movie theaters doubled (El Financiero, 2015b).

CONCLUSIONS: KIDZANIA AND CINÉPOLIS

Important lessons can be drawn from the successful internationalization experiences of KidZania and Cinépolis, both of which are leaders in the Mexican and global entertainment industry. These are summarized below.

The first lesson is the unique global education and perspective of their founders. The international study and work experience of both López Ancona (KidZania) and Ramírez (Cinépolis) undoubtedly influenced their global aspirations not only to start a business, but to create a business with true international scope and reach in lucrative, strategic markets that were culturally and geographically very distant from Mexico.

Of even greater relevance was the development by both firms of a highly differentiated service offering, which potentially drove their business's international expansion given the unique space it carved out for itself within the industry. In the case of KidZania it was the unique concept of "edutainment"; in the case of Cinépolis, the VIP movie theater and high technology applied to the cinema experience. Through unique service offerings, both companies created new market niches for themselves in traditional entertainment service industries. This allowed them both to grow their share of the market at home while competing successfully based on differentiated service offerings, instead of low prices, in international markets.

The second important lesson from KidZania and Cinépolis is how they have successfully sustained their international presence. Educational workshops, such as those offered by KidZania, or premium movie theaters, such as those run by Cinépolis, are not patentable innovations, and in theory they are susceptible to copying. Not only have both companies carefully registered and defended their intellectual property assets overseas, but they have achieved such a high level of excellence in service execution that it is nearly impossible for global competitors to replicate or compete in the long term with their outstanding service delivery. To achieve this, KidZania has carefully selected local franchisees who undergo extensive orientation and ongoing training at the company's corporate university. For Cinépolis, this involved the appointment of partners who were both intimately familiar with the original business concept for its replication overseas. These same individuals possessed the know-how and "know-who" to secure key commercial contracts, such as was the case with KidZania, or to identify and negotiate the purchase of key real estate or acquisition targets, such as was the case with Cinépolis.

Undeniably, both KidZania and Cinépolis have experienced a very rapid, diverse international expansion strategy in a short period of time. This was, no doubt, aided by the fact that, as private companies, they could sacrifice some short-term losses for medium- and long-term gains in global presence. This rapid international expansion allowed both companies to secure access to key strategic real estate locations, required to achieve the customer volume needed to make their service businesses profitable.

Moreover, financing of this rapid growth overseas was built into each company's business model. In the case of KidZania, corporate sponsors provided one-third of the company's income, and through a robust global franchise model, they could expand overseas quickly. In the case of Cinépolis, Ramírez has publicly committed to reinvesting 90 percent of the company's profits towards its growth, which again serves to finance its bold global ambitions.

Both companies also practiced an exhaustive international market selection and due diligence process. In many cases, their international site selections possess economic and demographic characteristics similar to those of Mexico: a growing middle class, urbanization, growing disposable income, etc. In the case of Cinépolis, many of its global market choices are regional, and hence also reflect a minimal cultural distance from the company's headquarters. Their know-how in Mexico can easily be transferred to other emerging market locations worldwide where the demand for services is on the rise and the competitive environment is less fierce. In developed countries, however, such as the USA, both companies have sought out external consultants to help them identify the appropriate joint venture partner (in the case of KidZania) or acquisition partner (in the case of Cinépolis USA). Their awareness and willingness to vary their choice of international entry mode based on the characteristics of each international market destination reflects a high degree of awareness of the formula for success of their unique business models across varying cultural, legal, and competitive environments.

REFERENCES

AECOM. 2013. Global Attractions Attendance Report. *AECOM.* www.aecom.com/deployedfiles/Internet/Capabilities/Economics/_documents/ThemeMuseumIndex_2013.pdf. Accessed March 15, 2015.

AdAge. 2013. KidZania. A Theme park for work, gears up for US debut in 2015. *Adage.* http://adage.com/article/cmo-interviews/ad-age-cmo-summit-speaker-cammie-dunaway-kidzania/241540/. Accessed December 28, 2014.

Anderson, B. 2015. Xavier Lopez Ancona: En México caben dos KidZanias más. *Milenio*. www.milenio.com/financial_times/ftmercados-kidzania-negocios_0_5 76542495.html. Accessed September 5, 2015.

Arteaga, R. 2013. KidZania quiere ser un Disney, pero a la mexicana. *Forbes*. www.forbes.com.mx/kidzania-quiereserun-disney-pero-a-la-mexi cana/. Accessed December 15, 2015.

Cinépolis. *Cinépolis Company Intranet*. https://intranet.Cinépolis.com/SitePage s. Accessed January 5, 2015.

CNN Expansión. 2014. Los empresarios que transforman a México. *CNN Expansión*. www.cnnexpansion.com/negocios/2014/11/04/los-empresarios-que-transforman-a-mexico. Accessed January 5, 2015.

CNN Expansión. 2013a. Alejandro Ramírez Magaña. *CNN Expansión*. www .cnnexpansion.com/especiales/2013/10/14/45-alejandro-ramirez-magana. Accessed March 22, 2015.

CNN Expansión. 2013b. Un líder de tercera generación. *CNN Expansión*. www.cn nexpansion.com/especiales/2013/05/14/un-lider-de-tercera-generacion. Accessed March 22, 2015.

Daspro, E. 2013. *KidZania: Global franchise development*. Centro Internacional de Casos. Tecnologico de Monterrey. Case # C2814–002.

Delo, C. 2013. KidZania, A Theme park for work, gears up for US debut in 2015. *Ad Age*. Accessed January 5, 2014. https://kzjournal.kidzania.com/2013/05/17/kid zania-a-theme-park-for-work-gears-up-for-u-s-debut-in–2015/

El Economista. 2014. Cinemex vs. Cinépolis que empiece la función. *El Economista*. http://eleconomista.com.mx/entretenimiento/2014/01/05/cine mex-vs-cinepolis-que-empiece-funcion. Accessed January 5, 2015.

Espinosa, E. 2015. Retrato hablado: Xavier López Ancona juega lo grande. *Excelsior*. www.excelsior.com.mx/nacional/2015/07/05/1032974. Accessed September 7, 2015.

Estrada, N. 2015. Xavier López Ancona: El Walt Disney Mexicano. *El Contenido*. http://contenido.com.mx/2010/03/xavier-lopez-ancona-el-walt-disney-mexicano/. Accessed September 8, 2015.

Euromonitor. 2013a. *Amusement Parks and Entertainment Services in Mexico*. London: Euromonitor.

Euromonitor. 2013b. *Movie Theaters in Mexico*. London: Euromonitor.

El Financiero. 2014. Cinépolis confirma adquisición de cine Hoyts en Chile. *El Financiero*. www.elfinanciero.com.mx/empresas/cinepolis-confirma-adquisi cion-de-cine-hoyts-en-chile.html. Accessed April 25, 2015.

El Financiero. 2015a. Cinépolis negocia dos compras en el extranjero. *El Financiero.* www.elfinanciero.com.mx/empresas/cinepolis-negocia-dos-compras-en-el-extr anjero.html. Accessed April 20, 2015.

El Financiero. 2015b. Cinépolis enfocará su crecimiento y expansion en países emergentes. *El Financiero.* www.elfinanciero.com.mx/empresas/cinepolis-enfo cara-su-crecimiento-y-expansion-en-paises-emergentes.html. Accessed April 20, 2015.

El Financiero. 2015c. Cinépolis compra segunda cadena de cines más grande de Expaña. *El Financiero.* www.elfinanciero.com.mx/empresas/cinepolis-compra-s egunda-cadena-de-cines-mas-grande-de-espana.html. Accessed August 10, 2015.

Forbes. 2014. Bollywood India's film industry by the numbers. Infographic. *Forbes.* www.forbes.com/sites/niallmccarthy/2014/09/03/bollywood-indias-film-indus try-by-the-numbers-infographic/. Accessed April 20, 2015.

Gutierrez, T. 2013. Ten lessons from KidZania for internationalizing a business. *AltoNivel.com.mx.* www.altonivel.com.mx/33366-las-claves-de- kidzania-para-lograr-el-exito.html. Accessed January 5, 2015.

Hernández, E. 2014. KidZania, a la conquista de nuevos mercados. *24 Horas Diario Sin Límites.* http://admin.24-horas.mx/kidzania-a-la-conquista-de-nue vos- mercados/. Accessed January 5, 2015.

Heskett, J. L., Reynoso, J. & Cabrera, K. 2015. *KidZania: Shaping a Strategic Service Vision for the Future.* Harvard Business School Case 916–402.

KidZania. 2017. *KidZania company webpage.* http://kidzania.com/history.php. Accessed May 12, 2018.

Martinez, G. 2012. Like child's play. *WOBI World of Business Online Magazine.* www.wobi.com/articles/childs-play. Accessed February 10, 2015.

19 MultiMexicans in the Television Industry

Televisa and TV Azteca

Xiomara Vázquez Guillén* and Mauricio
Ramírez Grajeda

INTRODUCTION

Televisa and TV Azteca are two major players within the global media industry. Both are focused on Spanish-language households in a wide variety of business such as television, radio, publishing, and music. Both firms are iconic cases of MultiMexicans, especially in the USA and Latin America. The former holds sound links with Univision, the largest broadcasting firm in Spanish within the US market. Through its US firm, Televisa's expansion strategy is based on providing content in Spanish mainly to the US market. On the other hand, TV Azteca is focused on the Mexican market in the USA. As with other cases of Mexican firms in foreign markets, both firms consolidated their competitive advantages locally, much like América Móvil and Cemex did, and then stepped into the global arena. In this light, both firms have enjoyed a non-competitive environment in Mexico. Both of them are iconic companies and are part of Mexican culture. Televisa has a long tradition stretching back to the very beginnings of television broadcasting. We show that its process of globalization features a clear path: a discrete beginning, a process of consolidation within the national market, and a stage of globalization. By contrast, TV Azteca followed a different path, starting as a private company followed by a strong presence within the Mexican community in the USA. In both cases, three pillars underlie their development: entertainment (music and soap operas), sports (soccer, American football, and baseball) and news. In 2016 a new company, Imagen TV, broke the traditional

* Corresponding author.

television duopoly. The way forward for this sector is complex due to new alternatives available to their traditional customers. In this chapter, we analyze the globalization of these media firms. We start by providing an overview of the television industry, followed by an analysis of Televisa and TV Azteca.[1]

TELEVISION INDUSTRY ANALYSIS

Mexican television traces its origins back to the 1940s within the radio industry. In particular, the television industry's origins are Telesistema Mexicano and Televisión Independente de México, which were eventually grouped together to form Televisa. It is worth mentioning that Televisa's expansion could be partially explained by the strong support of PRI (Partido Revolucionario Institucional), the ruling party until 1997. Under these conditions Televisa became one of the most successful companies in the country, and the largest media company in Latin America, with a presence in all media branches and broadcasting. There were no real competitors in the industry until 1993, when TV Azteca arrived as Televisa's main rival. Canal 13 and Canal 7, on the other hand, were public stations, which had represented low competition because both focused on educational and cultural programs for limited audiences. Canal 7 and Canal 13 were acquired in the early 1990s to become TV Azteca. The broadcasting regulations of 1960 and 1973 considered broadcasting a public service at that time.

Historically, the Mexican television market structure has been characterized as an oligopoly. In this light, the dissolution of such a concentrated industry began in the year 2000, when PRI lost the presidential election in which Vicente Fox from the conservative party took office. However, during the 2005–6 elections a set of reforms regarding federal laws on communications, known as "Televisa law," reversed the 2000 changes protecting the interests of the duopoly, Televisa and TV Azteca. In particular, the media created

[1]   ifM (2015).

a great dependency of the political system. In this way, both firms ensured their dominant position in the industry through the spectrum frequency allocation (95 percent to both firms) at no cost and the full control of their allocated frequencies. However, there was a constitutional inconsistency declared by the Supreme Court. Public television such as ONCE TV, Canal 22, and TV UNAM would have been seriously affected.

In 2013 a constitutional reform and a new Federal Law on Telecommunications and Broadcasting were approved in Mexico by the national legislative branch. The aims of these reforms were to increase and clarify more rights for custumers and stakeholders, to foster competition aiming at better service quality and lower prices. The reforms to the constitution, along with the new federal legal framework, regulate issues relating to the radio-electric spectrum, the open telecommunication networks, the access to infrastructure, the convergence of telecommunications and broadcasting, the customer's rights, and the market structure in these sectors.

TELEVISA: AN OVERVIEW

Televisa is the largest mass media firm in the world for a Spanish-speaking audience, in terms of market value within the Mexican Stock Exchange Index (IPC). In 2015, for instance, Televisa's stocks represented slightly more than 8 percent of the IPC. Therefore, it is an important player in the international entertainment business and telecommunications, and provides video, voice, and broadband services. It owns 60 percent of Sky, a satellite pay-television system operating in Mexico and Central America, and has a major role in five cable and telecommunications subsidiaries: Cablevisión (the largest network in Mexico), Cablemás, Cablecom, TVI, and Bestel. Televisa also provides telecommunication services through these companies. Another of its branches is Editorial Televisa, which is a major Spanish-language magazine publisher and distributor with a presence in more than two dozen countries in Latin America and with a network of slightly more than 100,000 selling points.

Regarding radio production and broadcasting, Televisa has 81 radio stations that reach more than 70 percent of Mexico's population. The company also offers professional sports and live entertainment, feature film production, and film distribution. Televisa Digital operates the website Esmas.com, offering videos, chat, forums, and email services. On the other hand, Televisa Home Entertainment produces and distributes the television and film production of the company on DVD; it also manages Televisa Music, and the licensing division markets all Televisa brands. Besides, Televisa owns three professional soccer teams as well as the world-famous Azteca stadium in Mexico City.

Emilio Azcárraga Jean and his relatives hold 15 percent of the voting share of Televisa's stocks and his family owns the bulk of the shares. Under Azcárraga Jean's administration, the management structures have been modernized. He changed the company's logo, and the revenues and profits have increased quite considerably due to his aggressive expansion plans. In 2014, for example, revenues were around US$2.2 billion. Televisa tried to acquire even more of Univision during a bidding war, but lost out to the German ProSiebenSat.1.

Pioneering Mexico's communications history, Televisa started in the 1920s when the radio broadcaster XEW, one of Mexico's first stations, launched operations under Emilio Azcárraga Vidaurreta. Televisa's best ally was the ruling party PRI (Partido Revoluacionario Institucional), which helped XEW's national expansion in radio in the 1930s. During the 1940s, Azcárraga had a strong position not only in radio but also in the film industry, with Churubusco Studios. In the mid-1940s, Radio Programas de Mexico bought out the Mexican radio operations of NBC and CBS.

Romulo O'Farrill won the first television concession granted by the government in 1942 and founded Television de Mexico, which operated Channel 4. Azcárraga stepped into the television industry until 1951 through Televimex and created Channel 2. In the following year, Guillermo González Camarena created Channel 5. After President Miguel Aleman Valdés granted a television concession to his own family, in 1955, the Azcárragas, Alemans, and O'Farrills merged their stations into a single network, called Telesistema Mexico. The families retained individual licenses, thus avoiding monopoly charges.

For more than a decade, Telesistema dominated the Mexican television industry. Nevertheless, when, in 1968, the government attempted to tax radio and television broadcasters with a 25 percent rate, the group struck back by influencing the public opinion during elections. The government cancelled the tax, but received in exchange 12.5 percent of each station's air time. In the same year, Channel 8 was created by a Monterrey business group under Televisión Independiente. In 1970, Teleprogramas launched "24 Horas" (24 Hours), a news program that supported PRI with a conservative and anti-communist view of Latin America. It quickly became the primary news program available in the Spanish language.

Televisa was created in 1973 with the fusion of Telesistema Mexicano and Televisión Independiente de México, and has coordinated, operated, and broadcast Channels 2, 4, 5, and 8 ever since. Then the Azcárraga family gained complete control and hegemony over Mexico's entertainment industry, with holdings in television, radio, film, and the recording industry. At this time, Emilio Azcárraga Milmo took control over Group Televisa and started working on synergies. For instance, the actors and advertisers were not allowed to perform in government-run stations; and Televisa developed its own "star-making" system with training schools. The company then reached more than a 90 percent market share in Mexico around a soap opera, a melodramatic but very successful program both in Mexico and all over the world, with dubbed and subtitled versions of its programs in Western and Eastern Europe, Africa, India, and China. In 1985, Channel 8 changed its signal to XEQ Channel 9 and changed from being a cultural channel into a commercial one. In September 1988, Televisa created the first Spanish-language satellite news system: ECO (Orbital Communications Company), broadcasting live 24 hours a day in Mexico, the United States, Central and South America, Western Europe, and Northern Africa.

The 1990s were times of privatization. The government sold two television networks, but Televisa was not allowed to buy them. Finally, Televisa was able to acquire a third network with six stations. 1996 was a complicated year for Televisa: the firm had to compete for advertising revenues against the new Mexican rival, TV Azteca, which had been building market share and even beating Televisa in some markets.

In 1997, Azcárraga Milmo died; then his son, Emilio Azcárraga Jean, who had worked for the company since 1988, assumed the leadership as President, Chairman, and CEO. At that time, Televisa's share of the prime-time audience had fallen below 60 percent and Azcárraga Milmo's legacy included $1.8 billion in personal and holding company debt. Gilberto Perez-Alonso was hired in 1988, as the first of Azcárraga Jean's CFOs, and under his command austerity began. The size of management was reduced by 4,000; the workforce was reduced from 15,400 in 1999 to 13,500 by the end of 2001; and a newspaper and three training schools were closed. The advertisers were paid for specific units in order to measure more clearly the profits generated. Azcárraga bought out other heirs and raised his share of Televisa's holding company, Televicentro, to 51 percent and consolidated control in his own hands. In 2000, the debt was restructured, the interest was reduced, and the company improved its grade rating.

Azcárraga Milmo once declared: "We are from the PRI, we always were from the PRI ... As a member of the party we will do all that lies in our power to make sure that our candidate comes out on top." However, Televisa recognized that its close links with the political system, in contrast with TV Azteca's greater political independence, would no longer be beneficial. In 2000, Televisa finally ended its open links with the PRI, putting an end to an era of service to the government, but also to the firm's political protection. In the same year, and after 71 years of ruling the PRI, Vicente Fox of the Partido Acción Nacional (PAN) won the presidential election in Mexico. After elections, new projects were launched, such as "En Vivo" (In Direct), a live entertainment division, and "Big Brother," a reality show.

In April 2001, Channel 4 became 4TV, and in June Channel 9 became Galavision. During the period of austerity, Televisa had decreased its investment in Univision to 5.8 percent, but in this year the company invested up to US$375 million, equating to an investment of 15 percent, giving priority to the US Spanish-language market. One year later, under the management of Azcárraga Jean, the transformation and modernization of the firm began. Televisa announced that it has signed a definitive agreement with Endemol Holding, the leading international content developer and producer for television and online platforms, to set up a new television and interactive production company focused primarily on the Mexican market. Based in Mexico City, the new company would be named Endemol Mexico and a 50/50 joint venture of the two companies.

In July 2010, the joint venture won an auction of mobile broadcasting frequencies by the Mexican government, under suspicion and claims of unfair conditions. Very soon, in October 2010, Televisa sold its 30 percent investment in the mobile network provider Nextel, a subsidiary of the American company. Shortly before the termination of the collaboration between Televisa and Nextel, a judge had stopped the usage of the frequency in question with an injunction. In April 2011, Televisa announced the purchase of 50 percent of Iusacell, the mobile provider, part of TV Azteca owner Ricardo Salinas's portfolio of companies, for a total of US$1.6 billion.

With the convergence of television, phone, and Internet (Triple Play), Televisa and TV Azteca started a war against Telmex, Carlos Slim's subsidiary and Mexican leader in the telephone market. Slim struck back by trying to enter the pay-television market, forbidden at that time because of the roaming policies. Telmex announced it would cease to broadcast adverts on Televisa and TV Azteca from July. This was a big hit against Televisa, because 3.8 percent of its advertising revenues were generated by Grupo Carso. At the same time, Televisa and TV Azteca were struggling to increase their market share in the Mexican mobile market. In December 2011, Televisa participated in the merger between Antena 3 and Gestora de Inversiones Audiovisuales La Sexta.

In 2014, Televisa was operating four nationwide channels in Mexico City through 258 regional stations that cover more than 90 percent of the population. The company produced content of more than 94,000 hours of soap operas, live entertainment, news, and professional sports. Its programs reached 70 percent of the national viewing audience. Televisa's content has universal appeal; 87,000 hours of original programming were exported to over 80 countries. Televisa also produced and distributed 25 pay-television brands in Mexico and the rest of the world, and exports its programs and formats to the USA through Univision and to other television networks in over 50 countries.

Televisa's Expansion

At the beginning of the 1960s the international expansion path of Televisa started when the company focused on the Spanish-language market within the USA through Univision. Specifically, in 1961, Rene Anselmo and Emilio Azcárraga Milmo founded the Spanish International Communications Corporation (SICC) by acquiring KWEX-TV in Los Angeles. Telesistema supplied SICC with financing and all its programming. Anselmo also became the president of the Spanish International Network (SIN), founded by the end of 1975, with 25 percent, and Telesistema held the other 75 percent of the ownership, with more than 350 affiliated stations, and eventually controlled practically all the Spanish-language television in the United States. In 1968, SIN had absorbed KMEX-TV in Los Angeles, WXTV in New York City, and KPAZ-TV in Phoenix, all of them ultra-high-frequency (UHF) stations, and also five Mexican stations into the network. These broadcasting stations were practically the only ones with programs in Spanish within the USA. It is worth noting that this market featured a seven-fold faster growth rate than the entire population.[2]

2   Univision's Quarterly Report.

In 1976 SIN started its satellite broadcasting. By 1980 SIN had reached 67 percent of the whole potential Spanish-speaking market in the USA, and by 1982, 33 out of the 35 Spanish stations were receiving SIN programming, of which 55 percent came from Televisa and the remaining 45 percent was produced within the United States. The shows included World Cup soccer and popular soap operas. SIN's revenue was US$45 million for 1984. In April of 1979, SIN founded Galavision, a cable television satellite service in Spanish, offered in some states of the US, such as New Mexico and Florida. Its contents consisted of films, sports, and soap operas. Its subscriber base went up from 60,000 in 1981 to 100,000 in 1984. The Azcárraga family owned 75 percent through Televisa's subsidiary, Univision.

In 1986, SICC lost the renewal of licenses because of a violation of the 20 percent legal limit on ownership by foreigners. A year later, ten television stations were sold to Hallmark Cards for US$300 million; SIN was launched as Univision Network and Hallmark purchased a majority stake for $265 million. A change in the programing started when Univision released Spanish-language clones of such English-language shows as "Saturday Night Live," "Entertainment Tonight," "The People's Court," and "Oprah Winfrey", among others. On the other hand, the company acquired more presence in Latin American hot spots such as wars in Central America. Then they came up with a new show called "Sábado Gigante" (Giant Saturday), a combination of variety, game, and talk show. However, the new style of programming was not to the taste of the subscribers. In 1992, Jerrold Perenchio bought Univision for US$550 million.

Perenchio received 75 percent of the station group and 50 percent of the network; Group Televisa and Venevision (Venezuela's largest broadcasting company) received the rest. Univision had annual revenues of more than $200 million and had 13 Spanish-language television stations. From 1992 to 1997, Univision's market share of Spanish-language television increased from 57 to 83 percent. A new era of acquisitions began with Chicago and Houston stations in 1994; and a Sacramento station in 1997. Televisa and Venevision provided

92 percent of Univision's programming. Univision's programming again was similar to US English-language shows, such as the "Today"-type early morning program "Despierta America" (Wake up America); some talk shows like "Cristina" (seen by 100 million people from Boston to Chile); the news at "Primer Impacto" (First Impact); a variety show, "Al Ritmo de la Noche" (Rhythm of the Night); and, the soap operas. By the end of the year, 14 of the 20 top prime time Spanish-language programs in the USA belonged to Univision, and the firm was one of the most trusted institutions among Hispanics. On the other hand, Galavision reached around 50 percent of the Hispanic households wired for cable service on more than 370 US cable systems.

Televisa decided to go public in December 1991 and sold 20 percent of the company for about US$807 million. The next step was to go international, and Televisa acquired 49 percent of a television network in Chile; 76 percent of a radio network in Peru; and 50 percent of PanAmSat; and purchased the *Editorial America* magazine, becoming the world's largest Spanish-language publisher with this acquisition. However, in 1994, the "Tequila Financial Crisis" began, and after the devaluation of the peso the company was losing money again. One year later, Televisa started being fully listed on the New York Stock Exchange and sold an additional 10 percent stake for about US $1 billion. On the other hand, the company sold off its holdings in PanAmSat.

In 1996, the firm's expansion continued with satellite programming ventures in Sky Entertainment Latin America and its television holdings in two English-language stations on the US border. Univision Communications made its initial public offering (IPO) and sold 19 percent of its common stock. Perenchio held 26 percent while Grupo Televisa and Venevision held 10 percent each. In financial terms, Televisa has featured increasing net profits, and an expansion of its labor force since 2000 (See Table 19.1).

In December 2001, Univision, Televisa, and Venevision announced a global alliance to penetrate the US Hispanic market.

Table 19.1 *Televisa's financial indicators*

	2000	2005	2010	2015
Revenue	2,000.4	3,104.2	4,583.2	5,559.8
Total assets	2,684	3,326.3	4,854.4	5,220.3
EBITDA	659.7	1,261.7	1,755.6	2,092.7
Gross profit	512.2	1,030.5	1,234.4	1,169.9
Net profit	–83.6	585.4	608.6	688.2
Foreign investment	N/A	N/A	N/A	N/A
Exports	400.7	359.7	606.3	538
Employees	14,738	12,284	24,362	32,047
Countries	5	5	5	5

N/A = not available
Data in millions of US dollars
Source: Bloomberg (2015) and Televisa's Annual Reports.

In 2007, Televisa made a buyout bid for Univision but lost out to Broadcasting Media Partners. In 2009, Televisa and Univision amended the current Program License Agreement, and the litigation between the parties was dismissed. By the end of 2010, Televisa and the NY-based Univision confirmed their business relations and extended a collaboration for the shared usage of program licenses to 2025. Televisa will invest US$1.2 billion in Univision and receive at least a 5 percent share in return and the option to grow that stake to 40 percent via convertible debt. Televisa will give Univision 50 percent of its TuTv joint venture and extend its content agreement from 2017 to 2020.

In 2014, Univision was the dominant media firm operating within the US for the Hispanic market, and its assets include: Univision Network, a top-five network that reaches 94 percent of Hispanic television households; UniMás, a leading Spanish-language broadcast that reaches 88 percent of US Hispanic television households; Univision and Galavision Cable Networks; Univision TVnovelas (soap operas); Univision Deportes (sports); ForoTV (news);

and additional cable offerings of movies and music; Univision Local Media (61 television and 67 radio stations in major US Hispanic markets and Puerto Rico); online and mobile bilingual apps and products; Uforia, Hispanic digital music service; Univision.com, the most-visited Spanish-language website in the USA; and Univision Partner Group, an advertising and publisher network. And a minority stake in "El Rey," a 24-hour English-language entertainment cable network; and a joint venture with Disney/ABC.

Televisa distributes its pay-television channels through Univision in the United States. In 2014, it produced approximately 24,500 hours of content for pay-television networks with 40.3 million pay-television subscribers. Televisa has equity and debt subject to approval from the Federal Communications Commission ("FCC"), that represents 38 percent of the equity capital in Broadcasting Media Partners, Inc. ("BMP"), the controlling company of Univision, headquartered in New York City. BMP owns a network of television and radio stations and sales offices in major cities throughout the USA. Current US laws prevent foreign companies from holding a 25 percent stake in a broadcasting company, and it's unclear how Televisa might structure an arrangement to get around that issue if it pursues a 40 percent holding.

In 2014, UCI continued its strategy of growing revenues and maximizing profitability while increasing the long-term value of the company. During the year, revenues increased by 10.8 percent to US$2.9 billion, fueled by the transmission of the World Cup 2014 and the continued growth of retransmission revenues. Televisa received US$313.7 million in the form of royalties from Univision, a 14.8 percent increase from the previous year. The US marketplace is a key issue in Televisa's expansion, and in the status of a leading media company in the Spanish-speaking world. Televisa's content is very appealing to Hispanic audiences in the United States, and to Univision's advertising clients. The soap operas have allowed Univision to become the most watched network on Friday nights, surpassing every other broadcaster in the USA, regardless of language. Under the current license agreement with Univision, Televisa receives a royalty of 11.91 percent of substantially all audio-visual revenue generated by Univision.

On July 2, 2015, Univision and Televisa agreed that certain subsidiaries of Univision and Televisa would enter an amendment to their existing PLA, and that they also extended to 2030. Univision's exclusive U.S. broadcast and digital rights to Televisa's programming including premium Spanish-language soap operas, sports, sitcoms, reality series, new programming, and feature films, will remain unchanged.

On January 1, 2018, the royalty rate will increase to 16.13 percent. Televisa will continue to receive an incremental 2 percent in royalty payments on such media networks' revenues above an increased revenue base of $1.66 billion, compared to the prior revenue base of $1.65 billion.

TV AZTECA[3]

TV Azteca, launched in 1993, is Televisa's most important rival within the Mexican market. Grupo Azteca is a holding company with a couple of subsidiaries engaged in television broadcasting, production, and advertising. One of them is TV Azteca, which operates two national networks: Canal 13 and Canal 7. TV Azteca also owns a professional soccer team in the Mexican league, a record company, two television stations in Central America, and a web portal. (See Table 19.2.) The other is Azteca America, which is a US broadcasting firm for the Spanish-speaking audience, in particular for the Mexican market.

TV Azteca's history began with Controladora Mexicana de Comunicaciones, the government corporation in charge of two out of seven VHF television stations in Mexico City, and a television transmission network. In 1969 Francisco Aguirre Jimenez was granted the concession of Canal 13, but returned it to the government in 1972. Then,

---

[3]   Televisa's Annual Report.

Table 19.2 *Televisa's events*

Year	Domestic Events	Year	International Events
1955	Azcárraga moved into television, forming Televimex, and created Channel 2. Four years later it became Telesistema Mexico.	1961	Telesistema supplied SICC (Spanish International Communications Corp.) with 20 percent of its financing and held 75 percent of SIN (Spanish International Network) in the USA.
1968	Mexican government attempted to tax radio and television broadcasters with a 25 percent rate; the latter group struck back by affecting the public opinion during election period.	1968	SIN had added KMEX-TV in Los Angeles, WXTV in New York City, and KPAZ-TV in Phoenix.
1970	Teleprogramas launched the news program "24 Horas," the primary news program available in Spanish-language.	1976	SIN started with the earth satellite network, the company increased the direct transitions from abroad while reducing transmission cost.
1973	Televisa was created as the fusion of Telesistema Mexicano and Televisión Independiente de México and passed into the hands of the second generation under the leadership of Emilio Azcárraga Milmo.	1979	SIN launched Galavision, a commercial-free pay cable television satellite service in Spanish offered in Arizona, Colorado, New Mexico, and Florida, owned by the Azcárraga family at 75 percent and the remaining 25 percent by Anselmo. A year later, SIN reached 67 percent of all Hispanics in the USA.
1985	Canal 8 changed its signal to XEQ Canal 9 and passed from a cultural channel to a commercial one.	1982	33 out of 35 all -Spanish station were receiving SIN programming, of which 55 percent came from Televisa and the remaining 45 percent was produced in the USA.

Table 19.2 (cont.)

Year	Domestic Events	Year	International Events
1988	Televisa created the first Spanish Language satellite news system: ECO (Orbital Communications Company).	1987	Ten TV stations were sold to Hallmark Cards Inc. for US $300 million; SIN was renamed "Univision Network."
1993	The government sold off two television networks to private bidders; Televisa was barred from bidding for these stations.	1993	Televisa purchased the Editorial America magazine arm of Miami-based America Publishing Company, making Editorial Televisa the world's largest Spanish-language publisher.
1997	Azcárraga Milmo died and his son Emilio Azcárraga Jean assumed the leadership. One year later, the latter restructured and downsized the company by 4,000 employees.	1997	Televisa and Venevision were providing Univision with 92 percent of its programming.
2001	Channel 4 became 4TV, and June Channel 9 became Galavision.	2001	Univision, Televisa, and Venevision announced a global alliance to penetrate the US Hispanic market.
2010	The company won an auction of mobile broadcasting frequencies by the Mexican government.	2010	Televisa and Univision extended the shared usage of program licenses to 2025. Televisa received at least 5 percent of Univision.
2015	Televisa was operating four nationwide channels through 258 regional stations that cover more than 90 percent of the population.	2015	Univision and Televisa agreed that certain subsidiaries of Univision and Televisa entered into an amendment to their existing PLA, and they extended to 2030.

Source: Televisa's Annual Reports.

both Canal 13 and Canal 7 were grouped in 1985 under the Instituto Mexicano de Television (Imevisión), which was almost off the air in 1988. In 1993, during the Mexican privatization era, the government put Canal 13 and Canal 7 up for auction. Ricardo Salinas Pliego, owner of Grupo Elektra, a chain of retail stores of electronic products, appliances, and furniture, purchased the station for US$642 million – by far the highest bid. The money came from Salinas Pliego and other owners of Elektra; a credit syndicate; Alsavicion Alberto Saba Raffoul's firm; and $30 million in loans from Raul Salinas.

Just after acquiring Imevisión, Salinas Pliego called off low-rated programs, launched new ones produced or acquired abroad, put Channel 7 into production, invested money in new studios and updated the transmission network, cut the work force from 1,500 to 750, and offered advertisers rates far below those of Televisa. By 1994 Channel 13 was reaching 85 percent of Mexican homes and Channel 7, 65 percent. The company's prime time weekday audience in Mexico City rose to 14 percent.

The new programming mainly consists of European and Latin American soap operas; exclusive rights to transmit NBC Nightly News, four television serials; and, the games of the professional football soccer teams in Veracruz and Morelia, owned by TV Azteca. By the end of 1995, Channel 13 was reaching 91 percent of all Mexican households with televisions, and Channel 7, 81 percent; revenues triplicated in a year to US$150 million. TV Azteca hired "Argos Comunicaciones" to produce a popular semi-documentary police show with a technical realization more similar to that of a film or theatrical production than television.

TV Azteca's Golden Years were 1996 and 1997. TV Azteca turned to Argos for its first soap opera, "Nada personal," a huge hit based on the seamy realities of Mexican public life, such as a politician assassination (a presidential candidate was recently murdered), drug dealers, and corrupt policemen, produced in public places in Mexico City. The second soap opera was "Mirada de Mujer" (Woman's Gaze), the story of a woman cheating on her unfaithful husband. Some other popular programs were "Ciudad Desnuda" (Naked City), a documentary with hidden cameras to expose crimes even as they occurred; "¡Te caché!" (I Caught You!), a version of "Candid Camera"; and a fresh way to present the nightly news. TV Azteca was making US$305 million and introduced Azteca Music, associated with Warner Music.

In 1997, TV Azteca went public and sold 21 percent of its stocks in Mexico City, and New York shareholder Saba Raffoul sold his stake of about 22 percent to Salinas Pliego, who increased his share of the company to 73 percent. The company's prime time weekday audience in Mexico City rose to 35 percent, focusing on high-income viewers. The main advertising customers were Bayer, Burger King, DHL, Tequila Jose Cuervo, Nissan, and Volkswagen.

The company lost 20 percent of its prime time viewers when "Mirada de Mujer" concluded in April, 1998. TV Azteca tried to strike back with two soap operas, but both were audience failures. Weekday prime time viewership in Mexico City dropped to 25 percent. Salinas Pliego decided to bring in a new CFO and spokesperson, 31-year-old New Yorker Adrian Steckel, who had worked for the company as Pliego's assistant and Vice President of Business Operations.

At the end of 1998, TV Azteca formed a joint venture to operate and provide programming for Channel 40: it negotiated an agreement to broadcast Disney movies, television series, and children's programming in Mexico to reposition Channel 7 for children and young adults; and, maintained Channel 13 as the flagship network. One year later, TV Azteca retained its share of the prime time audience, but its sales dropped by almost 20 percent; the advertising sales had decreased; there were no special events (such as the world soccer championships in 1998); and the Veracruz soccer team was sold. On the bright side, Channel 13's programming was available in 97 percent of Mexican households, while Channel 7's in 94 percent; TV Azteca produced 50 percent of its own programming, and sold about $20 million worth of it, including two telenovelas to Telemundo; and, Azteca Music released 32 recordings.

During the summer of 1999, popular game- and talk-show host Francisco (Paco) Stanley was murdered; cocaine was found in his pocket and he was linked with drug dealers. TV Azteca blamed Mexico City's government for the high crime rate; and city prosecutors struck back by arresting Stanley's colleagues and accusing them of the murder. The scandals continued when Salinas Pliego used company funds to buy 50 percent of Unefon, his low-cost fixed wireless telephone service. In contrast, the soap opera "El candidato" (The Candidate) depicted vote buying and the links between corrupt politicians and police and drug dealers; it finished three weeks before Mexico's presidential election and was a hit.

In 1999, The Salinas Pliego family controlled 62.5 percent of TV Azteca's shares, but the long-term liabilities came to $425 million. A year later, TV Azteca purchased 50 percent of another Salinas company, the Internet portal Todito.com. TV Azteca and Salinas Pliego entered into a credibility crisis while top management tried to restore trust in the company and stockholders. Efforts were focused primarily on new program development: game show and situation comedy formats.

In 2003, TV Azteca separated its investment in the telephone company Unefon and the provider of wireless broadband access to Internet Cosmofrecuencias. In 2010, the firm acquired 51 percent of the Football Club "Jaguares" and renewed three more years of broadcasting transmission rights of "Santos Laguna" football club.

In October 2015, a new era began, when the Board of Directors designated Benjamín Salinas Sada as the new TV Azteca CEO. Since 2010, net profits have decreased dramatically so that its stock price in 2016 is at historical low levels. See Table 19.3.

TV Azteca expansion[4]

In 1997, seeking more markets, TV Azteca purchased a 75 percent interest in an El Salvador station intended as the axis of a national network and 75 percent of a UHF station in Guatemala City.

[4]   TV Azteca's Annual Reports.

Table 19.3 *TV Azteca's financial indicators*

	2000	2005	2010	2015
Revenue	573.8	783.8	915.3	812
Total assets	1,935.2	1,727.1	2,258.8	2,121.4
EBITDA	226.9	353.1	374.2	95.1
Gross profit	166.8	318.1	332.4	37.4
Net profit	37.3	111.7	183.6	−166.3
Foreign investment	N/A	N/A	N/A	N/A
Exports	N/A	N/A	N/A	174.9
Employees	2,758	4,228	5,000	4,167
Countries	3	3	3	3

Data in millions of US dollars
N/A = not available
Source: Bloomberg (2015) and TV Azteca's Annual Reports.

In 2000 TV Azteca sold to EchoStar Satellite Corp. exclusive rights for three years to transmit Channel 13's programming to the United States via satellite. TV Azteca launched four popular soap operas, but broke up with Argos, who started working for Telemundo. TV Azteca then turned to Columbia Pictures Television Inc. to co-produce films and soap operas, and to Pearson to produce programs.

One year later, the company began operations at KAZA-TV Los Angeles and added Channel 68 in Reno, Nevada to its network. One year later, they had operations at Channel 31 in Miami, Channel 43 in West Palm Beach, Channel 55 in Fresno, and Channel 42 in Bakersfield, reaching 42 percent of the Hispanic market. Two years later, the firm added KTDF Channel 18 in San Antonio and KBGS Channel 51 in Victoria, Texas; one more Channel in San Diego; and KCIN-TV/Channel 27 in Denver Colorado, and KBKI-TV/Channel 9 in Yakima-Pascoe-Richland-Kennewick, Washington reaching 69 percent of the Hispanic market in the USA.

Table 19.4 *TV Azteca's events*

Year	Domestic Events	Year	International Events
1993	Ricardo Salinas Pliego bought Channel 13 and Channel 7 from the Government. One year later, Channel 13's coverage reached 85 percent of Mexican homes and Channel 7's 65 percent.		
1997	Shareholder Saba Raffoul sold his stake of about 22 percent to Salinas Pliego, who increased his share of the company to 73 percent. TV Azteca's Golden Years, 1996–8.	1997	Purchased a 75 percent interest in an El Salvador station intended as the axis of a national network and 75 percent of a UHF station in Guatemala City.
1998	Channel 40 was operated and provided TV Azteca programming.	2000	EchoStar Satellite bought exclusive rights for three years to transmit Channel 13's programming in the USA. Azteca America acquired the station WSAH in New York and ended its relationship with Telemundo.
2001	Purchased 50 percent of another Salinas company, Todito.com SA de CV, an Internet portal with the exclusive right to distribute TV Azteca content.	2001	Began operations in KAZA-TV Los Angeles and added Channel 68 in Reno, Nevada to its network. One year later, reached 42 percent of the Hispanic market with its operations at Channel 31 in Miami, Channel 43 in West Palm Beach, Channel 55 in Fresno, and Channel 42 in Bakersfield.

Table 19.4 (cont.)

Year	Domestic Events	Year	International Events
2003	Separated its investment in the telephone company Unefon and the provider of wireless broadband Internet access, Cosmofrecuencias.	2003	Added KTDF Channel 18 in San Antonio and KBGS Channel 51 in Victoria, Texas; one more channel in San Diego; and KCIN-TV /Channel 27 in Denver, Colorado, and KBKI-TV /Channel 9 in Yakima-Pascoe-Richland-Kennewick, Washington, reaching 69 percent of the Hispanic market in the USA.
2010	Acquired 51 percent of the Football Club "Jaguares" and renewed three more years of broadcasting transmission rights of "Santos Laguna" football club.	2008	Entered into an agreement with Pappas Telecasting to broadcast in Kaza-TV Channel 54 in Los Angeles, until 2012. Acquired 70 percent of Latitud TV in Guatemala.
2015	Board of Directors designated Benjamín Salinas Sada as TV Azteca's new CEO.	2013	Won a tender in Colombia for the construction and maintenance of fiber optic network and a tender in Peru to build and operate fiber optic network to provide telecommunications services.

Source: TV Azteca's Annual Reports.

In 2008, TV Azteca finally entered an agreement with Pappas Telecasting, the largest private owner of US television stations, to broadcast on Kaza-TV Channel 54 in Los Angeles, for the next four years. During the same year, the firm acquired 70 percent of "Latitud TV" in Guatemala. See Table 19.4.

In 2013, TV Azteca won a tender in Colombia for the construction and maintenance of a fiber optic network, and a tender in Peru to build and operate a fiber optic network to provide telecommunications services.

FINAL REMARKS

Televisa and TV Azteca have followed a strategy of international expansion over the course of their history based upon an increasing population of Spanish speakers within the USA. The common denominator is to export contents produced in Mexico to the rest of the world, and to run business in the USA through firms with their own seal. The result is a sound presence within Spanish-speaking households, and in different languages as well. Their strategy consists of consolidating in the local market with a dominant market share and close political links, and creates profits for expansion opportunities abroad.

On the other hand, Televisa and TV Azteca diversify their businesses in other fields such as cable television, publishing, telecommunications, film production, and music. It is worth mentioning that television technology has evolved over time from analog to digital. Also, households increasingly spend less time watching television due to more entertainment alternatives and greater competition.

The way forward points to more national television channels to compete against traditional firms. In Mexico, digitalization was introduced in December 2015, and in the same year regulators became more powerful. Thus, globalization could be the basis of the companies' business expansion. It is worth mentioning, on the one hand, that Grupo Televisa's share price has decreased by 50 percent from the summer of 2015 to the winter of 2017. As for TV Azteca, its share price has decreased by 66 percent from the spring of 2013 to the winter of 2017. On the other hand, Netflix's share price has increased by 300 percent from January 2012 to January 2015. Regarding the Mexican firms, 2017 is a critical point for changing their business models into a more diversified portfolio. Their financial structures depend heavily upon the exchange rate, and their audiences have been dramatically decreasing.

REFERENCES

ifM. 2015. International Media Corporation. Grupo Televisa. www.mediadb.eu/ en/data-base/international-media-corporations/grupo-televisa.html. Accessed in May, 2015.

Bloomberg. 2015. Company Overview Holdings, Inc. www.bloomberg.com/resear ch/stocks/private/snapshot.asp?privcapId=224555999. Accessed in April, 2015.

Univision. 2005–2015. Annual Reports. http://investors.univision.net/financial-reports/quarterly-reports/default.aspx. Accessed in May, 2015.

Televisa. 2000–2015. Annual Reports. www.televisair.com/en/reports-and-filings /quarterly/2016. Accessed in May, 2015.

TV Azteca. 2005–2015. Annual Reports. www.irtvazteca.com/. Accessed in May, 2015.

Company Histories. 2015. TV Azteca SA de CV. www.company-histories.com/TV-Azteca-SA-de-CV-Company-History.html. Accessed in May, 2015.

20 MultiMexicans in Information Technology
Binbit and Softtek[1]

Mauricio Cervantes-Zepeda

INTRODUCTION

The objective of this chapter is to analyze briefly how, within the IT industry in Mexico, Mexican entrepreneurs have taken advantage of the new opportunities and created global companies. The top global companies in the IT industry are analyzed. Surprisingly, these are young companies that in only a few years have reached amazing worldwide penetration. Thus, important lessons about entrepreneurship can be learned from this chapter.

According to the ranking of the top global firms in Mexico by importance and level of globalization (CNN Expansión, 2015b), the top firms in the IT industry are Binbit, Softtek, Neoris, Intellego, and Global Hitts, in that order. In this chapter, Binbit and Softtek's history will be analyzed. These young companies (founded in 2005 and 1982, respectively) focus on IT services. After a short period, they reached 67 countries in America, Europe, Asia, Africa, and Australia. Binbit mainly focuses on delivering entertainment through mobile phones, and Softtek is a provider of outsourcing in IT services.

Binbit and Softtek take advantage of technological changes by creating a business model completely centered around information technologies. Binbit is not a domestic company that adopted IT and became global, but rather a company that was born as a global IT firm. Similarly, Softtek's approach was to deliver the best IT service to Multinational Enterprises (MNEs). IT and Globalization are not accessories or parts of the firm's strategy; both must be the core foundation

[1] Thanks to Jose Manuel Lopez and Esthela Silva, from Binbit corporate communication; Gilberto Romero, Softtek marketing director; Nayeli Acevedo, Softtek public relations; and Jose Tam, former Softtek Peru office director. All provided insightful information.

of the business model for new companies if they want to survive and succeed in the current technological and dynamic environment.

Binbit and Softtek have taught us important lessons through the practices that have led them to success. Both have shown that flexibility and fast reactions to constant market changes have been key for growth in this competitive sector. Both exemplify how Mexican companies can become global players. They both demonstrate devotion to quality, great flexibility, a focus on the market, a highly specialized workforce, cutting edge technologies, strategic alliance, and global practice.

IT INDUSTRY IN MEXICO

The IT industry is very diverse and covers a lot of different sub-industries, including telephone operators, software developers, outsourcing services, and mobile entertainment developers. To compare the advance of one country to others in the IT industry, the most complete index is the World Economic Forum's Networked Readiness Index (NRI), which measures the propensity of countries to exploit the opportunities offered by the IT industry; it is published annually (Bilbao-Osorio, Dutta & Lanvin, 2014). The NRI seeks to better understand the impact of IT on the competitiveness of nations. According to the 2014 report, Mexico did not consolidate its place in the ranking and fell 16 places, being positioned 79th out of the 144 countries that were included in this ranking. Despite some progress in expanding and modernizing its IT infrastructure and absorption by individuals, this is not enough to catch up with advances in other economies, and therefore Mexico fails to converge digitally with more advanced economies.

The cost of access to Mexico's existing IT infrastructure remains high, but the quality of its education system remains its main Achilles heel; in this, Mexico ranks 119 out of 144. Mexico has a serious need to provide the country with the necessary skills required for a shift to a digital economy. This results in low levels of

IT use by individuals and businesses, despite the considerable efforts of the government to provide many of its services online.

According to Digital Statistic (2014), while 81 percent of the US population and 47 percent of the South American population uses the Internet, in Mexico only 38 percent of the population does so, which is similar to the rate in Central America (34 percent) and the world average (35 percent). Additionally, 43 percent of the population in Mexico participates in social networking: below the USA (56 percent) and South America (44 percent), but above Central America (34 percent) and the world average (26 percent). Mexico has a rate of 87 percent in mobile users: below the USA (101 percent), South America (124 percent), Central America (89 percent), and the world average (93 percent).

Larios (2010) argues that Mexico has not been characterized as a producer of IT. The development of IT is very heterogeneous. The government's efforts have not been reflected in the general population, and they have yet to address background elements such as low educational level, lower income, and lack of transformation of the economy in higher value-added areas. Additionally, the percentage share of micro, small, and medium enterprises in IT investment has declined. Large companies are the ones increasing their participation as users of IT (Select, 2003; AMITI, CANIETI & FMD, 2006).

However, there are niches where Mexico has achieved an international presence. The prestigious A. T. Kearney study of the top markets for locating offshore services (Laudicina, Peterson & Gott, 2015) examines the leading locations for IT outsourcing. India kept its place as the world leader, but other countries such as China, Mexico, Malaysia, and Poland are becoming attractive alternatives thanks to their skills availability, business environment, and financial attractiveness. India remains the leading choice for US companies, but Mexico is gaining ground – in the 2014 ranking Mexico appears in fourth place. Mexico offers language skills, strong IT expertise, and both physical proximity and time zone similarities. India is a leader in a wide range of IT services with more than 2 million employees in this sector and it has strong English proficiency. India has the world's largest IT suppliers: Tata Consultancy Services, Tech Mahindra, HCL, Infosys, Cognizant, and Wipro, in addition to international firms with a presence in India such as HP, IBM, Accenture, and CSC (Laudicina, Peterson & Gott, 2015).

However, Mexico is a fast-growing player, with a time zone advantage to attend to Latin American and North American organizations. Mexico's IT industry includes nearly 500,000 professionals, with low wage rates, and universities and technical schools that produce a steady source of new talent. Most major US IT firms have established delivery centers in Mexico, with HP and IBM as leaders. Furthermore, Accenture, T-Systems, Tata Consultancy Services, Stefanini, Carvajal, and many more provide strong competition. Softtek is a 100 percent Mexican firm, is the Mexican leader, and is among the five top players. Mexico's labor costs are not as low as India's, but for some buyers, proximity and service quality tip the balance in Mexico's favor. According to an infrastructure index, Mexico is above India but below China (Stettler, Mirza, Ali, Mohal & Jaiswal, 2014).

Another important niche of the IT industry where Mexico has excelled is mobile entertainment. This industry is very new compared to other industries; mobile phones began to penetrate all countries and social levels just a few decades ago. Also, technology allowing videogames, music, and movies through mobile phones has been in place for only a few years. According to the Mobile Entertainment Forum (MEF),[2] mobile entertainment includes a range of sub-industries associated with mobile phones. The division is subjective and constantly adjusting, but can include purely leisure activities, music, playing games, communications, social media, instant messaging, and activities that could also be defined as mobile commerce. According to Transparency Market Research (2015), the key growth factors for the mobile entertainment market include the continuous rise of

---

[2]   MEF is the global trade association for companies wishing to monetize their products and services via mobile phone. www.mefmobile.org.

smartphone users and the consequent rise in app downloads. The market is expected to reach US$54 billion in the year 2015. The segments of music, mobile gaming, and social media are the fastest growing segments of the mobile entertainment market. Other top segments of the mobile entertainment market include mobile personalization, mobile television, and access to premium content.

The market finds major brands that are ready to invest in it, due to the growing number of consumers who are using mobile entertainment platforms that are rich in media content. It is difficult to do a ranking or compare companies, since within the mobile entertainment industries there are many subcategories. Furthermore, it is worth mentioning that many of these companies are short-lived and the turnover is high, and that there are a lot of mergers and takeovers among these companies. But the key players that dominate the mobile entertainment market at the moment are: Apple, AT&T, Vodafone, Android (which belongs to Google), Blackberry, and Motorola Droid (Transparency Market Research, 2015).

Furthermore, the ME-Awards focus more on the mobile entertainment service sub-industries, with categories like games publisher, operator, D2C service provider, developer of a consumer app, developer of an enterprise app, video service provider, music service provider, gambling entertainment, adult entertainment, social games service provider, best games monetization service, cross-platform tools provider, and others.[3] Since many of these companies are private, they do not disclose sales or financial information, and furthermore their work in many of these fields is not usually easy to compare or rank by category. We will just mention some of the companies that are particularly distinguished (taking into account the ME-Awards): Unity, Samsung, O2, Gameloft, Golden Gekko, Saffron Digital, Spotify, Betfair, Cherry Media, Boostermedia, Tapjoy, Bango, Dotmobi, Inmobi, Amobee Pulse 3d, and Comscore, among others.

---

[3] The ME Awards is one of the biggest and most recognized events in the industry calendar, bringing together mobile content execs to celebrate the achievements of the past year. www.me-awards.com

However, within the Distributor-to-Consumers (D2C) service provider category, the key world players with a presence in Mexico and Latin America that are competing directly with Binbit are: Neomobile Commerce, IGN (subsidiary of J2 Global), Buongiorno (subsidiary of NTT Docomo), Zed Co., Acotel Interactive, and others.

Despite the strong global competition in the IT industry, some Mexican companies have managed to position themselves and build their strengths to become important players worldwide.

BINBIT

The Leader in Mobile Entertainment Services

Binbit is a company that was born with an international vision. The keys for its success have been alliance and acquisition. Binbit forms alliances with the key providers of content, from the top music companies and game developers to the most famous football teams. In addition, they form alliances with not only the best mobile phone operators, but also the best providers of technology, browsers, etc., to achieve a very efficient operation. Binbit has shown the Mexican firms that through alliances, an efficient operation, and focusing on the right markets for your product, an efficient global operation can be developed in a few years. A globalization of more than 60 countries on five continents in 10 years is achievable.

Binbit is a company in the IT industry, and its mission is to provide an entertainment focus to mobile operators, media groups, and end-user services. Its business model is based on a solid network of suppliers, and alliances, including the four major record companies in the world: Warner Music, 2009; EMI Music, 2009; Sony Music, 2010; and Universal Music, 2012. According to the CNN Expansión (2015b) ranking, Binbit is the most globally spread-out firm from Mexico in the field of IT. Binbit does not disclose either financial statements or sales, but does disclose total messages processed; using this information we can appreciate the exponential growth that the company had in its first decade (see Figure 20.1). According to Esthela Silva,

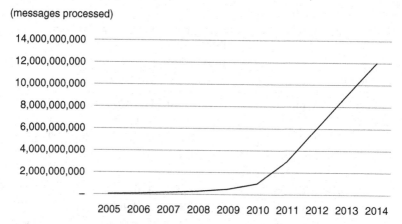

(messages processed)

FIGURE 20.1 Binbit Growth
Source: the author, based on Binbit website information www.binbit.com

Corporate Communication Director, as of June 2015, Binbit has offices in 31 countries, provides services in 61 countries (mainly in Latin America, Africa, Eastern Europe, and Asia), has sent more than 12 billion messages, and has alliances with 98 mobile carriers.[4]

Binbit provides services through which the consumer can enjoy a broad portfolio of content for his or her mobile phone. Furthermore, Binbit has been sensitive to the demands of different international markets; its Chairman and founder Antoni Muntaner stated, "Binbit has proved to be an excellent business partner through its capacity for innovation and constantly seeking opportunities to reinvent itself" (Businesswire, 2014c).

Following the leadership of Muntaner, Binbit is one of the leading publishers of entertainment in the world, specifically D2C, receiving many international awards. Binbit was nominated for best D2C in the world by Meffys 2009, and ME 2010 (Binbit, 2009a, 2010). "The negotiation power and the trust generated by Binbit have been the keys to multiply the number of agreements the company has with the

[4]   Interview conducted by the author on July 9, 2015.

Table 20.1 *Industry leaders*

Mobile Entertainment		Revenue in millions of US dollars	Outsourcing	
Top world leaders	Apple	224,340	Tata Consultancy Services	982,050
	AT&T	132,990	Tech Mahindra	226,210
	Android (Google)	69,610	HP	108,280
	Vodafone	65,500	IBM	86,910
	Motorola Droid	5,880	HCL Infosystems	62,700
	Blackberry	3,030	Accenture	30,940
			Cognizant Tech.	10,750
			Computer Science Corp.	12,170
			Infosys	8,830
			Wipros	7,530
Competitors in Mexico	Buongiorno (NTT Docomo)	35,380	HP	108,280
	IGN (J2 Global)	626	IBM	86,910
	Binbit	N/A	Tata C S	982,050
	Neomobile Commerce	N/A	Accenture	30,940
	Zed Co.	N/A	Softtek (1)	505
	Acotel Interactive	67	T-Systems (2)	10,406
			Stefanini (3)	913
			Carbajal	N/A
			Neoris	N/A
			Intellego (1)	142
			Global Hitts	N/A

Source: the author, based on Transparency Market Research, (2015); ME awards, www.me-awards.com; Laudicina, Peterson & Gott (2015). Revenues are *from Yahoo Finance,* http://finance.yahoo.com, key statistics, Revenue (Trailing Twelve Months, as first quarter 2015) (1) Estimated revenue for 2013 by CNN Expansión (2015b), exchange rate Mex$ 13.0/US$

(2) Estimated revenue for 2012, by www.nearshoreamericas.com/brazils-stefanini-expand-united-states/

(3) Disclosure by the company www.T-systems.com, exchange rate €1.2 1/usd

Note: The revenues are from the holding and are not desegregated for subsidiaries or for Mexico.

N/A = information is not available (private companies).

most important mobile operators in the world," said Muntaner (Binbit, 2013).

According to Silva, the main success factors of Binbit are: "a highly specialized workforce committed to implement effective online promotion and developing digital marketing strategies; constantly developing and acquiring cutting edge technologies; a specialized company branch that develops contents focusing on entertainment with the latest programming languages; partnership with some of the most important worldwide content providers and carriers; a global structure that allows Binbit to share best practices worldwide; operation oriented to customer care and satisfaction; marketing area that develops and optimizes our own media campaigns; office branches in 31 countries that develop strategies and actions to implement and adapt our global initiatives; an expert in-house design team, which develops high impact creative work adapted to local needs; Intelligent Offices at countries where a specialized Binbit team coordinates with sector suppliers in a direct way; it's driven on collaborators that develop and liberate their audacious and innovative ideas; finally, operational excellence is based on the slogan: There is just one way: be the best."

The globalization process in Binbit has been very fast and successful. One of the key requirements in this process is finding the right people for each region. Silva commented: "When we began operations in a country, we tried to make alliances with operators through a commercial director. However, we have established offices without a commercial director. In such cases, after formalizing an alliance we focus on finding the manager who can make the best deal with customers and office."

Binbit has largely succeeded in entering markets worldwide. However, this globalization process has not been free of challenges. Silva commented that they had to leave some countries, such as the United States, due to government regulations. Furthermore, Silva remarked that the main problems for globalization have been: "Cultural barriers on every continent and every country; we need to adapt to the infrastructure and the marketing decisions that every country demands. The time is a significant factor for the realization of partnerships with content providers, the opportunities depend on where the negotiations are conducted. Constant improvement of the technological capacity, adapting to the market requirements. Finally, a big challenge is the difference in government regulations in every country they work."

To overcome these difficulties, Silva commented: "Our key is to detect what is the crux of the situation in each market; we collect ideas, select carefully the best, and then incorporate to the strategic plan in order to provide better service targeted to the needs of each country. Perseverance has been a key to the success we have had in most countries where we operate. We do this work in teams, based on the achievement of common goals."

The global market is very volatile, and technological change is increasing rapidly; currently Mexico, Argentina, and Thailand are the most successful countries in achieving a higher volume of customers. "However, as the mobile entertainment business changes rapidly, each year highlights a new country with the highest volume and success, compared with others," said Silva.

To penetrate in all the continents, Binbit has sought markets little exploited by worldwide industry, but with large growth in demand for cell phones, as has been the case in Latin America, Southeast Asia, Poland, and Russia, where, unlike the USA, Canada, or the Western European market, mobile telephony has not yet reached the stage of maturity. It has also sought to concentrate on volume, as in the Philippines and Thailand. However, it has had the flexibility to adapt to smaller markets where competition is higher and firms have to focus on covering only certain segments, such as in Singapore. Binbit also has been known for its ability to detect markets where major phone operators have grown and consolidated their networks, motivating this increased competition, which in turn causes a drop in prices and increased use of more complex services via mobile devices, as in the case of Serbia. Another major challenge has been the cultural differences. Binbit has had the sensitivity to understand the culture and tastes of each nation, as in the case of Arab countries where there are huge cultural obstacles because users generally prefer local content and are very sensitive to religious aspects and international politics. This is a notable difference from other parts of the world where tastes are similar and where an artist can succeed in various countries within a region, such as Latin America. This is generally not the case in the Arab nations. Binbit has followed a flexible strategy, adapting to the regions and cultures. Binbit is an example of a young, international, innovative firm, as Muntaner states, "Binbit is part of a new generation of Mexican companies that base their competitiveness in new technologies and new global trends" (Businesswire, 2015).

History

Antoni Muntaner, founder and current Chairman of Binbit, began operations in Mexico in 2005 with José Luis Gralla as co-founder and CEO of Binbit. Both are the main shareholders. Gralla has been responsible for opening, operating, and managing the worldwide network of offices of Binbit. Muntaner and Gralla have directed and negotiated the main acquisitions of Binbit around the world. "Since the beginning they [Muntaner and Gralla] had clear where they wanted to go: to be a world leader in sales of mobile content. For this reason, they planned from the start to push Binbit worldwide; to achieve this goal they sought and explored new forms of business that are tailored to the economic development strategies of different countries," commented Silva.

Their strategy was to begin with Latin America through acquisitions and strategic alliances. In the first year, they acquired Nikter from Uruguay; this acquisition was very strategic because they appropriated its technological platform. In 2006, Binbit opened its first international office in Panama. They chose Panama because "it is a mature value-added services country and a small market that allowed us to learn without much risk," commented Silva. Between 2006 and 2009, Binbit achieved a rapid expansion in Latin America. In 2007, they began operations in the USA.

The Mobile Entertainment Forum (MEF) acknowledged this rapid expansion in 2009 by nominating Binbit for their prestigious "Meffy" award in the category "D2C Service"; the Meffys are one of the most recognized awards in the industry of mobile entertainment. Gralla declared: "Being nominated at only three years in the market next to such great companies in the mobile entertainment industry is a huge incentive to continue with the commitment of providing top-quality mobile entertainment" (Binbit, 2009a).

After consolidating a strong position and leadership in Latin America, in late 2009, Binbit also decided to go to Africa and Southeast Asia. Later, they expanded their operations to Niger, South Africa, Kenya, and Tanzania in Africa, and to Singapore, Thailand, Malaysia, Indonesia, the Philippines, and Vietnam in Southeast Asia. In the Philippines, Binbit had more than 800,000 subscribers after its launch, and in Thailand, it had more than 200,000 subscribers (Nieto, 2011). Latin America, Africa, and Southeast Asia were not enough, so at the end of 2009 Binbit began its expansion to Western Asia by entering Saudi Arabia. Additionally, in that same year Binbit signed exclusive agreements with international leaders in the music industry such as Warner Music and EMI Music, as well as the press firm Associated Press (AP) and the adult entertainment firm Playboy. With these agreements, Binbit's portfolio of products and services was enriched significantly.

To celebrate its first five years (2010), Binbit increases its operations in Latin America, beginning operations in Honduras, Uruguay, and the Dominican Republic. That year Binbit reached its first 1 billion messages processed and signed an exclusive agreement with Sony Music. More international recognitions appeared that year, this time including the "ME Awards Prizes." These are granted by the Mobile Entertainment Magazine within the mobile entertainment industry, and have become a very valuable prize (Binbit, 2010).

A year of great success and true global presence for Binbit was 2011; by February, Binbit was a main player at the Mobile World Congress and hosted the MEF Connects Party at the Picasso Museum in Barcelona. In June, the processing of 3 billion messages was achieved, an impressive figure considering Binbit's relatively young age. Furthermore, during this year, Binbit increased its presence in Latin America with Brazil, and in Asia with Hong Kong and Sri Lanka, and initiated its presence in Oceania by entering Australia and New Zealand (Binbit, 2011b).

Only six years after beginning operations, Binbit built a MySQL data warehouse, selecting Microstrategy for its business intelligence reporting tool and choosing Talend for its data integration solution.[5] The use of Talend is gradually eliminating the manual process of integrating data. "Talend has automated a time-consuming and manual process of integrating 11 million records of valuable customer information from our MySQL database into Microstrategy's business intelligence tool for trend analysis," declared Eduardo Paredes, Business Analyst at Binbit (Binbit, 2011a).

In 2012, CNN Expansión named Binbit the most globally spread-out Mexican company in the category of "Mobile Entertainment." With only seven years of operation it already had a presence in 36 countries and over 750 million users, more than América Móvil (Gasca & Nieto, 2013). In the same year Binbit

---

[5]   Talend Co. is a worldwide company leader in open source software, providing data integration, data management, enterprise application integration, and big data software and services. www.talend.com.

broadened its scope, its users, and its contents and began operations in Bangladesh, Bahrain, Jordan, Kuwait, Lebanon, Pakistan, Palestine, Qatar, Syria, and Iraq. Additionally, Binbit signed an exclusive agreement with the music firm Universal Music, included the service of "Load and Cash $" with major Latin American carriers, and did online marketing campaigns with over 110 networks. All these actions together led Binbit to reach six billion messages processed in 2012.

In 2013, Binbit consolidated its presence in Africa and the Middle East and began a penetration of Eastern Europe, entering Ghana, Egypt, Nigeria, Cyprus, United Arab Emirates, Yemen, Oman, India, Serbia, Russia, Croatia, Albania, Bosnia and Herzegovina, Montenegro, Macedonia, and Bulgaria. In March 2013, Binbit launched a new website in Arabic to meet the needs of the growing subscriber base in the Middle East and started expanding its business operations in the region, focusing its efforts mainly on offering its subscription service for ringtones, games, wallpapers, and screensavers. In April 2013, as part of its globalization strategy Binbit signed an agreement with Panama Music Corporation. Furthermore, Binbit created Club U+ to reach nine countries (Nicaragua, Panama, Peru, Colombia, Ecuador, Guatemala, El Salvador, Uruguay, and Mexico). Club U+ is part of the agreement with the firm Universal Music and represents the creative collaboration effort to provide special products to subscribers through which Binbit distributes Universal Music Latin America's exclusive content. Muntaner commented that "Strategic alliances of this type sum up experiences and expertise, especially in areas in which each one of the companies has great strengths, to begin with, the possibility of Binbit to reach nearly 750 million users of the 64 carriers with which we have agreements, and the reputation and quality of Universal's products (Businesswire, 2013b).

Also in 2013, Binbit launched its websites in Polish and Russian to directly meet the needs of its subscribers and corporate clients based in those nations. Binbit operations in Poland mean betting on a market where demand for content grows in an accelerated manner, because unlike other European markets, the mobile phone market in Poland still has not reached a mature stage (VOXs News, 2013).

In December 2013, Binbit began operating an office in Belgrade, Serbia, to coordinate its trade promotions throughout Eastern Europe, strengthening operations in Poland and Russia. Muntaner declared, "Binbit comes to Serbia at a special moment because in recent years the major phone operators have grown and consolidated their networks, this has led to greater competition, which in turn has led to a drop in prices and increased use of information via mobile devices" (Businesswire, 2013c).

Operating in five continents is a big challenge, so an adequate technological backend has been fundamental to achieving Binbit's worldwide growth. This is why the company values and seeks out the best technology partners that further contribute to its innovation process. Muntaner explains that, "As we looked for a US-based colocation partner, we found that Data Foundry's Texas 1 data center was an excellent strategic choice for us ... we not only have access to a world-class data center, but by utilizing their Managed Internet solution we also have tremendous network access that allows us to reach every corner of the globe," (Businesswire, 2013a). Additionally, Binbit made a strategic alliance with Opera Software Company. Opera is one of the world's leading mobile browsers, with users on all mobile platforms.

In 2014, Binbit continued its penetration in Eastern Europe and Asia by entering Slovenia, Kyrgyzstan, Kazakhstan, and Azerbaijan, and diversified its portfolio with new services like "Parking Movi," and "Global Movie." This year, Binbit reached 12 billion processed messages, quadrupling the achievement of 2011 in just three years. In February of that year, Binbit bought CellCast in Lebanon, which became its Middle East division. Pascal Dufour, CEO of CellCast (now Binbit Middle East), stressed the great opportunity that the Arab countries represent and the challenges that the group faces in the region. "There are huge cultural obstacles in the Arab countries, as users generally prefer local content. This is a great difference from other parts of the world, such as Latin America, where an artist can succeed in various countries within a region. This is generally not the case in the Arab nations" (Businesswire, 2014b).

In the same month, Binbit was a promoter of development within government and the IT industry and participated with ProMéxico (promotion agency of the Ministry of Economy of the Mexican Government) at Mobile World Congress in Barcelona, Spain, the most important forum in telecommunications worldwide (Businesswire, 2014a).

Binbit, constantly looking to add content to enrich its offerings for all ages, in August 2014 signed an agreement with FC Barcelona and in October 2014 with Real Madrid CF, both for the distribution of the contents of these famous Spanish football clubs exclusively through cellular and mobile devices in various regions of the world (Reuters, 2014).

In 2015, Binbit achieved an alliance with the prestigious magazine *Maxim*, which allowed an exclusive offering of its contents.[6] "At that same period, consolidated operations are affiliated in Africa launching Kenya, Nigeria, Tanzania, and Ghana, and with growth plans in other countries in the region," commented Silva.

Binbit is aware that technological changes, new products, and market trends in the IT industry move very fast. New competitors and new mergers and acquisitions among the big players change the market landscape constantly. Keeping the pace while competing in more than 60 countries is not an easy task. Great flexibility, adaptation, and the best people are necessary.

SOFTTEK

The Mexican Leader of Outsourcing

Softtek is an IT outsourcing global services company. It is a private firm that does not disclose financial or market information. However,

---

6   Maxim is an international magazine, devised and launched in the UK, but now based in New York, reaching nearly 9 million readers each month. Maxim Digital reaches more than 4 million unique viewers each month. Maxim magazine publishes 16 editions, sold in 75 countries worldwide. www.maxim.com.

Expansión magazine estimates the firm's sales in 2013 to be approximately US$505 million, with an increment of 13.9 percent over its estimated sales of 2012 (CNN Expansión, 2015a). This places Softtek as the 247th largest company in Mexico, with more than 9,000 employees as of April 2015, according to Gilberto Romero, Marketing Director of Softtek.[7] Furthermore, according to the CNN Expansión ranking (2015b), Softtek is the second most internationally spread-out firm in the field of IT services in Mexico and is number 15 in the top 100 global companies in Mexico. By May 2015, the company had 35 offices in Mexico (8), the USA (3), Canada, Costa Rica, Puerto Rico, Argentina (2), Peru, Uruguay, Brazil (3), Chile, Colombia, Paraguay, Venezuela, Spain (2), the United Kingdom, Netherlands, China (3), and India; 18 countries in total. It also has 12 Global Delivery Centers (GDC): in the USA, Mexico (4), Brazil (2), Argentina, Spain, China (2), and India. Throughout its 33 years of life, Softtek has been a preferred services provider for several Fortune 500 companies, and has been recognized by various organizations and industry analysts as one of the most important IT companies in Mexico and the world.

Softtek offers services for IT platforms, design, and test solutions. Its service models include delivery on-site, on-shore, and its trademarked Global Nearshore. Softtek has focused its service offerings primarily on financial services firms and governments, and in general for the industry it offers services like system integration company information (ERP), implementation and measurement of effective customer relationship management (CRM), and analysis and integration of information (BI), among other services (Softtek, 2015).

According to Romero, Softtek always delivers services of a high quality, focusing on high value projects, having highly trained personnel and very efficient processes. Romero states that the main factors in the company's success have been always thinking as a global company and being able to compete at all levels; having a unique corporate

---

[7] Interview by the author conducted on April 27, 2015.

culture; focusing on the human element and talent as the core of the organization; having continuous innovation; and having good financial health. All this has been rewarded with the highest certification in this industry, the CMMi Level 5; Softtek was the first Latin American company to obtain this certification. Furthermore, in 2006 and 2007 the firm was listed in the "100 Best Companies" by Global Services. Additionally, Softtek has been the only Latin American company included in the "Magic Quadrant" for two years, 2006–7. Softtek has achieved many other important distinctions because of its strategy and its high-quality services.

Softtek is playing an increasing role as a large organization that is moving to a more diversified multi-sourcing model, and the company has seen a 35 percent annual growth rate in recent years, according to Beni Lopez, CEO of Softtek's US division. Softtek has operations and GDCs in Mexico, Brazil, the USA, Argentina, Spain, China, and India. Despite rising costs in India, Latin America still does not have a wage cost advantage over India or China. Latin America's primary advantage is geography: it lies in the same time zones as North America, making collaboration and communication with support staff easier. Softtek's China operation may support projects in other countries. "There will always be work that can't be offshored easily and China wants more software" says Lopez (Mitchell, 2007).

According to Romero, in May 2015, approximately 40 percent of Softtek's revenue came from MNEs in the USA, and these clients are attended to mainly with the GDC in the USA, with 500 employees, and with the four GDCs in Mexico. Softtek in Mexico has 6,000 employees; approximately 3,500 attends to US MNEs and 2,500 attends to Mexican firms. 27 percent of the company revenue is concentrated in Mexico. Brazil has two GDCs with 1,000 employees; they attends to Brazilian firms and contribute 25 percent of Softtek's revenue. In Argentina, there is one GDC with 700 hundred employees, which contributes 3 percent of the company's revenue and attends to MNEs in the rest of Latin America excluding Brazil. Spain has a GDC with 200 employees and 2 percent of the company revenue. China has two GDCs, with 500 employees and 2 percent of the company revenue. Sixty percent of the employees are devoted to Chinese firms and the rest support MNEs of other countries, mainly from the USA. Finally, Softtek's newest acquisition is a GDC in India with 400 employees which currently contributes 1 percent of the company revenue, but the firm has expectations of strong growth there in the coming years. Summarizing, the GDC of the USA serves exclusively American firms. The Mexican GDCs support the Mexican firms and US MNEs. The Brazilian GDCs attend to Brazilian companies. The Argentinian GDC caters for the rest of Latin America. The Spanish GDC attends to Europe. And the Chinese GDCs support Chinese clients and the MNEs of other countries. The reason that the number of employees does not correspond to the country's income is because many of the global customers are billed by the US headquarters regardless of where they were attended to. US MNEs requested Softtek to attend to their facilities in other countries with a closer GDC; this is the model Softtek calls "follow the sun," and uses to serve the MNEs at the same time as the GDCs in Mexico, Brazil, Argentina, Spain, India, and China.

Softtek has made it very clear that it cannot compete directly against the huge Indian outsourcing companies in cost, but it is possible to do so in terms of services, speed, and quality. The firm focuses on valuable projects. One of the key advantages of Softtek's model is its operation management. Rather than a rigid pyramidal structure, with the CEO at the top making all the decisions, Softtek works like an umbrella of divisions. Softtek is a network of independent working units. This provides the flexibility of fast entry to new markets, new services, and new products. According to Romero, there was no strategy summit of the company on how it would go global. Softtek encourages its employees' initiatives and many projects flowed up from the bottom to the top of the company. Jose Tam, former director of the Peru office, said: "definitely the main factor for the rapid international expansion of Softtek was the empowerment and entrepreneurship encouragement that Softtek g[a]ve to all its employees and business units."[8]

About Softtek's organizational approach, Blanca Treviño declared: "Softtek began, rather than a company, as an umbrella for separate business units, that is, each shareholder focused their efforts toward different goals: one focused on the customer, in other technologies, others by industry, etc., which allowed these cells to provide a specialized business approach to each market" (Corona, 2009). Currently, the organization is led by a global corporate office and the President and CEO Blanca Treviño. Hierarchically, below her the firm management is divided by regions according to geographies and sizes. Thus, there is a CEO who manages the North American market composed of the USA and Canada. Mexico and Central America are conducted like a separate area with its own CEO, and another division is Spanish-speaking South America and Europe with its CEO in Spain. Brazil, China, and India are managed as unique markets and each has its own CEO.[9]

Another important factor for success in Softtek has been its policy to follow the client. The company is very sensitive to attending to the needs of its customers. Wherever its customers go – Europe, South America, or Asia – Softtek is there to provide excellent service delivery on time. According to the CEO of Softtek, Blanca Treviño, the key factor of success has been to work on value projects. "Since day one, we have been very focused on our target market – Fortune 50 and Fortune 100 companies – and have made it clear that we want to compete on value" (Haneine, 2015).

Softtek's History

The beginnings of Softtek date back to 1982, when it was founded by a group of five former employees of Alfa led by Gerardo Lopez and Blanca Treviño, among others. Gerardo Lopez was the first director

---

[8]   Interview by the author conducted July 8, 2015.

[9]   Interview with Nayeli Acevedo from Softtek's Public Relations department by the author, conducted June 6, 2015.

of Softtek until 1999, when he left the company. Blanca Treviño was appointed in 2000, and has been the company's CEO ever since. The company has experienced rapid growth since its inception: by the year 1988 it already had 100 employees. In 1994, it became an international company by opening its first office in Brazil. In 1996, the company had 1,000 employees. Romero declared, "at the beginning Softtek started to attend to the largest Mexican companies such as Alfa, Xerox, Aurrerá, Bancomer, Superama, and Somex, competing against the leading consulting firms like IBM and HP. After three years, the company had penetrated to Mexican companies nobody had bet they could. At that point they decided to broaden their scope to the Multinational Enterprises (MNEs) operating in Mexico. Working with these MNEs gave Softtek a global vision and decision to become an international company, starting to serve American MNEs around 1986."

Softtek began attending to US MNEs in Mexico, but its first international office was in Brazil at the initiative and vision of one of its employees. At the beginning, Softtek sent Mexican employees to serve Brazilian companies and subsequently hired Brazilian employees. Currently, Softtek has two GDCs in Brazil that exclusively attend to Brazilian customers; this is because of the language, the higher costs due to taxation, and labor cost. The Brazil project has been very successful, and as of May 2015, it is the third highest revenue country for the company, after the USA and Mexico, with approximately 25 percent of the company revenue. The entrance to the Chinese market followed a similar path; it was on the initiative of one of its partners. However, the foundation of the offices and GDCs in Spain and Argentina followed a different path: one of the important clients of Softtek opened facilities there and asked Softtek to support them on-site.

In 1997, Softtek registered "Nearshoring" as a form of outsourcing that relates to services provided from a center in close geographic proximity. With this characteristic of outsourcing and competing mainly with India, Softtek created its first GDC in Mexico and, with this GDC, Softtek began to attend to the United States. In the same year, the firm opened offices in the USA, Venezuela, and Argentina. In 1998, it opened an office in Colombia and created its first GDC in Latin America, located in Brazil, and a few years later opened the GDC in Argentina. With this infrastructure, Softtek consolidated a strong presence in the Mexican, North, Central, and South American markets.

In the twenty-first century, after Blanca Treviño was named president and CEO of the company, a new momentum toward international projects became part of the firm's philosophy. On December 19, 2003, Softtek announced an agreement with General Electric (GE) to acquire GE's GDC in Mexico, including a US subsidiary, GE Ddemesis (Terdiman, 2003). In 2004, the first GDC opened in Mexico City; in 2014, another opened in Guadalajara. Mexico became the strategic core to attend to Mexican and US MNEs.

In 2006, Softtek entered Europe, specifically Spain, following one of its clients that required its services on-site. The firm founded its GDC in La Coruña. With Spain as a base, Softtek began to search for clients in the rest of Europe. The strategy for Europe was based on three pillars: the first was to increase the participation of the GDC in serving global customers of the company; the second, to provide Spanish organizations with the cost and productivity benefits inherent in its Global Nearshore service model; the third was to increase penetration into the European market, using its presence in Galicia and Madrid as hubs and offices in the UK and the Netherlands as selling offices (Softtek; 2008b).

In 2007 Softtek opened a GDC in La Plata, Argentina. Daniel Scioli, Vice President of Argentina, led the ceremony. This office was part of its expansion plan in Latin America (Softtek, 2007b). According to Romero, they chose Argentina because of the good quality of its universities and the availability and low cost of labor. Since Brazil's GDC was devoted entirely to Brazilian clients, Argentina's was created to attend to the rest of (Spanish-speaking) Latin America.

In the same year, Softtek was included in the "Niche Players quadrant" by Gartner, Inc. (Softtek, 2007a). In August, following the initiative of one of its partners to penetrate the Chinese market, Softtek acquired China's IT United, which in 2008 became the Softtek Asia Company. This GDC has a cutting-edge access control and telecommunications infrastructure, including biometric identification devices, on-site 24/7 surveillance, triple-redundant Internet connections, and isolated network segments per customer. In 2008, Softtek Asia operated in Beijing, Shanghai, Xiamen, and Xi'an (Softtek, 2007c). "Since the union of these two teams (IT United and Softtek) we continue receiving great enthusiasm from our clients," said Cyrill Eltschinger, founder of IT United, who now serves as Executive Vice President of Softtek Asia and CEO of Softtek China (Softtek, 2008a).

In 2009 Softtek opened offices in Paraguay and was consolidated in the region. The company began operations with seven clients. Paraguay was its third subsidiary in the Southern Cone, along with those already consolidated, Argentina and Chile. Consequently, Softtek will attend to other countries in the region such as Bolivia, Peru, and Uruguay (Softtek, 2009).

In 2010, Softtek opened new facilities in La Coruña, Spain (Softtek, 2010). From the new facilities of Softtek's GDC in La Coruña, the company continued to serve corporate clients of Spain, in addition to companies in the United Kingdom, Italy, Germany, and France via its Nearshore model. In 2011, Softtek was placed in the 38th position in the Global Outsourcing 100 list, which is compiled by the International Association of Outsourcing Providers (IAOP). "We are thrilled that in such a competitive industry we have achieved a position among the top 40 in the list of IAOP's Global Outsourcing 100, for the third consecutive year," said Treviño. Additionally, Michael Corbett, IAOP Chairman, commented: "Companies included on the list 'The Global Outsourcing 100' have proven leaders and rising stars ... these are companies with which you want to partner to achieve success and better results by outsourcing" (Softtek, 2011a).

In 2011 Blanca Treviño became the first woman to be introduced into the IAOP Hall of Fame. 2012 was the 30th anniversary of Softtek and the 15th of its GDC in Argentina, and in that year Brazil became the second largest market, consolidating Softtek as an important technology partner for organizations such as Monsanto, Mercedes Benz, VW, Quilmes, Sanofi, L'Oreal, Mortgage Bank, Zurich, Bridgestone, Bunge, Pluspetrol, Cencosud, OSDE, Techint, HP, Ecogas, EDET, and others. "We have been privileged to have the trust of many of the most important companies in the region, facing with them abundance cycles and cycles of uncertainty," said Treviño (Softtek, 2011b).

In 2013, the Softtek offices in Beijing transformed into an "Enterprise Mobility-Specific Center of Excellence" dedicated to meeting the growing need for enterprise mobility solutions in Asia; from here, the company offers business solutions and interactive marketing for the Asian market on the major mobile platforms, including iOS and Android. According to the research study "Our Mobile Planet" (Our Mobile Planet, 2013), sponsored by Google, Asian countries are leaders in terms of market penetration and the use of smartphones. China, moreover, is the smartphone market with the fastest growth in the world.

Also in 2013, continuing its expansion plan to cover the world, Softtek ventured into India, opening a GDC. The idea of the Indian GDC was to support the rest of the centers with projects of high volume and low costs, explained Romero. This way, the firm can give MNEs the best service regardless of where their offices are located or their time zone.

In recent years, Softtek has kept its pace toward the internatio-nalization of the firm; in 2014, it inaugurated a new office in Colombia. With 15 years of history in the country, the MultiMexican reinforced its growth plans to more spacious and mod-ern facilities (Softtek, 2014b). Additionally, the firm also opened new offices in Guadalajara, Jalisco. The new facilities are part of the growth strategy of the company, which plans to convert the Guadalajara office into a GDC (Softtek, 2014a). In 2014, Softtek was once more positioned in the Global Outsourcing 100 ranking IAOP, this time in 37th place, as one of the best outsourcing providers in the world. This was the sixth consecutive year that Softtek was selected (Softtek, 2014c). Additionally, Blanca Treviño received the Mexican government's "Woman of the Year" award that is given to those carrying out work of social significance.

Discussion and Conclusion

Binbit and Softtek are two young companies that were born internationally, and interesting lessons can be derived from a summary of their history; see Tables 20.2 and 20.3.

Mexico is a country with a low level in the world rankings in the IT industry, but two Mexican companies have managed to position themselves among the best worldwide: Binbit and Softtek. Binbit had a clear strategy of globalization since the conception of the company. It made agreements with major content providers in the world, and the largest mobile operators in each country where it were penetrating. It made acquisitions wherever it was more convenient to penetrate faster. It took advantage of the position of Mexico in South America to penetrate these countries; it later continued penetrating developing countries, mainly in Southeast Asia, the Middle East, and Eastern Europe. Meanwhile, Softtek's internationalization started with the US's MNEs working in Mexico, offering IT outsourcing services, and taking advantage of the lower costs of Mexican engineers and the advantage over India of companies that have the same time zone as the USA. While Binbit reaches the end user, Softtek specializes in large corporations; many of its customers are in the Fortune 500. Softtek follows its customers, always locating near them, and thus its operational advantage over India is faster delivery due to being in the same time zone, for which Softtek opened GDCs in Mexico, the USA, Brazil, Argentina, Spain, China, and India, and this allows Softtek to optimize the strategy of each of its customers

Table 20.2 *Binbit timeline*

Year	Domestic Events	International Events
2005	Birth of Binbit.	Acquisition of Nikter in Uruguay, which became Binbit's technological platform.
2006		Entrance to Panama, Salvador, Guatemala, Costa Rica, Nicaragua. Central American expansion begins in five new markets.
2007		Entrance to USA, Colombia, Ecuador, Paraguay, and Bolivia. Acquisition of Cash Investment in Panama and Atinco in Colombia.
2008		Entrance to Argentina, Peru, and Chile. Acquisition of Easylabs SA in Uruguay, Easytel in Salvador, and Tecnova in Guatemala.
2009		Entrance to Niger, South Africa, Kenya, Tanzania, Vietnam, Singapore, Philippines, Malaysia, Thailand, Indonesia, and Saudi Arabia. Signs exclusive agreement with music firms Warner Music, EMI Music, the press firm Associated Press (AP), and adult entertainment firm Playboy.
		Binbit is nominated for 2009 Meffys Awards in the D2C category.

Table 20.2 (cont.)

Year	Domestic Events	International Events
		Antoni Muntaner, Chairman of Binbit, is selected as one of the 50 most important people in the mobile entertainment industry by ME's Top 50 Executives List.
		Acquisition of Cash Investment Atinco in South Africa and ACME Mobile (AMOB) in Singapore.
2010		Entrance to Honduras, Dominican Republic, and Uruguay. Binbit enters ME's Top 50 Executives List.
		Signs exclusive agreement with music firm Sony Music.
		Binbit reaches 1,000,000,000 messages processed.
		Binbit is nominated for 2010 ME Awards in D2C category.
2011	Binbit evolves its Business Intelligence with Talend Integration Suite.	Entrance to Brazil, Australia, New Zealand, Sri Lanka, and Hong Kong. Binbit hosts ME Connect Party at MWC 2011 Barcelona Picasso Museum.
		Acquisition of Forest Media International, Indonesia.

Table 20.2 (cont.)

Year	Domestic Events	International Events
		Binbit reaches 3,000,000,000 messages processed.
2012	Promoswap launched, working with 60 networks.	Entrance to Bangladesh, Bahrain, Jordan, Kuwait, Lebanon, Pakistan, Palestine, Qatar, Syria, and Iraq.
	Online marketing campaigns with over 110 networks.	Signs exclusive agreement with music firm Universal Music.
	CNN Binbit named as the most international company in mobile entertainment.	Load and cash $ with major Latam carriers.
	CNN Binbit named as the most international company in mobile entertainment.	Load and cash $ with major Latam carriers.
		Binbit reaches 6,000,000,000 messages processed.
2013	Strategic alliance with Opera Software Company.	Entrance to Cyprus, Egypt, Unites Arab Emirates, Yemen, Oman, Serbia, Russia, Poland, Croatia, Albania, Bosnia and Herzegovina, Ghana, India, Nigeria, Montenegro, Macedonia, and Bulgaria.
	Antoni Muntaner is elected by the board for America MEF.	Website in Arabic, Polish, and Russian.
	Selection of Data Foundry as database provider.	Agreement with Panama Music.
2014	New Services Parking Movi, and Global Movie.	Entrance to Slovenia, Kyrgyzstan, Kazakhstan, and Azerbaijan. Acquisition of CellCast in Lebanon.
		Participation with Promexico at Mobile World Congress in Spain.

Table 20.2 (*cont.*)

Year	Domestic Events	International Events
		Signs exclusive agreement with Football Soccer teams: FC Barcelona and Real Madrid C. F.
		Binbit reaches 12,000,000,000 messages processed.
2015		Alliance with Maxim and operation consolidation in Africa, Kenya, Nigeria, Tanzania, and Ghana, and with growth plans in other countries in the region.

Source: Author based on personal interviews and www.binbitgroup.com/es/noticias/

Table 20.3 *Softtek timeline*

Year	Domestic Events	International Events
1982	Foundation in Monterrey, Mexico.	
1988	First 100 employees.	
1994		First international office in Brazil.
1996		First 1,000 employees.
1997	Create *Nearshore* model.	Entrance to USA. Entrance to Venezuela and Argentina.
1998	Sap Award of Excellence (1998–2009).	Entrance to Colombia.
		Create first GDC in Latin America, in Brazil.
2000	Blanca Treviño is appointed President and CEO of Softtek. Achieve certification of CMMi Level 3.	

Table 20.3 *(cont.)*

Year	Domestic Events	International Events
2003	Acquisition of GE Ddemesis.	
2004	First GDC in Mexico DF. First Latin American company to achieve certification of CMMi Level 5.	
2006	"100 Best Companies," Global Services (2006–7).	Only Latin American company included in the "Magic Quadrant" 2006–7. GDC inaugurated in La Coruña, Spain for the European market. "Top Company to Watch in LA," (2006–8), Global Services.
2007	Largest generator of jobs for IT professionals in Mexico, (Consultant Select, 2007). "Super Company," Expansión 2007.	Acquisition of China IT United, starting its expansion into the Asian market. Open GDC in La Plata, Argentina. "Strong Performer" by Forrester Research (2007, 2009).
2008	"100 Major Entrepreneurs in Mexico" (Blanca Treviño) Expansión 2008.	"Stevie For Women in Business Award" given to Blanca Treviño.
2009	Obtains its 11th "Sap Award of Excellence."	Opening offices in Paraguay GDC opened in Wuxi, China Global Outsourcing 100 ranking, IAOP (2009–14).
2010		Best Latin company in IAOP's 2010 Global Outsourcing List.
2011		Three executives are included in the Nearshore Power 50 List, in "Nearshore Industry's more powerful Voices," Blanca Treviño first woman admitted to the "IAOP Outsourcing Hall of Fame."

Table 20.3 (cont.)

Year	Domestic Events	International Events
2012	For the third year recognized by the CEMEFI as "Socially Responsible Company." 30th anniversary.	Acquisition of SCAi specialists in SAP Brazil has become the second largest market.
2013	Licensing Solution Partner of Microsoft.	Acquisition of "Systech Integrators, Inc." New offices in Colombia. 30 offices in Latin America, USA, Europe, and Asia. Softtek offices in Beijing transformed into a "Center of Excellence specializing in Enterprise Mobility Services."
2014	Softtek opens new office in Guadalajara. Softtek expands technology partnership with RSA for Information Security, Governance, and Risk Management Services. Softtek receives requalification by SAP for its SAP® Business All-in-One Partner Solutions.	Softtek announces New Senior Vice President of Consulting Services for US Market. Softtek opens New GDC in Fortaleza, Brazil. Softtek opens new office in Colombia. Softtek positioned in 2014 Gartner Magic Quadrant for SAP Application Management Service Providers, Worldwide.
2015	Softtek is elected "Channel Partner of the Year 2014" in Latin America by Informatica.	Softtek is positioned within the rank of the "Best Consultants 2015" World Executive Magazine.

Source: Author based on personal interviews and www.softtek.com/es/a cerca-de-softtek/historia

depending on where its operation facilities or their offices are located.

Binbit and Softtek have taught us that Mexican companies need not be giants like Cemex or FEMSA, or be in an industry where Mexico has the technology to become a multinational company and noted worldwide. Both take advantage of the competitive advantages of the country and have made strategies that optimized their possibilities. They knew the world industry map and the timing to penetrate each country. Softtek started with US MNEs, Binbit with Latin America; Softtek penetrated China, Binbit penetrated Southeast Asia; Softtek Spain, and Binbit Poland and Russia. These are not vanilla strategies; successful companies should read the market waves and grab opportunities as they present themselves. They have very clear knowledge of the market's characteristics, analyze the possibilities of acquisitions, know their product/service and adapt it faster. Both companies have great flexibility and adapt to the markets; they make "in-market" decisions oriented to the special needs of each market. Both companies believe in and empower their employees and work more like a network than like a pyramidal, hierarchical organization. They share the best practices in each region but decide locally, by adapting world trends to their local culture. Both companies are examples of strategy and motivation for Mexican companies that want to become multinationals firms.

The main lessons that other companies could learn from Binbit and Softtek to compete in today's global scenario and become MNEs are:

a) Devotion to quality. Softtek only pursues valuable projects, and doesn't compete in low-cost-margin projects with small companies. Similarly, Binbit always make its alliances with the best companies in every sector. Its policy is based on the slogan: "There is just one way: be the best."

b) Great flexibility. The new business environment is very dynamic, so the way that the company organizes itself in order to make fast changes and adapt to new challenges is crucial to its survival. If you want to be a global company, the company's decisions cannot be centralized in the CEO or the owner; you need to develop a network of divisions and empower the leaders of each team. You need to develop a global strategy but change it as the technology, regulation, politics, and markets need it to change. The most important consideration is that your decisions must be faster than those of your competitors, if you want to be a global leader.

c) Focus on customers. Global leaders make their operational models oriented to their customers' satisfaction, and follow their customers' needs. Binbit and Softtek have shown us how the importance of their customers was clear to them. They developed global strategies but adapted to each region, culture, and regulation.

d) Highly specialized workforce. Companies should not save money by hiring a cheap, unqualified workforce. If you want to be a leader, you need to build a team of leaders.

e) Cutting-edge technologies. Equipment, software, network, and Internet services are changing every day. Global companies must be constantly developing and acquiring cutting-edge technologies, and renewing themselves.

f) Strategic alliances. You cannot be the best at everything; partners help to provide the best services. Alliances with your vendors, your potential clients, distributors, and IT providers are essential. Strategic alliances are crucial to compete in global markets.

g) Global practice, locally adapted. Binbit and Softtek follow a model that is a combination of global structures that allow sharing the best practices worldwide, but adapted to regional cultural needs. A team of empowered regional leaders and a very flexible global leader is necessary for the success of global companies.

The IT industry is currently one of the most dynamic; both Binbit and Softtek have shown devotion to quality, adaptability, and flexibility, and an ability to read the market and innovate, which has positioned them as global leaders, despite the major technological and educational disadvantages of Mexico. Both have shown Mexican companies that, with a global strategy, alliances, flexibility, and efficient operations, they can become global competitors.

REFERENCES

Amiti, Canieti & Fmd. 2006. *Public Policies for the Proper Use of Information Technology and Communication to Boost Competitiveness of Mexico: A View to 2020*. México D.F.: Amiti, Canieti & Fmd.

Bilbao-Osorio, B., Dutta, S. & Lanvin, B. 2014. *The Global Information Technology Report 2014. Rewards and Risk of Big Data*. World Economic Forum.

Binbit. 2009a. Binbit is Nominated for 2009 Meffys Awards. *Binbit*, May 17. www .binbitgroup.com/news/press-room/page/7/. Accessed March 4, 2015.

Binbit. 2010. Binbit is Nominated for 2010 ME Awards. *Binbit*, October 21. www .binbitgroup.com/news/press-room/page/6/. Accessed April 14, 2015.

Binbit. 2011a. Mobile Entertainment Industry Leader Binbit Evolves its Business Intelligence with Talend Integration Suite. *Binbit*, March 23. www.binbitgroup .com/news/press-room/page/5/. Accessed March 5, 2015.

Binbit. 2011b. Binbit Acquires Indonesia's Forest Media International. *Binbit*, August 23. www.binbitgroup.com/news/press-room/page/4/. Accessed April 15, 2015.

Binbit. 2013. Binbit Increases Alliances with Mobile Operators around the World. *Binbit*, July 15. www.binbitgroup.com/news/press-room/. Accessed April 15, 2015.

Binbit. 2015. Company website. *Binbit*. www.binbitgroup.com. Accessed June 24, 2015.

Businesswire, 2013a. Binbit Selects Data Foundry's Texas 1 Data Center for US-Based Colocation. *Businesswire*, February 25. www.businesswire.com/news/ho me/20130225005417/en/Binbit-Selects-Data-Foundry%E2%80%99s-Texas-1-D ata#.VYxgUUYqtQo. Accessed April 16, 2015.

Businesswire. 2013b. Binbit and Universal Music Launch Club "U+" in 9 Countries of Latin America. *Businesswire*, March 18. www.businesswire.com/news/home/ 20130318005502/en/Binbit-Universal-Music-Launch-Club-%E2%80%9CU%E 2%80%9D-9#.VYxd-EYqtQo. Accessed April 13, 2015.

Businesswire. 2013c. Binbit Formalizes Mobile Entertainment Operations in Southeast Europe. *Businesswire*, December 23. www.businesswire.com/news/h ome/20131223005007/en/Binbit-Formalizes-Mobile-Entertainment-Operation s-Southeast-Europe#.VOy2VS7Swmc. Accessed April 5, 2015.

Businesswire. 2014a. Binbit to Participate alongside ProMexico in the Mobile World Congress. *Businesswire*, February 25. www.businesswire.com/news/ho me/20140225006658/en/Binbit-Participate-ProMexico-Mobile-World-Congres s#.VZLPsEYqtQo. Accessed March 6, 2015.

Businesswire. 2014b. Binbit Acquires Company in the Middle East. *Businesswire*, March 4. www.businesswire.com/news/home/20140304006515/en/Binbit-Acq uires-Company-Middle-East#.VOy3xi7Swmc. Accessed April 13, 2015.

Businesswire. 2014c. Binbit Signs an Agreement with Real Madrid C.F. *Businesswire*, October 14. www.businesswire.com/news/home/201410130062 19/es/#.VOztRy7Swmc. Accessed 5, 2015.

Businesswire. 2015. Binbit Participate in the Mobile World Congress. *Businesswire*, March 2. www.businesswire.com/news/home/20150302006214/es/#. Accessed July 5, 2015.

CNN Expansión. 2015a. Interactive Ranking 2014, the 500 Companies Most Important in Mexico. *CNN Expansión*. www.cnnexpansion.com/rankings/inter activo-las-500/2014. Accessed March 28, 2015.

CNN Expansión. 2015b. The 100 Most Global. *CNN Expansión* 1157.

Corona O. 2009. Softtek Mexican Proudly 100%. *Infochannel*, September 12. www .infochannel.com.mx/softtek-100-mexicana-orgullosamente. Accessed May 20, 2015.

Digital Statistic. 2014. Estadísticas Digitales 2014. *Slideshare*, October 6. http://es.sl ideshare.net/it-soluciones/1-slideshare-it-indicador-socialmedia. Accessed March 6, 2015.

Gasca, L. & Nieto, G. 2013. Emerging Actors, scene. *CNN Expansión*, January 18. iwww.cnnexpansion.com/expansion/2013/04/15/actores-emergentes-a-escena. Accessed March 6, 2015.

Haneine, R. 2015. Mexico: The Competition is Stiff, Global, and Here to Stay. *At Kearney*. www.atkearney.com/communications-media-technology/ideas-insig hts/article/-/asset_publisher/LCcgOeS4t85g/content/mexico-the-competition-i s-stiff-global-and-here-to-stay/10192#sthash.vDiwj5qH.dpuf. Accessed June 10, 2015.

Larios, G. 2010. ICT diffusion in the territories of Mexico: an analysis of casual relations (Difusión de las TIC en los territorios de México: un análisis de relaciones casuales). *In IV Conference of ACORN-Redecom*, Brasilia.

Laudicina, P., Peterson, E. & Gott, J. 2015. *Global Services Location Index*. www .atkearney.com/es/research-studies/global-services-location-index. Accessed June 16, 2015

Mitchell, R. 2007. Mexico, Latin America and the Battle to Be the Next India. *Computerworld*, September 13. www.computerworld.com/article/2477683/it-management/mexico–latin-america-and-the-battle-to-be-the-next-india.html. Accessed June 9, 2015.

Nieto, G. 2011. Asia is More than China. *CNN Expansión*, September 20. www
.cnnexpansion.com/expansion/2011/09/14/asia-es-ms-que-china. Accessed April
13, 2015.

Our Mobile Planet. 2013. Our Mobile Planet Data Download. *With Google*. http://
think.withgoogle.com/mobileplanet/es/downloads/. Accessed June 9, 2015.

Reuters. 2014. Binbit Signs Agreement with FC Barcelona. *Reuters*, August 14. ht
tp://uk.reuters.com/article/2014/08/14/binbit-idUKnBw136281a+100+BS
W20140814. Accessed March 6, 2015.

Select. 2003. *Identifying Niches Economic Activity Potential Adoption of
Information Technology*. Mexico, D.F.: Ministry of Economy.

Softtek. 2007a. Softtek Positioned in Niche Players Quadrant for North American
Offshore Application Services, 2007. *Softtek*, August 17. www.softtek.com/news
room/news-releases/softtek-positioned-in-niche-players-quadrant-for-north-am
erican-offshore-application-services-2007. Accessed May 21, 2015.

Softtek. 2007b. Softtek Opens Regional Service Center in La Plata, Argentina.
Softtek, July 20. www.softtek.com/newsroom/news-releases/softtek-opens-regi
onal-service-center-in-la-plata-argentina. Accessed June 8, 2015.

Softtek. 2007c. NFVZone Softtek finalizes acquisition of China's IT United.
Softtek, August 20. www.tmcnet.com/usubmit/2007/08/20/2874627.htm.
Accessed June 9, 2015.

Softtek. 2008a. Softtek introduced Softtek Asia with Expansion of Global Delivery
Center in China. *Softtek*, January 28. www.softtek.com/es/sala-de-prensa/comu
nicados-de-prensa/softtek-introduce-softtek-asia-con-la-expansion-del-centro-gl
obal-de-entrega-en-china. Accessed May 22, 2015.

Softtek. 2008b. Softtek Appoints Francisco Alvarez-Cascos as President of Softtek
Spain. *Softtek*, November 20. www.softtek.com/newsroom/news-releases/softtek-
appoints-francisco-alvarez-cascos-as-president-of-softtek-spain. Accessed May 18,
2015.

Softtek. 2009. Softtek Opens Offices in Paraguay and is consolidated in the
region. *Softtek*, June. www.softtek.com/newsroom/news-releases/softtek-ope
ns-offices-in-paraguay-and-is-consolidated-in-the-region. Accessed May 22,
2015.

Softtek. 2010. Softtek Opens New Global Delivery Center Office in Corunna,
Spain. *Softtek*, October 1. www.softtek.com/newsroom/news-releases/softtek-
opens-new-global-delivery-center-office-in-corunna-spain. Accessed June 9,
2015.

Softtek. 2011a. Softtek Ranks Among Top 40 Outsourcing Companies in the
World. *Softtek*, May 17. www.softtek.com/newsroom/news-releases/softtek-ra

nks-among-top-40-outsourcing-companies-in-the-world. Accessed May 20, 2015.

Softtek. 2011b. President and CEO of Softtek Inducted into Outsourcing Hall of Fame. *Softtek*, May 31. www.softtek.com/newsroom/news-releases/president-a nd-ceo-of-softtek-inducted-into-outsourcing-hall-of-fame. Accessed May 20, 2015.

Softtek. 2014a. Softtek Comes to Guadalajara. *Softtek*, April 1. www.milenio.com/ negocios/Softteck_en_Guadalajara-Softtek_Mexico-inauguracion_Softtek_Guad alajara_0_272973186.html. Accessed May 20, 2015.

Softtek. 2014b. Softtek Opens Offices in Colombia. *Softtek*, April 3. www.softtek .com/es/sala-de-prensa/comunicados-de-prensa/softtek-inaugura-oficinas-en-co lombia. Accessed June 9, 2015.

Softtek. 2014c. Softtek Ranks Once Again as One of World's Best Providers by Prestigious IAOP 2014 Global Outsourcing 100 List. *Softtek*, June 9. www.soft tek.com/newsroom/news-releases/softtek-ranks-once-again-as-one-of-world-s-b est-providers-by-prestigious-iaop-2014-global-outsourcing-100-list. Accessed 9, 2015.

Softtek. 2015. Softtek webpage. *Softtek*. www.softtek.com. Accessed 20 February 2015.

Stettler, E., Mirza, F., Ali, I., Mohal, M. & Jaiswal, A. 2014. The Rising Starts. *At Key*, October. www.atkearney.com.mx/strategic-it/ideas-insights/featured-arti cle/-/asset_publisher/TR9cTHECBwma/content/the-rising-stars-of-it-outsour cing/10192?_101_INSTANCE_TR9cTHECBwma_redirect=%2Fstrategic-it%2F ideas-insights#sthash.LoHerWdB.dpuf. Accessed June 15, 2015.

Terdiman R. 2003. Softtek's Ddemesis Purchase Will Boost Mexico's Leading ESP. *Gartner*, December 22. www.gartner.com/doc/419880/Softteks-ddemesis-pur chase-boost-mexicos. Accessed May 20, 2015.

Transparency Market Research. 2015. Mobile Entertainment Market – Global Industry Size, Share, Trends, Analysis, and Forecasts 2012–2018. *Transparency Market Search*. www.transparencymarketresearch.com/mobile-entertainment-market.html. Accessed July 24, 2015.

VOXs News. 2013. Binbit Sets New Websites in Polish and Russian. *VOX*, May 13. www.vox.com.mx/2013/05/binbit-establece-nuevos-sitios-web-en-polaco-y-ruso. Accessed April 13, 2015.

21 MultiMexicans in the Telecommunications Industry
América Móvil and Iusacell

Xiomara Vázquez Guillén and Mauricio Ramírez Grajeda*

INTRODUCTION

Due to economic trends, such as good economic growth rates, increasing demand, and improving competitive regulatory framework within the product and service markets, Latin American economies have been investing and innovating to fulfill the information technology (IT) requirements of both households and firms in the last two decades. In this sense, stylized facts show that this sector has featured a steady growth path, turning the IT industry into one of the most appealing and dynamic markets among investors.[1] In most countries of the region, wireless and broadband telecommunications in particular have offered major business opportunities along with a higher level of competition. Mexico's mobile market revenues, for instance, were estimated to reach US$24 billion by 2015, and two of its major carriers emerging in this game are América Móvil and Iusacell.

In this chapter, we describe 15 years of globalization of América Móvil, and the contrasting history of Iusacell. The former's performance has been remarkable since the firm was spun out of Telmex in 2000. This company is one of the largest single privatization cases in Latin America in the early 1990s; it served as a benchmark experience for further privatizations and paved the way for reduced market constraints. América Móvil swiftly expanded its operations in South and Central America by exploiting the mobile communications market conditions; in the early stages it progressed by working with partners and, more recently, by acquiring assets from other firms. It is still

* Corresponding author.   [1]   GSMALA (2014).

involved in an incipient process of expansion into global markets. So far, Iusacell has been a local provider; however, AT&T acquired the company in early 2015, aiming at expanding Iusacell services to the rest of North America. This chapter explains the telecommunications industry and legal reforms in Mexico, provides a broad description of América Móvil, its origins and globalization strategy, and gives a brief description of Iusacell's inward path. Finally, we present some lessons about this industry. Generally, América Móvil has taken advantage of business opportunities mainly in emerging markets by acquiring local companies and setting up market dominance in such a way that potential entrants find it difficult to cope with "competition."

TELECOMMUNICATIONS INDUSTRY ANALYSIS

The history of the telecommunications industry in Mexico can be traced back to two companies: the American International Telephone and Telegraph Company, which started operations in Mexico in 1888, and the Swedish L. M. Ericsson in 1905. In 1947, in order to establish a single telephone operator in Mexico, a domestic company, Teléfonos de Mexico (Telmex), was set up, as result of consolidating the two companies operating at that time. From 1950 to 1958, Telmex was the main telephone company in the country. During the following 15 years, it operated as a private firm with strong links with the Mexican government to spread phone services nation-wide. For instance, in the 1960s a telephone service tax and a long-distance tax were created, and represented 60 percent of Temex's revenues by the end of the 1980s. These financial resources were allocated to unrelated government programs.

However, until 1972, the government's role at Telmex kept expanding until it took control of the company by purchasing slightly more than 50 percent of the company's voting shares. It is worth mentioning that in those years there was an open tendency to move private enterprises under the government's control. Furthermore, in Mexico in those years, the relationship between the private sector and the government was tense. Mexican and foreign citizens and other institutional holders owned the rest of Telmex's shares. From that year on, the company in practice ran its business as a state-owned asset (known as *paraestatal*). The government regulated tariffs impacting both on operating revenues and total costs, and made other business decisions not entirely based upon economic rationality. Telmex kept some of its private-company aims, though. For example, the government appointed shared seats on Telmex's board of directors with individuals belonging to the private sector. However, the government held most of Telmex's management after it took full control of the company.

As stated, Telmex operated as a private company during most of the 1970s. The CEO of the company from 1975 to 1987 was Emilio Carrillo Gamboa. During that period, the company expanded its telephone services at a rate of 6 percent annually, and the system was modernized. By 1980, operators no longer controlled Telmex's exchanges, and the company started installing only digital rather than electromechanical lines (from zero to 20 percent of the whole infrastructure). Similarly, Telmex's indicators on telephone service performance in comparison to other developing nations and other state-owned companies within Mexico ranked well. Nevertheless, political bias, operational inefficiencies, labor union interference, and fiscal mismanagement negatively affected Telmex's financial performance. The net effect, in terms of service quality and financial position, arose by the end of the mid-1980s: prohibitive long-distance tariffs and hookup fees, high rates of inoperable lines, overpaid or long waiting times of connection. The main performance indicators were poor in comparison to other markets in the USA, Europe, and Japan.

Even though there was an effort to improve Telmex's service during the late 1980s, inefficiency could not be minimized, and the company's performance remained well below international standards. Furthermore, it failed to adopt key technologies such as toll-free services and fiber optic transmission. Telmex continued to pay dividends on its stock because the firm was artificially supported by the State, though.

By 1982, the privatization of a small number of large public enterprises, including Aeroméxico and Mexicana, Mexico's two national airlines, began. At that time, the Mexican government, accounting for one-fifth of the Mexican GDP and employing around one million people, controlled more than a thousand state-owned enterprises. When Miguel De la Madrid Hurtado was in office (1982– 8), one-half of these were ousted; most of them were non-large firms in non-strategic areas where the government's direction was not essential. Of these divestitures, 294 were closed, 204 sold, 72 merged, and 25 transferred. However, there was a minor impact on government finances, which had small-scale macro- and microeconomic consequences. Moreover, the number of *paraestatal* workers has increased since, as some enterprises were divested and others from the private sector were incorporated. During the 1990s the government kept privatizing many of Mexico's hundreds of state-owned enterprises; one of the largest was Telmex.

In 1990, Telmex was sold as a monopoly to a consortium led by a Mexican conglomerate, Grupo Carso, with Southwestern Bell and France Telecom as minority foreign partners. Grupo Carso put up half of the US$1.76 billion and received a 10 percent equity stake in Telmex, while its partners financed the other half and shared the other 10 percent interest. The agreement was that Grupo Carso would take control of the company, Southwestern Bell would be responsible for improving operations and developing paging and cellular divisions, and France Telecom would concentrate on line expansion and modernization. This was one of the largest single privatizations in Latin America, and generated US$6 billion for the Mexican Treasury.[2]

Grupo Carso and its subsidiaries, the sixth largest company in Mexico at that time, operated in the retail, insurance, tourism, paper products, industrial and manufacturing, infrastructure and construction, mining, and energy sectors. It currently has a presence in the retail segment through department stores, boutiques, gift shops,

[2] Winter (2007).

record stores, restaurants, cafeterias, electronic and entertainment stores, and shopping malls through the Sanborns, Sears, Saks Fifth Avenue, Mix-up, and iShop brands. It produces cable products for use in the construction, automotive, energy, and telecommunications industries, copper, aluminum, automotive parts, and lighting solutions. It also has operations in highway construction and maintenance, water system and treatment plants, duct installations, fiber-optic, gas pipelines, oil well drilling, oil platforms and equipment, and real property construction.

Southwestern Bell increased its international focus throughout its subsidiary, Southwestern Bell International Holdings Corporation (SBIHC). One operation was the acquisition of 20.4 percent of the total equity and 51 percent of the shares with full voting rights in Telmex, Mexico's national telephone company. This participation gave SBC a chance to sell services, such as long-distance telephone communications, that it was prohibited from offering in the United States.

The third partner was France Telecom, recently independent in terms of budget, management, and organizational independence, but still with monopoly status; it started looking for alliances and mergers to achieve the scale necessary to compete in international and new markets.

Telmex was granted a concession – expiring in 2026 – to provide voice, data, text, sound, and video transmission services, but was not allowed to provide television services over its telephone/broadband network either directly or indirectly. Telmex was given a monopoly in the provision of long-distance and international service for seven years, to allow network expansion targets and "rebalance" its finance structure. In return, Telmex committed to expand the number of basic service lines by a minimum average annual rate of 12 percent during 1990–94 and drive down prices. For the first years, Telmex was an unregulated monopoly except for enforcement of the concession by the Secretaría de Comunicaciones y Transportes (SCT). In the early nineties, Latin American countries followed a list of policy recommendations known as the Washington Consensus, which included the selling of non-strategic firms.[3]

Telmex's privatization was not accompanied by an institutional design to guarantee its customers' satisfaction and reasonable mark-ups. Due to the lack of institutional capabilities, monopolistic rents were distributed among owners and employees. Consumers paid for monopolistic telecommunications services and Telmex's competitors were unable to lower their own prices because of high interconnection charges. For example, in 1989, 26 out of 30 OECD countries featured a monopoly market structure in the fixed network; in 2003 only one country kept the same structure: Mexico. In 2000, Mexico charged the highest tariffs for both business and residential users among OECD countries: US$5 versus US$0.5 in Norway, controlling for purchasing power parity.[4] In 1999, Telmex launched a process of acquisitions of international subsidiaries in the Americas.

On the other hand, in 1978, the government granted the first concession for a wireless telephone system for cars. In 1984 Publicidad Turística, founded in 1956 as an affiliate of Telmex and owned by the Mexican government, changed its name to Radiomóvil Dipsa, like the original company that gave birth to Telcel, and started operating wireless communications. From 1988 to 1990, Telcel expanded its cellular network to cover Mexico City and other major cities of the country. In 1989 the company began operating under the Telcel brand. One year later, Telcel started supplying cellular services all over the country. In 1995, Telcel had 57 percent of the market and was a pioneer of prepaid phone cards for the medium- and-low income segment. In 2000 Telcel had around 9 million out of 12 million cellular-phone subscribers in Mexico. In the same year, the Telmex spin-off América Móvil was announced. See Table 21.1.

América Móvil's large market share has motivated regulators in Mexico and abroad to review its practices. A 2012 OECD study (OECD Review of Telecommunications Policy and Regulation in Mexico) on

---

[3] González (2008).   [4]   OECD (2012).

Table 21.1 *Subscriber base in Mexico*

Year	Broadband	Fixed Lines	Cellular Phones
2000	103	12,331	14,077
2001	105	13,774	21,757
2002	212	14,975	25,928
2003	432	16,330	30,097
2004	1,090	18,073	38,451
2005	1,980	19,512	47,128
2006	3,136	19,861	55,395
2007	4,633	19,997	66,559
2008	7,638	20,491	75,322
2009	9,976	19,505	83,219
2010	11,817	19,918	91,383
2011	12,733	19,731	94,583
2012	13,560	20,587	100,727
2013	13,552	20,590	105,005
2014	12,970	20,900	101,800
2015–2Q	13,680	21,100	103,400

Data in thousands
Source: América Móvil quarterly reports

the Mexican telecommunications and media markets reported a below average performance of the two sectors due to insufficient competition. It caused an average annual welfare loss of US$129.2 billion or 1.8 percent of Mexican GDP between 2005 and 2009.[5] In 2014, the Federal Government promulgated a legal reform on the telecommunications industry, seeking to foster investment and competitiveness. The main objectives were to spread coverage, reduce prices, and improve quality of service. In terms of regulation, foreign investment

[5]   OECD (2012).

Table 21.2 *Mexican market share (%), 2Q 2015*

Celluar Phone		Fixed Lines		Broad Band	
Telcel (América Móvil)	69.5	Telmex-Telnor	62.7	Telmex-Telnor	62.8
Movistar (Telefónica)	21.5	GTM (Telefónica)	8.6	Televisa Group	18.7
Iusacell-Unefón (AT&T)	5.4	Axtel-Avantel	7.3	Megacable	11.4
Nextel (AT&T)	3.1	Televisa Group	6.9	Axtel-Avantel	3.4
Virtual Movil Operators	0.5	Maxcom	6.8	Total Play	1.4
		Alestra	2.9	Maxcom	1.2
		Megacable	1.4	Others	1.2
		Others	3.4		

Source: IFT

can reach up to 100 percent in telecommunications, including satellite transmissions; the legal framework of the telecommunications industry will provide better legal certainty; there will be more rights for customers. In terms of infrastructure, wider access, high-speed connectivity, and coverage through fiber optic will be provided, with the aim of "universal digital inclusion"; and Government will build a network for broadband access.[6,7] See Table 21.2.

Finally, the Federal Telecommunications Institute (IFT), created in 2013 as substitute of COFETEL, and the Federal Economic Competition Commission (Cofeco), are the antitrust authorities in the industry. IFT's main duties are to: provide or revoke operating licenses; limit concentration and market share; foster economic and free competition and content diversity; set costs for licenses; and establish fines. If IFT considers that the market indicators are not

[6]   IFT (2015).   [7]   Bejarano (2014).

moving toward a more competitive environment, it could enforce more pro-competitive measures. Like the EU model through the European Commission, the Mexican reform intends to build a competition-based regulatory architecture.

In 2014, as part of its exclusive responsibility for competition issues in the telecommunications and audiovisual sectors, IFT declared América Móvil a dominant player as its market share exceeded 50 percent of the provision of audiovisual or telecommunications services, measured by number of users, subscriber base, audience, and traffic or network capacity utilized. As a consequence of its 'preponderance' position, América Móvil must comply with several regulatory measures determined by IFT and review its practices. This puts América Móvil in an exceptionally weak position with respect to AT&T, which has recently acquired Iusacell and Nextel.[8]

América Móvil is quite complex to analyze in comparison to other firms. Most of its competitors in emerging countries are local and small, and its stocks are not traded on the international markets.[9]

Nevertheless, the services in the wireless communication industry seem to be changing dramatically because many new customers are not seeking long-term contracts; rather, they are willing to be under the scheme of prepaid services with minimum requirements. In the future, the wireless segment market will converge to competitive conditions that will reduce profit growth opportunities.

Based in Spain and larger than América Móvil, its main competitor is Telefónica and its subsidiaries, the world's third-largest telecommunications firm by access lines. This giant operates telecommunications, media, and contact center industries via three business branches: Telefónica Spain, Telefónica Europe, and Telefónica Latin America. It runs businesses in the UK, Germany, the Czech Republic, and Ireland with 100 million customers, and businesses in Argentina, Brazil, Chile, Colombia, Costa Rica, Ecuador, El Salvador, Guatemala, Mexico, Nicaragua, Panama, Peru, Puerto Rico, Uruguay, and Venezuela with

---

[8]   Noll (2013).   [9]   Sidak (2012).

200 million customers that represented slightly more than 51 percent of its overall revenues in 2013 and more than one third in 2014. In May 2015, Telefónica completed the acquisition of Brazilian fixed carrier GVT from Vivendi, and strengthened its presence in the Brazilian market with an increasing demand for fixed and wireless services.[10]

In recent years, the telecommunications sector has featured a highly competitive structure in almost all developed countries, where markets are saturated for new players; however, there are plenty of opportunities for expansion in emerging countries.

Within the mature markets, incumbent companies usually compete in the quality dimension. For example, in the USA, competition in the mobile telecommunications industry has increased dramatically over time. The four main telecommunications firms, Verizon, AT&T, Sprint, and T-Mobile, have been struggling for new subscribers. In contrast, the Mexican market is still growing in cellular, fixed line, and broadband services.[11]

América Móvil is currently the largest firm in Mexico; however, there is plenty of room to grow for the other competitors after América Móvil has been accused of monopolistic practices.

AMÉRICA MÓVIL: AN OVERVIEW

América Móvil is one of the most important carriers within the telecommunications industry worldwide (it ranked ninth in terms of its revenues in 2013). In 2014 it was the fourth largest global mobile operator in terms of wireless subscribers and fixed lines. The corporation operates in 28 countries in the Americas and Europe through many subsidiaries such as Telcel, Telmex, Claro, Embratel, Simple Mobile, Net, and TracFone.[12]

Based in Mexico City with around 190,000 employees globally at the end of 2014, América Móvil is the largest provider of wireless communications in Latin America, and the largest landline operator

---

[10] Santillana & López (2015).   [11]   PWC (2015).
[12] América Móvil (2015).

in Central America. In Mexico, the company controls around 70 percent of the mobile phone network and 80 percent of landlines. The company has usually reported above average returns based upon its particular market dominance within developing countries.

The firm has grown out of Telmex, which was a public telecommunications firm. In 2000, the spin-off América Móvil from Telmex, the largest mobile-service provider in Latin America with about ten million subscribers, was announced as an independent company for cellular and broadband Internet services.

The company mainly provides wireless and fixed voice services (30 percent of its revenues in 2015), including airtime, domestic, and international long-distance, as well as network interconnection and public telephone services. The company also provides data communications, such as messaging, web browsing, mobile entertainment, enterprise mobility services, and corporate network services, data transmission, email services, real-time messaging, content streaming, and interactive applications. Except in the USA, the corporation has the license to build, install, operate, and manage public and private networks.

Carlos Slim Helú (according to *Forbes* magazine, one of the world's wealthiest people), controls more than 200 companies, ranging from telecommunications to mining, construction, banking, and retailing, through his conglomerate, Grupo Carso. Along with certain members of both his immediate family (for instance, his children) and the Lebanese community, he holds a majority interest (62 percent) in América Móvil through the holding company América Telecom. This company also holds a controlling interest in Mexico's dominant landline telecommunications company, Telmex. It is worth mentioning that Wal-Mart de México, América Móvil, and Telmex are the largest private companies in Mexico, in terms of annual revenues. América Telecom has a remarkable management team. Although Carlos Slim has stepped down from regular operations, he is still the firm's largest shareholder and honorary lifetime chairman. He is 75 years old and dedicated to philanthropic activities.

América Móvil's strategy, as an entrant player in developing countries, is based upon scale economies (a vast network infrastructure): driving down competitive prices due to low costs (operating and interconnection) combined with quality services (speed, capacity, and coverage). Thus, its operations capture most market share. Additionally, this has allowed the company to generate one of the highest return rates among wireless operators globally, and to cover a vast population in Latin America. For instance, in Argentina the company's wireless networks cover approximately 99 percent of the population; in Chile, its networks cover 98 percent of the population, while in Uruguay it covers 97 percent of the population.[13]

In Latin America, América Móvil has carried out another business strategy throughout its subsidiaries, which operate with prepaid subscribers. These subscribers only purchase the number of minutes they need, either via a card in a particular selling location or online. Locations where cards are available may include places like service stations, convenience stores, phone stores, even street vendors. The customer does not need to sign a legal contract to commit to periodical payments. This attracts many low-income subscribers. Such figures are the result of state-of-the art technology innovation to increase market share and create a huge customer base as well.

In this light, América Móvil reported the following financial figures over recent years (see Table 21.3):

América Móvil's relatively solid Balance Sheet (Net debt/ EBITDA = 1.7) allows the financial support to exploit business opportunities. This allows targeting Latin American markets to return value to its shareholders through hostile acquisitions, dividends, and stock buybacks. It has featured an aggressive expansion strategy and built up a solid history of acquiring troubled companies and turning them into sound players. Robust demand for cellular services, along with aggressive pricing strategies, have allowed the company to become the largest wireless provider in the region, with more than

---

[13]   PWC (2015).

Table 21.3 *América Móvil's financial indicators*

	2010	2011	2012	2013	2014
Revenues	48	53	59	67	66
Total assets	71	68	77	79	87
EBITDA	19	20	20	22	21
Gross profit	29	27	33	33	31
Net profit	7.2	6.6	7	6	3.5
Foreign investment	N/A	10	10	10	10
Exports	N/A	N/A	N/A	N/A	N/A
Employees	150	161	169	173	191
Countries	19	18	19	20	20
0D/E percent	88	120	159	221	233
ROA percent	11	9	9	7	4
ROE percent	33	28	34	33	24

Data in billions of US dollars
Source: Bloomberg

330 million customers. As consequence of this expansion, América Móvil has generated attractive profits on its investments: invested capital return is above the cost of capital. Regarding small markets, dominant share and margin expansion are some of the issues the firm is still trying to cope with. In this vein, lack of scale diminishes profits in these markets. Therefore, the company is taking advantage of its foreign operations to achieve greater scale.

After IFT declared América Móvil a dominant player in Mexico, the company was instructed to share its infrastructure; open broadband access to other competitors with a new cost structure; allow interconnection for other companies in their local and long-distance networks with fees regulated by IFETEL; no charge for national roaming, controlled tariffs for the end user and agreed roaming tariffs for wholesale services for visiting users. Because of these measures, it has been increasingly difficult for Telcel to compete on price. América Móvil is considering selling off its assets (customer base and infrastructure) to reduce its market share of the Mexican telecommunications industry to below 50 percent. Nevertheless, if IFETEL considers that the market is not moving toward a more competitive environment, it could implement more pro-competitive measures. Therefore, América Móvil has been facing tighter controls in Mexico, after the new telecommunications law requires it to reduce its share of the market, getting rid of its assets since it was accused of having a dominant status.[14]

América Móvil seeks to enter the pay television market to be able to offer triple-play services. First, it would need to get out of the measures imposed as a dominant player in less than two years – the period that IFETEL had originally announced. América Móvil announced its intention to sell part of its assets in order to reduce its market share below 50 percent. In this operation, the company could obtain a minimum of US$10 billion by selling off 21 million out of 105 million mobile subscribers and 4 million out of 21 million fixed line subscribers.

América Móvil Expansion[15]

América Móvil swiftly expanded its operations in Latin America by exploiting communications development opportunities. This was originally done with partners and then, like its main competitor, Telefónica, through a challenging strategy of acquiring assets from other enterprises in the industry (BellSouth, Verizon, AT&T, MCI, TIM, and France Télécom). Later, it acquired assets in the broadband and television segments to reach sufficient coverage to allow it to provide combos of television, Internet, and phone services.

Its takeover of Telmex made América Móvil in 2000 the parent company of Telmex, Telcel, Claro, Embratel, Net, and Comcel, all of which provide services such as wireless, fixed telephony, broadband,

---

[14]   Hernández (2014).   [15]   América Móvil. Annual Reports.

and cable. By the end of the year, the company had a presence in Argentina, Brazil, Colombia, Ecuador, Guatemala, Puerto Rico, the United States, and Uruguay; and América Móvil started being listed on stock exchanges in Mexico City, Madrid, and New York; however, Carso Global Telecom (Telmex's holding) retained majority control.

América Móvil's principal markets of operations are Mexico and Brazil. In the latter country, the company operates under the brand names of Claro, Embratel, and Net, offering mobile and fixed telephony services, as well as pay-television. It provides wireless services under the brand name Claro in Argentina, Paraguay, Uruguay, Chile, and Colombia. In addition, América Móvil provides fixed telephony services in Guatemala, El Salvador, Nicaragua, and Panama; while in the United States it has operators Tracfone and SimpleMobile, owns several call centers, and has a comprehensive service agreement with Vodafone. It also has stakes in European companies Telekom Austria and Koninklijke KPN.

The Brazilian telecommunications industry in particular is mainly controlled by Spain's Telefónica, Mexico's América Móvil, and Oi (fixed line and mobile), which is controlled by Brazilian investors and Portugal Telecom. Brazil's mobile market is the fifth largest in the world and subscriptions continue to grow; this is a key market for América Móvil and where it derived 25 percent of its total revenues in 2013. América Móvil started international operations in Brazil through Telecom Americas, a joint venture with Bell Canada International and SBC. In 2001 the company had acquired 100 percent of Tess and controlling interests in Telet and Americel. During 2013, Claro Brasil's GSM network covered more than 3,600 cities and 92 percent of the country's population, including the most important tourist and business cities. Embratel owned the largest long-distance network in Latin America and the largest data-transmission network in Brazil. Finally, Net Servicos had an advanced network that provided services and products to 18.8 million homes in 164 localities. Due to the 2016 Olympic Games, held in Brazil, the demand for fixed and mobile broadband, mobile telephony, and other wireless products such as smartphones and mobile applications is expected to rise. According to industry estimates, Brazil's telecommunications market is expected to reach US$100 billion in 2017.

Three players dominate the Colombian mobile market: América Móvil's Comcel, Telefónica's Movistar, and Millicom-controlled Tigo. Broadband is growing due to a government initiative that seeks to close the 'digital divide,' and provides Internet access nationwide. América Móvil first entered the Colombia market in 2000 through its participation in Telecom Americas and controlling interests in Comcel and Occel, which together had 2.5 million subscribers. In 2003, América Móvil closed the acquisition of a 95 percent interest in Colombian wireless operator Celcaribe, which covered the Caribbean region of the country and attained nationwide coverage in Colombia, serving 22 million subscribers. In the same year, América Móvil launched its new GSM services in Brazil, Colombia, Ecuador, Mexico, and Nicaragua. América Móvil has inaugurated its undersea optic fiber cable system AMX-1 in Colombia. The submarine network had 11 landing points in seven countries, including the United States, Colombia, Brazil, Dominican Republic, Mexico, Puerto Rico, and Guatemala.

Peru is a very attractive country for América Móvil. Mobile Internet usage is expected to grow near to a percentage in the 70s per year. The main segments are prepaid customers that represent 75 percent of the market. The most popular services are entertainment subscriptions, music, games, ring tones, and "Ideas Idiomas," a service developed for users to learn English. Claro's strategy is to target mid- to low-income consumer segments usually represented by prepaid users, by using entertainment subscriptions.

In 2010, América Móvil was the largest or second-largest cellular phone company in every Latin American country except Chile, where it was third; and also, the fifth-largest telecommunications company in the world – behind China Mobile, AT&T, Vodafone, and Telefónica – with a market capitalization average of approximately US $97 billion. At that time, the company controlled 70 percent of the cellular telephone market, 80 percent of the fixed-line market, and an estimated 88 percent of the Internet service market in Mexico, the 13th largest economy in the World.[16]

In order to transmit data more rapidly, América Móvil improved its wireless and landline networks throughout Latin America by investing around US$10 billion annually over 2010 and for the next five years. This capital expenditure was intended for submarine cable, fiber optic networks, cable to home, fiber to sites, 3G and 4G LTE coverage, and satellites. The company also has an advantageous bargaining position when buying inputs and capital goods from its suppliers.

In the first quarter of 2011, América Móvil reported a wireless subscriber base of 65.7 million customers in Mexico, 53.4 million in Brazil, 30 million in Colombia, 18.5 million in both Argentina and the United States, and 17.5 million in Central America and the Caribbean.

In 2012, América Móvil took its first steps to play within the competitive European telecommunication market, investing US$5.5 billion as it sought to acquire stakes in KPN (a Dutch group) and Telekom Austria. However, only the second of these transactions was successful. At the end of 2013, the company controlled a 28 percent stake in KPN; however, its actions to take over the Dutch firm ultimately collapsed.

In 2013, the International Olympic Committee awarded América Móvil the right to broadcast on all media platforms across Latin America, except for Brazil, two major sports events: the 2014 Olympic Winter Games in Sochi, Russia, and the 2016 Olympic Games in Rio de Janeiro, Brazil.

At the beginning of 2014, América Móvil secured a shareholders' agreement, allowing it to launch a public tender offer through which it hopes to gain outright control of Telekom Austria (TKA). Once this transaction is complete, América Móvil will use TKA – which has operations in seven Central and Eastern European markets

---

[16]   América Móvil (2014).

(Belarus, Bulgaria, Croatia, Liechtenstein, Macedonia, Serbia, and Slovenia) – as a takeoff platform for expanding its operations in the European telecommunications market. Nevertheless, the European competition authority has shown a tougher position under the leadership of its new commissioner, Margrethe Vestager.

On the other hand, América Móvil faces further considerable economic (poor economic performance of Brazil), political, and currency risks, provided that most of its operations are in Latin America. América Móvil has a substantial amount of debt denominated in US dollars (38 percent in 2014), but most of its revenue is generated in currencies such as Mexican pesos and Brazilian real, which have been negatively affected.

It is worth mentioning that the 2015 depreciation events in the firm's operating currencies could imply a larger debt burden. The firm is also dealing with recurring operational challenges in Brazil due to brand positioning problems and integration issues. Its fixed-line business is eroding because of fixed-to-mobile substitution, and mobile termination rates are coming down in all of its key markets. Ongoing depreciation in the firm's operating currencies against the US dollar will lead to higher debt obligations. Mexico is supposed to hold a sufficiently wide radio frequency spectrum in 2015 as to allow for more competition within the main telecommunications industry. Their main competitors, Telefonica and Telecom Italia, are depending on Latin America for growth and similar price competition is expected in the USA. As a consequence, América Móvil is looking for investment possibilities in India with Videocon Telecom. This will be its first foray into Asia.

In 2015, the still-low Mexican competitive market represents 29 percent of subscribers but 36 percent of revenues. Other developing markets like Colombia, the Panama region, and the Andean region exhibit the opposite effect, because more firms are struggling for market share, which causes excess competition. The aim of the company is to dominate its new markets and turn them as profitable as its home market. See Table 21.4.

Table 21.4 *América Móvil's domestic and international events*

Year	Domestic	International
2000	Cover around 66 percent of 12 million cellular-phone users in Mexico.	Announced América Móvil as spin-off from Telmex, covering Argentina, Brazil, Colombia, Ecuador, Guatemala, Puerto Rico, the United States, and Uruguay.
2001	Launched mobile Internet, and had alliance with suppliers such as Palm.	Acquired minority shares up to 14 percent of the capital of Comcel in Colombia.
2002	Telcel invested US$950 million to build GSM for 300 thousand customers.	Sold 50 percent of Cellular Communications of Puerto Rico; bought 14 percent of Comunicaciones Celular in Colombia; and concluded the acquisition of stake in Bell Canada International en Telecom Americas.
2003	Had a boom and reported an increase in sales of 40 percent.	Closed the acquisition of 95 percent interest in Colombian wireless operator Celcaribe. Launched GSM services in Brazil, Colombia, Ecuador, Mexico, and Nicaragua.
2004	Carlos Slim stepped down as CEO, handing the reins to Carlos Slim Domit.	Acquired 41.3 percent of Compañía de Telecomunicaciones of El Salvador (CTE).
2005	Launched aggressive advertising in order to convince customers about its leadership in infrastructure and coverage.	Began operations and entered a license for the next 20 years in Peru. Signed a contract with Hutchison Telecom to acquire operations in Paraguay and Uruguay.

Table 21.4 (*cont.*)

Year	Domestic	International
2006	Reached 24 million subscribers in Mexico and 93.3 million in Latin America.	Comcel of América Móvil and Telefónica had to pay a penalty of US$1.1 million because of monopolistic practices in Colombia. Bought out 100 percent of Verizon Dominicana.
2007	The fusion of América Telecom (AMTEL) and América Móvil. Reached 137.2 million cellular phone subscribers and 141 million fixed lines.	Expanded operations into Guatemala, Jamaica, and Panama.
2008	Telcel signed an agreement of connectivity with Cablevision.	Claro, subsidiary in Brazil, reached second place in the country.
2009	Moved into the smart phones and laptops market, and started distribution of Motorola operating system "Android."	Prepaid service accounts for over 60 percent of US phone mobile service. Entel, subsidiary of América Móvil, invested US$100 million in Nicaragua.
2010	Moved into quadruple play technologies and reached out to 200 million subscribers.	Acquired 90 percent of the stake in Telmex International (Telint) and Carso Global Telecom (CGT).
2011	Moved into 4G technologies market and entered an alliance with the bank Bancomer to promote mobile banking services.	Became the biggest or second biggest cellular phone company in every Latin American country except Chile, where it was third.
2012	Launched IdeasMusik in order to compete with Apple and iTunes in the download music market.	Invested in assets outside the region for the first time, acquiring strategic interests in Telekom Austria and KPN of Holland.

Table 21.4 (*cont.*)

Year	Domestic	International
2013	Carlos Slim Helu increased his stake in América Móvil to 15.8 percent.	Got the rights to broadcast on all media platforms across Latin America, except the 2014 Olympic Winter Games in Sochi, and the 2016 Olympic Games in Rio de Janeiro.
2014	América Móvil rescinded Telsistes SAB and transferred some assets related to mobile operations infrastructure.	Launched a public tender offer through which it hopes to gain outright control of Telekom Austria, which has operations in Belarus, Bulgaria, Croatia, Liechtenstein, Macedonia, Serbia, and Slovenia.
2015	Offers wireless services, fixed line services, and data services as well.	Largest provider of wireless communications in Latin America and the largest landline operator in Central America, with around 190 thousand employees globally.

Source: América Móvil. 2015. Annual reports from 2002 to 2015. www .americamovil.com/investor-relations/financial-reports/annual-report. Accessed in May 31, 2015.

After trying unsuccessfully to sell part of its stocks, América Móvil took another asset-shedding strategy by spinning off part of its infrastructure into a tower rental company, Telesites, which was supposed to start operations in June. The company generates positive free cash flow each year while spending a significant and growing amount on capital expenditures, as well as paying off debt, buying back stock, and paying a dividend.

In the near future, América Móvil will continue to explore acquisition opportunities in Latin America, in particular in

Venezuela, Panama, Bolivia, and the Caribbean. It is also open to expanding into other regions if the price is reasonable.

In terms of technology, América Móvil has also launched an Edge-based push-to-talk service for individual clients in Mexico and has 3G services available in Mexico's largest cities. América Móvil is on the cutting edge of wireless technology, which is evident by the speed at which it delivers new products to the market. The company was the first telecommunications provider to offer 4G services in Mexico.

In emerging countries, considerable investments are expected in telecommunications and information technologies. Due to growing demand in mobile services, América Móvil, for example, will invest US$50 billion over the next few years. Traditional sectors like manufacturing and agriculture have a relevant role to play as well, to foster innovation and drive sophistication. Investors also expect a more favorable, market-friendly business environment in order to boost competitiveness.

Even though the Latin American mobile market is characterized by decreasing growth opportunities – improving market maturity and decreasing subscriber and revenue growth – there is still enough room within the region to expand at a relatively fast pace in the coming years. For example, broadband subscribers are expected to grow 30 percent annually. In the pay-television market the region is forecast to grow up to 100 million customers in 2018. In this way, América Móvil – with a large network infrastructure and competitive practices – is well positioned to take advantage of such a potential scenario. Nevertheless, 90 percent of Latin Americans already have wireless services, which means growth is going to have to come from outside, growing the customer base.

In sum, the firm has a well-structured acquisition strategy. It has been very good at taking control over other highly indebted companies during the information technology bubble. It then consolidates operations, improves management, and makes operations more profitable. However, América Móvil is intended to play in new markets through new acquisitions, which may involve a risk of buying above the market price.

IUSACELL

Currently, Iusacell operates concessions for mobile services in the central and southern regions of Mexico. The company supplies local and long-distance telephony, messaging services, mobile television, and wireless broadband services as well. The company traces its origins back to 1955, when it was founded as Servicio Organizado Secretarial (SOS).

Grupo Iusacell is a mobile telephone pioneer in the Mexican market, set up in 1989. During 2000, the company tried to increase its market share in the largest Mexican cities, offering radio services, local phone calls, and long distance calls. In 2001, the company invested in a nationwide infrastructure in order to gain a presence all over the country. In the same year, the British company Vodafone acquired 34.5 percent of Iusacell. Two years later, Verizon and Vodafone sold out all their shares in Iusacell, totaling 73.9 percent of the company; the company faced insolvency problems and lost 200,000 subscribers.

The company merged in 2007 with Unefón, which belonged to the conglomerate Grupo Salinas. The company had a 4 million subscriber base, which represented an approximate market share of 7 percent. Nevertheless, Grupo Televisa had a 50 percent share of Iusacell.

In September 2014 Grupo Salinas purchased Televisa's equity share in Iusacell for US$717 million. One year later, AT&T acquired the total shares of the company from its controller, Grupo Salinas, Mexico's third most important wireless operator, for US$1.7 billion in order to gain access to 8.6 million subscribers and wireless coverage of 70 percent of the country. It also spent about US$2.8 billion to acquire Nextel Mexico mobile network with 2.8 million subscribers. Mexico is AT&T's current target, due to the 105 million base subscribers that have grown at a rate of 7 percent for the last 7 years, 86 percent of mobile services penetration, and a big opportunity for the mobile broadband market with just 13 percent penetration.

Table 21.5 *Iusacell's domestic and international events*

Year	Domestic Events	International Events
1955	Servicio Organizado Secretarial (SOS) was founded.	
1989	Iusacell was set up as a mobile telephone player.	
2000	Globalstar and Grupo Iusacell entered into an agreement of a national connectivity hedge.	Iusacell signed an Internet contract with the US company "phone.com."
2001	Invested US$229 million to modernize and increase connectivity and infrastructure all over the country.	Vodafone acquired a share of 34.5 percent of Grupo Iusacell for a total of US$973.4 million. Iusacell signed an agreement with the Chinese company Unicom Horizon Mobile Communications in order to provide roaming service to Asia.
2003	Iusacell postponed the interest payment on its debt.	Verizon Communications and Vodafone Americas BV sold their shares totaling 73.9 percent. Ricardo Salinas Pliego took control of the company.
2005	Launched "Radio Plus" radio service.	Iusacell ADRs were unlisted in NYSE.
2007	Iusacell merged with Unefón, which belonged to the conglomerate Grupo Salinas. Entered into an agreement with Nextel México for mobile interconnection. Salinas Pliego took control.	
2008	Lost market and suspended operations.	
2009	Negotiated debt in foreign currency.	

Table 21.5 (*cont.*)

Year	Domestic Events	International Events
2011	Televisa bought 50 percent of Iusacell shares.	
2012	Changed strategy and focused on heavy users, not on volume customers.	
2013	Grupo Televisa had a 50 percent participation in Iusacell shares.	
2014	Grupo Salinas purchased Televisa's equity participation in Iusacell for US$717 million.	
2015	AT&T acquired the total shares of Iusacell from its controller, Grupo Salinas, for US$1.7 billion, plus US$2.8 billion to acquire Nextel Mexico mobile network.	

Source: Bloomberg. 2015. Company Overview Holdings, Inc. www.bloo mberg.com/research/stocks/private/snapshot.asp?privcapId=224555999. Accessed in April, 2015.

AT&T plans to invest about US$3 billion to build up its recently acquired Iusacell mobile phone network in Mexico, including voice and data services to cover about 90 percent of the total population before 2019. AT&T also plans to set up the first North American mobile service area covering more than 400 million consumers (households and firms) in Mexico and the USA.

In summary, the deal aims to increase market share where cellular penetration is relatively low and attractive for potential growth. AT&T is looking to tap into the growing cellphone market in Latin America's second economy now that the government is fostering international investment in the sector.

Table 21.6 *Iusacell's financial indicators*

	2001	2002	2003	2004	2005	2006	2007
Revenues	0.66	0.55	0.43	0.48	0.56	0.71	1
Total assets	N/A	N/A	N/A	0.98	1	1	1.2
EBITDA	0.27	0.18	0.03	0.05	0.09	0.12	0.2
Gross profit	N/A	N/A	N/A	N/A	N/A	N/A	N/A
Net profit	-0.1	-0.21	-0.43	-0.17	-0.06	0.35	-0.29
Foreign investment	N/A	N/A	N/A	N/A	N/A	N/A	N/A
Exports	N/A	N/A	N/A	N/A	N/A	N/A	N/A
Employees							
Countries	1	1	1	1	1	1	1

Further information is not available.
Data in hundreds of US dollars.
Source: Bloomberg

LESSONS FROM THE TELECOMMUNICATIONS INDUSTRY

América Móvil took advantage of the 2000 capital excess crisis within the information technology sector by acquiring assets of telecommunications enterprises below the original price, and became a prominent player in Latin America. At that time there were high expectations in the IT industry business cycle such that the industry capacity (for example, the excessive number of satellites launched in 1998) was above the demand. As was the case in Mexico, Carlos Slim's business expansion into Latin America was driven by his telecommunications investments. América Móvil is now the largest wireless telephone provider in the region, and also provides services such as fixed telephony, broadband, and pay-television, comprising 284 million accounts. It was a very strategic move to create a market for low-income households with a pay-as-you-go format with phone cards at several prices. Other strategies within this business model include using Telcel technologies to outperform local competitors, or to acquire dominant wireless communications firms in existing markets. The way forward is new markets reaching into Eastern Europe.[17]

América Móvil's extensive market share in Mexico generates economies of scale, which helps to fund the firm's expanding operations internationally. It is worth mentioning that, so far, América Móvil has operated in Mexico in a market with a very low competition level. Fortunately, for consumers, new regulations will allow for players to increase the supply of services, increase quality and reduce prices. Finally, the company runs business in a keiretsu fashion as in Japan or chaebol in South Korea.[18] All the firms associated with Carlos Slim are closely linked: financial services, retailing, media, and construction. Other companies such as AT&T (ranked number 1 in terms of revenues in 2013), Telefónica (ranked number 4 in terms of revenues in 2013), and TDC have expanded their business following América Móvil's steps: acquiring assets in its markets to reduce costs in order to increase its mark-ups. Nevertheless, strictly speaking, América Móvil followed the steps of Telefónica's internationalization process. It is worth mentioning that profits in US dollars generated in 2016 are below its historical trend because most currencies all over the world have depreciated with respect to the US currency.

On the other hand, Iusacell could not expand its business to international markets due to the lack of a sound position in the Mexican market. There are still attractive opportunities for globalization for this company as part of AT&T, though.

In this chapter we offer an overview of the evolution of two Mexican companies in the telecommunications industry. The figures that we present here are so dynamic because the sector is booming and constantly adopting better technology: New information is being released every day. However, the chapter aims to shed light on

---

17   PRS (2014).
18   In Japan, a keiretsu is a group of firms with close business links. In South Korea, this model of business is known as a chaebol.

the way América Móvil spectacularly expanded. For the future, we cannot yet reject the hypothesis that América Móvil could be a technological driver in the market, and interact with its main competitors.

REFERENCES

América Móvil. 2014. *Market Line*, September 20. www.marketline.com. Accessed May 31, 2015.

América Móvil. 2015. Annual reports from 2002 to 2015. www.americamovil.com/investor-relations/financial-reports/annual-report. Accessed in May 31, 2015.

Bejarano, O. 2014. *The Telecommunications Sector in Mexico: Present and Future in the Context of the 2014 Reform*. Working Paper. Rice University.

PWCs. 2015. Overview of the Telecommunication Sector in Mexico: Fixed and Mobile Lines. *Communications Review*. 16, No. 2.

González, R. 2008. *The Benefits of Privatization? The Mexican Experience in the Telecommunications Industry*. Paper to be presented at the Emerging Research on Political Economy and Public Policy Conference. The London School of Economics and Political Science.

Hernández, F. 2014. Mexico: The challenges of the new telecommunications and broadcasting law. *Hogan Lovells Global Media and Communications Quarterly*. Autumn.

IFT. Segundo Informe Trimestral Estadístico. 2015. www.ift.org.mx/sites/default/files/contenidogeneral/estadisticas/3ite16v4.pdf. Accessed November 8, 2015.

PRS. 2014. Country Report Updated as of December 2014. *PRS*, July. www.PRSgroup.com. Accessed May 31, 2015.

Noll, R. 2007. Priorities for Telecommunications Reform in Mexico. *World Bank*. Discussion Papers 06–035, Stanford Institute for Economic Policy Research. http://siteresources.worldbank.org/INTMEXICOINSPANISH/Resources/noll-paper.pdf. Accessed May 31, 2015.

Noll, R. 2013. *Assessing Telecommunications Policy in Mexico*. Discussion Papers 12–030, Stanford Institute for Economic Policy Research.

OECD. 2012. OECD Review of Telecommunication Policy and Regulation in Mexico. *OECD*. http://dx.doi.org/10.1787/9789264060111-enOECD. Accessed May 31, 2015.

OECD. 2013, *OECD Communications Outlook*. Paris: OECD Publishing.

Palacios, J. 2011. *Telecommunications Industry in Mexico: Performance and Market Structure Analysis, and Conflicts of Interest Prevailing between Operators and Authorities*. Mexican Institute for Competitiveness (IMCO).

Sidak, J. 2012. *The OECD's Proposal to Cartelize Mexican Telecommunications.* Competition Policy International.

Swarna, H. 2009. Mexican Telecom Industry: (Un)wanted Monopoly? *IBSCDC.* www.ibscdc.org. Accessed May 31, 2015.

GSMALA. 2014. The Mobile Economy Latin America. *GSMALA.* www.gsmala.com. Accessed May 31, 2015.

Winter, B. 2007. How Slim Got Huge. *Foreign Policy,* 163: 34–42. www.jstor.org/stable/25462229. Accessed May 31, 2015.

Santillana, I. & López, L. 2015. La internacionalización de Telefónica: reflexiones sobre un proceso. *El País.*

22 MultiMexicans in Professional Consultancy Services

Sintec and Feher & Feher

Lucía Rodríguez-Aceves and Angel E. Rivera[1]

INTRODUCTION

This chapter analyzes two Mexican consulting firms that expanded overseas in recent years. Sintec, founded in 1987 in Monterrey, Mexico, has developed more than 300 projects in commercial operations/supply chain strategies, with more than 100 leading companies in 14 Latin American countries over the last 25 years. On the other hand, Feher & Feher offers a full range of specialized services to entrepreneurs, businesses, and franchise networks. It has more than 750 clients, and in 2012 was recognized as the 17th highest impact incubator and the 21st best business accelerator by the Mexican Economic Ministry. Both Sintec and Feher & Feher have more than 20 years of experience and they have developed consulting projects in several countries. The internationalization process of this type of company presents interesting peculiarities, since its key resource is the knowledge that people have.

In order to get first-hand information, as well as to understand the viewpoints of the CEOs of the companies and explore the meanings they attribute to their experiences, understanding, and views about the internationalization process, four semi-structured in-depth

[1]   **Acknowledgements**
       We sincerely thank Oscar Lozano and Ferenz Feher, founders of SINTEC and Feher & Feher, respectively, and Ilan Ipelbaum, Feher & Feher's Commercial Chief Officer, for kindly agreeing to share their time and experience.
       Angel Rivera appreciates the support provided by the National Research System, at CONACYT, Mexico, as well as the Secretaría de Investigación y Posgrado and the program COFAA del Instituto Politécnico Nacional, México; particularly the projects SIP20161961 and SIP20151473 at IPN, México.
       Lucía Rodríguez-Aceves appreciates the support provided by the National Research System, at CONACYT, Mexico, as well as by the Tecnológico de Monterrey.

611

interviews were conducted face to face. The internationalization strategy used by these companies is based on exploiting the talent they possess and the talent available outside their structures.

Our findings allowed us to identify some lessons learned by the CEOs and CCOs interviewed from both companies. Some of the most important that can be mentioned are: the proper selection of people to run operating and strategic processes, creating strategic partnerships to enter in new markets, and the storage and transfer of best practices within companies to create an organizational memory. Such lessons can be useful to firms in the consultancy industry but also to companies in similar industries in order to create value and competitive advantages. This research contributes to the literature by breaking down the internationalization process into a more concrete concept from a people perspective, and it provides insights on the necessary elements and how they interact, in order to achieve the goals of emerging multinationals.

CONSULTANCY SERVICES INDUSTRY

Consulting is an industry that has been growing rapidly in recent decades due to the enterprise focus on understanding the market and the organization in order to become competitive and to ensure a company's survival and/or success in the marketplace. One peculiarity of companies in this industry is that knowledge is their core resource, and it is both the input and output in their production processes. In addition, three sources of sustainable differentiation have been identified.[2] First, greater specialist knowledge and expertise embedded into products and services. Second, closer and deeper client relationships, including a better understanding of what generates value for the customer. Lastly, greater knowledge transfer to the client, resulting in improved performance within the client organization.

---

[2]   Dawson (2000).

The first recognized management consulting firm was formed in 1886 by Arthur Dehon Little, a chemist from MIT, initially specializing in technical research. Frederick W. Taylor, an American mechanical engineer, was one of the first management consultants. He created his consulting practice in 1893. Some of their ideas about management improvement practices and the efficiency movement were published in his book, *The Principles of Scientific Management*. His business card read "Consulting Engineer – Systematizing Shop Management and Manufacturing Costs a Specialty."[3] In 1898, Coopers & Lybrand, as well as PricewaterhouseCoopers, were founded with a focus on accounting practice. In 1899, Harrington Emerson founded Emerson Company, which is probably the first company managed like a generalist consulting firm of today. Most of the other early consulting firms had an engineering orientation in this period.[4] In 1908, Harvard Business School was founded with a focus on professional management training. The first management consultancy to serve both industry and government clients was Booz Allen Hamilton, founded in 1914. In 1926, James O. McKinsey, an accounting professor at Northwestern University, founded McKinsey and Company. The firm called themselves "consultants and engineers" but mostly audited clients' books. Perhaps McKinsey is the first modern, pure management and strategy consulting company. After the Second World War, the growth in globalization aided the boom in consulting and saw the development of a number of tools, methods, and products. In 1963, Bruce Henderson founded Boston Consulting Group (BCG) and used experience curves, growth-share matrices, and some of the smartest graduates from US business schools as his tools. BCG became the first pure strategy consultancy. In 1973, William W. Bain Jr. left BCG to found Bain & Company, focusing on building heavy client relationships by sending dozens of consultants into companies. That was very new at the time and allowed Bain to grow very rapidly. On this same order of ideas, Marvin Bower, the CEO of McKinsey from

---

[3]   Gautier (2014).   [4]   Career in business (2012).

1950–67, developed the "professional" status of consultants, focusing on top MBA graduates.

Regarding consulting firms' contributions, from the 1940s to the 1960s they focused on structure and influenced the rise of "multi-departmental" models, which are still the spine of many great groups.[5] From the mid-1960s, consulting firms started to sell strategy rather than structure. By the end of the 1980s, consultants played a completely new role in firms: they would legitimize their strategy. During the 1980s, BCG created the experience curve and BCG Matrix for allocating resources within a portfolio of activities, and researchers like Michael Porter contributed to the creation and diffusion of the Industrial Organization model.

Recently, consultancy had continued to expand on the back of increasingly globalized companies, the information revolution, and cost cutting in government. In this sense, two important breaks in this trend have been the Dot-com crash (2000–2), which led to an increase in demand for consultancy services, and the Credit Crunch (2009–11), which represented the first decline in global consulting revenues for decades. Companies have developed advisory services in areas such as IT and strategic advice, in addition to their traditional auditing, accounting, or manufacturing services, such as, for example, IBM, Accenture, Deloitte, PwC, KPMG, and Ernst & Young. In order to get a sense of the importance of competitors, Table 22.1 presents the market share and revenues of the top consulting firms. It is noteworthy that only four of the companies account for 40 percent of the global consulting market. Such companies have a long tradition as described in the previous paragraphs.

Nowadays, the edges around the old distinctions between consulting, staffing, and outsourcing are fading. One of the major evolutionary trends is the progressive development of new collaborative frameworks, allowing a mix of large and small organizations to come together across specializations to create value for their clients (for

---

5   McKenna (2012).

Table 22.1 Consulting firms in Mexico

Firm	Country of origin	Year of foundation	Revenues	Services	Employees in the world	Geographical presence	First office in Mexico (year)	Offices in Mexico	Employees in Mexico
Accenture	United States, but headquarters in Dublin, Ireland	1989	US$30 billion (2014)	Global management consulting, technology services, and outsourcing company	323,000	120 countries	1990	Mexico City and Monterrey	N/A*
Boston Consulting Group (BCG)	United States	1963	US$4.55 billion (2014)	Post-merger integration, technology, operations, strategy, corporate finance, and development	9,700 (6,200 consultants)	80 offices in 46 countries	1993	Mexico City and Monterrey	N/A
Deloitte	United States (New York)	1845	US$34.2 billion (2014)	Enterprise Risk Services (ERS), business process outsourcing, human capital, operations, risks, strategy, technology	200,000	680 offices in 150 countries	1906	22 offices in Mexican territory	5,400

Table 22.1 (cont.)

Firm	Country of origin	Year of foundation	Revenues	Services	Employees in the world	Geographical presence	First office in Mexico (year)	Offices in Mexico	Employees in Mexico
Ernst & Young	United States & London, UK	1989	US$27.40 billion (2014)	Assurance services (45%); tax services (26%); advisory services (20%); Transaction Advisory Services (TAS) (9%)	190,000	Worldwide	1990	19 offices in Mexican territory	N/A
PricewaterhouseCoopers (PwC)	United Kingdom (London) / Merger of US, UK, and Canada	1998	US$34 billion (2014)	Audit and insurance, legal, family business services, tax, advisory	184,235	776 offices in 157 countries	N/A	21 offices in Mexican territory	N/A
McKinsey & Company	United States, Chicago	1926	US$7.8 billion (2013)	Business technology; corporate finance; marketing & sales; operations; organization; risk; strategy; sustainability & resource productivity	17,000	100 offices in 50 countries	1970	Mexico City and Monterrey	N/A
Sintec	Mexico	1987	N/A	Operations strategy, organizational transformation, customer	154	4 offices in 3 countries	1987	Mexico City and Monterrey	154

Table 22.1 (*cont.*)

Firm	Country of origin	Year of foundation	Revenues	Services	Employees in the world	Geographical presence	First office in Mexico (year)	Offices in Mexico	Employees in Mexico
				strategy, business analytics, and optimization					
Feher & Feher	Mexico	2002	N/A	Finance; internationalization; prevention and legal solutions; design; international franchise; business training	Around 70	4 offices in 3 countries	2002	Mexico City	N/A

*N/A = No data available

Source: Own elaboration with data from companies' websites and other sources.

example, collaborations between technology vendors and business consultants). Some of them are new structures of multi-party colla-boration to gain global coverage and capabilities in research, sales, and delivery of products and services. Also, consulting models such as the hybrid staffing/consulting models have overtaken the markets, where blended teams of permanent staff and contract labor are key.

It is noteworthy that in the emerging markets (Latin America, the Middle East, and others), the consultancy maturity level is less than one generation old.[6]

Consultancy Services Overview in Mexico

In Mexico, during the period 2002–9, the professional services sector grew around 4.1 percent per year. The industry is mainly comprised of firms in the following specialties: legal advice and representation, accounting, architecture, engineering, computer services, consulting services, research, and advertising.[7]

As in Latin America, in Mexico, the consultancy industry is an element barely present in the knowledge economic map. The statistics do not allow for precise descriptions of the Mexican markets in the professional service sector, and what is known must be treated carefully. From The National Institute of Statistics and Geography's (INEGI)[8] census, in 2004 and 2014, it is known that the economic units registered under the NAICS[9] code "5416 Management, scientific and technical consulting services" increased from 2784 to 5162. In other words, in ten years the number of busi-nesses dedicated to this kind of consulting services increased by 85.4 percent. Surprisingly, the number of employees in the subsector decreased by 8.3 percent in the same period. Regarding the total income, it had an important increase from Mex$19.3 billion in 2004 to Mex$24.6 billion in 2009, which is an increase of 27.4 percent. The opposite occurred from 2009 to 2014, with a decrease of 23.8 percent.

---

6   Consulting ideas (2010).   7   Accenture (2012).   8   INEGI (2014)
9   NAICS is the North American Industry Classification System.

It is difficult to attribute to one particular factor the large increase in 2009 and then the significant decrease in the total income. Nevertheless, it is evident that the global economic crisis had an important impact in the consultancy industry. After 2009, many companies that had running projects stopped them, since the main focus at that point was on survival. Besides, Federal Government expenditures were contracted and consequently the whole industry was affected. The main effect of the economic crisis was after 2009, since in 2008 the Scientific and Technical Professional Services sector produced a total income of US$1.6 billion, which was 1.25 percent of the Gross Domestic Product and provided direct jobs to 578,000 people.[10] In 2009, the National Business Consultancy Council (CNEC by its Spanish acronym)[11] estimated that the total demand for consultancy services was around US$5 billion, distributed in the following manner: US$1,500 million from the private sector, US$2,000 million from the federal government, and US$1,500 million from the local governments. Moreover, 450 firms were affiliated with this sector, and approximately 50 of those firms reported more than 100 employees.

Regarding the Mexican consulting market in 2013, the sectors of financial services and services in general were at the top in the ranking of nine, with a value of Mex$164.6 million and Mex$93 million, respectively. At the bottom, the healthcare sector had a value of Mex$13.3 million, and pharma and biotech a value of Mex$6.5 million. In 2014, Source Information Services Limited estimated, based on a research study, that "big consulting" market size, referring to consulting done by firms with more than 50 consultants globally and for clients with revenues more than US$500 million, was about US $550.1 million.[12] This number represents 70 percent of the Mexican market, making the entire market worth US$785.87 million.

It is worth mentioning that, regarding the services sector, in 2013 an increased demand for operations, financial management,

[10]   Casartelli (2010).   [11]   CNEC (2015).   [12]   Global Source (2014).

and technology consulting occurred. Operational improvement was the biggest consulting service in 2013. It is well known that, with changes in horizons, companies choose to invest internally, focusing on supply chain strategies and optimization projects, as supply chains grow international tentacles and increase in complexity. The market for financial management and risk consulting is the second consulting service in size. In this regard, the government's financial reforms and the introduction of new taxes have been keeping consultants busy, as clients seek to adapt their businesses to ensure compliance. Increased investment and new companies entering the Mexican market represent good news for consultants who can help businesses establish themselves in a new geography. In addition, due to governmental reforms aiming to increase competition, those in financial services, telecoms, energy, and resources must adapt their businesses to a changing landscape. This, certainly, is a fertile field for consultants, particularly those with expertise in these sectors.

As firms wake up to the strategic importance of opportunities in Mexico, the competition in the country's consulting market is intensifying. Although growing, the consulting market is still relatively small, and reputations matter a great deal in what some have described as a "relationship market." In some ways, large firms with global brands are at an advantage in terms of getting in front of clients; their all-important reputation precedes them, while smaller firms need to work harder to make connections with prospective clients.

The history of the consultancy industry in Mexico is not sufficiently documented. In order to contribute to this particular issue, Table 22.1 was elaborated. Table 22.1 presents information about the main consulting firms in Mexico nowadays. In particular, it contains the year in which each opened its first office in the country, as well as its geographical presence and the number of employees. Mostly, the firms started operations in Mexico at the beginning of the 90s, probably motivated by the North American Free Trade Agreement and the opening of the Mexican frontiers in general.

As shown in Table 22.1, in Mexico some of the most important global consultancy firms have offices in Mexico, such as Accenture, Boston Consulting Group (BCG), Deloitte Consulting, Ernst & Young, PricewaterhouseCoopers (PwC), McKinsey & Company, and others.[13] Nevertheless, there are some firms created by Mexican entrepreneurs competing against the global referents, and entering new markets such as the United States and Latin America, like, for example, Sintec and Feher & Feher. In Table 22.1, we compared the country of origin, year of foundation, annual revenues for 2014, services offered, number of employees, and geographical presence of the previously mentioned consulting firms.

It is our interest to get a deep insight regarding how those Mexican consultancy firms started. What was their process of internationalization? How did the firms decide which country to expand to? As Table 22.1 shows, Mexican firms are younger and considerably smaller in terms of revenues, number of employees, and geographical scope in comparison with the rest of the firms; nevertheless, they are successfully competing in Mexico and overseas.

CASES

The two cases described in this section are Sintec and Feher & Feher. Both are Mexican consulting firms with a presence overseas. On the one hand, Sintec has over 25 years of experience, during which time it has developed more than 300 projects with more than 100 leading companies in 14 Latin American countries. In this sense, Sintec occupies 19th place in the CNNExpansión ranking of Super Companies with fewer than 500 employees.[14] On the other hand, Feher & Feher has over 20 years of experience, more than 750 clients, and in 2012 was recognized as the 17th highest-impact incubator and the 21st best business accelerator by the Mexican Economic Ministry.

---

[13] Management Consulting Case Interviews (2015).   [14]   CNN Expansión (2009).

Sintec Consultancy Firm

Sintec is a consulting firm generating profitable growth in leading Latin American companies through its holistic customer and operations strategies. The firm bases its consulting model on the development of organizational core competencies that allow their clients to generate unique capabilities based on organization, processes, and IT. During the last 25 years, Sintec has developed more than 300 projects in commercial operations/supply chain strategies, with more than 100 leading companies in 14 Latin American countries. The consultancy firm has offices in Mexico City; Monterrey, Mexico; Bogotá, Colombia; and São Paulo, Brazil. Also, it is noteworthy that Sintec has important strategic alliances with SAP, Oracle, Rapid-I, and Gurobi Optimization.

Sintec's clients include Grupo Bimbo, the largest Mexican-owned baking company; Nestlé, the Swiss multinational food and beverage company; Coca-Cola FEMSA, the largest beverage company in Mexico and in Latin America; Cemex, the MultiMexican classified as one of the world's largest producers of building materials; GM, the automobile manufacturing company; and many others.

The firm's success is based on the excellence of its consulting team, its profound practice insight, its vast project execution experience, and the high involvement of its partners and directors in projects. Thus, Sintec was recognized by *Expansión* and *Top Companies* magazines as a Super Company. Also, in 2011 and 2012, Sintec was certified as a "Great Place to Work."

Sintec is not a public firm and, for reasons of confidentiality, it was not possible to obtain additional information about the evolution of financial data beyond that shown in Table 22.2. Nevertheless, in order to have a general context of the firm, Table 22.2 shows Sintec's constant growth in terms of income as a percentage of the total income in 2008.

In addition, Table 22.2 presents overseas income compared with the total, and makes evident the constant growth of the firm, except

Table 22.2 *Sintec income and number of employees (income growth versus year 2008)*

Year	Total income versus year 2008	Overseas income versus total income	Number of employees
2008	100%	12%	N/A
2009	77%	14%	72
2010	111%	18%	91
2011	185%	26%	107
2012	194%	34%	125
2013	228%	21%	153
2014	245%	42%	154

Source: Own elaboration with data obtained from interviews

for the year 2013. Additionally, Table 22.2 shows Sintec's growth in terms of the number of employees, and highlights the fact that the consultancy firm employed 80 people in 2009 and ended 2014 with 154 employees.

On the same order of ideas, Table 22.3 shows a timeline that describes the years when Sintec offices were opened, in Mexico and overseas. Table 22.3 proves the rapid growth of the firm after 2009. In three years, three new offices started successful operations in two different countries.

Sintec has developed strengths that have positioned it as a very competitive business consulting company. The vision of its leader, the formalization of its processes, and the talent of its people have led to its expansion and standardization in different offices around the world. The firm's monitoring and control processes and the exchange of best practices among all staff are coordinated by the department of knowledge management, which has given the firm a competitive advantage in the market.

Table 22.3 *Sintec timeline of key events*

Year	Local	International
1987	Sintec is founded in Monterrey by Oscar Lozano.	
1993	Sintec initiates the process of consolidation and expansion (e.g., strengthen market position, internal processes).	
1999		Sintec opens an office in Barcelona, with no success. The office closes after a year. The lack of demand, the presence of a strong competitor, and the incorrect selection of the office manager were the causes.
2004	Sintec integrates an advisory board with external experts. As the company grew rapidly, it was necessary to make wiser decisions.	
2008	The global economic crisis starts. This situation initiates the internationalization of the company.	
2009		Sintec opens an office in Bogotá, Colombia, to serve South America and the Caribbean. The location is selected based on the volume of clients already demanding Sintec services.
2011	Sintec opens a new office in Mexico City to serve as the headquarters for a number of clients in the domestic market. The location responds to the geographical proximity to key clients.	

Table 22.3 (cont.)

Year Local	International
2013	Sintec opens an office in São Paolo, Brazil, to serve the Brazilian market. In São Paolo, one important client had a contract with Sintec and the market represented a huge opportunity for the company.

Source: Own elaboration with data obtained from interviews and secondary data

Finally, social responsibility is a key topic at Sintec. In the last 10 years, the firm has helped over 20 non-profit organizations through financial donations and consulting projects under the umbrella of the Sintec Ser Campaign.

Sintec's History and Internationalization

Throughout Sintec's history, critical phases have been decisive in understanding what the consultancy firm represents today. Founded in 1987 in Monterrey, Mexico, the firm rapidly identified the regional market opportunities, and until 2009 was highly concentrated in the domestic market. During the first ten years of Sintec, the firm worked for regional companies in the north of Mexico, undertaking specific projects in some management areas. Clients got in touch with Sintec generally through word-of-mouth recommendations. In this period, the company implemented a model called "suitcase consulting." This business model provided personalized services to companies, but few projects were developed and people had to go door-to-door to promote the services of the company. In 1999, when the company had 15 employees based in Monterrey, the CEO started a deliberate effort to strengthen the name of the firm in the region, and he made the decision to expand and consolidate the company as a consultancy firm. In addition, he initiated a process of recruitment and selection of human capital, defined compensation policies, and approached three partners. In 2004, an advisory council with external experts was integrated.

According to Oscar Lozano, Sintec's CEO, the professionalization of Sintec lasted about ten years, and this allowed the firm to develop complex projects abroad. From 1987 to 2009, the company developed several projects overseas (e.g., Brazil, Colombia, Venezuela, and the Dominican Republic), mainly with customers previously attended to in the Mexican territory, such as Coca-Cola FEMSA and Panamco. "We did a project in the Dominican Republic, specifically a Telephone Company owned by an executive with whom we previously had developed projects here in Monterrey."[15]

Sintec's international experience began with the coordination of some projects in Latin America, in particular in Colombia. Nevertheless, the offices in that country served only to deliver services and to find prospective new clients. In these kinds of projects, Sintec did not have a consultancy team there, and only sent one person and an assistant to support and advise the company overseas. In all those early international experiences, the business model was to go abroad, support the clients, but maintain the base in Monterrey. Those projects did not represent an important part of Sintec's operations. According to Oscar Lozano, "Sintec also had other projects in the United States for Mexican companies with operations in that country ... at least two projects there ... That model was circumstantial rather than strategic ... if somebody called them to contract their services, they traveled where it was necessary," said Lozano.

In 2009, when the operations remained mainly in Monterrey, the well-known economic crisis affected all kind of industries, and consultancy services were no exception. The Mexican Gross Domestic Product dropped dramatically, by nearly 6.5 percent. This situation seriously affected Sintec's operations and motivated the

---

[15]   Interview with Oscar Lozano, Sintec founder and CEO, conducted by the authors on February 4, 2015.

CEO and founder to make radical changes, initiating the internationalization process that has continued to evolve since then. Sintec established a board of directors, who recommended expanding overseas. "At the end of 2009, one advisor of Sintec's board of directors suggested that I attend an event related to the consultancy industry. There I met two consultants ... of consultancy firms ... At that moment, I knew that staying still, static, was not an option ... we must expand overseas ... we had already experienced the economic crisis and the best option was to start the expansion ... we could not keep doing things as always ... If we had not made the decision to expand, we do not know what would be happening today."[16]

Since that day, the internationalization process was focused on exploiting Sintec's competences and capabilities to have success in other markets. It is noteworthy that it was not clear which market to select. Dallas in the United States was a temptation, since it is geographically near to Monterrey and would open a window to one of the strongest economies. In order to make the best decisions, Sintec and the board of directors developed a strategy to follow. "With these two people we developed a strategy to expand Sintec. We had to internationalize the firm, and we choose Latin America because our expertise was mainly related to companies' concerns in that region ... we also had good relationships with clients that had a presence in Latin America," said Lozano.

Once the decision to expand to Latin America was made, there were other important decisions to make inside the company. The first decision was to select the partners and employees that would relocate outside Monterrey. In this expansion plan, keeping 90 percent of the employees based in Monterrey was not an option. The decision was to keep two of the five partners of the firm in Monterrey and the rest went to Mexico City and to Colombia, and the company also recruited one new person to become the head of the office in Brazil. According to Sintec's CEO, "they wanted to expand Sintec to Latin America ... they

[16] Interview with Oscar Lozano, Sintec founder and CEO, conducted by the authors on November 26, 2014.

had to create offices, strengthen, and expand them ... to have the resources where they were required ... In order to do that, they had to relocate employees."

After studying and designing the strategy, Sintec decided to open offices in São Paolo, Brazil, and in Bogotá, Colombia. Each of the offices focuses on different strategic sectors. The decision to open these two offices overseas was supported by the existence of essential elements in those markets. Those elements are not present in every market, because of the variation in regional development, talent availability, infrastructure, and other factors. Due to the type of consultancy Sintec offered, the markets that they could expand into had to have peculiar characteristics. There had to be a critical mass of universities, available talent, a professional management culture, and other elements. "The markets where we can expand to, must have a sufficient size, density, and professional management culture, among other elements. Bogotá and São Paolo have all that, but no other cities in the region ... you have to select very well the market you are looking to enter," said Lozano.

Sintec's internationalization process considered exactly what were the minimum elements necessary to open an office. Nevertheless, the process was complex and took time. For example, in the case of Brazil, Sintec spent a year interviewing Brazilian people to recruit the head of the office. Then, it took another year for the new manager to learn about Sintec's work environment. Afterwards, the firm had to go through all the formalities to legally register the office and shape the business. Finally, it took another year and a half to start operations and let the market know Sintec was there. In the end, it took two to three years to open the new office in Brazil; then they just had to wait and expect to work well. "To open an office is one of the most complex processes in a city or a country. It is not easy ... you have to comply with legal, tax, labor, and general culture differences, but also work culture differences. You have to devote a lot of energy."[17]

---

[17]   Interview with Oscar Lozano, Sintec founder and CEO, conducted by the authors on November 26, 2014.

Even in the expansion process, there were errors that cost the firm money, but overall the firm gained great experience regarding what should not be done in the internationalization process. Prior to 2009, for just an accidental or circumstantial situation, Sintec opened an office in Barcelona in Spain, and it was not a good experience. When the firm went there, it had no clients, so the consultants started from scratch and tried to understand the market once it was there. In the end, the company realized that the market was a small one regarding the type of services it offered at that time, and in addition there was a strong competitor. "Prior to 2009, we opened an office in Barcelona in Spain. We sent the wrong person to manage the office, we did not have any clients there, the market did not have enough need for our services, and there was a strong competitor. A success in that office would have been a miracle. Everything was designed and ready to end in a failure," said Sintec's CEO.

Those mistakes helped to strengthen Sintec's internationalization strategy. The company tried to eliminate the mistakes when it opened the office in Brazil, and today the firm recognizes its early mistakes as critical factors of success in its subsequent internationalization process. When Sintec opened its office in Brazil, it hired a Brazilian manager who knew the market and had a great network, and sent two of the best managers in Mexico to form a team with the Brazilian manager. Also, it only opened the office once it had a good client there, which gave the business some certainty. According to Oscar Lozano, "When they opened the office in Brazil, they tried to avoid all the mistakes made in Spain. In general, the right decisions were related to human capital. The combination was hiring a Brazilian that knew the market and had a great network, as well as relocating two Mexicans, which by the way cost a lot."

The internationalization process is a complex one that should not be taken lightly. In this process, planning where to go and what to do is one of the most important issues. Sintec's growth abroad is an ongoing but steady process. In fact, the company is considering whether to enter industries where they have no existing involvement, as well as whether to enter countries with the right conditions to prosper. "In the future, I think that Sintec is going to have more people and knowledge ... We are going to have offices in other parts of the world ... We have to participate in specific industries ... We need to develop bigger and stronger offices," said Lozano.

Feher & Feher Consultancy Firm

Feher & Feher is a Mexican consulting firm offering a full range of specialized services to entrepreneurs, businesses, and franchise networks. In 2014, Feher & Feher was distinguished as a socially responsible company, because the wellbeing of its stakeholders is aligned with its strategic and operative processes. Feher & Feher clients include Bosch, the global leader in mobility solutions and consumer goods; Ilusion, a Mexican company dedicated to the manufacture of underwear; +Kota, a well-known Mexican pet care chain; Exxon Mobil, an American multinational oil and gas corporation; Sushi Itto, a Mexican food chain; and others.

Like Sintec, Feher & Feher is not a public firm. Therefore, it was not possible to obtain data relating to the financial evolution of the company. Nevertheless, the firm's history, as explained in the following lines, reveals interesting facts that make evident the success of the firm.

In 2002, Ferenz Feher founded the Feher & Feher Consultancy firm, aiming to offer integral solutions for the development and growth of the business sector. Initially, the firm was small and totally focused on developing franchises. The CEO had expertise in the franchise sector because he was the first franchise director of the electronics company Steren in Mexico. During the next six years, the company developed remarkable expertise in this area.

Soon, Feher & Feher realized that entrepreneurs seek not only to develop franchises, but in some cases also to strengthen their business in terms of the design, development, and implementation of strategic and operational processes before development of the franchise. Offering all these activities as a consultancy service was an area of opportunity for Feher & Feher, as well as a competitive advantage in the sector. In 2009, in order to respond to the market demand, the firm entered the area of business consultancy. In particular, clients wanted to start franchises from scratch, therefore the firm began to offer services like business plan elaboration, business conceptualization, market validation, copyrights, commercial plans, and so on. Afterwards, new opportunities opened for Feher & Feher. Bancomer, which is one of the most important banks in Mexico, hired the firm to standardize their processes, in order to operate as a franchise in different regions in the country. Later on, the Mexican Administration Service (SAT) hired Feher & Feher's services under the same principle as Bancomer. One of the most important projects in this area was with Coparmex, which is the most important union in Mexico, with more than 36,000 member companies throughout Mexico that are responsible for 30 percent of the GDP and 4.8 million formal jobs. Feher & Feher standardized all the Coparmex offices in the country. Consequently, since the company started, out of the total sales of the firm, 60 percent correspond to franchises and 40 percent to the business area.

Regarding the franchising area, in 2011 the firm decided to divide this branch depending on the sector it was serving, in order to encourage specialization. For example, the firm identified an important niche in the market in the food service industry – 31 percent of the franchises in Mexico are related to this industry – so Feher & Feher created a department entirely dedicated to this sector. Other divisions include retail and services, and the social franchising which is related to civil organizations that want to replicate their models. In 2012, Feher & Feher opened the Franchise Store to commercialize franchises. Through that entity, the firm works with more than 100 brands and continuously sells new units. Along the same lines, the firm also offers consultancy services to existing franchises that want to become more efficient and profitable, or want to accelerate their growth through expansion and diversification. Table 22.4 shows a timeline of the key events in Feher & Feher's history.

Table 22.4 *Feher & Feher timeline of most relevant events*

Year	Local	International
2002	Ferenz Feher, who previously had experience in successfully franchising an electronics business named Steren, founds F&F in Mexico City. He rents a big house in Polanco with the vision of a fast growth.	
2003–2008		F&F offers consulting services related to franchises. The company creates an identity and gains prestige as the experts in franchising in Mexico.
2008		F&F opens its first office in Sherman Oaks, in Los Angeles, USA. The company becomes the opener of the Latin American market for franchising American brands.
2009	F&F starts offering business-consulting services. Because of the different services required by the existing clients, F&F responds with the offering of consulting services in incubation and acceleration.	
2011	The firm creates divisions in the franchising area (e.g., retail, food service, and beverages). The rapid growth and the variety of industries attended to increases the necessity of specialization.	
2012	F&F opens the Franchise Store in order to seize the opportunity	

Table 22.4 (cont.)

Year	Local	International
	to commercialize brands with the potential for growth. F&F is recognized as an impact incubator and business accelerator.	
2013		F&F opens an office in Guatemala. Based on a strategic alliance with a renowned law firm in that country, F&F opens the door to introduce brands and develop new ones in the new market.
2014	F&F is recognized as a socially responsible company. F&F is constantly standardizing its internal processes.	

Source: Own elaboration with data obtained from interviews and secondary data

Public relations were and are one of the most important factors in the operation and success of the company. The human, personalized care and close contact with clients are some of the key activities that the firm undertakes in order to be different. The offered services are franchise consulting, business consulting, business incubation, business acceleration, business financial consulting, franchise development (franchise sales), international consulting (franchise & business), legal consulting (Mexico), design services, and corporate training. "We help our customers and friends to build their dreams ... we support them in order to potentiate, expand, and grow their companies ... whether this is related to franchising, incubation, acceleration ... the common denominator is the search for growth and creation of new jobs."[18]

Feher & Feher's expertise regarding franchising is one of its biggest advantages. It specializes in topics such as the legal framework, manual development, financial aspects regarding royalties and franchise fees, and even the evaluation of whether a business has the minimum elements to become a franchise.

Feher & Feher has offices in Mexico City; Los Angeles, California; Miami, Florida; and Guatemala. In addition, it has international alliances with important firms such as Edward Global Systems (EGS), Barbadillo & Associates (B&A), Cherto, and Asiawide Franchise. Moreover, it has important client firms such as Deloitte, Finmex, Smart Location, Endeavor, the Friedman Group, and others.

Feher & Feher's Internationalization Process

Nowadays, Feher & Feher owns subsidiaries in three different countries. Also, it has partial ownership of offices in Peru and Spain and an international presence in more than 15 countries through the International Franchise Consultants Network (IFCN).[19]

The internationalization process of a company responds to several factors and particular circumstances. In some cases, this process derives from a structured planning process, as is mostly the case for companies that are already consolidated in their home markets. Sometimes, it is an unstructured process perhaps motivated to seize a particular opportunity related to an economic crisis or frontier opening. In Feher & Feher's case, one of the most important factors influencing the decision to start the internationalization process was the way of thinking of the CEO and founder of the company. For him, Mexico is an important element in the consolidation process, but the real market is outside Mexico. All of the projects Feher & Feher plans

---

[18]   Interview with Ferenz Feher, Feher & Feher founder and CEO, conducted by the authors on April 14, 2015.

[19]   www.ifcn-international.com.

and implements take into account both the domestic market and the overseas market. "I travel twice a week in the Mexican territory and other countries, from one city to another, meeting new places and new people, learning from others' experience and accumulating my own expertise ... and that is where we can identify opportunities ... Mexico is a great market where we are consolidated today as a company, nevertheless, that does not mean it will be the same in the medium or long term ... for such reason, we have to move to other markets, to look for new opportunities and to see what others cannot ... that is the only way we can keep awake and alert," said Ferenz Feher.

Two factors strongly motivated Feher & Feher's international presence: the entrepreneurial mindset of the CEO, Ferenz Feher, and the constant connection and interaction with the industry environment. For example, the firm participated in international events, as well as a constant interchange of experiences at an international level. According to Ferenz Feher, Feher & Feher, "The International Franchise Consultants Network (IFCN) invited Feher & Feher to join the association, and twice a year they participated in such forum in order to learn and keep up with the best practices regarding the franchising industry overseas ... that knowledge motivated them to implement new projects in Mexico."

The CEO of Feher & Feher spends much of his time searching for new trade shows to participate in; therefore, the firm is always aware of what is going on in the industry. In this sense, Feher & Feher's internationalization process started with international networking.

One key element in Feher & Feher's internationalization process is without doubt the trust and confidence created with important clients in the domestic market. Such trust is the result of a close relationship, understanding, and compromise with client companies. One of Feher & Feher's strengths is that it deeply analyzes its customers' characteristics, and understands the companies and the way the clients think, so they are empathetic and act as if the clients' companies were their own. "An intrinsic characteristic of Feher & Feher is latent in our slogan: professionalism with warmth. This topic is essential. We make new friends instead of new customers ... therefore I believe that trust and confidence are fundamental issues in consultancy services and in Feher & Feher we seed that," said Ferenz Feher.

In addition, another strength is the active participation in the franchising industry that increases Feher & Feher's business knowledge, which allows it to solve real problems and develop real solutions based on expertise by practicing. For example, some of Feher & Feher's managers also own and run businesses. "We are not theoretical consultants, following a method. On the contrary, we are involved in business operations ... in my case, I have been a franchisor, a franchisee, and an investor ... we lead by example, we are franchisors, franchisees, and investors ... we are people involved in the operation and for this reason we are familiar with both sides of the equation" said Feher & Feher's founder and CEO.

In summary, trust is a key component of the success of Feher & Feher's projects, and several factors contribute to promoting and strengthening it. Among them are the firm's specialist knowledge about the franchise business, friendly and personalized service, and guarantee of confidentiality of information.

Another strength in Feher & Feher's internationalization process was the exploitation of its core business process: the development of franchises. The domestic market knowledge, as well as the trust and confidence created with its Mexican clients, enabled the expansion of the company overseas. Feher & Feher opened its first office in Los Angeles, in Sherman Oaks, with the idea of bringing American brands to Mexico, but also bringing Mexican brands to the United States. 95 percent of the brands that the company manages in the United States have a Mexican origin. The key to entering the American market was the trust and confidence that clients previously developed with Feher & Feher in Mexico. It was not easy to enter the United States, but the firm benefited from its long-term relationships with Mexican clients. "We sell experience and expertise ... that is what our customers buy from us ... when you buy a consultancy service, you pay for the experience. We have developed more than 750 franchises; therefore, we have seen a lot ... many different obstacles and troubles that can happen in a franchise. What you buy from Feher & Feher is experience to reduce your learning curve."[20]

COMPARISON AND CONCLUSIONS

Our results suggest that there are some lessons derived from these two experiences in the process of internationalization that can help other Mexican firms and other firms in emerging economies. Overall, our results confirm that an entrepreneurial mindset and managerial skills are two significant factors in a firm's internationalization.

The CEOs of the two companies examined here appear to have clear ideas about the importance of establishing people, clear markets, customers, and partners before going overseas. In this regard, the internationalization process seems to be most focused around improvements in strategic issues (e.g., monitoring and control practices) and in people's talent (e.g., the transfer of best practices).

In order to identify a pattern in the internationalization process or specific mechanisms to do it, we compared particular elements of each company. The establishment of differences is based on three factors: market selection, internationalization motive, and cooperative strategies. We also describe similarities between the two companies based on six factors: expansion strategy, entry mode, monitoring and control, transfer of best practices, entrepreneurial mindset, and talent (see Table 22.5).

The cases analyzed in this chapter have particular characteristics regarding the context of their internationalization, and for this reason we identified some of the barriers, enablers, and other peculiar aspects that emerged after the interview analysis. The main barriers include regulations, unions, and money transfer. The principal

---

[20] Interview with Ilan Ipelbaum, Feher & Feher Commercial CEO, conducted by the authors on December 3, 2014.

Table 22.5 *Comparison summary (differences, similarities, barriers, enablers, and peculiar aspects)*

Factor	SINTEC	Feher & Feher
Differences		
Market selection (first office opened)	Emerging market (Latin America)	Advanced economy (United States)
Internationalization motive	2009 economic crisis	1. Seize opportunities in a new market
		2. CEO's entrepreneurial mindset
Cooperative strategy	No cooperative strategies	Strategic alliance in Guatemala
Similarities		
Expansion strategy	Consolidation in the domestic market, to create long-term relationships. Afterwards, expand overseas.	
Entry mode	Open a new office overseas (subsidiary).	
Monitoring and control	Relocate employees and partners to consolidate offices overseas.	
Transfer of best practices	Send managers of the domestic market to the offices overseas in order to share experiences.	
Entrepreneurial mindset	CEO's vision; the domestic market was not enough.	
Talent	An essential factor is talent; both in the domestic market and overseas.	
Barriers	1. Regulations	1. Regulations
	2. Unions	
	3. Money transfer	
Enablers	1. Structured internationalization strategy	1. Networking overseas
	2. Long-term relationships with clients in the domestic market	2. Prestige
	3. Prestige	3. New market idiosyncrasy

Table 22.5 *(cont.)*

Factor	SINTEC	Feher & Feher
Peculiar aspects	1. CEOs and founders are graduates of the same university, which is a renowned private school in Mexico.	1. CEOs and founders are graduates of the same university, which is a renowned private school in Mexico.
	2. CEO considers that opening new offices is a big responsibility, more than a feeling of pride or satisfaction.	2. Professionalism and human consciousness is something present in the CEO and all the Feher & Feher community.

Source: Own elaboration with data obtained from interviews

enablers include a structured internationalization strategy, long-term relationships with clients in the domestic market, prestige, networking overseas, and new market idiosyncrasy (see Table 22.5). Summarizing the content of Table 22.5, we can argue that particularly in the consultancy industry, human resource is a crucial aspect when expanding overseas. Selection and recruitment requires at least three times more effort when opening an office in a new market. On the one hand, it is hard to relocate experienced employees to other countries. It is hard for employees either to leave their families or to take them to the new location. Sometimes, they will prefer to leave the company rather than relocate abroad. On the other hand, the company's name is not well known in the new market; therefore, talented people will not be enthusiastic about joining the company.

A company's success in the consultancy industry depends greatly on prestige and recognition. Therefore, long-time relationships based on trust and confidence are key to both surviving in a market and entering a new one. Furthermore, empathy, quality, warmth, efficiency, and great results are crucial. Moreover, in general, attending events related to the industry is important. In both cases, the CEO's regularly attend events in order to keep up with new trends, reinforce networks, and meet possible customers. It is important to mention that the success of some other services industries such as tourism, software, and food, among others, depends on intangibles like the consultancy industry. In these kinds of industries, the management of intangibles is the basis for generating continuous value over time. The first step is to recognize that intangibles are different from traditional resources, and therefore should be managed carefully. In some companies, specific departments have been created in order to respond to this challenge, as when Sintec created the position of a Chief Knowledge Officer.

In another vein, developing a structured international strategy is essential. Sintec's first attempt to enter Barcelona's market was a bad experience. The firm did not have clients, market knowledge, or previous relationships. It was a decision taken based on a hunch. The evidence suggests, at least in the two cases examined in this chapter, that cooperative strategies can open new opportunities in new markets and reduce the learning curve. Feher & Feher entered Guatemala with a strategic alliance. The partner selection was key, since the law office in Guatemala was the most prestigious and recognized in the country. Joining with a sound partner allowed Feher & Feher to strengthen its position.

The launching or implementing stage implies a set of subprocesses, including the definition of the internationalization strategy, the opening of the new office, adaptation to the environment, the improvement and feedback, and finally the expansion within the new market. In both firms studied here, the elements of each of the sub processes were developed according to the firm's capabilities and strengths. It is noteworthy to mention that in the last two stages of the launching process – this is, in the consolidation stage – we identify a continuous feedback loop in which both firms use a variety of tools in order to transfer best practices among their business units.

These findings allow us to suggest some recommendations for other managers. The success of a consulting business is based on the identification and transfer of knowledge, capabilities, and competences, and the way in which they are applied in order to generate value in organizations. Consequently, the best and most valuable resources of such companies are the employees' talent and knowledge. For internationalization, talent can be outside organizational boundaries, and therefore strategic alliances with recognized organizations that possess complementary talent are highly recommended. The finding of key actors in order to develop overseas projects is fundamental. The quality of relationships between participants in these alliances can generate favorable conditions for the company in unknown places.

Moreover, in the analyzed cases the way the firms manage their processes is crucial. The proper definition of administrative, operational, and support processes, the documents that support them, and the implementation and transfer of best practices of these processes are key elements in generating value. According to people from these two companies, the knowledge acquired over time through the practices of consultancy in various case studies has been the most important resource, since it has allowed the redesign of current practices and even extended the domain of new consulting application areas. In general, the internationalization process of both companies required two principal components, one of planning and the other of launching or implementing. In both cases, the talent of people inside and outside the company was the key to success.

Finally, it is important to consider Ferenz Feher's advice to companies that want to expand overseas: "First of all, avoid the fear of failure ... second, plan before opening a new business or office in another market ... today, distances are not a barrier, and neither are languages ... nevertheless, keep it simple and select a country where your idiosyncrasy and language are similar ... It is also relevant to consider doing business as close as possible to your headquarters ... But more important than everything else, we must learn to win based on what others let you win."

In conclusion, this study is intended to be useful in adding to the understanding of the internationalization process in Latin American companies. It is hoped that our findings provide some insights and will serve as a basis for future studies in this area.

REFERENCES

Accenture. 2012. Sustainable Energy for All: Opportunities for the Professional Services Industry. *Accenture.* www.se4all.org/sites/default/files/l/2013/09/Su stainable-Energy-for-All-The-Business-Opportunity.pdf. Accessed March 6, 2015.

Careers in Business. 2012. Management Consulting History. www.careers-in-business.com/consulting/hist1800.htm. Accessed April 10, 2015.

Casartelli, G. 2010. Desarrollo de la Industria Consultora de México: Direcciones Estratégicas, Agenda de Acciones y Política. *Inter-American Development Bank,* Technical Notes, IDB-TN-215: 1–65.

CNEC. 2015. National Chamber of Consulting Companies. http://cnec.org.mx/. Accessed May 15, 2015.

CNN Expansión. 2009. Ranking of Super Companies with Fewer than 500 Employees. *CNN Expansión.* www.cnnexpansion.com/expansion/2009/05/22/s uper-empresas-de-menos-de-500-empleados. Accessed April 13, 2015.

Consulting Ideas. 2010. The history of consultancy. *Consulting ideas.* http://con sulting-ideas.com/learn/the-history-of-consultancy. Accessed April 25, 2015.

Dawson, R. 2000. Knowledge capabilities as the focus of organizational development and strategy. *Journal of Knowledge Management,* 4(4): 320–327.

Gautier, T. 2014. Evolution of Business Consulting. *Alliance Progress.* October 19. http://alliancesprogress.com/strategic-alliances/evolution-of-business-consulting/. Accessed April 25, 2015.

Global Source. 2014. Information Services Limited 2014. www.sourceforconsulting .com. Accessed, May 20, 2015.

INEGI. 2014. Censos económicos. México, D.F. National Institute of Statistics and Geography. www.inegi.org.mx. Accessed November 1, 2015.

Management Consulting Case Interviews. 2015. List of consulting firms in Mexico City. *Management Consulting Case Interviews.* www.consultingcase101.com/l ist-of-consulting-firms-in-mexico-city-mexico. Accessed July 25, 2015.

McKenna. 2012. A brief history of strategy consulting. *Paris Tech Review.* February 2. www.paristechreview.com/2012/02/02/history-strategy-consulting. Accessed May 26, 2015.

23 MultiMexicans in Higher Education

National Autonomous University of Mexico and Monterrey Tec

Olivia Hernández-Pozas and Daniel Carrasco Brihuega

INTRODUCTION

Internationalization in Higher Education attracts the increasing attention of researchers and practitioners. This interest is not surprising when we look at the opportunities and challenges of recent decades for Higher Education institutions. According to Knight (2004), there are varied definitions of internationalization in Higher Education. While some definitions refer exclusively to student and faculty mobility, others refer to the delivery of courses abroad or the inclusion of the global and intercultural dimension in the curriculum. In this chapter, the main focus will be on the strategies to establish offices abroad.

Like other organizations, Higher Education institutions coexist within an industry with other institutions. In Mexico, institutions vary according to their funding and orientation (e.g., public, private, technological, teacher training, universities). Institutions also have stakeholders (e.g., students, professors, parents, government, corporations, investors), and both internal and external forces that may influence their international strategy.

In Mexico, some universities have achieved remarkable results in internationalization. In this chapter, two of those cases are presented: the National Autonomous University of Mexico (Universidad Nacional Autónoma de México, UNAM) and Monterrey Tec (Tecnológico de Monterrey, TEC), both ranked as the best universities in Mexico. Academic reputation, reputation with recruiters, accreditations, international prestige, research, and

643

publications have served to rank these two universities in the top-tier place.

These two cases illustrate two different ways to establish offices abroad. Location and type of office vary depending on the case results too. The expectations and future plans of each university, although seemingly similar, might trigger different planning. Mission, resources, funding, stakeholders, capabilities, previous experience, and experimentation result in different approaches. Other institutions or organizations that plan to go abroad may benefit from the lessons that these two cases present.

Both universities decided to establish an international presence, but their types of international presence and specific locations differ. Although both universities share similar interests – such as international agreements with other universities, student mobility, and joint research – the nature of those activities varies considerably. However, both have capitalized on their strengths in certain knowledge fields and have positioned themselves where they can find suitable partners.

This chapter presents two strategies that respond differently to different markets. They focus on different customer profiles. Disposable resources and competitors guide decisions in original ways. The strategy of TEC enables the institution to move faster and spend less money abroad. On the other hand, the strategy of UNAM enables the university to formally establish itself in the community.

These cases highlight lessons about the impact of stakeholders and mission on strategy, convenience of historical opportunities, importance of identification of customers and their needs; and also, about how to use resources and competitive advantage in international market niches, underlining the relevance of location, partnering right, and obtaining external validation and guidance.

INDUSTRY

Higher Education refers to the educational processes that include professional, specialized, and systematic formation in diverse knowledge fields. These processes aim to incorporate individuals into the social, economic, political, and cultural context, as well as into the activities and functions of creation, leadership, and management (De la Torre, 1996).

According to De la Torre (1996), in the Higher Education sector in Mexico, many diverse institutions coexist, cooperate, and compete. There are some institutions that were founded in the Colonial times; others have antecedents of the scientific and scholarly institutes of the nineteenth century, and there are younger universities of the twentieth century created as industrial schools. The history of this industry mainly responds to two types of public policy: on the one hand, the post-revolutionary policies of the State that aim to develop society towards a more democratic and scientific vision of the world; on the other hand, the State policies that aim to impact the productivity and economic welfare of the country.

Over time, the evolution of this complex system has not been homogeneous. At the beginning, the first educational project aimed to develop people culturally and socially. The post-revolutionary movement in education (1920–46) was more related to social justice than economic development. Later, during the 40s until the 70s, there was a shift in orientation towards modernizing education with a philosophy of a welfare state. Next, during the 80s and 90s, another change occurred towards a Neoliberal policy of education.

There are important differences (e.g., origin, orientation and philosophy, funding, academic quality, size, and internal policies) not only between public and private institutions, but sometimes also within each category of institutions and within schools of the same institution that might be located in different places.

The Higher Education system in Mexico has grown considerably in the last 100 years. At the beginning of the twentieth century, there were fewer than 10,000 students enrolled in the Higher Education system. Nowadays, there are more than three million people attending these institutions.

This industry is organized by the Ministry of Public Education. It is divided by level of studies in Technological, Teacher Training, and University (includes undergraduate and graduate studies). Also, institutions are grouped by type of funding (public or private). Public universities are those funded by the Federation, by the State, or Autonomous. Private institutions are schools established by a presidential agreement. They have official recognition and validity.

When one compares recent number of schools, the private sector stands out. In regards to enrollment, although public universities continue to be numerically dominant, enrollments in the private sector have grown by a factor of almost ten in the last two decades, while enrollments in the public sector have increased fivefold (Kent & Ramírez, 2008). Demographics, an increasing demand for educational programs, and a new legal framework explain the phenomenon.

Since 1991, technical studies have been included and offered by Technological Universities. The purpose is to have students closely linked to the job market and regional development (Malo, Valle & Wriedt, 1999). Most technical studies courses can be completed in two or three years.

Teacher training enables teachers to educate at the initial, pre-school, elementary, secondary, special, physical, artistic, technological, and intercultural and bilingual elementary levels. Since 1984, they have been part of the Higher Education group (Malo, Valle & Wriedt, 1999).

The university level includes undergraduate and graduate studies. The purpose is to create professionals in their corresponding fields and to prepare them for professional practice. Most undergraduate studies are completed in four to five years. Undergraduate programs are typically grouped into six areas: Natural and Exact Sciences, Education and Humanities, Agricultural Sciences, Health Sciences, Engineering and Technology, and Social and Administrative Sciences (ANUIES quoted by Malo, Valle & Wriedt, 1999). At the graduate level, the specialization and Master and Doctoral degrees are included.

In recent decades, student enrollment has been growing. However, nowadays it is no more than 30 percent of the population. Increasing enrollment requires collaboration between government agencies, universities, employers, and society as a whole.

In 2013–14, the Higher Education system in Mexico was composed of the following components: technological 4.3 percent, teaching training 3.9 percent, undergraduate university 85.1 percent, and graduate 6.7 percent. The distribution of institutions by type of funding is as follows: 37.3 percent are autonomous, 30.6 percent are private, 18.9 percent are funded by State, and 13.2 percent by the Federation.

At the national level, for Mexico, internationalization is essential. According to the 2013–18 National Development Plan, Mexico is a significant actor in the current international context and an obligatory reference in the region. Therefore, it is important to take advantage of this opportunity and to establish international cooperation mechanisms (Gobierno de la República, 2014).

At the institutional level, internationalization is crucial too. But, it involves a process of transformation that few universities have been able to achieve. This transformation normally integrates the international and intercultural dimensions into the mission, policies, culture, and developmental projects of the institutions (Gacel-Avila, 2005).

Most universities that consider internationalization strategically send representatives to other countries to negotiate agreements. Some go beyond that and establish Branch Campuses, Centers, Field Offices (FO) or International Liaison Offices (ILOs) and start operations in foreign countries.

According to El Economista (2016), UNAM and TEC are the two best universities in Mexico. See Table 23.1 for the ranking list. Their methodology includes quality of faculty, research, internationalization, postgraduate academic offers, prestige, and accreditations by others.

Table 23.1 *2015 El Economista ranking of Mexican universities*

RK 2016	RK 2015	University (Ownership)	2016 Prestige	2016 Professors (% PhD)	2016 Paper ISI/ researcher	2016 Internationalization	2016 Accreditation	2016 Quality Index
1	1	UNAM (Public) (28,311 Professors)	100	28,311 (13.7%)	3,712	100	90.1	89.51
2	2	TEC (Private) (8,560 Professors)	98.4	8,560 (15%)	285	88.8	100	66.64
3	3	IPN (Public) (10,843 Professors)	72	10,843 (13.6%)	1,137	77.4	62.2	65.91
4	4	UAM (Public) (5,641 Professors)	34.8	56,41 (36.9%)	653	40	44.7	55.03
5	6	UANL (Public) (6,039 Professors)	22.4	6,039 (25.1%)	454	35.1	70.2	48.05
6	8	UdeG (Public) (7,751 Professors)	28.3	7,751 (17.4%)	428	44.9	73.4	46.98
7	5	COLMEX (Public) (162 Professors)	18.6	162 (88.9%)	34	36.1	0	46.89

Table 23.1 (cont.)

RK 2016	RK 2015	University (Ownership)	2016 Prestige	2016 Professors (% PhD)	2016 Paper ISI/ researcher	2016 Internationalization	2016 Accreditation	2016 Quality Index
8	7	UDLAP (Private) (455 Professors)	37.8	455 (44.9%)	65	67.8	38.6	44.08
9	12	U Autónoma de Chapingo (Public) (640 Professors)	12	640 (45%)	99	29.5	59.5	40.07
10	9	ITAM (Private) (582 Professors)	40.9	582 (46%)	51	81.7	27.8	38.8

Source: El Economista, 2016.

QS University Rankings 2016 also ranks these two universities as the best ones in Mexico (QS, 2016). QS is a British agency which ranks world-class universities in areas such as teaching, internationalization, employability, innovation, infrastructure, and commitment to the community. TEC became the first university in Mexico to be awarded with this honor (TEC, 2014). In the 2016 assessment, UNAM also ranked with an overall score of 96.5, ranking in 128th place in the world university ranking and in fourth place in the Latam university ranking. On the other hand, TEC got five QS stars and an overall score of 93.7, ranking it in position 206 in the world university ranking and in seventh place in the Latam university ranking. Regarding specifics, UNAM leads the ranking in Mexico with a score of 100 in the category of Academic & Employer Reputation. On the other hand, TEC stands out with a score of 97.1 in Academic Reputation and 100 in Employer Reputation.

NATIONAL AUTONOMOUS UNIVERSITY OF MEXICO

UNAM is a public university in Mexico, founded in 1551 under the name of The Royal and Pontifical University of Mexico. Archbishop Fray Juan de Zumárraga, in the days of the Spanish colony, noticed the necessity to establish a university and Viceroy Antonio de Mendoza joined the project in 1547. It started operations in 1553 and was organized in the European style. Antecedents of the modern university can be found since 1881, when Justo Sierra presented the project to the Chamber of Deputies. Later, in 1907, the President approved the opening of The National University (UNAM, 2017a).

In 2016, UNAM reported 346,730 students: 28,638 are enrolled at the graduate level, 204,940 at the baccalaureate level, 112,229 in high school programs, and 923 in technical and propaedeutic courses. It has 39,500 professors, 12,172 of whom hold full-time positions in the university. UNAM offers 92 master and doctoral programs, 38 specialization programs with 234 orientations, 118 different bachelor degree programs with 206 educational options, 35 technical education programs, and three high school programs. UNAM has a national presence in the 32 Mexican federal entities. It has six campuses and 17 schools in the metropolitan area of Mexico City. Also, in six developmental regional poles: Michoacan, Queretaro, Morelos, Baja California, Yucatan, and Guanajuato (UNAM, 2016a).

UNAM is distinguished by the large number of professors who belong to the National System of Researchers (SNI). Currently, the institution has 4,314 members of the SNI. In order to be part of this recognized group, professors should demonstrate excellent annual research productivity. Regarding accreditations, 92 percent of the baccalaureate programs are accredited by COPAES, or have been evaluated by CIEES at level 1. Also, 86 percent of the graduate programs of UNAM are accredited by the Conacyt National Register of Quality for Graduate Education Programs. University rankings, such as El Economista and QS, steadily rank UNAM in the top-tier list (UNAM, 2016a).

Regarding internationalization, UNAM has 131 international agreements with higher education institutions. There are 3,404 students and 2,004 faculty members abroad. There are 6,342 foreign students, and 1,293 foreign scholars at UNAM. It has international presence in the USA, Canada, Spain, China, Costa Rica, France, and the UK (UNAM, 2016a).

History

In the late 1920s, Vasconcelos discovered that there was great interest by the Americans to know about Mexico and its culture. Thus, in 1921, UNAM's summer school was founded. The main purpose was to host those interested in the Mexican language and culture. It was in 1954 when UNAM's first Branch Campus outside Mexico opened in San Antonio, Texas. It was created primarily to meet the demand for education in the areas of history, culture, and languages. Later, the summer school was named "Teaching Center for Foreigners" (CEPE).

In 1955, the Office of Cultural Exchange and Scholarships started operating. In 1961, the Department of Cultural Exchange,

Public Relations, and Grants was created. In 1970, the Scholarship and Academic Exchange Commissions started working. Later, in 1995, UNAM initiated a more active role outside Mexico, opening another campus in Gatineau, Canada. In 2000, the Office of Interagency Collaboration started operating. Later, in 2005, the Los Angeles campus opened. The General Direction of Cooperation and Internationalization (DGECI) was created in 2009. DGECI aims to consolidate the internationalization of UNAM by promoting student and academic mobility, as well as by developing joint research projects and publications (UNAM, 2017b). In 2012, UNAM created a Center for Mexican Studies (CEM) in China. Later, in 2013, UNAM started operating at the Cervantes Institute in Madrid, Spain. The same year, it signed the agreement with the University of Costa Rica. In 2015, UNAM set up offices in France. See Table 23.2 for a summary of UNAM's key domestic and international events.

Support from the Mexican government is crucial for UNAM. It can come directly by funding initiatives of the university or by allocating economic resources for students. UNAM's total 2016 budget was Mex$39,381,976,365 (UNAM, 2016b).

Internationalization

Initially, UNAM's idea of internationalization focused on opportunities relating to teaching culture and language abroad. But soon, UNAM incorporated agreements to carry out research and to encourage the exchange of students and professors.

UNAM uses Teaching Centers for Foreigners (CEPEs), in which the Center for Mexican Studies (CEM) can be included. They are often located inside a partner university (e.g., in the University of Beijing, in King's College, in the Sorbonne). The CEPE's mission is to promote knowledge of the Spanish language and the Mexican culture, to academically support Mexican communities abroad, to link UNAM with other universities, and to strengthen student exchange (UNAM, 2017c).

Table 23.2 *Timeline of domestic and international key events for UNAM*

	Transformation	
Year	Domestic Events	International Events
1536	UNAM's foundation.	
1547	Spanish Crown approval.	
1553	The Royal and Pontifical University of México started.	
1881	Presentation to the Chamber of Deputies.	
1907	President approved The National University.	
1910	UNAM started.	
1921	UNAM's summer school started.	
1929	First CEPE creation.	
1954		UNAM's first Branch Campus abroad started.
1955	Cultural Exchange and Scholarships office started.	
1961	The Department of Cultural Exchange, Public Relations, and Grants started.	
1970	The Scholarship and Academic Exchange Commissions started.	
1995		The Gatineau campus started.
2001		The Chicago campus started.
2005		The Los Angeles campus started.
2009	GDECI started.	
2010		UK CEM started.
2012		China CEM started.
2013		Costa Rica & Spain CEM started.
2015		France CEM started.

Source: Elaborated by authors of this chapter

DGECI supports traveling expenses for scholars. Armando Lodigiani, director of DGECI, stated that "UNAM has been international since it has been UNAM ... An important factor that has contributed to internationalization is its research."[1]

To operate abroad, UNAM locates in cities that have a particular interest for Mexico. CEMs are an important source of income. Foreign universities often outsource courses with UNAM. It also offers online programs around the world, including Spanish, English, French, and Mexican culture lessons.

UNAM has been working since 1954 in the USA and Canada. Offices in Spain respond to a common interest in boosting cooperation projects. The interest in Costa Rica relates to historical ties with Costa Rican Florencio Castillo, cleric and politician, who had great influence in the Mexican political life. In China, the motivation also relates to cultural exchanges and research projects.

UNAM schools located in the USA are considered extension schools or Branch Campuses. They offer courses in varied languages, Mexican culture, preparation for accreditation exams and citizenship tests, as well as customized courses for local businesses. In addition, courses for high school, Bachelors, Masters, and PhD programs are offered via videoconference.

The largest presence abroad of UNAM is in the USA, where 11.7 million Mexicans resided in 2011 (SRE, 2013). This expansion is mostly accounted for by migration. Proof of this is that the location of international offices in the USA is in cities with the highest number of Mexicans.

UNAM has a presence in Los Angeles, where 4.3 million Mexicans reside (37 percent of Mexicans in the USA), and also in Chicago, where 684,000 Mexicans live (6 percent). The headquarters of UNAM in the USA are located in San Antonio, Texas, which is home to 2.5 million Mexicans (21 percent) (SRE, 2013).

---

[1]   Interviewed by Carrasco in 2015.

In Chicago, offices were founded in 2001. They are considered a Branch Campus and focus on Midwestern universities. UNAM in Chicago has its own building. Many of those attending courses in Chicago work in the construction industry, restaurants, and hotels (UNAM, 2013). In this city the Latino population is large.

UNAM's range of services and academic offerings has increased its penetration among the immigrant market in the USA. Many courses are customized according to the needs of four industries where Mexican workers abroad provide services: construction, gardening, hospitality, and restaurants. When students complete the program, they obtain a certificate of professionalization, increasing their opportunities to improve their salary or working conditions.

Javier Laguna Calderón points out that "UNAM has impacted so much of the market, that the University of Chicago negotiated an agreement with it, just as Northwestern University did so. These programs have been very successful with immigrant students. So, foreign institutions hire services from UNAM to teach them specialized courses."[2]

In Canada, UNAM started operations in 1995. It is located in the city of Gatineau. Offices are very close to Ottawa, the capital. This location is strategic because it is close to the provinces of Quebec (French-speaking region) and Ontario (English-speaking region). Initially, the administrative office was located with the municipality mayor and began teaching classes in rooms provided by the University of Quebec and the Museum of Civilization. Later, in 1996, they moved to their own building. In fact, this boosted the environment's transformation by promoting the economic growth of the zone.

The Gatineau offices are considered a Branch Campus. This campus enrolls approximately 1000 students each year. The history of UNAM's Extension School in Canada is divided into two stages. The first one starts with its foundation in 1995. This stage was characterized by the constant visit of commissioners of CEPE, who

---

[2] Interviewed by Carrasco in 2015.

collaborated to create plans and curricula. The second stage starts in 2008, when CEPE's academic staff was renewed, evaluating their strategies and creating new educational policies of internationalization (UNAM, 2018). Roberto Gutierrez Alcalá explains that this site serves to draw attention to UNAM as a place of study in North America.[3]

In Canada, UNAM offers courses in English and French too. Classes are taught not only by Mexican teachers, but also by professors from other Latin American countries. The operation is based on promoting academic trips to Mexico to study its history too. Cultural topics include, for example, muralism and figurines of Campeche or Mesoamerica passages. Another means of operation is for people to travel to Canada for a year to study languages. Gatineau's offices promote this exchange and the creation of joint professorships in both countries. Also, Gatineau's campus offers an online high school degree, mainly focusing on the Spanish-speaking market. In recent years, the campus has doubled its enrollment. In 2013, the number of students was fewer than a thousand; by 2014, it had increased to 1500 students. Revenues have almost tripled (UNAM, 2011).

UNAM has a Center for Mexican Studies in China. It is located in the Foreign Studies University of Beijing (*Beiwai* in Chinese). This office serves as a liaison between UNAM and Chinese institutions.

The idea of creating this center initially emerged in March 2008, when the Subcommittee of Cultural and Educational Cooperation of the Permanent Binational Commission Mexico–China submitted a proposal to open a center to promote the Spanish language and the Mexican culture in this country. The proposal was approved and commissions worked on the project. Later in 2012, Dr. José Narro Robles signed a cooperation agreement with the university (SRE, 2012).

UNAM's CEM in China aims to foster meaningful collaboration activities and joint projects between both universities, with special

---

[3]   Interviewed by Carrasco in 2015.

emphasis on the dissemination of Spanish and Mexican culture in this Asian country (UNAM, 2017d).

At the Cervantes Institute in Madrid, Spain, UNAM established a presence in 2013. Like other CEMs, this one aims to promote the Spanish language, Mexican culture, and cooperation. Offices of UNAM in Costa Rica are placed in the Center for Research in Public Administration (CIPAC) at the University of Costa Rica. The collaboration agreement between both universities was signed in 2013. Like other CEMs, the one in Costa Rica provides Mexican Culture courses, including classes on history, literature, art, and music. Also, it promotes international mobility and offers scholarships for graduate students and academic exchange to carry out joint research in all areas of knowledge. Online courses are available too.

MONTERREY TEC

TEC is a private university in Mexico. It was founded by a civil society of Mexican businessmen, led by Eugenio Garza Sada in 1943, and supported by 27 non-profit organizations. The objective was "to create a cutting-edge educational institution that would mature and eventually become one of the best" (TEC, 2005, 2015a).

Nowadays, TEC has 89,641 students, enrolled in 26 campuses throughout the country. It has 10,117 professors (TEC, 2017) and offers education at three levels: high school, undergraduate, and Graduate. The main source of income for TEC is student tuition fees.

TEC is accredited by the Southern Association of Colleges and Schools (SACS) and by Federación de Instituciones Mexicanas Particulares de Educación Superior (FIMPES). In 2014, TEC received the 5-star rating by Quacquarelli Symonds (QS, 2016). Nowadays, this university has 35 graduate programs listed in the Conacyt National Register of Quality for Graduate Education Programs.

For TEC, internationalization is a fundamental pillar. It has an academic relationship with 644 partner universities in 53 countries, 10,618 students have international experience abroad, and the university received 4,714 foreign students in its campuses (TEC, 2017).

TEC's global presence includes 14 countries: the USA, Canada, Panama, Ecuador, Colombia, Peru, Chile, the UK and Ireland, Spain, France, Switzerland, and China (TEC, 2014). TEC publicly acknowledges that today's society demands citizens with a global outlook, who show a sincere appreciation for diversity and who can adapt to a wide range of culturally diverse environments (TEC, 2013). One of the main values of TEC is Global Vision.

History

The creation of TEC was due to the urgent need to solve the problem of the lack of professionalism in the Northern part of Mexico at that time (García, 2013). TEC undergraduate programs have always been more pragmatic than ideological, influencing the curricula with a corporate culture and orientation (García, 2013).

The history and development of TEC is divided into four phases: initial, growth, consolidation, and transformation (TEC, 2015a). Table 23.3 presents a timeline of domestic and international key events for TEC.

The initial phase in the history of TEC runs from 1943 to 1960. During this stage, the university focused on student recruitment and the provision of initial infrastructure (TEC, 2011a). Student enrollment grew from 350 students in 1943 to 4,458 in 1960. The first campus was inaugurated in Monterrey. Since its earliest phase, TEC has been committed to academic quality. Therefore, it has searched for national and international guidance with accreditations and well-known rankings. It was in this earliest stage that the institution got its first international accreditation by the Southern Association of Colleges and Schools (SACS) (TEC, 2015a).

Since its creation, TEC has developed specific initiatives and devoted resources to becoming one of the best. Such initiatives include infrastructure and technological planning, faculty training, research support, internationalization, strong partnerships, and a state-of-the-art educational model. Internal processes, as well as structure, respond to priorities.

Table 23.3 *Timeline of domestic and international key events for Monterray Tec*

	Transformation	
Year	Domestic Events	International Events
1943	TEC started.	
1950		SACS accreditation.
1960	Growth phase.	
1967	Guaymas Campus.	
1968	Principles published.	
1970	General Statute published.	
1973	Obregón & Mexico City Campus started.	
1974	Saltillo campus started.	
1975	Eugenio Garza Sada, Laguna, Querétaro, and San Luis Potosi Campus started.	
1976	Chihuahua, State of Mexico, and Irapuato started operations.	
1978	Ignacio A. Santos Medical School started.	
1980	First personal computers are introduced and Colima, Chiapas, Guadalajara, Hidalgo, and Cuernavaca Campus started.	
1981	Tampico & Central of Veracruz started.	
1982	Toluca Campus started.	
1983	Juarez, Mazatlán, Sinaloa, and Sonora Norte Campus started.	
1985	First mission 1985–95 is defined. Practice of Annual meeting of trustees, Biannual campus evaluation meeting and Annual Planning started. Zacatecas Campus started.	

Table 23.3 (cont.)

	Transformation	
Year	Domestic Events	International Events
1986	Consolidation Phase started.	International collaborations started. Formal training of professors started.
1989	Virtual University started.	
1995	Mission statement is updated to 1995–2005. Internationalization is introduced in it.	
1996	Transformation phase started.	Offices in Quito, Ecuador and in Panama City started.
1998		Offices in Bogotá, Colombia; Lima, Perú; and Santiago, Chile started.
1998	The Vice-Rectory of International Affairs is created.	
1999		Offices in Singapore; Washington, DC; Boston; Shangai, Hangzhou; and Madrid started.
2000	Tec Milenio started	Offices in Paris and Vancouver started.
2001		Office in Miami started and joint project with UBC begun.
2002		Offices in Montreal and Dallas started.
2004		Office in Bratislava started.
2005	Mission statement is updated to 2005–15.	Office in Fribourg started.
2008		Office in New Haven started.
2010	Board of trustees approved a new organization. New presidents were appointed and a new era of reforms started again.	

Table 23.3 (cont.)

	Transformation	
Year	Domestic Events	International Events
2014	Educational model Tec 21 is launched.	Office in London started.

Source: Elaborated by authors of this chapter.

The Growth Phase of TEC was from 1960 to 1985. During this period, the university expanded to other locations in Mexico and started focusing on the use of technology in education. Campus Guaymas was the first campus outside Monterrey. It was founded in 1967. After Guaymas, many other campuses were inaugurated. Expansion was evaluated according to potential student enrollment and strategic positioning of the institution. In 1973, Campus Ciudad de México and Ciudad Obregón started operations. According to TEC (2011a), Campus Ciudad Obregón, in contrast to the Guaymas unit operation, had its own civil association. The association sponsored and supervised the operation of the campus. Later, this model was adopted by the rest of the campuses and supported the national expansion plan (TEC, 2011a). In 1974, Campus Saltillo started operations; in 1975, so did the High-school Campus Eugenio Garza Sada in Monterrey, as well as Campus Laguna, Queretaro and San Luis Potosi; in 1976, Campus Chihuahua, Estado de México and Irapuato also got underway.

By 1978, TEC had 25,000 students in 14 units spread out through the Mexican Republic. In 1980, the first personal computers were introduced and the university continued growing. In 1980, Campus Colima, Chiapas, Guadalajara, Hidalgo, and Morelos (currently known as Cuernavaca) started operations. Expansion continued in 1981 opening Campus Central of Veracruz and Tampico. In 1982, Campus Toluca and in 1983 Campus Juárez, Mazatlán, Sinaloa, and

Sonora Norte were inaugurated. Later, in 1985, Campus Zacatecas started operations (TEC, 2015a).

With the change of TEC's president in 1985 came the redefinition of organizational structure towards consolidation of out-of-town units. After 1985, the establishment of new campuses was intentionally slowed down, to give priority to consolidation. The third phase, consolidation, started in 1986 (TEC, 2015a). The main focus was to consolidate operations among all campuses, as well as to get ready to better assure the quality of education and services. First, an annual meeting of the TEC trustees was established, its purpose being to achieve operational cohesion at all campuses within the institution. Also, a Biannual Campus evaluation meeting started. Next, annual planning of activities based on mission and including strategies and derived programs started, too (TEC, 2011a). Now, accreditation and rankings are part of the normal activities of the institution and assure its quality standards. It was in this phase of consolidation that the institution launched initiatives to train professors in English as a second language, and to improve their academic credentials with Masters and PhD degrees abroad. Therefore, it provided scholarships and time for professors, who were looking forward to getting a PhD degree abroad.

The transformation phase started in 1996, with the declaration of the Mission Statement 1995–2005: "To educate individuals with community engagement, who are internationally competitive in their area of expertise, and to foster research and extension programs relevant to the country's development." During this stage, the university started broadening its reach to other Latin American countries. Sandra Ortiz, TEC Director for Latin American and the Caribbean,[4] points out that "FOs in Latin America contribute to the internationalization strategy of the institution by strengthening the presence of TEC in the region, connecting the institution with governments, universities, schools, and companies." It is in this phase that internationalization started

---

[4]   Interviewed by Hernández-Pozas in 2015.

being coordinated by a system-wide entity, the Vice-Rectory of International Affairs. Also, all offices abroad were opened in this phase.

During the transformation phase, the institution re-engineered the teaching and learning processes, and opened the Virtual University and a few other campuses. It was during this period that the Community Centers started operations too (TEC, 2015a). Also, to become a research university, TEC set up a strategic plan to create a research and innovation ecosystem in the university. It included organizational arrangements and provided the physical infrastructure to consolidate research work (Cantu-Ortiz, 2015). See Cantu-Ortiz (2015) for the 12 features recommended to develop research through an innovation ecosystem.

Through the years, influential domestic events for TEC continued happening, along with many international events. But, it was in 2010 that the university experienced another major domestic event. That year, the Board of Trustees approved a new organization for TEC. This included four entities: Monterrey Tec, Tec Milenio University, The Medical Institutes & Centers, as well as The Virtual University. The new organization brought another shift, too. Along with the organizational changes, new presidents were appointed and a new era of reforms started again.

In 2014, the new educational model Tec 21 was launched. Also, the organizational structure was redefined by value processes and the Vice-Rectories of High School, Undergraduate, and Graduate levels started operating. With these changes, the Virtual University was transformed and became embedded in all academic programs. Innovative pedagogical methodologies, the use of technology for education, the redesign of learning spaces and experiential academic activities, as well as the crucial role of professors, high-impact research and more internationalization, now propel the institution in the new millennium.

Internationalization

The internationalization of TEC started since the university's initial phase and has always been present in the minds of the decision-makers of the university. One of the first key international events occurred in 1950, when TEC got accredited by SACS. The earliest key international events also included collaboration agreements with universities in the USA and the international mobility of students and professors. Leticia Santos Dresel, former Dean of the International Programs Office in Monterrey and Director of International Programs for TEC and former Dallas Liaison Director,[5] explains that "TEC started very early with the internationalization process. Even before the 80s, there were already about eight international collaboration agreements in place for bilateral exchange purposes. Also, an international summer program was offered to international students, bringing about 1,000 students to Campus Monterrey every year, during summer time. The fact that the institution is accredited by SACS, since the early years has influenced it. But, after 1986, internationalization increased notably due to the need to train professors in English as a second language, and to improve their academic credentials with Master and PhD degrees abroad. The period from 1986 to 1990 is characterized by international collaborations with universities in the US and Canada, building of the infrastructure to increase the student's mobility, and facilitating international opportunities for the professors."[6]

The establishment of offices abroad started in the 90s, mostly triggered by priorities of the 1995–2005 Mission of TEC. Leticia Santos Dressel pointed out: "later, the decade of the 90s marked a change. Student mobility increased notably, especially during summer time. Internationalization of students became a strategy and an important part of TEC mission. International collaboration expanded first to Europe and later to Asia ... The collaboration with US and Canada strengthened and became reciprocal. The International Student Exchange Program (ISEP), the Mexican government scholarships as well as those from international Embassies and the advancement of technology facilitated the process ... Campuses at

---

5   Interviewed by Hernández-Pozas in 2015.
6   Interviewed by Hernández-Pozas in 2015.

Cuernavaca, Guadalajara, Mazatlán, Mexico City, Monterrey, Querétaro and the State of México among others got involved in a multi-campus initiative to attract international students and most Campus[es] increased their exchange programs."

Enrique Zepeda, former Vice-Rector of International Affairs of TEC, points out that "the joint process of internationalization started more than 20 years ago by the coordinated efforts of several International Program Offices of some campuses. At that time, some campuses had already in place international agreements and were having international mobility with partner universities. But, opportunities and achievements were dispersed and varied greatly by campus. Later, with the declaration of the 1995–2005 Mission of TEC, the internationalization of the institution became priority and the transformation across the campuses was formally organized and sped up."[7]

Zepeda explained that the 1995–2005 Mission of TEC acknowledged the national and international context of the time: "It was the decade of the 1990s. Mexico had just signed the North American Free Trade Agreement (NAFTA) in 1994, and was changing towards more open trade and economic national policies. Authorities, as well as trustees of the institution, were attentive to these changes and eager to explore opportunities. Additionally, China, was experiencing an impressive transformation too ... Therefore, Chinese universities were having important achievements worth being monitored." (TEC, 2005). In sum, globalization was becoming important for most the world and an imperative for education. Thus, authorities, counselors, students, and professors at TEC, when consulted about the upcoming mission, voted for internationalization to be set as one of the priorities. Then, the 1995–2005 Mission of TEC stated the relevance to prepare students to be internationally competitive. That statement is still present in the current mission.

The official declaration triggered the creation of the Vice-Rectory of International Affairs in 1998 to support TEC, in the pursuit

---

[7] Interviewed by Hernández-Pozas in 2015.

of becoming a global university. Zepeda explained: "priorities included the following: to increase the student mobility; to diversify destinations and country of origin of incoming students; to improve the quality of the international experience for students of all campuses; to improve the content of the programs and agreements; as well as, to improve the international awareness, prestige, and positioning of TEC. To properly execute these tasks at hand, the Vice-Rectory of International Affairs designed specific norms and tactics and closely coordinated with local International Program Offices in all campuses."

Offices Abroad

In 1999, TEC set up the first six ILO. Two were established in the United States: one in Washington, DC, and the other in Boston. A third one was in Singapore. Two more were set up in China: one in Shanghai and the other in Hangzhou; and the sixth ILO was established in Madrid, Spain. One year later, in 2000, TEC set up two new offices: one in Vancouver, Canada and another in Paris, France (TEC, 2011b).

In 2000–1, the joint project with the University of British Columbia (UBC) started. This office has a geographical scope in the West of Canada and the Northwest of the USA. This ILO in Vancouver has focus areas on relationships with the Asia-Pacific region and with North America, as well as relationships with specific topics such as educational technology and ecosystems and environmental studies.

By 2004, the ILOs in Eastern Europe and other places in Asia were established. Eastern Europe by that time also represented an opportunity as an emerging market.

In the International Student Mobility bulletin (2014), TEC reported an international presence in 14 countries: Canada, the USA, Panama, Ecuador, Colombia, Peru, Chile, the UK and Ireland, France, Switzerland, Spain, Germany, and China. In some countries, for example, the USA, Canada, and Spain, there is more than one office per country. It depends on the activities that each region demands. In Canada, there are two offices: one in Vancouver and another in Montreal. In the USA, there are four offices: Dallas, Miami, New Haven, and Boston. In Spain, there are two offices: one in Madrid and the other one in Barcelona. Offices abroad take care of needed activities in the nearby region. They are organized by geographical scope.

Activities of those working in an office abroad include the following: to negotiate agreements; to coordinate student and faculty mobility; to manage Honors programs abroad; to organize company internships; to foster summer programs; to supervise company visits; to attend university fairs; to connect with EXATEC activities; to support faculty training; to promote joint research; to supervise medical rotations; to offer seminars and certificates; to sell continuing education, executive courses, and online/blended courses; to recruit students; to design in-company courses; and to enrich public relationships on behalf of the university. Activities vary by office and time of the year; they depend on the needs of the specific location.

There are three main reasons that can justify the opening of an ILO. First, there must be increasing international mobility. Patricia Montaño, Director of International Planning and Cooperation in the Direction of Internationalization at TEC, says that "There are regions where the presence of the institution has grown considerably and it justifies a person to take care of operational activities in the region. The ILO in Madrid is an example of this type of office."[8]

Second, an office abroad can be justified by a dense population of key higher education institutions with which TEC wants to be connected and develop a strong relationship. Patricia Montaño said, "An example of this is the ILO in Boston. This office was created in collaboration with Harvard University and LASPAU in 1999."

A third reason to open offices abroad relates to the specific momentum, potential opportunities, or political purpose: "These types of ILO may stay open just for a while. Offices like these have

---

[8]   Interviewed by Hernández-Pozas in 2015.

the objective of monitoring policies with a potential impact on international education. Examples include the ILO in Washington and in Brussels. The first one was close to the Organization of American States office. It was attentive to new specific educational and developmental policies for Latin America. The second was crucial to understand and adjust to the upcoming changes in the educational models of Europe."

When opening an ILO abroad, TEC takes into consideration many variables. It pays attention, for example, to governmental policies (e.g., case of Venezuela), economic policies (e.g., case of Colombia), immigration policies (e.g., case of the USA), expenses and money transfers (e.g., case of the European Union), and logistics (e.g., case of China) (TEC, 2005).

Joaquín Guerra, former Director of Internationalization at TEC,[9] explained that "ILOs have to strengthen institutional relationships, promote mobility, support students, create new opportunities, monitor developments in the region, negotiate agreements and attend important international events on behalf of TEC." Nowadays, one of the most important resolutions of TEC, in regards to internationalization, is to continue increasing the percentage of students with international experience before graduation. Another important plan for the future is to facilitate and provide new opportunities for joint research and teaching in collaboration with prestigious universities. Guerra cited UC Berkley and Yale as successful examples of partner universities where this is already happening.

In addition to ILO, TEC also has FOs abroad. Nowadays, TEC does not have campuses outside Mexico and FOs are located only in Latin America. TEC has FOs in Panamá, Ecuador, Colombia, and Peru. According to Sandra Ortiz,[10] "Latin American offices of TEC strongly contribute to the internationalization strategy of the institution. Their operation is currently in transition to assure they adapt properly to current challenges of the region."

---

[9]   Interviewed by Hernández-Pozas in 2015.
[10]   Interviewed by Hernández-Pozas in 2015.

FOs in Latin America started operations in those countries from which the university was already receiving students. A combination of a deliberate strategy to position TEC in the region and a series of opportunities triggered decisions in Latin American FOs. Those countries with the greatest recruitment potential started first: Panama and Peru. Later, when the academic offer of online degrees and courses grew, other FOs started operations – among those, the offices in Ecuador and Colombia. Expansion in Latin America continued in countries such as Chile, Argentina, Venezuela, and Brazil. Expansion even triggered the opening of offices in more than one city in countries such as Colombia and Ecuador. Over time, not all offices in Latin America have remained. A learning curve, as well as different economic, legal, and political factors, influenced the closure of some FOs and new strategies of consolidation in Latin America.

In the Latin American FOs, Panama, Ecuador, Colombia, and Peru, TEC offers courses in three modalities: face-to-face, blended, and online. Courses can be for various Masters degrees or for continuing education. Academic offers of Masters degrees include MBAs and the Masters in Education, as well as in Engineering and Innovation. Continuing education courses can be in-company or from the institutional catalog. Profiles of participants are mostly characterized by professionals in educational institutions or governmental institutions, and executives working at companies. In 2014, Latin American FOs had 2,040 students of Masters programs and provided varied courses for 6,532 executives.

To internationalize properly, TEC has received support from individuals, too. To fully understand the internationalization case of TEC, it is important also to give credit to the large network of TEC alumni, better known as EXATEC. Since the mission of the Alumni office of TEC is to "contribute with the personal and professional development of alumni by creating effective networking, that can produce opportunities of employment, business, socialization and community support" (Bonilla-Rios, 2006), alumni are frequently involved and committed because the relationship with their Alma

Mater is a win–win situation. Carlos Romero, former Director of Relationships with EXATEC,[11] explained that "the EXATECs are spread throughout the world. They are active and collaborate to connect TEC with corporations, governments, and with non-governmental organizations (NGOs) in many international settings. The Network of Mexican Talent Abroad is also very useful to strengthen international projects and alliances."

LESSONS

UNAM and TEC have been ranked as the best universities in the country, and have been distinguished with international accreditations. Both have developed unique strategies of internationalization. The analysis of these two exceptional cases teaches us the following important lessons of international strategy.

First, the creation of value to stakeholders is a determinant of international success. According to Resource Dependence Theory, organizations must attend to the demands of those in the environment that provide key resources (Pfeffer, 1982). Stakeholders who provide critical resources should elicit more attention from decision-makers than stakeholders who don't provide them (Jawahar & McLaughlin, 2001). Primary stakeholders may include investors, employees, customers, suppliers, government, and communities that provide infrastructures and markets, whose laws and regulations must be obeyed, and to whom taxes and other obligations may be due (Clarkson, 1995). While UNAM is a public university and receives its main financial support from the Mexican government, TEC is a private university whose funding comes from tuition, paid by parents. UNAM is more exposed to social scrutiny since it receives federal funds. In addition, tax-paying society and Mexicans living abroad would demand certain services from it. On the other hand, TEC has pressures too, but from students and their parents who pay tuition fees and demand that students be prepared for a successful professional career, as well as

[11]   Interviewed by Hernández-Pozas in 2015.

from employees (e.g., corporations, NGOs, and Governments), who expect professionals to be capable of performing well at their jobs. Therefore, it would be expected that, when allocating resources for internationalization, each school would serve its group of primary stakeholders differently: UNAM, by disseminating knowledge about Mexico internationally and by training Mexicans abroad; TEC, by enabling its students to be internationally competitive and by impacting the performance of corporations. Over the years, both have excelled because both have been able to allocate resources where outcomes create value to the primary stakeholders.

Second, an effective mission statement sets an institution or business apart from the competition and serves as guidance for operations. Missions also communicate how the organizations see themselves and how they want others to view them (Palmer & Short, 2008). UNAM is, in many ways, iconic of Mexico. Its mission focuses on serving the country and humanity, forming professionals who can solve the problems of Mexico. Missions also serve as a vehicle of legitimization. When UNAM establishes offices abroad to disseminate knowledge of the Mexican culture and to train Mexicans who live in other countries, it is wisely connecting to its mission and legitimizing their educational role abroad. In the other case, the mission of TEC focuses on creating competitive international professionals. When TEC announces that it aims at competitiveness at the international level, TEC is also legitimizing its role, impacting Mexico's economic development. Strategic planning starts with the development of a mission statement. Devoting time to stating the mission accurately and then remaining loyal to that statement is crucial. In the cases in this chapter, the missions of both universities have guided differentiated operations that have contributed to their good performance.

Third, historical opportunities should be monitored and capitalized upon. Both universities capitalized on momentum in adapting their strategies according to historical opportunities. Deregulation of the Mexican state has favored the competitiveness and openness of these leading Mexican universities. It facilitated a legal framework as a starting point. At that time, Mexico was changing from a traditional economic model of Protectionism to a Neoliberal one. In the Neoliberal model, international trade and open market policies are crucial. This was evident in Mexico through NAFTA. In the 90s, NAFTA and the open market policies created new social needs for Mexico, its people, and its industries. Foreign interest in Mexican culture, its history, its language, and business opportunities increased. But also, migration to the USA increased, as well as threats and problems for those who were not well prepared for the changes. Again, UNAM and TEC responded with actions.

Fourth, appropriate identification of customers and their needs is crucial in finding international market niches. In the differentiated strategies, we can observe a clear focus on the type of customer each university services. Customer needs are different between the two. Thus, each university reaches a different market segment, offering differentiated products and services to specific niches. Pricing is linked to the type of market they serve, too.

Fifth, to be successful, organizations must not only have appropriate resources, but they also need to manage their resources effectively (Hitt, Bierman, Uhlenbruck & Shimizu, 2006). In these two cases, we can see larger differences regarding allocation of resources. International investment is managed differently in both cases. While UNAM has established branch campuses abroad and CEPEs, TEC preferred to established ILOs and FOs. However, it is clear that both universities have capitalized on their strengths in certain knowledge fields and have positioned themselves where they can find suitable collaboration and partners. Knowledge is the most important asset that universities have. UNAM uses its enormous capacity for research and knowledge development to leverage its opportunities abroad; especially in the dissemination of knowledge about the Mexican culture. On the other hand, TEC chooses to build on its extensive expertise and relational capital with the corporate world. This institutional behavior illustrates what the resource-based perspective teaches.

According to García (2013), the success of TEC is the result of its flexibility, as well as the fast reading of and adaptation to changes in the economic context. García (2013) explains that TEC typically aims to achieve administrative efficacy, maximization of current infrastructure, and a reduction of operational costs. On the other hand, the strategy of UNAM enables the university to formally establish in the community.

Sixth, location and partnerships, when choosing international endeavors, clearly matter. Both universities decided to have an international presence and explore opportunities abroad, but the type of international presence and specific locations abroad of both universities are different. However, both universities are close to where their customers, partners, and future opportunities are. Networking and alumni collaboration have been key.

Seventh, accreditations and rankings provide reputation, guidance, and credibility: all key for international expansion. Accreditation and rankings have helped both universities to demonstrate compliance with international quality standards. That compliance and external validation have helped them to establish their reputations. Reputation is crucial for international expansion. Also, accreditations and rankings have served them in focusing on the future and having clarity about their strategies.

Globalization has arrived to stay, and the opportunities of internationalization will keep on growing. There are many different ways in which organizations can internationalize, but the right strategy will depend on the organizational origin, stakeholders, mission, and capabilities. Organizations need to capitalize on historical opportunities and read the changes in their environments. They need to understand their customers and use their resources effectively. The lessons that these two cases have illustrated can be used by firms, other universities, NGOs, and governmental agencies.

REFERENCES

Bonilla-Rios, J. 2006. *Creating Value in the Relationship of EXATEC and TEC.* Mexico: TEC.

Cantú-Ortiz, F. 2015. A research and innovation ecosystem model for private universities, in Gregorutti, E. & Delgado, J. E. (Eds.), *Private Universities in Latin America: Research and Innovation in the Knowledge Economy.* New York: MacMillan-Palgrave.

Clarkson, M. 1995. A stakeholder framework for analyzing and evaluating corporate social performance. *Academy of Management Review,* 20: 92–117.

De la Torre, M. 1996. Educación Superior en el siglo XX. *UNAM.* http://biblioweb .tic.unam.mx/diccionario/htm/articulos/sec_8.htm. Accessed September 2, 2015.

El Economista. 2016. Las mejores universidades de México. Ranking 2016. *El Economista.* http://eleconomista.com.mx/especiales/2015/las-mejores-universidades-mexico-ranking-2015. Accessed February 22, 2017.

Gacel-Avila, J. 2005. Internacionalización de la educación superior en México, in de Wit, H., Jaramillo, I. C., Gacel-Avila & Knight, J. (Eds.), *La Educación Superior en America Latina. La dimensión internacional.* Colombia: Banco Mundial y Mayol Ediciones.

García, D. 2013. Aportaciones para el análisis de la cultura empresarial en la universidad mexicana. El caso del Tec de Monterrey. *Revista Mexicana de Investigación Educativa,* 18(56): 191–221.

Gobierno de la República. 2014. Plan Nacional de Desarrollo 2013–2018. *PND.* ht tp://pnd.gob.mx/. Accessed August 5, 2015.

Hitt, M. A., Bierman, L., Uhlenbruck, K. & Shimizu, K. 2006. The importance of resources in the internationalization of professional service firms: the good, the bad, and the ugly. *Academy of Management Journal,* 49(6), 1137–1157.

Jawahar, I. & McLaughlin, G. 2001. Toward a descriptive stakeholder theory: An organizational life cycle approach. *Academy of Management Review,* 26(3): 397–414.

Kent, R. & Ramírez, R. 2008. Private higher education in Mexico: Growth and differentiation, in Altbach, P. (Ed.), *Private Prometheus: Private Higher Education and Development in the 21st Century.* US: Greenwood Press.

Knight, J. 2004. Internationalization remodeled: Definition, approaches, and rationalities. *Journal of Studies in International Education,* 8(1): 5–31.

Malo, S., Valle, R. & Wriedt, K. 1999. Planning for the International Quality Review Process: The National University of Mexico. *Journal of Studies in International Education,* 3(1): 15–32.

Ortiz, S. 2012. *La implementación de la estrategia operativa en las universidades. Un estudio en las sedes del TEC en Sudamérica.* Mexico: TEC.

Palmer, T. & Short, J. 2008. Mission statements in US colleges of business: An empirical examination of their content with linkages to configurations and performance. *Academy of Management Learning & Education,* 7(4): 454–470.

Pfefier, J. 1982. *Organizations and Organization Theory.* London: Pitman.

QS. 2016. QS University Rankings Latin America 2016. *QS Top Universities.* www .topuniversities.com/university-rankings/latin-american-university-rankings/2 016. Accessed February 22. 2017.

Rangel, A. 1983. *La educación superior en México.* Mexico: Colegio de México.

SRE. 2012. Inaugura UNAM centro de estudios mexicanos en China. *SRE.* http:// saladeprensa.sre.gob.mx/index.php/es/comunicados-de-sala-de-prensa-global/2 147-embajada-chn. Accessed March 23, 2015.

SRE. 2013. Los Mexicanos en Estados Unidos: La importancia de sus contribuciones. *SRE.* http://consulmex.sre.gob.mx/mcallen/images/stories/201 3/contribuciones.pdf. Accessed March 23, 2015.

Silas, J. 2005. Realidades y tendencias en la educación superior privada mexicana. *Perfiles Educativos,* 27(109-110): 7–37.

TEC. 2005. *An Experience in Partnership and Development. Presentation of the Vice-Rectory of Internationalization to the European Consortium of Innovative Universities (ECIU) prepared by Patricia Montaño.* Mexico: TEC.

TEC. 2011a. *El Sistema TEC en 2011.* Mexico: TEC.

TEC. 2011b. *La internacionalización en el TEC. Presentation of the Vice-Rectory of Internationalization.* Mexico: TEC.

TEC. 2013. *International Student Mobility Report.* Mexico: TEC.

TEC. 2014. *International Student Mobility Report.* Mexico: TEC.

TEC. 2015a. History. *ITESM.* www.itesm.mx/wps/wcm/connect/ITESM/ Tecnologico+de+Monterrey/English/About+Us/What+is+Tecnologico+de+Mon terrey/History/. Accessed August 8, 2015.

TEC. 2015b. Visión Internacional. Strategic agreements in the world. *ITESM.* htt p://sitios.itesm.mx/vi/boletin/agreements.html. Accessed August 8, 2015.

TEC. 2015c. *Presentation of the Vice-Rectory of Internationalization.* Mexico: TEC.

TEC. 2017. Datos y Cifras. *TEC.* https://tec.mx/es/diferencia-tec/datos-y-cifras. Accessed February 22, 2017.

UNAM. 2011. Misión y objetivos de la UNAM. *UNAM Canadá,* www.canada .unam.mx/canada/programaUnamCanada.pdf. Accessed February 20, 2017.

UNAM. 2013. UNAM in Chicago, Illinois. *UNAM Chicago*. www.chicago.unam .mx/. Accessed February 20, 2017.

UNAM. 2016a. La UNAM en números. *Portal de Estadística Universitaria*. www .estadistica.unam.mx/numeralia. Accessed February 21, 2017.

UNAM. 2016b. Presupuesto 2016. *Consejo univeristario*. https://consejo.unam .mx/archivo-noticias-y-multimedia/comunicados-y-mensajes/350-presupuesto-unam-2016. Accessed February 22. 2017.

UNAM. 2017a. Cronología histórica de la UNAM. *Acerca de la UNAM*. www .unam.mx/acerca-de-la-unam/unam-en-el-tiempo/conologia-historica-de-la-unam. Accessed February 21, 2017.

UNAM. 2017b. ¿Quiénes somos? *DGECI UNAM*. www.global.unam.mx/es/quie nes_somos/historia.html. Accessed February 21, 2017.

UNAM. 2017c. ¿Quiénes somos? *CEPE*. www.cepe.unam.mx. Accessed February 21, 2017.

UNAM. 2017d. ¿Quiénes somos? *UNAM-CHINA*. http://unamenchina.net. Accessed February 21, 2017.

UNAM. 2018. Programa de trabajo 2011–2015. Escuela de extensión en Canadá. *UNAM-CANADA*. www.canada.unam.mx/canada/programaUnamCanada.pdf. Accessed May 14, 2018.

World Bank. 2015. School enrollment, tertiary (% gross). http://data.worldbank .org/indicator/SE.TER.ENRR. Accessed September 2, 2015.

24 Conclusions
Building Multinationals in Emerging Markets

Alvaro Cuervo-Cazurra

INTRODUCTION

MultiMexicans are becoming credible international competitors, and some of them have become global leaders in their industries. Surprisingly, they have received little attention in studies of multinationals, except for a few cases such as the bakery goods firm Bimbo or the cement producer Cemex. In this book, we address this oversight of an important set of international competitors by analyzing how MultiMexicans in a variety of industries have been able to overcome the limitations of operating in an emerging country and become successful multinationals, competing against what in many cases are much larger and more sophisticated rivals from advanced economies. To achieve this, local experts analyzed the upgrading and internationalization of two of the leading companies in a variety of industries, providing new insights and drawing implications from the comparison of those two companies. Table 24.1 summarizes the companies and industries studied.

In this concluding chapter, I now abstract from each of the within-industry comparisons and make a cross-industry comparison to summarize and integrate the insights of the chapters into a model that explains the transformation of domestic firms operating in emerging markets into successful multinationals that can compete in a variety of countries. This cross-industry comparison facilitates the identification of deeper lessons into this process, in part because the chapters contain not only firms in a variety of industries but also a diversity of companies regarding their ownership, size, technology, sophistication, managerial skills, etc.

Table 24.1 *Companies analyzed in this book*

Ch.	Industry	Companies	Created	Sales 2016 or latest, US$bn	Exports, % sales 2016 or latest	Foreign investments, 2016
3	Agriculture	Bachoco	1952	2.5	20	USA
		SuKarne	1972	2.25	N/A	Nicaragua, USA, Japan, China, South Korea, Canada
4	Mining	Grupo Mexico	1942	8.17	11	Peru, USA, Italy, Japan, Germany, Chile, Argentina, Ecuador
		Industrias Peñoles	1887	4.09	82	Europe and South America (Peru, Chile, Argentina)
5	Oil and gas	Pemex	1938	73.64	28	Europe (Spain, Ireland, the Netherlands, the Netherlands Antilles), USA
6	Iron and steel	Altos Hornos de Mexico	1942	2.59	10	USA, Netherlands, Canada, Israel
		Industrias CH	1934	1.84	12	Central America, Brazil, USA, Canada

Table 24.1 (*cont.*)

Ch.	Industry	Companies	Created	Sales 2016 or latest, US$bn	Exports, % sales 2016 or latest	Foreign investments, 2016
7	Food	Bimbo	1945	13.83	18	22 countries, among them Germany, Spain, Portugal, Argentina, Chile, China, Peru, Colombia, Guatemala, USA, Canada, Brazil
		Gruma	1949	3.67	73	112 countries (America, Europe, Asia, Oceania), among them USA, Spain, Costa Rica, France, Italy, Portugal, Malta, Russia, Malaysia, Guatemala, Honduras, El Salvador, Nicaragua, Venezuela, UK, Netherlands, Australia, China, Ukraine
8	Beverages	Grupo Modelo	1925	8.17	11	USA, Australia, New Zealand, Japan, Greece, Netherlands, Belgium, Germany, Canada, Russia, countries in Africa and Latin America, Hong Kong, Singapore, China

Table 24.1 (*cont.*)

Ch.	Industry	Companies	Created	Sales 2016 or latest, US$bn	Exports, % sales 2016 or latest	Foreign investments, 2016
		Cuauhtémoc Moctezuma	1890	2.49	N/A	63 countries, among them countries in Europe, Canada, USA, Brazil
9	Shoes	Andrea	1973	1	N/A	USA, Brazil, Colombia, Guatemala, Argentina, Spain, Asia
		Flexi	1935	0.77	N/A	USA, Canada, European Union, Asia (Vietnam, China, Japan) Latin America [Costa Rica, Guatemala, Honduras, El Salvador, Panama, Nicaragua, Peru], Middle East
10	Cement	Cemex	1906	14.25	75	Over 50 countries in South, Central, and North America, Caribbean, Europe, Asia, Africa, and Oceania: e.g., USA, Spain, Venezuela, Panama, Dominican Republic, Haiti, Colombia, Chile, Costa Rica, Puerto Rico, Nicaragua, Philippines, Indonesia, Australia

Table 24.1 (cont.)

Ch.	Industry	Companies	Created	Sales 2016 or latest, US$bn	Exports, % sales 2016 or latest	Foreign investments, 2016
11	Ceramic	Cementos Chihuahua	1941	0.75	N/A	USA, South America, Bolivia
		Lamosa	1890	0.67	10	North, Central, and South America, among them USA, Cuba, Canada, Guatemala
		Interceramic	1978	0.54	30	China, USA, Italy, Panama, Guatemala
12	Containers	Vitro	1909	0.89	29	34 countries in the Americas, Europe, and Asia, among them Bolivia, Brazil, Colombia, Costa Rica, Guatemala, Panama, USA
		Envases Universales	1993	N/A	N/A	Guatemala, Colombia, USA, Scandinavia, China, South Korea
13	Car components	Metalsa	1956	2.44	N/A	North and South America (USA, Argentina, Brazil), Australia, Europe, Japan, India, Russia, Thailand

Table 24.1 (*cont.*)

Ch.	Industry	Companies	Created	Sales 2016 or latest, US$bn	Exports, % sales 2016 or latest	Foreign investments, 2016
		Nemak	1979	4.47	37	USA, Canada, Germany, Europe, South Korea, Asia, Italy, Norway, Argentina, Brazil, China, Poland, Austria, Hungary, Spain, India, Japan, Russia
14	Appliances	MABE	1946	3.46	N/A	Canada, USA, Central and South America and the Caribbean (Venezuela, Peru, Chile, Costa Rica, Ecuador, Colombia, Brazil, Argentina)
		MAN Industries	1949	N/A	N/A	Cuba, Colombia, Peru, Nigeria, Senegal, Morocco, Tunisia, Ghana, Togo, Spain, Germany, Austria, Italy, Guatemala, El Salvador, Honduras, Costa Rica, Dominican Republic, USA
15	Retail	Elektra	1906	4.79	N/A	Brazil, El Salvador, Guatemala, Honduras, Peru, Panama, USA

Table 24.1 (*cont.*)

Ch.	Industry	Companies	Created	Sales 2016 or latest, US$bn	Exports, % sales 2016 or latest	Foreign investments, 2016
16	Restaurants	Coppel	1941	5.75	N/A	Argentina, Brazil
		El Pollo Loco	1975	N/A	N/A	USA, Japan, Philippines, Singapore, Malaysia
		Alsea	1989	1.21	N/A	Colombia, Brazil, Chile, Argentina, Spain
17	Hospitality	Hoteles City Express	2002	0.10	N/A	Costa Rica, Colombia, Chile
		Grupo Posadas	1967	0.43	N/A	USA
18	Entertainment	KidZania	1996	N/A	50	Asia, Middle East, UK, Portugal, United Arab Emirates, South Korea, Thailand, India, Kuwait, Brazil, Saudi Arabia, Philippines, Japan, Chile, Malaysia, Indonesia, Turkey, Dubai, Egypt, Singapore, Russia, Qatar
		Cinépolis	1971	N/A	N/A	Asia (India), Central and South America (Chile, Costa Rica, El Salvador,

Table 24.1 (*cont.*)

Ch.	Industry	Companies	Created	Sales 2016 or latest, US$bn	Exports, % sales 2016 or latest	Foreign investments, 2016
						Guatemala, Honduras, Panama, Colombia, Peru, Brazil), USA
19	Television	Televisa	1973	5.56	9	Latin America, Western and Eastern Europe, Africa, India, China, USA
		TV Azteca	1993	0.81	21	USA, Central and South America (Peru, Colombia, El Salvador, Guatemala)
20	Information technology	Binbit	2005	N/A	N/A	Over 60 countries in Latin America, Africa, Asia, Eastern Europe, among them Argentina, Panama, Niger, Kenya, Tanzania, Singapore, Malaysia, Indonesia, Vietnam, Saudi Arabia, Honduras, Uruguay, Dominican Republic, Brazil, Hong Kong, Sri Lanka, Australia, New Zealand, Bangladesh, Bahrain, Jordan, Kuwait, Lebanon,

Table 24.1 (*cont.*)

Ch.	Industry	Companies	Created	Sales 2016 or latest, US$bn	Exports, % sales 2016 or latest	Foreign investments, 2016
						Pakistan, Palestine, Qatar, Syria, Iraq, Poland, Russia, Philippines, Thailand, Ghana, Egypt, Nigeria, Cyprus, UAE, Yemen, Oman, India, Serbia, Nicaragua, Peru, Colombia, Ecuador, Guatemala, El Salvador, Croatia, Albania, Bosnia and Herzegovina, Montenegro, Macedonia, Bulgaria, Slovenia, Kyrgyzstan, Kazakhstan, Azerbaijan
		Softtek	1982	0.50	73	USA, Canada, Costa Rica, Puerto Rico, Argentina, Peru, Uruguay, Brazil, Chile, Colombia, Paraguay, Venezuela, Spain, UK, Netherlands, China, India
21	Telecom	AméricaMóvil	2000	66	N/A	28 countries in Europe and the Americas and the Caribbean, among them Argentina, Chile, Uruguay, Brazil,

Table 24.1 (cont.)

Ch.	Industry	Companies	Created	Sales 2016 or latest, US$bn	Exports, % sales 2016 or latest	Foreign investments, 2016
						Colombia, Ecuador, Guatemala, Puerto Rico, USA, Paraguay, El Salvador, Nicaragua, Peru, Venezuela, Panama, Bolivia, Belarus, Bulgaria, Croatia, Liechtenstein, Macedonia, Serbia, Slovenia
		Iusacell	1955	N/A	N/A	North America and Latin America, among them USA, Canada
22	Consulting	Sintec	1987	N/A	42	14 Latin American countries, among them Colombia, Venezuela, Dominican Republic, Brazil
		Feher & Feher	2002	N/A	N/A	USA, Peru, Spain, Guatemala
23	Education	Universidad Nacional	1551	N/A	N/A	131 international agreements, main operations in USA, Canada, Spain, China, Costa Rica, France, UK

Table 24.1 (cont.)

Ch.	Industry	Companies	Created	Sales 2016 or latest, US$bn	Exports, % sales 2016 or latest	Foreign investments, 2016
		Autónoma de México				
		Tecnológico de Monterrey	1943	N/A	N/A	Alliances in 53 countries. Campuses in 14 countries: USA, Canada, Panama, Ecuador, Colombia, Peru, Chile, UK, Ireland, Spain, France, Switzerland, China, Germany.

Source: Companies' websites

The selected firms provide insights that are useful not only for managers of Mexican companies in the same industries, but also for managers of firms in other industries and in other emerging markets. Mexico is a much more prototypical emerging country in terms of its relative size and development, and can be compared more easily to other emerging countries than the four largest emerging markets of Brazil, China, India, and Russia, which are typically investigated in most studies. The transformation of Mexico from a closed and relatively backward country in the 1980s into an open and modern economy in the 2010s, which has resulted in the emergence of many leading MultiMexicans, has been a remarkable change. Surprisingly, it is one that has received relatively little attention in comparison to the transformation of other emerging economies.

Nevertheless, Mexico is an important economy and one that has served as the basis for studies that have generated important implications. For example, when in 1994 Mexico joined the North American Free Trade Agreement (NAFTA), it became the first free-trade agreement that included both advanced economies and emerging ones. Before then, multi-country free trade agreements had only occurred among either advanced economies or emerging economies. NAFTA became an experiment that paved the way for many other free trade agreements among emerging and advanced economies. Similarly, the large contractor *maquila* factories built along the USA–Mexico border became a laboratory for understanding how to set up free-trade zones and benefit from differences in comparative advantage among countries. In this book, I contribute to this tradition by explaining how companies in a typical emerging country, underwent deep economic transformations and were exposed to deep competitive pressures, but were nevertheless able to overcome the limitations of the underdevelopment of their home country and become multinationals.

THE PROCESS OF UPGRADING CAPABILITIES TO BUILD AN EMERGING MARKET MULTINATIONAL

Abstracting from the cross-industry comparison of MultiMexicans, I develop a model that highlights some of the leading drivers of the internationalization of emerging market multinationals. The model integrates the usual arguments about the influence of the company's resources on its internationalization (Tallman & Yip, 2009) and external influences on the behavior of emerging market multinationals (Ramamurti, 2012), with ideas that emerge from the analysis of MultiMexicans. The starting point of the model is the home country, which has a direct influence on the company via the provision, or rather the limited provision in the case of emerging economies, of inputs such as skilled labor or sophisticated technologies. It also plays a role in the provision of hard infrastructure like reliable roads and airports and soft infrastructure such as pro-market institutions and regulations. The home country also has an indirect influence on the firm via its impact on the objectives, skills, and capabilities of managers, and on the types of competitors, competitive interactions, and regulatory framework of the industry. These four factors (emerging home country, managers, industry, and company) influence the ability of the company to upgrade capabilities, which in turn affects internationalization. Figure 24.1 illustrates the relationships among the key variables.

This model contributes a better understanding of the theory of the multinational in general, and of the models of emerging market multinationals in particular, by explaining the process by which companies upgrade capabilities before they internationalize. As I reviewed in the introductory chapter, the traditional models of the multinational tend to assume that the company has already achieved a competitive advantage at home and can transfer this advantage to other countries to sell more. In contrast, here I highlight how the international expansion of a company is contingent on its ability to upgrade competitive capabilities to international levels. This

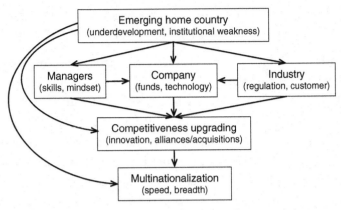

FIGURE 24.1 Relationships among the main influences on the
internationalization of emerging market firms

upgrading, in turn, is contingent on changes in the company that are
driven by transformations in managers and the industry as well as in
modifications in home country conditions. Thus, in essence, the
model takes competitive advantage as a driver of firm behavior, with
this competitive advantage being contingent on the context in which
the company operates, not only the industry as traditionally studied in
strategic management, but also the conditions of the home country.

Home Country: Underdevelopment and Institutional Weakness.
Abstracting from the experiences of the MultiMexicans analyzed, two
main dimensions of the home country – typical of emerging economies – affect firm behavior and subsequent internationalization: (1) the
level of underdevelopment of the economy, with consumers that have
limited income and skilled employees that are low cost; and (2) the level
of underdevelopment of the institutions, and the associated poor protection of contracts and property rights.

Emerging economies tend to be characterized by the underdevelopment of their economy, which includes not only a large segment of
poor citizens, but also an economy with fewer industries of high value
added, and a relatively unsophisticated infrastructure (Hoskisson
et al., 2000). All countries have poor people, but emerging countries

are characterized by larger segments of the population being considered poor; however, these people can still provide a market for creative companies that design products adapted to their needs (Prahalad, 2005). The large segment of poor people was viewed as an opportunity by some of the firms analyzed, which eventually developed business models and capabilities that, although initially designed to serve the needs of poor people in Mexico, became the basis of their global competitive advantage. For example, the retailers Elektra and Coppel developed a business model of financing the sale of a wide variety of goods to low-income consumers by offering convenient weekly or biweekly payments and used this model to expand abroad. Thus, the fact that Mexico had a large segment of the population with low incomes had a direct impact on the development of the core identity of the firms and their business models. The lower level of development of the country is also reflected in the lower cost of skilled labor that companies had to pay, which reinforced their ability to compete across markets. For example, the shoe producers Flexi and Andrea benefitted from the concentration of skilled and low-cost labor around León that enabled them to produce quality products that could be sold at relatively low prices.

The second characteristic of emerging markets, and one that has received the bulk of attention in the international business literature, is a relative institutional weakness. Emerging markets are characterized by fewer market-supporting rules and regulations and specialized intermediaries that support transactions (Khanna & Palepu, 2010). Although not all emerging economies suffer from institutional weaknesses, and some, like Chile, even have institutions that are more sophisticated than those in some advanced economies (World Bank, 2018), many emerging economies suffer from the unclear and in some cases unpredictable creation and application of pro-market rules and regulations in economic relationships. This particular characteristic seems to play a large role in the transformation of Mexican firms. Some of them suffered from the inability to rely on others, as contracts become difficult to enforce in a system of relatively ineffectual

judicial protection of rights. Thus, some of the firms had to incorporate activities that in other countries are undertaken by specialized
providers, and they therefore developed a wide variety of expertise.

It is this influence of the underdevelopment of the characteristics of the home country on the upgrading of the capabilities of the
company and its subsequent internationalization that sets the analysis of emerging market multinationals in general – and
MultiMexicans in particular – apart from traditional models. This
underdevelopment of the home market affects the way in which
managers understand the company and its market opportunities.
It also affects the way in which the industry where the company
operates is regulated and exerts competitive pressures. And it is
these characteristics of the home country, together with those of
managers and the industry, that determine how the company can
achieve a competitive advantage at home, and eventually an advantage abroad.

Managers: Skills and Mindsets. It is well known that managers
play a key role in the development of the competitive capabilities of
the firm as decision-makers that determine the resources and capabilities of the firm and how these are used in its growth and advantage
(Penrose, 1959). It is also well known that managers determine the
internationalization of the company since they are the decision-
makers, selecting the countries and entry methods based on their
knowledge and experience (Johanson & Vahlne, 1977). In the case of
MultiMexicans, two dimensions seem to have a large influence on
where and how the firms expanded: managerial skills and managerial
mindsets.

First, managerial skills and abilities are a key component of the
success of a company. Managers can be viewed as one of the key
resources of the firm as they are the ones who select other resources
and decide how they are used (Castanias & Helfat, 1991). For example,
the IT companies Binbit and Softtek were created by highly skilled
individuals who understood the needs of domestic and international
markets and how they could be better served by the firms.

Unfortunately, in emerging economies, the majority of the population does not have advanced education, and even colleges and universities are not sophisticated (McMullen, Mauch & Donnorummo, 2000). Education systems tend to be focused on the memorization of facts and figures with a limited development of creative and independent thinking (World Bank, 1999). This underdevelopment of the educational system limits the skills that managers can obtain from the formal education system, thereby harming the competitiveness of their firms. However, not all of the successful companies had highly skilled founders in the sense of individuals with advanced degrees; some had founders with limited formal education who nevertheless understood well the needs of customers and how to satisfy them to create successful companies.

In many of the firms, it was the second generation of family owners or professional managers rather than the founders who ignited a rapid transformation of the company to international levels of competitiveness, and later oversaw its wide international expansion. This was partly because these second-generation managers received a more sophisticated formal education that better prepared them to operate across markets, with a superior understanding of foreign languages as well as a deeper understanding of the needs of international markets. For example, Cemex started in 1906 in cement, grew to become the dominant cement producer, and then diversified in a variety of businesses, operating in machinery, mining, paper, petrochemicals, and tourism within Mexico. It was not until the mid-1980s that the new CEO, Lorenzo Zambrano, who had been educated at Stanford, focused the firm on cement and transformed it into a leading global competitor.

Second, the mindset of managers also plays a key role in the upgrading of capabilities and international expansion, because it changes the focus of managerial attention towards the need to improve to be able to serve foreign markets. Many of the companies were created in the country by entrepreneurs who understood the conditions of the home country and founded viable and successful firms adapted to take advantage of such opportunities. This mindset of how to upgrade to serve emerging markets can be developed over time as the need to internationalize arises. This is nicely illustrated by the case of the entertainment firm KidZania. The firm was initially branded *Ciudad de los Niños* (children's city), which was a name that conveyed what the company was offering its customers. However, this was a brand name created with a particular market in mind: Mexico. Although it could have been used in other Spanish-speaking countries, it was not a brand that could work well across languages. To expand abroad, the managers had to find a distinct name that worked well globally, and that could be registered as a trademark for the exclusive use of the company. The solution was the creation of a new word: KidZania.

These ideas serve as the basis for recommendations for managers of other emerging market companies that are considering turning their firms into multinationals. There is little that managers can do to solve the underdevelopment of the educational systems of their home countries, unless of course they create educational organizations. This was the case of the Tecnológico de Monterrey, which was created in 1943 by a group of managers affiliated with the Alfa conglomerate in Monterrey, who needed skilled engineers that were not being provided by the public university. On a more modest level, managers can address their limitations directly by undertaking an active assessment of their skills and mindsets and how these are constraining or enabling the upgrading of capabilities and internationalization of their companies. Managers can purposefully evaluate their skills and abilities to operate globally in terms of the knowledge of foreign countries and languages, understanding of differences across cultures and institutions, etc., to get a better sense of how they would be able to serve customers, face competitors, and interact with regulators abroad. If they perceive themselves to be lacking some of these skills, they can either undertake training to address the deficiencies or assess and identify other managers in the company who have the skills to operate globally. Additionally, they need to evaluate their mindsets to understand whether they have the appropriate attitudes to transform their firm into a multinational. This is a more challenging assessment because it is not as easily measurable as skills. It can nevertheless be studied by exploring their attitudes and views on the importance of foreign markets, for example, by identifying their willingness to put foreign customers or sales ahead of domestic ones if the company runs low on products. Managers who identify themselves as not having the appropriate mindset for running a multinational can either modify it via conscious training, or make sure that somebody who does have the required mindset is in charge of international operations. However, this is a common challenge for many family-owned firms, which are the majority in emerging markets, given that founders are rarely willing to give up control and may forgo the growth and international expansion of the company in exchange for their continued ability to lead the firm.

Industry: Regulation and Type of Customers. The industry in which the company operates always plays a large role in the ability and incentive of the company to compete and internationalize. The industry affects not only the profitability of the company and the competitive strategies it can implement (Porter, 1985; Tirole, 1988) but also the ability of the company to use similar sources of advantage across borders or the need to use different actions for each country (Prahalad & Doz, 1987). It also affects the types of competitors that the firm may encounter in international markets, as rivals keep track of what others do and follow each other abroad (Knickerbocker, 1973). In the case of MultiMexicans, two dimensions seem to play an important role: the regulation of the industry and the types of customers.

The regulation of the industry reflects the level of government control over the ability of companies to undertake the actions their managers deem best versus those that are required by the government. The implementation of pro-market reforms in emerging markets and the associated deregulation of industries has played a major role in enabling companies to internationalize (Cuervo-Cazurra, 2015).

The pro-market reforms resulted in the deregulation of the industry and the entry of new domestic and foreign competitors, forcing firms to upgrade capabilities. For example, the car component firms Metalsa and Nemak were pushed to upgrade their capabilities in preparation for the opening of the industry that was going to accompany the integration of Mexico into NAFTA. This experience with industry deregulation can create capabilities that are useful for operating in other countries. For example, the early experience gained at home with the processes of deregulation that accompanied pro-market reforms helped Chilean firms achieve an advantage over domestic firms in other Latin American countries that were undertaking reforms later (del Sol & Kogan, 2007). Thus, this experience with pro-market reforms can help firms use the same strategies across multiple countries instead of having to create country-specific strategies (Prahalad & Doz, 1987).

The type of customer that the company serves – either other companies or final consumers – influences whether or not the company needs to develop country-specific products and services, as consumer needs tend to differ more across countries than do company needs (Prahalad & Doz, 1987). As indicated before, emerging markets are characterized by a large segment of the population with low incomes, which leads companies to create products for these customers (Prahalad, 2005). However, this does not mean that emerging market multinationals only concentrate on low-income consumers. They can focus on developing innovations that serve the needs of higher-income customers and use these innovations to internationalize. For example, the cinema chain Cinépolis created new entertainment formats by adding more sophisticated experiences and food and entertainment to serve all market segments. It then used this experience to enter the US market, selling not only a sophisticated cinema experience but also the experience of watching sports in luxury cinemas with sophisticated food and drinks.

In the case of firms that sell to other businesses, the process of upgrading and internationalization differs, as customers tend to be more focused on functionality and price than perceptions of quality and brands. As a result, the negative impact that producing in an emerging market tends to have on customers in other countries, especially advanced ones, is less of an issue. Whereas final consumers may discriminate against products coming from emerging economies (Bilkey & Nes, 1982; Peterson & Jolibert, 1995), industrial customers tend to be more analytical and analyze the quality and costs of the emerging market product before deciding whether to purchase it. This facilitates the internationalization of emerging market firms, but at the same time requires them to achieve credible and tangible levels of competitiveness in their products. Thus, for example, the container firms Vitro and Envases Universales focused on upgrading capabilities to match the increasing expectations of their industrial customers.

The lesson for managers from this analysis is a push to analyze this dual influence of the industry: regulation and type of customer. First, all industries are regulated, as all require permits and are subject to inspections and paperwork. These regulations can be more onerous in some industries than in others, and vary in their dimensions. Thus, for example, in the food industry there is limited regulation regarding entry in the industry but a large number of complex regulations in place to ensure the safe handling and distribution of food to prevent consumers from becoming sick. In contrast, the television industry is highly regulated with a limited number of licenses being issued, but fewer controls regarding the production of programs and their content. And these regulations vary across countries significantly, requiring different sets of capabilities. For example, whereas the oil industry in Mexico is regulated to the point that only the state-owned oil firm Pemex is allowed to explore, produce, and distribute oil, in other countries, such as the USA, new firms can easily enter the industry. Thus, in cases in which the company is operating in a highly regulated industry, the manager needs to use consultants and local lawyers, and interact with regulators and politicians to understand industry requirements and ensure that their products meet such requirements. Unfortunately, this results in the development of regulatory and institutional capabilities that, although useful at home, may be of limited use in other countries, as rules and regulations and the regulatory agencies differ. For example, although Pemex controlled the exploration and production of oil in Mexico, its refining capacities were underdeveloped as a result of limited investments and low competitive pressures. Thus, it ended up exporting crude oil to US refineries and importing refined products.

In contrast, in a lightly regulated industry, the company can focus on improving its capabilities and the quality of its products so that it becomes the supplier of choice for customers. These more sophisticated capabilities can then be put to good use in foreign markets, exporting lower cost and higher quality products than host country competitors are producing. Thus, the cinema chain Cinépolis used its well-honed capabilities and sophisticated products to great effect in the US market.

Second, the type of customer matters – whether customers are final consumers or other businesses – and not just in terms of how to fulfill their needs, but also regarding how the firm upgrades capabilities and internationalizes. For firms that create products for final consumers, the sale of the products depends not only on their inherent quality but also, and in many cases mostly, on the perception of quality by consumers. Thus, efforts to improve competitiveness and quality need to be visible and perceived by customers, or communicated to customers when the changes are not tangible. These same improvements then need to be included in the internationalization efforts, especially since emerging market firms have to contend with the effect that consumers tend to discriminate against products from emerging economies. Additionally, consumer preferences tend to differ widely across countries, even those that are considered similar on the surface.

To understand this, managers need to do detailed market research to understand how the needs of consumers differ across countries, or find countries that have consumers with needs that are similar to those of the home country. For example, the restaurant franchiser Alsea did this as it expanded in Latin America, and it was surprising to find that consumer preferences in Brazil differed widely from those in Mexico, even though both countries are perceived as being similar because they are both Latin American countries. In contrast, when the company is serving other companies, the focus is more on signaling the quality of the products and establishing business partnerships, selling the customer not just the product but a continued relationship. One way to do this is to build on existing contacts with current customers to facilitate entry into new countries, as the consulting company Sintec did when entering the Colombian market.

Company Resources: Funds and Technology. The usual assumption when analyzing the internationalization of the company is to focus on the resources of the firm as the basis of its competitive advantage at home and abroad. A company is a bundle of diverse resources, or assets that are tied semi-permanently to the firm (Penrose, 1959). Among these, some have the potential to support the firm's competitive advantage and thus its internationalization, while others have limited influence on the advantage of the firm, and yet others may be a source of disadvantage (Montgomery, 1995). First, resources that support a firm's advantage are those that help the firm create value for customers, that few other companies have, and that are difficult for competitors to imitate and substitute (Barney, 1991). Second, resources that have a limited impact on the advantage of the firm are those that are common among competitors; however, a firm that lacks them may be at a disadvantage. Finally, resources that create competitive disadvantage are those that reduce the value to customers or create inefficiencies in other resources.

Although, in principle, any resource has the potential to serve as the basis of a firm's advantage, from the analysis of the cases, we found two main types of resources that had a higher influence on the ability of the firm to upgrade capabilities and become a multinational: funds and technology. The funds available to the company include both internally generated capital from existing operations in the home country, as well as access to external sources of finance, not only at home but also abroad. In principle, the generation of financial funds can be viewed as the outcome of the overall advantage of the firm, but in emerging markets, it takes a new meaning as it can become a source of advantage on its own. Even though in advanced economies finance tends to be seen as a second-level resource that is generic and widely available, in emerging economies access to funds for investment becomes a driver of change. The lower level of sophistication of financial markets in emerging economies increases the costs and limits the availability of funds (Booth et al., 2001). Thus, the achievement of a dominant position in the home market becomes the basis for the firm to ensure a stream of excess funds that can be used to invest in new technologies and expand abroad. For example, Cemex acquired competitors and achieved a dominant position in the home market that enabled it to generate the cash needed to invest in new information and communication technologies. It also used the funds to acquire the Spanish firms Sanson and Valenciana de Cementos. These acquisitions further enhanced the firm's access to funds because they enabled Cemex to reduce its cost of capital by issuing debt in Spain rather than in Mexico. However, such a dominant position is not necessarily a guarantee of excess funds as it depends on how the funds are used. Thus, for example, the state-owned Pemex has been constrained in its ability to invest not only in exploration and development but also in improving the exploitation of fields by the forced transfer of cash to support the general budget of the Mexican government.

The second type of resource is the level of technological sophistication of the company, which includes not only its ability to innovate products, but also its ability to establish new organizational processes and new business models. In the case of emerging market multinationals, these organizational and business model innovations tend to be the main sources of technological sophistication. Emerging markets suffer from weaknesses in their innovation systems and limitations in their intellectual property rights protection (OECD, 2017). These restrict the ability of companies to innovate products

(Awate, Larsen & Mudambi, 2012). This is unfortunate because technological sophistication of the company is the basis for its ability to outcompete host country competitors with a more sophisticated product or production technologies, and thus to compensate for the cost of doing business abroad (Hymer, 1976) and other liabilities of foreignness (Zaheer, 1995). Nevertheless, technological sophistication does not necessarily require large investments in R&D. It can be accomplished with a rethinking of the traditional business model used to compete in the industry and by finding and designing a new business model. Thus, for example, the tile manufacturer Interceramic altered its business model from a traditional producer of glazed ceramic tiles to become a more sophisticated competitor by first incorporating more advanced technology from Italy that enabled it to produce better products at lower costs. It then continued to upgrade its business model by adding franchise distribution systems that assisted it to further differentiate its products in terms of quality in the mindset of consumers.

However, the business model and underlying technology need protection at home and abroad. This protection at home can be achieved via secrecy and complexity, as intellectual property might not be properly protected (Zhao, 2006). However, many emerging market firms can take advantage of the stricter protections abroad and consider new ways in which to defend their advantage. For example, KidZania not only changed its name from *Ciudad de los Niños* to KidZania because the original name did not work well in other languages, but also because KidZania could be registered as a trademark and thus legally protected throughout the world. Additionally, KidZania guards its business model by identifying and registering the key characteristics that differentiate it to be able to constrain imitation by competitors.

The lessons that one can derive from the cases on how MultiMexicans use key resources are as follows. First, when analyzing funds, the manager needs to assess the ability of the company to finance the foreign expansion. This includes not only support at the initial entry into the country when the firm invests in operations abroad, but also support for sustained losses over time, which are likely to happen to a subsidiary until it establishes itself abroad and becomes well known among customers. Thus, the question is not so much whether the company has enough funds to invest abroad and establish an operation, which is a necessary condition for foreign expansion, but whether the company has enough funds to support both the foreign expansion as well as current domestic operations until the foreign operation is independently profitable. The manager needs to make sure that losses abroad do not jeopardize the home operations, and needs to establish a limit to how much money the company can afford to lose, i.e., for how long the manager is willing to subsidize foreign losses.

Second, when studying the technological sophistication of the company, the manager can analyze this not only in comparison with competitors in the home country, which is probably implicit in the mindset of the manager, but also in comparison to competitors in the host country. Such analysis includes a study of the product technology of host country competitors, which can be done relatively easily by reverse engineering their products. It also includes the analysis of process and organizational technology, which is much more challenging to analyze because these contain high levels of tacit knowledge that are not available to a new competitor in the host country. Thus, the manager needs to identify first the relevant competitors, second the level of technological sophistication of each of them in comparison to the company, and third the methods the company can use to protect its technology from being copied by host country competitors.

Capability Upgrading: Innovation and External Methods. The interactions among managers, company, and industry characteristics, and the conditions of the home country, create various ways in which the company can upgrade capabilities for internationalization. This upgrading is in many cases one of the prerequisites for the company to become a multinational and achieve success abroad. There are three main ways in which a company can upgrade its capabilities (Capron &

Mitchell, 2012): building capabilities internally through investments; borrowing capabilities from external partners through alliances and continued cooperation with other companies; and buying the capabilities of other companies via the acquisition of firms or the purchasing of technologies. However, from the analysis of the cases of MultiMexicans, there appear to be two key ways that support the success of upgrading and internationalization of emerging market multinationals: internal innovation, and the acquisition of technology from advanced country competitors.

In the case of internal innovation, companies that became successful multinationals were able to innovate processes internally to achieve higher levels of efficiency, or innovate their business models to do something that competitors were not offering in the home country. Such innovations were usually done intentionally, in many cases by the entrepreneurial founder of the company. The driver of innovation was mostly the business model and the interconnections among the different activities within the firm. Thus, for example, both the cinema chain Cinépolis and the theme park firm KidZania identified new customer experiences and developed ways to serve these. These innovations were built around a series of activities that were combined to create a novel service, i.e., being an immersive luxury entertainment venue with food and drinks, or role-playing adult activities for children, respectively.

In the case of acquisitions and alliances, MultiMexicans upgraded their capabilities to international levels by learning from the superior capabilities of companies from advanced economies via alliances in the home country or acquisitions of foreign companies abroad. Some of the companies established alliances with foreign companies in Mexico and acted as their domestic partners, providing access to and understanding of the domestic market in exchange for more sophisticated technology from the foreign partner. Other companies instead acquired firms in more advanced economies to access the more sophisticated technology of the target firm as well as the network of relationships and presence in a superior innovation

system. For example, the component firm Metalsa acquired companies in advanced economies with the stated purpose of accessing more
sophisticated technologies.

Managers can reinforce the upgrading of capabilities toward
international levels using these types of internal innovation and external sources of technologies. In the case of innovation, the focus on
process innovation seems to be the usual source of competitive advantage for emerging market multinationals. This is partly because there
tends to be limited product innovation in emerging markets, as an
outcome of the weaknesses in the innovation systems and the lower
protection of intellectual property rights, and partly because the most
sophisticated customer demands tend to be in advanced economies.
Nevertheless, there are large opportunities for product innovation in
areas that are distinctly typical of emerging markets, such as innovations for consumers who have very low levels of income, the so-called
bottom-of-the-pyramid consumers (Prahalad, 2005). Thus, some companies have created new business models that take advantage of such
opportunities, such as the retailers Coppel and Elektra, and these
innovations can be used in other countries. In other cases, innovations
come from solving limitations in consumer demands or the infrastructure of the country that prevents them from fulfilling their needs,
turning these limitations into opportunities. Hence, for example, the
cement company Cemex had to compensate for the lack of a good,
reliable telephone service in Mexico by creating its own telecommunications system, which later helped it achieve an advantage in coordination over advanced economy competitors. In the case of using
alliances and acquisitions to improve technology, managers can
focus on establishing alliances with foreign companies not just as
a market opportunity that enables the company to sell to a large client,
but also as a source of potential improvements for the firm. For
example, Bimbo benefitted from learning how to make bread of the
same quality and consistency from its alliance in Mexico with the
US firm Sunbeam, which helped it to counter the entry of the US firm
Wonder Bread in Mexico. Before establishing an alliance, managers

need to assess the technology status of the company and the areas in which it needs the most significant upgrading, and establish strategic alliances or strategic acquisitions that facilitated the firm to solve these upgrading gaps.

Multinationalization: Speed and Breadth. There is a long tradition in international business of analyzing multiple dimensions of internationalization (see reviews in Rugman, 2009). The cases studied in this book point towards two key dimensions of the internationalization of MultiMexicans that are particularly relevant: the speed at which companies expand abroad, and the breadth of the expansion of companies across multiple countries. First, the analysis of the speed of internationalization goes back to the debate in international business about the appropriate process of internationalization: that is, whether the company would be better off following a gradual internationalization process that enables it to learn from foreign operations and limits its exposure and thus potential downside risks (Johanson & Vahlne, 1977); or whether it is better off following a rapid internationalization process that allows it to conquer foreign markets and increase in size quickly, benefiting from innovations created in the home country that can be used across multiple countries (Oviatt & McDougall, 1994). The analysis of MultiMexicans seems to challenge both models. On the one hand, these firms, except IT ones, grew first domestically before venturing abroad. In many cases, they internationalized only after several decades of operating at home. And their internationalization was prompted by the upgrading of capabilities in response to the increase in competition after pro-market reforms. Thus, it appears that the born-global model of a rapid internationalization has a couple of unstated assumptions. One is that firms are assumed to be internationally competitive from their inception. Another is that firms have products or services that can be distributed easily across national borders. On the other hand, the experience of MultiMexicans seems also to challenge the incremental internationalization model, as many of them did not expand first to other Latin American countries that were similar to the home country and later to countries that were more distant. Instead, the attractiveness of the US market regarding economic size and geographic proximity appeared to be a strong magnet for expansion. Some firms entered the US with a focus on the Latino population rather than the larger and more diverse general population. So in this sense, the incremental internationalization model seems to work, with the caveat of having to go deeper into subsegments of the population with more fine-grained analyses of the characteristics of subnational locations. Thus, for example, the expansion of the television companies was aided by the presence of a large Latino population in the USA that became an attractive market segment for the firms and induced them to focus on achieving dominance in that subsegment.

Second, the study of the breadth of foreign expansion reflects the dilemma of management: whether the company can manage the wide diversity and complexity that comes with a large number of foreign countries and the associated learning benefits (Bartlett & Ghoshal, 1989); or whether it is better off focusing on a few countries and thus simplifying its foreign operations and the costs of managing diversity and complexity (Teece, 1977). In the case of MultiMexicans, this selection seems to be partly driven by the ability of the firm to transfer competitive advantage across multiple countries rather than by a particular decision to limit the breadth of internationalization. Companies that were assumed to internationalize narrowly, because they operate in industries that tend to be national as a result of the large differences across countries in terms of consumer preferences or barriers to transportation and distribution, were nevertheless highly global. For example, the cement firm Cemex, which sells a product that is bulky and low value-added and has high transportation costs that limit its distribution, became a leading global contender. Similarly, the food firms Bimbo and Gruma operate in an industry in which consumers have very different preferences across countries, but they nevertheless expanded across a large diversity of countries. In contrast, the oil and gas firm Pemex, which operates in an industry that is considered global, had a relatively limited international presence. Additionally, the analysis of the breadth of operations seems to be part of a process of expansion rather than one of end-game decisions. Depending on when one analyzes the international expansion of the firm, one can draw very different conclusions regarding the breadth of expansion. For example, if we were analyzing the internationalization of Cemex in the 1990s, it would appear that it was a regional company because most sales and operations were concentrated near its home market with an initial foray into Europe via Spain. However, the same analysis in the 2010s reveals a firm with a global presence in which the home market represented only a fifth of total sales.

To facilitate the internationalization of their firms, managers can derive a few lessons from this analysis. The first one is to investigate the level of competitiveness of their firms and how the resources and capabilities that underpin their competitiveness can be transferred to other countries, both regarding the speed of transfer of the advantage as well as the breadth of applicability of the advantage. Before considering entering other countries, managers need to have a deep understanding of not only what gives their firms an advantage at home, but also whether such sources of advantage can be transferred abroad, because the sources provide customers abroad with value above the offers of other firms or because they offer something better than what current competitors are offering. This requires going beyond the usual assessment of whether a foreign country presents appealing opportunities for expansion, and going deeper into analyzing in which countries the company can better transfer and apply its competitive advantage. The traditional approach is to seek countries that are similar to the home country and that offer attractive market opportunities because they are growing and have plenty of potential customers. However, the question is not whether the country has good market opportunities, but whether the country has good market opportunities for the particular company that is analyzing that market. Hence, the first step is to understand the company and its sources of advantage. Once this is done, the next assessment is whether such sources of advantage can be quickly transferred to the selected host countries, and what steps will enable a successful transfer. For example, managers can take actions to increase the speed and breadth of the internationalization of the company by rethinking the distribution channels of the products and relying on partners for logistics and distribution. Or they can rethink the need to control the distribution channels and use methods such as licensing and franchising instead of expanding through foreign direct investments. Finally, one important idea to mention is that there is a positive feedback loop between capability upgrading and internationalization, in the sense that companies that upgrade their capabilities to international levels can successfully internationalize, and those that have internationalized benefit from access to new knowledge and learning that enables them to upgrade their capabilities further. This was, for example, the approach that Cemex took with its acquisitions of companies in foreign countries. It developed a process, the "Cemex Way" (Lessard & Lucea, 2009), by which it analyzed private companies and determined in which activities the target companies would benefit from the use of current best-in-class industry practices that Cemex had developed. It also identified areas and practices in which the target company was superior to Cemex and transferred those to other operations.

CONCLUSIONS: UPGRADING STRATEGIES FOR INTERNATIONALIZATION: IMPROVEMENT, INTEGRATION, INSPIRATION, AND INNOVATION

The analysis of the transformation of Mexican companies from domestic firms into successful multinationals as studied in this book provides new lessons. These are interesting not only for understanding the behavior of these companies in particular, which have not been studied in detail despite their importance and success abroad, but also for comprehending the internationalization of emerging market multinationals in general. Each chapter contains suggestions and reflections on the internationalization of the company that take into account the particular conditions of the country and industry in which they operate. On the basis of these insights and their comparison across the different chapters, I developed a model that explains the process by which domestic companies in emerging markets become multinationals. At the foundation of this process is the idea that the conditions of the home country have a large influence on the characteristics and behavior of managers, companies, and industries, and on the subsequent processes of competitiveness upgrading and internationalization. As a result, the model presented here that explains how domestic companies become multinationals has at its core two main ideas.

The first idea is the importance of the home country in understanding multinationals. Not all of the behaviors of emerging market multinationals differ from those of advanced economy companies; there are many characteristics that they have in common (Ramamurti, 2012). The distinguishing characteristic of emerging market multinationals is their country of origin and how this affects certain dimensions of their behavior. Here I highlight how the development of the home country influences how managers, companies, and industries behave and thus the eventual upgrading and internationalization of firms.

The second idea is the importance of understanding how companies develop resources and capabilities that enable them to compete at home and that support their foreign expansion. Rather than assume that companies have already developed a competitive advantage at home and then analyze how this can be better applied in other countries, models and theories of the multinational need to take into account that this process of development of capabilities is not a given. The only requirement for a company to become a multinational is the willingness to spend enough money on the foreign expansion. However, this does not ensure that the company is going to be a successful multinational. To become a successful multinational, the company needs to be able to achieve a competitive advantage in other countries rather than assume that it will have an advantage because it has expanded abroad.

Hence, building on these two ideas, I introduce a typology of companies based on the strategies they have used to upgrade their capabilities towards international levels and that have eventually enabled them to become multinationals. Table 24.2 illustrates the four upgrading strategies. These are organized in a two-by-two matrix based on two dimensions. First, the locus of upgrading: whether the company is upgrading capabilities to achieve excellence in the processes that the company uses, or to achieve excellence in the products and services that it sells. Second, the focus of upgrading: whether the company is focusing on upgrading capabilities to the local level, or whether the focus of upgrading is to achieve global excellence.

Upgrading via improvement is characteristic of companies that concentrate their efforts on enhancing their processes and that focus attention on achieving excellence for the local market. Companies compete by renovating how they make products and services that better fulfill the needs of customers at a more attractive quality level or price point. For these companies, internationalization is a byproduct of the upgrading of processes as their focus is concentrated on the domestic market. They become multinationals as new market opportunities to sell products to similar markets appear. Thus, for example, the food firm Gruma focused on the domestic market and

Table 24.2 *Four strategies for upgrading capabilities for internationalization by emerging market firms*

		Locus of upgrading	
		Process	Product
Focus of upgrading	Local	Improvement	Inspiration
	Global	Integration	Innovation

on improving the way in which it produced corn tortillas. The product was a traditional staple of the Mexican diet, and the company modernized production by bringing in industrial methods to a sector that operated in a mostly artisan manner. It started its multinationalization in Costa Rica after the invitation of the Costa Rican government to set up a production facility there, and continued the expansion in other countries by replicating the sophisticated production processes it had refined at home.

Upgrading via inspiration is the strategy followed by emerging market multinationals that concentrate on introducing new products and services in the market, to fulfill some unmet needs of customers at home. These companies create a new product or service that differs from current offers in the home country, even if such a product or service may be similar to those of other countries. The firm uses a deep understanding of the characteristics of the home market to create something new that fulfills some unmet needs. This innovation can be a new product or service that is applicable in other countries as well, and which the company can take abroad as the basis of internationalization, offering something that customers in the other country come to value. For example, the cinema chain Cinépolis rethought the cinema service and introduced not only more comfortable seating but also more sophisticated food and beverages and new formats to upgrade the experience of moviegoers. These new services were then used in the international expansion of the firm in the USA, in which it had to create new services, such as offering sports games in the cinemas, as other movie chains already offered plush seating and large screens.

Upgrading via integration is the strategy of those firms that focus on improving the production processes that enabled them to achieve higher quality products by introducing ideas and seeking help from leaders, and doing so with the aim of achieving global excellence. These companies focus on enhancing their production processes and integrate ideas from other foreign and domestic companies. In so doing, they raise the level of competitiveness of their production process to international levels, enabling them to be highly competitive at home and abroad. For example, the bakery goods firm Bimbo focused on improving the production and distribution process of fresh bread and baked goods. It incorporated ideas developed in the US market by other companies that helped it increase the quality of its production process and ensure the distribution of fresh products throughout Mexico. These innovations enabled it to enter other countries in which it brought a better understanding of production processes and used domestic brands to facilitate market penetration.

Upgrading via innovation is followed by firms that concentrate their attention on creating new products or services that will fill unmet needs, and that do so by aiming to understand ideas and needs on a global level. In these companies, the thrust is to create a new product or service that is new to the world even though the initial focus may be on the domestic market. This new product can then be used as the basis for the expansion of the firm into new countries, ensuring that it maintains a level of innovation over that of global competitors who may imitate the emerging market multinational. For example, the theme park firm KidZania created a new type of entertainment park in which children could role-play the jobs of adults. They started in the Mexican market, collaborating with local companies that provided the supplies and training on how to role-play in exchange for marketing presence. The concept was eventually used not only in Mexico but also abroad, and thus the company refined and adapted its business model to fulfill new needs and collaborate with new local competitors. The firm also changed its name from *Ciudad de los Niños* to KidZania and trademarked its name and production process so that it could defend its competitive advantage abroad.

In sum, the analysis of MultiMexicans presented in this book helps to create a better understanding of how these particular companies have become global competitors, and thus fill the gap in our knowledge on emerging market multinationals from an important emerging country. The analysis also advances the models of the multinational by providing a better understanding of the influence of the home country on internationalization via upgrading strategies. The process identified – whereby the home country influences the characteristics and behavior of managers, companies, and industries, and these, in turn, affect the upgrading of capabilities and internationalization – helps us to understand better how companies in other emerging economies can become multinationals despite the limitations they face in the home country. The four identified strategies that enable the company to upgrade capabilities to support its internationalization (improvement, integration, inspiration, and innovation) provide a useful framework for managers of other companies that are also aiming to turn their domestic companies into multinationals. I hope that these insights inspire future analyses of emerging market multinationals and help improve the understanding and management of these companies.

REFERENCES

Awate, S., Larsen, M. & Mudambi, R. 2012. EMNE catch-up strategies in the wind turbine industry: is there a trade-off between output and innovation capabilities? *Global Strategy Journal*, 2, 205–223.

Barney, J. B. 1991. Firm resources and sustained competitive advantage. *Journal of Management*, 17: 99–120.

Bartlett, C. A. & Ghoshal, S. 1989. *Managing Across Borders: The Transnational Solution*. Boston, MA: Harvard Business School Press.

Bilkey, W. J. & Nes, E. 1982. Country-of-origin effects on products evaluations. *Journal of International Business Studies*, 13(1): 89–99.

Booth, L., Aivazian, V., Demirguc-Kunt, A. & Maksimovic, V. 2001. Capital structures in developing countries. *Journal of Finance*, 56(1): 87–130.

Capron, L. & Mitchell, W. 2012. *Build, Borrow, or Buy: Solving the Growth Dilemma*. Boston, MA: Harvard Business Review Press.

Castanias, R. P. & Helfat, C. E. 1991. Managerial resources and rents. *Journal of Management*, 17: 155–171.

Cuervo-Cazurra, A. 2012. How the analysis of developing country multinational companies helps advance theory: Solving the Goldilocks debate. *Global Strategy Journal*, 2(3): 153–167.

Cuervo-Cazurra, A. 2015. The co-evolution of pro-market reforms and emerging market multinationals, in Tihanyi, L., Banalieva, E., Devinney, T. M. & Pedersen, T. (Eds.), *Advances in International Management 28: Emerging Economies and Multinational Enterprises*. Emerald.

del Sol, P. & Kogan, J. 2007. Regional competitive advantage based on pioneering economic reforms: the case of Chilean FDI. *Journal of International Business Studies*, 38(6): 901–927.

Hoskisson, R. E., Eden, L., Lau, C. M. & Wright, M. 2000. Strategy in Emerging Economies. *Academy of Management Journal*, 43(3): 249–267.

Hymer, S. H. 1976. *The International Operations of National Firms: A Study of Foreign Direct Investment*. Cambridge, MA: MIT Press.

Johanson, J. & Vahlne, J. E. 1977. The internationalization process of the firm: A model of knowledge development and increasing foreign market commitments. *Journal of International Business Studies*, 8: 23–32.

Khanna, T. & Palepu, K. 2010. *Winning in Emerging Markets: A Road Map for Strategy and Execution*. Boston, MA: Harvard Business School Press.

Knickerbocker, F. T. 1973. *Oligopolistic Reaction and the Multinational Enterprise*. Cambridge, MA: Harvard University Press.

Lessard, D. R. & Lucea, R. 2009. Mexican multinationals: Insights from CEMEX, in R. Ramamurti & J. V. Singh (Eds.), *Emerging Multinationals from Emerging Markets*. New York, NY: Cambridge University Press.

McMullen. S. M., Mauch, J. E. & Donnorummo, B. 2000. *The Emerging Markets and Higher Education: Development and Sustainability*. New York, NY: RoutledgeFalmer.

Montgomery, C. A. (Ed.) 1995. *Resource-Based and Evolutionary Theories of the Firm: Towards a Synthesis*. Norwell, MA: Kluwer.

OECD. 2017. *OECD Science, Technology and Industry Outlook 2016*. Paris: Organization for Economic Cooperation and Development.

Oviatt, B. M. & McDougall, P. P. 1994. Toward a theory of international new ventures. *Journal of International Business Studies*, 25(1): 45–64.

Penrose, E. T. 1959. *The Theory of the Growth of the Firm*. Oxford: Oxford University Press.

Peterson, R. A. & Jolibert, A. J. P. 1995. A Meta-Analysis of Country-of-Origin Effects. *Journal of International Business Studies*, 26(4): 883–900.

Porter, M. E. 1985. *Competitive Advantage*. New York, NY: Free Press.

Prahalad, C. K. 2005. *The Fortune at the Bottom of the Pyramid: Eradicating Poverty through Profits*. Philadelphia, PA: Wharton Business School Press.

Prahalad, C. K. & Doz, Y. L. 1987. *The Multinational Mission*. New York, NY: The Free Press.

Ramamurti, R. 2012. What is really different about emerging market multinationals? *Global Strategy Journal*, 2(1): 41–47.

Rugman, A. M. (Ed.). 2009. *The Oxford Handbook of International Business*. New York, NY: Oxford University Press.

Tallman, S. B. & Yip, G. S. 2009. Strategy and the multinational enterprise, in A. M. Rugman (Ed.), *The Oxford Handbook of International Business*. New York, NY: Oxford University Press.

Teece, D. J. 1977. *The Multinational Corporation and the Resource Transfer Cost of Technology Transfer*. Cambridge: Ballinger.

Tirole, J. 1988. *The Theory of Industrial Organization*. Cambridge, MA: MIT Press.

World Bank. 1999. *World Development Report 1998/99: Knowledge for Development*. New York, NY: Oxford University Press.

World Bank. 2018. Worldwide governance indicators. http://info.worldbank.org/g overnance/wgi/#home. Accessed April 18, 2018.

Zaheer, S. 1995. Overcoming the liability of foreignness. *Academy of Management Journal*, 38: 341–363.

Zhao, M. 2006. Conducting R&D in countries with weak intellectual property rights protection. *Management Science*, 56, 1185–1199.

25 Research Strategy for Analyzing MultiMexicans

Alvaro Cuervo-Cazurra and Miguel A. Montoya

The insights presented in this book are based on the comparison of case studies. The case studies were selected by their ability to provide insights into MultiMexicans. In this book, we have followed a common procedure throughout the chapters to facilitate their analysis and the development of conclusions that can help managers and academics.

METHODOLOGY

We chose to use comparative case studies for several reasons. First, cases are appropriate for identifying processes and sequences of actions, which are rarely available in databases. Since our interest was in understanding how Mexican companies had been able to become multinationals, the use of case studies was the best technique for gaining such comprehension. Second, using multiple cases from a diverse set of industries not only helps us to better learn how companies have taken particular sets of actions, but also helps separate the uniqueness of actions taken by one company from actions that are common across several companies and across multiple industries. Third, in general, firms in emerging markets are less willing than companies in advanced economies to provide information about the actions they have taken. This is not just because some of the companies are private, and thus do not have to share as much information as publicly traded ones, but also because managers tend to be cautious about revealing information that could be used against them by competitors or the government. Finally, case studies not only provide detailed information on the actions and processes taken by the companies, but also present information in a way that managers of other

716

companies can understand more easily. The cases become examples that managers of other companies can use as they guide their firms abroad.

Nevertheless, despite case studies being the main source of information for this book, we also used other techniques. These include studies of the largest companies that appear in periodicals like the magazine *Expansión* as well as country-level data on foreign direct investment. These sources helped us get a better sense of whether the insights gained from the case studies were part of a general trend shared by many of the other large companies, as well as part of the general development experienced by the country as a whole.

DATA COLLECTION

The collection of data analyzed in the cases followed a common pattern across the chapters, with some leeway for the requirements of particular companies or industries. In general terms, we first identified the companies that seemed to be the most appropriate for analyzing in this book because they were examples of successful MultiMexicans. Unlike other books that have focused only on the largest multinationals, we provide a broad overview of the whole spectrum of MultiMexicans and include both large and small ones. We achieved this by first identifying industries that represented some of the key poles of economic activity in Mexico and then finding within each of the industries two of the top companies that were owned by Mexican investors and that had a large presence abroad. We identified some of these companies using the list of the most globalized Mexican companies that appeared in the magazine *Expansión* (CNN Expansión, 2015), and those companies that appeared in the list of the largest multinationals from developing countries in UNCTAD (2012) and BCG (2006, 2008, 2011, 2013).

In most of the chapters we were able to analyze two leading MultiMexicans that were similar in size to facilitate their comparison, but this was not always possible. In some industries we could

only study one company because there are no other Mexican companies that are multinationals; such is the case of the petroleum industry, which is under the control of a state-owned monopoly.
We nevertheless thought that this industry was too important to
leave out of the discussion, especially since it illustrates the influence
of the government in the industry, and thus included it. In other
industries we were not able to find multinationals that are currently
of Mexican ownership because the leading firms were recently purchased by foreign companies, as was the case in the beer industry; we
nevertheless included these because they illustrate the possibility
that successful MultiMexicans may become targets for acquisitions
by advanced economy competitors. Yes, in other industries we studied
companies that are relatively small in comparison to the world standards, such as information technology, consulting, and automobile
components, which are dominated by global foreign investors; we
included them because they exemplify the ability of small companies
to compete against much larger foreign rivals. Finally, in other industries, we included companies that are significantly different in size, as
was the case of the telecommunication and television industry in
which one of the rivals dominates the sector and the other is
a relative minnow; these illustrate the competitive interactions
among companies of different sizes within the same industry.

Once we had identified the industries and companies, we
assigned each of the chapters to experts in the industry. We used
information from the magazine *Expansión* to get a sense of which
were the leading players in each industry. *Expansión* has been publishing the list of the largest Mexican companies annually since 1987.
We used the list of the largest 500 Mexican companies in the 2010s to
identify those companies that appeared among the top contenders in
each industry. Within each industry, we analyzed which of those
companies were Mexican by ownership by going directly to company
directories and the company's websites, because *Expansión* lists the
largest companies operating in Mexico and not just the largest
Mexican companies. Once we had agreed on the companies to study,

the authors of each of the chapters then collected secondary information on the companies and industry from all available sources. Some of the sources were periodicals in the Spanish language such as *Expansión* or *Gazeta de los Negocios*, as well as in English such as *The Economist* or *The Financial Times*. We also used existing case studies on companies available from publishing houses like Harvard Business School, Ivey School of Business, IMD, Sloan School of Management, etc., as well as cases that appear in books like Casanova (2009), ECLAC (2006), Hoshino (2001), Ramamurti & Singh (2009), and UNCTAD (2006). We also used the company websites to obtain information, especially financial information from annual reports published there; in some cases, we were unable to present the financials because the firms do not disclose them. Information and statistics on the industry came from industry-specific sources such as industry associations, the Mexican government, and trade magazines.

With all these secondary information sources, the authors of each chapter first constructed a summary of the evolution of the industry in the twentieth- and twenty-first centuries, and an overview of the two companies that were compared. In some cases, the authors analyzed more than two companies and then selected the two that seemed the best for gathering insights on the transformation from domestic companies into successful multinationals.

Once we had a draft of each chapter with information at the industry and company level and a clear understanding of the actions of the firms, the authors set up interviews with current and former managers of the companies. These interviews were facilitated in some cases by personal contacts, or through the relationship between Monterey Tec and the managers, many of whom were graduates of the Tec. In some cases, the authors did not have a relationship and simply contacted the company directly and gained access to the managers. The interviews were designed to obtain additional information that was not available from secondary sources, to clarify the reasons explaining some of the actions of the companies, and to get a better understanding of what the firm had done in the past and its plans for the future. In a few cases, the interviews were the primary source of information on what the companies did; this was usually the case for firms that were relatively small or that were privately held, for which secondary data were scarce.

Table 25.1 presents a list of the interviews conducted. In some instances, we only reveal the position of the person because we were asked to maintain personal anonymity. We also conducted interviews with people who were not in the company but in industry associations, other companies in the same industry, or experts on the company not affiliated with it directly to gain additional insights. By using multiple data sources, we sought to achieve triangulation and saturation in data collection.

DATA ANALYSIS

The analysis of the cases was done in several stages. First, the authors of each chapter analyzed the cases within the industry to gain insights on how the two companies were able to upgrade their capabilities to international levels and become multinationals. The cases followed a common structure to facilitate their analysis and comparison within and across industries. Each chapter first provided an overview of the evolution of the industry in Mexico, describing the main events in the industry and providing some statistics to provide a better understanding of its importance. The analysis of the industry was then complemented with an overview of the main competitors, and the identification among those competitors of the two companies analyzed. A similar approach was then followed by the presentation of the two companies to be compared. Each case started with a brief summary of the history of the firm, from its founding to the present, including a discussion of its business model in Mexico and its success there, to provide a deeper understanding of the firm. After this, the case presented the company's internationalization process, discussing exports and investments abroad and an explanation of the progress and success in foreign markets. A table providing a long-term evolution of

Table 25.1 *List of interviews*

Industry	Company	Person	Location	Date	Duration in minutes
Mining	Grupo Mexico	Xavier García de Quevedo Topete (member of the Board of directors)	Company Headquarters (México City)	May 5, 2015	44
Oil and gas	Pemex	Sergio Guaso Montoya	México City	January 21, 2015	60
Beverages	FEMSA	Omar Canizales Soto (Former Sales Manager)	San Diego CA	May 20, 2015	120
Footwear	Flexi	Alejandro Vega (Former sales director)	Tec de Monterrey, Leon	March 17, 2015	85
Footwear	SDE	Francisco Allard (Assistant Director)	Secretaria de Desarrollo Econòmico (SDE) Leon	March 18, 2015	92
Footwear	Muñoz-López & Associates	Miguel Muñoz (Partner)	CICEG, Leon	March 25, 2015	45
Footwear	Consultants	Miguel Esquer (Consultant)	Tec de Monterrey, Leon	March 3, 2015	90

Table 25.1 (*cont.*)

Industry	Company	Person	Location	Date	Duration in minutes
Cement	Cemex	Don Rogelio Zambrano (Founder and Ex-CEO)	Company Headquarters (Monterrey)	May 11, 2015	58
Cement	Cementos Chihuahua	Don Federico Terrazas (President)	Company Headquarters (Chihuahua)	January 21, 2015	71
Car components	Metalsa	Oscar Espronceda	ITESM	March 17, 2015	80
Car components	Nemak	Carlos Herrera	ITESM, Monterrey	June 3, 2015	45
Appliances	Mabe	Luis Berrondo	México City	June 4, 2015	80
Appliances	Mabe	Rafael L. Nava y Uribe	México City	June 4, 2015	30
Appliances	Industrias Man	Oscar Pardo	México City	September 23, 2015	60
Retail	Elektra	Bruno Rangel (Director of Finance and Investor Relations) Daniel McCosh (Press Director, Grupo Salinas)	México City	March 11, 2015	120
Retail	Coppel	Jose Luis Ramírez (Director of Operations)	Culiacan, Sinaloa	March 19, 2015	90

Table 25.1 (*cont.*)

Industry	Company	Person	Location	Date	Duration in minutes
Restaurants	Pollo Loco	Don José Ochoa	Monterrey (headquarters of the group)	November 13, 2015	180
Restaurants	Pollo Loco	Don Francisco Ochoa/ Jorge Ochoa/Jaime Ochoa	Laredo, USA (headquarters of the Palenque group)	November 14, 2015	270
Entertainment	Kidzania	Andres Fabre (COO KidZania)	Phone	April 15, 2015	90
Entertainment	Cinépolis	Ramón Ramírez Guzmán (Cinépolis Institutional Relations Director)	Guadalajara, Jalisco Phone	April 16, 2015 April 6, 2015	210 90
Television	TV Azteca	Bruno Rangel (Director of Finance and Investor Relations) Daniel McCosh (Press Director, Grupo Salinas)	México City	May 1, 2015	120
Information technology	Binbit	Esthela Silva (Corporate Communication Director)	Phone	July 9, 2015	60

Table 25.1 (cont.)

Industry	Company	Person	Location	Date	Duration in minutes
Information technology	Softtek	Gilberto Romero (Marketing Director of Mexico)	Phone	April 27, 2015	60
		Jose Tam (former director of Peru office)	Phone	July 8, 2015	60
		Nayeli Acevedo (Softtek PR)	Phone	June 6, 2015	60
Telecommunications	Iusacell	Daniel McCosh (Press Director, Grupo Salinas)	México City	May 1, 2015	20
Consultancy	Sintec	Oscar Lozano (founder and CEO)	Company Headquarters (Mexico City)	November 26, 2014	75
			Company Headquarters (Monterrey)	February 4, 2015	82
Consultancy	Feher & Feher	Ilan Ipelbaum (CCO)	Company Headquarters (Mexico City)	December 3, 2014	48

Table 25.1 (cont.)

Industry	Company	Person	Location	Date	Duration in minutes
Consultancy	Feher & Feher	Ferenz Feher (Founder and CEO)	Company Headquarters (Mexico City)	April 14, 2015	36
Education	UNAM	Ramón Peralta y Fabi (Director of the UNAM site in Canada)	Gatineau, Canada	March 2, 2015	28
Education	UNAM	Javier Laguna Calderón (Director of the UNAM site in Chicago)	Chicago, Illinois	February 23, 2015	75
Education	UNAM	Armando Lodigiani (Director General of Cooperation and Internationalization)	México City	March 2, 2015	26
Education	Tecnológico de Monterrey	Joaquín Guerra (Director of Internationalization at Tecnológico de Monterrey)	Monterrey, México	February 5, 2015	45
Education	Tecnológico de Monterrey	Patricia Montaño (Director of International Planning & Cooperation)	Monterrey, México	February 6, 2015	45

Table 25.1 (cont.)

Industry	Company	Person	Location	Date	Duration in minutes
Education	Tecnológico de Monterrey	Carlos Romero (Former Director of Relationships with EXATEC)	Monterrey, México	February 6, 2015	30
Education	Tecnológico de Monterrey	Enrique Zepeda (Former Vice-provost of International Affairs)	Monterrey, México	February 13, 2015	75
Education	Tecnológico de Monterrey	Sandra Ortiz (TEC, Latin American and The Caribbean Director)	Monterrey, México	May 12, 2015	30
Education	Tecnológico de Monterrey	Leticia Santos Dresel (Former Director of International Programs & Former Dallas Liaison Director)	Monterrey, México	August 14, 2015	30

the key financials, and another showing the evolution of the key events in domestic and foreign markets, completed the picture of each firm.

The analysis of the information contained in the cases was done following suggestions explained in Eisenhardt (1989), Eisenhardt & Graebner (2007), and Yin (2003) on how to perform analysis and comparison of case studies to gain theoretical insights. Thus, with a deep and complete historical understanding of each of the cases, the authors compared similarities and differences between the two companies in their domestic and international expansions. This comparison of the two cases resulted in the development of conclusions that provided new insights on processes and firm actions useful not only to companies in the same industry but also to other companies in emerging countries. The objective of the comparison was to abstract from these two cases and identify patterns and influences on the foreign expansion of the firms, as well as factors that helped the firms succeed abroad, and some of the challenges encountered. The analysis of these cases was aided by three conferences at which each of the authors of the chapters presented the insights they were gaining to other authors and were questioned about the ideas they identified. With these presentations and queries, the authors then went back to the cases and improved their analyses. Additionally, the coeditors of the book provided detailed suggestions for improvement for each of the chapters and the comparisons of cases, pushing authors to think more deeply about the ideas they were discovering.

Later, the comparison across cases was done once the chapters were completed. In two further conferences, the coeditors and authors discussed the ideas learned from analyzing all the cases. This comparison across cases and industries helped separate conditions and actions that were specific to some of the companies and industries, from those that were common across multiple companies and industries, helping establish the conclusions of the book. The analysis of the cases across industries in the conclusions was designed to identify factors and influences relating to the manager, company, industry, and country that explained the process of upgrading capabilities for international competition and international expansion. This comparison had the objective of creating a generalizable model of multinationalization that spoke directly to theory and that provided useful lessons for managers. Additionally, the conclusions of each of the chapters, as well as those of the overall book, went beyond the summary of what Mexican companies had done individually. Rather, they provide new ideas and suggestions as to how companies in emerging markets can become successful multinationals.

REFERENCES

BCG. 2006. *The New Global Challengers: How 100 Top Companies from Rapidly Developing Economies Are Changing the World*. Boston, MA: Boston Consulting Group.

BCG. 2008. *The 2008 BCG 100 New Global Challengers: How Top Companies from Rapidly Developing Economies Are Changing the World*. Boston, MA: Boston Consulting Group.

BCG. 2009. *The 2009 BCG 100 New Global Challengers: How Companies from Rapidly Developing Economies Are Contending for Global Leadership*. Boston, MA: Boston Consulting Group.

BCG. 2011. *2011 BCG Global Challengers. Companies on the Move: Rising Stars from Rapidly Developing Economies Are Reshaping Global Industries*. Boston, MA: Boston Consulting Group.

BCG. 2013. *Allies and Adversaries: 2013 BCG Global Challengers*. Boston, MA: Boston Consulting Group.

Casanova, L. 2009. *Global Latinas: Latin America's Emerging Multinationals*. Fontainebleau, France: INSEAD Business Press.

CNN Expansión. 2015. Las 100 mas globales. *Expansión*, January 16–29: 88–89.

ECLAC. 2006. *Foreign Investment in Latin America and the Caribbean 2005*. Santiago de Chile: ECLAC.

Eisenhardt, K. M. 1989. Building theories from case study research. *Academy of Management Review*, 14: 532–550.

Eisenhardt, K. M. & Graebner, M. E. 2007. Theory building from cases: opportunities and challenges. *Academy of Management Journal*, 50: 25–32.

Hoshino, T. 2001. *Industrialization and Private Enterprise in Mexico*. Chiba, Japan: Institute of Developing Economies, Japan External Trade Organization.

Ramamurti, R. & Singh, J. V. (Eds.) 2009. *Emerging Multinationals in Emerging Markets*. New York, NY: Cambridge University Press.

Santiso, J. 2013. *The Decade of the Multilatinas*. Cambridge, England: Cambridge University Press.

UNCTAD. 2012. *World Investment Report*. Geneva, Switzerland: United National Conference on Trade and Development.

UNCTAD. 2006. *World Investment Report 2006: FDI from Developing and Transition Economies: Implications for Development*. Geneva, Switzerland: United Nations Conference on Trade and Development.

Yin, R. K. 2003. *Case Study Research. Design and Methods* (3rd edn.). Thousand Oaks, CA: Sage.

Index

Printed in the United States
by Baker & Taylor Publisher Services